Biological Psychology

Biological

Daniel P. Kimble
University of Oregon

Psychology

HOLT, RINEHART AND WINSTON, INC.
New York   Chicago   San Francisco   Philadelphia
Montreal   Toronto   London   Sydney   Tokyo

For Reeva, Matthew, Evan,
Sara, and Marian Kimble

Publisher Susan Meyers
Acquisitions Editor Susan Arellano
Developmental Editor Herb Kirk
Photo Researcher Nicollette Harlan
Special Projects Editor Jeanette Ninas Johnson
Text Design Leon Bolognese
Cover Design Louis Scardino
Cover Illustration Gustave Falk
Anatomical Drawings D. L. Cramer
Line Illustrations J & R Art Services
Calligraphy Reeva Kimble
Art Director Louis Scardino
Production Managers Pat Sarcuni/Stefania Taflinska
Field Editor Jim Lizotte

(Literary and photographic credits appear on page 481.)

Printed in the United States of America

Library of Congress Cataloging-in-Publication Data

Kimble, Daniel P. (Daniel Porter)
  Biological psychology.

  Bibliography: p.
  Includes index.
  1. Psychobiology. 2. Neuropsychology. I. Title.
[DNLM: 1. Psychophysiology. WL 103 K49b]
QP360.K49 1988   152   87-17633

8 9 0 1 039 9 8 7 6 5 4 3 2

ISBN 0-03-069636-4

Holt, Rinehart and Winston, Inc.
The Dryden Press
Saunders College Publishing

Preface

In the nearly quarter-century that I have been teaching biological psychology at the University of Oregon I have learned a great deal from my students, most of whom are not psychology majors, about what a textbook should and should not be. It should be accessible to the general liberal arts student, yet contain sufficient detail to communicate the basic principles of the subject matter. Finding the correct balance between readability and technical exposition is not easy. I have tried to accomplish these two goals in several ways.

First, I have read research reports and review articles from a variety of fields, talked with researchers, and looked for interesting and relevant material from as many sources as possible. Second, I have tried to write clearly and simply. Wherever possible, I have related technical material to relevant psychological problems. Third, I have incorporated several organizational devices to help the reader. Each chapter is preceded by an outline and a preview. Throughout the book you will find key words bold-faced, indicating a "running pronouncing glossary." (I find that most of us have difficulty learning new concepts if we do not know how key words are pronounced.) At the end of each chapter there are a summary and a list of suggested readings. At the back of the book you will find all the glossary items repeated, in alphabetical order. In reading this book you will learn a basic vocabulary that will allow you to read other material in this field, along with some of the fundamental concepts relating brain function and behavior. In addition, I hope you will become excited about this field and that at least some of you will contribute to the next generation of research. Although we know something about how the brain works and can make some tentative statements about how this knowledge can be applied to understanding our own behavior, we are still in the early days of this field and your generation will know more and discover much more than mine. I will be delighted if this book helps to further your interest and enthusiasm for biological psychology and related fields.

For instructors, several aspects of this book will make it particularly useful for courses in biological psychology. These include:

1. The material on development of the nervous system (Chapter 4) is more detailed than in most comparable texts. I have also tried to relate this material to the related topics of aging, brain injury, and learning. By placing this chapter fairly early in the book, I hope to present the idea that the brain is capable of profound changes and is not a static, "hard-wired" computer.

2. Considerable material is provided on the role of hormones in the regulation and modulation of behavior, including the development of personality characteristics, such as gender role and gender identity. In addition, the possible role of androgens in male aggressive behavior is discussed in detail. Most of this material is in Chapter 9.

3. An entire chapter is devoted to language and the brain. Most of this chapter is concerned with various aspects of aphasia. I believe that the study of language behavior by psychologists will continue and become even more important than it is now.

4. Several hundred references appear at the back of the book. In selecting articles to cite in this book, I have attempted to keep the list selective, and as current as possible. Thus this reference list should provide students with leads to finding their way into the scientific literature.

5. I believe I have addressed most of the basic topics usually taught in courses in biological psychology. In addition to the chapters just noted, there are chapters on neuron function and synapses, neuroanatomy, vision, the other senses, movement and the regulation of posture, thirst and hunger, sleep and dreaming, emotion, learning and memory, specializations of the human brain, and disorders of brain and behavior. (See the overview of the book in Chapter 1.)

I would like to acknowledge the help I received from many individuals in preparing this book. Part of this book was written while I was on sabbatical leave at Oxford University. I would like to thank people there, particularly Alan Cowey, Nick Rawlins, Edmund Rolls, and Lawrence Weiskrantz of the Institute of Experimental Psychology. In addition, I would like to thank Norman Adler, Huda Akil, Colin Blakemore, Jacob Beck, Gene Block, Ruth BreMiller, Larry Butcher, Suzanne Corkin, Christina Enroth-Cugell, Peter Donovick, Alan Epstein, Beverly Fagot, H. C. Fibiger, Deanna Frost, Michael Gazzaniga, Hill Goldsmith, Robert Goy, Robert Grimm, Philip Groves, Barbara Gordon-Lickey, Marvin Gordon-Lickey, Philip Grant, William Greenough, Charles Gross, David Gunner, Charles Hamilton, Doug Hintzman, Fred J. Hodges III, Harry Howard, Robert Isaacson, Wesley Jordan, Eric Kandel, Ray Kesner, Charles Kimmel, John Liebeskind, Michael Merzenich, Richard Marrocco, James McConnell, Mortimer Mishkin, John Money, Walle Nauta, David Olton, Charles Phoenix, Gary Pickard, Michael Posner, Ron Racine, Pasco Rakic, Benjamin Rusak, Marcus Raichle, Evelyn Satinoff, Elizabeth Schaughency, Paul Schinkman, Roger Sperry, Nico Spinelli, Donald Stein, Ann Streissguth, Philip Teitelbaum, Carl I. Thompson, Richard F. Thompson, Kathryn Tosney, Nathan Tublitz, Monte Westerfield, James Weston, Terence Williams, Sandra Witelson, and Irving Zucker.

I would like to acknowlege the steady and valuable assistance of Mary Frances Ross in various aspects of the preparation of this book. I thank my wife, Reeva, and my children, Matthew, Evan, and Sara for their cheerful support and encouragement. Finally, I would like to thank Susan Meyers, Herbert Kirk, Jeanette Ninas Johnson, Susan Arellano, Hilary Jackson, Lou Scardino, and Nicollette Harlan at Holt, Rinehart and Winston for their help in the development and production of *Biological Psychology*.

My appreciation goes to the following who reviewed all or portions of the manuscript for *Biological Psychology*:

William R. Clark, Ball State University
Verne Cox, University of Texas, Arlington
Alan N. Epstein, University of Pennsylvania
Stephen Goldberg, University of Miami (Fl)
Barbara Gordon-Lickey, University of Oregon
Marvin Gordon-Lickey, University of Oregon
Douglas L. Grimsley, University of North Carolina, Charlotte
Terence Hines, Pace University
Wesley P. Jordan, St. Mary's College of Maryland
Sheldon Lachman, Wayne State University
Jacqueline Liederman, Boston University
Carlton Lints, Northern Illinois University
Mark McCourt, University of Texas, Austin
William Metzger, Whitman College
Antonio Nunez, Michigan State University
Ronald Peters, Iowa State University
Robert Provine, University of Maryland
Lanna Rhody, State University of New York (Geneseo)
Paul Shinkman, University of North Carolina, Chapel Hill
Garth J. Thomas, University of Rochester Medical Center
Carl Thompson, Wabash College

Daniel P. Kimble
Eugene, Oregon

Brief Contents

Detailed Contents

Biological Psychology

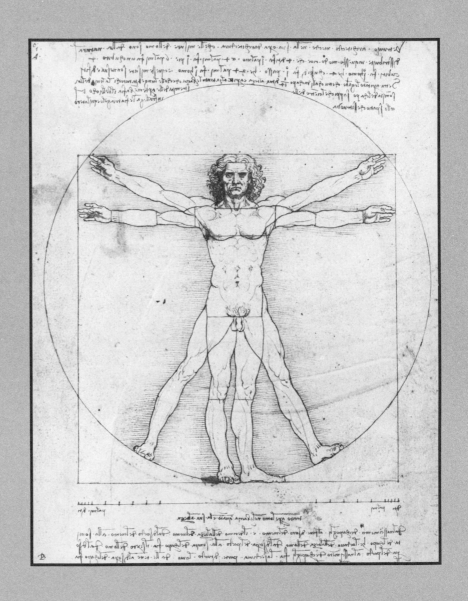

1

Introduction

The brain is wider than the sky,
For put them side by side,
The one the other will include
With ease, and you beside.

EMILY DICKINSON

Preview

Biological psychology has developed from physiology, psychology, and several other related disciplines. Its goal is to understand the function of the brain and the relation between it and behavior. An overview of the book introduces many of the specific topics to be discussed later, including sensory processing, learning and memory, sleep and dreaming, and disorders of brain and behavior.

A brief history of psychology and physiology illustrates some of the themes that still interest modern workers. Only within the past 40 years has there been a widespread effort to understand behavior from a biological standpoint, but there are now hundreds of undergraduate and graduate programs in biological psychology. Biological psychology is an area of neuroscience and is thus also termed *behavioral neuroscience*.

This chapter concludes with a discussion of some of the basic experimental tools used by biological psychologists—and the essential reminder that the most important tool of the scientist is still an informed curiosity.

A Computer That Dreams

Imagine a device capable of storing thousands, even hundreds of thousands of bits of information. Imagine that this device can not only store this information, but process it, rearrange items from one filing system to another, with virtually limitless flexibility. So far this may seem to describe any modern computer, but let us consider some additional characteristics of this device: Imagine that it can be tuned to sense different types of energy present in the environment, such as electromagnetic radiation, molecular movements in the air, and tiny amounts of certain chemicals in the water. Suppose that it is capable of generating coherent speech and language patterns, not only in response to input, but spontaneously. Moreover, assume that it can generate sentences never before spoken, given an arbitrary vocabulary, and maintain understandable grammatical constructions. Consider that this device is connected to an output system that is capable of moving with considerable strength and speed.

In describing some of the characteristics of the brain that make it the most remarkable biological system yet to evolve, we should mention its weaknesses as well. For one thing, vast ranges of energies are present in the universe to which this device is insensitive. For example, it cannot detect unaided the presence of such lethal gases as carbon monoxide. Moreover, it is almost continually dependent on a steady supply of oxygen and glucose. Deprive it for even 10 minutes of an air supply and its value to its owner will be severely and permanently diminished. Consider also that the remarkable information-processing capacity and analytical skills can be changed easily, not always in predictable ways, by conditions we call emotion and that these conditions in the brain are in some cases due to substances carried from other regions of the body through the bloodstream. Our brains are not always reliable; they can play tricks on us. We can't even turn them off when we go to sleep. Instead, the brain continues to rummage through its memory banks of images from the past day's events, from events of months or years ago; it even produces imagined events that never happened and never could happen, often with startling clarity. In short, this is a computer that can feel, love, and dream.

There have been many philosophical approaches to what is often referred to as the *mind–body problem* (or more precisely, the *mind–brain problem*), since virtually everyone now agrees that it is the brain, not the liver or the heart (as had been suggested in ancient days), that is responsible for mental events. The brain has been the main site for theoretical locations of mind ever since the time of the French philosopher and mathematician Réné Descartes (1596–1650). Descartes believed that two basic types of substances exist: physical material, which makes up our bodies, including our brains, and nonphysical substances, which include mind. In developing this notion, which we now refer to as a form of *dualism,* Descartes even identified the place in the brain—the pineal gland—where he believed these two different sorts of substances met and interacted.

Most modern biological psychologists would probably classify themselves not as dualists, such as Descartes, but as *monists*—subscribing to the general notion that only one sort of substance is found in the universe and that the brain and everything else are constructed from it. Opinions vary about such mental events as thinking, dreaming, and remembering. For example, mind can be considered as (1) simply a concept that we use to explain the workings of the brain; (2) a process that has as one of its characteristics *self-awareness;* (3) an *emergent property* of the organization of the network of billions of cells in a complex brain; (4) an unimportant byproduct of the workings of the brain (although most of us would probably find this alternative somewhat deflating).

We shall discuss many different aspects of the functions of the brain in this book, from how the individual cells of the brain transmit information

neuron (NUR-on) An individual nerve cell. Its main components include the cell body, nucleus, dendrites, axon, and end feet.

synapse (SIN-naps) Junction between neurons. Synapses can be either electrical or chemical. Most of the synapses in mammalian brains are thought to be chemical.

Alzheimer's disease (ALLS-high-mers) Severe mental and emotional deterioration due to brain changes. Occurs primarily in elderly individuals.

to what goes wrong with information processing when particular conditions occur in the brain, causing what we call mental illness. We shall examine how our brain uses energy changes in the environment to guide behavior and how the quick flood of emotion may be related to the activity in certain regions of the nervous system. We shall consider how we know we are hungry, how our brain develops, and what happens to the brain as it ages and when it is injured. We shall deal with the sorts of changes in the brain that underlie learning and memory, how our movements get organized, and many other topics relating to the way the brain generates behavior. You will not learn the "final answers" to questions about how the brain works, but I hope you will enjoy the search. As one of Christopher Fry's characters says in *The Lady's Not for Burning,* "the best thing we can do is to make wherever we're lost in look as much like home as we can" (Fry, 1950). At the present, biological psychology finds itself in a most interesting and exciting place indeed, and we are beginning to make it look more like home. Welcome.

Overview of the Book

The brain does not give its secrets away easily. Cells in the brains of mammals, which number in the billions, are very small and are interconnected in an incredibly complicated fashion. Chapter 2 discusses the main properties of **neurons,** the most important type of cell in the brain for processing and storing information. Much of this material may seem far removed from the study of behavior, but it is not, for it is the activity in neurons that generates our thoughts, emotions, and actions. For example, to understand how drugs may reduce the symptoms of mental illness, we must understand how neurons communicate with each other. This communication takes place at junctions called **synapses,** and it is here that most psychoactive drugs act. Research on the way in which the brain changes during learning has focused on changes at synapses. Learning and mental illness are only two of many topics that can be understood better if we understand something of the mechanism by which brain cells operate.

Chapter 3 provides an overview of the basic structures in the nervous system, including a discussion of the *autonomic nervous system* (ANS). Understanding the ANS is important if we are to understand emotional experiences (discussed in Chapter 11). Much of the material in Chapter 3, in fact, is useful background for later discussions.

The stages in the development of the brain are discussed in Chapter 4. Each of the billions of nerve cells in the brain must solve a series of developmental problems—what type of neuron to become, where to go in the brain, and what connections to make with other neurons. Neuroscientists have found brain development a fertile field for experimentation, and some of their research is discussed, along with some of the behavioral abnormalities that occur when the stages of development do not go according to plan. The effects of aging and attempts to combat the ravages of such conditions as **Alzheimer's disease** are also discussed in Chapter 4.

Philosophers and scientists throughout our literate history have asked, "How do we know the world?" Certainly one of our primary means of gaining knowledge about our world is through what we see. Knowledge of how the visual system of the brain works has increased greatly in the last twenty-five years, and Chapter 5 explores some of this knowledge and some of the current controversies in the field.

Vision is just one of our senses. Chapter 6 discusses the others: audition, balance, touch, temperature, olfaction, and taste. In these senses, as in vision, the brain must accomplish three main tasks—*transduction* of the relevant energy forms, *transmission* of nerve impulses to the appropriate regions of the brain, and *abstraction* of meaning from these signals.

Much of the brain is devoted to the reception and analysis of sensory information about the world, but considerable attention also goes to the control of movement and the regulation of posture. Chapter 7 discusses various aspects of movement control, from reflexes to more elaborate motor "programs" stored in neural circuits in the brain.

Like bright children, good scientists often ask questions that seem simple but are not. Chapter 8 addresses some of these "not-so-simple" questions, such as why we eat and drink. Most mammals regulate their food and water intake within quite narrow limits. We are slowly discovering the biological mechanisms that allow them to do so. Human beings do not always manage to limit their food intake effectively. The special problems of obesity are also discussed in this chapter, as is the growing problem of **anorexia nervosa,** termed by one researcher a "relentless pursuit of thinness."

Chapter 9 introduces the other main organ system that influences behavior—the *endocrine system.* The endocrine system includes those tissues that secrete the chemical messengers known as *hormones* into the bloodstream. The endocrine system and the nervous system are active partners in the regulation of behavior. Hormones can affect the activity of nerve cells, and nerve cells control or influence the production and secretion of hormones. In fact, some nerve cells actually secrete hormones, and many "hormones" are identical to the substances used as neurotransmitters by neurons at synapses.

We spend a third of our lives asleep, but the brain never really rests. The discovery of ways to measure the spontaneous electrical activity of the brain made possible the scientific study of sleep and dreaming. The electrical activity of the brain can be classified according to several stages of sleep and waking. One state in particular, *rapid eye movement (REM) sleep,* correlates highly with reports of dreaming. Sleep, dreaming, and biological rhythms are explored in Chapter 10.

Although much of the brain is devoted to processing and storing information, it also allows us to experience and express emotions. Chapter 11 deals with the way we feel pleasure, pain, and other emotions. In this chapter we discuss the recent discovery of substances within our bodies that are similar to such opiate drugs as morphine and opium. These so-called **endorphins** may be released during stressful situations and help us to endure temporarily what would otherwise be incapacitating pain.

anorexia nervosa (Ann-or-EX-e-ah nur-VO-sah) A disease characterized by insufficient eating, loss of weight, and other symptoms.

endorphins (en-DOR-fins) A word coined from combining parts of "ENDOgenous moRPHINes." Substances in the body that possess properties similar to the opiates.

Of all the intellectual puzzles that confront modern biological psychologists the question of what happens in the brain during learning is perhaps the most challenging. Chapter 12 includes two quite different approaches to this problem. The study of human amnesia is directed, in part, at discovering the *location* of the crucial neural circuits underlying learning. Another, quite different approach takes advantage of the huge neurons that certain invertebrates possess and studies those neurons as the animal learns. These studies have allowed us to gain information about learning at the level of individual nerve cells!

Is there something about your brain that clearly distinguishes it from that of, say, a chimpanzee? Chapter 13 explores this question in some detail. One way in which the human brain is specialized is that the right *hemisphere* makes somewhat different contributions to mental activity than does the left one. The extent and significance of this *functional lateralization* are debatable, but a number of fascinating experiments have been done. Some of the most dramatic results have been obtained with epileptic patients who have undergone neurosurgery that "disconnects" the two hemispheres. The functional differences between the left and right hemispheres can be observed more readily in these so-called *split-brain* individuals than in normal subjects.

Chapter 14 discusses some of what is known about the production of speech and language, including the problems of speech production and comprehension that occur with damage to specific areas of the brain.

Chapter 15 deals with the biological aspects of mental illness, particularly depression and schizophrenia. Most current treatments for these disorders involve the use of drugs, but the growing incidence of serious side effects, particularly with the drugs used to treat schizophrenia, has raised fundamental questions about the value of drugs in treating these diseases. Nevertheless, viewing mental illness as a brain disorder has led to some dramatic advances in treatment and to testable hypotheses.

The Historical Roots of Biological Psychology

Tracing the history of biological psychology involves tracing the history of psychology, biology, and medicine. Experimental approaches in these fields began less than 200 years ago, but scholarly curiosity about the functions of the brain and the nature of mental activity dates from far before that time.

As early as the fifth century B.C., in one of those glorious bursts of intellectual activity that occur from time to time, the Ionian philosophers considered many issues in ways that seem almost modern. For example, Hippocrates (460–380 B.C.) wrote that epilepsy was a "brain disease" and that "pleasures, joys, laughter, and jests as well as sorrows, pain, griefs, and tears originate in the brain." Three great Greek philosophers—Socrates (469–399 B.C.) Plato (428–348 B.C.), and Aristotle (384–322 B.C.)—pondered at length the problems of how we know the world and of the nature of thinking, feeling, and dreaming. The intellectual method used by the early Greeks was basically deductive, with particular cases being explained from assumed principles. But science as we now conceive it cannot exist without gathering new observations. Consequently, the contribution of these philosophers to modern neuroscience is not as great as it is for philosophy or logic.

Not until the Renaissance—with its rediscovery of Greek, Roman, and Arabic learning; the invention of the printing press; the expansion of world travel; and the general intellectual awakening from the Dark Ages—did the modern period of thought have its beginnings. From the decline of Greek culture to the Italian Renaissance, thought was dominated by Christian theology that focused primarily on the next world. There were, of course, exceptions, such as the great physician Galen (c129–c200 A.D.), whose writings on medicine and anatomy were the final authority until, in 1543, Andreas Vesalius (1514–1564) published a much more accurate anatomy text based not on a dogmatic acceptance of Galen, but on his own observations from the dissection of cadavers. Throughout the history of science, one great theme is that progress is rapid when the intellectual climate favors direct observation of nature and slow when uncritical reliance is placed on earlier authorities, no matter how brilliant those authorities may have been in their time.

Modern science can be said to have had its beginnings in the seventeenth century. Three men were primarily responsible: Johann Kepler (1571–1630), Galileo Galilei (1564–1642), and Isaac Newton (1642–1727).

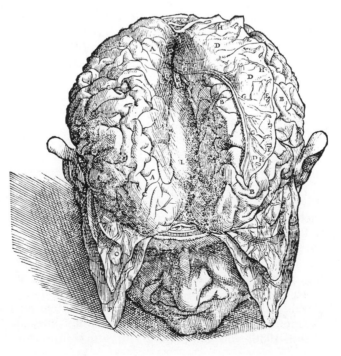

Figure 1.1 A drawing by the famous Renaissance anatomist Andreas Vesalius. Vesalius was one of the first anatomists to draw from actual observations of the human brain.

William Harvey (1578–1657), whose discovery of the circulation of the blood in 1628 was a landmark in biology, was also important. In addition, Francis Bacon (1561–1626) proposed the inductive method of logic in 1620. This method of arguing from the observation of many different instances to basic generalization replaced Aristotle's deductive methods as the main logic of science and provided the very essence of what has come to be known as the scientific method, the foundation of modern science.

Beginnings of Psychology

The "first man who without reservation is properly called a psychologist," according to Edwin Boring (1950), is Wilhelm Wundt (1832–1920). Wundt founded the field of experimental psychology, which, although he often referred to it as "physiological psychology," was, in fact, not based on physiology either in Wundt's laboratory or anywhere else until well into the twentieth century. Nevertheless, because of his own startling scholarly output (he published 491 items totalling 53,735 pages between 1853 and 1920) and his dominating personality, Wundt put psychology in the ranks of the experimental sciences. He founded the first formal laboratory in psychology in 1879 at the University of Leipzig (although William James is sometimes credited with starting the first laboratory because he set aside some space at Harvard for psychology work in 1875).

Wundt's techniques and most of his ideas now are of only historical interest. He taught that the analysis of consciousness into its "elements" was the main task for psychology. This was to be done through careful introspection by individuals trained for such tasks by Wundt himself. Since this approach is not open to independent verification, it could not survive the demands of modern science. Careful analysis of mental activity has survived, however, supplemented by more objective measures and is still useful in modern psychology.

Wundt's most famous student, Edward B. Titchener (1867–1927), was a key figure in the development of American psychology. Titchener came to Cornell University to plant the flag of introspectionism in the New World. His success was limited. Americans preferred the more dynamic, functional psychology proposed by John Dewey (1859–1952) at the University of Chicago. Dewey and other "functionalists" were concerned with the application of psychological knowledge, particularly in education. One consequence of this interest was an emphasis on studies of learning. Experimental animals such as rats were introduced into psychology laboratories in an attempt to uncover the "basic laws" of learning. This method of studying behavior survives in modern psychology.

The most famous of these early pioneers in the study of animal learning, a man whose ideas influenced a generation of psychologists, was Edward Thorndike (1874–1949) of Columbia University. He observed cats in puzzle boxes and described what he called their trial-and-error learning of escape maneuvers. At about the same time, in Russia, Ivan Pavlov (1849–1936) was developing laboratory procedures for studying conditioned reflexes in dogs. Both Pavlovian conditioning and the trial-and-error learning techniques of Thorndike are still used, in modified form, to study learning in humans and laboratory animals.

Beginnings of Physiology

Physiology developed earlier than psychology. William Harvey's discovery relating to the circulation of the blood was published in 1628, but the study of nervous tissue did not begin to yield results until the nineteenth century. Charles Bell (1774–1842) in London and François Magendie (1783–1855) in Paris independently (and nearly simultaneously) discovered that the dorsal roots of the spinal cord brought sensory information into the central nervous system and that the ventral roots carried movement commands. This seemingly simple fact, now known as the *law of roots* or the *Bell–Magendie law,* demonstrated that different functional regions of the nervous system exist. This realization encouraged others to seek additional facts about the brain and spinal cord.

In the years following Bell's and Magendie's discovery there were many important findings about the nature of the nervous system, but the most dramatic (although not the only, for he made many other major contributions, particularly in the area of vision) was that of Herman von Helmholtz (1821–1894). In 1850 Helmholtz discovered that the impulse in a typical motor nerve traveled not at the speed of light (as many contemporary authorities believed), but at a much more modest 20–50 m/sec. The ability to arrive at these figures (which turned out to be quite accurate) suggested that thought itself also might be studied. If the speed of nervous conduction took time, so might thought. Mental processes too could be subjected to experimental tests.

Darwin and the Theory of Evolution

In 1859 a quiet, scholarly Englishman named Charles Darwin (1809–1882) published a book that forever changed the way we think about ourselves: *On the Origin of Species.* Although Darwin knew his ideas would create controversy, it is unlikely he could have imagined the extent to which his ideas would penetrate modern thought. Probably no other modern book has so influenced thinking about human beings. The implications of Darwinian theory (and subsequent evolutionary theory) are found throughout modern neuroscience. In 1872 Darwin published another book, *Expression of the Emotions in Man and Animals,* which contains evidence (much of it anecdotal) on the continuity of facial expressions across widely varying cultures. This book remains a valuable reference for modern workers in the area of emotion.

The theory of evolution is firmly associated with Darwin's name, but it must be remembered that another man, Alfred Russel Wallace (1823–1913), sent a manuscript proposing virtually the same theory to Darwin before the publication of Darwin's 1859 book. Darwin resolved his crisis of conscience concerning Wallace's possible priority by publishing his own and Wallace's ideas simultaneously. Darwin's theory, better argued and documented, took center stage in the history of science. The idea that there is continuity among all animal forms encouraged biologists (and later psychologists) not only to look for the biological basis for such "human" attributes as emotion and thought, but also to look for more advanced aspects of behavior, such as learning and reasoning, in animals. After Darwin it became impossible to draw a firm line between what was human and what was animal. Since the publication of *The Origin of Species* many individuals have proposed alterations to Darwinian theory, but it remains the bedrock on which modern neuroscience stands.

Modern Biological Psychology

In the last 40 or so years scientific progress has accelerated at a rapid rate. For much of the first half of this century, psychology and physiology advanced separately, with only a few pioneers crossing over to work on problems in the other discipline. Not until after World War II did most psychologists begin to study the nervous system seriously. Similarly, only a few neurophysiologists were interested in studying behavior until recently. This isolation—which began to dissipate in the 1950s, when graduate students started to cross disciplinary lines and doctoral programs in physiological psychology and psychobiology were started—is now gone. Most of these programs have flourished, and departments and institutes devoted to the study of brain and behavior now exist throughout the United States, Canada, Great Britain, West Germany, France, Japan, and Australia. The 1986 listing of neuroscience training programs in North America, published by

A Neuroscience Hall of Fame

Several scientists whose work forms part of the present field of behavioral neuroscience have been awarded the Nobel prize. Although neuroscience did not exist at the time these awards first were made at the beginning of the century, neuroscience can claim several individuals who received the prize in physiology or medicine. Table 1.1 lists some of the Nobel laureates whose research is relevant to one or another of the topics in this book (Jasper and Sourkes, 1983). Many of these individuals are discussed in greater detail in subsequent chapters. The first name on the list is that of

Ivan Pavlov, who was honored for his work on digestive processes. This work led directly to his interest in the operation of the nervous system, particularly conditioned reflexes. Two years later the prize was awarded to Camillo Golgi (1843?–1926) and Santiago Ramón y Cajal (1852–1934) for work on the anatomy of the nervous system. Since these early awards, Nobel prizes have been awarded to many other individuals whose work we shall discuss. We can look forward to important additions to the neuroscience hall of fame in the future.

TABLE 1.1   Some Nobel Laureates Whose Research Is Relevant to Neuroscience

1904	Ivan Petrovich Pavlov. In recognition of his work on the physiology of digestion.
1906	Camillo Golgi and Santiago Ramón y Cajal. For their work on the structure of the nervous system.
1932	Charles Scott Sherrington and Edgar Douglas Adrian. For their discoveries on neuronal function.
1936	Henry Hallett Dale and Otto Loewi. For their work on chemical transmission at the synapse.
1944	Joseph Erlanger and Herbert Spencer Gasser. For their work on single neurons.
1961	George von Békésy. For his work on the basis of hearing.
1963	John Carew Eccles, Alan Lloyd Hodgkin, and Andrew Fielding Huxley. In recognition of their work on the nerve impulse and synaptic events.
1967	Ragnar Granit, Haldane Keffer Hartline, and George Wald. For their discoveries concerning basic processes in vision.
1970	Julius Axelrod, Ulf Svante von Euler, and Bernard Katz. For their discoveries concerning chemical transmission in the nervous system and between nerve and muscle.
1973	Karl von Frisch, Konrad Lorenz, and Nikolaas Tinbergen. For their discoveries in the field of ethology (animal behavior).
1977	Roger C. L. Guillemin, Andrew V. Schally, and Rosalyn S. Yalow. In recognition of their work on the discovery and assay for peptide hormones in the brain.
1979	Allan MacLeod Cormack and Godfrey Newbold Hounsfield. For their development of the CAT scan.
1981	David Hunter Hubel, Torsten Nils Wiesel, and Roger Wolcott Sperry. Hubel and Wiesel for their work on the response of single neurons in the visual system, Sperry for his research into specialized functions of the left and right cerebral hemispheres.
1986	Rita Levi-Montalcini and Stanley Cohen. For their discovery of nerve-growth factor and increasing our understanding of the development of the nervous system.

Dr. Roger Sperry of the California Institute of Technology receiving his shared Nobel prize in medicine from King Carl XVI Gustaf in Stockholm in 1981.

the Society for Neuroscience, lists 297 institutions offering training in neuroscience, with 328 different doctoral programs, an increase from 98 in 1978. Undergraduate programs have risen from 20 in 1978 to 97 in 1986.

Methods in Biological Psychology

The methods used by neuroscientists vary widely, depending on the nature of the problem under investigation and the background and interests of the investigator. Some research opportunities arise from an examination of people with diseases of the nervous system or endocrine system. Some of the diseases that have come to the attention of neuroscientists include Parkinson's disease and Alzheimer's disease, each of which seems to affect different parts of the brain and to produce different symptoms. Patients suffering from the aftermath of strokes or brain infections have given investigators the opportunity to study language and memory impairments associated with brain damage to specific areas of the brain. All these topics are explored in later chapters.

The tradition of studying disease to understand normal function dates from antiquity; in recent years, however, this technique has been dramatically improved by the invention of various devices that can better specify the exact location of brain damage in nonintrusive ways. (These methods are discussed in more detail in Chapter 14). The increasing precision with which brain damage can be located, together with careful psychological analysis, promises to enlarge greatly our knowledge about speech, language, memory, and other mental processes.

The Lesion Technique

A related experimental procedure destroys localized regions of the nervous system in laboratory animals and studies the behavioral and physiological effects. The functions that remain undisturbed following the experimental *lesion* or *ablation* (removal) of specific brain regions can be assumed to be handled primarily by the remaining, undamaged regions of the brain. The aspects of the animal's behavior that are changed by the lesion may suggest ways in which that part of the brain may function. It is important in such studies to make certain that the particular behavioral change is not a side effect of some other problem induced by the lesion.

The lesion technique has advantages and disadvantages. One advantage is that, unlike accidental or disease-caused brain damage seen in neurological patients, experimental brain damage can be varied systematically in different subjects, and precise lesions can be made to correspond with recognized anatomical divisions. In addition, the exact location of the damage can be determined, which cannot be done always with human patients, even with the more sophisticated scanning techniques. Another advantage to the lesion method is that the animals can be studied over an extended period of time in various behavioral situations to determine what the animal can and cannot do.

One disadvantage of the technique is that it takes careful and prolonged testing to begin to determine what behavioral changes have occurred. Also, brains respond to injury in a dynamic manner, sending off new sprouts from injured **axons,** perhaps making new and different synaptic connections. The brain may be capable of shifting its function in ways that are not yet understood. (Some of these changes following injury are discussed in greater detail in Chapter 4.) Despite the difficulties in interpreting lesion studies, they have provided considerable information regarding the function of the brain.

Localized brain regions can be lesioned in several ways. For example, discrete lesions can be produced by passing electrical current through a fine wire electrode that is insulated except at the tip. With the subject under anesthesia, the electrode is inserted into a specific brain region through a small hole drilled in the skull. The tip of the electrode is positioned in the desired region of the brain through the use of a *sterotaxic instrument.* This device holds the animal's head firmly in position. With the help of a sterotaxic instrument in combination with brain atlases (available for several different species), it is possible to place the electrode tip in the desired location. With the tip in position, application of direct current produces a lesion. The size of the lesion depends on the strength and duration of the current. Selected regions of the brain can also be removed by applying gentle suction through a small glass or metal pipette. Usually this is the preferred method when the tissue to be removed can be seen readily with the aid of an operating microscope. This *aspiration* technique is particularly suitable for making ablations on the surface of the brain.

One variation on the lesion technique is to apply chemicals that disrupt the activity of the cell bodies of neurons without interfering seriously with the nerve tracts in the same region. A surgical or electrically caused lesion destroys both cell bodies and their axons. However, a few chemicals selectively destroy cell bodies, sparing the axons. Two such chemicals are *kainic acid* and *ibotenic acid.* Small amounts of chemicals can be injected into a region of the brain in a manner similar to that described for passing electrical current. Instead of inserting an electrode, however, the experimenter places a hollow tube, or *cannula,* in such a way that its tip is in the desired location.

As will be discussed in Chapter 2, dozens of different chemical substances are used by the brain as *neurotransmitters.* These chemicals are released by neurons at their junctions with other neurons and interact with specialized receptors on these other neurons. This interaction underlies the passage of information from one neuron to another. Over the past few years several *neurotoxins* have been used to destroy selectively one or another of these neurotransmitter systems in the brain. For example, the chemical **6-hydroxydopamine (6-OHDA)** when injected into the brain is taken up by the fine terminal branches of the neurons that secrete the neurotransmitters *dopamine* and *norepinephrine.* It then kills the neurons,

axon (AKS-on) That part of the neuron that carries the nerve impulse. Usually a long process extending from the cell body.

6-hydroxydopamine (6-OHDA) (six-hi-droks-ee-DOP-ah-meen) A neurotoxin that is taken in by the axon terminals of neurons secreting dopamine and norepinephrine and that subsequently kills those neurons.

Ethics of Animal Experimentation

Neuroscientific research, like much of medical research, often depends on using experimental animals as subjects. Human neurological patients also provide us with information about the working of the brain, but these cases cannot always provide the information necessary to enlarge our knowledge. The right to use animals in experiments brings with it the responsibility to make sure that no unnecessary experiments are performed, that no unnecessary pain is inflicted on the animal, and that all possible care is taken in the housing and treatment of experimental animals. Professional societies such as the Society for Neuroscience, the American Physiological Society, and the American Psychological Association have all produced written standards of animal care. In addition, the federal government has passed legislation regulating the use of animals in research, legislation applicable to virtually every research institution in the United States. Most states and some local governments also have passed laws in this area. Moreover, internal review committees within universities must approve any research project involving vertebrates.

These regulations all aim at protecting the animal and the right of the experimenter. To do animal research experimenters usually must demonstrate that the problem they are investigating requires an animal model, that the proposed animal model is appropriate, and that the number of animals to be used is necessary. Living conditions for experimental animals are also regulated to ensure that discomfort and stress are kept to a minimum. Actually, of course, experimenters have been aware of the importance of such conditions as a prerequisite for reliable results for many years. The scientific community both welcomes and initiates rigorous standards for the treatment of experimental animals.

The decision to use animals in behavioral neuroscience research is based on the realization that to learn about the way the brain generates behavior, we must study both the brain and the behavior of the subject. We do not yet know enough about the brain to use computer simulations of brain networks. If we could produce such simulations, we would have already most of the information we are seeking. Most individuals agree that when animal research is done under regulated conditions, for research reasons that have been defended and approved, the benefits outweigh the costs. In medical research, of course, animal experimentation has been critical for virtually every advance from the treatment of rabies in the nineteenth century to more recent developments such as heart transplants and the prevention of smallpox and polio. Research, discussed later in this book, on the development of vision in kittens is paying off in the treatment of infant cataracts. Moreover, research on the implantation of small pieces of brain tissue may lead soon to a treatment for such conditions as Parkinson's and Alzheimer's diseases. (All these topics are discussed in greater detail in later chapters.) It has been demonstrated over and over again that the treatment and prevention of disease, including those in veterinary medicine, depend directly on a basic understanding of normal function, and in most cases such understanding depends on animal experimentation. Similarly, our basic understanding of how the nervous system operates requires animals in research.

5-6-dihydroxytryptamine (5-6-DHT) (five-six-di-hi-droks-ee-TRIP-tah-meen) A neurotoxin that selectively destroys neurons that secret serotonin.

with those that secrete norepinephrine being more severely affected than those that secrete dopamine.

Similar selective neurotoxins have been developed for other neurotransmitters. The substance **5-6-dihydroxytryptamine (5-6 DHT)** selectively destroys those neurons in the brain that secrete *serotonin*. The neurotransmitter *acetylcholine* can be destroyed selectively (by an irreversible inhibition of the process by which it is made) by a chemical with both a formidable name, *ethylcholine mustard aziridinium ion,* and an alphanumeric abbreviation, *AF64A*. This selective lesioning of neurotransmitter systems in the brain allows for testing the behavior of the animal deprived of the function of the particular neurotransmitter. This may allow for the development of "model disease states" in animals. For example, Alzheimer's disease (discussed in greater detail in Chapter 4) is considered by some scientists to be due in large part to a failure of the acetylcholine neurotransmitter system. With the use of AF64A, animal models of this hypothesis of Alzheimer's disease can be tested.

Eavesdropping on the Brain

Nerve cells communicate with each other by electrical and chemical signals. The electrical signals can be readily measured with modern electronic devices, which have allowed modern neuroscientists to eavesdrop on the activity of the nervous system. The nature of the conversation one can overhear in such experiments depends on the location of the recording "microphone."

Imagine you are in the Goodyear blimp high above a crowded football stadium. You are equipped with recording equipment that includes a microphone with a very long cord. If you lowered the microphone until it was a few hundred feet over the stadium, you could record the noise generated by the crowd. You might be able to tell something about the mood of the fans and perhaps even guess how the game was going from the swelling and ebbing of the crowd noises. But you could not record any actual conversations in this manner. Suppose, however, that you were to lower your microphone until it was only a few inches away from a particular individual. Now you would be able to single out from the thousands of voices the conversation of a single individual.

A similar situation exists in recording the electrical activity of the brain. If the recording "microphone" (the electrode) is placed high above the brain, as on the surface of the skull, the combined "roar of the crowd" can be recorded readily. This is basically what the EEG (electroencephalograph) machine can do. This record of the combined activity of hundreds of thousands of nerve cells sometimes can be very useful, providing the experimenter with information about the general activity of the underlying cortex. The EEG has been particularly helpful in distinguishing various functional states of the brain, such as those characterizing sleep and waking. Chapter 10 contains additional information on the invention and use of the EEG in studying the activity of the brain.

However, suppose you were interested not in the overall state of the brain, but in how an individual nerve cell responded to certain stimuli. It is possible to lower the recording electrode directly into the brain until it is very close to (or even penetrating) an individual nerve cell. Such recordings of "single units" have proved invaluable in discovering the response properties of neurons in various sensory systems of the brain as well as other brain regions.

Single-unit recording can be done under general anesthesia (although, of course, the activity of some neurons is suppressed under anesthesia). Such recordings also can be made using *chronically implanted* electrodes. With electrodes permanently implanted in the brain, secured to the skull, the activity of single neurons can be recorded in conscious, behaving animals. Such recording has rarely been done with human beings, since there are typically few neurological procedures for which such recordings would be appropriate.

Stimulation of Brain Tissue

A third major experimental technique, in addition to lesion and recording procedures, stimulates a localized region of the brain, either with electrical pulses of alternating current (direct current causes damage) or with some chemical that excites nerve cells. The brain can be stimulated electrically by using electrodes similar to those used for recording electrical activity. It can be stimulated chemically by injecting chemicals into the brain through implanted cannulas. It is not always obvious whether such stimulation mimics normal activity of the brain or "jams the system" by causing abnormal excitation, but careful experimentation and practice usually make it possible to determine what is happening. Chemicals such as local anesthetics or other drugs that inhibit neural activity can also be injected via implanted cannulas. Variations on all these procedures are continually being developed.

Histological Techniques

Most experiments in neuroscience require the examination of brain tissue. Starting in the nineteenth century, a variety of stains and dyes have been applied to brain tissue in the attempt to make cell structure more visible. The branch of neuroscience concerned with the study of tissues is called *histology.* Many different histological techniques have been developed, and new ones are being steadily added. We can categorize most histological stains as either *cell stains* or *fiber stains,* depending on whether they stain the protein material in the cell body or the fatty materials that compose the nerve axons. Figure 1.2 shows a section through a rat brain stained with a cell stain and another section stained with a fiber stain.

Figure 1.2 Sagittal sections through an entire rat brain, showing two different staining techniques.
The top section is stained to show the cell bodies; the section in the middle is stained to show myelinated fibers. The drawing at the bottom shows the major parts of the rat brain.

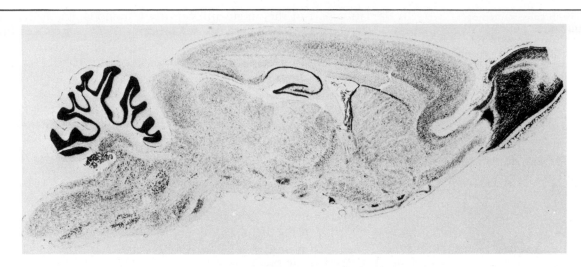

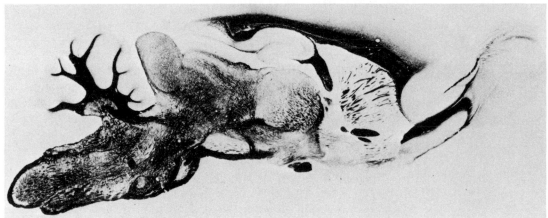

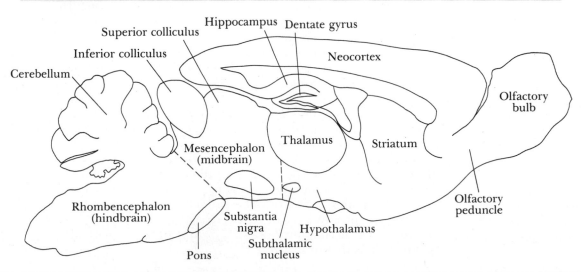

In the latter part of the nineteenth century Camillo Golgi, an Italian anatomist, developed a particularly useful procedure. The *Golgi stain*, in which neurons are impregnated with silver nitrate, is still one of the basic staining procedures. For reasons that remain unknown, even after a century of use, the Golgi stain results in the staining of entire cells, including cell bodies, dendrites, and axons. Interestingly, although the Golgi stain affects all of a particular neuron, it only works on about 1 percent of the cells to which it is applied. This turns out to be a tremendous advantage, as it allows for the staining of individual neurons, which then show up against a background of unstained cells. If all neurons, or even a much larger percentage of cells, were to be stained, the result would be a black mass similar to an overexposed negative. The Golgi stain, particularly in the hands of neuroanatomists such as Santiago Ramón y Cajal, has allowed for the detailed examination of neurons throughout the nervous system. There is some irony in the fact that Cajal used Golgi's stain to prove once and for all that the brain was made up of individual cells, thereby disproving Golgi's thesis that the brain was a network, or reticulum of tissue. The separation of neurons from one another by spaces has turned out to be one of the fundamental facts concerning the structure and function of the brain. Figure 1.3 shows one of Cajal's drawings, based on a Golgi stain of the cortex from a rat brain.

Another interesting question is, "Which brain cells have been most active in the past few minutes?" Activity in brain cells, as in all body cells, depends on the expenditure of energy. The fuel for the brain is *glucose*. The more active a cell, the more glucose it takes up from the brain's circulation. The chemical *2-deoxyglucose* (2-DG) is similar in structure to glucose, but the cell cannot metabolize 2-DG, although it is readily taken up from the blood. If 2-DG is injected into an animal, it is taken up along with glucose. The more active the cell, the more 2-DG (and glucose) that cell incorporates. Unlike glucose, however, which is used for energy, the 2-DG becomes trapped within the cell. If the injected 2-DG contains one radioactive carbon atom, the cells that have absorbed these 2-DG molecules can be identified by later cutting the brain into thin sections and exposing x-ray film to them. The more active a particular neuron has been, the more 2-DG it will incorporate, and the darker that cell will appear in the resulting *autoradiogram*. This technique, developed by Louis Sokoloff (1977), is particularly useful in showing which cells in the brain have been active recently.

The preceding histological procedures involve the examination of dead tissue. It is also desirable to be able to examine the regional activity of living brains, as in human neurological patients. A variation of the 2-DG technique known as **positron emission tomography** (PET scanning) has been developed for this purpose (Raichle, 1983). Patients are injected with small and harmless amounts of radioactive glucose and are then placed in a device containing a ring of radiation detectors that measure the emission of *positrons* (positively charged electrons) from the nucleus of the radioactive atoms. A computer draws a picture of the activity of the patient's brain such as that in Figure 1.4.

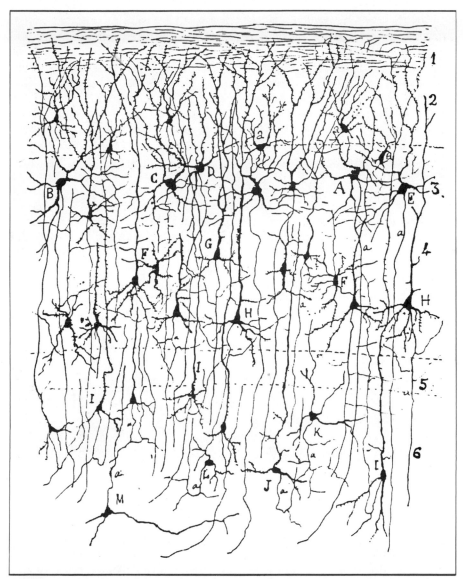

Figure 1.3 A drawing of neurons from the visual cortex of the rat, by Cajal, using the Golgi stain.
Cajal's superb drawings of neurons formed the base for modern neuroanatomy. (Numbers at right refer to cortical layers. Capital letters apparently refer to individual neurons. Small "α" refers to axon, "a" to a small cell type. This sketch was dated 1888.)

Many other techniques are used by biological psychologists, as will be discussed as they are relevant to the understanding of various topics in later chapters.

Figure 1.4   Positron emission tomography of the brain of a patient with Parkinson's disease on one side.
White arrows show abnormality in region of basal ganglia. (See Chapter 7 for more details.)

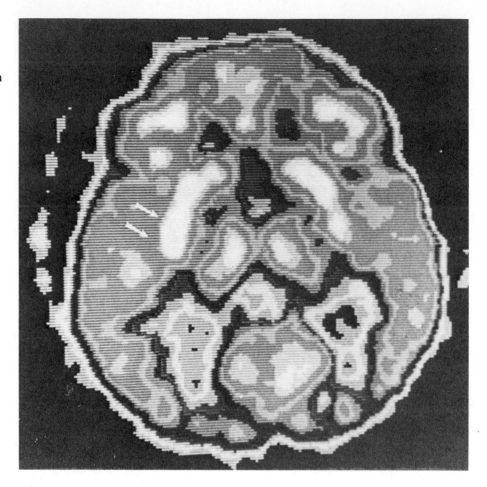

SUMMARY

1. The brain is the most highly evolved biological system known, with both remarkable abilities and limitations. This book explores many different aspects of the brain and how it generates behavior. An overview of the book discusses the contents of the remaining 14 chapters.

2. The historical roots of biological psychology are to be found in psychology, biology, and medicine. As early as the fifth century B.C. the Ionian philosophers were writing and teaching about the brain and mental events, but it was not until the Renaissance that the period of modern thought concerning nature is generally considered to have begun. Modern science itself began in the late seventeenth century with the work of Kepler, Galileo, Newton, and Harvey.

3. The beginnings of academic psychology can be traced to the activities of Wilhelm Wundt in Germany in the nineteenth century. Wundt's psychology was not to flourish in the United States, where a more dynamic,

functional psychology arose, stimulated by such individuals as Dewey and Thorndike.

4. Harvey's discovery of the circulation of the blood was an early landmark in the history of physiology, but it was not until the nineteenth century that study of the brain began to yield results. Important names in the history of the nineteenth century study of the nervous system include Bell, Magendie, and Helmholtz.

5. The publication in 1859 of the Darwin–Wallace theory of evolution forever changed the way in which we think about ourselves, and this theory remains the bedrock on which modern neuroscience stands. Modern biological psychologists use ideas and techniques from various fields, including experimental psychology, neurophysiology, and chemistry. The list of Nobel prize winners whose work is relevant to neuroscience began in 1904 with Ivan Pavlov and includes 1986 awards to Rita Levi-Montalcini and Stanley Cohen.

6. Various techniques used by researchers whose work is reported in this book include the study of brain-damaged humans, the study of animals with experimental lesions, the recording of the electrical activity of both single neurons and populations of neurons in the brain, and many other techniques. Animal experimentation is regulated by federal and state laws and by guidelines developed by professional scientific groups.

7. The examination of brain tissue stained to reveal one or another aspect of structural detail dates back to the nineteenth century and the work of Golgi and Ramón y Cajal. Modern techniques allow for glimpses of the living human brain in action, utilizing several different scanning procedures.

SUGGESTIONS FOR FURTHER READING

Boring, E. G. (1950). *A history of experimental psychology* (2d ed.). New York: Appleton-Century-Crofts.

Jung, R. (1984). Sensory research in historical perspective: Some philosphical foundations of perception. In J. M. Brookhart and V. B. Mountcastle (Eds.), *Handbook of physiology, Section 1: Neurophysiology* (vol. 3, pt. 1). Bethesda, MD: American Physiological Society.

Webster, W. G. (1975). *Principles of research methodology in physiological psychology.* New York: Harper & Row.

Wellman, P. J. (1986). *Laboratory exercises in physiological psychology (3d ed).* Boston: Allyn and Bacon, Inc.

2

Neurons and Synapses

*Electric wineskins filled
with ancient sea-secrets,
Generate the lightning
of our thoughts and dreams.*

D. P. K.

Preview

Specialized cells called neurons process, transmit, and store information in the brain. Neurons can perform these tasks because they are able to generate and conduct electrical signals and to secrete chemicals that alter the activity of other cells. These electrical signals, called nerve impulses, are caused by the passage of ions, which carry electrical current through the cell membrane of the neuron. The nerve impulses generated by this flow of ions travel from their place of origin to the axon terminals of the neuron, where they cause the release of small packets of special neurotransmitter chemicals that diffuse for short distances and contribute to the excitation or inhibition of other neurons. The junctions between the axon terminals of one neuron and the receptive areas of other neurons are called synapses. Individual neurons serve as decision-making points in the nervous system.

Structure of Neurons

Our brains are composed of several different kinds of cells, but it is the neurons that receive, process, and transmit information in our brains. We consider these information-processing abilities in this chapter. Neurons vary in shape, size, and other ways, but they all share some characteristics. Figure 2.1 shows some of the variety that can be found in the shape of neurons. In mammals, most neurons have a small cell body, measuring from 10 to 100 μm in diameter. However, the long extension from the cell body, the axon, can be very long, up to a meter in some cases. See Table 2.1 for some common units of length used in this book.

TABLE 2.1   Common Units of Length

Unit	Abbreviation	Equivalent
meter	m	about 39 inches
centimeter	cm	10^{-2} m (0.01 m)
millimeter	mm	10^{-3} m (0.001 m)
micrometer	μm	10^{-6} m (0.000001 m)
nanometer	nm	10^{-9} m (one-billionth m)

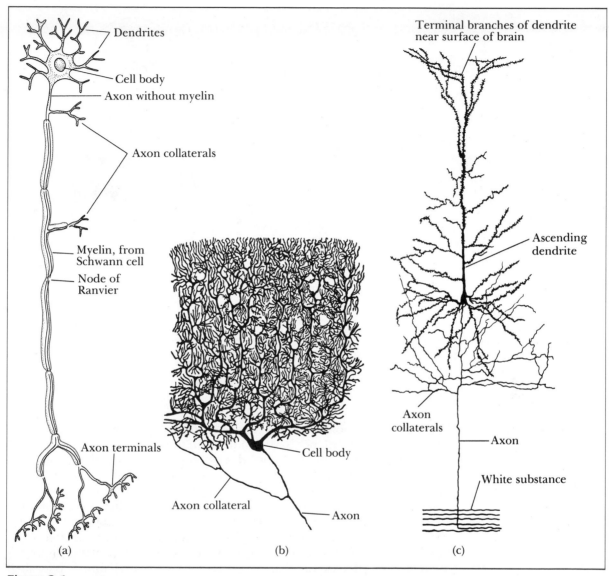

Figure 2.1
(a) Diagram of peripheral motor neuron. (b) Purkinje cell from cerebellum,
Golgi stain. The dendrites of such a cell may contain 200,000 synapses.
(c) Pyramidal neuron from cerebral cortex of rabbit. Golgi stain.

The number of neurons in most mammalian brains is staggering. No
one knows just how many there are in a typical human brain, but estimates
vary from 10 billion to well over 100 billion. The capacity of neurons to
process and store information depends on two fundamental properties—
their ability (1) to generate and conduct electrical signals and (2) to manufacture and secrete neurotransmitter substances.

nucleus (NEW-klee-us) A structure in the cell body containing the genetic material. The term *nucleus* is also used to refer to a cluster of neurons and their associated dendrites and glial cells.

endoplasmic reticulum (ER) (EN-do-plas-mik re-TIK-u-lum) A network (reticulum) of membranes within the cell body concerned with the production and transportation of cellular products. The prefix *endo* means "within" or "inner." ER with associated ribosomes is called *rough ER.* ER without associated ribosomes is called *smooth ER.*

ribosomes (RYE-bosomes) Structures associated with endoplasmic reticulum. Ribosomes are made of protein and ribonucleic acid (RNA). Important for protein synthesis.

ribonucleic acid (RNA) (rye-bo-new-CLAY-ik) Complex molecules within cells that are concerned with the transcription of genetic information.

dendrites (DEN-drites) Branchlike extensions of the neuron's cell body that form the main sites for synapses.

microtubules (mike-ro-TUBE-yools) Tube-shaped proteins within the cell body and axon of neurons. Important in the transport of nutrients and other substances within the cell. Other similar structures are called *neurofilaments* and *microfilaments.*

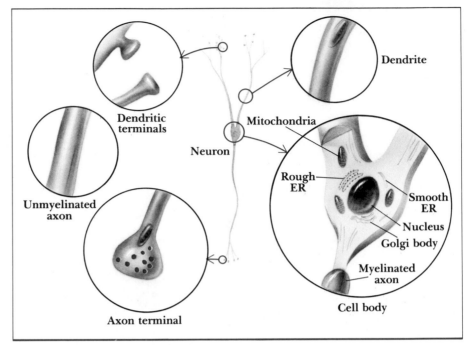

Figure 2.2 Diagrams of main parts of the neuron.
ER = endoplasmic reticulum (smooth or rough).

Figure 2.2 shows a representative vertebrate neuron. (Neurons of invertebrates usually do not have dendrites on the cell body. In invertebrates, the dendrites typically are more directly associated with the axon.) The neuron has several different parts. The cell body contains the **nucleus** and the apparatus for manufacturing most of the products the cell needs. This apparatus is found in the area just around the nucleus in the **endoplasmic reticulum (ER).** ER is made of membranes composed of lipid and proteins. (We shall discuss membrane structure in more detail shortly.) Associated with some of the ER are the **ribosomes,** complexes of proteins and **ribonucleic acid (RNA).** ER that has ribosomes associated with it is termed *rough ER;* ER without ribosomes is termed *smooth ER.*

Emerging from the cell body are the **dendrites** and the axon. The dendrites and cell body provide the main receptor sites for information coming to the neuron. Some neurons have dendrites studded with *dendritic spines* or *thorns* that contain synaptic sites (Figure 2.3). The axon is the output portion of the neuron and carries nerve impulses to the axon terminals. The junction of an axon terminal with another cell is known as a synapse. Axons often branch several times. Typically, there are many hundreds of axon terminals.

Microtubules, neurofilaments, and **microfilaments** are other important structures found in all parts of the neuron, including the dendrites and axon. These are all elongated proteins that guide the development of

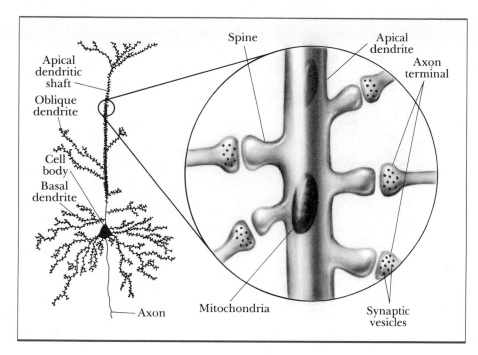

Figure 2.3 Drawing of a cortical neuron illustrating the dendritic spines. The spines can be seen magnified 30,000 to 40,000 times. Based on a Golgi stain preparation. *Bouton* is another term for *axon terminal*.

the cell and that help to form its structural support and transport cellular products. The size of each of these structures varies. Microtubules are the largest (20–30 nm in diameter), neurofilaments are next (10 nm in diameter), and microfilaments are the smallest (less than 10 nm in diameter). Other important cellular structures within the neuron are the **mitochondria,** which are important in providing energy for the cell, and the **Golgi body,** important in the cell's metabolism and in protein synthesis. The axon terminals enclose small vesicles that contain the neurotransmitter substance.

Glial Cells

The most numerous cells in the brain—amounting to many hundreds of billions—are satellite cells known as the *glial* cells, or **glia.** These cells are essential for the proper functioning of neurons and are important in the brain's response to injury. Several different types of glia, illustrated in Figure 2.4, have been classified.

One of the most important functions of glia is to produce the *myelin sheath* that surrounds the axons of many neurons. In the peripheral nervous system this myelin sheath is provided by the **Schwann cells.** During the development of the nervous system the Schwann cells wrap themselves around an axon. Each Schwann cell forms one section of the myelin sheath. Each section has a small space between it and the next section. These spaces—found in the brain, spinal cord, and peripheral nervous system—are called the **nodes of Ranvier,** after the French anatomist Louis-Antoine

mitochondria (my-toe-KON-dree-ah) Rod-shaped structures in cells. They are the principal sites of the generation of energy.

Golgi body (GOAL-gee) A series of membranes in the cell body important in the production of various substances. Synonymous term is *Golgi complex*.

glia (glee-ah); also *neuroglia*. Glia are satellite cells that, along with neurons, make up the two main types of cells in the nervous system.

Schwann cell (Sshwan) An accessory cell that forms the myelin sheath around the axons of peripheral neurons.

nodes of Ranvier (Ron-vee-AY) Gaps in the myelin sheath in myelinated axons.

myelin (MY-a-lin) A fatty substance, actually the cell body of a satellite cell (either glial or Schwann cell) that provides the "insulation" around myelinated axons.

lipid (LI-pid) Fat molecules that are insoluble in water and thus can be extracted from tissue only with a fat solvent such as alcohol. One of the main constituents of living things, lipids form the basic matrix of cell membranes.

deoxyribonucleic acid (DNA). (de-Ox-e-rye-bo-new-CLAY-ik) The molecule that contains the genetic information in virtually all cells. The genetic code is constructed from combinations of the four bases—thymine, cytosine, adenine, and guanine.

nucleotide (NEW-klee-o-tide) One of the units of DNA, containing a sugar, phosphoric acid, and a base

base A substance capable of giving up electrons. There are four bases in DNA from which the genetic code is composed—thymine, cytosine, adenine, and guanine. In RNA there are also four bases—cytosine, adenine, guanine and uracil.

cytosine (SY-toe-seen) One of the bases in DNA.

guanine (GWA-neen) One of the bases in DNA.

adenine (ADD-i-neen) One of the bases in DNA.

thymine (THIGH-meen) One of the bases in DNA.

protein One of the basic types of molecules in living matter. Proteins are synthesized from amino acids.

amino acids Basic components of proteins.

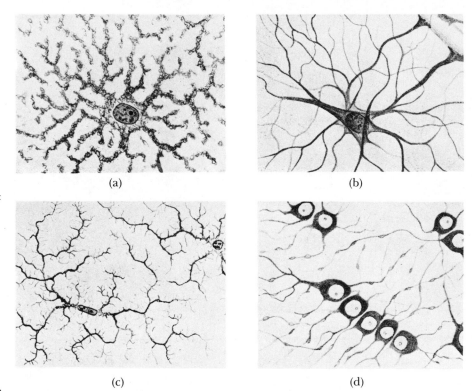

(a)   (b)

(c)   (d)

Figure 2.4   Drawings of the basic types of glial cells in the central nervous system.
(a) protoplasmic astrocyte; (b) fibrous astrocyte; (c) microglia; (d) oligodendroglia.

Ranvier (1835–1922), who first described them. At these nodes the nerve impulse is regenerated on its way to the axon terminals. Similar types of glial cells (although not called Schwann cells) form myelin within the brain and spinal cord.

The process of myelination takes several years to complete in humans. This myelination coincides with the gradual attainment of intellectual and motor skills by young children and partly accounts for them. **Myelin** is composed primarily of **lipids,** which are fatty substances that appear shiny white in unstained brains. Myelinated axons make up the "white matter" of the brain and spinal cord. By contrast, the "gray matter" is composed of the unmyelinated cell bodies and dendrites.

Myelination increases the speed with which nerve impulses can be carried in the axon. Normal myelination is crucial for proper timing and proper functioning of the brain. Such diseases as multiple sclerosis involve deterioration of the myelin sheath. In these diseases the damage to the myelin results in a loss of coordinated movements, sensory processing, and eventually, memory and other cognitive skills. Figure 2.6 (page 32) is an electron micrograph of myelinated axons in cross section.

A Genetic Library

Neurons, like virtually all animal cells, contain a variety of structures. Within the nucleus of the neuron is the **DNA (deoxyribonucleic acid)** containing the "library" of genetic information of the organism that governs growth, differentiation, and activity. Our understanding of the structure of DNA stems from the discovery by James Watson and Francis Crick in 1953 that DNA forms a double helix or spiral. The units of DNA are known as **nucleotides.** These nucleotides are attached to each other somewhat like rungs on a spiral ladder, giving the spiral helix shape to the DNA molecule. The individual rungs of the helix are formed by molecular attraction between those parts of the nucleotides known as **bases,** of which there are just four in DNA: **cytosine, guanine, adenine,** and **thymine.** In DNA, adenine is always attached to thymine and guanine is always linked to

cytosine, as shown in Figure 2.5.

The particular sequence in which these bases are attached in the DNA molecule forms the genetic code for that particular organism. This four-letter alphabet codes the information necessary for cells to produce the thousands of different **proteins** of which they are capable. Proteins form structural components of cells, and they serve as enzymes and other substances important for cell function. Proteins are composed of many **amino acids.** This code is transcribed ("read off") by another information molecule, messenger RNA (mRNA). The molecules of mRNA are then transported out of the nucleus. Together, the mRNA and other cellular structures in the cell body participate in protein synthesis. This process is true not only of neurons, but also of cells throughout the body.

Figure 2.5   Diagram of the DNA molecule.
The DNA is shown replicating at the right end. T = thymine; A = adenine;
G = guanine; C = cytosine.

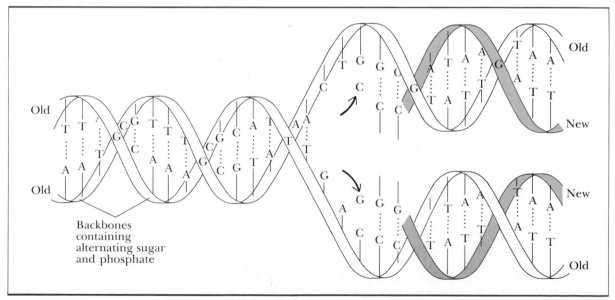

blood–brain barrier   A term given to the series of membranes and specialized capillaries that act as filters between the general circulation and the fluid that bathes the neurons.

cerebrospinal fluid (CSF) (sir-E-bro-spy-nal) Fluid in the ventricles and central canal of the central nervous system

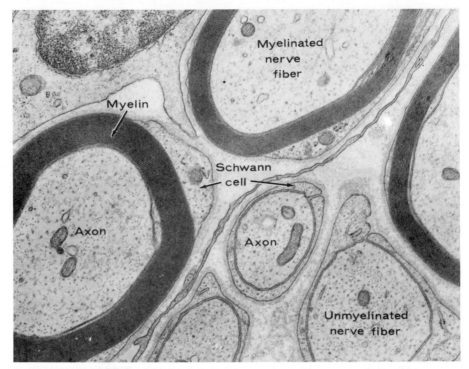

Figure 2.6   Electron micrograph of myelinated and unmyelinated axons, shown in cross section.

Glial cells are also important as metabolic "go-betweens" for the neurons, filtering out substances that might be harmful to the neurons, passing on nutrients such as glucose, and helping to rid the neurons of waste products. The filtering system, of which the glial cells are part, is known as the **blood–brain barrier.** The blood–brain barrier is formed primarily by a specialized type of capillary wall in the blood vessels that supply the brain. The cells that form these capillaries make very tight junctions with one another, preventing diffusion of most substances across the capillary wall. Actually, two cellular barriers exist in the brain, one between the blood and the fluid surrounding the neurons and glial cells (the blood–brain barrier) and another between the blood and the **cerebrospinal fluid (CSF),** termed the blood–CSF barrier. CSF is a clear fluid manufactured by specialized cells and secreted into the ventricles, which are the fluid-filled spaces in the brain. Substances in the CSF can enter more easily into the extracellular fluid immediately surrounding brain cells, but even this route is partially blocked by the cells that line the ventricles. Not all substances are prevented from passing from the blood to the neurons. Glucose, for example, is the main metabolic fuel for neurons and is granted easy access. Other substances have specialized systems to transport them between the blood and brain cells.

The Neuronal Membrane—A Fluid Mosaic

To understand how neurons generate the electrical signals that underlie mental activity, we must look more closely at the structure of the neuronal membrane. The cell membrane of neurons is very much like that of other animal cells, although certain specializations are found. Animal cell membranes are composed of a double layer of lipids, called a *bilayer,* to which are attached a variety of proteins. The particular mix of proteins associated with the lipid bilayer gives a region of membrane its particular properties. The lipid molecules are not tightly bound together, and the membrane is somewhat fluid. The lipid bilayer, together with its associated proteins, can thus be considered a *fluid mosaic.* Figure 2.7 illustrates one version of this fluid mosaic concept of the cell membrane. Actually, proteins have much more elaborate and defined shapes than can be easily illustrated. Often sugars are attached to the proteins that protrude from the membrane.

Lipids are self-organizing in a watery medium such as the brain. One end of each lipid molecule (the "head") is attracted to water molecules, whereas the other end (the "tail") is repelled by them. Because of these molecular interactions between water and lipid, the lipid molecules line up in rows with their heads nearest any available water molecules. The heads thus form the inner and outer surfaces of the membrane. The membrane is thus formed by two layers of lipids stacked tail to tail. The tails of the lipid molecules point away from any water molecules and form the middle of the bilayer. Because of the lipid composition of the membrane, water molecules and substances that are dissolved in water cannot penetrate through the lipid portion of the membrane. One important function of the transmembrane proteins is to form *channels* or passages through which certain substances can diffuse. The membrane is not uniform throughout the neuron. Special regions of membrane are formed by the insertion of different proteins, such as at the axon terminals, where the membrane is specialized for the release of the neurotransmitter, and on the receptor regions of the cell body and dendrites.

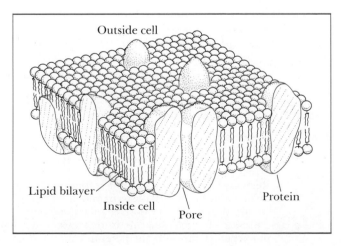

Figure 2.7 Schematic diagram of neuronal cell membrane.

ion (EYE-on) An electrically charged particle formed when a substance breaks apart or dissociates. The ions that are particularly important for neuronal signaling are Na^+, K^+, Cl^-, and Ca^{2+}.

cation (CAT-eye-on) Ion with one or more positive charges.

anion (AN-eye-on) Ion with one or more negative charges.

Electric Signaling by Neurons

How do neurons generate the nerve impulses that underlie behavior and mental activity? The answer lies in the ability of the neuronal membrane to generate and conduct electrical signals. These signals, in turn, release the chemical neurotransmitters from the axon terminals that influence the activity of other cells. The movement of **ions** across the neuronal membrane is important for both of these processes.

Several different kinds of ions occur in the brain, but four are particularly important for understanding the electrical signaling in neurons: sodium (Na^+), potassium (K^+), chloride (Cl^-), and calcium (Ca^{2+}). See Table 2.2. Inorganic ions such as these four are formed from the dissociation of molecules in a water-containing medium. Thus salt (NaCl) not only dissolves in water but *dissociates*, so that the sodium and chloride atoms move apart from each other, becoming electrically charged ions. This electrical charge occurs as the chloride ion carries with it one electron that had been shared with the sodium atom. This now gives the chloride ion one negative charge (Cl^-). The sodium ion, however, is missing one electron and thus carries a positive charge of 1 (Na^+).

Electrons are one of the fundamental constituents of matter. They carry one negative charge each. By convention, positive ions are also termed **cations,** because they are attracted to the negative pole of a battery, termed the *cathode*. Likewise, negative ions are also termed **anions,** because they are attracted to the positive pole of a battery, termed the anode. Na^+, Ca^{2+}, K^+, and Cl^- are not equally distributed on the two surfaces (inside and outside) of the neuronal membrane (see Figure 2.8, page 36). Since ions carry electrical charges, they attract and repel other ions, depending on the sign of the charges of the two ions. Specifically, cations always repel each other, as do anions ("like signs repel"), whereas anions and cations are attracted to each other ("opposite signs attract").

Our current understanding of how neurons produce signals is based on thousands of experiments conducted over the past 150 years. Several excellent accounts of nerve function are available, including those of Shepherd (1983) and Kandel and Schwartz (1985). For technical reasons much of this research has been done with neurons from a small number of species that offer such advantages as large size or ease of manipulation. The evidence suggests strongly, however, that the basic aspects of neuronal function are very similar across the entire animal kingdom.

TABLE 2.2 Some Ions Important for Nerve Activity

Ion	Importance
Na^+	Responsible for initiation of nerve impulse; involved in excitatory postsynaptic potentials
K^+	Responsible for restoration of resting potential during nerve impulse; involved in inhibitory postsynaptic potentials
Cl^-	Involved in inhibitory postsynaptic potentials
Ca^{2+}	Necessary for release of neurotransmitter at synapse; may be involved in excitatory postsynaptic potentials

Give the Squid the Prize?

The modern period of research on neurons rests primarily on the results of work by Andrew Hodgkin and Alan Huxley at Cambridge University in England. They worked extensively with the axon of the giant neuron from the squid. This particular neuron is one of the largest found in nature, with an axon of up to 1 mm in diameter. Because of its large size and the fact that it can survive for many hours if properly cared for, this neuron has been extremely useful in studying the properties of axons. Hodgkin and Huxley received Nobel prizes for their research in 1963, and Hodgkin subsequently acknowledged the importance of the squid neuron: "It is arguable that the introduction of the squid giant nerve fibre by J. Z. Young in 1936 did more for axonology than any other single advance during the last forty years. Indeed, a distinguished neurophysiologist remarked recently at a Congress dinner (not, I thought, with the utmost tact) 'It's the squid that really ought to be given the Nobel Prize.' " (Quoted in Kuffler and Nicholls, 1976.)

A squid.
The giant neuron of the squid has been invaluable in discovering the nature of the nerve impulse.

The Resting Potential

If they are treated properly, squid axons are rather forgiving. One can skewer them with recording micropipettes in such a way that the membrane seals itself around the micropipette, much as a self-sealing tire does around a nail. When this is done, as shown in Figure 2.9, an electrical voltage or potential can be measured across the membrane. This voltage, measured when the neuron is not actively producing a nerve impulse, is called the **resting potential.** The term *resting* is somewhat misleading, because neurons must continually expend metabolic energy to maintain this potential.

The resting potential in most neurons so far examined, from mollusks to monkeys, is between -40 and -90 mV, inside negative. Slightly more negative charges are spread over the inner surface of the axon membrane than on the outer surface. We shall use the giant axon of the squid as our example. The resting potential of this neuron is usually measured at about -60 mV. (The actual resting voltage depends on the exact conditions pre-

resting potential The electrical potential across the neuronal membrane when the neuron is not producing a nerve impulse.

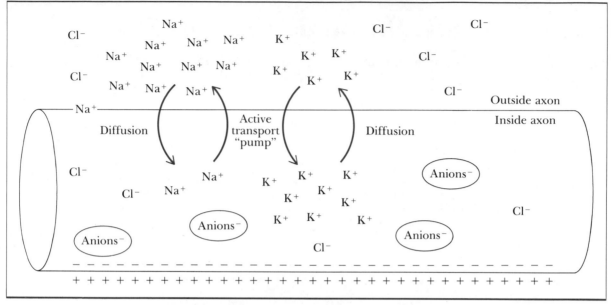

Figure 2.8   Diagram of axon segment of a neuron in resting state.
Sodium is being pumped out of the cell; potassium is being pumped in. The relative concentrations of the ions are represented, and the exact concentrations can be found in Table 2.3.

Figure 2.9   The micropipette and recording arrangement for recording from a neuron such as the giant neuron of the squid.

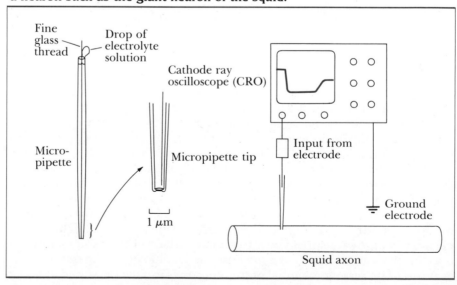

vailing in a particular experiment. The figure of -70 mV is also commonly used in textbooks.)

This resting potential can be thought of as similar to the voltage or potential energy that exists between the positive and negative poles of a storage battery before a conducting wire is placed between them. Just as an electrical current flows between the two poles of a battery when a conductor joins them, so too does current flow across the membrane if a conducting pathway is provided. Although wires are not involved in the normal functions of neurons, pathways for the flow of electrical current are important, as we shall see.

The current that flows across the neuronal membrane is *ionic current,* not a flow of electrons, as is true in the cable between the poles of a storage battery. Ionic current occurs when **ion channels** are opened across the membrane. This flow of current constitutes the *nerve impulse,* or *action potential.* Any reduction of the potential across the membrane toward zero is called **depolarization,** and any increase in the potential across the membrane is called **hyperpolarization.** Thus a change in membrane potential from -60 mV to -45 mV is depolarizing, while a change in membrane potential from -60 mV to -70 mV is hyperpolarizing. Depolarizations and hyperpolarizations are common events in the life of a neuron.

The resting potential reflects a balance of chemical and electrical forces that operate on those ions to which the membrane is permeable. Table 2.3 lists the main ions of the giant neuron of the squid, along with their concentrations inside and outside the cell. The concentration of these ions is expressed in millimoles per liter. (A millimole is 0.001 mole, which is the molecular weight of a particular element expressed in grams.) In Table 2.3 the symbol (A^-) stands for a collection of various large organic anions. Some of these anions are amino acids; others are proteins that carry one or more extra electrons. For our purposes the exact identity of the anions is unimportant. What is important is that they carry negative charge and that they are all located within the neuron, being too large to penetrate the membrane unless the membrane is ruptured. The other ions in the table are all small inorganic ions, Na^+, K^+, and Cl^-.

ion channels Passages in the neuronal membrane through which ions can pass under certain conditions.

depolarization A change in membrane voltage relative to the resting potential such that the new potential is less negative.

hyperpolarization A change in membrane voltage relative to the resting potential such that the new potential is more negative.

TABLE 2.3   Ionic Concentrations for the Giant Neuron of the Squid (Kandel and Schwartz, 1985)

Ion	Intracellular Concentration	Extracellular Concentration	Ratio (In/Out)	Equilibrium Potential
Na^+	50 mM	440 mM	1:9	$+55$ mV
K^+	400 mM	20 mM	20:1	-75 mV
Cl^-	52 mM	560 mM	1:11	-60 mV
(A^-)	385 mM			

voltage-gated ion channel
An ion channel whose
permeability to ions is
regulated by the voltage
across it.

**chemically gated ion chan-
nel**   An ion channel whose
permeability to one or
more ions is regulated by
the presence of certain
chemical substances such as
neurotransmitters.

Ion Channels

At rest, no net movement of the ions listed in Table 2.3 occurs. K^+ is 20
times more concentrated inside the neuron than in the extracellular fluid
immediately outside the neuron. On the other hand, Na^+ is nine times
more concentrated outside the neuron than inside. As we shall discuss
shortly, these imbalances in Na^+ and K^+ concentrations make it possible
for the neuron to generate signals. Ions are unable to pass directly through
the lipid bilayer. Under certain conditions, however, ions can and do pass
through special ion channels located throughout the membrane.

Ion channels may or may not be selective for particular ion species.
In the axon there appear to be channels that select either for Na^+ or for
K^+, but not for both. Elsewhere, in the dendrites, ion channels exist that
are not as selective and that allow the passage of both Na^+ and K^+ ions
under appropriate conditions.

Ion channels have more than one configuration. The proteins that
compose these channels can change their shape and thus alter the operating characteristics of the channels. Moreover, this change in configuration can be accomplished in a fraction of a millisecond. Most channels have
only two configurations, open and shut, but the Na^+ channels have a third
configuration, termed *inactivated.* The difference between shut and inactivated channels will be discussed shortly.

Ion channel configuration is controlled either by changes in the voltage
across the membrane or by certain chemical substances that interact with
the channel protein. The ion channels in the axon are regulated by voltage,
or **voltage-gated,** whereas both voltage-gated and **chemically gated** ion
channels are common in the dendrites.

Different types of ion channels differ in size as well as in their permeability to various ions. For example, one type of chemically gated ion channel that is activated by acetylcholine (a neurotransmitter discussed later in
this chapter) passes both Na^+ and K^+ ions when open. This is a type of
ion channel found on many muscle cells. These ion channels are rather
large in comparison with those ion channels in the axon that are selective
for Na^+, or those that are selective for K^+. In fact, even these two types
of voltage-gated ion channels are of different size, the K^+ channels being
smaller in area than the Na^+ channels.

Ion channels also differ in their response to various chemicals. Some
drugs may block voltage-gated Na^+ channels in the axon and have no effect
on the passage of Na^+ ions at chemically gated ion channels that are
permeable to Na^+ ions. For example, the poison found in the puffer fish
(see next paragraph) binds to and blocks the voltage-gated Na^+ channels
in the axon, but does not block the entry of Na^+ ions at chemically gated
channels.

Ion channels are scattered throughout the membrane, with concentrations that vary from one region to another. Myelinated axons contain
many channels at nodes and few in the internodal regions. Ion channels

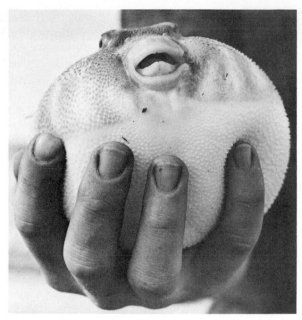

The tasty but sometimes deadly pufferfish.
The pufferfish contains the sodium channel blocking agent tetrodotoxin, which, if not carefully removed by the chef, can result in death to anyone
eating the fish.

are too small to be directly visualized with current techniques, but indirect
ways have been used to evaluate their density. For example, the chemical
tetrodotoxin (TTX) has been found to bind specifically to the part of the
protein that forms the outer surface of the Na^+ channel. Using techniques
that measure the amount of tetrodotoxin present in a given region of axon,
it has been found that there are in the squid giant axon an average 100–600
Na^+ channels per μm^2 of axon surface (Shepherd, 1983). (Incidentally,
although tetrodotoxin is a useful chemical in the laboratory, it can present
problems in real life. Certain animals, such as the puffer fish, considered
a great delicacy in Japan and elsewhere, contain it in large quantities. If
the puffer fish is not prepared properly to remove the TTX, it can be a
delicious but fatal meal, since the TTX binds to the Na^+ channels of the
diner, paralyzing many nerves, including those controlling breathing!)

tetrodotoxin (TTX) (te-
TRO-doe-TOK-sin) A sub-
stance found in a few animal species such as the
puffer fish. TTX selectively
blocks the Na^+ channels in
the neuronal membrane.

Electrical and Chemical Gradients

The resting potential results from the electrical and chemical forces that
operate on the ions to which the membrane is permeable. Let us consider
the two most important ions, Na^+ and K^+, separately. At rest, most of the
Na^+ channels in the axon are shut, but enough channels open from time

$Na^+–K^+$ pump (sodium–potassium pump)
An enzyme that causes the active transport or "pumping" of Na^+ and K^+ ions across the membrane from regions of lower concentration to regions of higher concentrations.

to time that there is a steady trickle of Na^+ ions into the axon. This fact raises several questions, including why the Na^+ leaks *into* the axon. Two physical forces, resulting from the electrical and chemical gradients that exist across the cell membrane, place an inward-driving pressure on the Na^+ ions.

Because there is a net negative charge on the inside of the membrane, an *electrical gradient* across the membrane exists that attracts all cations such as Na^+ to the interior of the neuron. Thus if an open Na^+ channel is available, Na^+ ions cross the membrane to the inside, attracted by this negative charge.

The second physical force operating on the ions on either side of the membrane is due to the *concentration gradient* for each ion. This concentration gradient is due to the difference in the concentration of the ions inside and outside the cell. Ions that in a solution are free to move will eventually distribute themselves equally throughout the solution, diffusing from regions of higher concentration to regions of lower concentration.

The situation for K^+ ions is slightly different. Some K^+ channels are open when the neuron is at rest. In fact, it is about 100 times easier for K^+ to cross the membrane during the resting state than is true for Na^+. Since K^+ is in greater concentration inside than outside, the concentration gradient forces K^+ to the outside. However, the electrical gradient drives K^+ ions back into the cell. The net result of these two conflicting forces is a slight outward leakage of K^+ during the resting state.

The Sodium–Potassium Pump

If not counteracted in some way, these steady leaks of Na^+ and K^+ would result in ion concentrations very different from those listed in Table 2.3. The counteracting force that maintains the ion concentrations seen in Table 2.3 is a metabolic process known as $Na^+–K^+$ pumping. Many ion pumps are present in the membrane of a typical neuron. They are made of proteins and found throughout the membrane in concentrations of from 100 to $1000/\mu m^2$. The average neuron may have over 1 million **$Na^+–K^+$ pumps**, capable of pumping several million ions each second (Stevens, 1979). Such pumps are not unique to neurons. All animal cells contain them, and several different varieties exist. One type pumps Na^+ ions back outside the cell and recaptures K^+ ions, forcing them back inside. The resting state of the neuron is the result of electrical forces, chemical forces, and active metabolic pumping of those ions, particularly Na^+ and K^+, to which the membrane is permeable. The $Na^+–K^+$ pumps use about 20 percent of the cell's available energy. Neurons work very hard to stay at rest!

What about the other two ion species listed in Table 2.3, Cl^- and (A^-)? The (A^-) ions cannot penetrate the membrane, because none of the channels are big enough for them to pass through. The Cl^- ions do have channels and are subject to both electrical and chemical gradients. Because the Cl^- ions are negatively charged, the electrical gradient at rest exerts an outward driving force on Cl^-. However, the concentration of Cl^- outside is greater and the concentration gradient opposes the electrical gradient, forcing the Cl⁻ ions back inside the cell. In the squid axon these two forces are evenly balanced when the voltage across the membrane is at −60 mV. At rest, then, no net movement of Cl⁻ ions takes place across the membrane. The voltage across the membrane at which there is no net movement of an ion species, even if open channels are available, is called the **equilibrium potential** for that ion species. In the giant neuron of the squid the equilibrium potential for Cl⁻ is about −60 mV, exactly coinciding with the resting potential.

The Nernst Equation: Predicting Equilibrium Potentials

We have determined that Cl⁻ is at equilibrium at a membrane voltage of −60 mV. Is there also some voltage at which Na⁺ would be at equilibrium? How about K⁺? Yes, there is some equilibrium potential for each ion to which the membrane is permeable. In 1897 Walter Nernst, a German chemist, published an equation that has been adapted so that it is possible to calculate the membrane voltage at which any ion will be at equilibrium for any given concentration difference across a membrane permeable to that ion. The simplest form of this **Nernst equation** is

$$E_{ion} = 58 \log \frac{[ion]_{out}}{[ion]_{in}} \, mV$$

where E_{ion} is the equilibrium potential, $[ion]_{out}$ specifies the concentrations of the ion outside the membrane, and $[ion]_{in}$ specifies the concentration inside a permeable membrane. The number 58 is a constant derived from several physical variables. This form of the Nernst equation is for ions carrying positive charge. For negatively charged ions, the constant is −58 rather than +58. If we insert the numbers for ionic concentrations from Table 2-3, we can calculate the equilibrium potential for each ion. For example, using the figures for K⁺, we find:

$$E_{K^+} = 58 \log \frac{20}{400} = -75 \, mV$$

Thus at a membrane potential of −75 mV, K⁺ would be at equilibrium. The inward-driving force due to the electrical gradient would balance the outward-driving force exactly because of the difference in K⁺ concentrations inside and outside the neuron. Therefore no net movement of K⁺ at −75 mV would result.

Likewise, using the Na⁺ concentrations from Table 2-3, we obtain:

$$E_{Na^+} = 58 \log \frac{440}{50} \, mV = +55 \, mV$$

For Na⁺ to be at equilibrium the voltage across the membrane would have to change by 115 mV from rest, from −60 to +55 mV. Thus at the

equilibrium potential   See *Nernst equation.*

Nernst equation   An equation based on the work of Walter Nernst, a German chemist. The Nernst equation allows for the calculation of the membrane voltage that would exist, given the internal and external concentrations of a particular ion, assuming the ion is free to move across the membrane. That membrane voltage is called the *equilibrium potential* for that ion.

resting potential of -60 mV, a much greater total "driving force" is exerted on Na^+ than on K^+. However, since most of the Na^+ channels are shut during the resting stage, the Na^+ ions cannot approach their equilibrium potential. But if Na^+ channels were suddenly to open, the inward rush of Na^+ would quickly approach the Na^+ equilibrium potential of $+55$ mV. *In fact, it is precisely a sudden opening of the sodium channels that starts the nerve impulse.*

Table 2.3 gives the equilibrium potentials for Na^+, K^+, and Cl^-, calculated with the Nernst equation. There is no equilibrium potential for (A^-), since the membrane is not permeable to these ions under normal conditions.

The Nerve Impulse

The fact that neurons generate and conduct electrical signals has been known for over a century, but only in the past 40 years have we come to understand the ionic movements underlying nerve impulses. Figure 2.10 shows a graphic representation of a nerve impulse. The nerve impulse is a reversal of the resting potential, such that the voltage inside the mem-

Figure 2.10 A nerve impulse as it would be recorded with one electrode (micropipette) inside the axon and the other just outside the membrane.

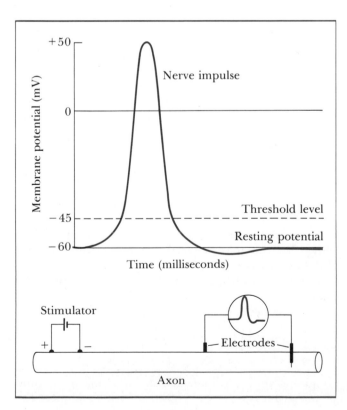

brane changes from −60 to approximately +50 mV. The exact size (amplitude) of the nerve impulse depends on that particular neuron and the recording conditions. A nerve impulse does not occur at the same time in all parts of a neuron. It starts in a particular region of the cell, termed the **spike-initiating region**. (*Spike* is another term for nerve impulse.) For example, in the motor neuron of the cat's spinal cord, the spike-initiating region is located just where the cell body tapers into the axon. In some very large neurons a "booster" region may exist in addition to the main spike-initiating region. Once a nerve impulse is initiated, it travels rapidly down the axon to the axon terminals, as well as "backfiring" into the cell body.

spike-initiating region
The part of the neuron that has the lowest threshold for producing a nerve impulse.

Changes in Na⁺ and K⁺ Permeability Underlie the Nerve Impulse

The basic events that underlie the nerve impulse were discovered by Alan Hodgkin and Andrew Huxley (Hodgkin and Huxley, 1952; Hodgkin, 1964). Nerve impulses result from a sudden increase in the permeability of the membrane, first to Na⁺ ions and then to K⁺ ions. The increase in Na⁺ permeability allows an inrush of Na⁺ ions, which moves the membrane voltage toward the equilibrium potential for Na⁺ (+55 mV). Then the Na+ channels are suddenly inactivated, and an increased permeability to K⁺ ions allows K⁺ ions to flow out, bringing the membrane voltage back toward the equilibrium potential for K⁺ (−75 mV). The movement of these two ion species thus accounts remarkably well for the voltage changes observed during the nerve impulse. Figure 2.11 shows the now classic sum-

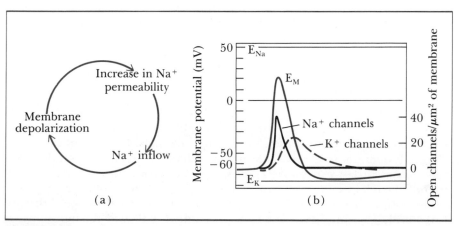

Figure 2.11
(a) Relationships among membrane depolarization, increase in the membrane's permeability to Na⁺, and Na⁺ inflow. (b) Relationship between voltage across the membrane (E_M) and the number of open Na⁺ and K⁺ channels/μm² of membrane. These relationships summarize the Hodgkin–Huxley model of the nerve impulse. E_{Na} = equilibrium potential for Na⁺; E_K = equilibrium potential for K⁺; E_M = membrane potential.

sodium inactivation A process in which the membrane becomes impermeable to Na⁺ ions due to change in shape of proteins associated with the inner surface of Na⁺ channels. Occurs with depolarization.

mary graph of Hodgkin and Huxley concerning these permeability changes and their relationship to the nerve impulse.

Under natural conditions input from other cells causes nerve impulses, but in the laboratory a convenient way to produce them is to pass current through the membrane. Various techniques are available for this, one of the most widely used of which is to inject positive ions (K^+, for example) into the cell through small glass micropipettes. Adding positive charge to the inside of the membrane partially depolarizes the membrane, bringing about the critical change necessary to produce a nerve impulse. This change is the increase in Na^+ permeability that occurs because the Na^+ channels in the membrane are voltage gated. The Na^+ channels open in response to depolarization. With depolarization the proteins forming the Na^+ channels change their configuration from shut to open. Na^+ can then flow into the cell in accordance with both its chemical and electrical gradients. An additional positive charge carried by the Na^+ ions is thus placed on the inside of the membrane, opening still more Na^+ channels until, very briefly, Na^+ can enter the neuron with almost no resistance.

Why doesn't the inrush of Na^+ cause the membrane voltage to reach the Na^+ equilibrium potential of $+55$ mV inside, instead of falling some 5 mV short? The answer seems to be that depolarization starts a process known as **sodium inactivation.** As the interior of the membrane becomes more positive due to the inward Na^+ current, proteins associated with the inner surface of the Na^+ channel undergo a conformational change which gradually inactivates these channels, causing them to become impermeable to Na^+ ions. This inactivated state outlasts the nerve impulse and is responsible for the absolute refractory period discussed later in this chapter. The actual number of Na^+ ions required to produce a nerve impulse is surprisingly small. For example, the squid axon needs only about 0.002 percent of the available Na^+ ions in the immediately surrounding extracellular fluid to produce one nerve impulse.

Restoration of the Resting Potential

The K^+ channels are also voltage gated, and depolarization also increases their permeability. However, the operating characteristics of the K^+ channels are different from those for the Na^+ channels. For example, the K^+ channels open more slowly than the Na^+ channels. As they open, K^+ ions move in accordance with the chemical and electrical forces operating on them. The K^+ ions flow outward. As the interior of the membrane becomes more positive because of the incoming Na^+, the outward electrical driving force on K^+ becomes even stronger. The outward flow of K^+ ions opposes the inward flow of the Na^+ ions, but initially, the inward Na^+ rush is much stronger. However, once sodium channels close, the outflow of the K^+ ions begins to return the membrane voltage to the K^+ equilibrium of -75 mV.

Still another difference between the effect of depolarization on the Na^+ and K^+ channels is that there is no process parallel to Na^+ inactivation for K^+. The K^+ channels remain open until the membrane voltage returns

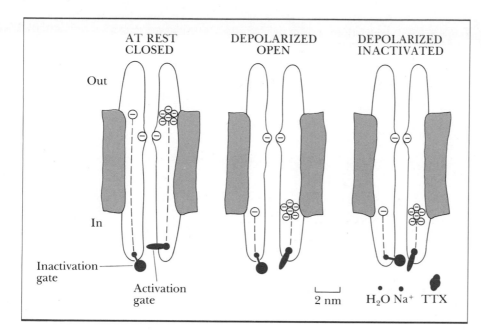

Figure 2.12 Voltage-gated Na$^+$ channels in their three configurations. Relative sizes of water molecule, hydrated Na$^+$ ion, and TTX molecule drawn approximately to scale. Na$^+$ ions are *hydrated* (surrounded by water molecules in a fluid environment).

to the resting voltage. The increase in permeability lasts longer for K$^+$ than for Na$^+$. In the squid axon the K$^+$ channels stay open about 2 msec longer than the Na$^+$ channels. During these 2 msec K$^+$ continues to flow out, but Na$^+$ ions are unable to flow in either direction. As the Nernst equation predicts, K$^+$ continues to move out of the neuron until the channels shut or until the K$^+$ equilibrium of -75 mV is reached. This K$^+$ outflow thus restores the membrane voltage to its resting level.

To summarize, depolarization initiates the nerve impulse and causes the Na$^+$ channels to open. As Na$^+$ rushes in along its electrical and concentration gradients, it reverses the membrane potential. As the interior of the membrane becomes increasingly positive, a second change in configuration occurs, inactivating the Na$^+$ channels and stopping any additional Na$^+$ flow across the membrane. After the nerve impulse ends, excess Na$^+$ ions are pumped out of the neuron. The Na$^+$ inactivation and the continued outward movement of K$^+$ restore the resting potential. In the Hodgkin–Huxley theory of the nerve impulse, no other ions are necessary to explain the voltage changes, although subsequent research has uncovered many additional facts concerning ionic movements during the nerve impulse. The work of Hodgkin and Huxley provided the foundation for this subsequent research (Shepherd, 1983).

Propagation of the Nerve Impulse

The Na$^+$ ions that enter the neuron during a nerve impulse also spread depolarizing current to regions of the axon near their point of entry, setting

**Figure 2.13
Propagation of the
nerve impulse in an
unmyelinated axon.**
The impulse is a travel-
ing wave of ionic cur-
rent produced by Na$^+$
inflow, followed by K$^+$
outflow.

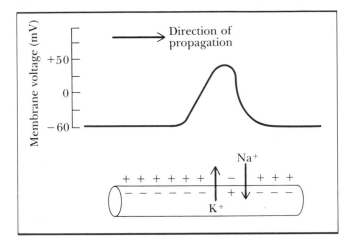

saltatory conduction
(SOL-ta-tor-ee) Conduction
of the nerve impulse in
myelinated axons. The im-
pulse jumps from node to
node, skipping the internodal regions.

up local currents. These local currents depend only on the physical properties of the membrane as a conductor, not on the opening of any ion
channels. However, they spread sufficient depolarization in both directions
from the site of impulse initiation to open other voltage-gated Na$^+$ channels in the vicinity. This process allows the impulse to spread in all directions from its point of origin as a traveling wave of inward Na$^+$ current
immediately followed by a wave of outward K$^+$ current, as illustrated in
Figure 2.13. In unmyelinated axons this is how the nerve impulse propa-
gates down the axon to the axon terminals. The rate at which a nerve
impulse proceeds varies in unmyelinated neurons with the diameter of the
axon. The larger the axon diameter, the faster the conduction speed. In
warm-blooded animals propagation speeds vary from less than 1 m/sec to
30–40 m/sec. In myelinated axons conduction speeds can reach 120 m/sec.

Figures 2.14 and 2.15 show myelinated neurons. The individual Schwann
cells that form the internodal regions of myelin serve as barriers to the
ionic currents. In addition, very few Na$^+$ and K$^+$ channels exist in the
internodal regions of the axon. At the nodes, however, both Na$^+$ and K$^+$
voltage-gated channels pack the membrane. The sciatic nerve of the rabbit
has about 25 Na$^+$ channels/μm^2 in the internodal regions, compared with
about 12,000 Na$^+$ channels/μm^2 at the nodes (Roots, 1984). The impulse
occurs at the nodes on its way down the axon of myelinated neurons.
Skipping the internodal segments causes the overall conduction velocity to
increase, as the opening of the Na$^+$ and K$^+$ channels takes some time.
When the impulse can jump from node to node, it can reach the axon
terminals faster than it can in unmyelinated axons of the same diameter.
This type of conduction in the myelinated axons is called **saltatory conduction** (from the Latin *saltare*, meaning "to jump or dance.") (Saltatory
transmission proceeds like an express train, traveling rapidly from its origin
to its destination without stopping. Transmission in unmyelinated axons,
on the other hand, would proceed in the manner of a local train.)

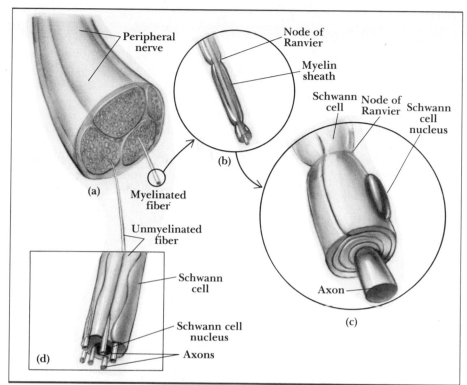

Figure 2.14 Drawings of peripheral nerve constructed from information revealed by light and electron microscopy.
(a) Myelinated nerve fiber extending out of a peripheral nerve (light microscope). (b) Myelinated nerve fiber (light microscope). (c) Myelinated nerve fiber (electron microscope).
(d) Several unmyelinated axons ensheathed by one Schwann cell (electron microscope).

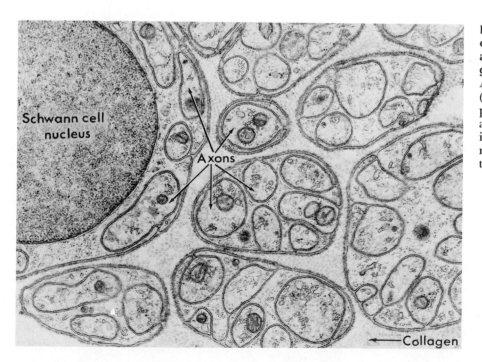

Figure 2.15 An electron micrograph of a lightly myelinated group of axons.
A single Schwann cell (nucleus shown in upper left) wraps itself around several different individual axons. Magnified about 25,000 times.

threshold The level of depolarization required to initiate a nerve impulse some percentage of the time (e.g., 50 percent).

all-or-none law The law that states that a nerve impulse either occurs or doesn't. When it does occur, it is of a fixed amplitude. This law does not hold for synaptic potentials.

absolute refractory period The time immediately following a nerve impulse during which a second impulse cannot be initiated at that site. Due to Na^+ inactivation.

relative refractory period The time following the absolute refractory period when another nerve impulse can be produced only if the second stimulus is of suprathreshold intensity. Due to combination of continued K^+ outward current and residual Na^+ inactivation.

Threshold

Some minimal depolarization is necessary to open the Na^+ and K^+ voltage-gated channels in the axon. The cat motor neuron, for example, needs about 15 mV. By convention, the level of depolarization required to produce a nerve impulse 50 percent of the time is termed the **threshold** for that neuron. Greater depolarizations increase the probability that the neuron will fire. Smaller depolarizations tend to produce only local currents that die out without generating an impulse. When a nerve impulse is generated, it produces more than enough depolarization (110 mV or so) to open the Na^+ and K^+ channels in adjacent sections of the axon, allowing the impulse to spread from the site of initiation. The spike-initiating region of the cell is that area of membrane that requires the least depolarization to produce a nerve impulse.

All-or-None Law

Once an impulse is generated, the amplitude of that impulse is constant for a given neuron. The amplitude of the impulse results not from the strength of the stimulus or from how the impulse was initiated, but from the characteristics of the particular neuron. Either a nerve impulse occurs at full strength or it does not occur at all. This fact is referred to as the **all-or-none-law**, which applies only to the axon, not to the kinds of potentials that occur at synapses, as we see later in this chapter.

The Frequency-Intensity Code

If impulses in a given nerve are of constant size, you may wonder how the nervous system can tell differences in the strengths of various stimuli. For example, how can we detect differences in the loudness of a tone at a particular pitch? The answer to such questions is complex, but part of the answer is that neurons can code for the intensity of the stimulus by firing more rapidly. However, because of the *refractory periods* of a neuron, a definite limit exists to the number of impulses that a neuron can produce in a given period. During these refractory periods, when the Na^+ channels are in the inactivated condition, no Na^+ can flow across the membrane; therefore no impulse can be generated. In the giant axon of the squid, Na^+ inactivation lasts about 1 msec. This time during which it is impossible to generate another impulse is termed the **absolute refractory period**. The absolute refractory period places a rigid limit on the frequency with which nerve impulses can be generated. In the squid axon an absolute refractory period of 1 msec imposes an upper limit of 1000 impulses/sec on that neuron.

Following the absolute refractory period is another period known as the **relative refractory period**, when impulses can be initiated only if the stimulus is quite strong. The relative refractory period occurs because the

K$^+$ channels are open, so that positive charge is being carried out, and because some of the Na$^+$ channels are still in the inactivated state. A strong stimulus can encroach on the relative refractory period and thus approach the upper limit of firing imposed by the absolute refractory period.

Synaptic Transmission

As the nerve impulse invades the axon terminals it initiates a series of events that allow the neuron to communicate with other cells. These other cells may be muscle cells, gland cells, or other neurons. Most neurons communicate only with other neurons. The junctions between the axon terminals of one neuron and the dendrites, cell body, or axon of another neuron are called synapses. Two types of synapses are found, electrical and chemical. At electrical synapses the impulse in the transmitting neuron is transferred to the next neuron through special channels that line up with one another, allowing for the passage of ionic current with very little signal loss. Electrical synapses are rather uncommon in nature, and chemical synapses are more prevalent throughout the animal kingdom. In discussions of synaptic events the neurons that are responsible for transmitting either chemical or electrical signals are termed *presynaptic* neurons, whereas the receiving neurons are called *postsynaptic* neurons. In reality, of course, virtually all neurons are both pre- and postsynaptic with respect to other neurons.

Chemical Synapses

Understanding chemical synaptic transmission is crucial to understanding both the way in which the brain works and normal and abnormal behavior. Most psychoactive drugs work by interacting with a component of chemical synapses in the brain, and many emotional disorders, such as depression and schizophrenia, are believed to involve abnormalities of chemical synaptic transmission. (Chapter 15 discusses these ideas in greater detail.) Figure 2.16 illustrates the main parts of a chemical synapse. Figure 2.17 shows an electron micrograph of a chemical synapse on a dendritic thorn.

The presynaptic terminal can take several shapes, but it is often a rounded enlargement of the axon. Within the terminal are *synaptic* **vesicles** that contain the neurotransmitter. Several different **neurotransmitters** are known and evidence for still other chemical transmitters is regularly published (see, for example, Schmitt, 1984). Moreover, many chemical substances occur naturally in the body and can influence neurons. Not all, however, are true neurotransmitters. Barchas et al. (1978) suggest that the term *neurotransmitter* be reserved for the compounds that "convey information between adjacent nerve cells." Those compounds that "amplify or dampen neuronal activity," such as some of the hormones, they suggest, should be called **neuromodulators**. Both neuromodulators and neurotrans-

vesicle (VESS-ik-ul) One of the small, round structures in the axonal end feet that contain the neurotransmitter.

neurotransmitter Chemical substance manufactured, stored, and released by neurons. Neurotransmitters are the messenger chemicals between neurons at chemical synapses.

neuromodulator Chemical substance that amplifies or dampens neuronal activity but is not strictly a neurotransmitter.

neuroregulator Any substance that affects neuronal activity. Includes both neurotransmitters and neuromodulators.

postsynaptic receptors Molecules on the postsynaptic side of a synapse that bind the neurotransmitter.

synaptic cleft The small space between the presynaptic end foot and the postsynaptic receptor site.

axodendritic synapses (AKS-o-den-DRIT-ik) Synapses on the dendrites of the postsynaptic neuron.

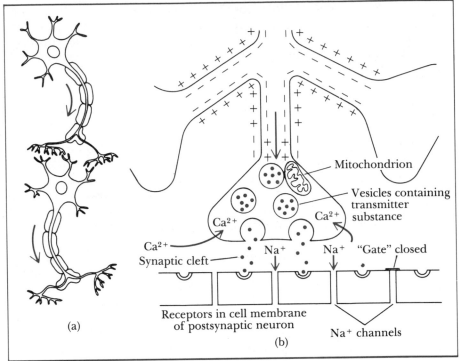

Figure 2.16 Transmission at a chemical synapse.
(a) Transmission is often (but not always) from axon terminals of the presynaptic neuron to the dendrites and cell body of the postsynaptic neuron. (b) The neurotransmitter is released by the entry of Ca^{2+} into the presynaptic end foot. The vesicles open up and release the neurotransmitter into the synaptic cleft, where it diffuses across and binds with the postsynaptic receptors. This results in the opening of chemically gated ion channels in the postsynaptic membrane (here they are Na^+ channels).

mitters belong to the larger class of **neuroregulators**. Table 2.4 lists the generally accepted neurotransmitters and some of the probable ones in vertebrate nervous systems. Neurotransmitters come from various chemical families, including the biogenic amines that contain an amine (NH_2) group, modified amino acids, and polypeptides. Polypeptides are composed of two or more amino acids.

The presynaptic terminals are aligned directly opposite a specialized region of the membrane on the postsynaptic neuron containing the **postsynaptic receptors**. These receptors are proteins formed into shapes that offer attachment sites for the neurotransmitter. Between the presynaptic terminal and the postsynaptic receptive site is the **synaptic cleft**, a space of 20–30 nm. The synapse has three basic components—the presynaptic ending, the cleft, and the postsynaptic receptive site. Synapses can be formed between axon terminals and various portions of the postsynaptic neuron. Synapses that end on the dendrites are termed **axodendritic synapses**.

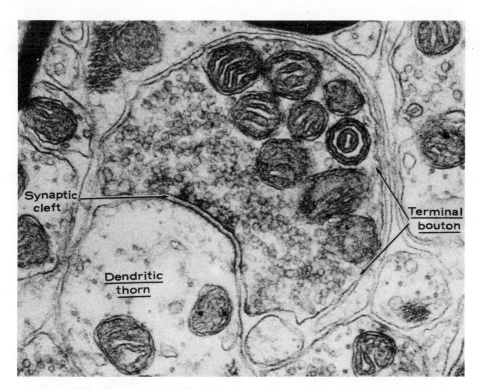

Figure 2.17 An electron micrograph of a chemical synapse showing terminal bouton ending on a dendritic thorn or spine.

TABLE 2.4   Generally Accepted and Probable Neurotransmitters

Generally accepted as neurotransmitters
    Acetylcholine
    Biogenic amines
        Norepinephrine (noradrenalin)
        Epinephrine (adrenalin)
        Dopamine
        Serotonin
        Histamine
    Amino acids or their derivatives
        Gamma-aminobutyric acid (GABA)
        Glutamate
        Glycine
        Aspartate
    Luteinizing hormone releasing hormone (LHRH)
Probable transmitters (supportive evidence exists; list not exhaustive)
    Substance P
    β-endorphin
    Oxytocin
    Vasopressin
    Somatostatin
    TRF (thyrotropin releasing factor)
    Taurine
    Met-enkephalin
    Leu-enkephalin
    Cholecystokinin
    Vasoactive intestinal hormone (VIP)

axoaxonic synapses
(AKS-o-ax-ON-ik) Synapses
on the axonal end feet of
the postsynaptic neuron.

axosomatic synapses
(AKS-o-som-a-tik) Synapses
on the soma (cell body) of
the postsynaptic neuron.

agonist (AG-o-nist) A substance that mimics the action of a naturally occurring neurotransmitter.

antagonist A substance
that blocks the action of a
neurotransmitter.

Other types of synapses include **axoaxonic** (from axon terminal to a receptive site on the postsynaptic axon), **axosomatic** (axon terminal to postsynaptic cell body), and even dendrodendritic (dendrite containing synaptic
vesicles to postsynaptic dendrite receptive site).

Chemically Gated Ion Channels

The sequence of events at a chemical synapse begins with the arrival of
the nerve impulse at the presynaptic terminal. This causes the release of
packets of neurotransmitter from the vesicles into the synaptic cleft. The
neurotransmitter then diffuses across the cleft and binds with receptive
sites on the postsynaptic membrane. This, in turn, opens ion channels in
the postsynaptic neuron for one or more ion species, allowing these ions
to move in or out of the postsynaptic cell. The direction of ion flow is
dictated by the existing electrical and chemical gradients for those ion species. Thus these ion channels, unlike those in the axon, are not voltage
gated, but *chemically gated*. Applying voltage to them has no effect, nor does
applying neurotransmitter to the voltage-gated ion channels in the axon.

Agonists and Antagonists

The neurotransmitter and receptor molecules fit with each other in a lock-
and-key arrangement. These fits are specific but not unique. Other chemicals in addition to the neurotransmitter can bind to the postsynaptic receptor. Such substances can either "jam the lock," blocking normal synaptic
transmission, mimic the effects of the natural transmitter, or prolong the
normal duration of synaptic activity. Substances that bind to the receptor
and that have biological actions similar to those of a naturally occurring
transmitter are termed **agonists** for that transmitter. Substances that bind
to the receptor molecule but that do not produce the normal postsynaptic
effects block normal synaptic transmission and are termed **antagonists**.
Many drugs that have an effect on the nervous system can be classified as
either agonists or antagonists for one or more transmitters.

Drugs and other chemicals can influence events at the synapse in many
different ways. Drugs can inhibit the synthesis of the neurotransmitter,
interfere with its storage in the vesicles, interfere with or accelerate the
release process, and interfere with the destruction of the transmitter or
with its uptake. Many drugs have more than one effect at a synapse. Drugs
may be selective, affecting only one type of neurotransmitter, or more
general, influencing chemical transmission at several different types of synapses. For added detail on these topics see Cooper et al. (1986). Often a
drug that can influence chemical synaptic transmission does so by either
increasing or decreasing the amount of neurotransmitter available in the
synaptic cleft. Table 2.5 lists a few of the more common drugs known to
affect synaptic transmission. The field of *psychopharmacology* deals largely
with the effects of drugs at chemical synapses.

TABLE 2.5   Some Drugs Affecting Chemical Transmission

Neurotransmitter	Drugs Increasing Availability of Neurotransmitter at Synapse	Drugs Decreasing Availability of Neurotransmitter at Synapse
Norepinephrine	Amphetamine	Reserpine
	Tri-cyclic antidepressants	Alpha-methyltyrosine
Dopamine	Apomorphine	Reserpine
	Amphetamine	Chlorpromazine
	Cocaine	
Serotonin	Iproniazid	Reserpine
Acetylcholine	Physostigmine	Atropine (muscarinic)
		Curare (nicotinic)
GABA	Muscimol	Bicuculline
		Picrotoxin

Importance of Ca²⁺ for Transmitter Release

In addition to Na^+ and K^+ channels, the axon terminals contain channels for Ca^{2+} ions. These Ca^{2+} channels are voltage gated and are opened by the invasion of the axon terminals by the nerve impulse. Ca^{2+} then rushes *into* the axon terminals, propelled by electrical and chemical gradients similar to those operating on Na^+. The inrush of Ca^{2+} causes the release of the neurotransmitter. If Ca^{2+} is removed from the fluid surrounding the terminals (which can be done in the laboratory), the nerve impulse will not release neurotransmitter from the terminals. If Ca^{2+} is restored to the fluid bathing the neuron, normal neurotransmitter release resumes. Similarly, Ca^{2+} injected directly into the axon terminals, even in the absence of any nerve impulse, will release neurotransmitter from the terminal. The major importance of the nerve impulse in the presynaptic terminal is to open the Ca^{2+} ion channels and thus bring about neurotransmitter release (Llinas, 1982).

It is not yet known just how the entry of Ca^{2+} causes the synaptic vesicles to release the neurotransmitter. One hypothesis is that there is some Ca^{2+}-activated contractile mechanism present in the terminals that moves the vesicles toward the cleft. Evidence suggests that the membrane of the vesicles then actually merges with the membrane of the terminal, forming a pocket with the open side facing into the cleft. The neurotransmitter is then released into the cleft. This process is known as **exocytosis**.

exocytosis (ex-o-cy-TOE-sis) The release of a substance from a cell through merger of a vesicle with the cell membrane.

Postsynaptic Potentials

The ionic currents produced by the interaction of the neurotransmitter and the postsynaptic receptor are carried in part by ions. Na^+ is the most important ion underlying *excitatory postsynaptic potentials* (*epsps*) while K^+ and Cl^- are most important in producing *inhibitory postsynaptic potentials* (*ipsps*). These ionic currents will be discussed in greater detail shortly. Even

TABLE 2.6   Comparison of Action Potentials and Postsynaptic Potentials

	Action Potentials	Postsynaptic Potentials
Amplitude	Approx. 110 *m*V, "all-or-none"	<1 to 15–20 mV, graded
Direction	Always depolarizing	Either depolarizing or hyperpolarizing
Duration	1–10 msec	Up to several minutes
Propagation	Without decrement	With decrement
Ion channels	Voltage-gated, Na$^+$, K$^+$	Chemically gated, Na$^+$, K$^+$, Cl$^-$

though the same ions may be involved, postsynaptic potentials are different in many ways from the nerve impulses that occur in the axon. Table 2.6 lists some of the most important differences in the two types of potentials. One important difference is that although the size of the nerve impulse is always constant, psps are graded in their amplitude. Moreover, psps can last much longer than most nerve impulses can. Perhaps most important, as we shall see shortly, psps can be either excitatory or inhibitory; nerve impulses are only excitatory. Figure 2.18 shows a typical epsp and ipsp.

Synaptic Delay

Synaptic transmission takes time. In one extensively studied synapse on the giant axon of the squid, there is about a 0.2-msec interval between the arrival of the nerve impulse at the terminal and the release of the neuro-transmitter. Much of this time is due to the time required for the Ca^{2+}

Figure 2.18 Postsynaptic potentials. Epsps are depolarizations; ipsps are hyperpolarizations.

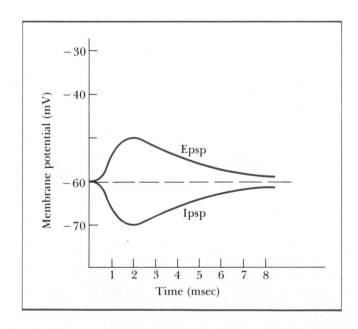

The Catecholamine Family

The term **catecholamine** appears throughout this book. Catecholamines are the chemical substances that have a *catechol* nucleus as well as an *amine* (NH_2) group. The catecholamines are important as neurotransmitters (e.g., dopamine and norepinephrine) and as hormones (e.g., norepinephrine and epinephrine). These substances are produced in various regions of the brain and sympathetic nervous system as well as in the adrenal gland. Catecholamines are believed to be involved in several psychological functions, including mental disorders, feelings of pleasure and pain, sleep, stress, and learning.

The catecholamines are all produced from a single amino acid precursor, **tyrosine**, which is taken from the bloodstream by catechol-amine-producing cells. In mammals, tyrosine also can be made from another amino acid, **phenylalanine**. Dopamine, norepinephrine, and epinephrine are all produced from tyrosine in steps, as shown in Figure 2.19. A different enzyme is responsible for each step in the synthesis of one catecholamine to another. Many drugs used in the treatment of mental disorders and other psychological treatments affect either the synthesis, release, postsynaptic reception, or metabolism of the catecholamines. Some of these drugs include the antidepressants, the antipsychotic drugs, and amphetamine (used in some cases with hyperactive children). Cooper et al. (1986) discuss the actions of the catecholamines.

Substance	Enzyme	Substance
(Formula)		(Name)

Tyrosine

Tyrosine hydroxylase

DOPA

DOPA decarboxylase

Dopamine

Dopamine β-hydroxylase

Norepinephrine

PNMT

Epinephrine

catecholamine (Cat-a-COLE-a-meen) A family of neurotransmitters derived from tyrosine. Includes dopamine, norepinephrine, and epinephrine.

tyrosine (TIE-ro-seen) One of the amino acids. The catecholamines are derived from tyrosine.

phenylalanine (Fen-ul-AL-a-neen) An amino acid.

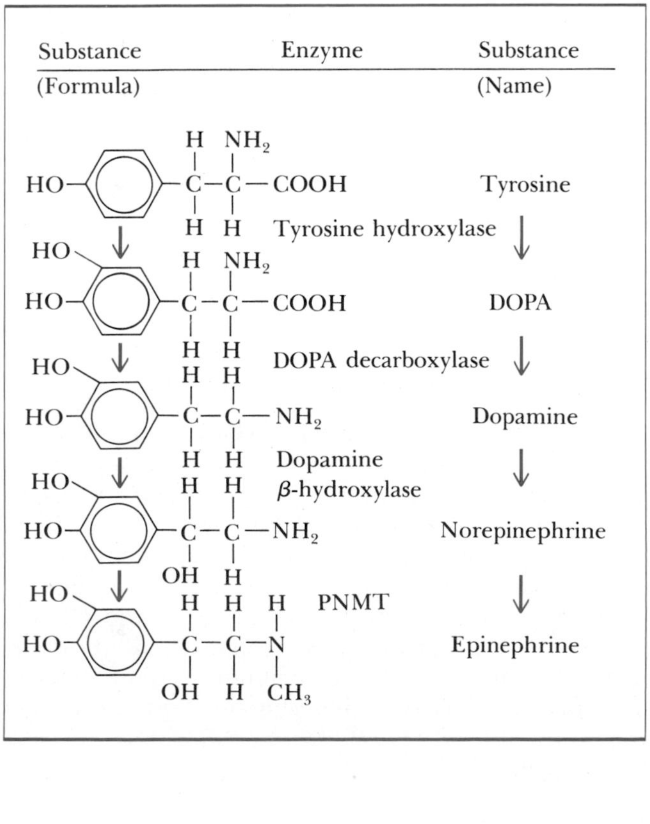

**Figure 2.19
Biosynthesis of the catecholamines.** Figure shows how the different substances such as dopamine and norepinephrine are derived from the amino acid tyrosine. PNMT = phenylethanolamine-*N*-methyl transferase.

excitatory postsynaptic potential (epsp)   Graded depolarization across the postsynaptic membrane at an excitatory synapse.

inhibitory postsynaptic potential (ipsp)   Graded hyperpolarization across the postsynaptic membrane at an inhibitory synapse.

channels to open (Llinas, 1982). Even more time is needed for exocytosis, for the diffusion of the neurotransmitter across the cleft, and for the binding of the neurotransmitter to the receptor molecule. These all add together to constitute the *synaptic delay*, the time from the invasion of the axon terminals by the presynaptic nerve impulse until a psp can be recorded. In mammals synaptic delay is typically about one millisecond.

Excitatory Postsynaptic Potentials

The main effect of the neurotransmitter is to open ion channels in the postsynaptic neuron. The nature of the psp depends on which ion channels are opened. Psps can be either **excitatory postsynaptic potentials (epsps)** or **inhibitory postsynaptic potentials (ipsps)**. Epsps can be produced by changing the state of different ion channels. For example, a neurotransmitter that opened Na^+ channels would produce an epsp. Also, a *decrease* in K^+ conductance could underly an epsp.

The number of ions exchanged across the membrane depends on how many ion channels are opened by the neurotransmitter and how long they remain open, which is determined by the number of molecules available in the synaptic cleft. Tracing cause and effect still further back in the sequence, the amount of available transmitter depends on a number of factors, one of which is the level of depolarization, and hence the amount of Ca^{2+} in the axon terminals.

Neurotransmitter action is eventually stopped by removing the neurotransmitter from the postsynaptic receptor and the cleft. Neurotransmitter removal is accomplished either by an enzyme that breaks down the neurotransmitter or by the *reuptake* of the neurotransmitter by the presynaptic axon terminals. In many synapses both processes take place. These mechanisms limit the duration of postsynaptic potentials and ensure that the neural circuits do not become jammed in "transmitting mode." The reuptake mechanism also allows the presynaptic neuron to recycle the neurotransmitter.

Inhibitory Postsynaptic Potentials

Not all synapses are excitatory. Many are inhibitory, with postsynaptic potentials that are *hyperpolarizing*. In these cases the ion channels opened by the action of the transmitter on the receptor molecule are selective for K^+, Cl^-, or both. The voltage changes recorded at such synapses are termed *inhibitory postsynaptic potentials* (ipsps), since they move the overall membrane voltage of the postsynaptic cell away from its threshold for generating a nerve impulse. For example, if the transmitter at an inhibitory synapse selectively opens K^+ channels, K^+ flows out, down its chemical gradient until it reaches its equilibrium potential of -75 mV or until the channels are closed. This results in a *hyperpolarization*, a move away from threshold. Hyperpolarizing potentials are thus always inhibitory. Surprisingly, the reverse is not always true; inhibitory potentials need not always be hyperpolarizing! What matters is the relationship between the membrane voltage due to the postsynaptic potential and the threshold of the postsynaptic neuron for generating a nerve impulse. Cl^- provides a good example.

You saw in Table 2.3 that the equilibrium potential for Cl^- in the giant neuron of the squid coincides with the resting potential of -60 mV. Thus if only Cl^- channels were opened, there would be no postsynaptic potential recorded in the postsynaptic cell, since even though Cl^- would now be free to move, it would be already at its equilibrium. However, if another synapse nearby on the postsynaptic cell were to begin to produce some depolarization, then the open Cl^- channels would begin to allow Cl^- to flow into the neuron as soon as the membrane voltage reached -59 mV. An inward Cl^- current would continue to flow as long as the membrane voltage remained depolarized with respect to the Cl^- equilibrium of -60 mV. In effect, opening the Cl^- channels retards excitation, keeping the overall membrane voltage at or near the Cl^- equilibrium. This is several millivolts hyperpolarized with respect to threshold, and thus inhibitory.

It is important to point out that usually each transmitter has two or more different types of postsynaptic receptors. For example, acetylcholine is known to have both **nicotinic** and **muscarinic** receptor types, so named because of their different responses to nicotine and muscarine. Moreover, it now appears that the muscarinic receptor has at least two subtypes (Snyder, 1984). The effect of a given transmitter on the postsynaptic cell can be quite different, depending on what combination of receptors it contains. From currently available evidence, it appears that virtually all neurotransmitters will turn out to have two or more different receptor types. Thus norepinephrine has four known receptor types, dopamine has two, and serotonin has two, possibly more. An individual neuron in the brain typically contains receptors for several different transmitters and two or more receptor types for some or all of these.

The richness of transmitter types and receptor types allows tremendous flexibility and diversity of action within an individual neuron and within the nervous system as a whole. The next few years are sure to bring discoveries of previously unrecognized neurotransmitters and previously unknown receptor types.

Synaptic Integration

Whether or not the combined excitatory and inhibitory input onto a neuron causes it to generate one or more nerve impulses depends on whether sufficient depolarization occurs at the spike-initiating region. Psps can change the membrane voltage only at relatively short distances from the synaptic site. Unlike nerve impulses, they cannot regenerate themselves; thus psps

nicotinic (nik-o-TIN-ik) Denoting a type of postsynaptic receptor for acetylcholine.

muscarinic (musk-ah-RIN-ik) Denoting a type of postsynaptic receptor for acetylcholine.

temporal summation The algebraic addition of post-synaptic potentials across some period of time.

diminish in size and effectiveness with distance from their origin. Even if a particular synapse is located directly on a spike-initiating region, its effects may be too small to affect the firing rate of that cell unless still other synapses are simultaneously active. The location of synapses is crucial—the closer the synapse is to the spike-initiating region, the more influential that particular synapse will be. The effects of an excitatory synapse close to the spike-initiating region may outweigh several more distant ones. One pattern that has been observed is the location of excitatory synapses further away from the spike-initiating region, and inhibitory synapses closer to the spike-initiating region, in a position of greater "veto power." This is only one of many possibilities, but such an arrangement would keep the neuron from being in a constant state of excitation.

Some psps last a long time, up to several minutes. Long durations allow for the depolarizations and hyperpolarizations to add together in time, a process termed **temporal summation**. Summation, both in time and within related parts of the postsynaptic membrane, is important, if routine. *Spatial summation* is also important, as several psps may add their effects if they are close together on the postsynaptic cell surface. The importance of these graded potentials is probably not as yet fully realized, and they may be much more directly involved in the brain's activity than currently acknowledged. Kuffler et al. (1984) is a good source for more discussion of graded potentials. This is an area where future research is likely to alter our current ideas dramatically. In the complexity of brain circuitry, individual neurons act as decision makers, responding to the net sum of a never-ending stream of excitatory and inhibitory input.

SUMMARY

1. Neurons are the information-processing cells in the nervous system. The human brain has billions of neurons. The basic parts of a neuron are cell body, dendrites, axon, and axon terminals.

2. Glial cells are satellite cells that surround neurons, providing them with nourishment and responding to injuries. Even more glial cells are found in the brain than neurons, but the role of glial cells in information processing, if any, is not known. One type of glial cell provides the myelin sheath that allows for more rapid conduction of the nerve impulse down the axon.

3. The neuronal membrane is composed of a double layer of lipids and associated proteins. These proteins form membrane receptors for various substances, give structural definition to the neuron, and compose the ion channels through which ions can pass from one side of the cell membrane to the other. Still other proteins form ionic pumps that are important in maintaining the proper ionic composition of the neuron.

4. The capacity of neurons to send messages depends on the passage of ions, particularly Na^+ and K^+, across the cell membrane. These ions pass through ion channels, dependent on the state of the channel (open or closed), and the driving forces on that particular type of ion. These driving forces come from both electrical and chemical gradients that exist across the membrane. Two additional ions that are critical for information processing in the nervous system are Ca^{2+}, important for the release of chemical neurotransmitters, and Cl^-, involved in inhibitory synaptic potentials.

5. When the neuron is not carrying a nerve impulse, it is said to be at rest. During this resting phase there is a steady electrical potential across the membrane of approximately -60 mV, inside negative. This potential is maintained by the different permeabilities of the membrane to various ions and by the active pumping of some ions, such as Na^+ and K^+. The equilibrium potential, the membrane voltage at which no net movement of an ion would occur, given the existing concentrations inside and outside the neuron, can be calculated using the Nernst equation. In the squid axon the equilibrium potential for Na^+ is about $+55$ mV, inside positive; for K^+ it is about -75 mV, inside negative; and for Cl^- it is about -60 mV, inside negative.

6. The critical event in the initiation of the nerve impulse is a change in the shape of the Na^+ channels in the cell body and axon such that Na^+ is allowed to flow down its electrical and chemical gradients into the neuron, producing a sudden reversal of the electrical potential across the neuronal membrane. The nerve impulse is terminated by an inactivation of the Na^+ channels to further passage of Na^+ ions. The original resting potential of the neuron is restored by the outflow of K^+ ions. According to the Nobel-prize-winning work of Hodgkin and Huxley, the movements of Na^+ and K^+ are primarily responsible for the nerve impulse, although other ions are probably involved in the nerve impulse in some neurons.

7. The nerve impulse is propagated in an all-or-none fashion down the axon, the Na^+ channels being opened by the positive ions that flow into the neuron. Propagation speeds depend on the diameter of the neuron and whether or not it is myelinated. In small, nonmyelinated axons nerve impulses may travel at speeds of less than 1 m/sec, whereas in large, myelinated neurons, the impulse may travel at rates of over 120 m/sec.

8. Some minimal amount of depolarization (e.g., about 15 mV) is required to trigger a nerve impulse. The degree of depolarization required to produce an impulse some agreed-on percentage of the time (e.g., 50 percent) is termed the threshold of that neuron. The region of the neuron that contains membrane with the lowest threshold is termed the spike-initiating region of the cell.

9. Once an impulse is generated in the axon, the amplitude of that im-

pulse is constant for any given neuron. This is called the all-or-none law. This law holds only for the axon, not for synaptic potentials.

10. In general, the more intense the stimulus, the higher the frequency with which a neuron will fire, up to some limit imposed by the absolute refractory period. This provides the nervous system with the ability to code for intensity of stimulation with frequency of neuronal firing. The absolute refractory period is due primarily to Na^+ inactivation.

11. The junctions between neurons where information can pass from one neuron to another are called *synapses*. Synaptic transmission can be accomplished either by electrical or chemical means. In chemical transmission, thought to be the main way in which vertebrate neurons communicate with each other, the release of a chemical neurotransmitter from the axon terminals is initiated by the nerve impulse as it invades the terminals or end feet. The influx of Ca^{2+} ions is necessary for neurotransmitter release.

12. Many different neurotransmitters exist. Some of the better-studied neurotransmitters include acetylcholine, norepinephrine, dopamine, serotonin, and GABA, but the final list of chemical neurotransmitters may include well over 100 substances. Substances that can mimic the effects of a neurotransmitter are termed *agonists*, whereas substances that block a particular transmitter are termed *antagonists*. Naturally occurring substances that can alter synaptic transmission but that are not themselves believed to be neurotransmitters (such as some of the hormones) are termed *neuromodulators*.

13. Neurotransmitters produce either excitatory or inhibitory potentials in the postsynaptic neuron by opening or closing ion channels in the membrane of the postsynaptic neuron. These channels can be either on the dendrites, cell body, or axon terminals of the postsynaptic neuron. These channels are referred to as chemically gated channels to distinguish them from the voltage-gated channels for Na^+ and K^+ in the axon and cell body.

14. Chemically gated channels are associated with protein receptors for neurotransmitters. Chemically gated ion channels are typically not responsive to changes in voltage, and voltage-gated ion channels are insensitive to neurotransmitters.

15. The resulting changes in the voltage across the membrane of the postsynaptic neuron are either excitatory or inhibitory, depending on which ion channels were opened and closed. Whether the postsynaptic neuron generates one or more nerve impulses in response to the presynaptic input depends on whether sufficient depolarization is produced by the postsynaptic potentials to exceed the threshold of the cell. Some postsynaptic potentials can last for many seconds or even minutes, whereas a nerve impulse rarely lasts for more than a millisecond or two.

SUGGESTIONS FOR FURTHER READING

Kandel, E. R., and Schwartz, J. H. (Eds.) (1985). *Principles of neural science* (2d ed.). New York: Elsevier/North Holland.

Kuffler, S. W., Nicholls, J. G., and Martin, A. R. (1984). *From neuron to brain* (2d ed.). Sunderland, MA: Sinauer.

Shepherd, G. M. (1983). *Neurobiology*. New York: Oxford University Press.

Stevens, C. F. (1979). The neuron. *Scientific American, 241*, 54–65.

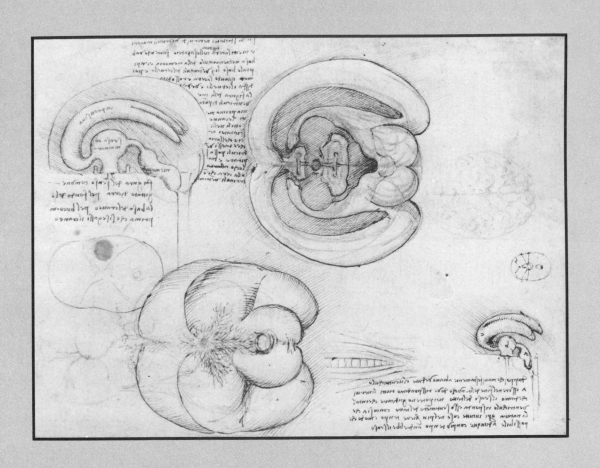

3

Anatomy of the Nervous System

*Living threads
more numerous than stars
frame the universe of my mind.*

D. P. K.

Preview

Neuroanatomists view mammalian nervous systems as composed of two main parts: a peripheral nervous system and a central nervous system. The peripheral nervous system consists of two networks: one that activates the skeletal muscles and another, known as the autonomic nervous system, that regulates such internal organs as the heart and intestines and becomes noticeable during states of arousal and emotion. However, 99 percent of our neurons belong to our central nervous system, which consists of the brain and the spinal cord. The human brain is the most complex organ found in nature. Its crowning glory, the cerebral cortex, is the most recently evolved part of our nervous system. The organizational principles of the nervous system shed some light on its manifold functions.

The Peripheral Nervous System

Our nervous system has two basic components: the central nervous system (CNS), which consists of the brain and spinal cord, and the peripheral nervous system (PNS), which includes the peripheral nerves and the autonomic nervous system. Although the PNS and the CNS function together in an integrated manner, we discuss these two systems separately.

Three groups of nerves form the PNS: cranial nerves, spinal nerves, and the autonomic nervous system (ANS). According to the direction in which the nerves transmit impulses, they can be classified further as either **afferent, efferent,** or mixed nerves. Afferent nerves conduct impulses from the periphery to the CNS. Efferent nerves conduct impulses from the CNS toward the periphery. Mixed nerves conduct impulses both to and from the CNS.

Cranial Nerves

There are 12 pairs of cranial nerves, which merge with the CNS at or above the neck. Traditionally, the cranial nerves are designated by Roman numerals, and they are sometimes referred to by number rather than by name.

I. *Olfactory* nerves. Bringing sensory information into the CNS from smell receptors in the nose, the olfactory nerves are afferent.

II. *Optic* nerves. Responsible for vision, these afferent nerves are the axons of ganglion cells in the retina.

III. **Oculomotor** nerves. These efferent nerves distribute to the muscles in and around the eye that alter the size of the pupil and control eye movements.

IV. **Trochlear** nerves. Efferent nerves whose action is coordinated with III and VI and is directed toward one of the muscles that moves the eyeballs in their sockets.

V. **Trigeminal** nerves. Divided into three branches each—ophthalmic, maxillary, and mandibular—the trigeminals are mixed nerves. The afferent component carries sensory information about temperature, touch, and pain to the CNS from the skin of the face, the cornea of the eye, the membranes of mouth and nose; from the teeth; and from the outer covering of the brain itself. The efferent component of the trigeminals activates the muscles involved in chewing.

VI. **Abducens** nerves. Like III and IV, these efferent nerves are concerned with the control of eye movement. In humans, as in many other primates, vision and the control of eye movement are important evolutionary developments, so a substantial amount of our nervous system is devoted to processing visual information and controlling movements of the eyes.

VII. *Facial* nerves. The afferent axons of these mixed nerves come principally from the taste buds on the forward two-thirds of the tongue. The efferent axons go to mucous glands in the nose, to tear glands in the eyes, to some of the salivary glands, and to facial muscles involved in laughing, smiling, and frowning.

VIII. *Auditory* nerves. Also called vestibulo-cochlear nerves or acoustic nerves, these primarily afferent nerves carry sensory input from the inner ear to the brain. Split into two branches each, the VIII nerves are instrumental in hearing and in maintaining the body's equilibrium (see Chapter 6).

IX. **Glossopharyngeal** nerves. The efferent components of these mixed nerves go to the parotid salivary glands and to the throat muscles involved in swallowing. Their afferent axons come from the taste buds on the back third of the tongue.

X. *Vagus* nerves. Of all the cranial nerves, these have the widest distribution. Their efferent axons go to tongue and throat muscles and to many of the internal organs, including the heart, the liver, and the stomach. The afferent components of the vagus nerves transmit input from a wide variety of tissues, including the throat, the heart, the stomach, and the gastrointestinal tract.

XI. *Accessory* nerves. These are efferent nerves supplying neck muscles and the vocal cords.

XII. *Hypoglossal* nerves. These efferent nerves supply the tongue muscles and are therefore involved in talking and swallowing.

oculomotor nerve (OCK-u-lo-MO-tor) Third cranial nerve, which regulates eye movements and pupil size.

trochlear nerve (TRO-klee-ar) Fourth cranial nerve, which regulates eye movements.

trigeminal nerve (try-JEM-in-al) Fifth cranial nerve, associated with the face and mouth.

abducens nerve (ab-DEW-sens) Sixth cranial nerve, associated with eye movements.

glossopharyngeal nerve (GLOSS-o-far-in-JEE-al) Ninth cranial nerve, associated with mouth and throat.

cervical nerves (SER-vi-kal) Group of the spinal nerves.

The Spinal Nerves

There are 31 pairs of spinal nerves, which we group and name after the spinal region from which they emerge. Eight pairs are **cervical** nerves; 12 pairs, *thoracic* nerves; five pairs, *lumbar* nerves; five pairs, *sacral* nerves; and

coccygeal nerves (kok-SI-jeel) Last pair of spinal nerves.

dermatome (DER-ma-tome) A body segment associated with a particular spinal nerve.

SUMMARY TABLE *The Cranial Nerves at a Glance*		
Nerve		**Main Functions**
I	Olfactory	Afferent: perception of smell
II	Optic	Afferent: vision
III	Oculomotor	Efferent: eye movements
IV	Trochlear	Efferent: eye movements
V	Trigeminal	Mixed: facial sensations chewing movements
VI	Abducens	Efferent: eye movements
VII	Facial	Mixed: taste sensations facial movements
VIII	Auditory	Afferent: hearing equilibrium
IX	Glossopharyngeal	Mixed: taste sensations swallowing movements
X	Vagus	Mixed: internal organ sensations regulation of internal organ functions such as heart rate
XI	Accessory	Efferent: vocal cord and neck movements
XII	Hypoglossal	Efferent: tongue movements

one pair **coccygeal** nerves. Each spinal nerve has a dorsal root as well as a ventral root. These two roots merge a short distance from the spinal cord to form the spinal nerve. The nerve's dorsal root is afferent; its ventral root is efferent. Figure 3.1 illustrates a representative spinal nerve. The dorsal root's afferent neurons have their cell bodies in the spinal ganglion. For that reason the spinal ganglion is also known as the dorsal root ganglion. In the surrounding body there are networks of nerves called *plexuses*, which also are part of the peripheral nervous system.

Each spinal nerve is responsible for a specific segment of the body. The dorsal root transmits sensory information from a particular area of the body. Likewise, each ventral root supplies a delineated, specific body area. Any such area is called a **dermatome** (see Figure 3.2, page 68). The boundaries between adjacent dermatomes are not precise, and there is some overlap between neighboring dermatomes. Nevertheless, the fact that a particular spinal root supplies a restricted body segment provides neurologists with a useful guide to the location of spinal nerve abnormalities.

The Autonomic Nervous System

Scene: A college campus, 30 minutes before your final exam in Western Civilization.

You have studied, but not enough, you fear; and your instructor has

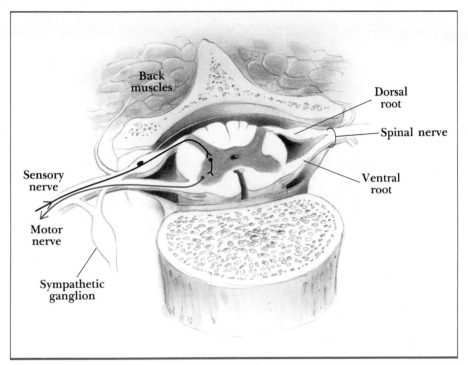

Figure 3.1 Branches of a spinal nerve.

a reputation for hard exams. As you nervously flip through your class notes on the steps outside the classroom, you feel a mounting sense of panic. Your heart is racing and seems to be thudding against your ribs. Your palms are sweaty and you have "butterflies" in your stomach. You have taken introductory psychology; so you know that being anxious is not likely to help you perform the complex tasks ahead.

You try to calm down by breathing deeply and stretching your neck and shoulder muscles. This helps a little, but only momentarily. Your pounding heart, sweaty palms, and queasy stomach seem to be beyond your control. You are in the grip of test anxiety. Also named stage fright or pregame jitters, this combination of bodily responses characterizes anxiety and is commonly experienced as we approach a situation in which we are expected to perform at top level. In actual fact, these bodily responses are largely beyond our control. They are *involuntary* and result, for the most part, from neuron activities in the sympathetic nerves of the autonomic nervous system (ANS). Figures 3.3 and 3.4 (pages 69 and 70) show the main components of the ANS: its sympathetic system and its parasympathetic system.

The Sympathetic Nervous System

Two large nerve trunks run alongside the spinal column, one on each side. Along with their associated axons, these trunks constitute the sympathetic

**Figure 3.2
Arrangement of
dermatomes.**
A dermatome is that
area of the skin sup-
plied by a single pair
of spinal nerves.
S = sacral; L = lumbar;
T = thoracic;
C = cervical

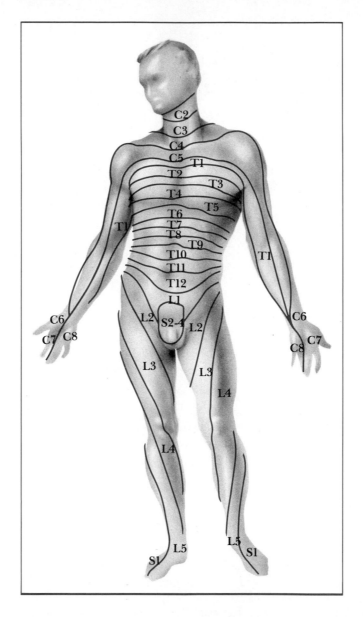

nervous system of the ANS. At intervals these trunks have enlargements called *sympathetic ganglia*. The ganglia contain collections of cell bodies with synapsing axon terminals or dendrites. Neurons that emerge from the spinal cord and then enter the sympathetic ganglia are termed *preganglionic neurons*.

All the preganglionic axons of the sympathetic division originate in the two upper lumbar spinal nerves and the 12 thoracic nerves. Some of them send collaterals to other ganglia in the sympathetic trunk. Some send collaterals to sympathetic ganglia scattered in the interior of the body. From the sympathetic ganglia, their axons run in the spinal nerve until they reach the internal organ that they innervate.

As noted, the activities of the sympathetic nervous system become very noticeable in stressful or anxiety-producing situations. Walter B. Cannon (1871–1945) characterized the overall function of the sympathetic system as preparing the animal for "fight or flight." This preparation includes

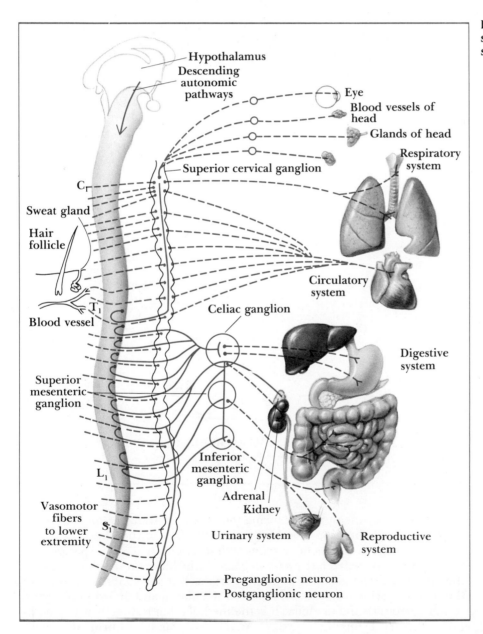

Figure 3.3 The sympathetic nervous system.

Figure 3.4 The parasympathetic nervous system.

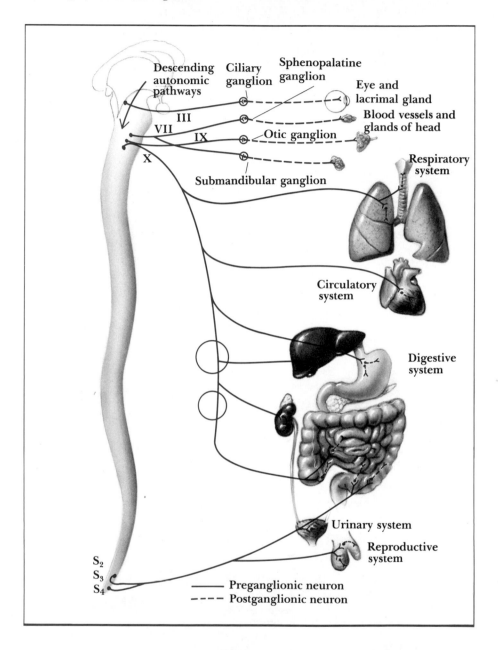

Descending autonomic pathways

Ciliary ganglion

Sphenopalatine ganglion

Eye and lacrimal gland

III

VII

Blood vessels and glands of head

IX

Otic ganglion

X

Submandibular ganglion

Respiratory system

Circulatory system

Digestive system

Urinary system

Reproductive system

S₂
S₃
S₄

—— Preganglionic neuron
- - - Postganglionic neuron

adrenaline (a-DRE-na-lin)
See *epinephrine.*

chromaffin cells
(KROME-a-fin) Secretory
cells in the adrenal med-
ulla.

such emergency measures as making more energy available, increasing the heart rate, and shunting blood from the intestines to the muscles.

One of the sympathetic nervous system's fight-or-flight responses is to release **adrenaline** from the *adrenal glands,* which are on the dorsal side of the kidneys. These glands are complex organs composed of two basic parts: the medulla, which is the central part of the gland, and the adrenal cortex, which surrounds the medulla. It is the medulla that is directly activated by preganglionic sympathetic axons. Within the medulla **chromaffin cells** manufacture adrenaline; when they are activated by the sympathetic system, they release their adrenaline into the bloodstream. Actually, what the adrenal medulla releases is a mixture of adrenaline **(epinephrine)** and *noradrenaline* **(norepinephrine).**

This "adrenaline rush" we experience when frightened or startled results from the effect the adrenaline mixture has on the blood vessels, the heart, and other tissues. It causes the heart to beat faster and more forcefully, and it releases stored-up energy from muscle tissues and from the liver, in the form of glucose. Such sympathetic activation can be triggered by unknown fears and tensions, a condition often termed *nonspecific anxiety.* It has been estimated that about 5 percent of the population suffers from chronic anxiety, or almost continual high sympathetic activation, which may contribute to tension headaches, cardiovascular disorders, and other complaints.

The Parasympathetic Nervous System

The parasympathetic nervous system consists of a small number of preganglionic neurons whose axons originate in four of the cranial nerves—III, VI, IX, and X—and two of the sacral nerves (see Figure 3.4). Most internal organs receive both sympathetic and parasympathetic innervation. Parasympathetic activity tends to conserve and restore energy reserves. Thus parasympathetic activation of the heart slows the heart rate down and decreases the force of the heart's contractions.

Although parasympathetic activation often counters sympathetic activation, the two can work together to bring about certain results. One example of this is erection and ejaculation. Erection is caused by a rush of blood into the spongelike tissue of the penis, coupled with changes in the veins that normally drain the penis. The blood that is trapped engorges the vessels, making the penis both larger and harder. This process is under the control of the parasympathetic system.

Sympathetic activation inhibits the erection process, which explains why men may have difficulties in achieving or maintaining an erection when they are anxious or afraid. It is not difficult to understand how failure to achieve or maintain an erection can develop into a vicious circle. The experience of failure can engender the fear of failing again, and this anxiety can bring about the very thing that is feared. But with most men such episodes pass and erections return in response to sexual excitement, memories of pleasant encounters, and gentle stimulation.

Although erection results from parasympathetic input, ejaculation results primarily from sympathetic input. Ejaculation is brought about by contractions of involuntary muscles in the seminal vesicles and prostate gland, along with some voluntary muscles of the penis. Thus, although sympathetic activation interferes with the early stages of sexual activity, it is essential for its completion.

In the sexual responses of women, parasympathetic activity is responsible for engorgement of the clitoris and for vaginal lubrication. Orgasm in women is a complex response characterized by rhythmic contractions of the uterine and vaginal musculature.

epinephrine (ep-ee-NEF-rin) A neurotransmitter and hormone secreted by the adrenal medulla, adrenaline.

norepinephrine (NOR-ep-ee-NEF-rin) A neurotransmitter and hormone secreted by the adrenal medulla, noradrenaline.

rostral (ROS-trul) Toward the front of the head.

caudal (CAW-dul) Of the tail or tail end.

Voluntary Control of Involuntary Responses

In general, the ANS is not under our conscious control, but there are some exceptions. For example, the ANS controls bladder function. Urination results from parasympathetic stimulation, which causes the bladder to contract. Urination is inhibited by sympathetic activation, which prevents this contraction. Despite the fact that urination is thus mediated solely by the ANS, it is routinely brought under voluntary control. There has been a great deal of interest in the degree to which such ANS functions as the heart rate and blood pressure also can be brought under some voluntary control.

The Central Nervous System

Widespread and important as it is, the peripheral nervous system contains less than 1 percent of our neurons. The other 99 percent are in the CNS, which consists of the brain and spinal cord. The spinal cord is a long tube of neural tissue extending from the brainstem at its **rostral** end to the coccygeal nerves at its **caudal** end. Figure 3.5 shows a representative cross section of the spinal cord in the lumbar region. The cord is composed of gray matter and white matter. The gray matter, made up of cell bodies, dendrites, glial cells, and axon terminals, is organized into many different

Figure 3.5 Cross section of the human spinal cord.

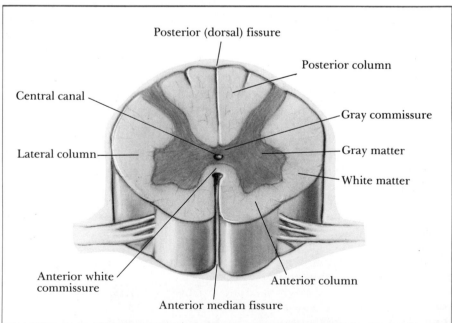

Posterior (dorsal) fissure

Posterior column

Central canal

Gray commissure

Lateral column

Gray matter

White matter

Anterior white commissure

Anterior column

Anterior median fissure

nuclei. In Figure 3.5 the gray matter can be seen as a butterfly-shaped region. The white matter, composed of myelinated axons, is organized into ascending and descending nerve tracts.

Ascending Pathways

The ascending nerve tracts in the spinal cord are organized into three recognizable systems: the anterolateral, the dorsal column–medial lemniscus, and the spinocerebellar systems. All nerve tracts in the cord are bilateral. The names of the individual nerve tracts usually indicate where any given tract originates and where it terminates—in that order. Thus the lateral spinothalamic tract goes from the spine to the thalamus, and the spinotectal tract goes from the spine to the tectum, the roof of the midbrain.

Most ascending pathways are composed of at least three sets of neurons. The primary sensory neurons, with cell bodies in the dorsal root ganglion of the spinal nerve, make synaptic contact with particular nuclei in the cord, often sending axon collaterals to other nuclei. These sensory neurons are the first-order neurons. The axons that receive these synaptic contacts are second-order neurons. Often these second-order neurons cross over, or **decussate,** to the opposite side of the cord. But neurons in the spinocerebellar system do not decussate, nor do the efferent axons from the cerebellum that are concerned with movement and posture. The third-order neurons of the ascending systems have their cell bodies in various thalamic nuclei. Their axons terminate on neurons of the cerebral cortex. Some ascending pathways require only two sets of neurons from the dorsal root to the thalamus.

Descending Pathways

Neurons from widespread areas of the brain send axons down to synapse on spinal cord neurons. Two of the main descending tracts are the right and left *corticospinal* tracts. Most of these axons decussate in the medulla. Just before they do so, they form the *medullary pyramids*—hence the corticospinal tracts are also referred to as *pyramidal tracts.* Axons from many tracts converge onto spinal cord neurons. The *ventral horn* cells, the main motor neurons of the spinal cord, receive between 2000 and 10,000 synaptic contacts.

The Meninges of the Brain

The brain is surrounded by a series of membranes, or **meninges** (see Figure 3.6). The outermost of the three meninges layers is the **dura mater** (*dura* means "hard" or "tough" in Latin). The dura mater is a tough, fibrous sheet of cells. The inner membrane, on the other hand, is a filmy, delicate

decussate (de-KUS-sate) Cross over to the opposite side.

meninges (me-NIN-jees) Membranes covering brain and spinal cord.

dura mater (DUR-ah MAH-ter) Outermost membrane covering of brain and spinal cord.

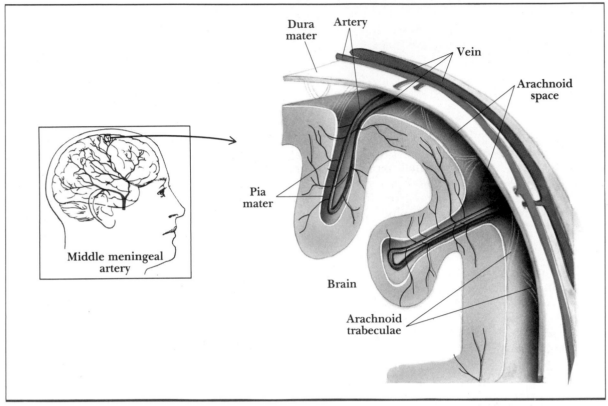

Figure 3.6   Drawing of meninges of the brain and associated blood vessels.
Arteries (lighter red) are shown as they pierce the dura mater and run in the
subarachnoid space, which is filled with cerebrospinal fluid.

pia mater   (PEE-ah MAH-
ter) Innermost membrane
covering brain and spinal
cord.

arachnoid layer   (a-RAK-
noid) Middle layer of membranes covering brain and
spinal cord.

trabeculae   (tra-BEK-yu-
lie) Strands of connective
tissue in the arachnoid
layer.

sulci   (SUL-si) Fissures in
the cortex.

covering called the **pia mater** (*pia* in Latin means "tender"). Between the
dura mater and the pia mater is the **arachnoid** ("weblike") **layer,** made of
connective tissue strands called **trabeculae.** The space between the pia mater and the arachnoid layer—the subarachnoid space—is filled with
cerebrospinal fluid. Blood vessels that penetrate the meninges supply oxygen, glucose, and other important substances to the brain and remove its
waste products.

Major Structures in the Brain

Figure 3.7 shows a photograph of the human brain's left hemisphere without its dura mater and arachnoid layer. The fissures in the cortex are
known as **sulci** (singular, *sulcus*), and the ridges between the sulci are known

as **gyri** (singular, *gyrus*). Individuals vary widely in the configuration and location of these sulci and gyri; but the major ones, indicated in Figure 3.8, are sufficiently constant to serve as landmarks for neurosurgeons.

By long-standing convention, each cerebral hemisphere is divided into four lobes, as indicated in Figure 3.9. Figure 3.10 shows the planes of reference used by anatomists. Figure 3.11 (page 78) shows the medial surface of the left hemisphere. This plane of section is termed a *sagittal section*. Notice the broad band of white matter dorsal to the thalamus. This is the **corpus callosum,** the main link between the two hemispheres, composed of approximately 200 million axons. Some extremely interesting effects can be observed when the corpus callosum is severed in human beings, as has been done occasionally in the treatment of intractable epilepsy. Such patients have been an important source of information about the functional organization of the human brain (details in Chapter 13).

Also visible in the medial view is the *cerebellum*, tucked up under the cerebral hemispheres (see Figure 3.12, page 78). The cerebellum is important for the initiation, modification, and guidance of body movements and postural adjustments (see Chapter 7). Farther forward, just rostral to the cerebellum, are the **superior colliculi, inferior colliculi,** and the **pineal gland.** [*Colliculi* (singular, *colliculus*) means "little hills."] There is a superior and inferior colliculus on each side of the midline. The superior colliculi are part of the visual system and play a major role in orientation to visual stimuli. The inferior colliculi are part of the auditory system.

The pineal gland is an unpaired organ, a fact that so impressed René

gyri (JIGH-rye) Ridges of the cortex.

corpus callosum (KOR-pus ka-LO-zum) Axon band connecting right and left cerebral hemispheres.

superior colliculus (kol-LIK-yu-lus) (plural, *colliculi*) Midbrain region associated with response to visual stimuli and orientation.

inferior colliculus (kol-LIK-yu-lus) (plural, *colliculi*) Midbrain region associated with hearing.

pineal gland (pin-EAL) Unpaired brain organ with largely unknown function.

Figure 3.7 Photograph of the left human cerebral hemisphere.

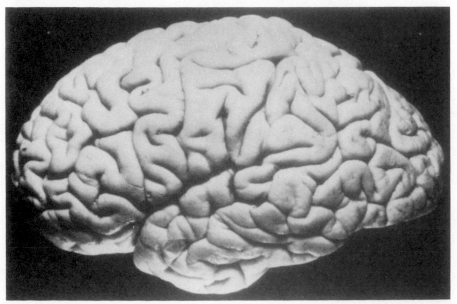

Figure 3.8 Outline drawing of the left human cerebral hemisphere shown in Figure 3.7.
The gyri are labeled. The sulci are indicated by leaders.

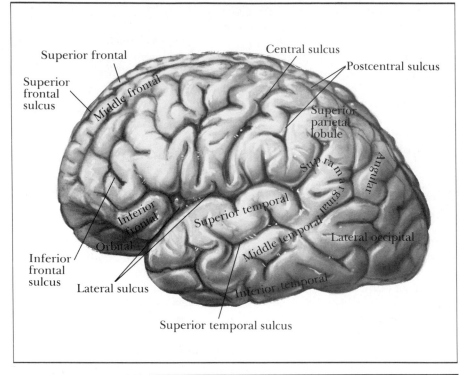

Figure 3.9 The four lobes of the human brain.

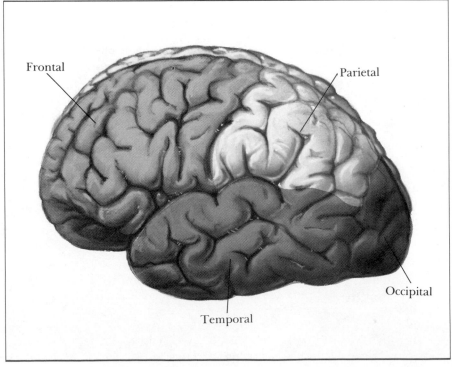

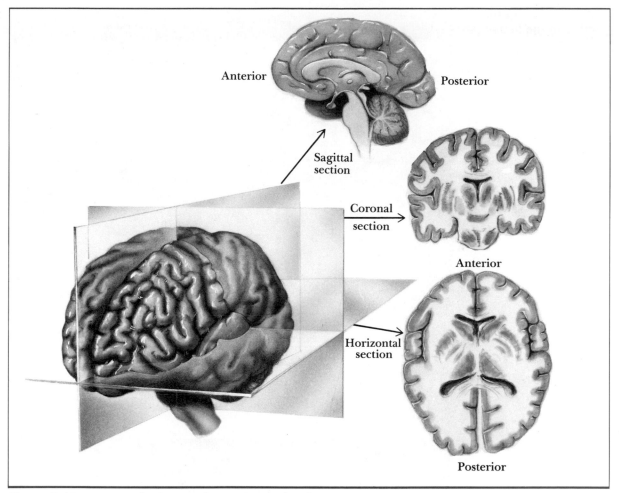

Figure 3.10 Planes of reference for anatomic drawings.

Descartes that he proposed the pineal gland as the site where mind and body interact (see Chapter 1). In hamsters the pineal gland participates in the control of the annual reproductive cycles, and some evidence exists that in some birds it plays a role in setting daily activity rhythms.

The **thalamus** is buried in the center of the brain, like the pit in a peach. It is a complex collection of nuclei that perform a variety of functions, including sensory processing, movement control, and the activation of the rest of the forebrain. It may also play a major role in the perception of pain. The thalamus is particularly well developed in primates, and its evolution seems to be closely related to that of the cerebral cortex.

Directly beneath the thalamus is the **hypothalamus,** a region of nerve tracts and nuclei bounded by the optic chiasm at the rostral end and by

thalamus (THAL-a-mus) Complex collection of nuclei in the center of the brain.

hypothalamus (high-po-THAL-a-mus) Brain region regulating hunger, thirst, sexual function, and temperature.

Figure 3.11 Sagittal section of the human brain showing the medial aspect of the left hemisphere.

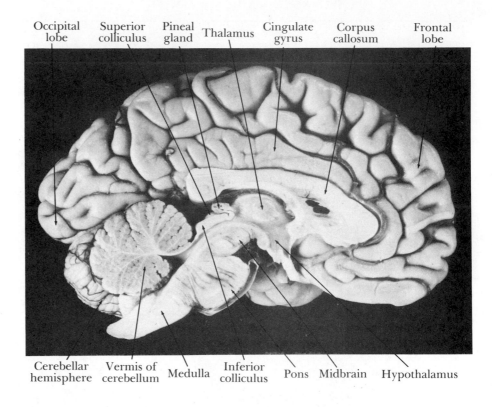

Occipital lobe   Superior colliculus   Pineal gland   Thalamus   Cingulate gyrus   Corpus callosum   Frontal lobe

Cerebellar hemisphere   Vermis of cerebellum   Medulla   Inferior colliculus   Pons   Midbrain   Hypothalamus

Figure 3.12 Sagittal view of the human cerebellum.

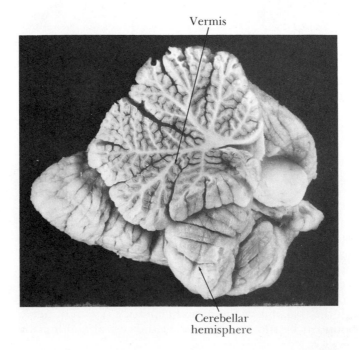

Vermis

Cerebellar hemisphere

the mammillary bodies at the caudal end. The hypothalamus contains neural circuitry involved in controlling the body's temperature and water balance, its sleep and wakefulness, hunger and thirst, and sexual behavior. Attached to the hypothalamus is the pituitary gland, a major component of the endocrine system.

Farther forward, and partly surrounding the thalamus and hypothalamus, is a group of large nuclei known collectively as the **basal ganglia.** Although it is not likely that all these structures have similar functions, we know that the basal ganglia are involved in the initiation and regulation of body movements. Caudal to the thalamus and hypothalamus is the brainstem, which is instrumental in a variety of vital body functions, including respiration. Running along the midline of the brainstem is the *brainstem reticular formation,* which is involved in such basic functions as controlling the level of consciousness and integrating activity in the entire brain (more details in Chapter 10).

The **limbic system** is so named because it forms a border, or *limbus,* around the brainstem just below the cerebral cortex (see Figure 3.13). The limbic system consists of several individual brain structures, such as the **hippocampus,** the **septal nuclei,** and the **amygdala.** All of these are paired structures, with one member of each pair being on the left side of the brain and the other on the right side. Parts of the hypothalamus and its surrounding cortical ridge may also be included in the limbic system.

The hippocampus is a highly organized structure, named by an imaginative anatomist, J. C. Arantius, in 1587 for its supposed resemblance to a seahorse. The hippocampus has been a primary focus for research. One hypothesis is that it is involved in either the maintenance or the manipulation of memory, or both. The hippocampus is connected to the adjacent septal nuclei as well as to the hypothalamus and the brainstem via the **fimbria/fornix.** The amygdalae are tightly clustered nuclei in the medial temporal lobe. The amygdalae appear to be involved in the activities of the hypothalamus and in the experience and expression of emotions (see Chapter 11).

The Cerebral Cortex

The most striking evolutionary aspect of primate brains is the massive development of their cerebral cortex, and nowhere is it more impressive than in the human brain. This cortex is also known as the *neocortex* (new cortex) to distinguish it from "older" cortices such as the hippocampus. Several different measurements have underscored the relationship between the evolution of the neocortex and the parallel evolution of complex behaviors. For example, Heinz Stephan (1972) developed a "progression index" that gives numbers to the evolution of major brain structures. The higher the number given to a particular brain region, the larger that brain region has become relative to other brain regions. In this scheme the reference brain is that of a primitive insectivore. Comparative numbers for the neocortex of various primates attribute 60 to the neocortex of chim-

basal ganglia (BAY-sal GANG-lee-ah) Brain structures involved with regulating movements.

limbic system Group of brain structures including hippocampus, septal nuclei, and amygdala.

hippocampus (hip-po-KAM-pus) A region of the brain whose functions, although probably concerned with memory, are still under active investigation.

septal nuclei Clusters of cell bodies in the septum.

amygdalae (ah-MIG-dah-lie) Group of brain nuclei with connections to olfactory system, affecting mood and recent memory.

fimbria-fornix Major nerve tract connecting the hippocampus and other parts of the brain.

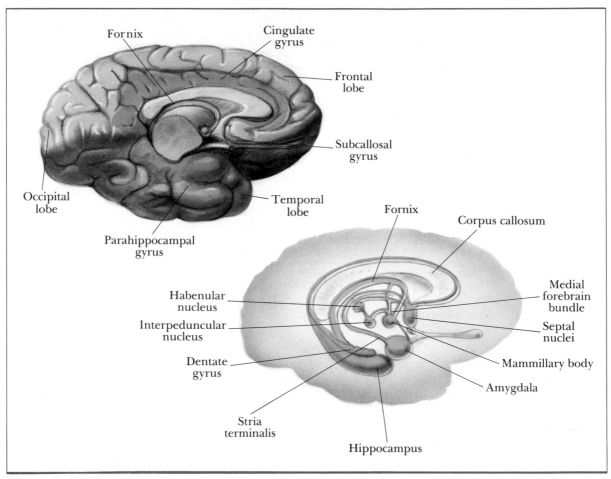

Figure 3.13 The limbic system.
Upper left: Medial view of human brain, showing cingulate gyrus, parahippocampal gyrus, and fornix. Lower right: View of limbic system structures ordinarily covered by other parts of the brain.

panzees—often considered our closest living relatives among primates—and 156 for the human neocortex. Other human brain regions also have grown larger, but at a lesser rate. Although our neocortex scored 156 on the progression index, our hippocampus scored 17; our cerebellum, 4; and our olfactory bulbs, 1.

Because of its extensive differential evolution, the neocortex has been forced to fold in on itself, forming fissures (sulci) and ridges (gyri). This folding allows for a much greater surface area without a tremendous increase in skull size. Severe evolutionary pressures have worked to keep skull size relatively small because the head must pass through the mother's pelvis during birth. The full extent of the human neocortex is about 3000 cm^2. If it were to be unfolded and laid flat, the neocortex would be only slightly smaller than a double page of an average newspaper (Hubel and Wiesel, 1979). The thickness of the neocortex varies somewhat from one region to another, from about 1.5–4.0 mm, with an average of about 2.5 mm.

Brodmann numbering system System identifying regions of the cortex on the basis of their cell structure.

Brodmann's System

As neuroanatomic techniques improved in the early part of this century, several different maps were published to show the differences in cell structure in different regions of the cortex. In many cases the regional differences they showed are questionable, and most of these schemes are of historical interest only. However, one of these systems, the one Korbinian **Brodmann** published in 1909, is still in use—at least in part. Brodmann gave numbers to 52 different cortical regions, some of which can be seen in Figure 3.14.

Layers in the Cortex

Six layers of cells may be seen in the neocortex after it has been appropriately stained. However, it is more by consensus than overwhelmingly convincing anatomical criteria that the number 6 has been adopted. Many descriptions conform to this number only by subdividing one or more of the layers. A widely accepted view of cortical layers is shown in Figure 3.15 (page 83). Starting with the surface of the brain, the cortical layers appear in the following order.

I. *Plexiform* layer. This outermost neocortical layer contains very few cell bodies and is primarily characterized by dendrites from neurons whose cell bodies are in underlying layers.

II. *External granular* layer. A layer of small pyramidal neurons, so named because their cell bodies are roughly pyramidal in shape (see Figure 3.17).

III. *External pyramidal* layer. A layer of medium to large pyramidal cells.

IV. *Internal granular* layer. A layer containing many small neurons, pyramidal as well as the star-shaped stellate neurons (see Figure 3.17, page 86).

V. *Internal pyramidal* layer. A layer of large pyramidal cells.

VI. *Spindle cell* layer. A layer of elongated neuronal cell bodies.

Pyramidal cells tend to be larger than stellate cells, and the distribution of their dendrites is somewhat different. The dendrites of the stellate cells tend to extend outward from the cell body in all directions. The large apical dendrites of the pyramidal cells come from the apex of the cell body, branch extensively, extend—often through two or more layers—in a dorsal direction, and are studded with dendritic spines. The basal dendrites of

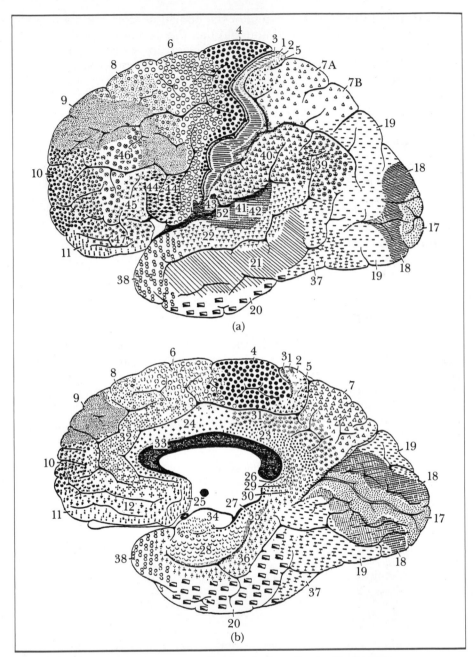

Figure 3.14 The Brodmann numbering system for cortical regions.
(a) Lateral view of left hemisphere. (b) Medial view of the right hemisphere.

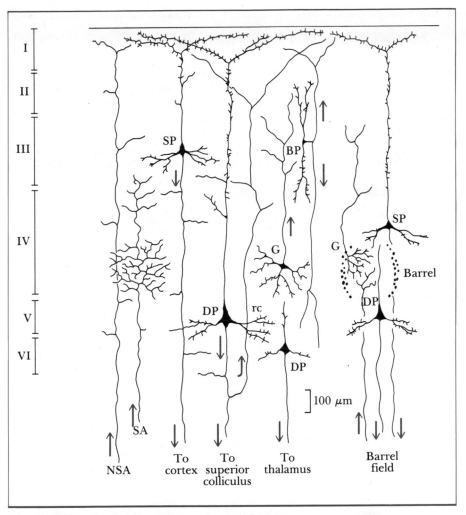

Figure 3.15 Neuronal cell types in visual cortex.
Inputs: specific sensory afferents (SA); nonspecific sensory afferents (NSA). Principal cell types: superficial pyramidal neurons (SP); deep pyramidal neurons (DP); recurrent axon collaterals (rc). Intrinsic neurons: granule cell (G); bipolar cell (BP). The various layers I–VI are shown on the left, together with drawings of the main cell body types seen in the various layers. The somatosensory barrel field is shown on the right for comparison.

pyramidal neurons emerge from the base of the cell body and extend horizontally and somewhat tangentially. Their axons also emerge from the base of the cell body and descend into the underlying white matter, though axon collaterals may extend laterally or upward into neighboring areas.

Whatever the pattern, the dendrites of any given neuron define the

Bumps on the Skull

One of the more colorful chapters in the history of psychology dealt with *phrenology*. This pseudoscience proposed to localize various mental "faculties"—such as cautiousness, self-esteem, and spirituality—in different regions of the brain, based on slight variations in the individual's skull. Although this idea now seems preposterous, at one time phrenology was taken very seriously and generated considerable scientific controversy. For much of the nineteenth and early twentieth centuries the theory enjoyed widespread public popularity and was undoubtedly a source of many pleasant evenings of "bump reading" throughout the world. It even foreshadowed modern ideas concerning the localization of functions in the brain.

The idea that small variations in the shape of the skull revealed underlying differences in the brain came primarily from Franz Josef Gall (1758–1828) and Johann Casper Spurzheim (1776–1832). Both men were accomplished neuroanatomists who had made many accurate observations of brain structure. However, when they began to follow the trail of the "bumps on the skull," they lost their scientific objectivity, finding nevertheless a place in history.

Gall was the driving force in the early days of phrenology. He had apparently been impressed from childhood that his classmates who had particularly good memories had protruding eyes. The idea came to him that this might be true because the "faculty of memory" was localized in the frontal region of the brain and, by growing and becoming overdeveloped, this brain region pressed outward and caused the eyes to bulge. No evidence exists that Gall actually tested any of his ideas objectively. Once he (and later Spurzheim) became convinced that phrenology was basically correct, he looked not for evidence, but for further examples and for converts. Figure 3.16 shows a representative "phrenology map" of the skull, illustrating the location of various mental faculties. The localization of "amativeness" came from Gall's examination of a woman who became known as "Gall's passionate widow," whose skull apparently protruded in the region of the cerebellum. (The details of Gall's examination of this individual are lost.)

It is likely that Gall's and Spurzheim's ideas never gained widespread acceptance among nineteenth-century scientists, and eventually phrenology fell even from popular favor. Phrenology failed for several reasons (Kolb and Whishaw, 1985). First, no relationship exists between structural variations of the brain and the shape of the outside of the skull. Second, the "faculties" Gall and others proposed had no independent status that could be agreed on and measured, and no attempts to define such objective criteria were made. Perhaps the most fatal error was that Gall and Spurzheim were interested not in testing their ideas, but in confirming them. Although phrenology long ago fell into disfavor, it is important to note that the idea of the localization of mental functions has not only survived, but flourished. Evidence for such localization, of course, comes not from skull variations, but from observations of patients with localized brain damage, results of electrical stimulation of different areas of the brain, and other more direct evidence, as we shall see later in this book.

region in which it can receive synaptic input from other neurons. Pyramidal neurons are usually oriented perpendicular to the plane of the brain surface (see Figure 3.18, page 87). Their apical dendrites may extend to layer I, a distance of 2.5–3 mm. Their basal dendrites may extend as much as 200 μm from the cell body. The dendritic spread of stellate cells, on the

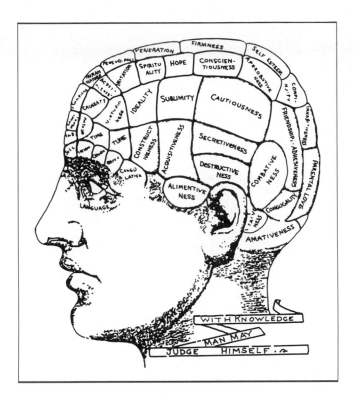

Figure 3.16   A phrenology chart showing the supposed mental faculties and their locations.
This particular drawing comes from the ideas of Johann Spurzheim.

other hand, is usually confined to a much smaller area, giving rise to the idea that the pyramidal cells are the main "long-distance" or "output" cells of the neocortex, while the stellate cells perform "local circuit" duties, processing information within a restricted region.

Input Channels to the Neocortex

Input reaches the mammalian neocortex via channels of four main types: specific sensory channels, nonspecific or diffuse channels, commissural channels from the opposite hemisphere, and intrahemispheric channels from the same hemisphere.

Specific sensory channels contain the axons of neurons within the various specific sensory systems, such as those for sight and hearing. The cell bodies of these axons are in various thalamic nuclei. Most of these axons synapse in layer IV, primarily on pyramidal cells; but some axon terminals can be found in the lower part of layer III; and some terminals synapse with stellate cells.

Nonspecific or diffuse channels relay input from neurons whose cell bodies are in the brainstem reticular formation and some of its associated nuclei in the thalamus. The axons of these cells have short collaterals and terminals at every level of all regions in the neocortex. This system of afferents

locus coeruleus (se-ROO-le-us) A nucleus in the brainstem thought to be concerned with the regulation of consciousness.

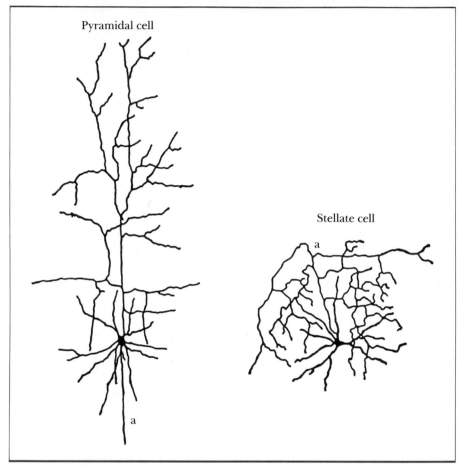

Figure 3.17   The two main types of cortical neurons.
Despite their variety, all cortical neurons may be classified as pyramidal or stellate cells. In general, pyramidal cells serve as the main output cells of the cortex, whereas stellate cells serve local processing functions. a = axon.

is thought to be involved in regulating the overall level of activation of the cortex, mediating the various states of consciousness from deep sleep to alertness. The **locus coeruleus** of the brainstem is an important component of this system.

Commissural channels are axon bundles that cross from one cerebral hemisphere to the other through one of several commissures, such as the anterior commissure, posterior commissure, and the corpus callosum. In many cases these interhemispheric connections are symmetrical, bringing mirror-image portions of the right and left hemispheres into synaptic contact; but some asymmetrical connections also are found.

Intrahemispheric channels come from neurons in the same hemisphere. Often they are axon collaterals from nearby neurons. An individual neuron can indirectly affect its own activity through collaterals that synapse on interneurons, which in their turn synapse with the original neuron.

Figure 3.18   A representative cortical pyramidal neuron.
Note that the cell's length almost equals the depth of the cortex.

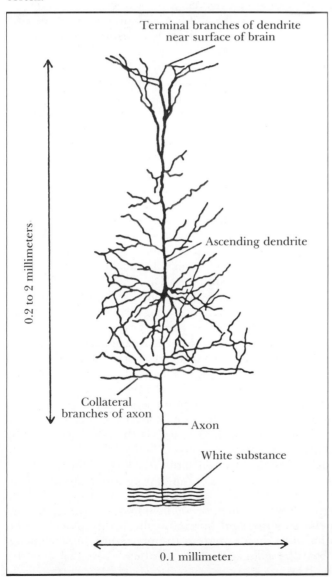

SUMMARY

1. The nervous system is composed of two basic parts, a central component that includes the brain and the spinal cord and a peripheral component, which includes the peripheral nerves and the autonomic nervous system.
2. There are 12 pairs of cranial nerves that bring information into and out of the central nervous system. These include the olfactory, optic, oculomotor, trochlear, trigeminal, abducens, facial, auditory, glossopharyngeal, vagus, accessory, and hypoglossal nerves.
3. Humans have 31 pairs of spinal nerves, 8 pairs of cervical nerves, 12 pairs of thoracic nerves, 5 pairs each of lumbar and sacral nerves, and 1 pair of coccygeal nerves. Each spinal nerve is responsible for a specific segment of the body termed a *dermatome*.
4. The autonomic nervous system (ANS) is made up of the sympathetic division and the parasympathetic division. For the most part the responses of the ANS are considered involuntary, but this is not strictly true, as some of the ANS responses can be brought under voluntary control.
5. The functions of the sympathetic division of the ANS have been characterized by Cannon as preparing the individual for "fight or flight," causing such responses as increased heart rate and increased supply of blood to the muscles. We are often aware of sympathetic responses as indicators of emotional states such as fear and anger. In actuality, both sympathetic and parasympathetic responses occur in most emotional states. For example, both divisions are crucial for the responses of the body during sexual arousal and orgasm.
6. The central nervous system contains over 99 percent of our neurons. The ascending nerve tracts in the spinal cord are classified as belonging to one of three systems, the dorsal column–medial lemniscus, the anterolateral, and the spinocerebellar. Most of the ascending neural pathways consist of three sets of neurons: primary sensory neurons and two sets of interneurons, a first-order and a second-order set. Many of the second-order neurons cross over or decussate to the opposite side of the cord, providing the basis for the sensory representation of the left side of the body in the right half of the brain and vice versa.
7. Neurons from widespread areas of the brain send axons down to synapse on spinal cord neurons. Most of these axons decussate, accounting for the control of movements of the left side of the body primarily by the right side of the brain and vice versa.
8. The brain and spinal cord are covered with three layers of membranes, the outer dura mater, inner pia mater, and an intermediate layer, the arachnoid layer.
9. The major structures in the human brain include the corpus callosum, the cerebellum, the superior and inferior colliculi, the pineal gland, thalamus, hypothalamus, limbic system (hippocampus, septal nuclei, and amygdala), basal ganglia, and cerebral cortex.

10. The most striking aspect of the primate brain is the development of the cerebral cortex, a six-layered structure that covers the surface of the cerebral hemispheres. One proposal of distinguishing different cytoarchitectural regions of the cortex, that of K. Brodmann, is still used.

11. The six layers of the cortex are termed (from dorsal surface downward) the plexiform layer, the external granular layer, the external pyramidal layer, the internal granular layer, the internal pyramidal layer, and the spindle cell layer. Two basic types of neurons are found in the cortex, pyramidal cells and stellate cells. These two basic types differ in form and probably in function.

12. Four different types of input channels to the cortex are found: specific sensory channels, nonspecific or diffuse channels, commissural channels from the opposite hemisphere, and intrahemispheric channels.

SUGGESTIONS FOR FURTHER READING

Angevine, J. B., and Cotman, C. W. (1981). *Principles of neuroanatomy.* New York: Oxford University Press.

Nauta, W. J. H., and Feirtag, M. (1986). *Fundamental neuroanatomy.* New York: W. H. Freeman.

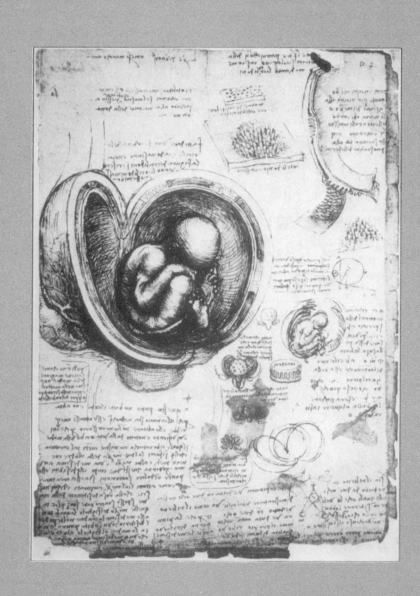

4

Brain Development, Growth, and Aging

*Ten thousand million tendrils
delicate as cloud
Tenacious as the tide . . .
seek and find their place.*

D. P. K.

Preview

A single fertilized egg gives rise to all the cells in the human brain and body. At birth, the brain consists of about 100 billion cells. The growth and development of the brain pose some interesting questions: How do the neurons manage to connect with each other so that the brain functions properly? What happens to neurons that do not make the proper connections? How do neurons find their appropriate place in the brain? These and other related questions are discussed in the first section of this chapter.

Neurons in the mammalian brain do not generally retain their capacity to divide after birth. With the exception of olfactory receptor cells, brain cells that die are not replaced. Nonetheless, brain damage can produce a variety of responses from the injured cells or their neighbors, such as the sprouting of new axon terminals and, under some conditions, extensive synaptic changes. Certain neurons continue to grow slowly throughout life, but restoration of normal circuitry following injury has not been seen as yet in the brain of a mammal.

Some of our brain cells are dying all the time, but this process causes only minimal mental or behavioral changes unless cell loss becomes extensive. Severe brain changes occur more frequently in the elderly and accompany such conditions as Alzheimer's disease, which is characterized by both mental and emotional changes.

Stages in Brain Development

There are eight principal stages in the development of the brain:

1. *Induction* of the neural plate
2. *Proliferation* of cells destined to become neurons and glial cells
3. *Migration* of neurons and glial cells to their ultimate locations
4. *Aggregation* of neurons destined to become part of particular circuits

5. *Differentiation* of neurons into particular types
6. **Synaptogenesis**—the formation of functional connection with other cells
7. *Selective cell death* of neurons, especially those that failed to reach their destination
8. *Functional validation*—the stabilization and elimination of synaptic connections through use or disuse

synaptogenesis (sin-nap-toe-JEN-uh-sis) The forming of synapses.

mitotic cycle (my-TOT-ik) The cell division cycle.

Induction of the Neural Plate

During the third week after conception the tissue that will become the nervous system begins to form a sheet of cells on the dorsal surface of the human embryo. This sheet of cells is known as the *neural plate*. Once the neural plate forms, its cells and all their descendants are destined to be brain cells. Shortly after the neural plate has formed, it raises a pair of bilateral ridges (see Figure 4.1, a and b). The so-called *neural groove* between the two ridges becomes enclosed as the ridges join together at the top and thereby form the *neural tube* (see Figure 4.1,c). This tube, which now contains about 125,000 cells, forms the basis of the nervous system. It retains its basic tube shape despite the massive enlargements and changes that will take place. The central canal in the spinal cord and the cerebral ventricles are derived from the space within the tube. Some neural cells migrate away from the neural tube to form the *neural crest*, which becomes the source of the cells that form most of the peripheral nervous system and portions of the adrenal medulla.

Proliferation

At birth the human brain contains an estimated 100 billion neurons. Based on an average 270-day gestation period, this means that new neurons must be generated at the rate of about 250,000 per minute during the time the embryo is developing (Cowan, 1979a). For the most part, neurons in mammalian brains stop dividing before or shortly after birth. A small number of neurons is apparently added to the brain for a considerable time after birth in rat and cat brains (Altman, 1967). On the other hand, there appear to be definite limits to the degree to which new neurons can form after birth in primate brains. Pasko Rakic (1985) has found that except for a few neurons in the cerebellum and hippocampus, no new neurons are formed in the rhesus monkey brain after birth. Related research suggests that human brain cells have similar limitations.

The **mitotic cycle,** the cell division cycle, consists of four recognizable phases. In the *mitotic phase* the maternal cell divides into two daughter cells. Following the mitotic phase, there is a pause called the *postmitotic gap*. This gap lasts from minutes to forever, since many cells withdraw from the mitotic cycle at this point. A cell that does not drop out of the mitotic cycle then enters the *S phase*, in which it synthesizes DNA. The S phase is followed by the *premitotic gap*, which precedes the next round of the cycle. By

**Figure 4.1
Development of the
neural plate, groove,
and tube in the chick
embryo.**
(a) neural plate;
(b) neural groove;
(c) neural tube.

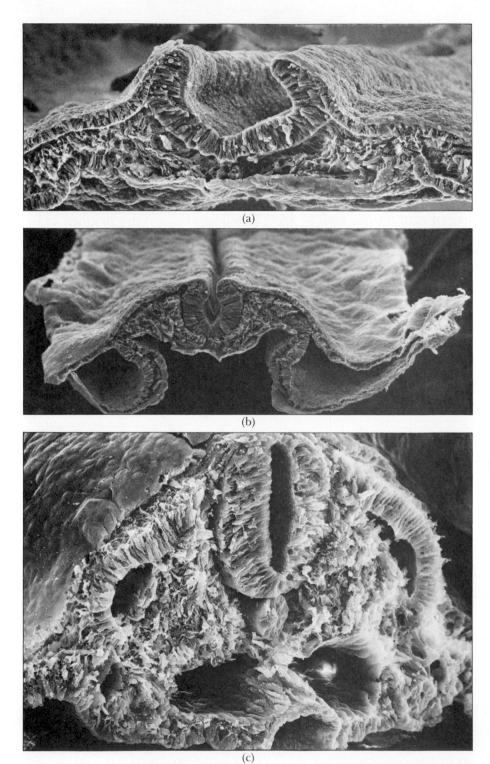

(a)

(b)

(c)

New Neurons for New Songs

The evidence currently available suggests that, except for an immediate, short period after birth, no new neurons are added to the primate brain. But this limitation does not apply to canaries—and maybe not to other songbirds either. Fernando Nottebohm and his colleagues (Goldman and Nottebohm, 1983; Paton and Nottebohm, 1984) have found evidence that male canaries generate new brain neurons throughout their lives.

In general, only male canaries sing, developing their first adult song at the age of about nine months. In the late summer of each year, they stop singing; and in the fall, they start to practice a new song for the next breeding season. Their singing is associated with the male hormone testosterone. When female canaries are given testosterone, they too sing; and when males are castrated before they learn to sing, they do not learn adult song. Both singing and testosterone levels are high during the spring breeding season, and both decline in the late summer. Strangely enough, the canary's brain region that responds to sound also grows and shrinks seasonally, with its size in the spring twice as large as its size in the fall. This structure, the **nucleus hyperstriatum ventralis pars caudalis** (HVc),

appears to have seasonal increases and decreases in the number of new neurons in adult male and testosterone-treated female canaries. Using an autoradiographic technique that can identify cells that have recently synthesized DNA, John Paton and Nottebohm (1984) were able to confirm the existence of new neurons in the HVc.

Paton and Nottebohm also recorded nerve impulses from the newly formed neurons in the HVc and found that these neurons responded to sound. The responses of these neurons and their appearance in microscopic sections seemed to indicate that they were small interneurons, which had apparently been added to the HVc during the six-week period of the experiment. The HVc also projects to other parts of the canary brain involved in song production. It is very likely that these HVc neurons play a key role in the learning of new songs each fall.

Other parts of the canary brain also add new neurons during the life of the bird. Nottebohm estimates that canaries may produce as many as 20,000 new neurons a day. Since the total number of neurons does not increase throughout the canary's lifetime, about the same number must die each day.

---

definition, the "birthday" of a cell is the day on which it undergoes its last division. This birthday can be determined by autoradiography.

The process of cellular proliferation has been studied in a number of species, and a few generalizations have emerged:

nucleus hyperstriatum ventralis pars caudalis (hy-per-stree-A-tum ven-TRAH-lis PARS kaw-DAH-lis) A brain region of songbirds.

1. The proliferation of larger neurons—such as the ganglion cells of the retina or pyramidal cells of the hippocampus and cerebral cortex—appears to precede the proliferation of smaller cells—such as bipolar cells and granule cells. Typically, the larger cells are those with long axons. In fact, the size of the cell body seems to be related to eventual axon length. The smaller neurons tend to have shorter axons and are destined primarily for "local circuit" duty, as opposed to the long-distance functions of the larger neurons.
2. Within the brain most of the proliferation occurs in the layer that forms the inner wall of the neural tube. Each region of the brain seems to have its own pattern of development. In the cerebral cortex, for example, the

neuroblasts (NEW-ro-blasts) Undifferentiated neurons.

fascicle (FAS-si-kul) A bundle of fibers.

mutant (MEW-tant) An organism that has one or more abnormal genes.

ectopic (ek-TOP-ik) in the wrong place.

neurons that are born first occupy the innermost layers of the cortex, and later-born neurons migrate past the earlier-born to occupy ever more superficial layers. In the retina, on the other hand, first the large ganglion cells form the outer layer and then the later-born interneurons and receptors form the inner layers (Cowan, 1979b).

Migration

Before they have differentiated, we refer to the neurons-to-be as **neuroblasts.** When neuroblasts have finished dividing, they migrate to their ultimate locations. Exactly what triggers this migration is not known, but it is closely linked in time with the cell's withdrawal from the mitotic cycle, and this withdrawal may serve as the initiating event. Evidence shows that most neuroblasts migrate in much the same way an amoeba travels: by extending a part of itself and then pulling the rest of the cell along (Cowan, 1979).

How do migrating neuroblasts know where to go? In the cortex, for instance, all neuroblasts must travel several millimeters from their birthplace to their particular destinations in the cortex. They have to find the right layer and must orient themselves so as make the appropriate synaptic connections with other neurons. Pasko Rakic and his colleagues investigated this problem in rhesus monkeys. Rakic (1981) suggests that three major factors determine a neuron's final position in the cerebral cortex: the position of its precursor cell in the proliferative zone, its time of birth, and its rate of migration.

Migrating cortical neuroblasts appear to be guided, in part, by a particular type of glial cell, the *radial glia.* Radial glial cells are present only during the fetal period of brain construction and disappear toward the end of gestation (Rakic, 1981). They seem to act as a scaffolding on which the migrating neuroblasts crawl toward their destinations. These radial glial cells constitute an orienting device around which the cellular columns of the cortex can form (details in Chapter 14). Radial glia are banded together in **fascicles** (bundles). Thus the basic columnar structure of the cortex is due, at least in part, to differences inherent in the proliferative zone. Such differences are preserved as migrating neuroblasts slide along their own particular fascicle to arrive at their designated home in the cortex.

A striking example of the relationship between the radial glia and the structure of the cerebellum is seen in the *weaver mouse.* Weavers are neurologically **mutant** mice, so named for their abnormal, weaving gait. In fetal weaver mice the radial glial cells disappear too early to provide the migrating cortical neuroblasts with a proper scaffolding. Thus many neuroblasts fail to migrate to their proper location in the cerebellum and fail to make the synaptic connections needed to support normal movements (Rakic and Sidman, 1973). Figure 4.2 illustrates a radial glial cell and associated migrating neuroblasts. Figure 4.3 contrasts the cerebellar tissue of a normal mouse with that of a weaver mouse, illustrating the abnormalities that arise when neurons fail to migrate to their correct locations.

There are more than 140 known neurologically mutant mouse strains (Sidman et al., 1965). In many of them neurons "get lost" through incorrect migration. Some of these **ectopic** (out-of-place) neurons are removed dur-

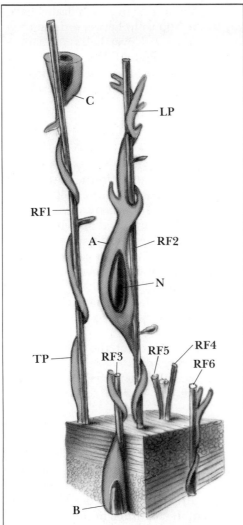

Figure 4.2 Migrating neurons on radial glia "scaffolding." Three different neurons are shown, labeled A, B, and C. Six radial glia fibers are shown, labeled RF1–RF6. LP=leading process; TP=trailing process; N=nucleus of migrating neuron. Reconstruction based on electron micrographs, semiserial sections (Rakic, 1978).

(a)

(b)

Figure 4.3 Semischematic drawing of neuronal arrangement in cerebellar cortex of normal (a) and weaver (wv/wv) mutant (b) mouse. Ba=basket cell; CF=climbing fiber; GII=Golgi type II fiber; P=Purkinje cell; PA=Purkinje cell axon; MF=mossy fiber.

ing the period of selective cell death (which will be discussed shortly). W. Maxwell Cowan (1979a) reports that in normal brains 3 percent of migrating neurons go astray during migration. Failures of proper migration show up as neurological syndromes in some of the human brains that come to autopsy, and they are usually accompanied by other abnormalities (Rakic, 1978). An abnormal arrangement of cells in the brains of a few dyslexics (individuals with a profound reading disability) has been reported (Geschwind and Galaburda, 1985). We do not know whether this abnormality is due strictly to a failure of migration or to a lack of proper aggregation (see below), nor do we know why these abnormally placed cells did not die. Perhaps some did. In any event, only four or five such brains have been examined; so conclusions about the relationship between these anatomical findings and dyslexia still remain tentative. Nevertheless, they provide an interesting lead, and as Norman Geschwind and Albert Galaburda (1985) point out, "The brains of all cases of childhood dyslexia so far studied contain cortical regions whose structure is anomalous as a result of disturbances in utero."

Aggregation

A migrating neuron must not only go to the right place in the cortex, but it must orient itself properly and become associated with other cells within its functional unit. This process is referred to as *aggregation*. Presumably, different cells can "recognize" one another by means of identifying membrane proteins. It has been known for many years that if neurons of a particular type—such as retinal, hippocampal, cerebellar, or cortical cells—are removed from the brain of an experimental animal, placed in a tissue culture, and then separated, they will "reaggregate" with cells of their own type (Kuffler et al., 1984). It is possible that similar mechanisms exist in the fetal brain, enabling specific cell types to aggregate into the characteristic layers and nuclei of the brain. Failure to aggregate properly seems to underlie the abnormality of another neurological mutant, the reeler mouse, named for its reeling gait. Unlike normal cortical cells, those from a reeler mutant do not reaggregate in a tissue culture (DeLong and Sidman, 1970).

Differentiation

Once a neuron has arrived at its destination, it starts to become a neuron of a particular type, with its own characteristic dendritic pattern, its specific number of axon collaterals, and its own chemical transmitter. The growth of neuronal processes into axons and dendrites is accomplished through the development of *growth cones* at the end of the neuronal branches. Figure 4.4 shows a growth cone. The first to observe such growth cones was Santiago Ramón y Cajal, almost a century ago. He was thrilled with this discovery and described a growth cone as "a living battering ram, soft and flexible, which advances, pushing aside mechanically the obstacles which it finds in its way, until it reaches the area of its peripheral distribution" (Ramón y Cajal, 1917, cited in Jacobson, 1978).

The membrane of the growth cone is known to be able to sustain Ca^{2+}-mediated nerve impulses. Rodolfo Llinas (1982) has suggested that Ca^{2+} channels later develop into the Ca^{2+} channels found in the axon terminals, which start off as axonal growth cones. When observed with time-lapse photography, the growth cones of axons and dendrites in a tissue culture seem to be in a frenzy of extensions and retractions. As the axon incorporates nutrients and grows out into the culture medium, it "samples" the

Figure 4.4 A neuronal growth cone in an artificial medium.

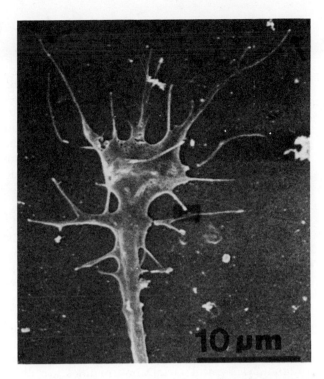

10 μm

cells with which it comes in contact, withdrawing from some and taking another "taste" of others. When the axonal growth cone finds the appropriate contact, synapses are formed with the acceptable cell. How neurons recognize each other is not certain; but presumably there are "recognition molecules" on the growth cone membrane and on the membrane of the contacted cell.

As for the axon sprouts of the differentiating neuron, "Many are called, but few are chosen." A lot are retracted and never develop fully. The "calling" may be done by other developing neurons that secrete *trophic* (growth-promoting) factors. An assumption that such substances can attract other cells from a considerable distance would help to explain why growth cones tend to grow in the proper direction. One substance of this kind has been observed to influence the development of adrenergic neurons in the sympathetic nervous system; it is a large protein called **nerve growth factor** (NGF), discovered by Rita Levi-Montalcini and Viktor Hamburger in 1951. Nerve growth factor has been shown to effect a dramatic increase in the growth of axons from the sympathetic ganglion toward the source of NGF (Campenot, 1977; Levi-Montalcini, 1966). Thus NGF is both a growth-promoting and a direction-giving protein. As mentioned in Chapter 1, Levi-Montalcini received the Nobel prize in 1986 for her research. It is almost certain that other, similar trophic factors exist in the nervous system (Thoenen and Edgar, 1985).

nerve growth factor (NGF) A naturally occurring protein that stimulates the growth of some neurons.

cretinism (KREE-tin-ism) Physical and mental stunting caused by insufficient thyroid secretion during fetal development.

fetal alcohol syndrome (FAS) Mental retardation, facial and other abnormalities in the offspring caused by mother's alcohol intake during pregnancy.

Environmental Factors in Fetal Development

The final form an individual neuron takes is determined by genetic instructions. But modulation of those instructions can occur as a result of factors in the environment of the developing cell. Malnutrition can alter the development of cells. Myelination, for instance, is vulnerable to a lack of appropriate nutrients. Since myelination continues for several years after birth in human beings, malnutrition in infancy can permanently affect the development of the nervous system. Recovery can occur, though. Korean orphans who had suffered varying degrees of malnutrition early in life did recover—in terms of IQ and school achievement—subsequent to their adoption by American middle-class families, who provided proper nutrition (Rosenzweig and Leiman, 1982).

Hormonal imbalances too are known to affect brain development. The severe stunting of the nervous system seen in **cretinism** is primarily due to insufficient thyroid secretion (Eayrs, 1964). An alarmingly long list of substances can cause abnormalities of fetal development. Alcohol can cause abnormalities in the nervous system and consequent deficits in mental and behavioral functions. The **fetal alcohol syndrome** (FAS), first identified and named by Kenneth Jones and David Smith (1973), is an example of foreign substances interfering with the normal development of the fetus. The extent of an infant's physical and mental abnormalities appears to be related directly to the amount of alcohol ingested by the mother during pregnancy. Typical facial abnormalities are illustrated in Figure 4.5. A

Figure 4.5   Child with a diagnosis of FAS photographed at birth, at eight months, and four and a half years.
The child's IQ was 40–45 at each evaluation from eight months on.

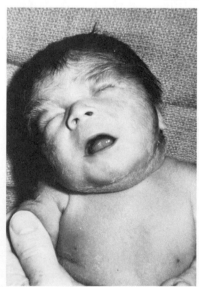 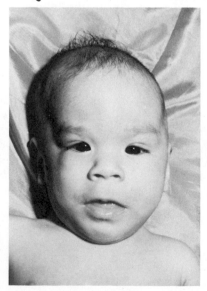 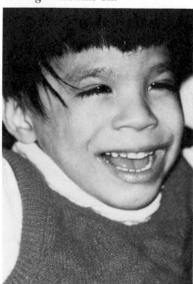

more recent review of this subject can be found in Colangelo and Jones (1982).

Choosing a Transmitter

One of the important "decisions" the differentiating neuron must make is its choice of transmitter. Each cell has genetic instructions for producing any or all of the neurotransmitters; but each neuron secretes only a small number, perhaps only one, after it has differentiated. Experiments with neurons of autonomic nervous systems indicate that the local environment of the differentiating neuron plays a critical role in determining which particular transmitter the cell actually secretes (Patterson et al., 1978; Le Douarin et al., 1975). Using embryonic rat cells derived from the neural crest, Patterson and colleagues discovered that when these cells were exposed to fluid from a culture medium to which nonneuronal cells had been added, they tended to become cholinergic—like those that normally serve to slow the heart rate via the vagus nerve. On the other hand, when such cells were *not* exposed to substances from nonneuronal tissue, they differentiated into noradrenergic cells—excitatory neurons that normally innervate the heart via the accelerans nerve. The influence of the nonneuronal cell substances in the culture medium appeared to change the inherently noradrenergic cells into cholinergic cells.

This hypothesis could not be completely correct, as Patterson and his associates realized, since all of these cells normally would be exposed to nonneuronal cells while they developed in the uterus. How were the cells destined to become noradrenergic cells "protected" in their natural environment and kept from becoming cholinergic? The answer seems to be that depolarization of the developing cells (and the accompanying Ca^{2+} entry) prevents the majority of them from becoming cholinergic, even in the presence of nonneuronal cells. In the animal this depolarization is normally provided by synaptic input from spinal neurons that grow out to make contact with these developing cells. The flowchart in Figure 4.6 shows how the differentiation of transmitter type is thought to proceed in these neurons.

Synaptogenesis

The activities of the brain are expressed through its synaptic circuits. In the process of synapse formation, called *synaptogenesis,* differentiating neurons must interact with other neurons so as to recognize appropriate partners and reject inappropriate ones. Not all the synapses formed during this stage of development survive, and some synaptogenesis is accomplished after birth while the brain continues to grow and develop. In animals with a relatively short gestation period a considerable amount of synaptogenesis takes place after birth. Thus in the cerebral cortex of the rat the number of synapses increases tenfold between postnatal days 12 and 30 (Jacobson, 1978).

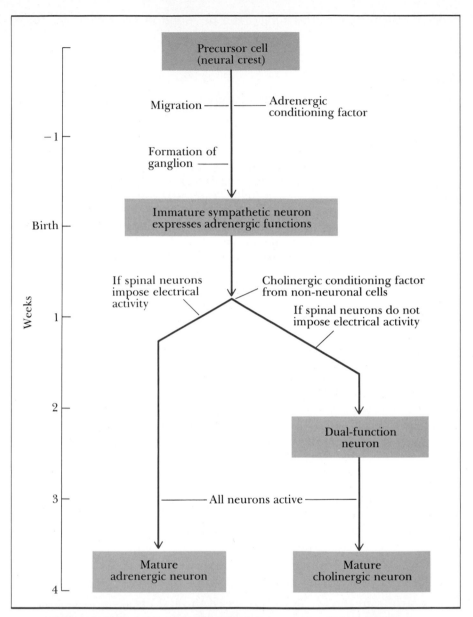

Figure 4.6   Flowchart of developmental steps proposed to underlie transmitter differentiation of a sympathetic neuron.
According to this hypothesis, the environmental factors that influence whether the neuron will become cholinergic or adrenergic include both nonneural secretions and neural activation. Time axis is approximate (Patterson et al., 1978).

In rodents and cats new neurons enrich the brain circuitry for some time after birth. Joseph Altman and his colleagues (1967) discovered, using autoradiography, that in a few restricted areas of the brain, a low level of neuronal mitosis continues after birth. Most of these newly formed neuroblasts eventually differentiate into small, short-axoned "microneurons," destined to be incorporated into existing circuits, especially into the circuits of the hippocampus, olfactory bulbs, and cerebellum. It may be that in these areas of cat and rodent brains this process of addition or replacement continues for a long time following birth. The functional significance of such postnatal neurogenesis is not certain, although Altman suggests that the addition of new neurons to the cerebellum of these animals is related to the development of adult-type movements.

chemoaffinity hypothesis (KEY-mo-a-FIN-ni-tee) The proposition that chemical differentiation allows neurons to make appropriate synaptic connections.

The Chemoaffinity Hypothesis

How do neurons make the correct synaptic connections? How, for example, do the axons of retinal ganglion cells make the correct synaptic connections in the brain? The fact that the visual system in mammals and other vertebrates is organized in an orderly, point-to-point manner has been used by various researchers in their attempts to discover how the visual system makes such connections in the first place. Although there is still considerable controversy about details, the **chemoaffinity hypothesis** of Roger Sperry (1963) serves as a major guide to research in this area.

Sperry proposed that the basis for selective synaptic connections was a chemical differentiation of each neuron. According to this hypothesis, neurons develop their own particular chemical identity. Furthermore, Sperry suggested, each projection neuron, such as a ganglion cell from the retina, has the capacity to detect and match up with appropriate neurons in the brain. The data supporting the chemoaffinity hypothesis have come largely from studying the neurons in the optic tectum of frogs and the connections made by the axons of ganglion cells during regeneration of the optic nerve after it had been cut or otherwise manipulated.

Amphibians have a remarkable capacity for regenerating neural tissue. This regeneration in the adult animal is the regrowth of neural tissue and the reestablishment of appropriate synaptic connections. Severing the optic nerve results in permanent and total blindness with mammals; but in a frog or a salamander, it is followed by regeneration of the optic nerve and reestablishment of synaptic connections with neurons of the optic tectum, which is the amphibian equivalent of visual cortex. Regeneration of these connections takes about a month in frogs. When optic nerves are simply cut and left in their normal position, normal vision seems to return in about a month, and as far as anyone can tell, the frogs see as well as ever. Such a finding is not definitive, though, for it is possible that the regrowing optic nerves make more or less random connections with the optic tectum and that normal vision returns as the frog relearns. A relearning hypothesis, however, could not accommodate the following findings.

In a series of experiments, Sperry manipulated the eyes of frogs in different ways. In one experiment he cut the optic nerves and rotated the eyeballs 180 degrees, so that what had been the dorsal half of the retina was now located on the ventral half of the eye socket, and what had been the anterior half of the retina was now located in the posterior half of the eye socket. After letting a month or so elapse to allow for regeneration of the connections between the cut optic nerve and the optic tectum, the frogs' vision was tested by introducing lures (flies) into various parts of the visual field. The frogs consistently showed striking responses—unrolling and flicking their long, sticky tongues—exactly 180 degrees in the wrong direction (Figure 4.7). No amount of practice seemed to change this result. There was, in fact, no evidence of relearning. These animals continued to show vision reversed 180 degrees, exactly matching the reversal of the eyes.

The most plausible explanation for this and similar findings is that the axons of the regenerating ganglion cells grew back and made synaptic connections in the same region of the tectum in which they had made the connections initially. In their new position, however, retinal signals from

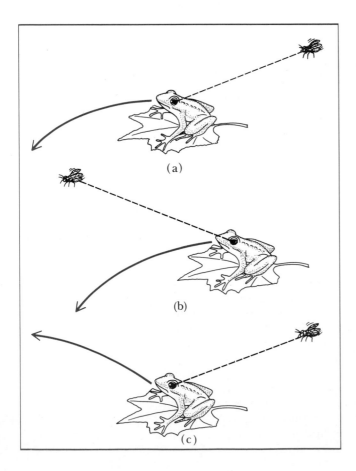

(a)

(b)

(c)

Figure 4.7 Misguided striking responses following rotation and inversion of the frog's eye.
(a) With eye rotated 180 degrees, frog strikes at a point 180 degrees from the fly lure.
(b) After dorsoventral inversion of the eye, frog strikes correctly with reference to the nasotemporal dimensions of the visual field, but inversely with reference to the dorsoventral dimension. (c) After nasotemporal inversion of the eye, frog strikes correctly with reference to the dorsoventral dimensions of the visual field, but inversely with reference to the nasotemporal dimensions (Sperry, 1951).

the anterior half of the retina were now interpreted by the frog as originating in the posterior half of the retina. The frogs struck where they perceived the lure to be.

Similar results were obtained by cutting the optic nerves and transplanting the right eye to the left socket and vice versa. Depending on just how the eye was placed, vision was misguided in precisely the way one would predict if one assumed that the regenerating neurons grew back to their original termination sites in the tectum. Later experiments with the regeneration of optic nerve connections have yielded results that suggested some changes in Sperry's original hypothesis, but the basic idea has survived (Gaze, 1970; Jacobson, 1978).

Selective Cell Death

Billions of neurons do not survive the developmental process. Extensive cell death is part of the normal developmental process. Neuron groups in which accurate counts are available show that from 15 to 85 percent of the cells formed during the fetal period die before birth, with an average death rate of about 50 percent (Cowan et al., 1984). Although it may seem strange, even wasteful, to produce so many neurons merely to have them die before the animal is born, selective cell death is actually quite a reasonable way to complete the organization of neuronal circuits.

Neurons that do not make the appropriate synaptic connections are particularly vulnerable and usually do not survive. In many cases, survival depends on some type of transsynaptic stimulation from one neuron to another (Jacobson, 1978). Selective cell death can preserve the important cells and their connections and eliminate cells that are unnecessary or even detrimental to the proper organization within the brain. When a neuroblast has gone astray during migration, its deletion is likely to improve the function of the surrounding brain area.

Whiskers and Barrels

The final developmental process is that of *functional validation,* which stabilizes the synaptic connections of circuits that are in use and weakens or eliminates unused synapses. A vivid example of neurons that disappear if they are not validated has been demonstrated in the somatosensory cortex of the mouse. If the sensory neurons that normally innervate the whiskers of the mouse are destroyed early in life, then the barrel-shaped rings of cortical neurons with which they normally synapse will disappear completely. These cortical cells cannot survive without normal synaptic contacts from the peripheral sensory receptors (see Figure 4.8). Such dependence is remarkable, since at least two other neurons, interposed in the chain between the whisker receptors and the cortical neurons, die as a result of whisker removal (Van der Loos and Woolsey, 1973). It is not clear just how general this sort of dependence is throughout the nervous system. Trans-

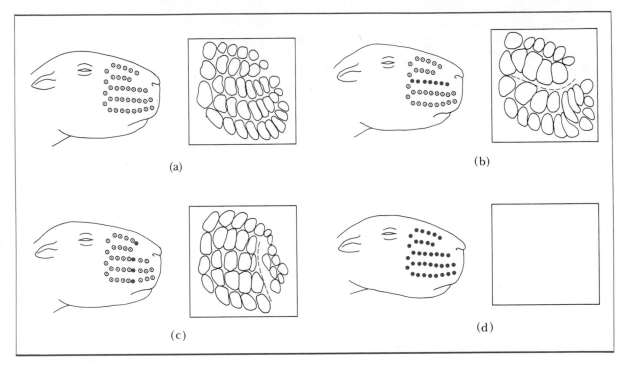

Figure 4.8 Whiskers and barrels.
(a) Each whisker in the snout of the mouse has its own barrel of responsive cortical neurons, which are activated when the whisker is touched. (b) If one row of whiskers is destroyed shortly after birth, the corresponding row of barrels in the cortex will later be found to be missing, and the adjoining barrels will be enlarged (b, c). If all the whiskers are removed, the entire group of neurons which form the barrels will disappear (d) (Cowan, 1979).

synaptic stimulation is clearly an important factor in allowing neurons to survive the developmental period, although many of the earlier stages of neuronal development do not involve such stimulation (Jacobson, 1978).

Enriching the Brain

The structural plasticity of the brain has been demonstrated by a series of experiments in which rats were housed in either standard conditions, impoverished conditions with few stimuli, or enriched environments with several cage mates and with objects to explore. (Figure 4.9 illustrates the three different rearing conditions.) Although other parts of the brain did not differ in weight among the three groups, the cortex of animals in the enriched condition was found to be about 5 percent heavier than the cortex of environmentally impoverished rats and about 2 percent heavier than the cortex of rats reared under standard conditions. These differences have

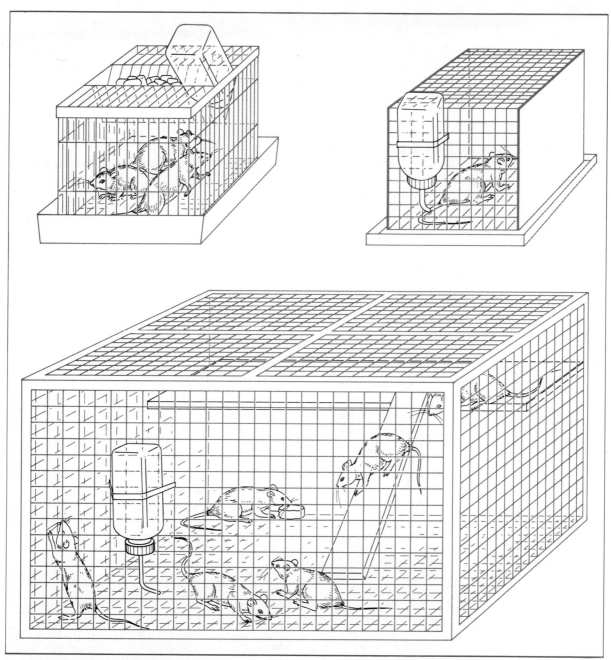

Figure 4.9   Three laboratory environments that produce differences in the thickness of the cerebral cortex in rats.
The standard condition is shown in the upper left; the impoverished environment is shown in the upper right; and the enriched environment is shown in the bottom drawing. Food and water are freely available in all three environments.

proved quite reliable and statistically significant (Rosenzweig and Leiman, 1982). The weight of the occipital cortex, in particular, is increased by enrichment. This additional weight is largely due to increased growth of basal dendrites on the cortical neurons (Greenough, 1975). There is some evidence that these cortical gains are due to informal learning about the environment by the animals, not to some general sensory stimulation (Rosenzweig and Leiman, 1982).

Thus, by a series of stages from proliferation to synaptogenesis, the basic organization of the brain is accomplished. If the environment permits normal functioning, the basic circuits that have been dictated by genetic information are validated and survive. However, the processes of dendritic growth and synaptic modifiability allow the brain to adjust to changing environmental events. These processes may be the basis of learning and memory, a topic discussed in greater detail in Chapter 12.

Responses of Nervous Tissue to Injury

Once a neuron has withdrawn from the mitotic cycle, it does not reenter the cycle—unlike a glial cell, which can reenter the cycle. It would be very interesting to know what causes this difference, for that knowledge might lead to a means of unlocking the reproductive capacity of mature neurons in cases of brain damage. So far as we know at present, once a mature neuron in the brain of a mammal dies, it is not replaced (unless it is an olfactory neuron; see Chapter 6). Cell death goes on continually throughout life, accelerating somewhat with advancing age. Behavioral effects of this cell loss in normal, aging humans are not clear. In advanced old age and in degenerative neural diseases, neuronal loss contributes to mental and behavioral changes.

SUMMARY TABLE
Stages of Development of the Nervous System

Developmental Stage	Main Feature of Stage
Induction	Production of cells that will become nervous tissue
Proliferation	Cell reproduction (mitosis)
Migration	Location of cells in appropriate brain areas
Aggregation	Clustering of cells that will form functional units
Differentiation	Development of neurons into particular type
Synaptogenesis	Formation of appropriate synaptic connections
Cell death	Elimination of mislocated cells and cells that failed to form proper synaptic connections
Functional validation	Strengthening of synapses in use, weakening of unused synapses

---

Responses to Axonal Damage

If the cell body of a neuron is destroyed or damaged beyond recovery, the entire cell will die—dendrites, axon, and all. But if the cell body survives, damaged axons may produce a variety of regenerative responses. If, for example, an axon is severed at some distance from the cell body, reactive changes will take place in the axon, in the cell body, and in the synaptic connections on the cell body and the dendrites, and even in the postsynaptic cell (the cell that synapsed with the severed axon).

Anterograde Changes

The segment of axon that is no longer connected to its own cell body begins to deteriorate almost immediately. Within a few hours it dies, unable to survive without nourishment from the cell body. In the brain, if the axon is myelinated, its myelin sheath deteriorates also. The debris is removed by specialized glial scavenger cells. In mammalian—unlike amphibian—brains, functional regeneration has not been documented. While the myelin sheath of neurons within the central nervous system deteriorates, the myelin sheath of efferent peripheral neurons survives and may act as a guide for the regenerating axon.

If the postsynaptic cell is a muscle cell, it will become paralyzed. Within a short time, it will also lose "tone" or elasticity, and if it is not reinnervated within a few weeks, the muscle will **atrophy.** If you ever had an arm or a leg in a cast, you have experienced some temporary atrophy of muscles that have been deprived of normal activity. This atrophy has been attributed in part to a decrease of some important trophic (nourishing) factor secreted by the presynaptic neuron. At most junctions between neurons and skeletal muscles, the transmitter is acetylcholine, and there is evidence that acetylcholine is the trophic factor as well as the neurotransmitter. Thus virtually all the effects of cutting a nerve can be produced by applying a drug that blocks the effects of acetylcholine at the neuromuscular junction (Jacobson, 1978). However, atrophy can be prevented by direct electrical stimulation of the muscle, so it appears that trophic factors may not be necessary if the muscle can be caused to contract directly.

Neurons in the visual system undergo a similar reaction. If the optic nerve is cut, the neurons in the lateral geniculate nucleus of the thalamus on which the optic nerve axons terminate undergo severe atrophy, and some of the lateral geniculate neurons die. This **anterograde** transsynaptic degeneration can even be seen at the next level in the visual system—the neurons in layer IV of the cerebral cortex on which the lateral geniculate cells terminate. This cascading of degenerative effects is most clearly seen in sensory systems but may not occur in all brain regions (Kelly, 1981b).

Retrograde Effects

If an axon is severed close to the cell body, the entire neuron almost certainly will die. If the cut is farther away from the cell body, the axon will

atrophy (AH-tro-fee) To waste away.

anterograde (ANN-TER-o-grade) Forward going.

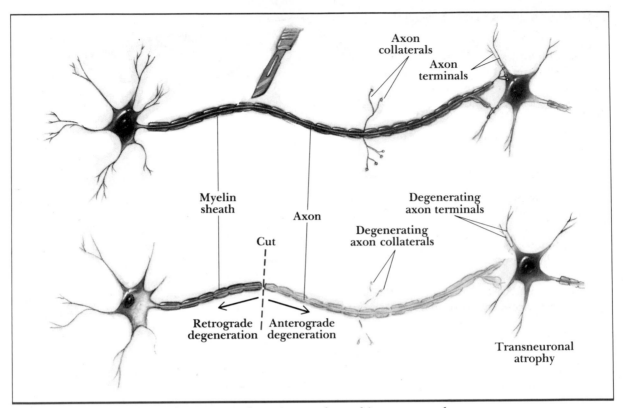

Figure 4.10   Diagram showing retrograde, anterograde, and transneuronal atrophy following cutting of a myelinated axon.

chromatolysis (kro-ma-TOL-i-sis) Disintegration within protein-producing regions of nerve cells.

die back to its next junction with an axon collateral. At this junction the axon will seal over and begin to form tiny axon sprouts. In addition, the following series of changes will take place in the cell body. The cell body will take in water and triple in size; the nucleus will move to one edge of the cell; and a complex series of events will take place in the endoplasmic reticulum of the cell body. These changes, which may be preparatory to sprouting and attempts by the cell to regrow its axon, involve the synthesis of RNA and new proteins. These can be seen when you stain the cells with thionine, which turns the protein blue. The term **chromatolysis** is given to the general degenerative changes that take place in the cell body of a neuron whose axon has been cut. Retrograde changes in the axon and cell body may take two or three weeks to develop. Figure 4.10 shows some of the retrograde changes in the cell body of an injured neuron.

Retrograde Transneuronal Changes

Axonal damage results in a retraction of the injured cell's dendrites from their synaptic contacts. Glial cells invade the vacated space, and the cell is thus removed from much or all of its normal synaptic connections. Neurons may or may not survive the period of chromatolysis. Recovery seems to depend in part on the restoration of synaptic connections (Kelly, 1981b). This is another example of the interdependence of synaptically coupled cells in the nervous system.

Axonal Sprouting and Synaptic Remodeling

If a neuron survives the damage to its axon, its proximal stump will begin to regrow by producing a number of sprouts at the cut end of the axon. In peripheral neurons these sprouts tend to die back once the neuron has regenerated to near normal length and has reestablished synaptic connections with a peripheral target cell. Original synaptic connections in the brain have not been seen to reestablish themselves after the severing of an axon. Axonal sprouting within the brain is something of a puzzle. It might have no effect, harmful effects (if it resulted in miswiring), or beneficial effects (if the sprouts produced useful synaptic connections). Although the puzzle is still unsolved, a few of its pieces have been put together. The work of Geoffrey Raisman and colleagues, for instance, established that through a process called *synaptic remodeling*, axonal sprouting can result in new synaptic connections (Raisman, 1969; Raisman and Field, 1973).

Raisman and Pauline Field studied electron micrographs of more than 50,000 synapses. They were examining rats' septal nuclei—neuronal clusters that serve as junctions between the hippocampus and the hypothalamus. Two main nerve tracts synapse in the septal nuclei: the *medial forebrain bundle* (MFB), which comes from the hypothalamus, and the *fimbria-fornix* (fimb), which carries axons from the hippocampus. Raisman and Field ascertained that both of these nerve tracts synapse on septal neurons, but they do so in different patterns. The axon terminals from the MFB make synapses on the cell body as well as on the dendrites of the septal neurons. But the axon terminals from the fimbria make synapses on only the dendrites of septal neurons.

Having determined this pattern, Raisman and Field cut one or the other of these two nerve tracts in various rats. To give the rats' axons time to sprout, they waited several weeks before they cut the other tract. After allowing two to three days for degeneration of axon terminals, they sacrificed the animals and stained their brains so as to show the degeneration products of the more recently severed axons. (The degeneration products of the earlier operation had already been cleared away by scavenger glia.) In those animals whose MFB had been cut before their fimbria, they found that the fimbria terminals had filled in synaptic sites that had been vacated as a result of cutting the MFB. Where the cutting sequence had been the reverse, MFB sprouts had filled in vacant synaptic sites caused by the earlier cutting of the fimbria.

In other words, as a synaptic site was vacated by the degeneration of the first tract to be destroyed, that site was filled in by the nearest available axon sprout, even though it came from the "wrong" tract. The overall result was a synaptic remodeling of the septal nuclei following the destruc-

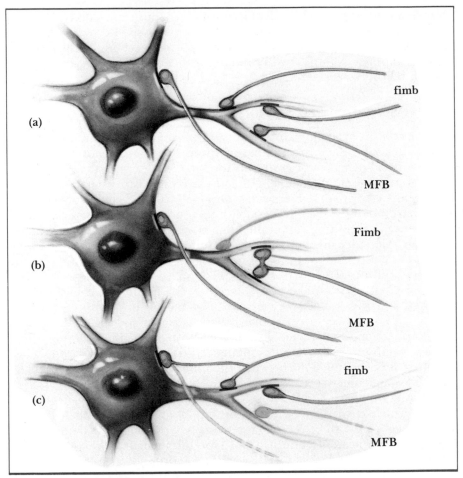

Figure 4.11   Synaptic remodeling after a cut through one of two main nerve pathways to the septal area.
(a) Normal arrangement: afferents from the medial forebrain bundle (MFB) terminate on the cell soma (S) and on dendrites; fimbria fibers (fimb) terminate only on dendrites. (b) Several weeks after a lesion to the fimbria: the MFB terminals extend from their own site to the vacated site, forming double synapses. (c) Several weeks after a lesion of the MFB: the fimbrial fibers have established a terminal on the somatic site the severed MFB afferent vacated. (Raisman, 1969).

tion of one of its main input channels. This was the first clear evidence of such synaptic alterations in the brain of a mammal. What makes this evidence even more remarkable is that these two nerve tracts use different neurotransmitters. The fimbria-fornix cells are cholinergic, whereas those of the medial forebrain bundle are noradrenergic. The recipient septal neurons appear to have undergone some sort of dedifferentiation that adapted their synaptic receptor membrane to the new neurotransmitter. Figure 4.11 illustrates this synaptic remodeling.

Synaptic remodeling has also been observed in the dentate gyrus of the hippocampus, where it has been termed **reactive synaptogenesis,** to emphasize that there must be a stimulus (some event triggered by the injury) to cause the sprouting and subsequent change in synaptic connectivity (Cotman and McGaugh, 1980). In several experiments (Cotman and Lynch, 1976; Cotman and Nadler, 1978) denervation of dentate gyrus cells was followed by a filling in of vacated synaptic sites by axon terminals from surviving neurons in the region. The new synapses were formed by neurons that already had made some synaptic contacts with the dentate cells, but the exact location of the synapses was different. It has not been determined whether an animal's behavior is altered by such synaptic remodeling. In rats the capacity to form new axonal sprouts decreases with age (McWilliams and Lynch, 1983). This fact may or may not be related to the observation that in most cases younger animals (and human beings) recover better from brain damage than do older ones. (See the discussion on recovery from brain damage in Chapter 14.)

reactive synaptogenesis (sin-nap-toe-JEN-e-sis) Synapse formation in response to axon terminal degeneration at nearby receptor sites.

Aging

In much of the world more people are living longer than ever before. On average, a baby born in the United States today will live to the age of 74. People aged 65 and over now constitute the fastest-growing segment of our population, and this has focused more attention on the phenomena of aging.

Normal Aging

The body ages, and so does the brain. As it grows older, it loses neurons and becomes slightly smaller. Actually, it begins to lose neurons even before birth. But until the age of 35 or so, this loss is not very great. With increasing age, however, and particularly after the age of 75, cells are lost at an accelerating rate. The number of neurons in the brains of individuals in their nineties can be less than half the average number found in an infant (Brody, 1955). This cell loss is also reflected in the weight of the brain, which declines steadily after the age of about 45 (Samarajski, 1976).

Nonetheless, there are some neurons in the cortex that seem to keep on growing all one's life. Stephen Buell and Paul Coleman (1979) examined the extent of dendrites in the brains of people who had died from causes other than brain disease: normal adults whose average age was 51; normal, aged adults whose average age was 80; and patients with an average age of 76 who had been diagnosed as suffering from senile dementia. In the aged, normal brains Buell and Coleman found the most extensive apical dendrites. They calculated that in normal brains, the growth rate of these dendrites is about 0.21 μm per year over the age span measured (ages 44–92). Evidence of this growth process was not seen in the brains of senile dementia patients. This suggests that there are at least two subpopulations

Fetal Brain Tissue Transplants

In the last few years a remarkable experimental technique has been developed that allows pieces of brain tissue from fetal animals to be grafted successfully into the brains of host animals. Most of the experimental work has been done with rats and mice, but some preliminary research has been done with primates as well (Gash et al., 1985). There seem to be several reasons fetal tissue survives in such grafting procedures. One of them may be that fetal brain cells retain their ability to undergo mitosis and can therefore proliferate in the environment of the host animal's brain. Another factor contributing to the success of these procedures may be that the brain seems to be a privileged site with respect to the immune system, which normally causes the rejection of foreign tissue. The reason for this is not yet understood completely, but it may be due to the obstacles the blood brain barrier presents to various elements of the immune system.

Modern research into brain grafting began in the 1970s with experiments in the United States and Sweden (Das and Altman, 1971; Lund and Hauschka, 1976; Stenevi et al., 1976). Since then over 200 studies have involved transplanting fetal tissue into adult brains. Brain grafting has been used to investigate whether problems related to brain damage could be corrected by such transplants. Recent experiments have demonstrated that

some partial restoration of function is indeed possible. Virtually all the research so far has been conducted on rodents. Improvement has been seen in rats with motor difficulties produced by chemical toxins, with hormonal deficiencies, and with various learning deficits produced by brain damage or aging (Dunnett, et al., 1985; Gage and Björklund, 1986). Figure 4.12 shows an example of fetal brain tissue grafted into the brain of an adult rat that had suffered a bilateral hippocampal lesion. In this study fetal brain grafts were instrumental in partially correcting a maze-learning deficit caused by a hippocampal lesion (Kimble et al., 1986).

To date, these techniques have been used on only two groups of human beings. In Sweden a few patients with Parkinson's disease have been given autografts, consisting of tissue from their own adrenal medulla. These adrenal cells secrete small amounts of the neurotransmitter dopamine, which is deficient in Parkinson's disease. The adrenal tissue was inserted close to the basal ganglia in these patients. Only some slight and transient improvement was observed, but these patients were in an advanced state of the disease. Similar studies on two younger patients with Parkinson's disease in Mexico have proved far more encouraging. (See Chapter 7 for a fuller discussion of Parkinson's disease.)

of cortical neurons: diers and survivors. In the latter group not only do the neurons survive, but they continue to grow and expand their dendritic domain.

Cells in the cerebral cortex that appear to be particularly vulnerable to the aging process are the large pyramidal Betz cells of the motor cortex. Madge Scheibel et al. (1977) examined the brains of seven elderly patients who had died between the ages of 74 and 102 and found that as many as 75 percent of these cells showed age-related changes, such as progressive loss of dendritic spines and atrophy of the basilar dendrites. By contrast, only about 30 percent of their neurons in the surrounding cortical tissue

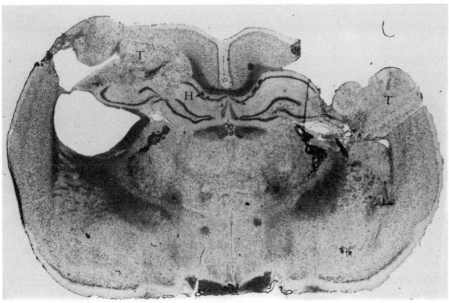

Figure 4.12   Implantation of fetal rat brain tissue (T) into adult rat's brain in the region of the hippocampus (H).
The hippocampal lesion is partly filled in by the fetal implant, and the maze-learning deficit is partly eliminated by the transplant.

An older athlete. His nervous system must still be operating rather effectively. Some research suggests one population of neurons in the brain continues to grow throughout life (see text)

dementia (de-MEN-sha) Deteriorated mental abilities.

Alzheimer's disease (ALLS-hy-merz) Severe mental and emotional deterioration associated with changes in the brain.

showed such degenerative changes. The Betz cells mediate the relaxation of the extensor muscles involved in smooth, rapid movements, particularly of the lower extremities. Scheibel and colleagues suggest that the age-related deterioration of Betz cells bears considerable responsibility for the pain, stiffness, and slowing of movements that characterize the elderly.

Mental Processes in the Elderly

In the last few years a great deal of research has been devoted to comparing the cognitive functions of young adults with those of older people. Much of this research has focused on learning and memory. As will be discussed in Chapter 12, most theorists assume that there are at least three types of memory: immediate memory, short-term memory (which, for example, allows one to remember a telephone number long enough to dial it), and long-term memory. Two kinds of long-term memory may exist: *semantic* memory—remembering how to do things and knowledge of the world—and *episodic* memory—memory for the events in one's own life.

Neither immediate memory nor short-term memory seems to suffer very much in normal aging, at least not before the age of 70 or so. (Studies of people aged 75 and older are more difficult to interpret, since a variety of sensory and attentional problems may interfere with the accurate measurement of memory capacity.) It is long-term memory that seems to be affected in advanced age—especially the ability to *recall* material, as opposed to simply recognizing material. The elderly tend to recall fewer details of a news article or story a week or so after they have read it. In extreme old age, other aspects of memory, such as short-term memory, may also decline.

Abnormal Aging

Although the majority of elderly people do not manifest a great loss of mental capacity, some do. About 5 percent of individuals over the age of 65 suffer from some type of **dementia** (severe impairment of cognitive functions). Another 10 percent of people 65 years old or older show mild to moderate dementia (Coyle et al., 1983). Among those who are diagnosed as having dementia, about 70 percent have **Alzheimer's disease** (Cote, 1981). Prominent among the early symptoms of dementia is an impairment of recent episodic memory, although longer-term episodic memories, such as childhood events, are usually retained. Progressive impairments in Alzheimer's disease include a loss of the ability to read and write correctly, general confusion, loss of normal speech, and inability to perform arithmetical calculation. Dementia patients often become irritable, and some experience hallucinations and delusions of a paranoid type (Coyle et al., 1983).

Brain Changes in Alzheimer's Disease

The brains of patients with Alzheimer's disease have come to autopsy often enough to give us rather a clear picture of the brain changes that accompany this disease. They fall into the following five categories.

Cell Loss

Alzheimer's patients show a more dramatic loss of neurons, particularly in the cerebral cortex, than age-matched nondemented individuals. Although healthy aged individuals may lose as much as 30 percent of the cortical neurons they had as young adults, people with Alzheimer's disease show cortical neuron losses of 50 percent or more (Samorajski, 1976). These losses affect primarily the frontal and temporal cortical regions of the brain.

Dendritic Degeneration

Examination of brain tissue from Alzheimer's disease patients has revealed severe degeneration of the dendrites of cortical neurons. One such study (Scheibel et al., 1975) showed the degeneration to be more closely related to the patients' degree of dementia than to their calendar age. Dendritic degeneration was particularly marked in layer III of the cortex and was most noticeable in the basilar or horizontal dendrites (see Figure 4.13). These dendrites synapse primarily on neurons within the cortex, and they are the last ones to differentiate in the infant. Thus there is a last-in-first-

Figure 4.13 Simplified drawings of cortical dendrites in (a) normal young adult brain, and (b) senile brain.
Note the loss of horizontal dendrites in the senile brain.

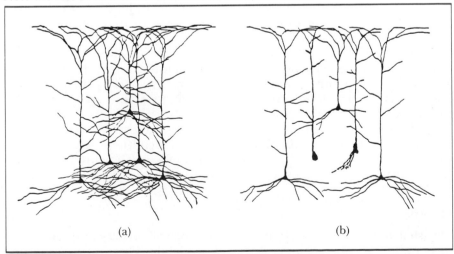

(a)   (b)

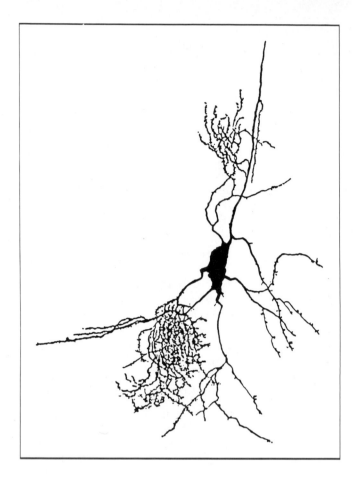

Figure 4.14   Drawing of a pyramidal cell from the temporal lobe of a 47-year-old patient who died of Alzheimer's disease. There is an irregular swelling of the cell body, dendritic spine loss on both basilar and apical dendrites, and "lawless" dendritic growth in lower left part of figure.

neurofibrillary tangles (new-ro-FIB-ri-la-ree) Distorted brain neurotubules and neurofilaments typical in Alzheimer's disease.

out degeneration of these dendrites. Scheibel and colleagues speculate that these dendrites may be directly involved in such cortical activities as reasoning, sophisticated thinking, and memory.

It is possible that the dendrites become progressively distorted and degenerate as the cell's neurotubules and neurofilaments deteriorate. In one form of Alzheimer's disease, which typically attacks patients in their late forties or early fifties, Arnold Scheibel and Uwamie Tomiyasu (1978) found yet another abnormality in dendritic structure. In these brains they found not only the dendritic degeneration characteristic of older patients, but also what they termed a "lawless growth of dendrites," which included haphazard dendritic bundles. Figure 4.14 shows such a neuron. Its abnormal structure would almost certainly distort its function.

Tangles

Twisted and distorted neurotubules, called **neurofibrillary tangles,** are another abnormality seen in patients with dementia. These tangles are common in the brains of Alzheimer's patients, but they also show up in other neurological conditions, such as Down's syndrome. They are occasionally seen also in aged normal brains (Cote, 1981).

Senile Plaques

Also found frequently in very old brains and in the brains of patients with Alzheimer's disease are *plaques*. With Golgi cell staining techniques these plaques show up as small dark spots. Such plaques, probably formed as axon terminals degenerated, have a core of **amyloid,** a complex protein thought to be similar to the immunoglobulins produced by the immune system.

Neurotransmitter Deficits, Abnormalities

The list of abnormal neurotransmitter levels in the brains of Alzheimer patients is probably not yet complete. What have been found so far are abnormally low levels of acetylcholine, noradrenaline, serotonin, and somatostatin (Winblad et al., 1985). Of all of these the most profoundly reduced neurotransmitter is acetylcholine.

Acetylcholine levels are usually measured by evaluating levels of **choline acetyltransferase** (ChAT), which is the enzyme responsible for synthesizing acetylcholine from its precursors, choline and acetyl-coenzyme A (see Figure 4.15). Levels of this enzyme are 60–90 percent lower in patients with Alzheimer's disease than in their age-matched controls (Coyle et al., 1983). The cell bodies of one critical population of cholinergic neurons are clustered primarily in a small region of the basal forebrain called the *basal forebrain cholinergic system* (Price et al., 1985). Neurons from the basal forebrain cholinergic system send axons to widespread regions of the cerebral cortex and hippocampus. The main structures in this basal forebrain cholinergic system include the medial septum, the diagonal band of Broca (dbB), and the **nucleus basalis of Meynert** (nbM). The medial septum and dbB project primarily to the hippocampus, whereas the nbM projects diffusely to various regions of the neocortex. It is now known that cell loss of neurons in the nbM is particularly important in producing the decrease in ChAT seen in widespread areas of the brain. This loss in cortical ChAT occurs as the axons of the nbM neurons degenerate.

Loss of neurons in the nbM is also seen in other types of dementia. For example, a subgroup of Parkinson's disease patients shows dementia, and this subgroup also shows selective cell loss in the nbM. Evidence also exists linking degeneration of cholinergic neurons in this and closely related areas of the brain with the mental impairments seen in elderly patients with **Down's syndrome** (Price et al., 1985). Although it is quite likely that other brain abnormalities can be found in Alzheimer's disease, the dramatic cell loss in the basal forebrain cholinergic system and the consequent degeneration of cholinergic axons throughout the cortex and hippocampus are thought to be very important in producing the mental impairments characteristic of Alzheimer's disease.

amyloid (AIM-i-loyd) A protein found in the senile plaques.

choline acetyltransferase (ChAT) (KO-leen ah-see-tul-TRANZ-fu-race) Enzyme involved in the synthesis of acetylcholine.

nucleus basalis of Meynert (nbM) (NEW-klee-us ba-SAL-is of MAY-nurt) A region of the forebrain with a concentration of cholinergic neurons.

Down's syndrome A condition marked by mental retardation and physical abnormalities due to an extra chromosome.

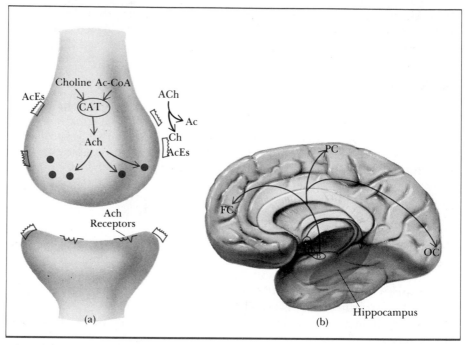

Figure 4.15 **(a) Diagram of acetylcholine synapse showing synthesis of acetylcholine. (b) Cholinergic pathways innervating hippocampus and cerebral cortex in human brain.**
ACh = acetylcholine; CAT = choline acetyltransferase; AcEs = acetylcholine esterase; Ac = acetate; Ch = choline; Ac-CoA = acetyl co-enzyme A; FC = frontal cortex; PC = parietal cortex; OC = occipital cortex; H = hippocampus; S = septal nucleus; D = diagonal band of Broca; B = nucleus basalis of Meynert.

Therapy Attempts Based on the Cholinergic Hypothesis

choline (KO-leen) A precursor of acetylcholine.

lecithin (LEH-si-thin) The main dietary source of choline, found in egg yolk and liver.

The proposition that the diminished cholinergic innervation of the cerebral cortex and hippocampus is responsible for many symptoms of Alzheimer's disease is known as the *cholinergic hypothesis.* Not surprisingly, several attempts have been made to restore patients' cognitive functions by increasing the supply of brain acetylcholine. Acetylcholine itself cannot be administered, however, because it breaks down in the bloodstream and in the digestive system. The most common procedure, therefore, has been to add **choline,** the precursor of acetylcholine, to the patient's diet. A similar tactic has been to increase the amount of **lecithin** in the patient's diet. Lecithin is the usual dietary form of choline. With an increased supply of the precursor, it was hoped that the patient's surviving cholinergic neurons would manufacture more acetylcholine and increase the amount of this neurotransmitter in the synaptic circuits.

To date, the results have not been encouraging. Reviews of dozens of such studies (Corkin, 1981; Bartus et al., 1982; Bartus et al., 1985) have been almost unanimous in reporting that such treatment failed to improve the memory functions of Alzheimer's patients; only one or two studies reported some moderate improvement. Of course, many possible reasons can be found for the ineffectiveness of such "precursor loading." For instance, the cholinergic nbM neurons may be too few or too incapacitated to use the extra supply of choline. Or the choline uptake system of these neurons may not work properly, and so the extra choline simply may not be taken into the cells in sufficient quantity. Also, even if more acetylcholine were synthesized, there may be problems with its release or its interaction with the postsynaptic receptors. The urgency of the problem, with an estimated $6 billion per year spent in the United States on nursing home care for dementia patients, suggests that research in this area will continue.

Drug therapy for Alzheimer's disease has involved several different substances. One that has been widely used is **physostigmine,** which inhibits **acetylcholinesterase,** the enzyme that inactivates acetylcholine at the synapse. In experimental animals it has prolonged the synaptic effectiveness of acetylcholine, but not enough studies have been done with physostigmine or related drugs to indicate whether such drugs can effect cognitive benefits for Alzheimer's patients (Bartus et al., 1982; Crook, 1985). Unlike precursor loading, where side effects are not a serious problem, drug treatments involving acetylcholinesterase antagonists like physostigmine do present side effects, making their experimental use with human patients riskier. Current preparations of physostigmine are not suitable for therapy on a regular basis, since they must be given by injection, and their effect on the brain lasts only about an hour (Growdon and Corkin, 1980).

One drug, **piracetam,** is not an anticholinesterase but works by increasing the release of acetylcholine from presynaptic terminals. This drug has been used by itself or in combination with choline in experimental work with rats. Preliminary results indicated that rats who had been given the piracetam choline combination performed better on memory tasks than the controls (Bartus et al., 1982).

physostigmine (fy-zo-STIG-meen) A drug that inhibits acetylcholinesterase.

acetylcholinesterase (ah-SEE-tul-ko-leen-ESS-ter-ace) An enzyme that inactivates acetylcholine in the synaptic cleft.

piracetam (pir-RAS-si-tam) A drug that causes presynaptic terminals to release acetylcholine.

SUMMARY

1. The development of the brain can be divided into eight stages, beginning with the induction of the neural plate and ending with the functional validation of brain circuitry through the stabilization of some synapses and the elimination of others. This process may continue throughout life.
2. The induction of the neural plate is followed by the curling up of the plate into a neural groove and the closing of the groove, forming the neural tube from which the brain and spinal cord are formed.

3. Although some species may produce new neurons after birth, proliferation of new neurons after birth in the brains of primates is thought to be extremely limited.

4. Most neurons must migrate from the region where they arise to their correct location in the brain. In some cases this migration covers distances of several millimeters. Radial glia appear to be important in guiding the migration of many cortical neurons.

5. Following aggregation of appropriate groupings of neurons, final differentiation of different neuronal types occurs. This process of differentiation includes the development of the neurotransmitter or neurotransmitters to be manufactured and released by that neuron as well as the synaptic contacts to be made.

6. The chemoaffinity hypothesis proposes that neurons find their proper place in the brain and make the correct synaptic connections because of particular chemical substances that distinguish one type of neuron from another. Although the details of how such a chemical guidance system works are not known, there is no rival hypothesis at the present.

7. If synapses are not used, they tend to become less effective, and neurons that do not make or sustain normal synaptic connections are likely to die. Cell death is a normal part of the development of the brain, eliminating neurons that have migrated to the wrong location or failed to make appropriate synaptic connections.

8. Neurons that have had their axons severed typically put out new axonal sprouts. Under some conditions peripheral neurons can reform their original connections. Neurons in the brain and spinal cord are thought to be unable to do this. Brain neurons may make new, and in some cases quite unusual, synaptic arrangements following injury, however. The degree to which such synaptic remodeling can result in functional consequences is a subject of current research. The brain appears to be a favorable location for the transplantation of foreign brain tissue, and implants of fetal brain tissue into brain-damaged rats can partially restore behavioral and physiological deficits.

9. The brain changes with age, although not all these changes are harmful, and the dendrites of at least one population of cortical neurons continue to grow throughout life. In general, however, aging is marked by death of neurons without replacement, along with other changes that eventually contribute to losses of memory and mental functioning in extreme old age. Not all individuals suffer such problems.

10. As more and more people live into old age, Alzheimer's disease has become an increasingly common problem. Although we now understand some of the brain changes associated with Alzheimer's disease, such as the deterioration of the acetylcholine neurotransmitter system originating in the basal forebrain, effective therapies for this disease are yet to be developed.

SUGGESTIONS FOR FURTHER READING

Cowan, W. M. (1979). The development of the brain. *Scientific American, 241,* 112–133.

Coyle, J. T., Price, D. L., and DeLong, M. R. (1983). Alzheimer's disease: A disorder of cortical cholinergic innervation. *Science, 219,* 1184–1190.

Jacobson, M. (1978). *Developmental neurobiology* (2d ed.). New York: Plenum.

5

Vision

*Reflections caught by
my eyes' dancing nets,
Transmuted, create your face.*

D. P. K.

Preview

Vision begins in the eye, where the energy present in light waves is converted into the electrical energy of nerve cells, a process termed *transduction*. Nerve impulses travel from the retina to various regions of the brain. Many of these areas have been explored with recording microelectrodes to discover the response characteristics of the neurons at various stages in the processing of visual input. Such experiments have given us insight into how the brain codes for the shape, color, and location of visual stimuli.

Two major theories attempt to explain the overall organization of the visual system. The *serial processing* theory suggests that complex visual processes, such as the recognition of a particular face, depend on a cascading of nerve impulses from one region of the brain to another, with each region containing neurons that have increasingly "facelike" response properties. The *parallel processing* theory proposes instead that the perception of complex stimuli such as faces results from the near simultaneous activation of different, "parallel" regions of the brain to different aspects of the visual stimulus.

Nature of the Visual Stimulus

The receptors in our eyes respond to only a narrow band of energy in the electromagnetic spectrum (see Figure 5.14). Electromagnetic radiation, such as that coming from the sun or other light-emitting body, can be considered to consist of quantal particles called *photons*. For many purposes electromagnetic energy also can be thought of as traveling in waves. (The term *wavicles* is sometimes used to illustrate this somewhat ambiguous view of the nature of light energy.) The wavelengths that human beings can see are in the 400–700 nm range, representing a very small fraction of the total spectrum. The waves of electromagnetic energy either come from a light-emitting body or are reflected from some object.

Structure of the Eye

retina (RET-in-ah) The sheet of cells in the eye in which transduction of light to nerve activity occurs.

Vertebrate eyes contain a thin sheet of cells responsible for changing light energy into neuronal activity: the **retina**. Although it is only 300–400 μm thick, the retina contains many millions of cells, organized into complex synaptic networks. Nerve impulses from the eyes are carried into the brain by the axons of the optic nerve. The brain interprets this stream of nerve impulses, and the result of that interpretation is what we call vision.

The retina is attached to the back of the eyeball (see Figure 5.1). In front of the retina is a gellike substance, the **vitreous humor**. The lens lies between the vitreous humor and the anterior chamber of the eye and is attached to several small muscles that control its shape and allow light to focus on the retina. The anterior chamber of the eye is filled with a watery fluid called the **aqueous humor**. On the outer surface of the eye is the *cornea*, a clear, curved structure approximately 1 mm thick at the edges and 0.5 mm thick in the center. The pigmented iris (which makes you brown or blue-eyed) is actually a thin sheet of delicate muscle tissue that controls the size of the opening in the middle of the iris, the *pupil*.

As light enters the eye, it goes through the cornea, aqueous humor, pupil, and vitreous humor before it strikes the retina. The actual photoreceptors (the rods and cones) are located at the back of the eye. Light must therefore pass through the other types of cells in the retina before it

vitreous humor (VIT-ree-us) A gellike material just in front of the retina of the eye.

aqueous humor (AH-kwee-us) A waterlike material in the anterior part of the eye.

Figure 5.1 **Drawing of the human eye in cross section.**

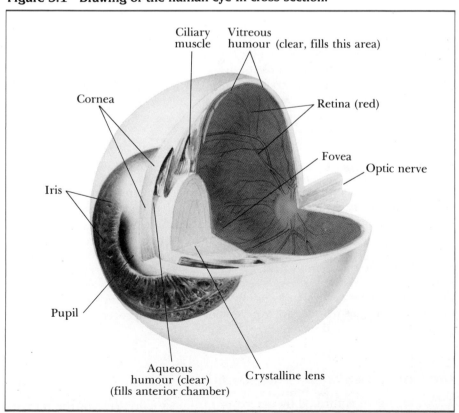

Figure 5.2   The blind spot.
Although we are ordinarily unaware of the blind spot, it can be shown readily.
To demonstrate its existence, close your left eye and focus your right eye on the
cross. Then move the book back and forth until the image of the dot disappears.
When this happens, the image of the dot has fallen on the blind spot.

encounters them. Since most of these cells are virtually transparent, not
much energy is lost. This arrangement may allow for more efficient initial
growth and development of the retina and for better maintenance.

The Blind Spot

One interesting consequence of the placement of the retina is the blind
spot found in each eye. The blind spot occurs at the *optic disk*, the region
of the retina where the axons that form the optic nerve leave the eye. No
receptor cells are present in this spot; therefore vision here is impossible.
We do not normally notice the blind spot because our brain "fills it in,"
but it can be demonstrated readily (Figure 5.2). The blind spot has been
known for a long time and was the topic of a very early scientific report.
The procedure for demonstrating the blind spot, as well as a reasonably
accurate explanation for it, was contained in a letter written by Edme Mar-
iotte in 1668 (Dennis, 1948).

Anatomy of the Visual System

Much of the brain is involved in processing visual information. Recent work
using 2-deoxyglucose, which reveals neurons that have been particularly
active recently, shows that many parts of the brain previously considered
to have no relation with vision are, in fact, activated by visual stimulation.
These brain regions include parts of the frontal lobe and the caudate and
putamen of the basal ganglia (Macko et al., 1982). We discuss various components of the visual system, concentrating on the lateral geniculate nucleus and various cortical regions. Before discussing each of these regions
in more detail, let us take an overview of the main processing regions in
the mammalian visual system.

The Lateral Geniculate Nucleus (LGN)

The optic nerve is formed by the axons of the ganglion cells of the retina.
About 1 million axons are found in each optic nerve in the human being

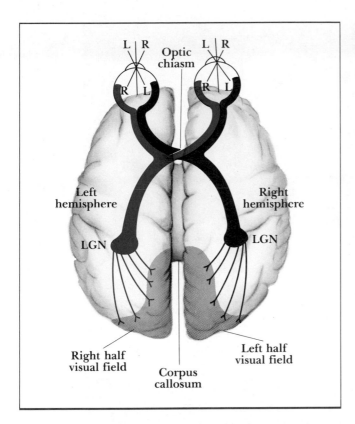

Figure 5.3 Diagram of the visual pathways in the human brain.
The partial crossing of each optic nerve causes the right half of each visual field to be relayed to the left hemisphere and vice versa.

or rhesus monkey brain. (The two species have very similar visual systems.) Most of the axons of the optic nerve travel to the LGN, where they synapse. A smaller number of axons go to other regions of the brain, such as the *superior colliculus* in the midbrain and the **suprachiasmatic nuclei** (**SCN**) of the hypothalamus, structures that are discussed later in the chapter.

As shown in Figure 5.3, the connections between the retina and the LGN are complex. The axons of those ganglion cells located on the nasal side of the retina project to the LGN on the opposite side of the brain. This projection is termed *contralateral*. The ganglion cells located on the temporal (outside) half of the retina send their axons to the LGN on the same side of the brain in *ipsilateral* projection. Although this projection scheme is found in virtually all mammals, the proportion of contralateral and ipsilateral projections varies in different species. In primates the ratio is about 50–50. The place on the ventral surface of the brain where the axons cross over is known as the *optic chiasm*. Figure 5.4 shows the human brain seen from the ventral surface. The optic nerves and optic chiasm can be clearly seen.

The result of this curious anatomic arrangement is that images of objects located in the left visual field (those to the left of the midpoint as one looks straight ahead) are initially processed by the right half of the brain, whereas images of objects in the right half of the visual field are

suprachiasmatic nucleus (SCN) (SOOP-rah-KY-as-mat-ik) One of a pair of nuclei located just dorsal to the optic chiasm. Involved in the regulation of various circadian rhythms.

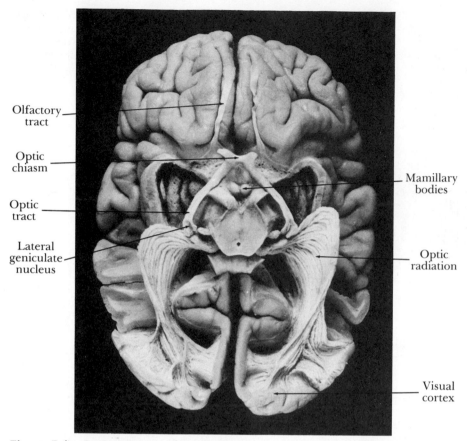

Olfactory tract

Optic chiasm

Optic tract

Lateral geniculate nucleus

Mamillary bodies

Optic radiation

Visual cortex

Figure 5.4   A photograph of the human brain as seen from the ventral surface.
The overlying tissue has been removed to show the optic radiation from the lateral geniculate nucleus to the visual cortex.

initially processed by the left half of the brain. This fact has enabled investigations of left-brain and right-brain functions, particularly in a small number of patients who have undergone surgery for severe epilepsy—an operation that involves cutting the connections between the two cerebral hemispheres. (The results of such operations are discussed in detail in Chapter 13.)

Each LGN is a highly organized collection of a million or more neurons, arranged in the primate brain into six distinct layers. The cells in the two deeper layers (layers 1 and 2) are larger than the cells in the four more dorsal layers (layers 3, 4, 5, and 6). Cells in the LGN receive synaptic input from only one eye, and the input is segregated in such a way that contralateral optic nerve axons synapse in layers 1, 4, and 6 of the LGN, whereas those from the ipsilateral optic nerve synapse in layers 2, 3, and 5 (see Figure 5.5).

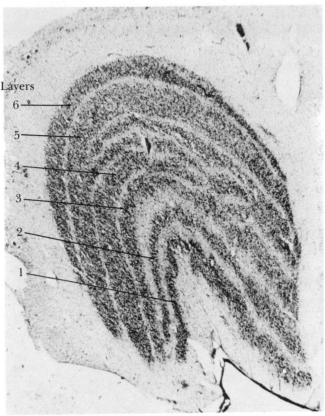

striate cortex   (STRY-ate)
Visual cortex, area 17.

Figure 5.5   The lateral geniculate nucleus of a rhesus monkey, shown in frontal plane.

Visual Regions of the Cerebral Cortex

Most LGN neurons project to the occipital lobe of the cortex. In the monkey brain about 99 percent of these axons synapse in the primary visual cortex. This region of the occipital lobe was given the number 17 by Brodmann and is also referred to as **striate cortex** because of the striped appearance of this region of cortex when stained. A few LGN axons go to nearby regions of the occipital lobe, numbered by Brodmann as 18 and 19. As the axons from the LGN penetrate the cortex, they branch many times, synapsing with many different cortical neurons. Most of these synapses take place in layers IV and VI.

The neurons in area 17 project, in turn, to a variety of other cortical regions, such as areas 18 and 19, and to subcortical components of the visual system, including the LGN and the superficial layers of the superior colliculus. Even though area 17 projects to at least 10 other regions of the cortex, Vernon Mountcastle (1979) observes that it may be the most isolated of all the cortical regions, underscoring the high level of interconnections among various regions of the cerebral cortex.

rhodopsin (ro-DOP-sin) The photosensitive substance in rods.

opsin (OPP-sin) The protein component of rhodopsin.

retinal (RET-in-al) A component of rhodopsin, derived from vitamin A. Also called *retinene*.

Transduction in the Retina: Straightening Retinal's Tail

Vision begins when light strikes the photoreceptors in the retina. The rods and cones are the only cells in the retina that can respond directly to light. All the millions of other cells in the retina are in turn influenced by neural activity generated in the rods and cones, but these other cells are insensitive to light. Our understanding of the conversion of light energy into neural activity is due largely to the research of George Wald and his co-workers (Wald et al., 1963; Wald, 1968).

The immediate effect of light hitting the rods and cones is to alter the molecular structure of a photosensitive chemical in these cells. This substance is also referred to as the *photopigment*, since color changes accompany the structural changes in the molecule. In rods the photosensitive substance is called **rhodopsin**. Most research has been on rhodopsin, but similar substances exist in the cones.

Rhodopsin is made up of two basic parts, a complex protein called **opsin** and a smaller component called **retinal** or *retinene*. Retinal is structurally similar to vitamin A, from which it is made by the rods. The molecules of rhodopsin are contained in a series of membranous discs in the outer segment of the rods, as shown in Figure 5.6. These discs are con-

Figure 5.6 Drawings of the outer segments of a rod and cone showing the disks that contain the photopigment.

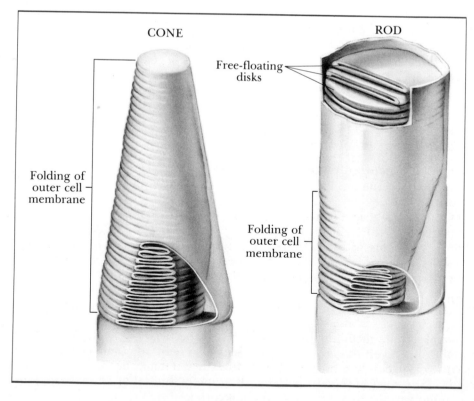

stantly being shed by the rods and replaced by newly formed discs. A similar process takes place in cones. These shed discs are normally digested and carried away, but in certain diseases, such as **retinitis pigmentosa**, the shedding process is abnormal, causing severe difficulties with vision.

retinitis pigmentosa (ret-in-EYE-tis pig-men-TOE-sah) An eye disease in which debris shed by rods is not removed, as is the case in normal eyes.

photon (FOE-ton) Elementary particle of radiant energy.

isomer (ICE-o-mer) One of two or more different chemical compounds with the same molecular formula. Isomers differ because of the different spatial arrangement of identical atoms.

Isomeric Changes in Retinal Underlie Vision

A quantum of light energy is called a **photon**. When a photon of light strikes a molecule of rhodopsin in the outer segment of a rod, the energy of the photon causes the retinal portion of rhodopsin to change shape. Retinal can exist in several isomeric forms. **Isomers** are different forms of the same molecule, containing exactly the same atoms but arranged in different spatial relationship to each other. Isomers have different chemical and physical properties. Wald's research in the 1960s showed that the crucial step in transduction in the rods occurs when photons of light change the retinal from the "bent-tail" isomer to the "straight-tail" isomer. The bent-tail form is called the 11-cis isomer, and the straight-tail form is called the all-trans isomer. This is the only step in vision for which light is necessary (Figure 5.7).

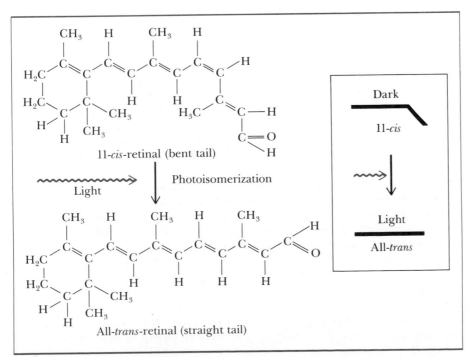

Figure 5.7 The structure of the main isomers of rhodopsin.
The net effect of light is to transform the 11-cis isomer to the all-trans isomer.

disinhibition Release
from inhibition.

In the dark the 11-cis isomer is bound tightly to the opsin portion of rhodopsin. The all-trans isomer does not bind very well to the opsin and separates from it. What happens next is still not very well understood, but somehow this separation of retinal from the opsin results in an electrical response in the rod. In every case so far examined in vertebrate photoreceptors, the electronic response to light is a shift of the resting membrane potential toward a more hyperpolarized level. (Some invertebrate photoreceptors respond to light with a depolarizing current.) In the dark, the membrane of the outer segment of a vertebrate rod contains open Na^+ channels, resulting in a steady influx of Na^+ into the outer segment. K^+ ions are also steadily leaking outward from the inner segment of rod, creating a small electrical current known as the "dark current." The Na^+ channels are held open by a substance called cyclic GMP (cGMP). As light strikes the rhodopsin molecule and causes it to change shape, this change activates another protein called *transducin*. Transducin then activates another substance, *phosphodiesterase*. Phosphodiesterase in turn breaks down cGMP, causing the Na^+ channels to close, stemming the inward flow of Na^+. Since the outward K^+ flow continues, and is no longer balanced by an inward Na^+ flow, the membrane potential now moves from its resting potential in the dark (about -40 mV) nearer to the K^+ equilibrium potential (about -75 mV). The response to a light is thus a *hyperpolarization* of the rod membrane. In the turtle rod, for example, a flash of bright light can produce a hyperpolarization of as much as 20 mV, moving the membrane potential to -65 mV (Schnapf and Baylor, 1987).

The fact that the response of rods to light is hyperpolarizing can be somewhat disconcerting, since we have discussed hyperpolarization as being associated with inhibition (as it often is). But in the rods, things are different. It appears that rods in the dark constantly secrete low levels of neurotransmitter onto those cells with which they synapse. No nerve impulse is necessary for this neurotransmitter release. In fact, rods and cones do not produce nerve impulses.

The neurotransmitter secreted by rods can be either inhibitory or excitatory, depending on the nature of the postsynaptic receptor. If it is normally inhibitory, the hyperpolarization of the rod by light and the resultant diminished flow of neurotransmitter can produce a **disinhibition** of the postsynaptic cell functionally equivalent to excitation (see Figure 5.8). If the interaction of the rod neurotransmitter with a postsynaptic receptor molecule normally produces excitation, the effect of light will be to produce a net inhibition of that postsynaptic cell.

The Duplicity Theory

Primate eyes have two different types of receptors: the rods and the cones. The duplicity theory states that rods and cones perform different tasks in vision, such that we have a "double" or two-receptor visual system. Although just one type of photopigment is found in the rods—rhodopsin—three different types of cones, each with a different photopigment, exist.

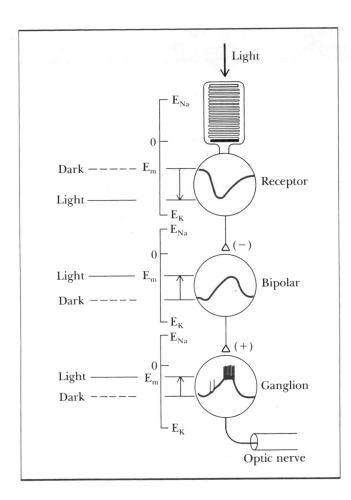

Figure 5.8 Potentials in the retina.
In the dark there is a steady leakage of Na^+ into the receptor. A flash of light (arrow) reduces the membrane permeability to Na^+, resulting in a hyperpolarization. This in turn causes a decrease in the release of an inhibitory neurotransmitter, $(-)$ from the receptor to the bipolar cell, resulting in a disinhibition of the bipolar cell. This results in an increase in the amount of an excitatory transmitter $(+)$ released by the bipolar cell onto the ganglion cell. The net effect is an increase in the firing rate of the ganglion cell. E_{Na} = equilibrium potential for Na^+; E_K = equilibrium potential for K^+; E_m = Membrane potential.

The different cone photopigments differ in the opsin portion; retinal is a constant feature of primate photopigments. The existence of three different photopigments in cones allows the cone system to respond to different wavelengths (and thereby lets us see color), which rods cannot do. Another difference between rods and cones is that rods are effective only in dim light and become almost useless in bright light. Cones are effective in daylight but cannot function well in dim light. The cone system is much better than the rod system at visual *acuity* (the ability to see the fine details of a stimulus), whereas the rod system is more *sensitive* (able to detect the presence or absence of light).

Overall, each human eye has about 100 million rods, about 5 million cones, and only about 1 million ganglion cells (Shepherd, 1983). On average, the convergence ratio of photoreceptors onto ganglion cells is about 100:1 for rods, and about 5:1 for cones. In the center of the retina, in the region called the **fovea,** there are almost no rods, and the cones tend to have convergence ratios of about 1 to 1. This maximizes visual acuity, and

fovea (FOE-vee-ah) A cone-rich region of the central retina in which most daylight vision is initiated in animals with both rods and cones.

amacrine cell (AM-ih-krin) A major cell type in the retina.

the fovea is responsible for most daylight vision. The fovea contains about 50,000 cones. More peripheral regions of the retina contain more and more rods. In the most peripheral regions of the retina the photoreceptors are all rods.

The rods in the periphery have high convergence ratios. These rods make particularly good "light-catchers," increasing the sensitivity of the peripheral regions of the retina. Let us assume that some small number of photoreceptors (say five) must be simultaneously excited in order to create sufficient activity in the optic nerve to create a signal above the baseline noise, allowing the individual to say, "I see the stimulus." Since light falling on several photoreceptors that all converge on a single ganglion cell is more likely to excite that ganglion cell, the greater the convergence ratio, the more likely it is that that photoreceptor "net" will be able to create a noticeable signal in dim light.

Other Cell Types in the Retina

In addition to the rods, cones, and ganglion cells, there are three other major classes of cells in the retina—horizontal cells, bipolar cells, and **amacrine cells.** Figure 5.9 shows these cell types in the primate retina. Much of the anatomy behind this diagram was done by John Dowling and colleagues (Dowling and Boycott, 1966; Dowling, 1979). The cells in the retina are interconnected in complex ways. One simplifying idea is to consider cells in the retina as oriented either "vertically" or "horizontally" (Shepherd, 1979) (see Figure 5.10). Vertical cells include those cell types that form the main line of transmission from photoreceptors to brain. The vertical cells include the rods and cones, bipolar cells, and ganglion cells.

In addition, two classes of cells are horizontally oriented, the amacrine cells and the horizontal cells. These two cell types are arranged to allow the lateral spread of neural activity across the photoreceptor layer and across the ganglion cell layer. The effect on vision from these lateral communication channels is to contribute to the formation of *receptive field* properties for cells elsewhere in the visual system. The primate retina contains about 5 million horizontal cells and from 10 to 100 million amacrine cells (Shepherd, 1979). Not all horizontal or amacrine cells have true axons (see Figure 5.11).

Retinal Potentials

Primate retinal cells are so small and so tightly packed that until recently no one was able to record directly from them. That has now been done, however (Nunn and Baylor, 1982). The technical difficulties are less severe in other organisms, and much of our knowledge about the kinds of receptor potentials that occur in the retina is based on work done in such amphibians as the mudpuppy (Dowling, 1979) and the toad (Baylor et al., 1979). In the retina only amacrine and ganglion cells normally produce nerve impulses. The other cells in the retina display potentials that are

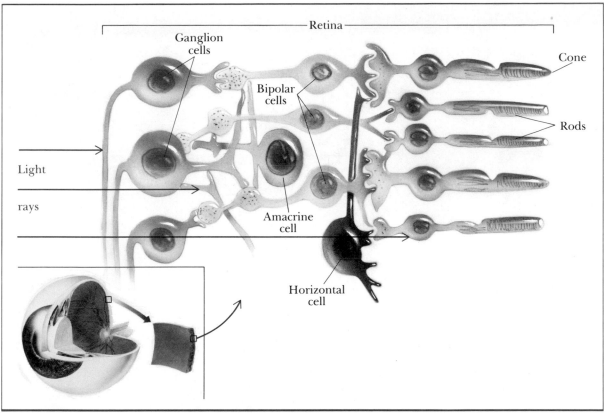

Retina

Ganglion
cells

Bipolar
cells

Cone

Rods

Light

rays

Amacrine
cell

Horizontal
cell

**Figure 5.9 A summary diagram of the main cell types and some of the
major types of synaptic arrangements in the primate retina.**

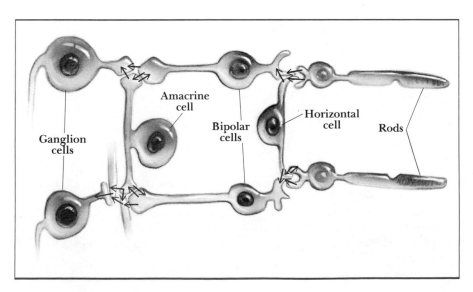

**Figure 5.10 Vertical
and horizontal
elements in the
primate retina.**

Amacrine
cell

Horizontal
cell

Bipolar
cells

Rods

Ganglion
cells

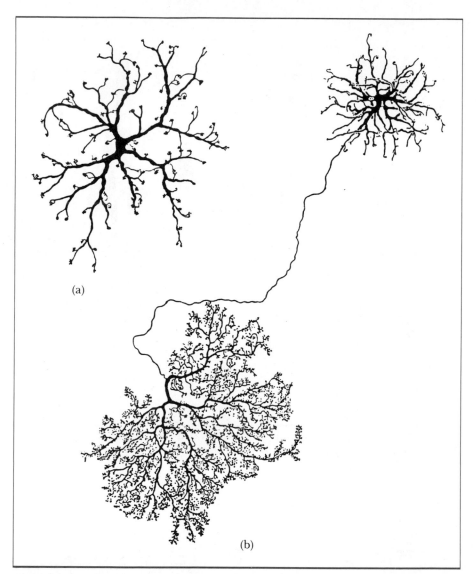

Figure 5.11 Horizontal cells from cat (Golgi stain).
(a) axonless type; (b) type with axon.

similar in many ways to the postsynaptic potentials discussed in Chapter 2. Transduction in a particular photoreceptor can have opposite effects on the firing rates of adjacent ganglion cells because of differences in the synaptic connections of the horizontal and bipolar cells that come between the photoreceptors and the ganglion cells. Figure 5.12 illustrates a little of this complexity.

SUMMARY TABLE
Cell Types in the Retina

Cell Type	Horizontal or Vertical	Graded or Nerve Impulse
Rod	Vertical	Graded
Cone	Vertical	Graded
Bipolar	Vertical	Graded
Horizontal	Horizontal	Graded
Amacrine	Horizontal	Impulse
Ganglion	Vertical	Impulse

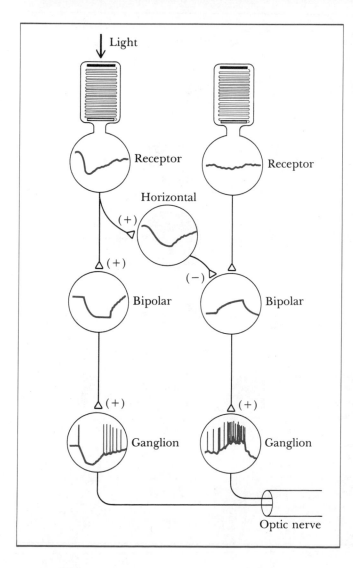

Figure 5.12   Diagram illustrating how light striking one receptor can have excitatory effects on one ganglion cell and simultaneous inhibitory effects on another ganglion cell.
Excitatory synapses indicated by (+), inhibitory synapses by (−).

Vision

receptive field The receptive field of a neuron is that region of a sensory surface in which appropriate energy changes produce an alteration in the firing rate of that neuron.

Receptive Fields

Although it is still difficult to record directly from individual cells in the retina of mammals, it is not particularly hard to record from the axons of the retinal ganglion cells that make up the optic nerve. This was first done in 1953 by Steven Kuffler (1913–1980), who used cats as subjects. His experiments revealed the type of **receptive fields** these cells possess. The receptive field of a neuron in the visual system is defined as that area of the retina from which the firing rate of that cell can be influenced by light. If the spontaneous firing rate is very low, inhibitory effects can be discerned only by their antagonistic action on simultaneously produced excitation. Figure 5.13 summarizes Kuffler's most important findings.

Figure 5.13 Responses of on-center and off-center retinal ganglion cells to light. X = excitatory region of receptive field; △ = inhibitory region of receptive field.

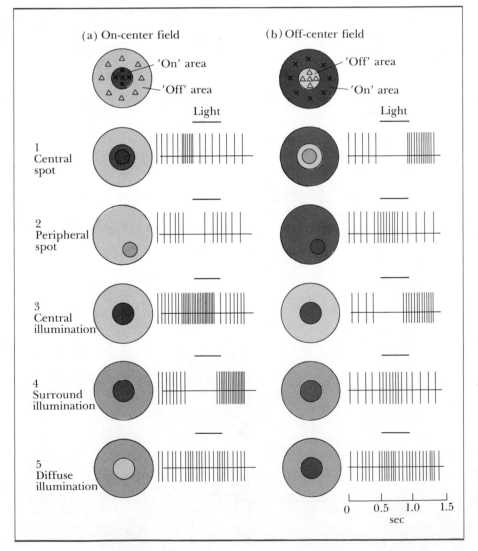

TABLE 5.1   Responses of On-Center and Off-Center Cells

	On Center		Off Center	
	Center	*Surround*	*Center*	*Surround*
Illuminate	Excite	Inhibit	Inhibit	Excite
Remove illumination	Inhibit	Excite	Excite	Inhibit

The typical receptive field of a cat ganglion cell is roughly circular, divided into a *center* and a *surround.* Kuffler used a 0.2-mm spot of white light as a stimulus. He shone the spot on different regions of the retina while monitoring the firing rate of individual neurons in the optic nerve, and he found two basic types of cells. The first type he called *on-center, off-surround.* For these cells illumination of the center of the receptive field produced excitation, while illumination of the surround produced inhibition. In addition, removal of illumination of the surround produced excitation, while removal of illumination from the center produced inhibition.

The second type of cell Kuffler called the *off-center, on-surround* type. Its response characteristics were opposite to those of the first type. Table 5.1 summarizes the properties of these two types of cells. Each ganglion cell has a slightly different receptive field location from others, although the amount of overlap between these fields is considerable. The concept of the receptive field has been applied to neurons throughout the visual system.

X, Y, and W Cells

It now appears that at least three subpopulations of ganglion cells exist and that they differ in several ways. The first two types, called X and Y, were identified by Christina Enroth-Cugell and John Robson (1966). W cells were classified by Jonathan Stone and Klaus-Peter Hoffman (1972). Table 5.2 lists the major differences among these three types of cells. The most common are the X cells, which make up about 55 percent of the total. Next most common are the W cells (40 percent). Y cells account for about 5 percent of the total in the optic nerve. X, Y, and W cells also have been identified in the lateral geniculate nucleus.

X cells are of medium size, with relatively restricted dendritic fields and comparatively slow conduction speeds. They synapse primarily in the LGN. One particular characteristic of X cells is *linearity,* or spatial summation. X cells sum the influences from various parts of the receptive field evenly. Thus there is always a null position or balance point such that an X cell shows no response to a stimulus that is presented in its receptive field so that excitation and inhibition are equally balanced. X cells are medium-sized, conduct nerve impulses slowly, and have restricted dendritic

TABLE 5.2   Response Properties of X, Y, W Ganglion Cells in Cat

	X	Y	W
Size (cell body)	Medium, 14–22 μm	Large, 30–40 μm	Small and medium, 8–22 μm
Extent of dendritic tree	Restricted	Extensive	Varied
Percentage of optic nerve axons	55%	5%	40%
Conduction speed	Slow, 15–23 m/sec	Fastest, 30–40 m/sec	Slowest, 2–18 m/sec
Discharge characteristic	Sustained	Transient	Varied
Movement sensitivity	Small	Great	Varied
Projection site(s)	LGN	LGN and superior colliculus	Superior colliculus
Mode of summing light signals	Linear	Nonlinear	Mixed

trees. Such characteristics allow us to infer that X cells are particularly important in detecting the fine features of visual stimuli. In the primate lateral geniculate, X cells are thought to be involved in color vision.

Y cells are large, have extensive dendritic fields, and conduct impulses at high speeds. They project both to the LGN and to the superior colliculus. Y cells do not display linearity; a stimulus in any part of the receptive field of a Y cell produces some sort of response. Y cells respond well to moving stimuli and are believed to be important in the perception of motion and changes in intensity.

W cells—about 40 percent of the total in the optic nerve—are either small or medium sized, conduct impulses slowly, and have dendritic fields of various sizes. They project primarily to the superior colliculus and to restricted regions of the LGN. W cells may also be important in the visual pursuit of moving objects. Some W cells show linearity or spatial summation; others do not. In fact, W cells have been found to be so variable in their properties that some investigators doubt that they really form a separate category.

The existence of different cell types in the optic nerve and lateral geniculate nucleus has given rise to the hypothesis that several parallel processing pathways or channels occur in the visual system, so that different aspects of visual stimuli, such as form, location, movement, and color, are processed by different sets of neurons. These channels are thought by many to remain independent all the way from the retina to the cerebral cortex. (We shall return to this topic later in this chapter.)

Response Characteristics of LGN Neurons

The main input to the LGN is from the ganglion cells of the retina. In primates it appears that the ratio of ganglion cells to LGN neurons is about

1 to 1. But this does not typically result in just one ganglion cell synapsing with just one LGN cell. Instead each ganglion cell axon divides to form several branches that are distributed to several different LGN cells. This type of synaptic arrangement is called *divergence*. The degree of divergence in the LGN is limited to about 100–200 μm (Shepherd, 1979). This arrangement maintains a close correspondence between the area of the retina served by a particular ganglion cell and a particular region of the LGN.

This "point-to-point" mapping of the sensory surface (retina, in this case), onto a region of the brain (LGN in this case) is seen in other senses as well. In fact, it seems to be a general principle of sensory processing that *neurons that are involved in the processing of related information tend to be clustered together* (Kuffler et al., 1984). In addition to divergence seen in the LGN, each LGN neuron receives input from several different ganglion cells, a pattern termed *convergence*. Neurons in the LGN also receive input from other brain regions, including visual cortical regions. This cortical input is capable of modulating the response characteristics of LGN neurons (McClurkin and Marrocco, 1984).

Spontaneity

LGN neurons have been the subject of much research, and we know as much about the response properties of neurons in the cat and monkey LGN as about any mammalian neurons. Nevertheless, much remains to be discovered. Most LGN neurons fire spontaneously, even in the dark. Typical spontaneous discharge rates are 5–60 impulses/sec (Barlow, 1982). The term *spontaneous* is used because we really don't know just why cells fire without apparent cause. In the LGN, spontaneity may actually be the result of excitatory input coming from the 100,000 or more cortical cells that project to the LGN. Hormones or other blood-borne substances may cause LGN cells to fire. Some neurons may have thresholds close enough to their resting potential that minor fluctuations in the opening and closing of Na^+ channels may result in a true spontaneous discharge rate.

LGN Receptive Fields

The receptive fields of LGN neurons are similar to those of ganglion cells. In fact, sometimes the only way to tell if one is recording from a ganglion cell or a LGN cell is to measure the response latency, which is slightly longer in the LGN neurons because of synaptic delay. LGN neurons have circular or oval receptive fields, usually organized in a center–surround fashion. The center–surround organization in LGN neurons is "sharper" than that of ganglion cells, and the inhibitory regions are more effective. Inhibitory regions of LGN neurons can cancel out the excitation caused by stimulation of the on region (at least in X cells). Diffuse light is therefore not an effective way to influence most LGN neurons.

Color Vision

One of the miracles of our daily life that most of us take for granted is our ability to see color. Although neurons throughout the visual system are involved in color vision, the way in which LGN neurons contribute to color vision is more clearly understood than is the case with most parts of the visual system. Human beings can distinguish about 200 different colors, ranging from bright red to violet blue (Gouras, 1981). Some other primates appear to have very similar color vision (much of the work on the role of LGN neurons in color vision, for example, has been done with the rhesus monkey, whose color vision system is very similar to our own), but not all mammals have true color vision. Nevertheless the ability to discriminate wavelengths of light (i.e., see color) is distributed widely among the animal kingdom, including some birds, fish, and even invertebrates.

A langur monkey. The visual systems of many primates such as the one pictured are very similar to our own.

For many purposes electromagnetic energy is considered to exist as waves of energy. The distance between two peaks of successive waves of energy is termed the *wavelength*. (It is the ability to distinguish between wavelengths of light that results in seeing color.) The entire spectrum of electromagnetic energy runs from waves with very short wavelengths, such as gamma rays and x rays, to the long radio waves that have wavelengths longer than a football field. As shown in Figure 5.14, we can only perceive energies between 400 and 700 nm. Energies in the shorter wavelengths

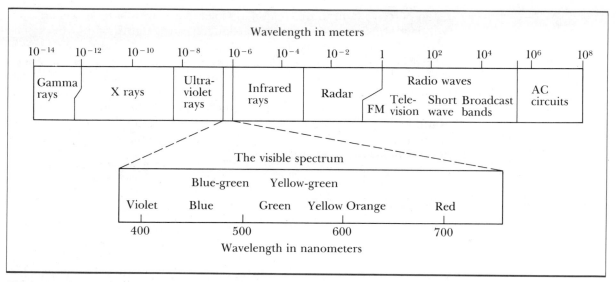

Figure 5.14 The electromagnetic spectrum of energies.
The rods and cones are sensitive to only a small fraction of the spectrum, shown
in the lower part of the figure as the visible spectrum.

appear in the blue–violet range, whereas longer wavelengths in the visible
spectrum appear red.

Three different types of cones are found in the primate eye, with three
different kinds of photopigments. Each photopigment has its peak sensitivity in a different portion of the visible spectrum. Figure 5.15 shows
sensitivity curves for cones in the primate retina. One cone type has its
peak sensitivity to light in the shorter wavelengths, with its peak at about
440 nm. This is called the blue cone, since individuals with normal color

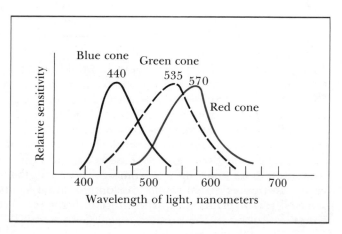

**Figure 5.15 Relative
sensitivity of the three
types of cones in the
primate retina.**

vision perceive light in this region as violet to greenish blue. A second cone type is more sensitive to somewhat longer wavelengths, with a peak sensitivity of about 535 nm. This is the green cone. The third cone type is primarily sensitive to the longer wavelengths, with a peak at about 570 nm. This is the red cone. Its peak sensitivity is actually in the yellow–orange region of the spectrum. The sensitivity curves of these three cone types overlap considerably. Intense light in the 500-nm range, for example, influences all three cone types. For some insight as to how our brains extract the experience of color from nerve impulses, let us return to our discussion of LGN neurons.

Color Opponent Cells

With white light, which contains energy from wavelengths throughout the visible spectrum, it is impossible to determine whether a given neuron in the visual system can respond differently to various wavelengths. But if one uses light from a restricted bandwidth of the spectrum ("colored" light), it turns out that the LGN contains neurons that can distinguish among different wavelengths.

Important early research in this area was done by Russell DeValois and his colleagues (DeValois and Jacobs, 1968; DeValois and DeValois, 1975). They discovered that individual LGN neurons in the rhesus monkey responded differently to light of different wavelengths. For example, a particular LGN neuron with a spontaneous firing rate of 25 impulses/sec might generate 50 impulses/sec when the monkey's visual field was flooded with red light. The same neuron, on the other hand, might fire only 1 or 2 impulses/sec or even fall silent when the visual field was illuminated with green light. The size of the response, either inhibitory or excitatory, depends on a number of factors, such as the degree to which the animal is dark-adapted, the intensity of the light, and the exact wavelengths used.

Overall, this work and subsequent research have demonstrated that most LGN neurons tend to be turned on by one bandwidth of wavelengths and turned off by a different bandwidth. These neurons are now called *color opponent* cells. They make up about 75 percent of LGN neurons. DeValois concluded that such neurons received inputs from ganglion cells that in turn were influenced by two of the three cone types in the retina. For example, an on-red, off-green neuron would receive excitatory input from red cones and inhibitory input from green cones. No input would be present from blue cones. Subsequent research uncovered a few LGN neurons that receive excitation from blue cones. In these cells both red and green inputs are inhibitory. Other neurons are on-green, off-red cells. Input from blue cones is not very common, particularly in neurons whose receptive fields are in the fovea. Evolutionary reasons for this may exist. Blue light tends to scatter more than light with longer wavelengths, and light scattering results in poorer visual acuity. Since high visual acuity has probably been selected for in primates, this may account for the fact that very few blue cones are found in the primate fovea (Gouras, 1981).

Dual-Purpose LGN Neurons

Each LGN neuron has a small and distinct receptive field, responding only to stimulation in a restricted part of the retina. Thus these cells can code for *spatial location* in the visual field. Such response properties are also used in detecting the *shape* of the stimulus. From the work of DeValois and others we know that LGN neurons can also code for color. Can they perform all these coding tasks simultaneously? An answer was provided by research conducted by Torsten Wiesel and David Hubel, who received Nobel prizes in 1981 for their work on the response properties of neurons in the visual system. When Wiesel and Hubel started this work in the early 1960s, they knew of DeValois' work on the color opponent cells and had themselves found LGN neurons in the spider monkey that were clearly coding for spatial location. Thus they reasoned: "Given the existence of two opponent mechanisms in the monkey visual system, one for the spatial variable and the other for color, it is natural to ask whether these occupy the same channels, or are confined to separate groups of cells" (Wiesel and Hubel, 1966). The answer, they discovered, was "Both." They examined the response characteristics of 244 LGN neurons in 16 rhesus monkeys. Most of these cells (213) were from the four dorsal layers of the LGN. They presented evidence for three distinct categories of cells in the LGN. Figure 5.16 shows a summary of these three categories.

Type I combination cells were most common, making up 77 percent of the total. These cells showed the center–surround organization as well as color opponent properties. For example, the center of the receptive field of such a cell would be excited by one bandwidth of wavelengths, whereas the surround region would be inhibited by a different bandwidth. Several varieties were discovered, including red on-center, green off-surround (35 percent of the total); red off-center, green on-surround (18 percent); green on-center, red off-surround (16 percent); green off-center, red on-surround (6 percent); and one cell that had a blue on-center and green off-surround. These combination cells can code for location and shape, due to their center–surround organization as well as for color, because of their opponent color inputs. Thus a red on-center, green off-surround neuron would be maximally excited by a spot of monochromatic light with wavelengths limited to the red portion of the spectrum and limited to the center of its receptive field. This same cell would be maximally inhibited by a doughnut of green light falling on the surround region of its receptive field.

About 16 percent of the cells examined by Wiesel and Hubel lacked the center–surround organization of the Type I cells but did display color opponent responses. These were termed Type II cells. Two main subtypes were seen, green-on, blue-off and green-off, blue-on cells.

The least common cells (7 percent) were those with only a center–surround organization. These cells (Type III) were not differentially sensitive to different wavelengths. As illustrated in Figure 5.16, Wiesel and Hubel surmised that these cells received input from all three cone types, with more or less equal proportions of the various cone types contributing

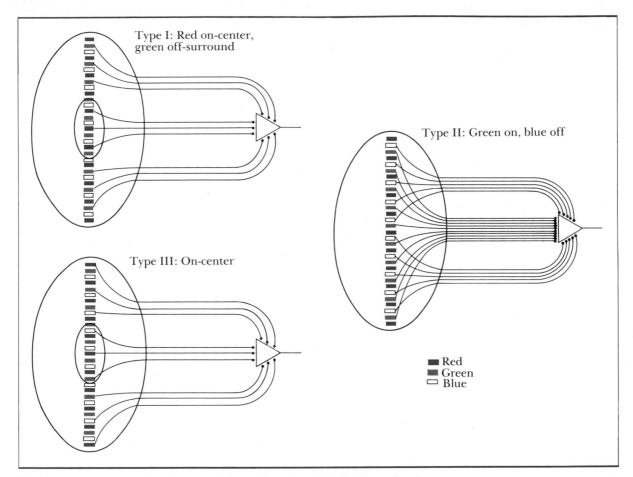

Figure 5.16   Schematic diagrams illustrating the contribution of various cone types to the LGN neurons studied by Wiesel and Hubel (1966). For purposes of simplicity the intervening bipolars, horizontal, amacrine, and ganglion cells are omitted.

to the center and to the surround of the cell's receptive field. Such cells can code only for shape and location.

Later research has revealed that there are also neurons responsive to color in the visual cortex (Zeki, 1980). In fact, some individuals have become color-blind as a result of cortical brain damage (Meadows, 1974). LGN cells undoubtedly contribute to color sensitivity at the level of the cortex, because the axons of LGN cells synapse primarily in the visual cortex.

Cortical Neurons: Feature Detectors or Spatial Frequency Analyzers?

Currently some controversy centers on how best to describe the response characteristics of neurons in the visual areas of the cortex. These two ideas are generally referred to as the "feature detector model" and the "spatial frequency model." The feature detector model was the first to be developed, and we will examine it first.

Hubel and Wiesel, whose basic techniques have been widely adopted, performed a long series of experiments examining the response characteristics of neurons in several different visual areas of the cortex (Hubel and Wiesel, 1962; 1965b; 1979). Their early research was done on cats; later work was on rhesus monkeys. Although there are differences in the results from these two species, the similarities across species in the response characteristics of visual cortical neurons are impressive. Hubel and Wiesel found different types of cells, depending in part on which layer of the cortex their electrode tip was in. As discussed in Chapter 3, the cortex is organized into six layers. The axon terminals of the LGN neurons that project to area 17 end primarily in layers IV and VI. In Layer IV the cortical neurons display response characteristics similar to those of the LGN, having circular receptive fields with clear center–surround organization. However, in layers II, III, V, and VI, we see quite different receptive fields.

Edge Detectors

In layers other than IV (and I, where there are virtually no cell bodies) the neurons recorded by Hubel and Wiesel tended to respond best to *line segments or slits oriented at specific angles.* These cells are often called *edge detectors,* since a leading edge of a stimulus is a good way to stimulate them. Hubel and Wiesel first happened on the use of edges as effective stimuli when they noticed a cell responding vigorously to the straight-line shadow cast by the edge of a slide they were using:

> We were inserting the glass slide with its black spot into the slot of the ophthalmoscope when suddenly, over the audio monitor, the cell went off like a machine gun. After some fussing and fiddling, we found out what was happening. The response had nothing to do with the black dot. As the glass slide was inserted its edge was casting onto the retina a faint but sharp shadow, a straight dark line on a light background. That was what the cell wanted, and it wanted it, moreover, in just one narrow range of orientations [Hubel, 1982].

Edge detectors in area 17 are very sensitive to the particular tilt or *orientation* of the stimulus as well. Most cells in this area respond only when the stimulus is oriented within 10–20 degrees of its "preferred orientation." (There are 360 degrees in a circle. Thus there are 30 degrees between each hour numeral on a standard clockface.)

Simple and Complex Cells

In exploring various visual cortical regions with their recording microelectrodes, Hubel and Wiesel found consistent differences in cells that led them to describe several subtypes. They identified two main subtypes—simple and complex. Simple cells, which in the monkey are located primarily in layer III, respond best when the stimulus is located in a particular region

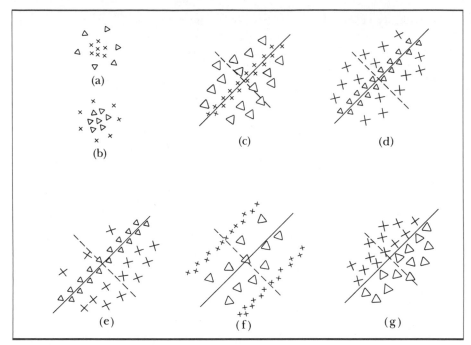

Figure 5.17 Receptive field properties of cells in cat visual cortex.
(a) and (b) circular receptive fields in layer IV. (c) through (g) various types of
edge detectors as seen in other layers of visual cortex. X = excitatory responses;
△ = inhibitory responses. The preferred orientation for the edge detector receptive fields is shown by the continous lines. Although all the cells shown have
"2:00" preferred orientations, all orientations have been observed in approximately equal proportion.

of the cell's receptive field, and oriented at the preferred angle. Moving
the stimulus around in the receptive field results in reducing the response,
since there are off regions either on both sides of a center strip or in
adjacent regions (see Figure 5.17). As is true for other center–surround
cells in the visual system, both excitatory and inhibitory regions were seen.

More numerous were neurons labeled *complex,* which were found
throughout layers II, III, V, and VI in areas 17, 18, and 19. Complex cells
are less fussy about the exact location of the stimulus. If the orientation is
within 10–20 degrees of the preferred angle, complex cells respond to
edges anywhere in their receptive fields. Complex cells do not usually have
on or off areas. A particularly good stimulus for a complex cell is an edge
or slit of light moving across the receptive field. In many cases movement
in one direction is more effective than movement in the opposite direction.

Hypercomplex cells, which have even more specialized stimulus preferences in terms of the length of the optimal line segment, were also found.
Cells that fired preferentially to stimuli in which two line segments met at
a particular angle (corner detectors) were also observed. Each neuron in
areas 17, 18, and 19 appears to be tuned to respond to edges with a par-

ticular orientation, ceasing to respond when the tilt of the stimulus is outside the preferred range. Different neurons have different orientation preferences, and all possible orientations are about equally well represented. The feature detection model requires the existence of many cortical neurons, but since the primate cortex contains 100 million or more cells, this does not appear to present a problem for the model.

A methodological point is worth emphasizing here. In Hubel and Wiesel's studies the animals were anesthetized with barbiturates or other drugs and immobilized with paralytic drugs. Such drug treatments eliminate the pain sensations that might otherwise occur. As far as can be determined, these drugs also eliminate any perceptual awareness of the stimuli being presented. These studies thus report on neurons from a cortex operating in a nonconscious mode. It is possible that information gathered under such conditions has little relevance to the way in which such cells respond under normal conditions. Fortunately, subsequent studies have shown virtually identical response characteristics for visual cortex neurons in monkeys with chronically implanted electrodes tested in wide-awake, undrugged conditions (Wurtz, 1969).

The fact that the edge detectors in the cortex continue to operate in basically normal ways even under deep barbiturate anesthesia raises some questions about just what conditions in the brain are necessary for perceptual awareness. As we shall see in Chapter 10, the active participation of neurons deep in the brain stem that project to the cortex may be critically important in this regard. It is thought that these brain stem neurons may be particularly vulnerable to anesthetic agents, whereas neurons in the information-processing parts of the brain continue to respond to input, even under surgical levels of anesthesia.

Recently it has been discovered that figures in which human subjects perceive "illusory contours," such as the one in Figure 5.18, also can evoke responses in presumed edge detectors in cells of area 18 of awake rhesus monkeys. Manipulations of the stimulus that weaken the illusion of lines also weaken the neuronal response (von Der Heydt et al., 1984).

Figure 5.18 Illusory contours or edges. Stimuli similar to this evoke responses in monkey edge detectors. When the stimulus is altered to reduce the illusion, such cells show diminished response.

Spatial Frequency Analyzers: An Alternative Model

The Hubel and Wiesel feature detection model is not the only way of characterizing the response of visual cortical neurons. In recent years an alternative model has been put forward. Two of the leading proponents of the spatial frequency model are Fergus Campbell (Campbell, 1974) and Russell DeValois (DeValois and DeValois, 1980). Consider the visual pattern in Figure 5.19. This figure is a grating composed of parallel lines. All visual stimuli can be considered to be composed of some number of light–dark alternations that occur within some specified distance across the visual field. Visual space is measured in degrees of arc. There are 180 degrees from one side of the visual field to the other, that is, from the far left-hand side of what you can see when looking straight ahead to the far right-hand side.

Figure 5.19   A grating stimulus illustrating the concept of spatial frequency.
The frequency of any particular stimulus is determined by the number of light–dark alternations in each degree of visual angle. This in turn depends on the distance between the stimulus and the observer.

A stimulus such as that shown in Figure 5.19 can be characterized in terms of its *spatial frequency*—the number of light–dark alternations in each degree of the visual field.

Human observers vary in their ability to perceive different spatial frequencies, depending not only on the actual frequency but also on the degree of contrast between the light and dark regions, and other factors. Most subjects seem to be most sensitive (can detect lowest levels of contrast) when the spatial frequencies of a grating stimulus are between one and five cycles per degree. Visual acuity can be evaluated as the upper limit of the spatial frequency that an individual can detect. This is usually about 48 cycles per degree (Campbell and Robson, 1968). Rhesus monkeys show almost identical responses to human observers when tested in similar ways (DeValois et al., 1974).

Individual cells in the visual cortex, the same cells that can be classified as simple or complex when tested with Hubel and Wiesel type stimuli, can also be classified as frequency analyzers when tested with grating stimuli. This is true for cats (Maffei and Fiorentini, 1973) and monkeys (DeValois and DeValois, 1980). Figure 5.20 shows the results of such an experiment. Thus evidence exists to support both the feature detection model and the spatial frequency model. It is somewhat premature to tell which of these approaches will prove most useful in the future development of theories of vision.

Evidence from perceptual demonstrations also exists for separate channels in the human visual system. These channels are usually thought to be separate pathways in the visual system, each channel performing some different analysis on visual input. Look at Figure 5.21. If you follow the directions in the figure caption, you should perceive changes in the test stimulus on the left after staring (i.e., adapting some of your spatial frequency channels) to the pattern on the right. Demonstrations of this sort suggest that the frequency analyzer model is relevant to understanding the results of some perceptual experiments with human subjects.

Binocularity

Under the drug conditions typically used in the sort of animal experiments we have been discussing, the two eyes have separate visual fields. Normally,

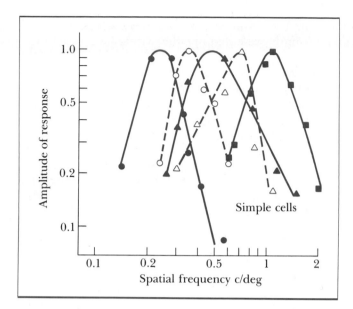

Figure 5.20   Response of simple cells in the cat visual cortex to different spatial frequencies.
Stimuli used were similar to that shown in Figure 5.19 (Maffei and Fiorentini, 1973).

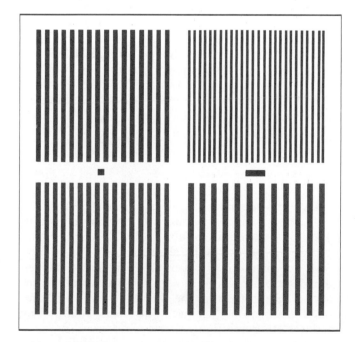

Figure 5.21
Place the book on a desk or table and view this figure from about 2m. First look at the small square in the middle of the left-hand side. The upper and lower gratings should appear to be the same. Now shift your gaze to the right-hand side and look back and forth at the small rectangle for at least one minute. Now again shift your gaze back to the left-hand side and fixate on the small square. Note the change in the appearance of the gratings on the left-hand side. These effects are thought to be due to adaptation of spatial frequency channels in your visual system (Blakemore and Sutton, 1969).

they are focused to allow for clear binocular vision. In anesthetized animals, however, the neural and muscular apparatus that allows both eyes to focus on a single point in space is inoperative. Each eye then looks out on its own visual field, except for a slight overlap along the midline. A neuron

strabismus (strah-BIZ-mus) A deviation of one eye.

amblyopia ex anopsia (am-blee-OPE-e-ah ex an-OPE-see-ah) A deterioration in vision in one eye due to the underutilization of that eye.

that responds to stimulation of only one eye is termed *monocular*. If a neuron can be influenced by stimuli presented in either visual field, it is called *binocular*.

There is considerable convergence of input from the two eyes on individual neurons in the cortex. In cats about 80 percent of all cells in area 17 are binocular. In monkeys far fewer simple cells are binocular, and about 50 percent of the complex cells are binocular. Even in binocular cells, one eye is usually more effective in driving the cell than the other, a condition known as *ocular dominance*.

Hubel and Wiesel devised a seven-category system, ranging from "monocular-contralateral" to "monocular-ipsilateral," to describe the various degrees of ocular dominance they encountered in the cat cortex. Only about 20–25 percent of the cells they saw were equally influenced by either eye (category 4, "equal influence"). Figure 5.22 shows the results of a number of cortical cells with respect to the degree of ocular dominance. The overall distribution is termed an ocular dominance histogram.

The degree of binocularity can be altered by environmental events in the first few "sensitive" weeks of the kitten's life. If a kitten is deprived of the normal use of one eye in this time, for example, by applying an opaque contact lens, the ocular dominance in that kitten will be abnormal when tested later in life. Although the occluded eye itself is functional, very few cells in the cortex respond to stimuli presented to the deprived eye even after removal of the occluder. An abnormally large percentage of the cells will be driven by the nonoccluded eye. The elimination of input from one eye results in the other eye gaining unusual advantage over those cortical neurons that would normally respond to both eyes. Related experiments with cats and monkeys have supported these findings.

Blindness from Disuse

The visual condition known as **strabismus** is a deviation in gaze that the patient cannot control. In these patients the two eyes are not aligned in parallel as is normal. In adults strabismus results in double vision. Some children with strabismus use their eyes alternately, but others consistently disregard the input from one of the eyes. Eventually, in these children vision in the ignored eye deteriorates, even though the eye remains optically normal. This condition of lost vision in the ignored eye is called **amblyopia ex anopsia,** "blindness from not seeing." This disuse followed by dysfunction raises some interesting questions.

Hubel and Wiesel have examined strabismus experimentally. They created an artificial squint or strabismus in four kittens by cutting one of the eye muscles responsible for normal parallel focusing (Hubel and Wiesel, 1965b). All four of these kittens adopted the habit of fixating objects with first one eye, then the other. As far as could be determined, vision was normal in both eyes when the kittens were tested at three months of age. However, when Hubel and Wiesel recorded from neurons in the visual

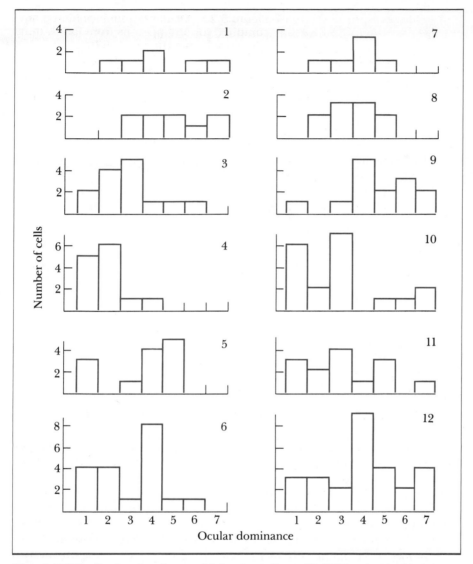

Figure 5.22   Ocular dominance histograms from 12 different experiments.

cortex of these kittens (when the kittens were several months old), they found that 79 percent of the cells were monocular, a reversal of the normal 80 percent binocular cells in the visual cortex (see Figure 5.23). In strabismus the input from each of the two eyes is normal; what is abnormal is the fact that the two eyes do not work together. Apparently, the absence of normal cooperation between the two eyes is the cause of the abnormal ratio of monocular to binocular neurons in the visual cortex.

The hypothesis that an absence of synchronous input resulted in fewer binocular cells led Hubel and Wiesel to perform a follow-up experiment.

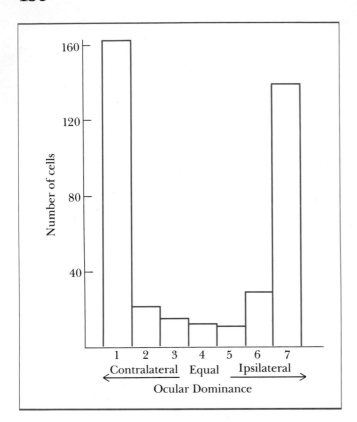

Figure 5.23 Ocular dominance histogram compiled for 384 neurons from four kittens with strabismus (Hubel, 1967).

In this experiment they did not cut the muscles of the eyes at all; they simply raised kittens with occluding contact lenses. On one day the left eye would be occluded, on the next the right eye would be occluded, and so on, for three months. At the end of this time, although vision was normal in both eyes, the ocular dominance histogram was virtually identical to that seen in the earlier experiment, in which the eye muscle had been cut to create an artificial squint. These results strengthen the conclusion that normal binocularity of the neurons in the visual cortex depends on the two eyes being focused on the same point in space.

Neurons in the visual cortex do not remain vulnerable to such dramatic changes throughout life (although some residual vulnerability may remain). In cats the first five to six weeks seem to constitute the most vulnerable time. In monkeys vulnerability begins to decline between six and ten weeks (LeVay et al., 1980). In human beings it has been reported that the sensitive period begins several months after birth and peaks between one and three years of age (Banks et al., 1975). Martin Banks and colleagues studied 24 subjects who had undergone corrective surgery for convergent strabismus (squint) at various ages. The times of onset of strabismus for these subjects were different. Using standard laboratory measures of binocular function, these investigators found that the later the onset of the strabismus, the more normal the subjects were on these tests. When the onset of strabismus was prior to age two, binocular function was permanently abnormal, even after surgery to correct the convergent strabismus.

Development of Orientation Specificity

Are the anatomic connections that underlie orientation preferences also genetically programmed and subject to environmental manipulation, as seems to be the case with binocularity? The answer is still not agreed on, although some similarities are found with the situation for binocularity. For example, it appears that one can find neurons with orientation preferences in the visual cortex of visually inexperienced kittens (in which neurons are sampled before the kittens' eyes are open). However, these neurons are somewhat less selective with respect to binocularity than those of normal adult cats (Hubel and Wiesel, 1963; Stryker and Sherk, 1975).

Evidence exists that abnormal visual experiences can change the cortex in a way that reflects these abnormal experiences. For example, if one rears kittens for several weeks with goggles such that one eye sees only vertical lines and the other eye sees only horizontal lines, the visual cortex neurons that receive their input from a given eye are primarily responsive only to the orientation to which they have been exposed (Hirsch and Spinelli, 1971). Figure 5.24 is a photograph of a kitten with such goggles. In this experiment virtually no neurons had orientation preferences other than those to which they had been exposed.

Similar findings were reported almost simultaneously by Colin Blakemore and Graham Cooper (1970), who worked with two kittens. Each kit-

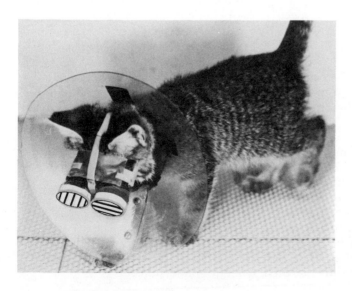

Figure 5.24 Cat in restricting goggles. One eye is exposed only to horizontal lines, the other eye only to vertical lines.

ten was placed for a few hours each day in a tall cylinder painted with black and white stripes of various widths, but all of one orientation. For one kitten the stripes were vertical; for the other kitten the stripes were horizontal. Both kittens, while in the cylinder, wore cardboard ruffs around their necks to prevent them from seeing their own bodies. The kittens were kept in a dark room until they were over five months old.

Blakemore and Cooper then recorded from neurons in the visual cortex of these kittens and found that most neurons they encountered responded best to lines or edges that corresponded to the orientation of the stripes to which that kitten was exposed. Many subsequent experiments have supported the conclusion that the early visual environment is an important determinant of response properties of visual cortex neurons.

Donald Mitchell (1980) has studied children with uncorrected astigmatisms (abnormalities in the lens) that cause lines of certain orientations to be permanently out of focus. Mitchell found that even when the astigmatism was later corrected with glasses, these children could not see lines at the affected orientations as well as children with normal vision, suggesting that the early experience had caused neurons responsive to those orientations that had been out of focus to become less effective in detecting lines, even when the eyes were optically corrected. Experimental work with kittens has led to new and better understanding of some of the visual difficulties such as cataracts and strabismus encountered by young children.

Are Visual Neurons Instructed or Preprogrammed?

The fact that neurons in the visual cortex seem to be more responsive to those orientations that are seen clearly has prompted two rather different hypotheses. One of these ideas can be thought of as an *instructional* hypothesis, the other as a *preprogrammed and validated* hypothesis. According to the instructional hypothesis, cells in the visual cortex are not genetically programmed to be responsive to lines or edges of any particular orientation but are "instructed" early in life by visual experience, becoming committed to respond to the orientations in the visual world to which they are exposed during some sensitive period. This hypothesis does not explain very well how some neurons become committed to one orientation and other neurons to other orientations. This idea can explain, however, results of experiments such as that of Helmut Hirsch and Nico Spinelli (1971) discussed earlier.

The preprogrammed hypothesis, on the other hand, assumes that the anatomic connections that specify orientation preferences are genetically preprogrammed. This hypothesis would account very well for the presence of orientation selective neurons in the cortex of visually inexperienced kittens. This preprogramming, it is suggested, must be validated by appropriate visual experience with lines or edges of the correct orientation for the neuron to retain its genetic programming. In the restrictive goggles experiment of Hirsch and Spinelli, only horizontal and vertical orientations were validated, and neurons with orientation preferences other than horizontal and vertical thus lost their synaptic connections.

Visual Regions outside the Occipital Lobe

It is now known from a variety of experiments that many other regions of the primate brain participate in vision. One such area is the inferior gyrus of the temporal lobe. The recognition that this region of the brain is important in vision comes in part from experiments by Heinrich Klüver and Paul Bucy (1939). These investigators were interested in where in the brain hallucinogenic drugs such as mescaline had their effects. They reasoned that the temporal lobes might be involved, since temporal lobe epilepsy often produces brief hallucinations preceding attacks. Bucy therefore removed the temporal lobes from several monkeys. Following the animals' recovery from the surgery, Klüver and Bucy were doing some routine training when, to their total surprise, they found that although these animals were clearly not blind, they had apparently lost all ability to recognize or identify objects by sight. This phenomenon, which they called *psychic blindness,* is now known to be due to the removal of the inferior temporal gyrus. Their original report gives the flavor of these striking findings.

> In the "concentration" test, in which a piece of food or a metal object passes the experimental cage every thirty seconds, the monkey picks up both the food and the metal object until it ceases reacting to both. The food is eaten, whereas the nail or the steel nut is discarded after an examination by mouth. In some experimental periods, both the food and the inedible object are picked up in 100% of the trials. Even after as many as 260 successive trials the monkey may remove the nail each time it passes, so that finally more than a hundred nails may lie on the floor of its cage. As a rule, however, the monkey is not content with removing and examining the metal object in all or practically all trials; it will frequently pick up a nail or a steel nut from the floor of the cage in the intervals between removing an object every thirty seconds. It should be pointed out that the normal monkey in this test situation will let the nail pass by in all trials or pick it up only after the first few times [Klüver and Bucy, 1939].

Actually, similar results had been reported in 1888 in England by Sanger Brown and E. A. Schaeffer, but they had been ignored or forgotten until Klüver and Bucy rekindled interest in the visual functions of the temporal lobe. More modern findings have enlarged our knowledge of the visual properties of the temporal lobe. For example, Charles Gross and co-workers have recorded from neurons in the inferior temporal gyrus and found some neurons with intriguing properties. As often is true in science, a little luck can help. (Although, as Louis Pasteur observed, "Chance favors only the prepared mind.")

> One day, when having failed to drive a unit with any light stimulus, we waved a hand at the stimulus screen and elicited a very vigorous response from the previously unresponsive neuron. We then spent the next 12 hours testing various paper cutouts in an attempt to find the trigger features for this unit. When the entire set of stimuli used were ranked according to the strength of the response they produced, we could not find a simple physical dimension that correlated with this rank order. However, the rank order of adequate stimuli did correlate with similarity (for us) to the shadow of a

The Klüver–Bucy Syndrome

Although the "psychic blindness" observed in monkeys with temporal lobe removals was one of the most striking symptoms, Heinrich Klüver and Paul Bucy observed several other dramatic changes in the behavior of these monkeys. Together with psychic blindness, these other symptoms are referred to as the **Klüver–Bucy syndrome.** A second symptom was described as "oral tendencies," defined as strong, almost compulsive tendencies to examine all objects by placing them in the mouth. This symptom, of course, is related to psychic blindness, since if an animal cannot recognize an object by sight, it is likely to put it in the mouth and attempt to recognize it by taste. Klüver and Bucy found this orality extended even to feces. These animals often ate large amounts of food and would eat virtually anything, including raw meat, which is rarely eaten by this species.

A third symptom Klüver and Bucy labeled *hypermetamorphosis,* a rather long word for the tendency to examine compulsively and to react to virtually everything in the environment. Tiny specks of dust, a whiff of smoke, a scratch on a piece of the testing apparatus—nothing was too small or insignificant to be inspected. Common objects such as a nail might be picked up, examined, placed in the animal's mouth, dropped, picked up again, examined, placed in the animal's mouth, and so on, 100 times or more.

A fourth symptom was a significant lack of emotion. Rhesus monkeys are normally quite emotional, and often very excitable, but following the removal of their temporal lobes,

these animals became placid, almost indifferent to events, showed little fear or avoidance of objects (such as a toy snake) which before surgery would send them shrieking to the back of their cages. This particular symptom, along with the orality, has been linked to damage to the amygdala. Sometimes these animals would begin to show emotional behaviors, but they typically did not "follow through" and an "attack" behavior would suddenly end with the monkey licking the examiner's fingers.

The last major symptom of the Klüver–Bucy syndrome was hypersexuality, manifested by a tendency to mount and attempt to copulate with almost any object too big to be put in the mouth. Monkeys would mount stuffed animals, cats (much to the cats' annoyance), and other inappropriate objects. This symptom too can be related to the animal's inability to identify objects by sight. Even after two years, and in some cases longer, these symptoms were still present.

Klüver–Bucy Syndrome in Humans

Although some of these symptoms have also been observed in human beings suffering from brain damage in and around the temporal lobe, a true "full-blown" case of a Klüver–Bucy syndrome has been found only rarely. The most convincing case was reported by Wendy Marlowe, Elliott Mancall, and Joseph Thomas in 1975. These investigators examined a 20-year-old male who had suffered a severe viral brain infection that had resulted in permanent destruction of parts of both temporal lobes,

---

Klüver–Bucy syndrome (CLUE-ver Bhu-see) Psychic blindness and emotional changes seen after temporal lobe removal.

monkey hand. The relative adequacy of a few of these stimuli is shown [see Figure 5.25]. Curiously, fingers pointing downward elicited very little response as compared with fingers pointing upward or laterally, the usual orientation in which the animal would see its own hand [Gross et al., 1972].

Follow-up research from the same laboratory has uncovered another interesting type of neuron in the inferior temporal gyrus and in brain tissue located nearby in the superior temporal gyrus (Bruce et al., 1981). These

particularly the left one. Prior to this viral infection, this man had been perfectly normal, a good athlete, a high school graduate with better than average grades, well liked, exclusively heterosexual, and engaged to be married at the time he became ill. The infection left him permanently and profoundly changed. The examination took place a few months after the onset of the illness, but little or no recovery was seen two years later, and the individual was in custodial care at the time of the report.

The symptoms matched those seen by Klüver and Bucy in monkeys with temporal lobe removals. Although this young man could walk and move normally and showed no gross disturbances in vision or other senses, he was profoundly impaired in his recognition of common objects. For example, when handed his razor, he had no idea of what it was or what to do with it. When he was shown another patient using a razor, he was able to copy the other patient exactly, even adopting the precise order of movements used by that patient, and was thus able to shave himself. He could, when tested nonverbally, be trained to tell the difference between geometric designs, and although he got lost in the hospital, he showed no "blindness," did not walk into walls or closed doors, and so on. He also suffered from a severe form of aphasia, which made communication with him difficult. This was also due to damage to the left temporal lobe (discussed in more detail in Chapter 14).

Emotionally, he displayed an indifference to people and situations and would often say and do socially inappropriate things, such as mimicking the gestures and actions of others. He also showed the change in both sexuality and oral tendencies characteristic of the Klüver–Bucy syndrome:

He engaged in oral exploration of all objects within his grasp, appearing unable to gain information via tactile or visual means alone. All objects that he could lift were placed in his mouth and sucked or chewed. He did not attempt to pick up objects directly with his mouth, using his hands for that purpose, but was observed to engage in much olfactory behavior. When dining he would eat with his fingers until reprimanded and a fork placed in his hand; he was thereafter able to imitate use of a fork, but failed to remaster the task of eating with utensils spontaneously. He would eat one food item on his plate completely before turning to the next. Hyperbulimia was prominent: he ingested virtually everything within reach, including the plastic wrapper from bread, cleaning pastes, ink, dog food, and feces. Although his tastes were clearly indiscriminate, he seemed to prefer liquids or soft solids.

The patient's sexual behavior was a particular source of concern while in hospital. Although vigorously heterosexual prior to his illness, he was observed to make advances toward other male patients by stroking their legs and inviting fellatio by gesture; at times he attempted to kiss them. Although on a sexually mixed floor during a portion of his recovery, he never made advances toward women, and in fact, his apparent reversal of sexual polarity prompted his fiancée to sever their relationship [Marlowe et al., 1975, p. 56].

"face detector" neurons appear to be selectively responsive to faces, those of either monkeys or human beings. Figure 5.26 illustrates the response of one such neuron and stimuli to which it was and was not responsive. This neuron responded better to faces than to all other stimuli presented. Distorting the face reduced the response. The precise role of such neurons is still a matter of debate, but it is known that in human beings damage to the temporal and occipital areas of the brain occasionally produces a very

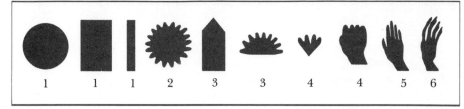

Figure 5.25   Stimuli used to excite a neuron in the inferior temporal lobe of a monkey.
The stimuli are arranged from left to right in order of their increasing ability to excite the neuron. 1 = little or no excitement; 2–6 = increasing ability to excite (Gross et al., 1972).

curious visual deficit—an inability to recognize the identity of faces, even those of close relatives. In fact, in a few cases such patients do not recognize their own face in photographs or in a mirror! The technical term for this phenomenon is **prosopagnosia.**

The ability to recognize faces quickly and reliably is important in maintaining the complex social interactions of primate societies. Perhaps a special class of neurons dedicated to face recognition has evolved. In experiments such as that of Charles Bruce and colleagues the response properties of any given neuron can only be tested with so many stimuli, and the possibility always exists that some untested nonface stimulus would also produce a vigorous response in these cells. The evidence, however, supports the conclusion that face recognition cells exist in the temporal lobes of the primate brain. Such face selective neurons are not common, constituting only about 7 percent of the neurons examined. At least two other laboratories have found such face selective neurons in the temporal lobe in the rhesus monkey (Rolls, 1984; Perrett et al., 1985). Edmund Rolls also found face selective neurons in the amygdala, to which the temporal lobe sends afferents.

Brain Damage and Vision

Cases of human brain damage have contributed to our knowledge of the visual system. Damage in such cases never coincides exactly with the divisions recognized by neuroanatomists. Nevertheless, a large number of cases now exists; by comparing the regions of overlap of damage with the clinical signs and symptoms, it is possible to make some tentative conclusions. For example, damage to the primary visual cortex (area 17) produces blindness for the regions of the visual field related to the area of cortical damage. Such lesions can produce virtually complete blindness if the damage encompasses all of area 17. If only small regions are damaged, such as from a small-caliber bullet wound, then small areas of blindness in the visual field, called **scotomata,** are found.

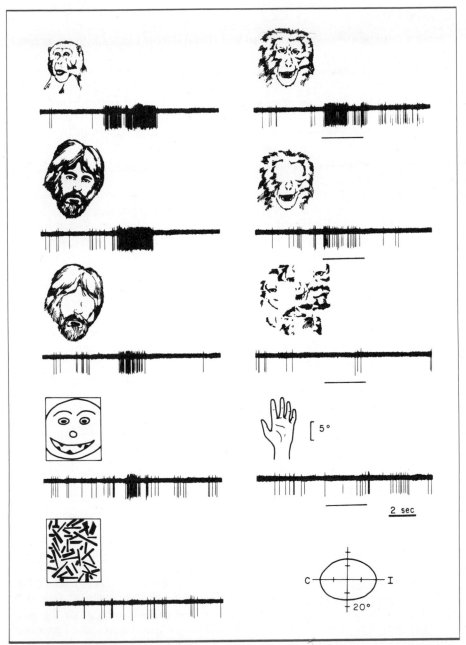

Figure 5.26 Stimuli and responses of a neuron in the temporal lobe that responded best to faces.
Removing the eyes or rearranging the parts of the face decreased the response (Bruce et al., 1981).

blindsight   Ability of some individuals to guess, at better than chance levels, the identity of stimuli in parts of their visual field that correspond to their scotomata.

retinohypothalamic tract (RET-in-o-hy-po-thal-AM-ik) A small bundle of axons that emerge from the optic tract and innervate the suprachiasmatic nuclei.

Blindsight

The generalization that damage to the visual cortex causes blindness must be qualified. Some residual visual function occurs even within scotomata, but the patient may not be conscious of any visual sensations (Pöppel et al., 1973). Lawrence Weiskrantz and his colleagues in England studied a patient who had had a substantial portion of his visual cortex removed as the result of surgery for a brain tumor (Weiskrantz et al., 1974). This patient was blind even with very high levels of illumination in those portions of his visual field corresponding to the region of damage. Nevertheless, when asked by the experimenters to guess where a stimulus presented in this blind area might be, he could do so at a level well above chance. Moreover, he could determine whether a stimulus was an X or an O at better than chance levels, despite continuing to report that he could not see anything. This **blindsight** appears to be a type of visual discrimination that is not accompanied by any conscious visual experience. It is possible that such blindsight is mediated by the superior colliculus.

As noted earlier, damage to the temporal lobe also produces visual problems, but not blindness. Monkeys with lesions in the inferior temporal gyrus do not appear to be visually impaired on casual inspection. They do not bump into things, and they reach and grasp things without error. The deficit seems to be in visually recognizing the significance of objects, not in locating them in space. In monkeys both the left and right temporal lobes must be lesioned in order to see this phenomenon. In human brain damage patients it appears that a similar deficit is seen following damage to just the *right* temporal lobe. Patients with such injuries can see objects normally but have unusual difficulty in recognizing what they are seeing. (This example of apparent lateralization of function in the human brain is discussed in more detail in Chapter 13.)

Other Visual Regions of the Brain

Many regions of the brain are influenced by light; not all are involved in image formation, however. Some parts of the visual system use visual information to regulate or guide other aspects of behavior. For example, the *suprachiasmatic nuclei* (SCN) of the hypothalamus receive input from the eye and apparently use this information to synchronize various circadian rhythms with environmental events such as the light–dark cycle. The SCN in the golden hamster receive input from less than 1 percent of the ganglion cells in the retina. This input is carried by the collaterals of axons of ganglion cells that also innervate a small nucleus in the thalamus called the *intergeniculate leaflet* (IGL). The IGL in turn sends axons to the SCN (Pickard, 1985). The collaterals of the ganglion cell axons that go directly to the SCN are collectively known as the **retinohypothalamic tract.**

Damage to the retinohypothalamic tract does not interfere with visual discrimination, but it does destroy the ability of hamsters to synchronize their activity rhythms with environmental light cues. On the other hand, if the retinohypothalamic tract and SCN are left intact and the main "image formation" system that goes through the LGN and visual cortex is destroyed, hamsters become behaviorally blind but can still synchronize their activity rhythms with environmental light cues. Further discussions of circadian rhythms and the functions of the SCN appear in Chapter 10.

saccade (sah-KAD) Rapid voluntary eye movement.

The Superior Colliculus: Organ of Orientation?

Another very important part of the visual system is the superior colliculus. It is located on the dorsal surface of the midbrain, in a region called the *tectum.* Just rostral to the tectum is another region involved in visual function, the *pretectal area,* which contains circuitry required by the pupillary reflexes to light.

Each superior colliculus can be divided into two regions, a superficial part and a deeper part. The cell layers that compose the superficial division receive visual information directly from the retina (mainly from Y and W cells). In addition, the superior colliculus receives input from the primary visual cortex, the cortex immediately adjacent to the primary visual cortex, and a region of the frontal lobes termed the *frontal eye fields.* The deeper layers of the superior colliculus do not receive direct input from the retina, but they do receive input from a wide variety of other brain regions, including visual, auditory, and motor cortical regions and an extremely large number of subcortical nuclei.

According to Robert Wurtz and Joanne Albano (1980), the two divisions of the colliculus have different functions. Briefly, the superficial layers appear to be primarily concerned with vision, whereas the deeper layers contain neurons that seem related to orientation of the animal to various stimuli and that fire in relation to *eye movements,* particularly **saccades.** Saccades are small, rapid eye movements that change the point of visual fixation, bringing the eyes to bear on a new target of interest in the visual field.

In the superficial layers of the superior colliculus of monkeys, recordings from individual neurons have revealed cells with receptive fields that vary in size from less than 1 degree to more than 10 degrees and that are not "fussy about stimulus size, shape, direction, or speed of movement" (Wurtz and Albano, 1980). Interestingly, the number of nerve impulses a particular neuron produces in response to a stimulus is influenced by the significance of that stimulus to the animal. In an awake, behaving monkey, Michael Goldberg and Robert Wurtz (1972) found that if the preferred stimulus for a cell is used as a visual target for directed saccades, the response rate of that cell increases to that stimulus as the animal learns to pay attention to it on successive trials.

The superior colliculus is involved in orienting to stimuli of various modalities. Most of the efferent neurons of the deeper layers (which are thought to be involved in orienting the eyes to stimuli in the environment) also *respond* to input from one or more sensory modalities. These are the neurons that fire in relation to saccades. M. Alex Meredith and Barry Stein

(1985) found that over 70 percent of these cells are multimodal, responding to two or more different sensory modalities. The combined evidence suggests that the superior colliculus is an organ of orienting, not just to visual stimuli, but to attention-demanding stimuli of various kinds.

Serial Versus Parallel Processing Revisited

In our discussion of the visual system we have traced events from the effects of light energy on the photoreceptors of the retina to face selective neurons in the temporal lobe. The input to one part of the visual system is the output of the preceding part. Traditionally, the visual system has been viewed as a *serial processing system,* in which raw information is transmitted from the retina to the LGN, and increasingly more "digested" information is passed on, first to area 17, then to areas 18 and 19, and finally to other regions of the cortex, such as the temporal lobes. The neural events that underlie visual perceptions have been thought to take place in these higher brain regions.

Several other assumptions are commonly associated with the idea of serial processing. For example, such a view is consistent with the idea that there is only one primary cortical receptive area (area 17) for vision. The other cortical regions, such as 18 and 19, are considered as secondary processing regions. Still another idea that is compatible with a serial processing hypothesis is that the cortical input from the LGN is more or less homogeneous, varying primarily in the region of the visual field with which it is concerned. Finally, the serial processing hypothesis usually considers those regions of cortex not classified as either primary or secondary sensory cortex as *association cortex.*

Association cortex is usually defined anatomically by the absence of direct input from the thalamus. It has often been assumed that these areas increase in relative size in primates, particularly in the human brain. Thus, according to this line of thought, rats have very little association cortex, carnivores more, and primates the most. To its credit, the serial processing hypothesis, which developed out of a long line of sound research, did a good job of accounting for most of the experimental data up until a few years ago. However, it now appears that there is an even better way to view the visual system. The *parallel processing* hypothesis takes into consideration recently discovered facts about the mammalian visual system.

The Merzenich and Kaas Model

The data and arguments supporting the parallel processing hypothesis have been marshaled by Michael Merzenich and Jon Kaas (1980). The fundamental principle of their parallel processing hypothesis of vision is, "Perception is a product of a nearly simultaneous activation of a number of topographic sensory representations." The Merzenich–Kaas model arises

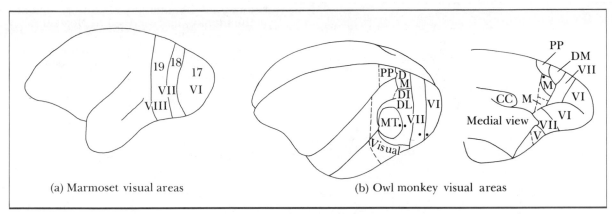

Figure 5.27 Traditional (a) and current (b) views of the organization of the visual areas of the cortex in the monkey (Merzenich and Kaas, 1980). MT = middle temporal; DI = dorsointermediate; DM = dorsomedial; M = medial; PP = posterior parietal; MV = medial ventral; VI, VII, VIII, visual areas corresponding to Brodmann areas 17, 18, and 19, respectively (Merzenich and Kaas, 1980).

from the results of experiments using new neuroanatomic techniques. From these studies it is now known that many more representations of the retina in the cortex exist than was previously known. For example, the owl monkey has been shown to have 10 distinct topographical retinal maps in the occipital lobe. Figure 5.27 illustrates these visual areas. Data on the rhesus monkey also demonstrate multiple visual fields (Van Essen and Maunsell, 1983). The notion of a single primary region of cortex for reception of visual input has been disconfirmed by these findings.

Other senses also appear to have multiple cortical fields. There are seven or more for somesthesis and four or more for hearing (Merzenich and Kaas, 1980). Thus multiple cortical receptive regions are found for each of the three senses for which there is a spatial aspect to the sensory surface. Taste and odor also have cortical receptive fields but do not have a true spatial aspect for their sensory receptive surfaces. We shall have more to say about all the other senses in the next chapter.

These newly recognized receptive fields are not simply copies of one another. Although there is some redundancy, the available evidence now suggests that each visual cortical region has its own particular pattern of anatomic connections and contains neurons with particular response properties. Considerable overlap probably exists among the various fields for both anatomic connections and response properties of its neurons. Each area is reciprocally connected with most or all of the other areas. It would appear to be beyond the capacity of any serial processing model to cope with this newly discovered anatomic complexity.

These anatomic findings also have seriously undermined the concept of association cortex. It now appears that virtually all the cortex behind the central sulcus (see Figure 5.28) is made up of one or another sensory

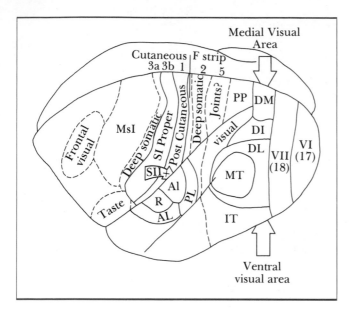

Figure 5.28　A summary of cortical regions in the monkey as described by Merzenich and Kaas (1980).
Abbreviations as in Figure 5.27 and R = rostral auditory field; AL = anterior lateral auditory field; PL = posterior lateral auditory field; MsI = motor-sensory area I; IT = inferior temporal region.

receptive field, leaving virtually no "blank spaces" to be classified as association cortex. Like the Cheshire cat in *Alice in Wonderland,* association cortex has virtually disappeared, leaving only its smile. Thus the idea that association cortex has increased in more advanced brains has been replaced largely by the hypothesis that instead an increase occurs in the number of cortical receptive regions dedicated to sensory processing.

To See a Tree

The two different hypotheses lead to different conclusions regarding the likely nature of brain activity underlying perception. For example, when we look at an apple tree, the serial processing hypothesis would suggest that the final percept of *apple tree* is due to the activation of a very small number of neurons. These neurons would be recipients of multiple converging pathways from retina to some higher visual center in the brain. Thus the light reflected from the tree would stimulate the cells of the retina, causing a series of impulses in the optic nerves, which in turn would activate LGN neurons. Then LGN neurons would influence various edge detectors and color-coding cells in area 17. From here the higher-order processing regions and association cortex would be activated. Finally, a serial processing hypothesis would say that all the various visual inputs for color, edges, and angles would have to activate a few tree detectors somewhere in the brain that would then be responsible for our visual perception of the apple tree. (This brief summary ignores the necessary contribution of memory, which allows us to recognize and name the tree, factors that are not easy for any existing theory of perception to explain.) The serial processing hypothesis assumes that perceptions are due to the cascading of converging input onto a small number of complex object receptors located in the temporal lobe or other higher order cortical regions.

A parallel processing hypothesis does not assume that such a cascade of converging input underlies complex percepts. Instead, since multiple representations of the retina are found in the cortex, different aspects of the tree could be recognized, nearly simultaneously, in *different* regions of the cortex. Under this hypothesis different aspects of the visual stimulus would be handled by different channels from retina to cortex. Our overall experience of a unified percept of the tree would not be the result of a small number of closely located neurons, but the result of a much larger number of more widely scattered neurons, activated simultaneously, or nearly so. Thus the green color of the leaves or the red of the apples would be mediated by different cells, spatially removed from those responding to the lines and angles formed by the distinctive shape of the branches.

These two hypotheses seem to have different implications for the development of theories of perception. At the present time the parallel processing hypothesis seems to have a stronger experimental base. However, it should not be assumed that we have now discovered how the visual system of primates is organized. The parallel processing hypothesis has only sharpened the focus of the search.

SUMMARY

1. Our eyes respond to a narrow band of wavelengths in the electromagnetic spectrum. Light passes through many different structures in the eye before it comes in contact with the photoreceptive cells of the retina, the rods and cones.

2. Vision begins with a change in the photosensitive molecules in the rods and cones. Much of what we know about the nature of the response of the visual system has come from recording nerve impulses from individual neurons. The structures that have been studied particularly well in this way include the lateral geniculate nucleus, the visual cortex, and the inferior temporal lobe.

3. Because of the arrangement of the mammalian brain, the images of objects in the left visual field are processed initially by the right side of the brain and vice versa.

4. The primate eye has two different types of photoreceptors, rods and cones, which are important for vision during dim light conditions and daylight conditions, respectively. The eye has many more rods than cones, but our peak visual acuity depends on a relatively small number (50,000) of cones located in the fovea of the retina. Rods are more sensitive to the presence or absence of light, but the cone system is capable of far greater acuity.

5. Other cell types are found in the retina, the most important being horizontal cells, bipolar cells, amacrine cells, and ganglion cells. The

axons of the ganglion cells form the optic nerves. In the retina it appears that only amacrine cells and ganglion cells actually produce nerve impulses; the other cell types communicate by means of graded potentials that either increase or decrease transmitter release.

6. Cells throughout the visual system can be characterized in terms of their receptive fields. The receptive field of a cell can be defined as that area of the retina from which the firing rate of that cell can be influenced by light. In the lateral geniculate nucleus receptive fields tend to be circular and consist of a center and a surround. The center and surround responses are opposite (e.g., on-center, off-surround).

7. Ganglion cells have at least three subpopulations, termed X, Y, and W. These cell types vary in function and structure. These different populations support a parallel processing model of vision.

8. The response properties of neurons in the lateral geniculate nucleus reflect the input from three different populations of cones in the retina, providing the basis for color vision. Some lateral geniculate neurons show an opponent process type of response, being excited by light of one band of wavelengths and inhibited by light of another band of wavelengths. Other cells display only a center–surround organization, but most lateral geniculate cells show both center–surround and opponent process responses.

9. Two rival models have been developed to account for the observed properties of neurons in the visual cortex and surrounding cortical regions in the occipital lobes. These hypotheses are usually referred to as the *feature detector model* and the *spatial frequency model*. Both ideas are worthy of our consideration at the present. In support of the feature detector model are the findings of Hubel and Wiesel on edge detectors in the cortex. DeValois and others have proposed that a better way to interpret these responses and other findings is by considering the visual system as a spatial frequency analyzer. Some data are more readily explained with this model.

10. Another important response property of visual cortex neurons is that most cells respond more to stimulation from one eye than from the other, but most cells respond at least somewhat to both eyes, that is, they display binocularity. The degree of binocularity is in part determined by the visual experience of the individual during the early part of life. Orientation specificity of edge detectors is also thought to be determined in part by early visual experience.

11. The inferior temporal lobe of primates also contains neurons that are sensitive to visual stimulation. A small number of neurons have been discovered that respond preferentially to stimuli that resemble hands or faces. Removal of the temporal lobes produces a bizarre set of symptoms including "psychic blindness," emotional changes, and hypersexuality. This condition is called the Klüver–Bucy syndrome, after the individuals who first described it in detail in 1939.

12. Destruction of the visual cortex in human beings typically leaves individuals blind for those areas of the visual field corresponding to the damaged cortical areas. However, a curious phenomenon of blindsight has been noted in a few such individuals in which some visual identifications can be made, even though the person is not aware of seeing anything.

13. The superior colliculi, which receive visual input from the retina and from the visual cortex, appear to be important for orienting to both visual and nonvisual stimuli in the environment.

14. Two different theoretical approaches to the physiology of vision are dominant today, a serial processing model and a parallel processing model. Data regarding multiple visual receptive areas in the cortex, as well as other considerations, tend to favor the parallel processing model, although much remains to be learned about the way in which our brains process visual information.

SUGGESTIONS FOR FURTHER READING

DeValois, R. L., and DeValois, K. K. (1980). Spatial vision. *Annual Review of Psychology, 31,* 309–341.

Hubel, D. H., and Wiesel, T. N. (1979). Brain mechanisms of vision. *Scientific American, 241,* 150–162.

Kuffler, S. W., Nicholls, J. G., and Martin, A. R. (1984). *From neuron to brain* (2d ed.). Sunderland, MA: Sinauer Associates.

Merzenich, M. M., and Kaas, J. H. (1980). Principles of organization of sensory-perceptual systems in mammals. In J. M. Sprague and A. N. Epstein (Eds.), *Progress in psychobiology and physiological psychology* (vol. 9). New York: Academic Press.

6

Our Other Senses

*From a swirling sea of energies
each sense selects its own.*

D. P. K.

Preview

Our ability to respond to any form of energy depends on the *transduction* of that particular energy form into neural activity, the *transmission* of nerve impulses to appropriate regions of the brain, and the *abstraction* of meaning from these signals. Human beings, in addition to being able to see, can respond to energy forms that stimulate the senses of hearing, touch, temperature, taste, and smell. Further, our sense of balance (our *vestibular* sense) allows us to monitor the position of our bodies in space.

Some of the sensory input coming into our brain does not reach consciousness, but instead evokes automatic reflex responses. For each sense we shall consider the critical stimuli, the construction of the sense organ, the nature of the transduction, the main pathways into the brain, and the abstraction of meaning from these signals by higher brain regions.

Hearing

Our ability to hear is due to receptors in the ear that send signals in the auditory (VIIIth) nerve to various processing centers in the brainstem, thalamus, and neocortex. The energy changes responsible for sound are mechanical disturbances propagated through an elastic medium such as air, water, or bone. Vibrations that produce sound can be represented as waves, as shown in Figure 6.1.

Figure 6.1 shows an idealized, or pure, wave form. The wave forms of naturally occurring sounds are much more complex, but all waves, simple or complex, have three fundamental parameters: *frequency, amplitude,* and *complexity*. Frequency is the number of complete waves per second. The unit for frequency is the *hertz* (abbreviated Hz), named for the German physicist Heinrich Hertz (1857–1894). Young adults with normal hearing can detect sounds from 20 to 20,000 Hz; older individuals become less able to hear the higher frequencies as they age. Many animals, such as bats, whales, and dolphins, can detect sounds up to 100,000 Hz.

The amplitude of a wave form is the distance from the trough to the peak of a given wave. It is correlated with its intensity or pressure, measured in **decibels** (abbreviated dB). The decibel scale is a measure of the ratio of the sound in question to a standard pressure. Sound intensity is measured

decibel (DES-ih-bel) Unit of measurement for the intensity of the pressure in sound waves. Abbreviated dB.

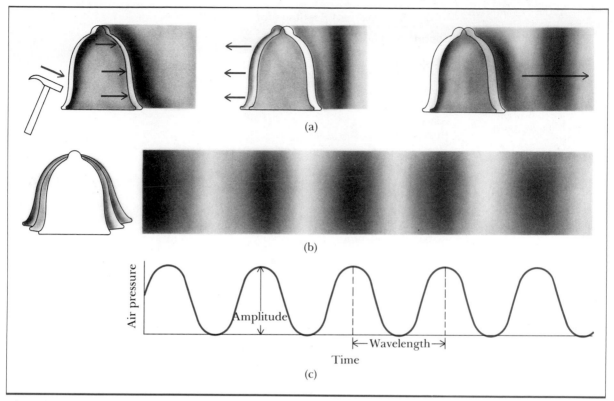

Figure 6.1   The production and propagation of sound as represented by waves produced by a vibrating object.
(a) Striking a bell sets up vibrations in the bell and alternate compression and rarefaction of air molecules surrounding the bell, as shown in (b).
(c) Diagrammatic representation of compression and rarefaction of air molecules, showing amplitude and wavelength of resulting sound waves. Rarefaction is a reduction in density of air molecules.

with sound level meters. Decibel levels for some familiar sounds are given in Table 6.1. Another commonly used term, *wavelength,* refers to the distance between corresponding points on two successive waves.

SUMMARY TABLE *Dimensions of Sound*	
Psychological Dimension	**Main Physical Determinants**
Pitch	Frequency
Loudness	Intensity
Timbre	Frequency overtones

sone   A unit of loudness; the loudness of a 1000-Hz tone at 40 dB above a listener's threshold.

timbre   (TIM-ber, TAM-br) The musical quality of a sound. The quality that allows a listener to tell the difference in two sounds having the same pitch and loudness.

tympanic membrane (Tim-PAN-ik) The eardrum.

ossicles   (OS-sik-uls) The three tiny bones involved in hearing: the malleus, incus, and stapes.

TABLE 6.1   Decibel Readings for Familiar Sounds

Sound	Decibels
Quiet room	40
Average home	50
Normal conversation	60
Freeway traffic, (from 50 meters)	70
Alarm clock	80
Busy street	85
Heavy truck, shouted conversation	90
Subway train	97
Motorcycle, jackhammer	100
Power mower	110
Rock music, amplified	115
Jet plane at ramp	117
Rocket at launching	180

SOURCE: Hoyt (1975).

Psychological Correlates of Frequency and Intensity

The main psychological correlate of intensity is *loudness*. Although intensity can be measured with a sound level meter, loudness can be measured only with a hearer (usually a human being but sometimes animals). Loudness is measured in **sones.** One sone is defined as the perceived loudness of a 1000-Hz tone at 40 dB above the listener's threshold for hearing. Intensity is the main determinant of loudness, but frequency is also important. *Pitch* is the main psychological correlate of frequency. **Timbre** is the quality of sound that allows the listener to tell the difference between two steady signals with the same pitch and loudness (e.g., the same note played on a violin and on a piano). Timbre depends primarily on the complexity of the full spectrum of the stimulus.

Anatomy of the Ear

The human ear is composed of three main parts: the *external ear*, the *middle ear*, and the *inner ear* (see Figure 6.2). The external ear includes the pinna (or auricle) and the ear canal. As sound waves penetrate the ear, they strike the eardrum, or **tympanic membrane,** which seals the auditory canal and marks the transition from the outer ear to the middle ear.

Prominent in the middle ear are three tiny bones, the **ossicles,** which transmit the vibrations of the eardrum to the oval window of the inner ear. These three bones are (in order from the eardrum) the *malleus* (hammer), the *incus* (anvil), and the *stapes* (stirrup). They are tightly coupled together with muscles that can alter their position slightly. The ossicles do not simply transmit vibrations from the eardrum to the oval window; they also are important in *impedance matching* in the ear.

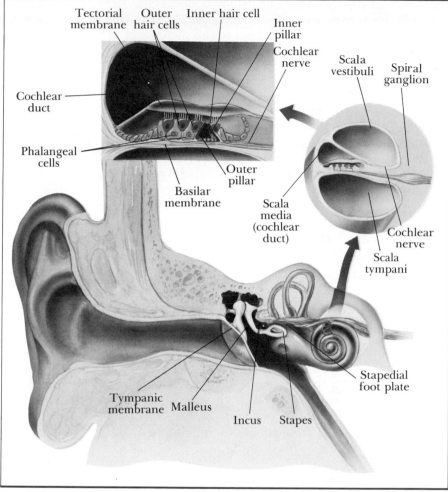

impedance (im-PEED-ance) Resistance to the flow of energy.

Figure 6.2   The external ear, middle ear, and inner ear of the right ear as seen from the front of the head.
A cross section through the organ of Corti is shown in the drawings at the top of the illustration.

Impedance is resistance to the flow of energy. The concept can be applied to the flow of electrical current and to mechanical vibration. In the ear the resistance to vibration is much greater in the fluid that fills the inner ear than in the air of the middle ear. Thus the fluid of the inner ear is said to have more impedance than the air of the middle ear. If there were not some way of at least partially equilibrating these different impedances, about 97 percent of the energy of the sound waves striking the eardrum would be reflected and only about 3 percent would be transmitted to the inner ear (Evans, 1982a). However, because of impedance matching, about 60 percent of the energy striking the eardrum is transmitted to the inner ear.

Unlike human beings, some animals can move their external ears in order to better focus sound. Animals such as the rabbit are dependent upon acute hearing for survival and have evolved large, moveable external ears.

cochlea (KOKE-lee-ah) That portion of the inner ear concerned with hearing.

utricle (U-trik-ul) A sense organ in the inner ear concerned with the sense of balance.

saccule (SACK-yule) A sense organ in the inner ear concerned with the sense of balance.

basilar membrane (BAZ-i-lar) The membrane to which the base of the hair cells are attached in the organ of Corti.

organ of Corti (KORE-tee) The actual sense organ of hearing in the cochlea.

tectorial membrane (tek-TOR-ee-al) The membrane into which the cilia of the hair cells in the organ of Corti are embedded.

Much of the impedance matching is due to the fact that the area of the eardrum is approximately 17 times greater than that of the oval window. This difference in area allows for an increase in the intensity of the vibration, as the pressure on the oval window is concentrated on the smaller area. Impedance matching is also due in part to the fact that the ossicles act as levers, providing a mechanical advantage of about 1.3 (Kelly, 1981a). The total gain is a factor of about 22 (17 × 1.3). Contractions of the muscles attached to the ossicles can alter the impedance-matching characteristics of the middle ear, reducing the intensity of the vibrations of the oval window. This sound attenuation, which is reflexive and is triggered by very intense sounds, can be as much as 30 dB at 100 Hz and is an important protective mechanism. The muscles of the ossicles are supplied by neurons of the Vth and VIIth cranial nerves.

The Inner Ear: The Snail Shell and the Canals

The inner ear contains the **cochlea,** the structure containing the organ of hearing; the **utricle;** the **saccule;** and the semicircular canals. The utricle, saccule, and semicircular canals are responsible for the sense of balance. They will be discussed shortly. The cochlea looks very much like a tiny snail shell (the Latin for snail shell is *cochlea*). The cochlea in the human ear has about 2.5 turns and would be about 3.5 cm long if laid out flat. It is divided into three main compartments by various membranes: the *scala vestibuli,* the *scala tympani,* and the *scala media.* (*Scala* means "staircase" or "passage" in Latin.) At one end of the scala tympani is a thinner, more elastic region known as the round window, which serves as an outlet for the pressure exerted on the oval window by the stapes.

Located in the scala media (middle passage) is the array of sensory receptors responsible for the transduction of the vibrations in the cochlear fluid into nerve impulses. The receptors, called *hair cells,* together with their supporting cells, are embedded in the floor of the scala media, called the **basilar membrane.** Figure 6.2 shows the main components of the **organ of Corti,** the sense organ for hearing. This structure was named for its discoverer, the Italian anatomist Alfonso Corti (1822–1876). The basilar membrane is, surprisingly, wider at the apex (500 μm) than at its base (100 μm). Thus it gets wider as the cochlea in which it is located gets narrower! The basilar membrane is also somewhat stiffer at its base. The receptor cells of the organ of Corti consist of four rows of hair cells, named for the 30–150 *cilia,* or hairlike projections, that reach upward from these cells and that are embedded in the overlying **tectorial membrane.**

Hearing through Shearing: Transduction in the Cochlea

The vibrations initiated by the movement of the stapes on the oval window are transmitted almost instantaneously by the fluid of the cochlea to the basilar membrane. Our understanding of the role of the movements of the basilar membrane in hearing is due in large part to Georg von Békésy

(1899–1972), who received the Nobel prize for his work in 1961. Békésy carefully removed the cochlea from human cadavers and by ingenious experiments was able to determine that the movement of the stapes on the oval window set up a series of *traveling waves* in the basilar membrane.

The traveling wave in the basilar membrane can be likened to the movement of a rope attached at one end and given a shake at the other. The speed of the wave slows down somewhat as it travels from the base to the apex of the basilar membrane. Thus the wave begins traveling at about 160,000 cm/sec at the base and slows down to about 15,000 cm/sec along the membrane and to 1000 cm/sec near the apex (Green, 1976). This traveling wave excites the hair cells, producing the necessary neural activity for hearing.

The neural activity required for hearing results from a shearing force exerted on the hair cells by the movements of the basilar membrane, combined with the force exerted on them by the overlying tectorial membrane in which the cilia are embedded. Imagine you are standing on a swaying rope bridge with your shoes tied tightly to the bridge. Your hair, on the other hand, is firmly entangled in a rigid ceiling overhead that is not attached to the bridge. As the bridge undulates, your hair is pulled and twisted because the ceiling does not move with the bridge. The hair cells are in a similar position, with the base of the cell firmly embedded in the undulating basilar membrane and the cilia that emerge from the apex of the cell firmly embedded in the overlying and separate tectorial membrane.

The deformation of the cilia of the hair cells as they are pulled and twisted by the unequal movements of the basilar membrane and the tectorial membrane produces an electrical response in the hair cells called a *receptor potential*. Receptor potentials are similar in many ways to postsynaptic potentials (see Chapter 2). It is not completely clear how this receptor potential occurs, but it is likely that the shearing force on the cell opens ion channels (probably for K^+ and Ca^{2+}) and that the resulting ion flow slightly depolarizes the hair cell (Hudspeth, 1983). The hair cells are not true neurons: They do not have axons and they do not produce nerve impulses. Instead the receptor potential causes the release of neurotransmitter from the hair cells, which synapse with neurons of the cochlear nerve that make contact with the base of the hair cells. The cochlear nerve, the vestibular nerve, and some efferent axons compose the auditory nerve.

Von Békésy also discovered that the peak of the traveling wave in the basilar membrane depends on the dominant frequencies in the stimulus. For example, using relatively pure tones, the peak amplitude of the wave for tones of 6000 Hz or higher is near the base of the basilar membrane, whereas low-frequency sounds produce a peak amplitude close to the apex of the basilar membrane, where it is wider (see Figure 6.3). Von Békésy's evidence suggested that for virtually all sounds, however, most of the basilar membrane would be displaced somewhat.

The Place Theory

The fact that the basilar membrane undergoes different peak displacements with different frequencies forms the basis for one of the two main

Figure 6.3
(a) Drawings showing the vibration of the basilar membrane to sounds of three different frequencies. (b) Illustration of the traveling wave in the basilar membrane as if the membrane were spread out into a flat sheet.

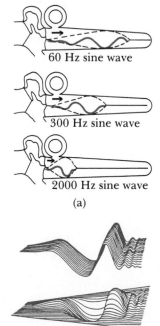

60 Hz sine wave

300 Hz sine wave

2000 Hz sine wave

(a)

(b)

theories concerning the perception of pitch, the *place theory*. However, although the basilar membrane does undergo different displacements with signals of different frequencies, the peak of the traveling wave is thought to be too broad to account for the remarkable acuity of pitch discrimination of which humans are capable. People with normal hearing can usually distinguish between two tones with fundamental differences in frequency of as little as 3 or 4 Hz. The traveling wave appears too broad to allow for different displacements for two such tones, particularly in the lower frequencies (below 800 or 900 Hz). At higher frequencies (above 4000–5000 Hz), the peak of the traveling wave in the basilar membrane is much sharper and the place theory becomes more convincing. Recently, S. M. Khanna and D. G. B. Leonard (1982) have shown that the "tuning" of the basilar membrane to various frequencies is even sharper than von Békésy's earlier studies had suggested. Thus the place theory could account for pitch perception, particularly for signals at higher frequencies.

The Volley Theory

The other main theory of pitch perception is based on the idea that different neurons in the cochlear nerve fire in response to tones of different frequencies. This idea might work for signals of up to a few hundred Hz, but at some point faithfully following the frequency would be impossible because of the refractory period of neurons. You will remember from Chapter 2 that the refractory period of a neuron sets an upper limit to the frequency with which any neuron can generate nerve impulses. For example, if the absolute refractory period lasts 1 msec, that neuron could fire at a maximum rate of 1000 Hz. If the refractory period lasted 2 msec, that neuron could fire at a maximum rate of only 500 Hz, even at very intense signal strength. Clearly, a simple frequency-following idea is not very useful.

A way out of the difficulty was offered by Ernest Wever (1949), who suggested that neurons could code for frequency by firing in volleys, so that an individual neuron would fire *in synchrony* with the signal but only produce a nerve impulse, for example, every second, third, or tenth wave. The theory, known now as the *volley theory*, proposes that different frequencies are coded for by volleys in closely associated groups of neurons in the cochlear nerve, firing as illustrated in Figure 6.4. The loudness or intensity of the tone could also be coded for in this way by increasing the firing rate of the individual neurons. Some direct evidence exists for such a process in experimental animals, but suggests that neurons in the auditory nerve probably can fire only in volleys for signals of up to about 5000 Hz, and at higher regions of the brain the upper limit for such coding is much lower, perhaps only 1000 Hz (Goldstein, 1984).

It would appear, then, that the place theory works fairly well for higher frequencies, say above 1000 Hz, just the point at which the volley theory begins to look weak. Conversely, the volley theory seems to account well for the perception of pitch for auditory signals with dominant frequencies considerably below 5000 Hz. The theory works particularly well at frequencies below 1000 Hz. The complementary nature of the strengths and

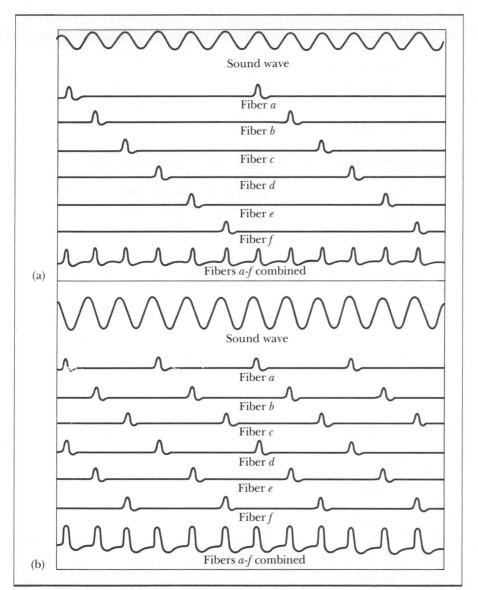

Figure 6.4   The coding of frequency and intensity according to the volley theory.
The frequency of the signal is the same in both (a) and (b), as the pattern of nerve fibers a–f is the same in both cases. The intensity, however, is greater in (b), as each of the fibers in the volley fires at a greater rate than in (a).

weaknesses of these two theories in accounting for pitch perception across the audible range of frequencies suggests that both theories may be partly right and that we code for frequency (pitch) using both a volley and a place principle. Thus the volley principle could account for pitch perception at frequencies below 1000 Hz; the place principle, for frequencies above 5000

tonotopic (TONE-o-top-ik) Adjective referring to the orderly projection from particular locations in the basilar membrane on higher auditory centers.

Hz; and some blend of the two principles, between 1000 and 5000 Hz. Although this seems plausible, it is not yet possible to account for all the known phenomena of pitch perception. Plenty of room still exists for improvement in our theories of pitch perception.

For any type of place coding to work, of course, particular regions of the basilar membrane must project in a systematic, orderly fashion to the auditory processing stations of the brain. Good evidence exists that such **tonotopic** mapping of the basilar membrane onto neuronal populations in the brain is a fact. This mapping is complex. The auditory sensory neurons diverge considerably in the brain. The human cochlea has only about 23,500 hair cells (Shepherd, 1983), and only about 25,000–30,000 neurons make up the auditory nerve, some of which are efferent neurons going to the cochlea. As each auditory neuron penetrates the first processing station, the cochlear nucleus, each axon forms multiple collaterals and synapses with several neurons in the cochlear nucleus. The result is the creation of multiple maps of the basilar membrane in the cochlear nucleus. The cochlear nucleus is composed of two parts, a dorsal and a ventral portion. (Figure 6.5 is a diagram of the main auditory pathways in the mammalian brain.)

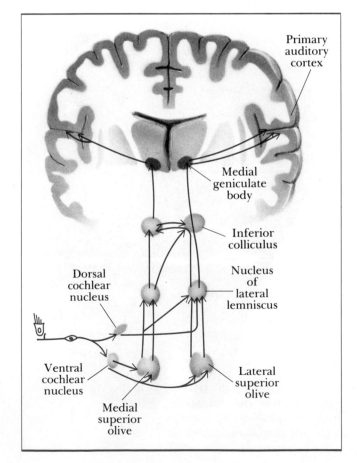

Figure 6.5   The main auditory pathways. View is of the dorsal surface of the brainstem (cerebellum and cerebral cortex not shown).

Both contralateral and ipsilateral connections exist from the cochlea to the rest of the brain. In human beings, as we shall discuss in Chapter 13, usually a slight functional advantage exists for the contralateral pathways. The ascending connections of the auditory system involve many different regions of the brain, including the cerebellum, inferior colliculi, portions of the pons and medulla, medial geniculate nucleus of the thalamus, and various cortical projection areas. These cortical regions are located primarily in the temporal lobes, particularly in the transverse gyrus of Heschl (Brodmann areas 41 and 42).

As is true for the visual system, multiple representations of the sensory surface (the basilar membrane) are found at the level of the neocortex. This comes about primarily from the systematic divergence of axon collaterals onto more and more neurons in higher auditory areas. The monkey auditory system has 30,000 or so neurons in the auditory nerve, 190,000 in the cochlear nucleus, 400,000 in the medial geniculate nucleus of the thalamus, and at least 10 million at the level of the neocortex (Green, 1976). In addition, efferent connections are found from higher auditory centers to lower ones, including a bundle of axons from neurons of the superior olive that synapse on the hair cells of the basilar membrane. It is not yet understood what these efferent axons do. One current hypothesis, for which there is only preliminary evidence, is that these efferent systems serve to reduce activation of the auditory system in response to sounds generated by the organism such as animal calls or human speech (Green, 1976).

Abstraction in the Auditory System

Neurons in the auditory system display response specificity, one of the clearest examples of which is frequency tuning (see Figure 6.6). Neurons in the auditory system are more responsive to certain frequencies than others. Typically, they have a broader range of response to frequencies below their best frequency and a much sharper cutoff for higher frequencies, producing the asymmetrical *tuning curves* seen in Figure 6.6. At the level of the neocortex, neurons with similar response specificities are arranged into columns. About 10 percent of the cortical cells in the monkey auditory cortex respond only to tones whose frequency is changing. Still others respond only to clicks. In the squirrel monkey some neurons respond exclusively to squirrel monkey calls (Evans, 1982b).

To summarize hearing: Our perceptions of sound depend on the displacement of the basilar membrane in the cochlea. These displacements are set up by the vibrations in the fluid of the cochlea transmitted to it from the vibrations of the eardrum. Signals from the hair cells of the cochlea are transmitted to neurons in the cochlear nerve and from these neurons to millions of others in the brain. Individual neurons in the auditory system are sensitive to different frequencies. The perception of pitch probably results from both a volley principle (particularly for signals below 1000 Hz) and a place principle (for signals with dominant frequencies above 5000 Hz). Between 1000 and 5000 Hz both volley and place principles probably contribute to our identification of pitch.

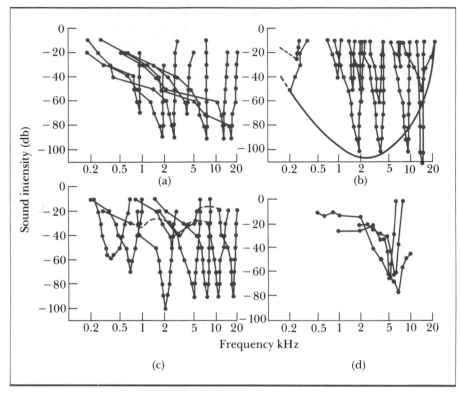

Figure 6.6 Response curves for single neurons in the auditory system.
(a) cochlear nerve; (b) inferior colliculus; (c) trapezoid body; (d) medial geniculate body.

Balance: The Vestibular System

Imagine trying to take a photograph of a flying bird from the deck of a small boat in rough water. Such a task would severely test a system that usually performs its functions swiftly and accurately, without intruding on our consciousness. Known as the *vestibular* system, it allows us to maintain an upright posture with respect to gravity and helps guide our eye movements.

The Vestibular Organ

Attached to the cochlea is the rest of the apparatus of the inner ear, which consists of the three semicircular canals, each with a tiny sense organ, and two nearby sensory organs, the *utricle* and the *saccule*. The semicircular canals are particularly important for detecting rotations of the head. Along with the utricle and saccule, the semicircular canals keep the nervous system continually informed of the position of the head.

These acrobats depend upon many different senses in order to perform such balancing acts, but none is more important than the vestibular system.

ampulla (am-PUL-lah) [plural, *ampullae* (am-PUL-lie)] A jar- or flasklike enlargement in a tubular structure. In the semicircular canals the ampullae contain the sense receptors for balance.

crista (KRIS-ta) (plural, *cristae*) The sensory organs in the semicircular canals. Formed from a cluster of hair cells.

cupula (KOOP-you-lah) The gelatinous mass in which the cilia of the hair cells in the vestibular organs are embedded.

kinocilium (kine-oh-SIL-ee-um) A large cilium (extension of the cell body) in "hair" cells of the vestibular organs.

Each of the semicircular canals is oriented in a different plane, so accelerations of the head in any direction affect one or more of the sensory organs within the canals. Each canal contains an enlarged region called the **ampulla.** Within each ampulla hair cells are clustered together into the sense organ of the canal, termed the **crista.** The cilia of these hair cells are oriented toward the roof of the canal and are embedded in a gelatinous mass called the **cupula.**

The canals are filled with a fluid called *endolymph.* The outer edges of the cupula are free to swing, like a hinge, from the roof of the canal. The cupula is not attached to the walls of the canal. When the head turns, the cupula swings, bending and deforming the cilia of the hair cells embedded in it. This process, quite similar to that in the hair cells of the cochlea, produces receptor potentials in the hair cells.

What is particularly remarkable about the hair cells in the vestibular apparatus is that the receptor potential is either depolarizing or hyperpolarizing, depending on the direction in which the head is moved. One of the cilia in each hair cell, the **kinocilium,** is much larger than the others and is set off to one side. The smaller cilia are called *stereocilia.* If the head movement results in a deflection of the stereocilia *toward* the kinocilium, the receptor potential in the hair cell is a depolarization. This causes transmitter release and an increase in the base firing rate of the associated neuron in the vestibular nerve. If, on the other hand, the head movement results in a deflection of the stereocilia *away* from the kinocilium, the re-

macula   (MAK-u-la) The sensory surface in the utricle and saccule of the vestibular organ.

otoconia   (Oh-toe-CONE-ee-ah) (singular, *otoconium*) Crystals of calcium carbonate atop the otolithic membrane in the semicircular canals.

ceptor potential is a hyperpolarization, resulting in a decrease in the normal rate of transmitter release onto the associated neuron in the vestibular nerve and a decrease in the base firing rate of that neuron.

The base firing rate of the neurons in the vestibular nerve is quite high (100–300 impulses/sec), which is necessary if inhibition of firing rate is to be used as a signal (Shepherd, 1983). How movement of the head in one direction produces depolarization and movement in the opposite direction produces hyperpolarization has so far not been discovered, although it may involve ion channels that are partially open at rest and either open more or close with movement.

The other part of the vestibular organ is composed of two additional membranous sacs, the utricle and saccule. Each cluster of hair cells in these structures is called a **macula.** These clusters of hair cells are very similar to those in the semicircular canals, but the overlying gelatinous mass in which the cilia of these cells are embedded is quite special. Lying on top of this membrane is a layer of crystals of calcium carbonate, **otoconia,** that increases the density of the membrane on which they are located, thereby increasing the sensitivity of the hair cells to head movements (see Figure 6.7).

The vestibular nerve has about 20,000 neurons that receive signals from the hair cells in the vestibular organ. The axons of these neurons are in the VIIIth nerve and synapse in the brainstem in various vestibular nuclei. Neurons from these vestibular nuclei are then sent both down into the spinal cord and up into the forebrain. These neurons form one of three main projection systems (Shepherd, 1983; Kelly, 1981a).

Vestibulo-ocular system

The neurons from the vestibular nuclei that make up the vestibulo-ocular system are involved in the control of eye movements. Eye movements that occur when the head is held still and the eyes move are called *saccadic* movements (see Chapter 5). Movements of the eye to compensate for head movements, such as keeping one's eye on a target as the boat is rocking, depend on input from the vestibulo-ocular projection system. These adjustments of eye movements are reflexive and do not require any conscious effort on the part of the perceiver.

Vestibulo-spinal system

The neurons that constitute the vestibulo-spinal system project into the spinal cord, where they synapse with motor neurons throughout the length of the cord. This system makes reflexive adjustments in posture to compensate for changes in the position of the head. An example of this system in action is provided by the remarkable ability of many animals to right themselves in air and land on their feet.

Vestibulo-cerebellar system

The vestibulo-cerebellar system connects the cerebellum and the vestibular nuclei. The input from the vestibular system is important in the regulation

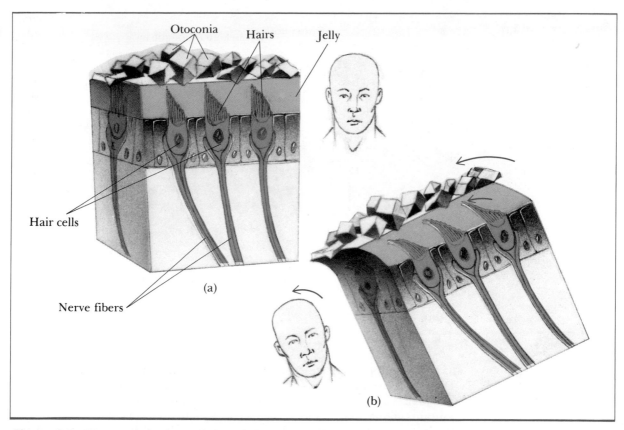

Figure 6.7   The vestibular apparatus of the saccule and utricle.
Changes in head position from (a) to (b) result in distortion of the cilia of the
hair cells as gravity affects the otoconia differently from the underlying jelly,
bending the cilia.

of balance. As is true for the vestibulo-ocular system and the vestibulo-
spinal system, the input into the cerebellum does not reach consciousness.

We do have some awareness, of course, of the position of our body in
space, and vestibular input can thrust itself into our consciousness in an
unpleasant way in the form of motion sickness, which many individuals
experience when they cannot control the motion to which they are subject
(e.g., when they are passengers in a car or on board a ship). From a neurological standpoint little is known of the cause of such motion sickness, but
it is believed that vestibular input is largely responsible, particularly when
there is a mismatch between vestibular and visual input.

Taste

From the most primitive bacterium to the most highly developed primate,
animals respond to chemical substances in their environment. In mammals

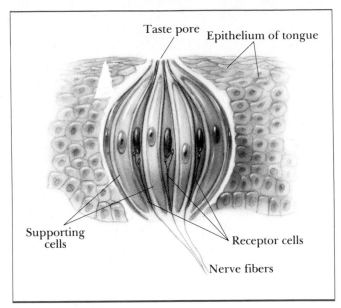

Figure 6.8   Taste bud.

the taste receptors are concentrated in the mouth, particularly on the tongue. Taste receptors are grouped in clusters, along with supporting basal cells into *taste buds,* as illustrated in Figure 6.8. In human beings each taste bud contains about 50 receptor cells, each of which has a very short life of about 10 days. They are replaced by new receptors that differentiate out of the supporting basal cells. Elderly individuals replace receptors more slowly and have fewer taste buds, which may account for the common complaint among elderly patients in nursing homes and hospitals that food needs more seasoning.

Taste receptors are stimulated by substances that dissolve in the saliva. Much of our taste perception also depends on stimulation of olfactory receptors in the nose. Although it is generally agreed that taste sensations result from an interaction of some part of the molecule with receptors in the membrane of the taste receptors, the transduction process leading to taste sensations is still not understood.

It has been useful to consider all tastes as mixtures of four sensations: sweet, salty, sour, and bitter—often referred to as the "basic taste sensations." However, it is now clear that it is *not* true that there are four basic receptor types, one for each basic sensation. In research on taste sensation, a sour taste seems to be related to the presence of the hydrogen ion (H^+), and saltiness seems to be related to Na^+ and K^+ ions. Quinine is a potent stimulus for the bitter taste. Sweetness can be evoked by a variety of sugars and other substances. However, if these substances are applied selectively to taste receptors and the responses of individual neurons in the taste pathway are recorded, no "pure type" taste receptors can be found.

For example, Carl Pfaffman (1959) recorded from the neurons in the chorda tympani, the nerve associated with the taste receptors, and found that most of the neurons responded to all the stimuli he used (dilute hydrochloric acid, which provided the H^+ ion; NaCl; KCl; quinine; and sucrose). Some cells did have what Pfaffman described as "best stimuli," to which they were particularly responsive, but he found no neurons that responded to only one taste stimulus. Similar tests on the taste receptors themselves have shown that the receptors lack pure specificity, although they did display different "response profiles" to the various stimuli used (Kimura and Beidler, 1961). It has been suggested that even this degree of specificity does not exist.

Recently, other researchers have also recorded from single neurons in the chorda tympani, as well as in the nucleus of the solitary tract, a major station in the taste pathway. They found no evidence for "taste types" (Erickson et al., 1980). The neurons from which they recorded responded to virtually all the stimuli they used. They suggest that when a large array of different stimuli are used, gustatory neurons show a continuum of responses and that "types" appear only if small groups of quite similar stimuli are used. Similar conclusions were reached by Susan Schiffman and Robert Erickson (1980).

Taste Pathways

Individual neurons in the chorda tympani synapse with more than one taste receptor, and each receptor synapses with more than one neuron. The chorda tympani joins the facial (VIIth) nerve, which projects to the main nucleus in the brainstem for taste, the nucleus of the solitary tract. From here, second-order neurons project to various parts of the brain. For example, in the monkey, solitary tract axons go to the ventral posterior medial nucleus of the thalamus. Neurons from this nucleus then send axons to the posterior region of the frontal lobe in a region known as the insula, as well as to the "face" area of the somatosensory cortex in the parietal lobe. Projections also go from the nucleus of the solitary tract to subcortical regions such as the hypothalamus and (in some species) the amygdala. Figure 6.9 illustrates the taste pathways in the human brain.

Olfaction

Like taste, the sense of smell—olfaction—results from the interaction of molecules with receptors in the membrane of the olfactory receptor neurons. The olfactory receptors are true neurons, with axons. In human beings they are contained within the nasal cavity in a small area called the olfactory **epithelium** (see Figure 6.10). In species with a more highly developed sense of smell (tracker dogs, for example) the olfactory epithelium is usually proportionately larger. The epithelium is made up of several

epithelium (ep-uh-THEE-lee-um) The sheet of cells covering some particular surface. The olfactory epithelium is the sheet of receptor cells for olfaction in the nose.

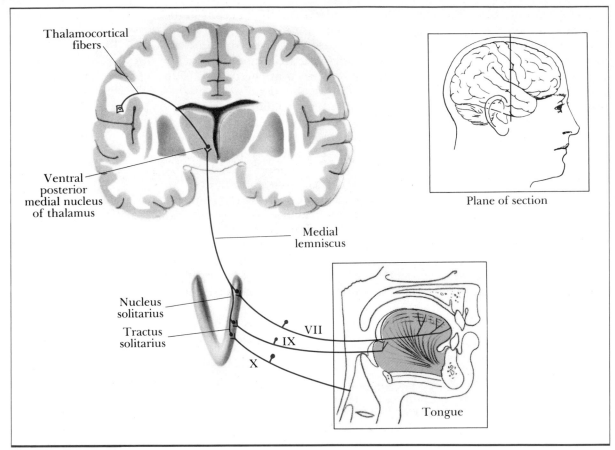

Thalamocortical fibers

Ventral posterior medial nucleus of thalamus

Medial lemniscus

Nucleus solitarius

Tractus solitarius

VII

IX

X

Plane of section

Tongue

Figure 6.9   Neural pathways for the sense of taste.
Taste sensations from the tongue are brought into the brain along the VIIth, IXth, and Xth cranial nerves. The first station in the brain is the V-shaped nucleus solitarius.

types of cells, including the receptor cells themselves, and supporting basal cells that differentiate into receptors on a continual basis as the receptors themselves die. The average lifespan of the olfactory receptors is about 60 days. This continual turnover of receptors is an exception to the general rule that no new neurons are formed in the mammalian brain following birth.

The olfactory receptors are equipped with six to eight cilia that extend up into the mucus covering the epithelium. The mucus is secreted by the supporting cells and allows air-borne substances to dissolve and thereby come into direct contact with the receptors. Human beings have about 10 million olfactory receptor cells (Noback and Demarest, 1975). The nature of the transduction process in olfaction is unknown. Most speculation centers around the interaction of the substances that dissolve in the mucus (termed *odorants*) with the membrane of the cilia of the olfactory receptors. This interaction is thought to alter the properties of ionic channels.

It is unlikely that there are many "odor specialists" in vertebrates. Gordon Shepherd (1983) found only "odor generalists" in the salamander olfactory system. These receptors responded to 10 or more different odorants. However, different odors do cause neural activity in different regions of the olfactory bulb. The different spatial distribution of neural activity for different odorants could provide the basis for an olfactory "place theory." If different odors excite different neurons in the olfactory bulb and these neurons follow separate pathways to higher regions of the brain, the basis for place coding would exist.

Chromatographic Theory of Olfaction

How could such a differential spatial distribution of odorants evolve? One interesting idea is that of Maxwell Mozell (1970), who suggests that the olfactory mucosa acts to separate different substances that dissolve in it

Figure 6.10   Location and structure of the olfactory epithelium.

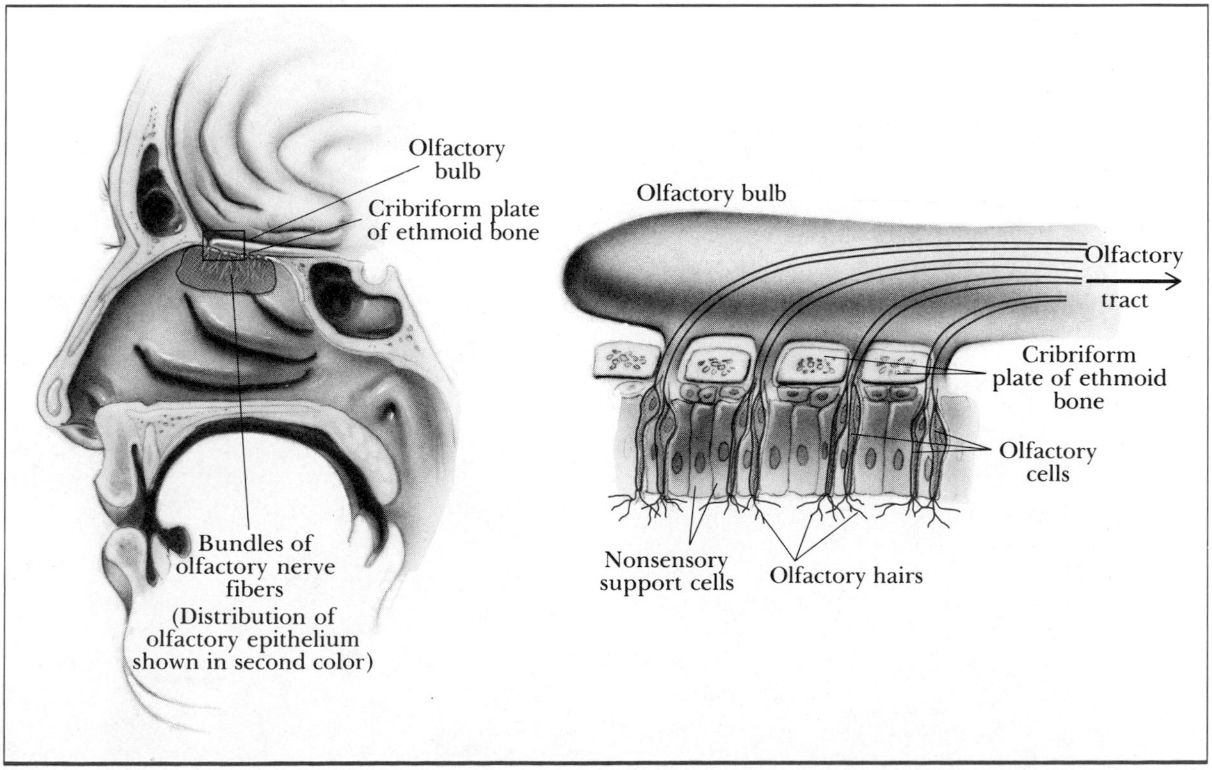

Wildlife Management through Conditioning?

One interesting phenomenon is *taste aversion learning.* If an animal is given a particular taste and then made sick (e.g., with injections of lithium chloride or apomorphine, which causes stomach and gastric distress), the animal will avoid that taste thereafter (Garcia et al., 1974). One remarkable aspect of such learning is that quite long times can elapse between the taste experience and the introduction of the illness. This is unlike most conditioning situations, in which the times of the conditioned stimulus (in this case the novel taste) and the unconditioned stimulus (in this case the gastrointestinal illness) must be close together. (Chapter 12 details other conditioning procedures.) It is not clear how general taste aversion learning is, although it has been obtained in several different species, including human beings (Logue, 1985).

One application of this procedure is in wildlife management. Conditioned taste aversion may be a successful way to reduce sheep predation by wild coyotes without permanently harming the coyotes (Gustavson et al., 1974). Freshly killed lambs, impregnated with some illness-causing substance are left out for coyotes to eat. Evidence exists that the coyotes that eat such meat are less likely to eat lamb again. The reliability of these effects is still uncertain, but this technique has been applied successfully to prairie dogs, blackbirds, baboons, wolves, raccoons, crows, wild dogs, ferrets, hawks, and bears (Gustavson and Gustavson, 1985).

Coyote howling near an elk carcass near Jackson Hole, Wyoming. Predation on sheep can be partially controlled with taste aversion conditioning techniques as described in the text.

much as the material in a gas chromatograph column separates the substances passed through it. This material in a chromatograph is termed the *sorbent*. In a gas chromatograph the different types of molecules in the sample to be analyzed are attracted in different degrees by the sorbent and thus travel either more slowly or more rapidly through the sorbent, causing different components of the sample to spread throughout the column. Mozell suggests that the olfactory mucosa acts as a biological sorbent, spreading different odorants across different regions of the olfactory mucosa, where they excite different receptors. Different odorants then produce different spatial patterns of receptor activity not because of any differences in the receptors themselves, but because of the way in which the mucosal sorbent has acted on the mixture of odorants. Mozell and colleagues have published some evidence to support this *chromatographic theory* of olfaction (Goldstein, 1984).

1. The reversal of the direction of flow of odorant-containing air across the olfactory mucosa in frogs changes the pattern of neural activity in the two main branches of the olfactory nerve.
2. The olfactory mucosa of the frog actually can be used as a sorbent in a chromatograph column.
3. A differential distribution exists across the olfactory mucosa of a powerful odorant, butanol, when measured with radioactively tagged samples.

Olfactory Pathways

The axons of the receptors penetrate the olfactory bulbs at the base of the brain. In human beings the olfactory bulbs are located under the frontal lobes (see Figure 6.11). In the olfactory bulbs the axons of the receptors

Figure 6.11 Diagram of the olfactory pathways in the human brain.

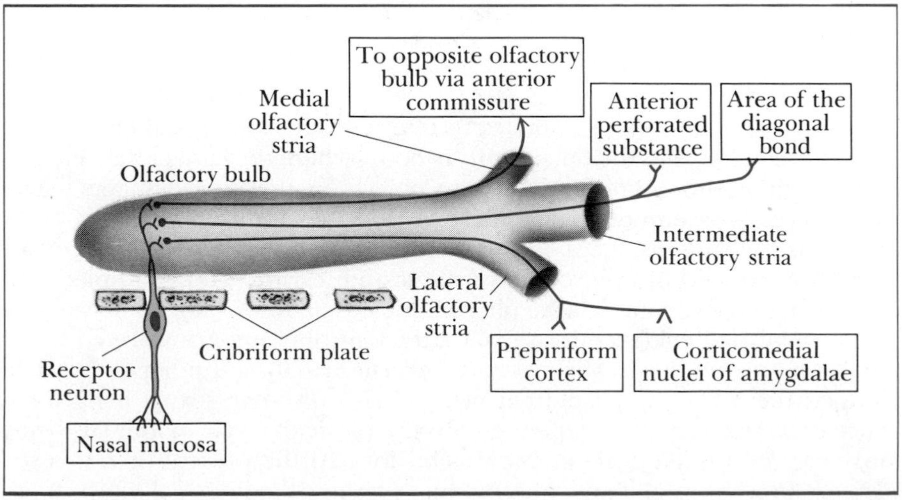

glomerulus (glo-MARE-u-lus) [plural, *glomeruli* (glo-MARE-u-lie)] A cluster or ball of cells.

vomeronasal organ (VOME-er-o-naze-al) Accessory olfactory organ present in some species.

pheromone (FEAR-oh-moan) A chemical substance secreted by an animal that carries a specific message to others of its species.

enter into a cluster of cells, termed a **glomerulus** (little ball), where synaptic contacts among the cells of the glomerulus are made in a very complex way. The main cell types in the olfactory bulb are the mitral cells and the tufted cells. In primates the axons of these cell types form the output of the olfactory bulbs, carrying impulses along the lateral olfactory tract to the prepiriform cortex. From the prepiriform cortex neurons project to the lateral hypothalamus and to the dorsal medial nucleus of the thalamus. From these regions impulses travel to the orbitofrontal cortex of the frontal lobe (Tanabe et al., 1974; Keverne, 1982). In other species, such as the rat, other connections exist from the olfactory bulb to the hypothalamus and to the corticomedial nucleus of the amygdaloid complex, as well as to regions of the forebrain, such as the anterior perforated substance and the area of the diagonal band in the septum.

Our ability to identify different odors weakens with age. In a study of almost 2000 human subjects more than half of the subjects between 65 and 80 showed a major impairment in a standard smell identification test. After age 80 more than 75 percent of those tested had an impaired sense of smell (Doty et al., 1984).

The Vomeronasal Organ

Carnivores, cattle, several rodent species, and elephants have a second, or accessory, olfactory organ called the **vomeronasal organ.** It is located so that it communicates with both the oral and nasal openings. Odors of special significance for the species, such as pheromones, which signal the nearness of a sexually receptive female, for example, are thought to be detected by this organ. The receptors of the vomeronasal organ, which appear to be very similar to those in the main olfactory epithelium, send axons to the accessory olfactory bulbs. From here projections go to the amygdala and hypothalamus.

Pheromones

Both invertebrates and vertebrates secrete message-bearing substances from specialized glands to the outside of the body, where they are either released directly into the air or rubbed onto objects in the environment. These substances, **pheromones,** are usually very volatile and can be carried by air currents for long distances. Pheromones have been discovered that convey messages concerning reproductive status and territory, for example.

Whether primates secrete pheromones is still uncertain. Some workers have published evidence for sexual attractant pheromones secreted by female rhesus monkeys (Michael and Keverne, 1970), but others have challenged these findings (Goldfoot et al., 1976). Primate sexual behavior is very complex and quite dependent on the particular pair of animals being investigated (unlike rodent sexual behavior). At the present time it is still uncertain what role, if any, pheromones play in primate social interactions.

No compelling evidence exists that human beings secrete pheromones, although a few scattered reports have suggested this (Rogel, 1978).

Somethesis

Skin consists of at least two basic components, the epidermis (outer layer) and the underlying dermis. Skin is also considered to be either hairy or **glabrous** (without hair). The skin sense receptors, of which there are a rich variety, are usually categorized as *mechanoreceptors,* preferentially sensitive to pressure; *thermoreceptors,* sensitive to changes in temperature; and **nociceptors,** which respond to injury. These skin sense receptors, along with other receptors located in the viscera, muscles, tendons, and joints of the body, are known collectively as the **somesthetic system.**

Skin receptors are either capsulated or uncapsulated. Uncapsulated receptors, usually called *free nerve endings,* have modified dendrites that spread out into the area of skin they innervate. Encapsulated receptors have a specialized "cap" around the receptive portion of the cell, aiding transduction. (These basic types are shown in Figure 6.12.) Receptors in the somesthetic system vary in modality sensitivity (touch, temperature, etc.), the rate at which they conduct impulses, and the rate at which they adapt to an unvarying stimulus.

Free Nerve Endings

Free nerve endings are found throughout the body, in hairy and glabrous skin, in muscles, and in the viscera. Some respond to touch, some to temperature, some to injury, and some (called *polymodal receptors*) to two or three of these stimuli. For the most part, free nerve endings are slowly adapting, small-diameter, lightly myelinated neurons with relatively slow rates of conduction. However, some are more heavily myelinated, with larger axons and correspondingly faster rates of impulse conduction. These are the A-delta fibers, which can conduct impulses at speeds of up to 30 m/sec. The smallest-diameter axons in the free nerve ending group are the C fibers, which conduct impulses at rates of less than 1 m/sec.

These two populations of receptors are believed to underlie the two different types of pain we experience, for example, when stuck with a needle. The immediate "fast pain" is mediated by the larger A-delta fibers, whereas the "slow, burning" pain that lingers afterward is mediated by the C fibers (Shepherd, 1983). The correlation of sensation and the neural activity in sensory receptors can be approached more directly in human beings than is generally true for the other senses. Recording electrodes can (with a little discomfort) be inserted into the skin of conscious subjects who then report on their sensations as various stimuli are applied to the skin. (To their credit, most of the experimenters in this area have used themselves as subjects rather than sticking pins and needles into their students.)

somesthesis (som-ess-THEE-sis) Collective term for receptors in the skin muscles, tendons, and joints.

glabrous (GLA-brus) Hairless

nocioceptor (NO-see-o-sep-tor) Receptor sensitive to noxious or pain-related stimuli.

Pacinian corpuscle (Pa-SIN-ee-an KOR-pus-ul) A sense receptor for the sense of deep touch or pressure.

Free nerve endings have been demonstrated repeatedly to be capable of conveying all the skin sensations. Sensations of warmth, cold, touch, and pain can all be elicited from the cornea of the eye, which has only free nerve endings (Ganong, 1977). Free nerve endings thus can be specialized to respond to slight mechanical deformation (touch), temperature changes, or injury. Actually, the exact stimuli that produce pain can vary from actual injury, such as a cut, to chemical stimulation, as in a beesting. We shall return to the discussion of pain in Chapter 11.

Encapsulated Receptors

Several varieties of encapsulated receptors exist, one of which is the **Pacinian corpuscle,** found in the dermis underlying both hairy and glabrous

Figure 6.12 (a)   Main receptor types in glabrous skin.

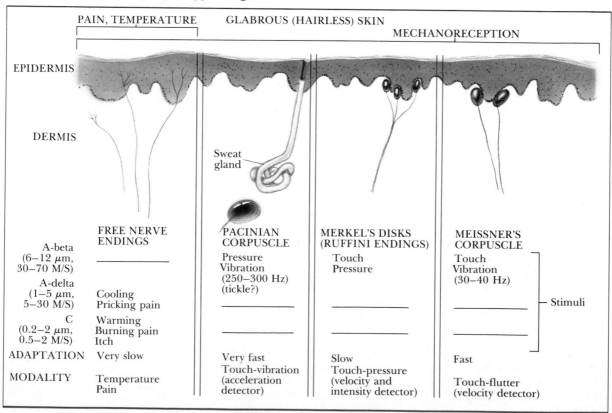

skin and in the connective tissue of the muscles and the viscera (see Figure 6.13). The Pacinian corpuscle is a specialized neuron with a pressure-sensitive neural process surrounded by a multilayered cap. Werner Lowenstein (1971) recorded directly from the process of the Pacinian corpuscle after carefully stripping off the overlying cap. Pressure on the process produces a depolarization, which, if strong enough, directly initiates a nerve impulse in the first node of the myelinated process. The impulse is then carried into the spinal cord along the second process of the corpuscle. All the skin receptors are bipolar cells, with one process (the receptive end) in the skin and the other process projecting into the spinal cord.

The Pacinian corpuscle is very good at responding to repeated stimulation, mediating sensations of vibration. Michael Merzenich and Thomas Harrington (1969) investigated vibratory stimulation in the hairy skin of monkeys and humans. They found evidence in both species that two sets

Figure 6.12 (b)   Main receptor types in hairy skin.

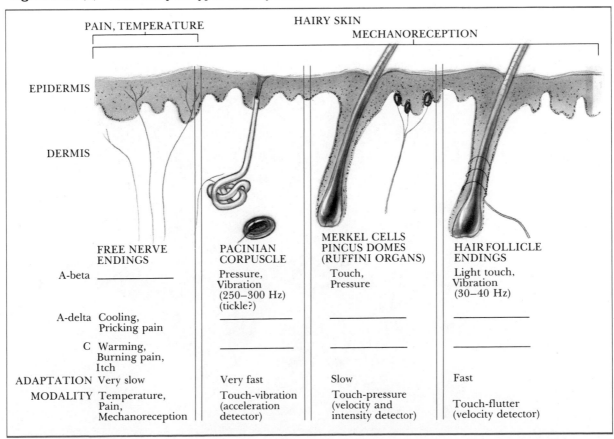

	FREE NERVE ENDINGS	PACINIAN CORPUSCLE	MERKEL CELLS PINCUS DOMES (RUFFINI ORGANS)	HAIRFOLLICLE ENDINGS
A-beta		Pressure, Vibration (250–300 Hz) (tickle?)	Touch, Pressure	Light touch, Vibration (30–40 Hz)
A-delta	Cooling, Pricking pain			
C	Warming, Burning pain, Itch			
ADAPTATION	Very slow	Very fast	Slow	Fast
MODALITY	Temperature, Pain, Mechanoreception	Touch-vibration (acceleration detector)	Touch-pressure (velocity and intensity detector)	Touch-flutter (velocity detector)

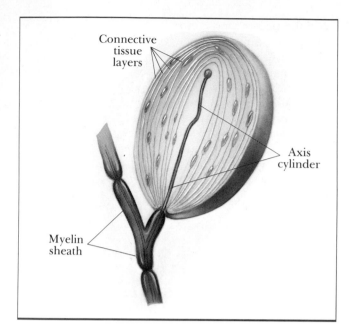

Figure 6.13 Drawing of the Pacinian corpuscle.
Note that the myelin does not extend into the capsule very far. The tip of the neuron's process is thus in direct contact with the extracellular fluid inside the layers of connective tissue.

The sense of touch is very important for infants in learning about the world. Here a baby girl of about six months is using both her eyes and her sense of touch to investigate a leaf.

of receptors are involved in vibration. Low-frequency vibration (flutter) sensations seem to be due to activation of free nerve endings in or around the hair follicles. These receptors adapt rapidly. High-frequency vibration, on the other hand, is due to the activation of the Pacinian corpuscles in both species. The Pacinian corpuscles are unresponsive to low frequencies of vibration, but they are very responsive to high frequencies of vibration and can follow vibratory stimuli well beyond 200 vibrations/sec. The ability to respond so well to high-frequency vibration is due in large part to the properties of the layers of connective tissue that compose the capsule itself.

The capsule, when pressed, filters out slow changes due to the continuing pressure and passes on to the nerve ending only the rapid changes in pressure that occur at the onset and the offset of the pressure. This was demonstrated by Lowenstein (1971), who carefully peeled off the capsule surrounding the nerve ending and found that pressure applied directly to the nerve ending of the Pacinian corpuscle produced a continuous response.

Kinesthetic Receptors

Within the joints of the body, in the tissue that covers the bones, and in associated tissues are free nerve endings and other types of receptors that send input into the central nervous system regarding the position of the joints. This input, along with information concerning the state of contraction of the muscles and tension on the tendons, is used in the control of movement and postural adjustments.

Somesthetic Pathways

The processes of the skin receptors join together and enter the spinal cord in the dorsal roots. Once within the spinal cord, however, the somesthetic system can be divided into two systems: the **anterolateral system** and the **dorsal column–medial lemniscal system** (see Figure 6.14). The neurons in these two systems are postsynaptic to the primary afferents coming into the spinal cord.

The anterolateral system is thought to be phylogenetically the more ancient of the two systems, having evolved in animals now long extinct. One component of this system consists of neurons with small-diameter, lightly myelinated, slowly conducting axons. These neurons make multiple synapses as they course upward. The anterolateral system contains neurons predominantly concerned with sensations of heat, cold, and pain, although sensations of touch are also represented. The system gets its name from the fact that after the receptors have synapsed with spinal cord neurons near their point of entry, the postsynaptic spinal neurons send their axons upward toward the brain in the *anterolateral* quadrant of the spinal cord. These axons cross the midline of the cord and ascend in the contralateral half of the cord. One part of this system makes multiple synapses in the

anterolateral system One of two major nerve tracts serving somesthesis.

lemniscal system (lem-NISK-al) One of two major nerve tracts serving somesthesis.

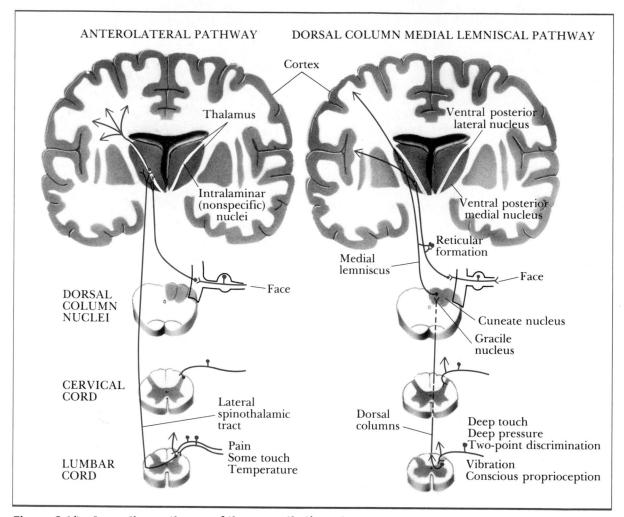

ANTEROLATERAL PATHWAY

DORSAL COLUMN MEDIAL LEMNISCAL PATHWAY

Cortex

Thalamus

Ventral posterior lateral nucleus

Intralaminar (nonspecific) nuclei

Ventral posterior medial nucleus

Reticular formation

Medial lemniscus

Face

DORSAL COLUMN NUCLEI

Face

Cuneate nucleus

Gracile nucleus

CERVICAL CORD

Lateral spinothalamic tract

Dorsal columns

Deep touch
Deep pressure
Two-point discrimination

LUMBAR CORD

Pain
Some touch
Temperature

Vibration
Conscious proprioception

Figure 6.14 Ascending pathways of the somesthetic system.

substantia gelatinosa (sub-STAN-sha je-LAT-uh-nos-ah) A region of the dorsal spinal cord in which pain-related impulses are processed.

brain stem reticular formation (the spinoreticular tract). Other axons synapse primarily in the intralaminar nuclei of the thalamus. Axons of the anterolateral system also terminate in a region of the spinal cord called the **substantia gelatinosa.** Considerable evidence exists that this collection of cells is concerned with the neural mechanisms in pain transmission, discussed further in Chapter 11.

The axons that form the dorsal column–medial lemniscal system are of more recent phylogenetic origin, larger in diameter, more heavily myelinated, and more rapidly conducting. Impulses in these axons can travel at rates of up to 70 m/sec. In the spinal cord neurons of this system travel in the dorsal portion of the cord (dorsal column) and synapse at the level of the medulla. These medullary neurons then form the *medial lemniscus,* hence the rather long name for this system. The neurons of the medial lemniscus cross the midline and project to the ventral posterior lateral nucleus and the lateral nuclear group of the thalamus, the main thalamic processing center for the somesthetic system. The thalamic neurons project to the somesthetic regions of the cortex in the parietal lobe. Since the afferent axons of the somesthetic system cross over and eventually project to the opposite hemisphere, representation of the body surface is contralateral.

Cortex: Multiple Body Maps

As is true for vision and audition, the sensory surface in the somesthetic cortex has several maps. These regions have been explored with recording electrodes while various regions of the body surface were stimulated. The primary receptive areas for somesthesis are in the anterior part of the parietal lobe, in Brodmann areas 1, 2, and 3. Area 3 is subdivided into 3a and 3b. Each of these four areas contains a separate and complete representation of the body surface in the various primate brains for which substantial information exists: the owl monkey, squirrel monkey, cebus monkey, and macaque monkey (Kaas et al., 1981). These four areas are not simply copies of each other, however; they differ in the details of their internal organization, response properties of the neurons, and connections with other brain regions.

One of the organizing principles in the somesthetic system is that those portions of the body surface most richly supplied with sensory receptors also have the most cortical tissue devoted to them. The lips, tongue, face, and fingertips are all very rich in receptors and all have large cortical regions devoted to them, whereas relatively insensitive regions of the skin, such as the back, have relatively small regions of cortex devoted to them. The cortical projection areas do not form exact maps of the body surface, although there is a rough correspondence of body surface relationships onto the cortex.

Updating the Cortex

Recently it has been reported that the projection of the somesthetic system onto the cortex can change dramatically if changes occur in the receptors in the skin. Michael Merzenich and colleagues (1984) have found that following amputation of a single digit on a monkey's paw, the cortical area that had been devoted to processing the input from that digit disappears and the neurons in that small region respond to the two digits on either side of the missing one, enlarging the cortical area responsive to the existing digits. For this to occur there must be considerable alteration of synapses in the cortex, demonstrating that neural connections in the cortex can change to accommodate changes in sensory input.

Columns in the Cortex

One of the anatomic principles to emerge from various examinations of the responses of neurons in the cortex is that the cortex appears to be organized into *columns*. The columnar organization of the somesthetic cortex was discovered by Vernon Mountcastle in 1957 and confirmed by T. P. S. Powell and Mountcastle in 1959. They found that if the response properties of neurons were determined by lowering the recording electrodes perpendicular to the cortical surface, these neurons showed very similar functional properties. For example, nearly all the neurons in these cortical columns would respond to light touch, to deep pressure, or to the rotation of a joint. If the electrode penetration were made at other angles, a mixture of cell types was found.

SUMMARY

1. All our sensory systems must accomplish three basic tasks: transduction of an energy form into nerve impulses, transmission of these impulses to appropriate regions of the brain, and abstraction of meaning from these signals. The transduction process in hearing is done by the hair cells of the cochlea, which transduce mechanical vibrations in the fluid of the inner ear into nerve impulses in the auditory nerve.
2. The pitch of sound is determined mainly by the frequency of the physical stimulus; loudness, by the intensity; and timbre, by the frequency of the overtones present. The intensity of sounds can be arranged along a decibel scale, with normal conversation at about 60 dB and amplified rock music at 115 dB.
3. Impedance matching is important to prevent loss of signal in the auditory system. It results largely because the eardrum is much larger than the oval window.
4. Transduction in the cochlea is due to a shearing motion exerted on the hair cells because of the movements of the basilar membrane and the overlying tectorial membrane. These two membranes move independently, with the hair cell stretched between them. The movement of the basilar membrane can be described best as a series of traveling waves.
5. A place principle of pitch perception could account for our ability to detect frequencies above 5000 Hz, whereas a volley principle works well for frequencies below 1000 Hz. Between 1000 and 5000 Hz some combination of the two principles may account for our remarkable ability to distinguish different frequencies.
6. Multiple orderly representations of the cochlea are found at various locations in the auditory pathway, including the neocortex. The response characteristics of individual neurons in the neocortex reveal vertical columns of cells with similar response specificities.

7. We can maintain our balance because of the input from the vestibular system of the inner ear. This system is composed of tiny sense organs in the semicircular canals, the utricle, and the saccule. Much of this sensory input does not enter our consciousness. Vestibular input is concerned with the regulation of head and body movements with respect to gravity and with the modulation of eye movements.

8. Both taste and smell depend on the interaction of molecules with specialized receptors in the mouth and nose. The exact transduction mechanisms for taste and smell are unknown. The chromatographic theory of olfaction suggests that the olfactory mucosa acts to separate spatially different substances that dissolve in it, causing different molecules to interact with different receptors and providing the basis for discrimination.

9. Pure receptors apparently do not exist for either taste or smell, but it has been useful to consider all tastes as mixtures of four basic sensations: sweet, salty, sour, and bitter.

10. Some animals have a second, accessory olfactory system called the *vomeronasal organ*. The vomeronasal organ appears to be specialized to receive olfactory signals important for reproduction, recognition of territory, and other species-characteristic behaviors. The olfactory signals that carry these specific messages are called *pheromones*.

11. The somesthetic system consists of a collection of receptors in the skin, muscles, joints, and viscera. No clear-cut relationship exists between receptor types based on structure and the particular sensation conveyed by that receptor type. Somesthesis is a term covering the senses of touch, pressure, vibration, temperature, joint position, and pain.

12. The somesthetic cortex is arranged to preserve the spatial relationship of receptors on the body surface. Vertical columns of neurons are found in the somesthetic cortex with similar response properties. The response properties of neurons in the somesthetic cortex can be changed with alterations in the sensory input.

SUGGESTIONS FOR FURTHER READING

Barlow, H. B., and Mollon, J. D. (Eds.) (1982). *The senses.* Cambridge: Cambridge University Press.

Goldstein, E. B. (1984). *Sensation and perception* (2d ed.). Belmont, CA: Wadsworth.

Katsuki, Y., Norgren, R., and Sato, M. (1981). *Brain mechanisms of sensation.* New York: Wiley.

7

Movement

" . . . to move is all mankind can do . . ."

C. S. SHERRINGTON

Preview

Movements, even the most complex and graceful, can be analyzed in terms of their underlying components. One of C. S. Sherrington's contributions to our understanding of movement was the analysis of reflexes, which play an important role in even the most elaborate sequence of movements. In normal movements reflexes are often mediated by circuits in the spinal cord and integrated as automatic subroutines in other movement patterns.

Many diseases of the nervous system are characterized by abnormality of movement. Parkinson's disease, a good example, affects both the initiation and execution of movements and postural adjustments. Studying this disease and similar conditions has increased our knowledge of the regulation of movement by the brain.

Reflexes

When we watch a ballerina's pirouette or a double gainer off the high board, we are looking at the integration of many different neural "programs" composed of circuits in brain and spinal cord. In normal movement all these subroutines are synchronized into the sequence of movements. To analyze how the nervous system produces complex movements, investigators have looked at some of these subroutines in isolation. One important set of subroutines is that of the *spinal reflexes,* which Sherrington (1906) was one of the first to investigate.

The Stretch Reflex

A normal muscle, when stretched, automatically contracts, which is an example of the *stretch reflex.* If the motor neuron that supplies that muscle is cut, however, this stretch reflex is abolished, demonstrating that it is indeed a *reflex* contraction, not just a reflection of the elasticity of the muscle tissue. Moreover, and somewhat surprisingly, if the sensory nerves that go *from* the muscle *to* the spinal cord are cut instead, leaving the motor neuron still connected to the muscle, the reflex is also abolished. This demonstrates the critical importance of *sensory input* in the production of reflexes. Both sensory and motor nerve activity are necessary for normal reflex movements.

One well-known stretch reflex is the knee jerk reflex. When the tendons just below the knee are tapped, the muscles to which they are attached

Mikhail Baryshnikov, the great dancer, illustrating the grace, power, and flexibility that human beings are capable of showing in their movements.

(the quadriceps muscles above the knee) contract, jerking the knee forward. This reflex has only about a 50-msec delay. This short delay is due to the fact that the signals from the tendons are transmitted directly to the motor neurons that activate the quadriceps muscles. (By comparison, the fastest *voluntary* response times to a signal are about 200–250 msec.) The knee jerk reflex is a **monosynaptic** (one-synapse) **reflex.** Most reflexes involve two or more sets of synapses and are termed **polysynaptic.**

monosynaptic reflex (MOAN-o-sin-AP-tik) Reflex involving only one set of synapses.

polysynaptic reflex (POLLY-sin-AP-tik) Reflex involving two or more sets of synapses.

Reciprocal Inhibition

Not only does a muscle contract when it is stretched, but the muscles that oppose the movement caused by this contraction simultaneously relax. Op-

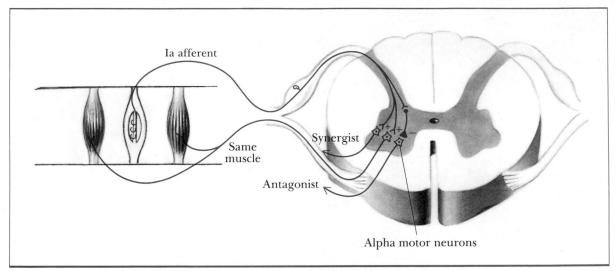

Figure 7.1 Simplified diagram of the neural circuitry underlying stretch reflex.
The Ia afferents from the muscle spindle organ excite the motor neuron going to the same muscle as well as exciting motor neurons going to synergist muscles. Reciprocal inhibition of antagonist muscles is also produced via an interneuron. Although the muscle spindle organ is actually embedded in the muscle, as shown in Figure 7.2, it is shown here beside it for clarity.

antagonist (ann-TAG-o-nist) A muscle opposing the movement under consideration.

synergist (SIN-er-jist) A muscle cooperating in the movement under consideration.

neuronal oscillator (OS-sil-a-tor) Term for neural circuitry underlying the production of rhythmic activities such as walking, swallowing, and flying.

Golgi tendon organs (GOAL-jee) Sense organs in the tendons attached to muscles, concerned with signaling degree of tension in the muscle.

posing muscles are termed **antagonists.** Muscles that cooperate in moving a limb are termed **synergists.** (Figure 7.1 illustrates the circuitry underlying the stretch reflex and the reciprocal inhibition of the antagonist muscles.) Reciprocal inhibition is due to the activation of *inhibitory interneurons* in the spinal cord, which inhibit the motor neurons supplying the antagonist muscles. Reciprocal inhibition is essential for such coordinated actions as walking, where the flexors of the leg must relax as the extensors contract, and vice versa. Walking is not simply a reflex, however. Evidence exists that rhythmic actions such as walking and flying are produced by **neuronal oscillators** composed of neural circuits that use subroutines such as the stretch reflex and reciprocal inhibition. We shall return to this point shortly.

Sense Organs in the Muscle

How does a muscle signal the state of its contraction to the central nervous system? Two basic types of sense organs are associated with muscles. They both send information into the spinal cord, informing spinal neurons about the *length* of the muscle and about the *degree of tension* the muscle is under. Both length and degree of tension of the muscle are taken into account by the reflex programs in the spinal cord. The degree of tension developed in the muscle is signaled by **Golgi tendon organs,** located in the tendons attached to the muscles. Muscle length is monitored by the **muscle spindle organs.**

Two different types of muscle tissue are found in what we think of as a "muscle": big muscle fibers, which move the limbs, and little muscle fibers, located *within* the muscle spindle organ. The muscle spindle organ is a sense organ tucked inside the big muscles. (The muscle spindle organ is shown in Figure 7.2.) The big muscles are termed **extrafusal muscles** and the little ones in the muscle spindle organ are called **intrafusal muscles.** Although the little intrafusal muscles are very weak and contribute nothing directly to the movements of the limbs, they do contract. Each of the two categories of muscles is activated by different sets of motor neurons from the spinal cord.

muscle spindle organs Sense organs embedded in the muscles, concerned with signaling the length of the muscle.

extrafusal muscles (EX-tra-fuse-al) The main muscles that produce movement; they are activated by the alpha motor neurons.

intrafusal muscles (IN-tra-fuse-al) Small muscle fibers in the muscle spindle organs; they are activated by gamma motor neurons.

Figure 7.2   Mammalian muscle spindle organ.
(a) Location of organ within body of muscle. (b) Simplified diagram of intrafusal muscle fiber and innervation. There are two types of intrafusal muscle fibers in the spindle organ, nuclear bag fibers and nuclear chain fibers.

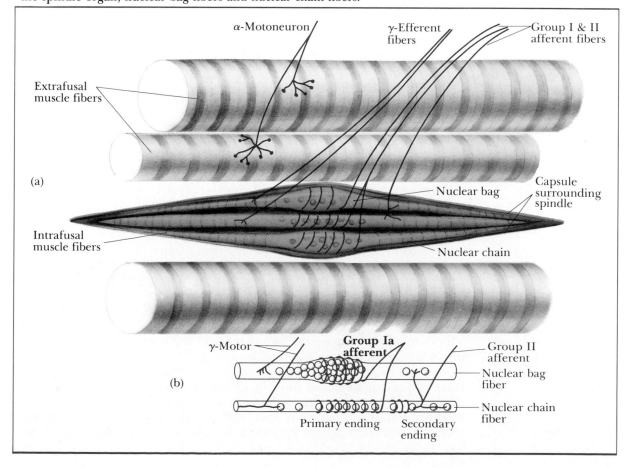

The muscle spindle organ has two groups of sensory neurons. The larger neurons are termed Group Ia afferents and the smaller are termed Group II afferents. Both groups send their axons into the spinal cord. Once within the cord these axons branch and synapse with the motor neurons going to the same muscle from which the afferents came (Carew, 1981). These afferents have endings that are connected to the weak intrafusal muscle fibers. Both Group Ia and Group II afferents are activated when these intrafusal muscles are stretched. Since the muscle spindle organ is attached to the larger extrafusal muscles *in parallel,* every time the big muscles are stretched, the small intrafusal muscles in the spindle organ are also stretched. This stretch activates the sensory neurons in the spindle organ, sending a burst of excitatory nerve impulses into the spinal cord and activating the large extrafusal muscles, which then contract. When the extrafusal muscles contract, the small intrafusal muscle fibers go slack (since the tension on them is relaxed when the larger muscles around them shorten). The firing rate of the muscle spindle receptors decreases, thus *reducing* the excitatory input onto the motor neuron. The decreased input from the muscle spindle organ allows the big muscles to relax. During relaxation the muscles lengthen, which again activates the muscle spindle organ, triggering excitation in the motor neuron.

This built-in automatic feedback arrangement helps keep the length of the muscle within a limited range (see Figure 7.3). This, roughly speaking, is what we call *muscle tone,* the partial state of contraction seen in relaxed muscles. Figure 7.1 illustrates the relationship between the Group Ia afferents and various neurons in the spinal cord. (For purposes of clarity the Group II afferents are not shown.)

Golgi Tendon Organs

In contrast to the muscle spindle organs, the Golgi tendon organs are placed *in series* with the muscle with which they are associated. The nerve endings of the Golgi tendon organs are embedded in the tendons that attach muscle to bone. The Golgi tendon organs are sensitive to the degree of tension developed in the muscle and are activated when the muscle actively contracts, pulling on the tendon. They signal the degree of tension during active muscle contraction via their afferent axons, the Ib afferents, which enter the cord through the dorsal root, send off axon collaterals, and terminate on *inhibitory interneurons.* These interneurons in turn inhibit the motor neurons to the extrafusal muscles, thus reducing the degree of excitation of those neurons and the degree of contraction of the muscle. The Golgi tendon organs are "safety brakes," serving to reduce the stretching or tearing of tendons and muscles during states of extreme contraction.

Just as there are two different types of muscle fibers, the large extrafusal muscles and the tiny intrafusal muscles, so too are there two classes of motor neurons that activate these two muscle types. All the motor neurons are bundled together in the ventral root. Most motor neurons are relatively large and activate the extrafusal muscles. These large motor neu-

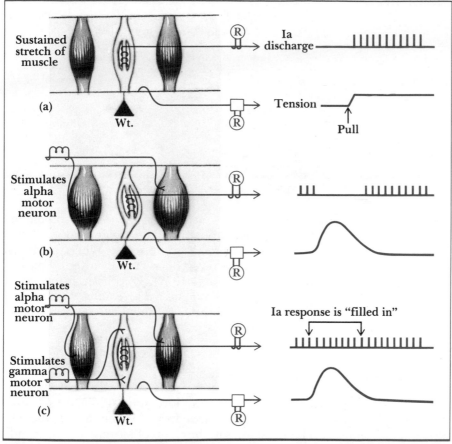

Figure 7.3 Firing rate of muscle spindle afferent under different conditions of stretch.
(a) Steady firing under steady stretch. (b) Pause in firing rate when extrafusal muscles contract, releasing tension on intrafusal muscles. (c) "Filling in" of pause by stimulation of gamma motor neuron to intrafusal muscle of spindle organ. R = recording device.

alpha motor neurons (AL-fa) The main motor neurons to striated muscles.

gamma motor neurons (GAM-ma) Motor neurons in the ventral root that activate the intrafusal muscles of the muscle spindle organs.

rons are the **alpha motor neurons.** About a third of the neurons in the ventral root, however, go to the intrafusal muscles of the muscle spindle organ. These smaller motor neurons are called the **gamma motor neurons.** Their activation causes the intrafusal muscles to contract but has no direct effect on the state of contraction of the extrafusal muscles. Such gamma motor neuron activation does have an indirect effect on the larger muscles, however. As the intrafusal muscles contract, the muscle spindle organ sends impulses into the spinal cord, activating the alpha motor neurons and causing the large muscles to contract. The exact role of the gamma motor activation is still uncertain, but it does provide a mechanism by which the

motor unit One alpha
motor neuron and the
muscle cells it innervates,
which all contract simultaneously.

SUMMARY TABLE — Function of Muscle Fiber Types		
Muscle Type	**Innervated by**	**Function**
Extrafusal (in main muscle)	Alpha motor neurons	Causes movement of limbs
Intrafusal (within muscle spindle organ)	Gamma motor neurons	Signals degree of extrafusal muscle length, maintains muscle "tone"

central nervous system can adjust the sensitivity of the muscle spindle organ (Kuffler et al., 1984). Without input from the Golgi tendon organs
and the muscle spindles, normal movement is impossible. When the dorsal
root carrying the impulses from these receptors is cut, the affected part of
the body is partially paralyzed (Ganong, 1977). One basic principle of
movement is that the *spinal reflexes can be considered to constitute basic units of
movement*. Reflexes are, however, typically incorporated into more elaborate
movement and posture programs.

The Final Common Path

Several billion neurons are concerned with movement. All the actual commands to the muscles, however, are carried out by only about 400,000
alpha motor neurons. These last links in the chain of movement commands
are also termed *ventral horn* cells, since their cell bodies are in the ventral
horn of the spinal cord. Recognizing their importance and position in the
sequence of nervous system activities underlying movement, Sherrington
termed these alpha motor neurons the "final common path" for movements. Shepherd (1983) estimates that, on average, over 5000 synapses are
to be found on each ventral horn cell, reflecting the many different influences channeled onto final common path neurons.

Motor Units

An individual alpha motor neuron goes to more than one muscle cell. One
motor neuron and the muscle fibers that it activates are referred to as a
motor unit. The number of fibers in a motor unit varies and determines
the precision of movements of which that muscle is capable. For example,
in the muscles that control fine eye movements, each motor unit has only
about three to six muscle fibers. However, in some of the large muscles of
the legs, the motor units may contain as many as 2000 muscle fibers (Rowland, 1981). When a motor neuron is activated, all the muscle fibers in its

unit contract. Relaxation of a muscle in vertebrates is achieved by reducing the firing rate of the motor neuron. No direct inhibition of muscle cells is found in vertebrates (although such inhibition does occur in invertebrates). Inhibition of vertebrate muscles is accomplished by circuitry within the nervous system. The smaller the motor unit, the greater is the degree of control over that set of muscles. In general, smaller motor units are found in the fingers and lips; larger motor units occur in the legs, arms, and back. The ventral horn cells innervate **striated** (striped) **muscles;** the *smooth* muscles of the intestine and blood vessels are innervated by neurons belonging to the autonomic nervous system.

striated muscle (STRY-ate-ed) "Striped" muscle, such as those that move the limbs.

Higher Command Centers for Movement

If the ventral horn cells are the final common path for movement program commands, where and how are such programs constructed and how are they modified to take account of changing conditions? In other words, how is integrative action of the nervous system developed? The regions that are particularly important are diagrammed in Figure 7.4. Four major regions

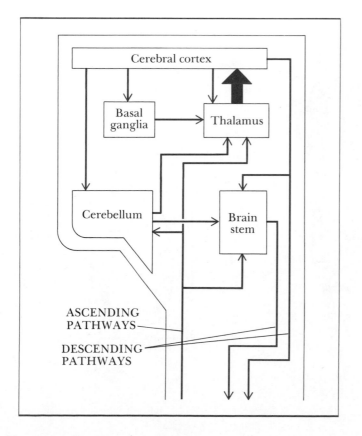

Figure 7.4 Major motor systems in the brain above the level of the spinal cord. Arrows do not imply monosynaptic connections. Crossing of pathways not indicated.

are found above the level of the spinal cord: brainstem, cerebellum, basal ganglia, and cerebral cortex. In addition, the thalamus serves as an important part of the circuits connecting these regions. All these regions of the brain send axons to the ventral horn cells, to interneurons in the spinal cord, and to each other, constructing a complex network out of which emerge coordinated movements.

Brainstem Controls on Posture and Locomotion

The brain region closest to the spinal cord is the brainstem. The brainstem contains the medulla oblongata, the pons, and the midbrain (see Figure 7.5). Sherrington discovered by sectioning the spinal cord that the brainstem contains neurons that modulate spinal reflexes. For all regions of the

Figure 7.5 Lateral view of the human brain stem.
The lentiform nucleus includes the putamen and globus pallidus. The crus cerebri is composed of descending nerve tracts.

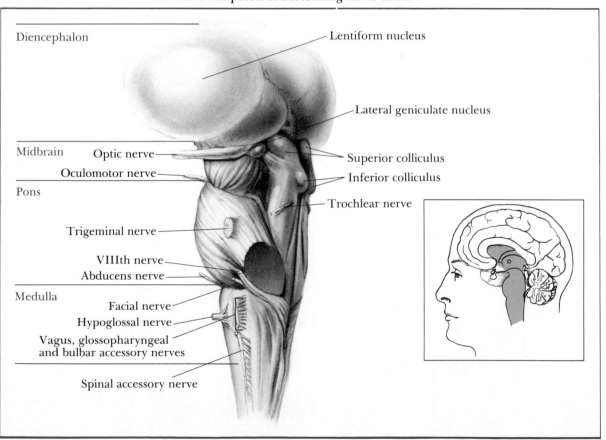

body whose nerve supply is below the cut, severing the spinal cord at the *caudal end* of the brainstem causes (1) the immediate loss of all voluntary movements, (2) the loss of sensation, (3) the loss of reflexes for some period of time, varying from minutes to weeks in different species (short times for cats and dogs, much longer for primates). The period of loss of reflexes is called **spinal shock;** after this period the spinal reflexes recover, and **hyperreflexia** (exaggerated reflexes) may be seen.

Decerebrate Rigidity

As discovered by Sherrington in the 1890s, if the transection is made more rostrally, between the inferior and superior colliculi, at the level of the anterior pons, **decerebrate rigidity** occurs. This condition involves an abnormal excitation of the alpha motor neurons that innervate the antigravity muscles, which allow animals to maintain their upright posture. For most animals these are the extensors; thus the animal's neck and limbs are rigidly and continually extended. That it is the antigravity muscles per se that are affected is revealed by modern experiments using tree-dwelling sloths. The antigravity muscles of sloths are their *flexors* (which allow them to combat gravity by hanging upside down from branches). In sloths the flexors become abnormally rigid with transection in the pons region (Mountcastle, 1968).

Decerebrate Rigidity as a Reflex

Although their spinal and brainstem circuits for walking are still intact, decerebrate animals do not walk spontaneously and cannot right themselves or sit or stand unaided. Decerebrate rigidity is reflexive, which can be demonstrated by cutting the dorsal root, thereby eliminating the sensory input from the muscles. If the dorsal roots from a limb of a decerebrate animal are cut, the limb becomes flaccid (loses muscle tone). Much of the activation of the alpha motor neurons that is so exaggerated in decerebrate rigidity actually occurs reflexively via the gamma motor neurons. Brainstem neurons are responsible for both excitation and inhibition of the alpha and gamma motor neurons. In the decerebrate preparation the excitation is stronger, because of the elimination of still higher brain centers that normally tend to activate the brainstem inhibitory region.

An upright posture is, of course, critical to the survival of animals in nature, and several control systems have evolved to ensure its maintenance. One such system of control is provided by excitation from the vestibular nuclei of the brainstem, which contributes to the increased contraction of the antigravity muscles. These nuclei receive input from vestibular sense organs in the inner ear and are important in maintaining normal posture with respect to head movements. Destruction of the vestibular nuclei in animals with decerebrate rigidity *decreases* the rigidity by eliminating this tonic excitation. Another system of postural control is provided by the cerebellum, which contributes input to the ventral horn cells concerned with posture. Postural adjustments with respect to gravity provide a good example of another basic principle of movement control: Maintenance of a particular state of firing of key neurons (in this case the alpha motor neurons to the extensor, antigravity muscles) is accomplished by the *combined excitation and inhibition of several different neural circuits,* each monitoring some different aspect of the environment.

Neural Oscillators

Most movements are not reflexive but voluntary, that is, initiated by the organism. Neural circuitry for one type of movement program, that of walking, exists in the spinal cord and in the brainstem. If the hind legs of a cat with a spinal cord transection are placed on a treadmill, walking movements will be elicited. Even if the dorsal roots are cut, these movements will continue, demonstrating that they are *not* reflexive but produced by a rhythmic *neural oscillator* in the cord (Pearson, 1976). This does not mean that the sensory input from the legs is unimportant in an animal's walking movements, but it does demonstrate that the sensory input from the muscles or paws is not *necessary* for the rhythmic, alternating contractions of extensors and flexors.

Neural programs for walking are influenced by sensory input as well as by impulses coming down from higher regions in the brain. The circuit in the brainstem was discovered by a group of Soviet scientists (see Carew, 1981), who produced rhythmic walking by electrically stimulating what they termed the *mesencephalic locomotor region* (MLR) in decerebrate cats. The pattern of walking is independent of the pattern of electrical stimulation, which simply turns on the MLR walking program. The exact pattern of such walking depends on the speed and angle of incline of the treadmill. The key distinction between a reflex, such as the knee jerk reflex, and a motor program or neural oscillator such as that for walking is that reflexes depend on sensory input from the muscles, and motor programs do not.

Evidence exists for a motor program, located in the brainstem, for swallowing (Doty, 1951; Doty and Bosma, 1956). Many such motor programs probably exist—for birdsong, for grooming behaviors, and for many aspects of reproductive behavior—that are independent of sensory input for their expression. (The exact form of such movements, however, is influenced by sensory input.) These motor programs can be either innate, which can be significantly altered by learning, or learned. Another principle of movement control is that *there are neural circuits, termed oscillators, in the spinal cord and brain that produce basic rhythmic movements. These movements are not dependent on sensory input for their occurrence.*

The Cerebellum

The cerebellum is located just dorsal to the pons and is marked by many lobes and fissures (see Figure 7.6). It receives sensory input from all the

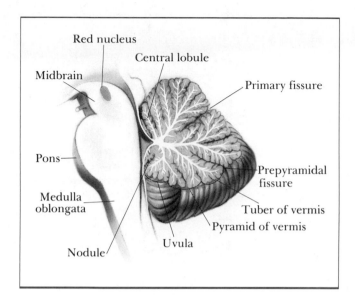

Figure 7.6 Sagittal section through the cerebellum.
Labels refer to various regions of the cerebellum.

senses and is involved in at least three general functions: maintenance of posture and balance, maintenance of muscle tone, and coordination of voluntary movements (Shepherd, 1979). Unlike the sensory input to the cerebral cortex, the sensory information going to the cerebellum does not enter consciousness. This is illustrated in patients with cerebellar damage, who have great difficulty with such coordinated movements as walking. Although they may stagger and fall, they do not feel dizzy!

Input from the various senses is processed by the cerebellum, and the output, which is via the **Purkinje cells,** goes to many places in the nervous system. The output of the Purkinje cells is inhibitory and is thought to modify motor programs initiated elsewhere and make them more precise. The Purkinje cell (of which there are about 7 million in the human brain) with its fan-shaped dendrites provides synaptic receptor sites for thousands of incoming axonal terminals, many of which end on one or more of the 100,000 dendritic spines on each Purkinje cell (Shepherd, 1979). Many synaptic contacts come from the *granule* cells whose axons, known as the parallel fibers, run through the Purkinje dendrites at right angles, making synaptic, excitatory contacts as they do so. Each parallel fiber excites about 50 Purkinje cells, and each Purkinje cell receives synaptic input from about 200,000 parallel fibers. The interlacing of these two cell types involves considerable divergence and convergence (Ghez and Fahn, 1981). The other types of neurons found in the cerebellum are shown in Figure 7.7.

Purkinje cell (purr-KIN-jee) The main output neuron of the cerebellum.

Kornhuber's Theory of Movement

The almost geometric arrangement of the neurons in the cerebellum has stimulated several hypotheses about the functions of the cerebellum (Marr,

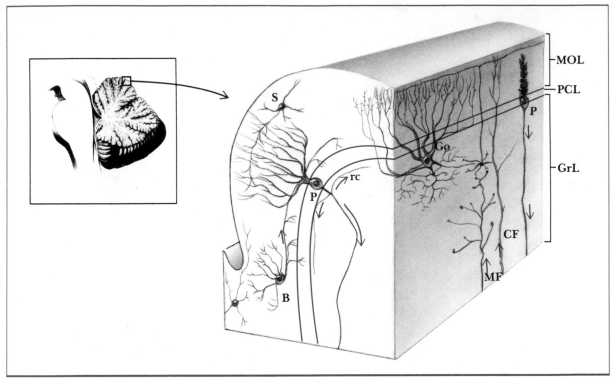

Figure 7.7   Various types of neurons in the cerebellum.
Inputs: mossy fibers (MF) and climbing fibers (CF). Principal neuron: Purkinje
cell (P) with recurrent collateral (rc). Intrinsic neurons: stellate cell (S); basket
cell (B); Golgi cell (Go). Three layers are recognized and shown on the right.
These include the molecular layer (MOL), the Purkinje cell body layer (PCL),
and the granule layer (GrL).

ballistic movements (ball-ISS-tik) Movements made rapidly to a particular point in space, too fast for feedback to be an effective guide.

saccadic movements (sah-KAD-ik) Rapid fixation movements of the eyes.

basal ganglia (BAYZ-al) Term given to a collection of subcortical structures including the caudate nucleus, the globus pallidus, and the putamen.

1969; Ito, 1970). Hans Kornhuber (1974) has proposed an extensive theory of movement in which the cerebellum is seen as being important for the initiation of preprogrammed **ballistic movements,** such as the fast **saccadic movements** of the eyes. Saccades are much too fast for feedback from the ocular muscles of the eyes to alter their trajectory. We use saccades in reading and other visual tasks that involve scanning the visual stimulus. Saccadic eye movements can become jerky and slower because of injury to or deterioration of the circuits in the cerebellum. This can happen in the elderly and has been linked with vitamin B1 deficiency.

The Basal Ganglia: The Comet, the Globe, and the Peachstone

The **basal ganglia** are crucial components of the mammalian motor system. Three related clusters of neurons make up the basal ganglia: the **caudate** (comet) **nucleus,** the **globus pallidus** (pale globe), and the **putamen** (peachstone). The globus pallidus and putamen together are referred to as the lentiform (lens-shaped) nucleus. These forebrain structures anterior to and surrounding the thalamus play an important part in the initiation and regulation of movements (see Figure 7.8). Much of our insight into the functions of the basal ganglia has come from study of patients with diseases of these structures. The two most common diseases are Parkinson's disease and Huntington's disease (both named after the physicians who first described them). About half a million people in the United States are affected with **Parkinson's disease,** and another 10,000 or so have **Huntington's disease** (Cote, 1981b). Parkinson's disease is characterized by involuntary tremors of the limbs and body, rigidity caused by overcontraction of muscles, slowness in initiating and performing motor acts, and a shuffling walk.

caudate nucleus (CAW-date) One of the basal ganglia.

globus pallidus (GLOBE-us PAL-i-dus) One of the basal ganglia.

putamen (pew-TAY-men) One of the basal ganglia.

Parkinson's disease Disease characterized by deterioration in motor control and movement initiation.

Huntington's disease Disease of the basal ganglia, produces uncontrollable movements and dementia.

Figure 7.8
(a) Lateral and views of the basal ganglia. (b) Frontal section through the brain at the plane shown in (a).

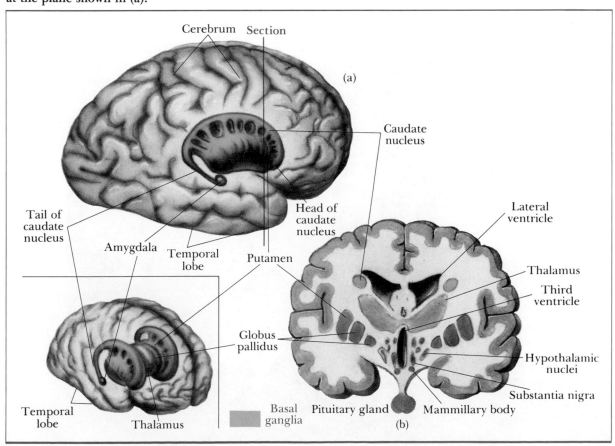

Ivan

The inability to initiate movements can be profound, causing the individual to be motionless for minutes at a time. Parkinson's patients often have to make whatever movement they can to get into action and perform the task they actually have in mind. As one courageous patient with this disease has put it,

> When carrying a drink to the breakfast table, if I allow myself to think of, say, the need to hurry because I've got to catch a train, tremor may break out in my hands. I then have to stoop quickly and place the drink on the floor before shaking it all around the room. I have to engage in self-deception, whereby any personal interest in the fulfillment or goal of an action must be removed from consciousness. The action is converted into something trivial or incidental [Vaughn, 1984].

Figure 7.9 is a photograph of this patient, Ivan Vaughn, who has volunteered as a subject in the study of Parkinson's disease.

Ivan jogs several miles each day, and to get going he falls forward until he starts to run. (Perhaps this type of running depends on the patient's undamaged cerebellum and neural oscillators for locomotion). Trouble occurs when the straightforward rhythmic running is interrupted. As he says:

Figure 7.9   Ivan, the Parkinson patient discussed in the text.

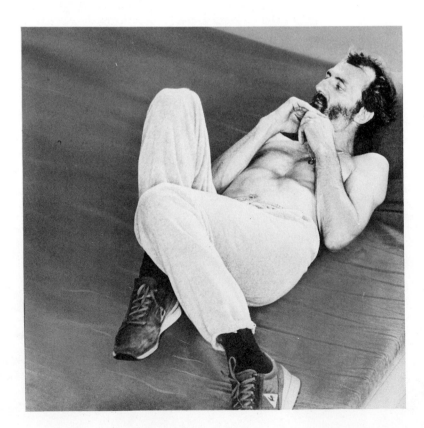

"if I meet someone while out running, I may begin to stumble and fall; if a dog comes up to me when I'm walking, I may grind to a halt and stand frozen to the spot. In order to get moving again I will probably have to fall forward into a run. Falling gives up postural control and thereby frees resources for initiating movement of the legs" (Vaughn, 1984). This patient is describing how he copes with his disease when he is *not* taking medication. Medication is available for Parkinson's disease (**L-DOPA**) that brings considerable relief, but this relief is short and the effectiveness of the drug lessens with time; moreover it has extremely unpleasant side effects, including involuntary writhing movements of the muscles in the neck, face, and other regions of the body.

L-DOPA is a precursor of the neurotransmitter dopamine. Parkinson's disease is considered a dopamine deficiency disease. Dopamine is drastically reduced in the basal ganglia of Parkinson's disease patients. In normal brains 80 percent of the brain's dopamine is concentrated in the basal ganglia, even though these structures make up less than 0.5 percent of the brain's weight (Côté, 1981). The cell bodies of the neurons that release the dopamine onto neurons in the basal ganglia are in a brainstem nucleus called the **substantia nigra.** These neurons deteriorate and die in patients with Parkinson's disease.

One quite radical treatment for Parkinson's disease, in which cells from the medulla of the patient's adrenal gland have been transplanted into the basal ganglia of the patient, has been tried recently in Sweden and in Mexico. These cells secrete small amounts of dopamine. Experimental work with chemically produced Parkinsonlike movement disorders in laboratory rats has demonstrated greatly improved movement following the transplantation of fetal brain tissue containing dopamine neurons into the basal ganglia (Bjorklund and Stenevi, 1984). Appropriate neural cell lines might be developed in tissue culture and used in such transplants.

The other main disease of the basal ganglia is Huntington's disease, characterized by rapid, uncontrolled "flicking" movements of the limbs and facial muscles. This disease is also due to an abnormality in the basal ganglia, but in Huntington's disease the neurons that are believed to malfunction include those that secrete GABA and acetylcholine. No effective treatment is known for this cruel disease, which is genetically transmitted and is always fatal. The disease usually begins in the patient's late thirties or early forties and death usually occurs within 10–15 years of its onset. Patients with Huntington's disease also become severely demented and in the past often were misdiagnosed as schizophrenic. The Huntington's disease gene has been located on chromosome 4, and a test is now available that allows the disease to be diagnosed long before any symptoms appear.

Cerebral Cortex

The last component of the motor system we discuss is the cerebral cortex. Although it is the most recently developed phylogenetically and the most anterior anatomically, the cerebral cortex is not the sole command center

L-DOPA A precursor of the catecholamines.

substantia nigra (sub-STAN-sha NYE-gra) Nucleus in the brainstem containing the cell bodies of dopamine-secreting neurons that project to the basal ganglia and other forebrain structures.

Parkinson's Disease Produced by Designer Drugs

Recently it has been discovered through the unfortunate experience of some drug users that Parkinson's disease also can be produced by synthetic heroin-type drugs (Langston et al., 1983). When a few users of such street drugs developed severe (and irreversible) Parkinsonlike symptoms, physicians tried L-DOPA as a treatment and achieved substantial (but temporary) improvement. These unfortunate "frozen drug addicts," who without medication are virtually paralyzed, provided an important clue that there was a substance in the synthetic heroin that could destroy nerve cells and the ability to initiate movements.

In their search for drugs similar to heroin but still labeled legal by some state laws, illicit drug manufacturers have produced a stream of so-called designer drugs that differ from heroin in minor ways. One substance appeared in one of these designer drugs. Called **MPTP** (short for **methylphenyltetrahydropyridine**), it is converted by the enzyme monoamine oxidase into **MPP$^+$** (**methylphenylpyridine**). Monoamine oxidase is found throughout the body, including the brain (see Chapter 15). MPP$^+$ selectively attacks the neurons in the brain that contain **neuromelanin,** a substance that appears black and gives the substantia

nigra its name (D'Amato et al., 1986). As MPP$^+$ attacks the neurons in the substantia nigra and kills them, it produces the symptoms of Parkinson's disease—severe tremors and virtual inability to make voluntary movements, leaving its victims frozen. At present, other than the temporary relief brought about by L-DOPA, there appears to be little or no hope for these frozen drug addicts. The ability of MPP$^+$ to produce Parkinson's disease has been demonstrated in primate experiments, although curiously, it has little or no effect on rats, demonstrating an important species difference in brain function.

Since MPP$^+$ may also occur in other chemical reactions, it, or substances very similar to it, may exist as environmental pollutants and contribute to the gradual destruction of the substantia nigra in individuals as they age and accumulate more and more such pollutants in their brains. With such increased contamination, more and more substantia nigra cells would be destroyed, thereby increasing parkinsonian symptoms. This hypothesis suggests that Parkinson's disease may be not just a "disease of old age," but a disease of environmental pollution.

MPTP (methylphenyl-tetrahydropyridine) (meth-ul-FEN-ul-tet-rah-high-dro-PEER-uh-deen) A substance found as a contaminant in some "designer drugs." Causes Parkinson's disease by destroying neurons in the substantia nigra after being converted into MPP$^+$ in the body.

MPP$^+$ (methylphenylpyridine) (meth-ul-FEN-ul-PEER-uh-deen) A substance produced in the body from MPTP. Selectively destroys neurons in the substantia nigra, causing Parkinson's disease.

for movements. Its role is still being investigated, but it is already clear that it is a part of a widespread, integrated system, receiving as well as sending messages concerning movements and postural adjustments. (The region of the cortex known as the *motor area* is shown in Figure 7.10.)

In 1870 two German investigators, Gustav Fritsch and Edouard Hitzig, discovered that they could produce movements in dogs and monkeys by electrical stimulation of certain restricted regions of the frontal cortex, just anterior to the central sulcus. Subsequent experimenters refined these early results. In particular, Wilder Penfield and his colleagues in Montreal performed many such stimulations during the course of human neurosurgical procedures. The motor **homunculus** (little man) that summarizes their basic findings is shown in Figure 7.11. The distortion of the figure reflects another principle of movement control: *The number of neurons in the cortex devoted to movements of a particular part of the body is related to the precision with* *which that part of the body can move.* The fingers and lips of the homunculus are drawn large to emphasize that we are capable of a wide variety of fine movements using our face and hands. The legs, back, and trunk of the little man are much smaller because our ability to make fine, coordinated movements of these body parts is much more limited. The region from which these body movements can be elicited is roughly the same as Brodmann's area 4. Moreover, many of the axons that form the pyramidal tract come from this cortical region. However, the motor area is not the only cortical region associated with motor functions, nor the only source of fibers to the pyramidal tract. Nevertheless, it is the area most closely concerned with the control of motor neurons (Shepherd, 1979).

Some of the axons that descend to the brainstem and spinal cord from the cortex become part of the **pyramidal tracts** (so named because they form the medullary pyramids as they cross over to the opposite side of the brain in the brainstem). Axons that do not go through the pyramidal tract are classified as part of the **extrapyramidal system.** The distinctions between these two systems are not convincing, and considerable overlap exists in the cortical areas that contribute axons to both systems; nevertheless the terminology survives. The pyramidal system is also referred to as the *corticospinal tract.* Each hemisphere has a pyramidal tract, and each tract contains about a million axons. Of these about 60 percent come from area 4; the rest are from nearby area 6, from a supplementary motor region down

neuromelanin (nur-o-MEL-ah-nin) A black substance in certain neurons, such as in the substantia nigra.

homunculus (huh-MUN-kew-lus) "Little man" cartoon representing the proportion of the motor cortex devoted to the regulation of various muscles in the body.

pyramidal tract (peer-AM-i-dal) The axons that cross over in the medulla, forming the medullary pyramids.

extrapyramidal system (EX-tra-peer-AM-i-dal) The neurons concerned with movement that are not part of the pyramidal system.

Figure 7.10   Diagram of the lateral surface of the right hemisphere of the human brain showing the primary motor area and premotor area.

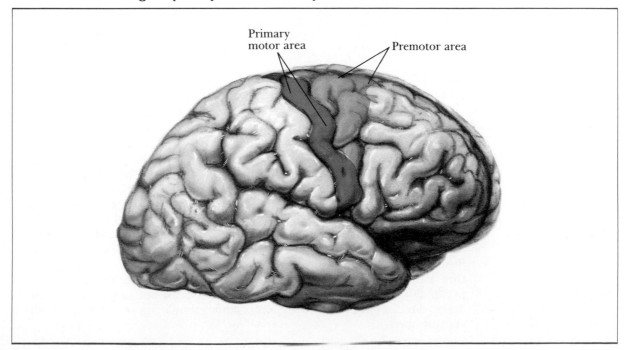

Betz cell (BETS) A type of large neuron in the motor cortex whose axons descend in the pyramidal tract. Also called *giant pyramidal cell.*

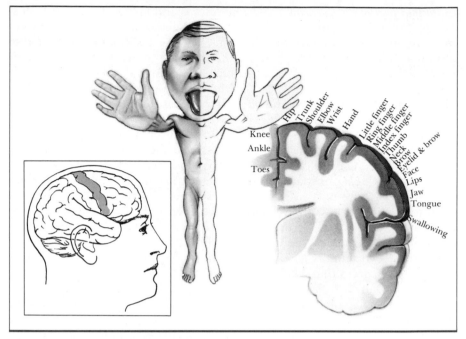

Figure 7.11   The motor homunculus.
The size of the various body parts in the figure reflects the amount of tissue in the primary motor area devoted to control of that body part. The left side of the brain controls the right side of the body. The labels refer to different regions of a cross section (frontal plane) through the primary motor cortex.

the medial side of the hemisphere, and from areas 3, 2, and 1 of the postcentral gyrus.

One type of cortical neuron that contributes to the pyramidal system is the giant pyramidal neuron, or **Betz cell.** Only about 34,000 of these neurons send axons in the pyramidal system. The other neurons of the pyramidal system are smaller, 90 percent being less than 4 μm in diameter. About half are unmyelinated (Ganong, 1977). About 80 percent of the axons in the pyramidal system cross over to the opposite side of the brain in the medulla, forming the *medullary pyramids.* The rest descend on the ipsilateral side until shortly before they synapse with spinal neurons. They then also cross over to the opposite side of the spinal cord. Motor control is thus basically contralateral, particularly for fine, precise movements of the fingers and toes. Human beings also have some ipsilateral motor control, particularly of movements of the hips and shoulders. Most of the pyramidal tract neurons synapse on interneurons, but at least 10 percent make direct connections with alpha and gamma motor neurons in the ventral horn.

Corollary Discharge

Many collateral axon branches of pyramidal system neurons synapse with brainstem neurons, which in turn send input into the cerebellum. This cortical–cerebellar pathway may be important in informing the cerebellum of movement commands being sent out by the cortex so that the cerebellum can be informed *in advance* of intended movements. This "preview of coming contractions" would be of particular value in adjusting head and eye movements so that greater stability of the visual world can be maintained. Such information is termed a **corollary discharge.**

Damage to the pyramidal tract does not cause permanent paralysis. In fact, the long-term effects are not as striking as those resulting from damage to either the cerebellum or basal ganglia. Nevertheless there are clear effects: Fine, coordinated movements become clumsier, slower, and weaker. An immediate flaccid paralysis follows ablation of area 4, although partial recovery occurs within a few days. Responses to sensory input from the somesthetic system are ended permanently. Moreover, damage to the motor area or the pyramidal tract results in a permanent deficit in placement of the limbs onto ledges (tactile placing), hopping behavior, and grasping reactions to objects. Kornhuber (1974) stresses the importance of somatic and vestibular sensory input for normal functioning of the motor areas of the cortex. In his theory of motor systems the motor regions of the cortex do not simply initiate movements; the cortical commands must be "con-

corollary discharge (KORE-o-lar-ee) Hypothetical signals from motor cortex to cerebellum and possibly other brain regions informing those regions of coming movement commands.

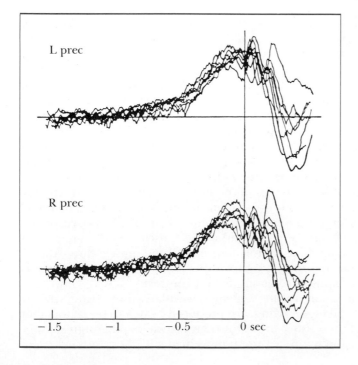

Figure 7.12 Readiness potential as recorded from the human scalp.
These potentials begin about 800 msec prior to the initiation of a voluntary rapid flexion of the right index finger. The traces are from eight different experiments with the same subject on eight different days. Traces are superimposed to show reliability of the potential. Top records (L prec) are from the left hemisphere, precentral motor region. The bottom records are from the right hemisphere (R prec), precentral motor region.

verted by the basal ganglia and cerebellum into spatiotemporal motor patterns." The cortex is particularly important in his scheme as a device for the adjustment of motor patterns in response to tactile input.

Neural activity in the cortex precedes the movements themselves by almost a second. Figure 7.12 shows electrical activity recorded from the scalp of a subject making voluntary rapid flexion movements of the right index finger. The large negative potential (upward in the figure) that starts 800 msec prior to the finger movement is termed the *readiness potential.* Pyramidal tract neurons also begin to change their activity before the movements with which they are associated occur. Many thousands of neurons in the motor area are involved even in very small movements (Evarts, 1979).

SUMMARY

1. Neurons throughout the nervous system are involved in the production of movements. Spinal reflexes, which can be considered as basic units for movement, are almost always incorporated into more elaborate motor programs. Sensory input is critical for the occurrence of reflex movements, as demonstrated by the elimination of spinal reflexes when the dorsal sensory nerves to the spinal cord are cut.

2. Reflex controls assure that when a particular muscle is contracted, antagonistic muscles are relaxed. This reciprocal inhibition is produced by inhibitory interneurons that are activated during the contraction of the original muscle and that inhibit the firing of motor neurons going to the antagonists. Reciprocal inhibition underlies walking and flying movements.

3. Sense organs in the muscles and tendons signal the degree of tension (Golgi tendon organs) and muscle length (muscle spindle organs). The muscle spindle organs receive input from the ventral root via the gamma efferent system of motor axons. The operation of the muscle spindle organ helps to keep the degree of contraction of the muscle within a normal range, maintaining muscle tone. Golgi tendon organs serve as "safety brakes," keeping the muscles from overcontracting and tearing.

4. The firing rate of key neurons in the motor system, such as the motor neurons of the ventral horn (the final common path), is regulated by both excitatory and inhibitory neural input from various parts of the brain and from sense organs such as the muscle spindle organ and Golgi tendon organ. The motor neuron and the muscle fibers that it activates are referred to as a motor unit. When that motor neuron is activated, all the muscle fibers in its unit contract.

5. Some neural programs for movement, particularly for rhythmic movements such as walking or flying, are produced by neural oscillators that do not depend on sensory input for their activation, although sensory input can alter the nature of these movements.

6. Sensory input into the cerebellum, although important for the modulation of various movements and postural adjustments, does not typically enter conscious awareness. Kornhuber's theory of movement proposes that the cerebellum is involved primarily in the initiation of preprogrammed, ballistic movements that are too fast for feedback to alter their trajectory.

7. The basal ganglia include the caudate nucleus, the globus pallidus, and the putamen. Kornhuber proposes that the basal ganglia produce slower, "ramp"-type movements that are subject to feedback control. Parkinson's disease is due to the malfunctioning of the basal ganglia produced by the deterioration of dopamine neurons whose cell bodies are in the substantia nigra and which send axonal projections to synapse on neurons of the basal ganglia. Parkinson's disease is characterized by tremors, rigidity of the muscles, and difficulty in initiating and performing motor acts. Temporary improvement can be achieved by administering L-DOPA, a precursor for dopamine, but the improvement is short-lasting and diminishes with continued treatment; moreover, L-DOPA has unpleasant side effects.

8. The cerebral cortex is involved in the modulation and further programming of motor commands coming from the cerebellum and basal ganglia. The number of neurons in the cortex devoted to the control of a particular part of the body is related to the precision with which that part of the body can move.

9. A "corollary discharge" of anticipated head and eye movements is sent by the brain regions that initiate these movements so that a stable visual field can be maintained, even when the individual is moving rapidly through space.

10. Electrical activity related to anticipated movements can be observed in scalp recordings almost a second before the occurrence of the movement itself.

SUGGESTIONS FOR FURTHER READING

Kornhuber, H. H. (1974). Cerebral cortex, cerebellum, and basal ganglia: An introduction to their motor functions. In F. O. Schmitt and F. G. Worden (Eds.), *The neurosciences; third study program* (pp. 267–280). Cambridge, MA: MIT Press.

Kuffler, S. W., Nicholls, J. G., and Martin, A. R. (1984). *From neuron to brain* (2d ed.). Sunderland, MA: Sinauer.

8

Thirst and Hunger

J came upon no wine
So wonderful as thirst.

EDNA ST. VINCENT MILLAY

Preview

Like all animals, human beings must constantly replenish their body fluids. How this is done and what neural activities constitute thirst and satiation are matters of enduring interest to behavioral neuroscientists. One major theory is the *double depletion theory* of thirst, a proposal that takes into consideration both the volume of fluid in the extracellular spaces and the water content of the cells in the body. Both of these fluid compartments are monitored in some way that is communicated to the brain, so that water conservation responses and thirst are triggered when fluid levels in either compartment fall below some critical value.

Organisms must also replenish their energy stores; for the most part, food intake and body weight are closely regulated. Much of the research in this area has centered on a search for the signals for hunger and satiety. One theory proposes that glucose is the important substance monitored by the brain, but the relevant evidence is mixed. Some evidence supports the hypothesis that we regulate our basic body weight around some *set point*. It is obvious that not all of us regulate our weight perfectly. The problem of obesity and its possible causes is discussed, along with the abnormal weight gain and change in eating patterns produced in experimental animals by damage to the hypothalamus.

Thirst

After three sets of tennis under a hot sun, a glass of cool water really hits the spot. In fact, in such a situation your need for fluids is likely to dominate your thoughts to such an extent that if the nearby fountain is not working, you may go down the street to buy a soft drink. If you cannot find a cold drink, you may buy an unrefrigerated bottle. In short, as your thirst grows, it drives you to take whatever steps are necessary to find relief. From reports of shipwreck survivors and individuals stranded in the desert, we know that thirst rapidly becomes more than just an annoying dry mouth; it becomes the center of consciousness, and rightly so, since without sufficient water, death is inevitable.

What signals thirst? Do the sensations from a dry mouth and tongue tell us we need to drink? Do fluid level monitors cause thirst when levels become low? These questions have been asked in the laboratory, and some of the answers are quite surprising.

Most animals regulate their fluid levels precisely; under normal circumstances the amount of body fluid fluctuates less than 1 percent. Many animals display a **circadian** rhythm in drinking. For example, the golden hamster does most of its drinking at night, and if kept under dim illumination it shows a true circadian rhythm of water intake. *Circadian* means "about a day" (from the Latin words *circa,* meaning "approximately," and *dies,* meaning "day"). (Chapter 10 has a more detailed discussion of such rhythms and the neural circuitry underlying them.) A typical 150-lb (70-kg) human being "turns over" about 2.5 quarts (2.7 liters) of fluid a day, drinking about half of this amount and extracting the rest from food. A little over half of the fluid lost is eliminated in the urine; the rest is lost in feces, evaporation of perspiration from the skin, and as water vapor from the lungs. Some animals never drink water, extracting all their fluid needs from the food they eat (e.g., sea mammals, such as walruses and seals, and several desert-living creatures).

Primary and Secondary Drinking

James Fitzsimons (1971) has drawn attention to the distinction between primary and secondary drinking. Primary drinking occurs in response to depletion of body fluids because of water deprivation, substantial bleeding, or sweating and in response to ingesting a hypertonic salt solution. The proportion of Na^+ and Cl^- ions in the blood plasma is about 0.9 percent. Any solution that contains a higher concentration of these ions (or other ions that act in similar fashion) is termed **hypertonic.** A solution containing less than 0.9 percent Na^+ and Cl^- ions is called **hypotonic.**

Secondary drinking occurs as a result of conditions that do not involve any fluid imbalance (e.g., electrical stimulation of certain regions of the brain). People drink when they eat dry food because it facilitates swallowing, and they drink for social reasons and out of habit at meals, even when they do not need additional fluids. There are even rare cases of pathological water drinking by mentally disturbed patients. Explanations of drinking are not likely to account for all these different secondary drinking situations, and most theorists have concerned themselves with primary drinking and with two basic questions: What starts drinking? What stops it?

The Dry Mouth Theory

Most people would identify a dry, bad-tasting mouth and throat as one of the conditions that makes them thirsty. A dry mouth is one of the cues that contributes to the sensation of thirst and to drinking, but a theory of thirst that relies solely on this idea is doomed to failure. A dry mouth theory of thirst was formally proposed by Walter Cannon in 1919. Cannon postulated that as salivary flow decreased, the resulting dry mouth produced

circadian (Sir-KAY-dee-an) Endogenous rhythmic changes in some process or behavior, occurring once about every 24 hours, even in the absence of environmental changes.

hypertonic (high-per-TON-ik) Denoting a solution that is more concentrated with respect to dissolved substances than the comparison solution. Often refers to a solution with more than 0.9 percent concentration of Na^+ and Cl^- ions, the concentration in blood plasma.

hypotonic (high-po-TON-ik) Denoting a solution that is less concentrated than a comparison solution. Often refers to a solution with less than 0.9 percent concentration of Na^+ and Cl^- ions, the concentration in blood plasma.

fistula (FIS-tue-la) An abnormal passage in the body, generally made to divert the flow of material from its normal course, typically to the outside of the body.

the sensations of thirst and triggered drinking. This theory was really not much more than a restatement of common sense, and as has turned out to be the case more than once, when commonsense ideas are rigorously tested in the laboratory, they leave a great deal to be desired. In support of Cannon's idea, it is true that many conditions that produce drinking also reduce the amount of saliva in the mouth and throat (e.g., water deprivation, hemorrhage, and eating dry or salty foods). A dry or unpleasant-tasting mouth is likely to produce some drinking; thus some correlation exists between the presence of a dry mouth, sensations of thirst, and drinking. But correlation is not causality. Several conditions occur in which a dry mouth does not trigger drinking, and others are known in which even constant wetting of the mouth and throat does not stop drinking. Let us take a closer look at these two stumbling blocks for the dry mouth theory.

According to the dry mouth theory, anything that decreases the amount of salivation should be thirst producing. Philip Teitelbaum and Alan Epstein (1962) noticed that lesions in the lateral hypothalamus of rats severely reduced their salivation, yet they drank *less* than normal rats. In addition, Rolls and Rolls (1982) tell of a young man born without salivary glands who sipped small amounts of water every hour or so while awake but had a normal total intake of water. Such observations severely weaken a dry mouth explanation for the *amount* of water drunk, although some weak support does exist for a dry mouth as a contributing factor in explaining *when* drinking may occur.

Another challenge to the dry mouth idea comes from various experiments in which animals are allowed to take water into their mouth, wetting their mouth and throat, but are not allowed to absorb the water into their body. These experiments involve *open* **fistulas,** either in the esophagus or further down the alimentary canal. Various types of fistula placements are illustrated in Figure 8.1.

Figure 8.1 The three main types of openings or fistulas that have been used to study sham drinking.

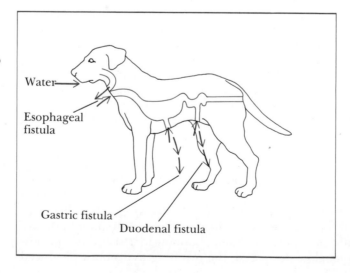

Fluids taken into the mouth and throat of a dog with an esophageal fistula keep the mouth and throat tissues wet but do not reach the stomach, since they flow out the open fistula. Such animals drink enormous quantities of water, despite an almost continually wet mouth and throat. (These animals cannot survive, of course, unless water is placed into their stomachs through the lower part of the esophagus.) Such experiments were actually performed as long ago as 1856 by the French physiologist Claude Bernard (1813–1878), but Cannon either overlooked or did not know of Bernard's results.

Later experiments, such as those of R. T. Bellows (1939) and Edward Adolph (1950), refined these experiments, measuring the amount of water drunk. When water-deprived dogs with open fistulas are allowed to drink, they drink about the normal amount, stop, and then return a few minutes later for a second drink. This process continues unless water is placed in the dog's stomach. Similar findings have been obtained with monkeys (Maddison et al., 1980). Thus, although sensations arising from a dry mouth and throat may influence the time at which water is drunk, other, more central mechanisms must be at work determining the amount of water drunk.

interstitial fluid (In-ter-STISH-al) The fluid of the body located between the cells.

The Double Depletion Theory of Thirst

The fluid in our bodies is in one of two basic "compartments." Water can move from one compartment to the other, but at any given time, water is either inside the cells of the body in the *intracellular compartment* or outside the cells in the *extracellular compartment* (see Figure 8.2). The extracellular compartment is further divided into the fluid between the cells, called the **interstitial fluid,** and the fluid in the blood plasma. About 67 percent of our total body water (40–45 percent of body weight) is contained in the intracellular compartment; the other 33 percent is in the extracellular compartment (20–25 percent of body weight). Most of the extracellular fluid is in the interstitial spaces between the cells.

The fluid in the blood plasma is very carefully monitored. Although blood constitutes only 7 percent of total body water, even small changes in blood volume elicit changes in drinking and fluid conservation. The *double depletion theory* of thirst proposes that changes in the water content of *both* the cellular and the extracellular components influence water intake and that these influences combine to produce the urge to drink (Epstein et al., 1973).

Cellular Dehydration

Most of the body fluids are in the cellular compartment, and fluid losses here produce thirst and drinking. In addition, physiologic responses occur that tend to conserve water. A hormone (antidiuretic hormone, or ADH)

osmotic pressure (oz-MOT-ik) See *osmosis.*

osmosis (oz-MOE-sis) The flow of water from the region of lesser concentration of the substance to the region of higher concentration, when two solutions varying in concentration of some substance are separated by a membrane permeable to water but not to the dissolved substance. The pressure required to stop this flow completely is the *osmostic pressure* of the solution.

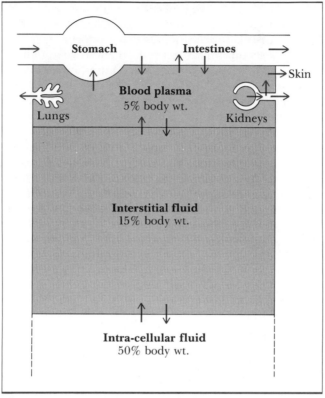

Figure 8.2   The main compartments for body fluids.
Body fluid is either within the cells (intracellular) or outside the cells in the interstitial fluid or the blood plasma (extracellular).

is released from the posterior pituitary and acts on the kidney to concentrate the urine, thereby retaining body water. Such conservation is useful during water deprivation, of course, but it cannot increase the total amount of water in the body. Thus thirst and (if water is available) drinking also occur in response to cellular dehydration.

The signals for cellular dehydration have long been thought to affect neurons in the brain, but it was not until 1953 that direct evidence for this hypothesis was found. Bengt Andersson (1953) caused avid drinking in water-satiated goats by placing small amounts of hypertonic salt solution directly into the anterior hypothalamus. Hypertonic solutions cause cellular dehydration by pulling fluids from the cells through osmotic action. Molecules of a dissolved substance that cannot flow freely across cell membranes (such as sodium ions) increase the **osmotic pressure** on the side of the membrane where they are more concentrated, which results in water molecules being pulled through the membrane to the side of the greater concentration until the pressure is equalized. This flow of water is termed **osmosis.**

Pulling water from the cells causes them to shrink. This shrinking, or reduction in cell volume of specific cells in the brain, termed **osmoreceptors,** is thought to explain why the administration of hypertonic solutions directly to the brain causes drinking. Likewise, hypotonic solutions result in water being pulled into these cells, causing them to swell, which reduces drinking. Substances that pass rapidly and freely through cell membranes do not exert significant osmotic pressure and thus should not have an effect on drinking. Urea is one such substance, and injecting it into the brain has no effect on drinking. These results all support the concept that cellular dehydration can cause thirst and drinking.

Andersson's results have been extended and confirmed in rats by several investigators, such as Jeffrey Peck and Donald Novin (1971), who found that other hypertonic solutions would also produce drinking when injected directly into the hypothalamus. Sucrose is a useful substance to use, since it turns out that hypertonic saline is a nonspecific excitant for neurons, clouding the interpretation of Andersson's original results. Cells that respond to cellular dehydration have been found only in the *lateral preoptic* (LPO) area of the brain, just anterior to the hypothalamus. Although these LPO receptors probably respond to cellular dehydration rather than to the osmotic pressure itself, they are still generally referred to as *osmoreceptors.*

As mentioned earlier, in addition to initiating thirst and drinking, cellular dehydration causes the release of an **antidiuretic hormone (ADH)** from the posterior pituitary. ADH acts on the distal tubules of the kidney to make them more permeable to water, which is thus reabsorbed into the bloodstream. This process causes more concentrated urine and increased water retention. The neurons that make and release ADH are different from the LPO osmoreceptors, although they may be influenced by them. Cellular dehydration accounts for most of the drive for drinking in mammals. Various experimental manipulations that remove only those stimuli concerned with cellular dehydration reduce the amount of water drunk each day in every species so far studied by at least 64 percent. In rats cellular dehydration accounts for 64–69 percent of drinking following water deprivation; in dogs, 72 percent; and in the rhesus monkey, 85 percent. Precise data for human beings are not yet available (Rolls and Rolls, 1982).

Hypovolemia

Although cellular dehydration probably accounts for most of the drinking in mammals, there is another important stimulus for thirst. Fluid loss from the extracellular compartment with no cellular dehydration, such as is found with hemorrhage, is also a potent stimulus for thirst. Another thirst-producing stimulus, sweating, reduces the extracellular component to a greater degree than it does the intracellular component. In the laboratory the common procedure to produce selective reduction in blood volume, known as **hypovolemia,** is to inject a **colloidal** substance such as polyethelene glycol under the skin or into the abdominal cavity. Such materials cannot get into the cells, but they pull fluids from the extracellular spaces, causing a reduction in blood volume.

osmoreceptors (OZ-mo-re-cep-tors) Neurons in the brain (thought to be primarily in the lateral preoptic region) that are sensitive to cellular dehydration and that can signal changes in osmotic pressure.

antidiuretic hormone (ADH) (AN-tie-die-ur-ET-ik) Another name for vasopressin. A posterior pituitary hormone that acts on the kidney to cause more concentrated urine, thus conserving body water.

hypovolemia (high-po-vol-EEM-ia) Reduced blood volume.

colloid (KOL-oyd) A gelatinous substance that does not diffuse through cell membranes but that can absorb water.

renin (REN-in) An enzyme produced by the kidney. When released into the general circulation, renin converts a liver hormone, angiotensinogen, into angiotensin II.

angiotensinogen (anj-ee-o-ten-SIN-o-jen) A liver product converted into angiotensin II by renin.

angiotensin II (anj-ee-o-TEN-sin two) A hormone made from the action of renin on angiotensinogen.

subfornical organ (SFO) (sub-FORN-ih-kal) Structure in the brain that projects into the lateral ventricle below the fornix.

baroreceptors (BARE-owe-re-sep-tors) Pressure receptors in the heart and large arteries that respond to changes in blood volume.

Hypovolemia can also be caused by depriving animals of sodium in their diet. This causes the blood plasma to become hypotonic and fluid to be pulled out of the bloodstream into the cells and the interstitial spaces, which produces significant drinking. It is interesting to note that drinking occurs in such conditions even though the intracellular fluid levels are *higher* than normal. Under these conditions hypovolemia apparently overrides cellular overhydration.

At least two different signals exist for hypovolemic thirst, one of which is produced as the blood volume to the kidney is reduced (Fitzsimons, 1971). The kidney responds to a reduced volume of blood by secreting an enzyme called **renin.** When released into the circulation, renin converts a liver product **angiotensinogen** into the hormone **angiotensin II.** Alan Epstein and colleagues (1970) demonstrated that small amounts of angiotensin II applied directly to the brain produced immediate and dramatic drinking in water-satiated rats. In 1973 John Simpson and Aryeh Routtenberg presented evidence that the critical receptor in the brain for angiotensin II was a small structure just below the fornix that projected into the ventricle, known simply as the **subfornical organ (SFO).**

Since these initial findings many different research efforts have attempted to discover if the SFO is really the main receptor for angiotensin II and if angiotensin II plays an important role in normal drinking. In general, the research supports both of these conclusions, although some controversy still exists as to whether the SFO is the only receptor in the brain for angiotensin II. Angiotensin II also has direct effects on the adrenal cortex, causing it to secrete another hormone, aldosterone, which acts to increase sodium ion retention by the kidney. The increased Na^+ retention in turn pulls water back into the bloodstream.

Hypovolemia also produces a second set of signals. Sensitive pressure receptors, called **baroreceptors,** are found in the walls of the heart and the carotid arteries, the main blood vessels supplying the brain. They are sensitive to the degree of stretch of the wall of the vessel or heart in which they are located. When blood volume falls, because of the loss of fluid, these baroreceptors signal this event to the brain via the vagus nerves. Such signals cause drinking as well as the release of ADH. Figure 8.3 summarizes the double depletion theory of thirst.

Hunger

Just as the fluids of the body must be replenished continually, so too must animals eat to replace energy stores and materials needed to sustain life. Although many different reasons are given for people eating the food they do, and the quantities they do, in this section we are concerned primarily with the biological influences on hunger, food consumption, and weight regulation.

Much of the research on the regulation of food intake has dealt with the initiation and cessation of eating—that is, hunger and satiation. Weight

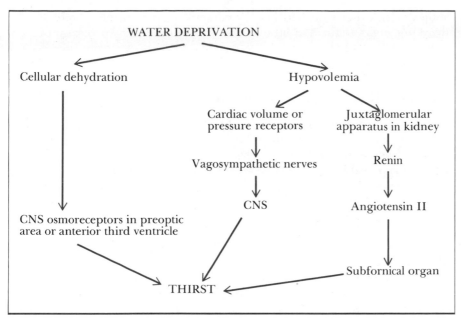

Figure 8.3 The double-depletion theory of thirst—summary diagram.

homeostasis (home-ee-oh-STAY-sis) The tendency of a system to maintain internal stability.

regulation is a related topic. Animals usually maintain their weight within narrow limits even when given unlimited amounts of food. However, obesity is a problem for many individuals in the developed countries. In our discussion of these various topics, one general idea recurs, the concept of **homeostasis,** introduced by Claude Bernard in the nineteenth century. Homeostasis is the tendency of a system to maintain internal stability. In terms of weight regulation, it is usually assumed that various physiologic processes combine to maintain body weight close to some baseline "set point." If food is not readily available, this theory predicts that various processes will be set into motion that will conserve bodily stores of energy and that weight loss will slow down. This can be a problem for some dieters, because some obese individuals continue to maintain abnormal levels of body fat even though their food intake is no greater than that of normal-weight individuals (Braitman et al., 1985).

Many things can interfere with homeostatic regulation of eating. Human beings, along with many other animals, eat more of a preferred food than of less palatable ones. The taste of food, independent of its food value, is a powerful determinant of eating and thus of body weight. The subjective evaluation of how good a particular food tastes seems to vary with the subject's hunger. Michel Cabanac (1971) demonstrated that the rating an individual gives a sweet taste or smell depends in a systematic way on how hungry that individual is and on the individual's body weight. For example, sweet tastes are rated as much less pleasant after subjects drink sugar water than when they are hungry. But if this same experiment was done with

glycogen (GLY-ko-jen) A form of stored glucose.

adipose tissue (ADD-ih-pose) Fat tissue.

insulin (IN-sool-in) Hormone secreted by the pancreas.

subjects on a diet who had lost 10 percent of their prediet body weight, drinking sugar water had little or no effect on the judged pleasantness of sweet tastes or smells.

The Two Basic Phases of Metabolism

Before we continue our discussion of the controls of eating, let us consider what happens to nutrients while they are being absorbed from the intestine during what is termed the *absorptive* phase and how the body responds when this phase is over and the *fasting* phase has begun.

Absorptive Phase

In the absorptive phase nutrients in the diet that enter the bloodstream after digestion are used as energy or as building blocks in various tissues, or they are stored, mostly as fat. The main energy source for the body is *glucose,* which is derived from carbohydrates and excess protein in the diet and is either burned as energy or stored. Excess glucose and amino acids are stored in the form of **glycogen** in the muscles and adipose tissue. Glycogen can also be converted into fat in **adipose tissue.** Fats in the diet are stored in adipose tissue (except in untreated diabetics who use fats as fuel, since they cannot use glucose or amino acids in a normal fashion) (Carlson, 1986). The entry of glucose and amino acids into the cells of the body depends on the presence of **insulin,** a hormone secreted from the pancreas in response to nutrients in the bloodstream and in *anticipation* of eating. Insulin is not needed for glucose to enter most brain cells.

Fasting Phase

Once the nutrients from a particular meal have been processed, the body begins to live on its stored energy reserves, during the fasting phase. (This phase may not last long in individuals who tend to overeat.) During this time, when no nutrients are available in the intestine, most of the body cells use energy in the form of *free fatty acids* (FFA) and glucose, derived from stored fat. The brain can use only glucose, not FFA. Under prolonged fasting, the brain can use ketones, which the liver makes from FFA, but normally it feeds exclusively on glucose. The fact that the brain feeds almost exclusively on glucose has been important to the development of theories of eating.

The Search for Hunger and Satiety Signals

It is widely assumed that food-related signals are important in initiating and stopping eating, particularly on a short-term basis. These short-term signals are thought to be important in regulating the size of individual meals and to be different from those that control body weight over longer periods of time. As he did for thirst, Walter Cannon formalized some commonsense assumptions into a theory based on stomach sensations as the signals for short-term hunger and **satiety.**

Cannon and Washburn (1912) performed an experiment in which human subjects swallowed an uninflated balloon attached to a device that could record the movements of the stomach after the balloon was inflated inside their stomachs. They found that stomach contractions were somewhat (but not perfectly) related to reports of hunger pangs by the subjects. Subsequently, however, considerable evidence has accumulated to suggest such stomach contractions probably play little or no role in most hunger sensations or in the control of eating. For example, cancer patients who have had their stomachs surgically removed still get hungry (Wagensteen and Carlson, 1931). The vagus nerves are the only neural connections between the stomach and the brain. Cutting them (an operation termed **vagotomy**) does not eliminate hunger sensations or the regulation of food intake (Thompson, 1980). Finally, hunger and eating occur in the absence of any stomach contractions.

satiety (Sah-TY-ih-tee) The feeling of having had enough, particularly of food or water.

vagotomy (Vay-GOT-ah-me) Cutting of the vagus nerve.

Glucose as a Signal

Glucose has been implicated repeatedly in the control of eating. As mentioned earlier, it is the only fuel used by brain cells, except during a prolonged fast. Other body cells can use either free fatty acids or ketone bodies. Brain cells cannot store significant amounts of energy and require a steady stream of glucose to function normally. In fact, the overall physiology of the body places the brain in a favored position, since it is supplied with glucose even when the rest of the body is starving. Another important difference between brain cells and cells in other parts of the body is that the great majority of brain cells do not need insulin in order to take up glucose from the bloodstream. The brain is preferentially supplied with glucose when nutrient levels fall because insulin levels fall with hunger. Thus only the brain can use the glucose that is made available from conversion of fats during fasting.

The central role of glucose in the economy of the brain has placed it at the center of a major theory of hunger, the *glucostatic* theory of Jean Mayer (Mayer, 1953; 1955). According to this theory, hunger and satiety depend on the rate of glucose utilization in the body. Immediately following a meal, when adequate glucose is available to the cells in the body and glucose utilization is high, satiety should prevail. Conversely, as the hours go by without additional food, most of the glucose is used or stored, insulin levels drop, the rate of glucose utilization goes down, and hunger recurs.

Mayer proposed that a useful measure of glucose utilization would be to compare glucose levels in the arteries, which deliver materials to the cells, with glucose levels in the veins, which drain the cells. This measurement is usually termed the A–V (artery–vein) ratio. If much more glucose is in the arteries than in the veins (high A–V ratio), glucose utilization should be adequate and satiety should occur. If, however, only slightly more glucose is in the arteries than in the veins (low A–V ratio), then not much glucose is utilized by the cells and hunger should occur. Several experiments have shown that this is indeed the case (Thompson, 1980).

Moreover, Mayer's theory seems to account for the increase in hunger in untreated diabetics. Although diabetes covers a complex family of diseases, still incompletely understood, it is known that many diabetics produce an insufficient amount of insulin. Since insulin is necessary for body cells to absorb glucose, untreated diabetics have abnormally high blood glucose levels, even though the cells of the body are starved for glucose. Thus although the absolute level of glucose in the arteries is high, the A–V ratio is low, because little or no glucose has been removed by the body cells. Mayer's theory predicts that untreated diabetics should be constantly hungry, despite high absolute levels of glucose in the arteries, and this is generally the case.

Mayer further proposed that particular cells in the hypothalamus are responsible for monitoring glucose levels and for triggering hunger sensations and eating behaviors. The proposal that hunger and eating are triggered by the hypothalamus was controversial, since brain cells do not need insulin to take up glucose and thus would not reflect the situation in the rest of the body. Fortunately for Mayer's theory, he also found evidence (which recently has been supported) that a few cells in the hypothalamus do seem to require insulin to incorporate glucose. These cells are influenced by glucose levels in the arteries and alter their responses in the presence or absence of insulin, in a fashion similar to body cells (Oomura et al., 1979).

Not all the evidence relevant to Mayer's theory is supportive, however. Preloading hungry animals with glucose, according to the theory, should reduce subsequent food intake, which it does not do reliably. Moreover, injections of glucose directly into the areas of the hypothalamus thought to contain glucose receptors do not reliably reduce food intake (Novin, 1976). Several theorists have pointed out that the glucose supply to the brain does not fluctuate much between meals and that it seems unlikely that the small fluctuations in blood glucose levels could account for eating behavior.

Recent findings by Donald Novin (1979) put a new twist on the glucose theory. It is not easy to generalize about the effects of glucose administration, for as he reports, "depending upon a complex interaction of factors such as nutritional state, route of infusion, time of day and amount given, glucose can depress, enhance or have no effect on subsequent food intake." For example, glucose administration actually can *increase* food intake in the rabbit. Moreover, the amount of glucose administered seems significant, for although 10 ml of a 5 percent glucose solution suppressed feeding, 30 ml *increased* it! Novin speculates that this seemingly paradoxical finding may be due to excessive insulin secretion produced by the larger glucose load, resulting in a "rebound" lowering of blood glucose as it is driven into the cells by the surge of insulin.

Liver Glucose Receptors

In addition to the glucose receptors in the hypothalamus, glucose-sensitive neurons are found in the liver (Niijima, 1969) and in the duodenum of the small intestine (Novin, 1979). Mauricio Russek (1971) emphasized the importance of the liver receptors, proposing that the liver is important for monitoring blood glucose levels and sending satiety signals to the brain.

By controlling the site of glucose infusions, it is possible to determine whether the liver or duodenal receptors are more effective in altering food intake in response to glucose. The liver is supplied with blood primarily through the hepatic-portal circulation, and substances injected into this system are carried directly into the liver. Glucose can be introduced into the duodenum with cannulas placed directly into the small intestine. Both the duodenal and the liver receptors respond to different glucose levels, but they differ in their effect on food intake, depending on how hungry the animal is. For example, in rabbits allowed free access to food, the receptors in the duodenum appear to be more important in suppressing food intake in response to glucose infusions than do the liver receptors. However, the same duodenal infusions of glucose are relatively ineffective in suppressing food intake if the rabbits are deprived of food for 24 hours (Novin, 1976). The importance of glucose as a satiety signal thus seems to depend on its proportion in the diet and on how hungry the animal is.

Cholecystokinin: A Satiety Substance?

In the past few years a hormone, **cholecystokinin (CCK),** secreted from the duodenum of the small intestine has been reported to have hunger-reducing properties in several different species, including human beings. The term *cholecystokinin* is actually applied to a heterogeneous group of hormones. The original substance isolated from the small intestine contains 33 amino acids, but it is now thought that shorter strings of CCK are also effective as hormones. In particular, CCK-8 and CCK-4 are eight- and four-amino acid hormones, respectively, which are part of CCK-33. (Chapter 9 has more information on hormones.) In the experiments on hunger reduction CCK-8 and CCK-33 proved to be most effective.

It was first reported in the early 1970s that CCK could reduce the amount of food eaten by rats, in comparison with control rats that had been deprived of food for equivalent periods of time. Evidence that this was not simply a result of making the rats ill came from an experiment by Joseph Antin and colleagues (1975). They found that CCK-33 injected into the abdominal cavity not only caused the rats to eat less than controls, but CCK-33 also elicited the normal satiety sequence of grooming and sleeping normal rats show after meals.

Subsequent experiments demonstrated that reduction in food intake followed CCK injections in several different species, including mice, rabbits, sheep, and monkeys. Reports on the effect of CCK with human subjects have been mixed. Both decreases and increases have been reported. It appears, however, that low doses of CCK-8 injected slowly into the blood-

cholecystokinin (COLA-sis-toe-kine-in) A term for several hormones secreted by the duodenum of the small intestine that have satiety-producing effects in several species, including human beings.

stream do decrease food intake in human subjects and that this decrease is not caused by feelings of illness. This result has been reported for normal, nonobese men (Kissileff et al., 1981) and for obese men (Pi-Sunyer et al., 1982). If these results are replicated and if no unwanted side effects are found, CCK-8 (which is a natural secretion of our intestines) could be significant in the treatment of obesity.

It appears that CCK does not signal satiety directly to the brain but instead activates receptors in the intestine, which in turn send nerve impulses to the brain via the vagus nerves. This conclusion is based on experiments that demonstrated that the satiety effect of CCK in rats is eliminated by cutting the vagus nerves (Smith et al., 1981; Lorenz and Goldman, 1982).

Overeating Without Increased Hunger

It has been reported from time to time since the nineteenth century that gross disturbances in food intake and weight regulation (as well as personality changes) sometimes occur as a result of brain tumors or other damage near the base of the brain in the region of the ventral medial hypothalamus (see Figure 8.4). As is true for most naturally occurring lesions, the damage is not localized to anatomically precise boundaries. In 1942 A. W. Hetherington and S. W. Ranson reported that experimental lesions in the ventral medial nucleus of the hypothalamus in rats produced a startling change in eating and weight regulation. Their basic finding has been replicated several times, although a precise explanation for this *VMH (ventromedial hypothalamus) syndrome* still eludes us.

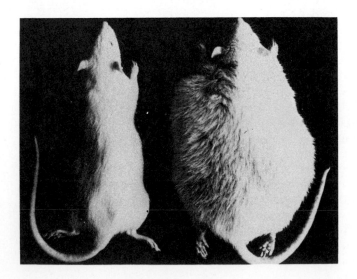

Figure 8.4   Obesity produced by hypothalamic hyperphagia.
Rat on the right had bilateral lesions of the ventromedial region of the hypothalamus four months previously. It is in the static phase and weighs 640 g. The control animal on the left is the same age and fed on the same diet. It weighs 290 g.

Although the details of the syndrome vary somewhat with different experimental conditions, there is general agreement on its basic features. If palatable food is available, rats with VMH lesions begin to eat voraciously, sometimes even before they are completely recovered from the anesthesia of surgery. Such animals continue to overeat for several weeks, often doubling their preoperative weight. This excessive eating is called **hyperphagia;** after this initial phase of hyperphagia food intake drops to levels only slightly higher than before surgery. Thus the VMH syndrome has two phases, a *dynamic* phase, in which animals overeat and gain weight rapidly, and a *static* phase, in which the rate of weight gain and of food intake decreases to just above preoperative levels. The rapid weight gain is due primarily to increased body fat. The fat in VMH rats can approach 74 percent of body weight, compared with 5–10 percent for normal rats (Grossman, 1967).

hyperphagia (high-per-FAYJ-ee-ah) Overeating.

Are VMH Rats Not Really Hungry?

In addition to hyperphagia, VMH rats display *finickiness.* Terry Powley (1977) defines finickiness as the "behavioral trait of food intake being inordinately influenced by the sensory, as opposed to the caloric, or post-ingestional, aspects of foodstuffs." VMH rats fed on a high-fat diet or a sweet-tasting diet tend to eat much more than VMH rats fed on standard lab chow. If the diet is bitter or too salty, VMH rats actually eat less than normal rats. It is thus hard to conclude that they are simply hungrier than normals. The finickiness of VMH rats extends to the texture of the food. They eat much less laboratory chow if it is powdered, a texture rats do not favor. Their hyperphagia seems unrelated to their simply being hungrier.

The VMH Syndrome and Human Obesity

Obesity in human beings is typically defined as a body weight of 15 percent or more over ideal body weight as determined from life insurance tables. Several investigators have wondered if there is any relationship between such an overweight condition in human beings and the symptoms seen in the VMH syndrome. Obesity in humans is rarely caused by actual damage to the hypothalamus, although such cases do exist. Jules Hirsch (1984) has presented evidence that some forms of obesity may occur as the aftermath of viral infections of the nervous system that leave subtle but long-lasting effects on the hypothalamus.

The observation of finickiness in VMH rats has suggested to some researchers that obese human beings might also be "inordinately influenced by the sensory aspects of foodstuffs." This finickiness might contribute to overeating and obesity if good-tasting food is continually available. Stanley Schacter (1971) and his colleagues performed a number of experiments with mildly to moderately obese people (15–25 percent overweight) to test this hypothesis. In a typical study Schacter and his co-workers found that obese individuals did consume more of a good-tasting milkshake than did normal-weight subjects. However, when the experimenters adulterated the milkshakes with quinine to make them taste somewhat bitter, the obese subjects consumed only about half the amount drunk by control subjects.

In recent years, however, support for this hypothesis has weakened. Judith Rodin, a former colleague of Schacter, has reviewed the research on this subject and concluded that the evidence suggests that some people in all weight categories, not just the obese, are highly responsive to external food cues (Rodin, 1976; 1978; Novin, 1979). Moreover, when group averages are used, a surprising relationship is revealed. Although several experiments support the idea that *moderately* obese people (15–25 percent overweight) tend to be more responsive to external food cues than normal-weight individuals, *extremely* obese people (50 percent or more over norms) are, on average, *less* responsive to external food cues than moderately obese persons.

Is Insulin the Link?

If some people are indeed more responsive than normal to external food cues, how might this be related to increased appetite and greater eating? One answer may be they *secrete more insulin in response to food cues.* Increased insulin secretion is known to increase appetite.

In a test of this idea Judith Rodin (1976) found that individuals who are more responsive to external cues than normals (as determined by several perceptual measures) did secrete significantly more insulin than normal subjects as they watched, heard, and smelled their luncheon steak sizzle and pop on the stove. Such individuals, overweight or not, also were found to secrete more insulin in response to the taste of various pastries. Still more support for the idea of hypersecretion of insulin by obese individuals has been presented by William Johnson and Hal Wildman (1983). They compared insulin levels in four obese individuals and six normal-weight subjects. Insulin responses were measured to the presentation of an actual meal (which the subjects were not allowed to eat until measurements were made). In addition, subjects were instructed to imagine a highly desirable meal, and their insulin levels were measured as they thought about it. The experimenters found that obese subjects secreted more insulin in response both to actual food and to their own imagined meal. Interestingly, obese subjects tended to secrete slightly more insulin to the imaginary meal than to the real one.

Increased secretion of insulin has a number of effects on the body. The most relevant for our discussion is the facilitation of glucose entry into cells, thereby lowering blood glucose levels and increasing hunger. Thus if individuals secrete insulin at the beginning of a meal, appetite should increase, particularly if the food is rich in "good food cues." As Rodin points out, this may limit the effectiveness of good-tasting low-calorie diet foods, since the food cues serve to increase insulin secretion, thereby driving glucose into the cells, increasing appetite, and causing the person to eat more.

We have moved from the finickiness of VMH rats to the possible role of increased insulin secretion in human beings who are overly influenced by external food cues. Can we move back to a consideration of the VMH rats and apply a similar logic? That is, is there an increased secretion of insulin in VMH rats in response to food or food-related cues? The answer seems to be yes, VMH rats do seem to secrete more insulin than normals in response to food cues, and this may be related directly to their overeating and weight gain (Thompson, 1980).

Insulin has long been suspected as a possible signal for hunger and satiety, but its role has been unclear, since the circumstances under which it is released are complicated. Terry Powley (1977) has emphasized that a series of bodily responses are involved in the digestion of food. These responses start before the food actually reaches the stomach. Powley has termed these **cephalic** responses, to emphasize the role of cephalic (head) receptors (located in the eyes, nose, and mouth) in initiating the digestive responses of increased secretion of saliva, gastric juices, and insulin. In addition to these digestive responses, there are reflexive ("wired in") cephalic responses of rejection for bad-tasting or disgusting substances. Powley suggests that the primary effect of VMH lesions in rats is to cause an exaggeration of both positive and negative cephalic digestive responses, resulting in a heightened response to the sensory aspects of food—in a word, finickiness. As a result of these increased cephalic responses, VMH rats eat more of good-tasting foods but less of bad-tasting foods.

Another aspect of insulin secretion is the increased entry of glucose and other nutrients into cells in the body, particularly fat cells. Insulin injected into normal animals reliably increases eating. If insulin injections are continued, animals become obese. Thus if insulin secretion is increased in VMH rats, more glucose should enter fat cells and these animals should become obese, if they are provided with a palatable diet. If the diet is unpalatable, obesity should not occur. These are precisely the results generally observed. From this perspective finickiness, hyperphagia, and obesity—the three cardinal features of the VMH syndrome—can be related to the increase in the cephalic digestive responses and particularly to insulin secretion (Powley, 1977). In other words, the lesion appears to lock animals into the absorptive phase of digestion.

Other theorists have also emphasized the metabolic and physiologic responses that result from VMH lesions. Insulin secretion appears to be greater in VMH rats, in response not only to the sight and smell of food but to the presence of food in the stomach (Friedman and Stricker, 1976). Since this increased insulin facilitates glucose entry into cells, it deprives the VMH animal of the normal satiating effect of glucose in the arteries. From this point of view one could say that rather than VMH rats getting fat because they are eating too much, they eat too much because they are getting fat. Likewise, human beings who are overresponsive to the smell, sight, taste, and thought of food, because of either their genetic makeup or conditioning, may secrete too much insulin and face problems similar to those encountered by VMH rats.

Other physiologic changes with VMH lesions may also contribute to

cephalic (suh-FAL-ik) Pertaining to the head.

prandial drinking
(PRAN-dee-al) Drinking initiated by eating dry food.

weight gain. For example, Duggan and Booth (1986) found that rats with VMH lesions show more rapid emptying of the stomach than normal rats, which would also be likely to short-circuit the normal processes of satiety.

The Lateral Hypothalamic Syndrome: Rats That Won't Eat or Drink

About 10 years after it was reported that VMH lesions could unleash voracious eating, B. K. Anand and J. R. Brobeck (1951) reported the "mirror-image" syndrome from lesions in the lateral hypothalamus. They found that after such lesions rats would neither eat nor drink, although if properly nursed through the first few weeks, some recovery would occur. The initial reports of this syndrome emphasized the effects on eating and drinking, but subsequent research has demonstrated that the behavioral effects are, in fact, much more widespread, and these lesions produce a dramatic decrease in the responsiveness of animals to virtually all motivating stimuli, including food, water, prospective sexual partners, and potentially dangerous stimuli. These animals are not comotose or unable to move; they just appear unresponsive to most external stimuli.

The "recovery" process has attracted the most attention. (It is not really accurate to speak of the recovery of these animals, for they never regain their ability to regulate their body fluids, nor do they respond normally in other ways with respect to food.) Alan Epstein (1971) divides recovery into four stages (see Figure 8.5).

The final stage of the lateral hypothalamic (LH) syndrome is marked by a permanent failure to eat when the animals are deprived of glucose by insulin injections or to maintain even reduced body weight levels when the food available is only minimally palatable. What drinking these animals do is related to the eating of dry food, termed **prandial drinking** (from the Latin *prandium*, "meal"), which is the sipping of water in order to wet the mouth and throat so that dry food can be swallowed more easily. This is about the only drinking that LH rats do, even in the final stages of "recovery." The amount of salivation in normal rats is sufficient so that they do not need to drink as they eat. Instead normal rats drink their water supply either before or after dry-food meals.

However, LH rats do not secrete normal levels of saliva, and they become prandial drinkers if fed on a dry-food diet. If they are fed on a liquid diet, they never drink water. On dry lab food, they take a sip of water with virtually every bite of food, 400–600 tiny sips and bites each day. If LH rats are deprived of what saliva they can produce by removing their salivary glands, they increase their prandial drinking. But this apparent improvement in water intake is deceptive; LH rats do not regulate their water intake according to their body fluid needs, and if they are deprived of water, they do not drink more when it is again available. It appears that LH rats have permanently lost the urge to drink, and only the prandial drinking forced on them by a chronically dry mouth allows them to drink enough to survive.

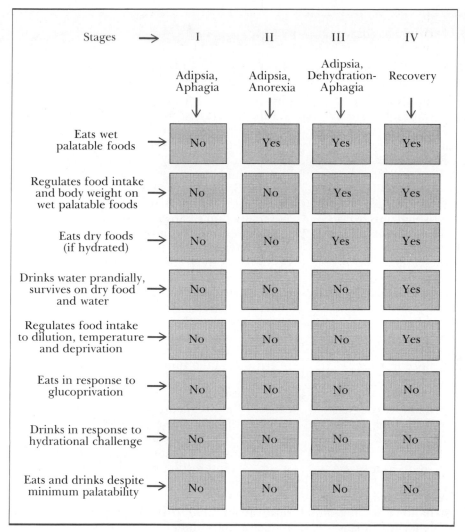

Stages →	I	II	III	IV
	Adipsia, Aphagia ↓	Adipsia, Anorexia ↓	Adipsia, Dehydration-Aphagia ↓	Recovery ↓
Eats wet palatable foods →	No	Yes	Yes	Yes
Regulates food intake and body weight on wet palatable foods →	No	No	Yes	Yes
Eats dry foods (if hydrated) →	No	No	Yes	Yes
Drinks water prandially, survives on dry food and water →	No	No	No	Yes
Regulates food intake to dilution, temperature and deprivation →	No	No	No	Yes
Eats in response to glucoprivation →	No	No	No	No
Drinks in response to hydrational challenge →	No	No	No	No
Eats and drinks despite minimum palatability →	No	No	No	No

Figure 8.5   The stages of recovery of the lateral hypothalamic syndrome.

"Recovered" LH rats do not return to normal eating either. If nursed, they eventually reach a stage at which they survive on dry food and water, but at reduced weights. Richard Keesey and his colleagues have suggested that LH rats have a lowered "set point" for body weight (Keesey et al., 1976; Keesey and Powley, 1975). In support of the lowered set-point hypothesis these investigators have reported that if the body weights of normal rats are lowered *before* the lateral hypothalamus is lesioned, these rats undergo a much shorter period of aphagia and occasionally show *increased* eating following surgery. In one such experiment LH lesions in normal body weight rats resulted in animals that maintained their weight at the 90

Anorexia Nervosa:
A Relentless Pursuit of Thinness

Anorexia nervosa is an eating disorder in which the patient displays a morbid fear of gaining weight, does not eat properly, and suffers a variety of physical problems associated with an inadequate diet. Although it is generally considered to be a recent phenomenon, an English physician named Richard Morton described a woman who refused to eat properly and resembled a "skeleton only clad with skin" in 1689 (Garfield, 1984). It is not known if this woman would meet modern diagnostic criteria for anorexia, however, as pathological eating can also be seen in patients with mental illness and in some patients with hypothalamic or pituitary disease. The term *anorexia nervosa* was invented by another English physician, William Gull, in the 1870s. Actually, the term, which means "nervous loss of appetite," is misleading, since in most cases it is the patient's eating, not his or her appetite, that is abnormal.

Not all physicians and psychologists agree on the diagnostic criteria for anorexia, but in general, they include a fear of weight gain, an unrealistic body image, refusal to eat enough to maintain normal weight, and serious weight loss, usually somewhere around 20–25 percent of normal body weight. In addition, in women, cessation of menstruation is a symptom of anorexia. Although the majority of diagnosed cases of anorexia are adolescent females, males account for 5–10 percent of cases. It is estimated that as many as one in 200 teen-age girls is anorexic. Until recently, most anorexics were white adolescent females from the middle and upper socioeconomic classes, but this disease is now being reported in all social classes, in men and women past adolescence, and in children.

What brings about this "relentless pursuit of thinness," as Hilda Bruch (1973) has called it? We really don't know. Several different hypotheses have been proposed. Bruch stresses that anorexics typically have a sense of personal ineffectiveness and that by controlling their diet and body weight, they can gain some mastery over themselves. In addition, anorexics can use their extreme dieting in power games within the family. Still other theorists believe that anorexia is a form of depression. The possibility of an abnormality in hypothalamic function has also been suggested. However, no single hypothesis seems to account for all the facts, and the causes of anorexia are still not understood.

Some theorists have stressed the popular image of the desirability and "sexiness" of thinness of models, movie stars, rock stars, and so on. An interesting study by Garner and colleagues (1980) showed that the "vital statistics" in *Playboy* centerfold models went down from 1960 to 1980. The models chosen tended to be thinner, more "tubular" in body shape than had been the case previously. This may be representative of a general emphasis on thinness in our society.

anorexia nervosa (ann-or-EKS-ee-ah nur-VOSE-ah) Condition in which patients do not eat enough to sustain normal body weight. Cause unknown.

percent level. Other animals that were reduced to 80 percent of body weight before surgery actually ate *more* than normals after surgery until they too reached the 90 percent body weight level, which they then defended.

The reduced food intake in LH rats appears to be due to an active rejection of food in the early postoperative stages, which gives way to a heightened finickiness later on. LH rats do not increase their food intake when challenged with insulin and thus do not return to normal eating.

The LH syndrome is probably due in part to the interruption of axons that ascend to parts of the forebrain, traveling through the lateral hypo-

The weight loss and inadequate diet produce a variety of symptoms in anorexics. As mentioned earlier, menstruation typically ceases in anorexic women. The hormones that control reproductive function decrease to prepubertal levels, and the pattern of the secretion of these hormones comes to resemble that of girls of 8–10 years of age. With appropriate weight gain the adult pattern and levels are regained. Male anorexics have low sperm counts and low levels of testosterone. In about 25 percent of female anorexics, menstruation ceases before there has been any significant weight loss, which has caused some theorists to suggest that at least in some individuals the maturation of the hypothalamus that triggers puberty may not have been quite normal.

Other physical symptoms of anorexia include an abnormal sensitivity to cold (patients often shiver and wear sweaters even on warm days), abnormally low heart rates and blood pressure, and in some cases a condition in which a fine, downy hair (**lanugo hair**), similar to that seen during fetal development, grows all over the body. In anorexics who vomit to control their weight (and even in some anorexics who do not), the loss of potassium in the body fluids can lead to serious heart problems and can contribute to death from heart failure. Several other hormonal abnormalities are common, but most of these problems disappear with weight gain to normal levels, although normal function may lag the return to normal weight by months or even years.

A condition related to anorexia is **bulimia,** characterized by rapid "binge" eating, often followed by induced vomiting. Bulimia can also occur in individuals of normal weight and is recognized as a separate condition that can occur without the other symptoms of anorexia. As is true for anorexia, bulimia is not understood, although many therapists find that it is associated with depression. It is unknown whether the bulimia is a cause of the depression, the depression causes the bulimia, or both are a result of another underlying condition.

Treatment for anorexia generally requires some program that will bring the patient's weight back toward normal. Behavioral control programs that reward weight gain (not just eating, because anorexics can often eat and vomit to stay thin) are common. Some drug therapy is used, particularly if the anorexia is seen as part of a more pathologic condition. Hospitalization is required in severe cases until some significant weight gain has been achieved. Surveys of various therapeutic programs reveal that about 40 percent of the patients show good progress, another 30 percent show fair progress, and about 30 percent show little progress. The death rate is about 5–10 percent, often from heart failure or infectious disease.

thalamus from their origin in the brainstem. Much of the LH syndrome can be produced with neural toxins that selectively destroy norepinephrine and dopamine neurons. The tract most commonly implicated is the nigrostriatal bundle, which projects from the substantia nigra in the brainstem to terminals in the basal ganglia (also termed the *striatum*) (Stricker and Zigmond, 1976). The importance of neurons in the lateral hypothalamic nuclei themselves is still undetermined. The LH syndrome can be produced with knife cuts that sever the axons running through the lateral hypothalamus without seriously affecting the nuclei themselves. On the

lanugo hair (lah-NU-go) A fine, downy hair often found on the skin of fetuses. Sometimes also found in anorexia nervosa patients.

bulimia (bu-LEEM-e-ah) Binge eating.

When does a concern with staying slim become anorexia nervosa? This young woman may be seeing her image in the mirror as that of someone who still needs to lose more weight. If so, she may be in danger of developing anorexia, a condition marked by unrealistic perception of one's own body image and drastically reduced food intake, along with other problems

other hand, Sebastian Grossman and colleagues (1978) have seen aphagia and adipsia following kainic acid lesions of lateral hypothalamus. Such lesions are thought not to impair fibers of passage, preferentially destroying only nerve cell bodies. However, since even this issue is uncertain, conclusions about the exact neural substrate underlying the LH syndrome remain tentative.

Set Point and the Regulation of Body Weight

Although obesity is a problem for a large number of people, most organisms, including human beings, actually maintain their weight within fairly narrow levels once they have become adults. Weight regulation can break down in illness or with obesity, but it is remarkable how well most organisms maintain a particular weight level without much conscious effort and in the presence of plentiful and good-tasting food. Since fluctuations in body weight are due primarily to additions or deletions from the body's fat deposits, many theorists have suggested that some sort of signal regarding the state of those fat deposits must be involved in the long-term regulation of eating and weight levels. One of the best known of these suggestions is the hypothesis of G. C. Kennedy (1950; 1966), who proposed that the level of fat in the body is monitored by lipostats somewhere in the brain. He suggested that when fat deposits reach a certain point, food intake is reduced, and when fat deposits become depleted (as in prolonged fasting or starvation), the lipostats trigger increased hunger and eating until normal weight levels are regained. Normal weight levels are considered to fluctuate around some set point, determined by genetic instructions, but modifiable by experience.

A set-point theory of weight regulation has not gone unchallenged. David Wirtshafter and John Davis (1977) have pointed out some of the weaknesses of the set-point idea and offer a theoretical model that accounts for existing data without reference to any set point. One additional value of their model is that it accounts for changes in food intake with changes in palatability of the diet, which is a problem for most set-point theories.

How can the brain know how fat the body is? Fat itself does not circulate through the bloodstream, and thus whatever is monitored must be some substance that reflects fat levels. Although glucose is the primary fuel for the brain, the body stores extremely tiny amounts of energy as glucose. Most of the energy reserves of the body are stored as fat, on which the body feeds when other energy sources are not available, as during fasting. Only when the fat reserves are quite low do other tissues, such as muscles, begin to be metabolized for energy.

Fat is stored in various parts of the body in the form of triglycerides and is released into the bloodstream as free fatty acids and glycerol. These substances are released from fat depots by the action of hormones such as epinephrine. The liver then converts glycerol into glucose, which is used to keep the brain well supplied even during fasting. Thus we have at least two candidates for a bloodstream substance that could be monitored to reflect the state of the fat deposits in the body—free fatty acids and glycerol.

The popular image of thinness as desirable brings a host of over-the-counter dietary aids to public attention.

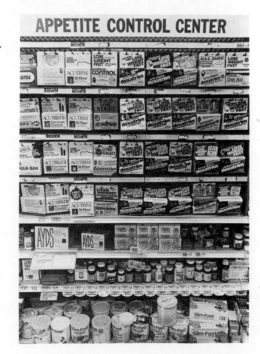

The level of free fatty acids increases in the bloodstream under a variety of conditions, including hunger (fasting phase), exercise, stress, and exposure to cold (Thompson, 1980). The idea that free fatty acids could be useful as signals was supported by Yutaka Oomura and colleagues (1979), who discovered neurons in both the medial and lateral hypothalamus that changed their firing pattern to alterations in free fatty acid levels.

It is still not understood what signals may be used by the brain to monitor fat levels, if indeed such levels are monitored at all. No single theory can account for the facts of long-term weight regulation or the absence of such regulation. One approach that shows some promise is the multifactor hypothesis of Mark Friedman and Edward Stricker (1976), who reject the idea that glucose can be the only signal controlling hunger and satiety, largely because the glucose levels in the brain probably do not fluctuate as much as is true for the rest of the body. They suggest that it is more likely that hunger is a response to a decrease in the utilization of *all* available food fuels, including glucose, free fatty acids, and amino acids.

SUMMARY

1. Proper levels of both food and water are critical for survival, and organisms have built-in controls that regulate food and water intake.
2. A dry mouth and throat may serve to tell us when to drink, but experiments have demonstrated that they are not important in regulating how much water we drink.
3. Thirst and water intake seem to depend on the fluid levels in both the intracellular and extracellular compartments of the body. Cellular dehydration is thought to be signaled by osmoreceptors located primarily in the lateral preoptic area, just anterior to the hypothalamus. Extracellular dehydration, or hypovolemia, is signaled in part by the release of the hormone renin by the kidney. Renin converts angiotensinogen into angiotensin II, which triggers thirst and drinking. Hypovolemia can also produce thirst, drinking, and the release of antidiuretic hormone (ADH) from the posterior pituitary. The signals for these responses are sent by stretch receptors sensitive to blood volume in the walls of the heart and carotid arteries.
4. Two basic phases of metabolism occur, an absorptive phase and a fasting phase. In the absorptive phase nutrients enter the bloodstream and are used as energy, incorporated into cellular structures such as proteins, or stored (mostly as fat). In the fasting phase, when no nutrients are available in the intestine, the body cells derive their energy needs from stored fats in the form of either free fatty acids or glucose. Under all but extreme fasting circumstances the brain uses glucose only.
5. The search for hunger and satiety signals has followed several different paths. The ratio of glucose levels in the arteries to those in the veins has been proposed as one such signal. Cholecystokinin, a hormone secreted by the intestine, has also been proposed as a satiety signal.

Sensory receptors in the liver may be important for transmitting information about nutrient levels in the blood to the brain, as both glucose and cholecystokinin regulation of food intake are disrupted by cutting the vagus nerve which connects the liver and the brain.

6. Lesions in the hypothalamus can produce dramatic effects on eating and weight regulation. Both obesity and self-starvation have been observed in rats following lesions in different parts of the hypothalamus. A disturbance in the secretion of the hormone insulin by the pancreas following damage to the ventromedial nucleus of the hypothalamus may account for the overeating and weight gain that follow such damage.

7. Damage to the lateral hypothalamus causes rats to lose much of their desire to eat and drink. Even in the "recovered" stage, they tend to drink only in order to swallow dry food and do not eat in response to glucose deprivation or drink in response to water deprivation. These changes may be part of a more general loss of responsiveness to all motivating stimuli produced by the brain damage.

8. It appears that human subjects who show increased responsiveness to food cues may do so partly because they secrete higher than normal levels of insulin in the presence of food-related cues, real or imagined. The increased insulin secretion would serve to clear the blood of nutrients and make the individual more hungry. Such increased hunger in the presence of good-tasting food is a recipe for overeating and gaining weight.

9. Anorexia nervosa is characterized as a "relentless pursuit of thinness" and is marked by voluntary restriction of food intake, loss of weight, cessation of menstruation in women, and a variety of hormonal changes. Anorexics may engage in "binge eating," consuming large amounts of food in a short time, followed by self-induced vomiting. Even with intensive therapy, from 5 to 10 percent of anorexic patients die from complications brought about by poor nutrition and weight loss.

10. It has been proposed that organisms regulate their body weight around some basic set point, but this idea has been challenged, and set-point theory has encountered difficulty accounting for changes in weight regulation with changes in the palatability of the diet. Signals that inform the brain about body weight or fat levels are not known, but both free fatty acids and glycerol have been proposed as important indicators of body fat levels.

SUGGESTIONS FOR FURTHER READING

Novin, D., Wyrwicka, W., and Bray, G. A. (Eds.) (1976). *Hunger, basic mechanisms and clinical implications*. New York: Raven Press.

Rolls, B. J., and Rolls, E. T. (1982). *Thirst*. Cambridge: Cambridge University Press.

Thompson, C. I. (1980). *Controls of eating*. New York: SP Medical and Scientific Books.

9

Hormones and Behavior

Preview

Hormones
Target Tissues
Hormone Families
Steroid Receptors
Polypeptide Hormones
Miscellaneous Hormones
Some Factors New: The Hypothalamic Hormones

Sexual Dimorphism in Brains and in Behavior
Cyclicity of Hormonal Secretion: A Female Characteristic
Ovaries in the Eyeballs
Dimorphic Sexual Behavior
Hormones and Female Sexual Behavior
Ovarian Cyclicity
Nursing and the Posterior Pituitary
Hormones and Male Sexual Behavior
Testosterone and Sexual Vigor

Developmental Effects of Hormones on Sexual Behavior
Rat Studies
Primate Studies

Fetal Effects of Testosterone on Human Behavior
The CAH Syndrome
The Androgen Insensitivity Syndrome
The Guevedoces of Salinas [BOX]
Male–Female Differences in Nonreproductive Behavior
Structural Differences in Male and Female Brains

Summary

Suggestions for Further Reading

Up in my head just over my tongue,
a little thing from my brain is hung.
To make it work there are factors new
that tell it when and how much to pitu.

M. SAFFRAN

Preview

Hormones are substances secreted into the bloodstream by various specialized tissues. They affect behavior in two ways. One is by influencing the development of the fetus, including the central nervous system. In particular, hormones from the fetal testes cause the fetus to develop along male lines, whereas the absence of such hormones causes the fetus to develop along female lines. Abnormal hormone levels during fetal development can partially override genetically determined male and female characteristics. Fetal hormones may play a subtle role in the development of gender-related behaviors and feelings in human beings.

The second way in which hormones can affect behavior directly is by interacting with target cells, including neurons (target cells contain receptors sensitive to a particular hormone that cause the cell to respond to the hormone), in the juvenile or adult animal. Sexual behavior in most animals is influenced by hormones; the possible importance of hormones for human sexual desire and behavior has stimulated considerable research. There are no simple answers in this area, and the influence of hormones on human sexual behavior remains uncertain.

Hormones

As computers become more sophisticated, comparisons between the human brain and computers often are made. In at least one important respect, however, such comparisons are misleading. Unlike the microchips in a computer, which operate solely on the basis of electrical signals, the neurons in the human brain are constantly being supplied with a rich soup of different substances delivered to them by the bloodstream. Among these substances are *hormones,* defined as "chemical messengers which travel via the blood to specific target tissues where they cause changes in the activities of the target tissue cells" (Norris, 1980). Hormones influence the activity of cells of virtually all types, including neurons. One main source of hormones is the anterior pituitary gland, which in turn is regulated by hormones secreted by neurons in the hypothalamus of the brain and carried to the anterior lobe of the pituitary gland in a specialized loop of the bloodstream. The fact that the brain itself regulates the anterior pituitary has many implications for understanding the effects of hormones on behavior.

Several different tissues in the body secrete hormones; together they are referred to as the **endocrine system.** Figure 9.1 illustrates the location of these hormone-secreting tissues, which include the pituitary gland, the thyroid gland, the adrenal glands, the pancreas, parts of the intestine, the heart, the gonads, the pineal gland, and neurons in the hypothalamus. The fact that the hypothalamus is part of both the endocrine system and the nervous system underscores the intimate interconnections between them. The connection from the hypothalamus to the pituitary gland can be considered as the final common path through which the brain can influence the rest of the endocrine system. Table 9.1 lists the major components of the endocrine system and some of their representative hormones.

endocrine system (END-o-krin) The collection of glands in the body that secrete hormones into the bloodstream.

Target Tissues

Most cells in the body respond only to some hormones. A cell that responds to a particular hormone is called a *target cell* for that hormone. Whether a

---

TABLE 9.1   Major Endocrine Tissues and Some of Their Representative Hormones

Anterior pituitary	*Adrenal cortex*
ACTH (adrenocorticotropic hormone)*	cortisol
β-endorphin*	corticosterone
GH (growth hormone)	aldosterone
FSH (follicle stimulating hormone)	*Testes*
LH (luteinizing hormone)	androgens
prolactin	estrogens
TSH (thyroid stimulating hormone)	*Ovaries*
Posterior pituitary	estrogens
vasopressin [antidiuretic hormone (ADH)]	progestogens
oxytocin	androgens
Thyroid gland	*Pancreas*
thyroxine	insulin (from β-cells)
triiodothyronine	glucagon (from α-cells)
thyrocalcitonin	*Small intestine*
Parathyroid glands	cholecystokinin
PTH (parathyroid hormone)	*Pineal gland*
Adrenal medulla	melatonin
epinephrine (adrenaline)	*Heart*
norepinephrine (noradrenaline)	ANF (atrial natriuretic factor)

*Both β-endorphin and ACTH come from a hormone precursor, proopiomelanocortin.

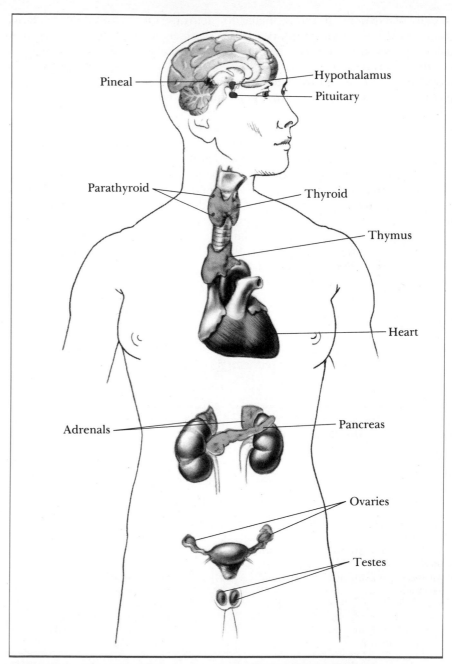

Figure 9.1   Location of the major endocrine organs of the body.
Other tissues, such as the duodenum of the small intestine, also secrete hormones.

particular cell is a target cell for a hormone depends on the presence or absence of a specific *hormone receptor* in that cell. These receptors are proteins, located either within the cytoplasm of the cell or in the cell membrane. Some cells contain receptors for several hormones and have both cytoplasmic and membrane receptors.

Hormone Families

All hormones belong to one of three chemical families: the **steroids, polypeptides,** or a *miscellaneous* family, most of which are modified amino acids. Figure 9.2 illustrates representative members of each of these three fami-

steroid (STE-royd) One of three main chemical families of hormones. Includes the reproductive hormones such as testosterone and estrogen.

polypeptide (polly-PEP-tide) A molecule composed of two or more amino acids.

Figure 9.2   Chemical structure of representative hormones from the three major hormone families.

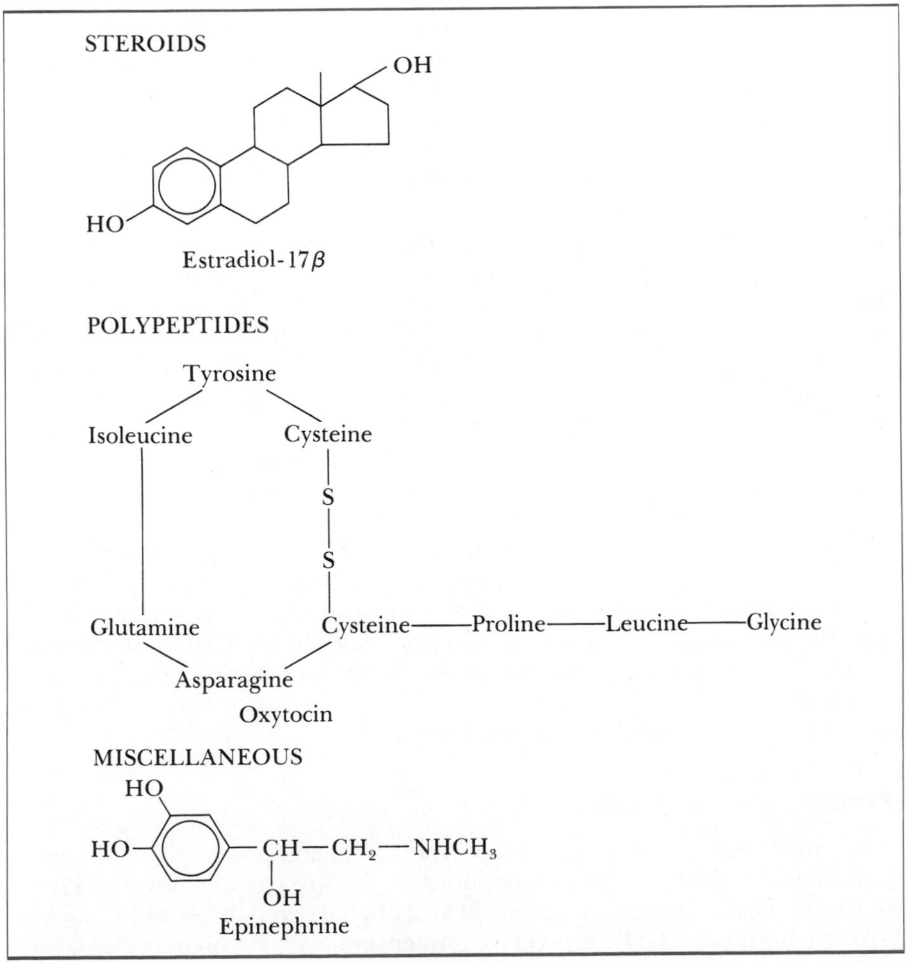

STEROIDS

Estradiol-17β

POLYPEPTIDES

Oxytocin

MISCELLANEOUS

Epinephrine

androgens (AN-dro-jens) Hormones that produce masculinizing effects. Distinctions between androgens and estrogens have become somewhat blurred with new discoveries, and the two types of hormones are closely related chemically.

estrogens (ESS-tro-jens) Hormones that produce feminizing effects. See also *androgens*.

progestins (pro-JES-tins) Steroid hormones such as *progesterone*. Progestins affect the walls of the uterus to prepare for implantation of the fertilized egg.

corticosteroid (kor-ti-ko-STE-royd) Any of the steroids produced by the cortex of the adrenal gland.

lies. The steroid hormones share a characteristic four-ring structure. Steroids are secreted from the gonads and from the cortex of the adrenal glands. Within the steroid family the hormones that are associated primarily with masculinizing effects, such as stimulation of the growth of the prostate gland and male genitals, are called **androgens.** Hormones primarily associated with feminizing effects, such as stimulation of vaginal and uterine tissue, are called **estrogens. Progestins** stimulate the growth of the walls of the uterus in ways different from that of estrogens, in preparation for the implantation of the fetus. Steroids secreted from the adrenal cortex are termed **corticosteroids.** All steroids are synthesized from cholesterol. With the exception of progestins (secreted only by females), both males and females regularly secrete all the preceding hormones, but females secrete more estrogens than androgens and males secrete more androgens than estrogens.

Steroid Receptors

Steroids are generally attached to carrier proteins in the blood, but they readily come loose from their carriers and, being lipid soluble, enter cells simply by diffusing across the lipid portion of the membrane. In target cells for steroid hormones receptors in the cytoplasm bind the hormone, trapping it (Jensen and DeSombre, 1973). In nontarget cells no receptors are found and the steroids diffuse back out of the cell and reassociate with their carrier proteins.

Once the hormone has been captured by the cytoplasmic receptor, the hormone–receptor complex migrates to the nucleus of the cell, where it binds to an acceptor site associated with the DNA. It is believed that here the hormone–receptor complex activates specific genes that alter the rate of synthesis of some cell product. (Figure 9.3 illustrates the Jensen–DeSombre model of steroid hormone action.) This process may take several hours before the maximum rate of synthesis is achieved. Thus the effect of an increase in bloodstream levels of a steroid hormone may not be seen for some time. Steroids also have direct effects on neurons. Various steroid hormones are known to alter the firing rate of neurons in the brain with much shorter latencies than would be possible if this effect were to be mediated by the genes. (Recent evidence has challenged the idea that the steroid receptors are located in the cytoplasm and then migrate to the nucleus after binding with the steroid hormone. Instead, these studies find that the receptors are primarily in the nucleus to begin with [e.g., King and Greene, 1984]. If these studies prove to be correct, there will have to be a revision of the Jensen-DeSombre model.)

Polypeptide Hormones

Most mammalian hormones are polypeptides, composed of two or more amino acids. Most smaller polypeptides, such as oxytocin (shown in Figure 9.2), are linear strings of amino acids; but larger polypeptides, such as growth hormone (GH), are very complex molecules. Polypeptides over a

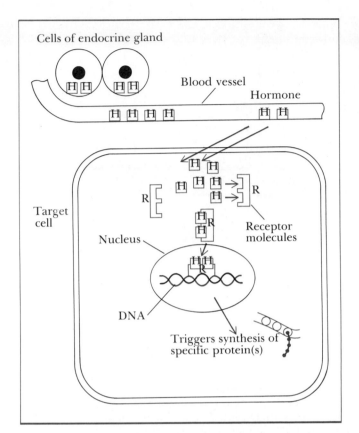

Figure 9.3 Mode of action for steroid hormones.
Being fat-soluble, the steroids pass freely through the lipid portion of the membrane. Inside the cell they combine with receptor molecules and are transported to the nucleus where the hormone-receptor complex alters the rate of synthesis of one or more proteins. H = Hormone; R = receptor.

certain size (about 100 amino acids) are called proteins. Because of their large size and because they are not soluble in lipids, polypeptides do not usually enter cells. Instead they bind to specific receptors located in the membrane. This process was first outlined in 1972 by E. W. Sutherland, who termed the way in which polypeptide hormones acted on cells the *second messenger* system. According to his hypothesis, polypeptides bind to a receptor in the membrane and thereby increase levels of **cyclic AMP (cAMP)** within the cell. Intracellular levels of cAMP are caused by the activation of an **enzyme** in the membrane called **adenylate cyclase** (see Figure 9.4). Thus cAMP, which can trigger various cellular responses, is the second messenger. The hormone itself is the first messenger. Other *second* messengers such as cyclic GMP (cGMP) have been identified. Both cAMP and cGMP can coexist in a given cell.

Miscellaneous Hormones

A few hormones belong to a miscellaneous family, including the thyroid hormones (thyroxin and triodothyronine), **melatonin** (secreted by the pineal gland), and the hormones of the adrenal medulla (epinephrine and

cyclic AMP (cAMP) (SY-klik) An enzyme found in many cells. It is activated by adenylate cyclase. cAMP is the second messenger for many hormones, carrying out the activities within the cell that are initiated by substances utilizing the second messenger system.

enzyme (N-zyme) A substance that speeds up a biochemical reaction.

adenylate cyclase (ad-ee-ni-late sy-KLASE) An enzyme in the membrane of target cells for hormones using the second messenger system. When activated by a hormone, adenylate cyclase activates cyclic AMP, the second messenger.

melatonin (mel-ah-TONE-in) A hormone made and secreted by the pineal gland.

pituitary gland (pih-TOO-ih-tare-ee) A complex gland closely associated with the hypothalamus. Manufactures and secretes a variety of hormones.

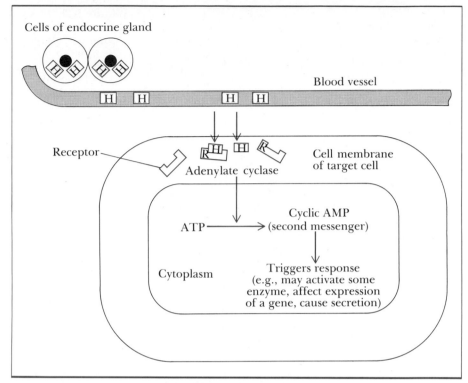

Figure 9.4   The second messenger system for hormone action.
This is the way most polypeptides affect cells. The hormone (the first messenger) combines with a receptor within the cell membrane, which results in the activation of adenylate cyclase and causes an increase in the amount of cyclic AMP (the second messenger) within the cytoplasm of the cell. Cyclic AMP then causes the cell to respond in some way. H = hormone.

norepinephrine). The thyroid hormones, like the steroids, are lipid soluble and enter cells through the membrane. They are bound to receptors in the cell nucleus (Norris, 1980). Melatonin is a modified amino acid. Its receptors are unknown. Epinephrine and norepinephrine are modified amino acids and appear to use a second messenger system.

Some Factors New: The Hypothalamic Hormones

In human beings, just below the hypothalamus, suspended from the brain by a slender tissue stalk, is an organ about the size of a pea—the **pituitary gland** (see Figure 9.5). The pituitary gland was named by the Renaissance anatomist Andreas Vesalius, who believed that its function was to collect mucus from the brain and distribute it as a lubricant to the nose and throat (Goodman, 1974). In human beings the pituitary is composed of an anterior lobe and a posterior lobe. Many species also have an intermediate lobe in the pituitary gland. The anterior and posterior lobes are derived from different embryonic tissues and are regulated differently. The posterior lobe is actually an extension of the hypothalamus. Neurons make and manufacture the two posterior lobe hormones, **oxytocin** and **vasopressin.** The cell bodies of these neurosecretory neurons are in the hypothalamus, but the axons project into the posterior lobe, where they terminate and release their hormones into the bloodstream.

Until a few years ago it was not clear how the anterior lobe, which is not brain tissue, was regulated. During embryonic development it is derived from tissue that comes from the roof of the mouth. This tissue forms a small pocket that migrates from its original location to attach itself and partially surround the developing posterior lobe. Geoffrey Harris (1955)

oxytocin (ox-e-TOSE-in) One of the two hormones secreted by the posterior pituitary.

vasopressin (vas-o-PRES-in) One of the two hormones secreted by the posterior pituitary.

Figure 9.5   Diagram of the hypothalamic–pituitary connections.
The hormones of the posterior pituitary are manufactured by neurosecretory cells in hypothalamic nuclei. The axons of these neurons descend down the pituitary stalk and end close to the venous drainage of the posterior pituitary. The anterior pituitary receives messages in the form of hypothalamic hormones via the pituitary portal veins.

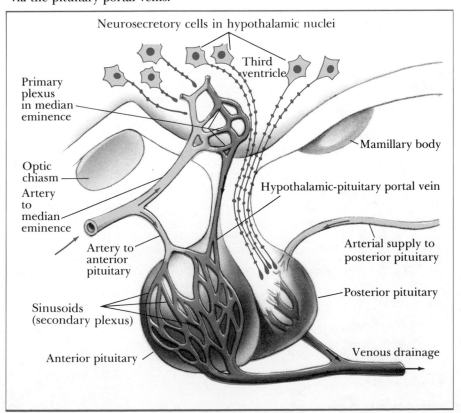

hypothalamic–pituitary portal system (hi-poe-tha-LAM-ik–pih-TOO-ih-tare-ee) The private circulatory system between the hypothalamus and the anterior pituitary.

thyrotropin releasing hormone (TRH) (thigh-ro-TRO-pin) A hypothalamic hormone that causes the production and release of the hormone thyrotropin from the anterior pituitary. A tripeptide.

first correctly proposed that the brain regulated the anterior pituitary by means of chemical factors carried from the brain to the anterior pituitary by the **hypothalamic–pituitary portal system.** This portal system is a highly specialized "private" part of the blood supply, formed by a dense network of capillaries that allow for the circulation of substances from the brain to the anterior pituitary (and, possibly, to a lesser extent, the other way as well; see Figure 9.6).

Not until 1968 was direct proof of Harris's idea obtained and the first *hypothalamic hormone* isolated from brain tissue. The hormone was **thyrotropin releasing hormone (TRH),** which causes the release of thyrotropin from the anterior pituitary. TRH is a tripeptide (three amino acids) and is present in the brain in very small amounts. The co-discoverers of TRH, Roger Guillemin and Andrew Schally, worked independently. Each laboratory had to process tons of brain tissue in order to obtain enough of the presumed hormone to analyze properly. "We scaled up our extraction process

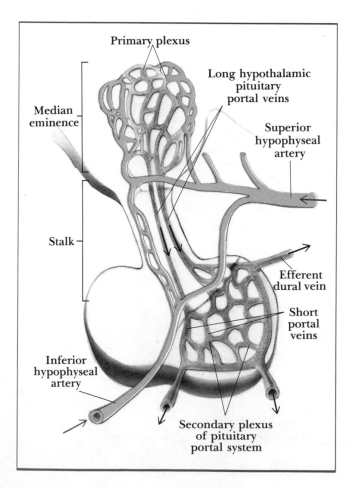

Figure 9.6 The hypothalamic–pituitary portal system (also termed hypothalamic–hypophyseal), responsible for carrying the hypothalamic hormones from the brain to the anterior pituitary.
The portal system is supplied with blood from the superior and inferior hypophyseal arteries and drained via the efferent dural vein and other veins.

Primary plexus

Long hypothalamic pituitary portal veins

Median eminence

Superior hypophyseal artery

Stalk

Efferent dural vein

Short portal veins

Inferior hypophyseal artery

Secondary plexus of pituitary portal system

TABLE 9.2 Some Hypothalamic Hormones and Their Respective Anterior Pituitary Hormones

Hypothalamic Hormone	Anterior Pituitary Hormone
GnRH (gonadotropin releasing hormone)	FSH, LH
CRH (corticotropin releasing hormone)	ACTH, proopiomelanocortin
GHRH (growth hormone releasing hormone)	GH
GHRIH (growth hormone release-inhibiting hormone; also called somatostatin)	GH
PRH (prolactin releasing hormone)	Prolactin
PRIH (prolactin release-inhibiting hormone)	Prolactin
TRH (thyrotropin releasing hormone)	TSH

to nearly industrial proportions. Some five million fragments of sheep brains, weighing a total of more than 500 tons and containing 50 tons of hypothalamic fragments were collected and processed. By late 1968, 1.0 mg of pure TRH was isolated from 300,000 of these sheep fragments" (Guillemin, 1980). Within 10 years it was recognized that all the anterior pituitary hormones were either released or inhibited by such hypothalamic "factors," inspiring the verse at the beginning of the chapter. These "factors new" are now generally referred to as hypothalamic hormones.

Most of the hypothalamic hormones so far identified are small polypeptides, although dopamine, which is also a neurotransmitter in the brain, is an inhibiting factor for prolactin. Table 9.2 lists some hypothalamic hormones and their associated anterior lobe hormones. The neurons in the hypothalamus that manufacture and secrete these hormones are themselves subject to synaptic influence from other neurons in the brain and form the last link between the brain and the anterior pituitary. Thus the activities of the brain can be brought to bear on these neurons that can influence directly the secretion of hormones throughout the body. This fact makes it somewhat easier to understand that the amount of daylight can influence the time an animal ovulates, that certain odors can trigger hormonal changes, that anxiety or worry can alter a woman's menstrual cycle, and that stress can lower a man's testosterone levels, even though the precise reasons for these phenomena remain to be discovered.

Sexual Dimorphism in Brains and in Behavior

Hormones can influence our behavior mainly in two ways. Some hormones, particularly the androgens, are important in fetal development in influencing the organism to differentiate along a male pattern. Later, at puberty and for most of the rest of life, hormones can influence a variety of behaviors more directly, through actions on tissues throughout the body, including the brain itself. The effects of hormones early in fetal life are called *developmental* effects, and those at puberty and beyond are called *activational* effects.

Sexual dimorphism in lions. In many animal species, the male and female differ in various bodily characteristics. Sexual dimorphism can also be observed in the pattern of hormonal secretion, behavior, and brain structure (see text).

sexual dimorphism (di-MORF-ism) Refers to differences in structure or behavior that distinguish male and female patterns.

cyclic (SY-clik) On a regularly occurring basis.

estrus (ESS-trus) Period of sexual receptivity in female mammals. Not applicable to human beings. The associated adjective is *estrous*.

The developmental effects of hormones on the fetus help to determine the maleness or femaleness of the individual. The term **sexual dimorphism** refers to the many differences that occur in the structure and behavior of males and females. In mammals sexual dimorphism can be seen in the pattern of hormonal secretion, in sexual behavior, and in the structure of the body, including the brain.

Cyclicity of Hormonal Secretion: A Female Characteristic

One fundamental characteristic of female mammals, including human beings, is that they secrete several of the anterior pituitary hormones as well as the gonadal steroids such as estrogen and progesterone on a rhythmic or **cyclic** basis. Males show no such cyclicity. In addition, in most mammalian species these hormonal rhythms are closely associated with episodes of increased sexual activity in females, termed **estrus.** Ovulation, the expulsion of ripe eggs (ova) from the ovary, occurs about the same time as estrus. This coordination of ovulation with the peak of sexual activity greatly increases the probability of the female's becoming pregnant.

Females in species in which ovulation is due to inherent hormonal cyclicity are called *spontaneous ovulators.* Human beings are spontaneous ovulators. Other species, such as rabbits and cats, have periodic estrous cycles, but ovulation occurs only in response to stimulation of the vaginal wall. Females of such species are called *induced ovulators.* In both spontaneous and induced ovulators, ovulation depends on a sudden surge of

luteinizing hormone (LH) from the anterior pituitary. The search for an answer to the question of why males and females secrete hormones on such radically different patterns goes back many years. We shall begin our discussion of this story with the work of Carroll Pfeiffer, published in 1936.

luteinizing hormone (LH) (LU-tin-eyes-ing) Anterior pituitary hormone responsible for ovulation in the female. Stimulates testosterone production in the male.

Ovaries in the Eyeballs

Pfeiffer was interested in the problem of sex differences in hormone secretion and chose to study ovulation in laboratory rats. Ovulation is an indirect but reliable indicator of cyclicity, since it depends on the LH surge. (Modern researchers would measure LH directly, which was impossible in Pfeiffer's time.)

In trying to discover what determined female cyclicity, Pfeiffer manipulated the hormonal status of both male and female rats at various times during their development. In a series of experiments Pfeiffer showed that male rats *castrated at birth* and later given an ovary transplant showed the normal *female* pattern of cyclicity and ovulation from this transplanted ovary. These transplanted ovaries went through the normal four-day cycle, ovulating every fourth day, as do those of normal female rats. Pfeiffer could observe the ovary because he transplanted it into the anterior chamber of the eye in these albino rats. Since these animals have no pigment in their eyes, he could see the ovary clearly through the transparent fluids of the eye. Within the eye the ovary became attached to the bloodstream, from which it received nutrients and the anterior pituitary hormones necessary for normal ovarian function. Male rats deprived of normal testicular hormones by castration shortly after birth displayed a cyclic female hormonal pattern, despite the fact that they were genetic males.

Pfeiffer discovered that other male rats, castrated as adults, retained the male acyclic pattern of hormone secretion. Ovaries transplanted into the eyeballs of such males remained healthy, but did not ovulate, an indication that no LH surge had occurred. Pfeiffer concluded from the observations of the rats castrated at birth that he had removed some masculinizing agent present in the testes, thus allowing for the expression of an "inherent hormonal cyclicity" characteristic of female mammals. Removal of the testes later in life, however, did not allow for this cyclicity, presumably because some critical period or sensitive period in which rats could be influenced by hormonal changes had passed. We now know that this vital masculinizing agent is testosterone and that the sensitive period generally lasts only a few days after birth in rats and is over prenatally in human beings and other primates.

Pfeiffer also found when he implanted testes into the neck of female rats within a few hours of birth that they lost their capacity to secrete hormones on a cyclic basis and failed to ovulate, even though their ovaries appeared healthy. The ova in such ovaries develop but ovulation does not occur, since the LH surge never comes. As a result of these experiments, as well as later, more refined ones by other investigators, we now know that the cyclicity of hormonal secretion in female mammals is inborn. This

sella turcica   (SEL-lah tur-KEE-ka) The pocket of bone in which the pituitary gland is encased.

capacity is suppressed at some early stage in development in males by the secretion of testosterone from their testes.

The relationship between the brain and the anterior pituitary was poorly understood in Pfeiffer's time. He assumed that the pituitary was a master gland, initiating and terminating its own hormonal secretions. Pfeiffer thus proposed (logically but incorrectly) that the vital masculinizing agent from the infant testes acted directly on the pituitary. We now know that the main effect of testosterone on the control of hormonal cyclicity is due to its influence on the brain.

How do we know that the brain and not the pituitary is influenced by testosterone early in life? Pfeiffer's experiments did not resolve the issue, but subsequent experiments have done so. Using delicate surgical techniques, Geoffrey Harris and Dora Jacobsohn (1952) removed the pituitary gland from a male rat and transplanted it into the sella turcica of a female rat that had already had its own pituitary gland removed. The **sella turcica** (Turkish saddle) is the small pocket of bone at the base of the skull in which the pituitary is located. When the transplanted "male" pituitary developed sufficient portal bloodstream connections with the overlying "female" hypothalamus, the female rat began to ovulate normally again. This demonstrates that the pituitary is regulated by the brain and that *it is the sex of the brain that dictates hormonal cyclicity or acyclicity in rats.* Harris and Jacobsohn also did the reverse procedure, transplanting a "female" pituitary into the sella turcica of a male rat. This animal, when the graft took hold, began to secrete the hormones of the anterior pituitary in the normal acyclic male pattern.

A few years later, Sheldon Segal and Donald Johnson (1959) demonstrated that the pituitary of a female rat that had been given testosterone was still capable of cyclic secretion and could produce the LH surge when it was removed and transplanted into the sella turcica of a normal female that had had its own pituitary removed. Several other experiments support the conclusion that it is the brain itself, not the pituitary, that is masculinized by exposure to early testosterone (Gorski and Barraclough, 1963; Mennin et al., 1974). Roger Gorski and J.W. Wagner (1965) suggest that the critical neurons that determine cyclicity are in the preoptic area, just anterior to the hypothalamus. Figure 9.7 illustrates their model. Additional modulation of the cyclic release of GnRH, the hormone that releases both FSH and LH, may come from the amygdala (Feder, 1981a).

Dimorphic Sexual Behavior

Male and female mammals display clear and reliable differences in their sexual behavior. Although many different species have been studied in this regard, including our own (Kinsey et al., 1948; 1953), we shall use the laboratory rat as our representative mammal, since the sexual dimorphism in the behavior of laboratory rats is quite striking, and, unlike the situation with human beings, there is a clear relationship between hormonal fluctuations and sexual behavior.

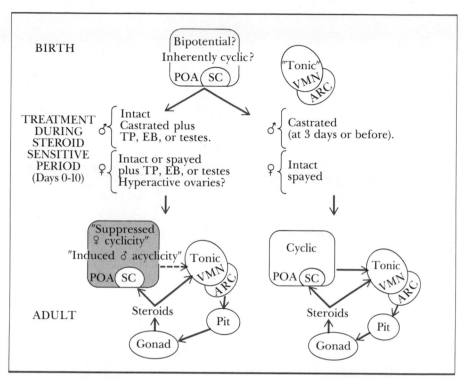

diestrus (di-ESS-trus) Period of sexual unresponsiveness in the female rats estrous cycle.

Figure 9.7 **Gorski–Wagner model of the sexual differentiation of the hypothalamus of the brain.**
TP = testosterone propionate; EB = estradiol benzoate; POA = preoptic area; SC = suprachiasmatic nuclei; VMN = ventromedial nuclei of the hypothalamus; ARC = arcuate nuclei of the hypothalamus; PIT = anterior pituitary (Gorski and Wagner, 1965).

Female rats typically have four-day estrus cycles, although some strains have a five-day cycle. The main difference between four- and five-day cycles is an extra day of nonestrus, or **diestrus,** in five-day cycles. (Figure 9.8 shows the hormonal fluctuations in a typical four-day cycle.) During the first two days of the cycle the female is not sexually responsive. However, in the early evening of the third day, the day termed *proestrus,* a dramatic change in the behavior of the female occurs. She becomes much more active. If she has access to a running wheel, she may increase her activity severalfold. She eats very little for the next 24 hours, and if housed with or near an adult male she begins to show signs of sexual interest and responsiveness. If the male shows interest, she responds to his investigations of her genitals with a characteristic hopping and darting behavior. She darts off a short distance and wiggles her ears rapidly (apparently a major attraction for the male). The male then follows and she repeats the darting, hopping, and ear-wiggling routine.

proceptive behavior
(PRO-sep-tive) Behaviors initiated by the female that increase the likelihood of sexual contact.

lordosis (lore-DOSE-us) [plural, *lordoses* (lore-DOSE-ease)] The posture adopted by some sexually receptive female mammals, such as rats and cats.

lordosis quotient (LQ) (lore-DOSE-us KWO-shunt) The number of times the female adopts the lordosis posture divided by the number of mounts by the male. A standard measure of female receptivity in laboratory rats.

intromission Penetration of the vagina by the penis.

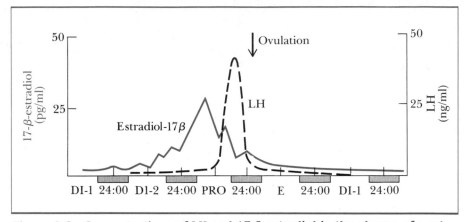

Figure 9.8   Concentrations of LH and 17-β estradiol in the plasma of a rat during a four-day estrus cycle.
DI-1 = Diestrus, Day 1; DI-2 = Diestrus, Day 2; PRO = Proestrus; E = Estrus.

These enticement behaviors have been termed **proceptive behaviors** by Frank Beach (1976), a pioneer researcher of sexual behavior. He defined proceptive sexual behaviors as those that are initiated by the female that increase the likelihood of sexual contact. Although the exact details of proceptive behaviors vary from species to species, virtually all female mammals display them. Female cats, for example, as they approach the peak of their estrus period, roll on their backs in the presence of the male, purr, and knead the ground with their front paws. Female rhesus monkeys come and sit nearer to males, groom them, and present their genitals to them.

In the rat, as the evening of proestrus goes on, proceptive behaviors are replaced by *receptive behaviors,* which Beach (1976) defined as those that allow the male to mount the female, insert his penis in her vagina, and ejaculate. The main receptive behavior in both cats and rats is **lordosis,** in which the female arches her back downward and crouches with her tail to one side to allow easier mounting and penetration. Workers in this area have quantified this response with the **lordosis quotient (LQ).** This is the number of lordoses by the female divided by the number of mount attempts by the male. At peak periods of receptivity, a female rat may reach an LQ of 0.8 or more (Bermant and Davidson, 1974). This peak usually occurs about six hours after the female shows the first proceptive behaviors. This typically happens in the early morning of the fourth day of the cycle, the day known as estrus. Robert Kuehn and Frank Beach (1963) found an average duration of estrus in laboratory rats of 19 hours. Some time during this period ovulation occurs.

As proestrus blends into estrus, some of the male mounts are marked by **intromission,** the penetration of the vagina by the penis. After a few rapid pelvic thrusts, the male typically dismounts, then remounts a few minutes later. Ejaculation occurs at the end of one of these mounting sessions and is marked by a deeper than average pelvic thrust and a slower dismount. Following an intercopulatory interval of several seconds to several minutes, the entire sequence of mounts and ejaculation is repeated. Male rats usually ejaculate four to ten times within a few hours. An estrous female accepts males throughout her time of peak receptivity.

estradiol (ESS-tra-DY-all) A potent estrogen.

However, if we were to observe this same pair of animals one day later (on day 1 of the new cycle), we would see very different behaviors. The male would still be interested (at least at first), but his advances would not be answered with hopping, ear wiggling, or lordosis. The female would be much more likely to "chatter" her teeth at the male (a sure sign of hostility if you are a rat). If the male were to be slow to grasp her meaning, she might turn away from him and kick him in the head, mule fashion. Clearly, it is over between them (but only for another two days). These repeated, stereotyped behaviors constitute clear-cut sexual dimorphic patterns. Other species also display species-characteristic sexual dimorphism in their reproductive behaviors. (Human beings are the least stereotyped species in their sexual behavior.)

Hormones and Female Sexual Behavior

What accounts for the changes in behavior of the female rat across the estrus cycle? Levels of various important hormones, particularly the estrogens, influence various tissues in her body, including the brain, to bring about these changes. Estrogens begin to be secreted in increasing amounts about 24 hours before proceptive behavior begins to occur (about 36 hours prior to ovulation). Progesterone peaks in the bloodstream about 20 hours after the estrogen peak, about four hours before the peak of receptivity (Feder, 1981).

The most potent of the estrogens for producing estrus behavior is **estradiol.** Progesterone seems somewhat secondary for receptive behaviors but more important for proceptive behaviors. For example, it has been known for many years that *ovariectomized* (ovaries-removed) rats are sexually inactive. However, if given estradiol alone, a few hours later they begin to show lordosis behavior. If the estradiol injections are accompanied, a few hours later, by progesterone injections, the lordosis responses are of "better quality." In addition, although estrogens alone produce *receptive* behaviors, such as lordosis, proceptive behaviors are minimal or absent unless progesterone is also administered. This suggests that in the natural course of events, the mix of estrogen and progesterone acts on different neural circuits in the brain to activate receptive and proceptive behaviors (Glaser et al., 1983). The main sites for estradiol action appear to be in the hypothalamus, the nearby preoptic region and parts of the amygdala (McEwen, 1980). Other researchers (Tennant et al., 1982) found that the behavioral effects of injections of progesterone could be duplicated by implanting small amounts of progesterone in the midbrain.

ovulation   (ov-u-LAY-shun) Expulsion of the ripe ovum (or ova) from the ovary.

ovarian follicles   (o-VAR-ee-an FOL-ik-uls) Many-celled structure in the ovary that contains and nourishes the ovum (ova). Also produces hormones such as the estrogens.

menstrual cycle   (MEN-stral) Cyclic sloughing off of the uterine walls. Occurs only in primates.

prolactin   (Pro-LAK-tin) A protein hormone secreted by the anterior pituitary. Supports lactation in the female.

alveoli   (al-VEE-o-ly) (singular, *alveolus*) Sacs or ducts surrounding the nipples.

Ovarian Cyclicity

The female exhibits not only behavioral cyclicity but also ovarian cyclicity. **Ovulation** is timed to occur at or near the peak of sexual receptivity. The processes of ovum development and ovulation are due to four main hormones: FSH, LH, estrogen, and GnRH. In the rat, levels of these hormones are low on the first day of diestrus. FSH levels begin to rise late on the second day and reach a peak a few hours before ovulation. As FSH levels rise, they act on the **ovarian follicles** and on the ova they contain and cause the follicles to grow and develop until they are ready to rupture. Ovulation consists of the rupture of the wall of the follicle and the expulsion of the ova. The LH surge itself appears to depend on a critical estrogen level being reached. In the rat estrogens increase the level of GnRH directly, thereby increasing the levels of FSH and LH secreted by the anterior pituitary. In many species, including human beings, estrogens increase the *sensitivity* of the anterior pituitary to GnRH, so that more LH and FSH are secreted in response to a given amount of GnRH. Figure 9.9 shows some of the main events in the human **menstrual cycle,** which directly reflects events occurring in the ovary, pituitary, and brain.

Nursing and the Posterior Pituitary

If a female mammal becomes pregnant, changes in her mammary glands prepare her for milk production. The hormones that underlie milk production and secretion are oxytocin and **prolactin.** Oxytocin is composed of eight amino acids and is secreted from the posterior pituitary. Prolactin, a very large polypeptide from the anterior pituitary, stimulates the mammary glands to produce milk. Once it is produced, milk passes into the **alveoli** (ducts surrounding the nipple). For it to be released from the nipple in more than tiny amounts, muscle cells surrounding the alveoli must contract vigorously, actively squirting the milk into the mouth of the suckling infant. This is milk ejection and is a *neuroendocrine reflex*. Stimulation of the nerve endings in and around the nipple produces nerve impulses that activate those neurons that secrete oxytocin into the circulation. When oxytocin reaches the contractile cells surrounding the alveoli, it causes them to contract, ejecting the milk (see Figure 9.10). The nursing reflex can be conditioned to stimuli associated with nursing, such as the chair in which nursing regularly takes place or the sight of the infant making nursing movements with its mouth.

Hormones and Male Sexual Behavior

One major difference between males and females of many mammalian species is that females display repeated cycles in sexual receptivity whereas males do not. It is true that most species have seasons during which males are sexually active, but throughout these mating seasons males are more or less constantly ready to copulate.

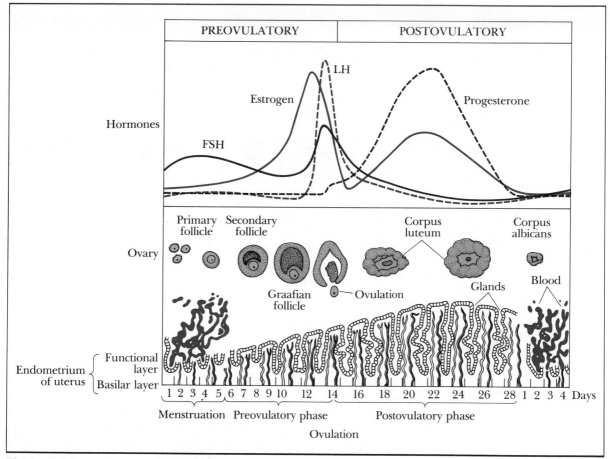

Figure 9.9 The primate menstrual cycle.
The second half of the cycle (from ovulation to the first day of uterine bleeding) is about 14 days. The first half is more variable, but averages about 14 days. Corpus luteum becomes corpus albicans at the end of the cycle.

The relationship between hormones and male sexual behavior is less clear than that for females. In general, males do cease copulating after castration (removal of the testes), but some aspects of sexual behavior, such as mounting or investigation of female genitals, may continue for a long time. In fact, in rhesus monkeys, some aspects of sexual behavior, including mounting, intromission, pelvic thrusting, and the behavioral ejaculation pattern, are still present several years following castration (Phoenix, 1976).

The clearest evidence for the reliance of male sexual behavior on hormones comes from experiments with laboratory rats. Following castration, male sexual behavior in rats declines over a period of several weeks. The behavior seems to decline in a "backward" fashion. Ejaculation stops first, then intromission. Mounting is the last part of the sequence to disappear.

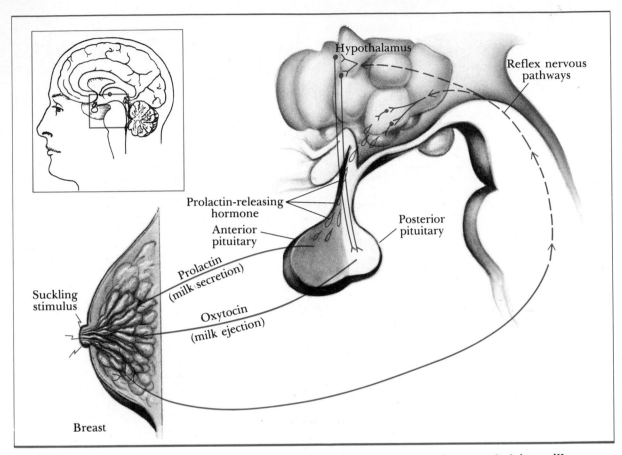

Figure 9.10   Diagram of the neurohormonal reflexes underlying milk ejection and milk secretion.

testosterone (tes-TOS-ter-own) A major androgen.

The remaining behaviors cannot be directly dependent on **testosterone** or any other testicular hormone, since these hormones are virtually gone from the bloodstream within hours following castration. Although small amounts of testosterone are secreted from the adrenal glands, experiments in which the adrenal glands were also removed from previously castrated animals demonstrate that these surviving sexual behaviors do not depend on adrenal testosterone either (Davidson, 1980). Eventually, sexual behavior in castrated rats ceases. In animals that have ceased copulating following castration, androgen therapy can usually reinstate normal sexual behavior after some recovery time.

Testosterone and Sexual Vigor

Although the popular literature often states that levels of testosterone are related to levels of sexual activity, no convincing evidence exists to support this notion. It is true that sexual behavior declines following castration and can be reinstated with injections of testosterone, but within normal ranges, no solid evidence supports the contention that sexual behavior is directly driven by testosterone levels.

One study with college students found a "general lack of relationship between testosterone levels and questionnaire items related to sexual activity and interest" (Monti et al., 1977). Peter Monti and colleagues did find a positive relationship between testosterone levels and frequency of masturbation, but they found no correlations with other forms of sexual activity. Laboratory rats show little correlation between sexual vigor and levels of testosterone in the bloodstream (Damassa et al., 1977). Blood levels of testosterone in men who are impotent (unable to achieve or maintain an erection) are typically normal, although in a very small number of cases, extremely low levels of testosterone can cause impotence. It is unlikely that in the great majority of cases of impotence any hormonal dysfunction exists (Schwartz et al., 1979; Pirke and Kockett, 1982). Some diseases, such as diabetes, however, can cause impotence because of circulation problems.

Although hundreds of men have undergone legal castration for sex-related crimes, both in Europe and in the United States, the reports on such individuals do not address many of the critical questions concerning sexual or aggressive behavior following castration (Davidson et al., 1982). For most individuals surgical castration dramatically reduces or eliminates most sexual behavior, but for a substantial number it does not prevent erections and sexual activity, although such individuals are unable to ejaculate. It is unclear what sorts of sexual feelings castrates have and whether the capacity for orgasm is retained.

In recent years surgical castration has been replaced largely by "chemical castration." Various drugs, such as **cyproterone** and **medroxyprogesterone,** act as antiandrogens, decreasing testosterone production by the testes. These drugs also act on other testosterone-sensitive tissues, such as the prostate gland and the penis. It is not yet clear how effective chemical castration is in preventing sexual activity. The main advantage of the drug approach is that its effects are reversible. These drugs do appear to reduce the frequency and intensity of sexual fantasies. Coupled with appropriate behavioral therapy, they may prove useful in treating sex offenders. Many sex offenses are actually crimes of violence. The possible relationship between testosterone levels and violent behavior in human beings is further discussed in Chapter 11.

Human sexual behavior appears to depend less on hormones than does that of other primates. Despite a substantial number of studies, no convincing evidence exists that either male or female human sexual behavior can be related to hormones in any systematic fashion, at least when the hormones are within normal levels. Very low levels of gonadal hormones are typically associated with decreased sexual desire, and in some of these cases treatment with appropriate hormones can restore sexual interest.

Much of the research with normal individuals has been flawed by one or another methodological problem, and the various studies disagree widely

cyproterone (Cy-PRO-ter-own) A chemical with antiandrogen properties.

medroxyprogesterone (med-ROK-see-pro-JES-ter-own) A chemical used as an antiandrogen. Also a synthetic progesterone.

(Feder, 1984). Human sexuality is influenced by many different factors, including cultural, religious, and personality differences. Although it is impossible to rule out hormonal influences, they do not seem to be significant for most individuals. Of course, with better techniques and more appropriately designed studies, some modulating influence of hormones on human sexual behavior may emerge. It is true that the onset of puberty, which is characterized by a dramatic upsurge in the levels of gonadal hormones, is also the time at which most individuals begin to experience adult-like erotic feelings and thoughts. Studies of children who enter puberty abnormally early (prior to age 10 or so) tend to support the concept that for boys (but not typically for girls), such *precocious puberty* is also accompanied by an increase in erotic fantasies and behavior (Money and Ehrhardt, 1972). The scientific study of human sexual behavior is still new, and a great deal more will be learned in the future.

Developmental Effects of Hormones on Sexual Behavior

As discussed earlier in this chapter, Carroll Pfeiffer found dramatic effects on hormonal cyclicity as a result of manipulating the early hormonal environment in rats. Pfeiffer did not report on the behavior of these rats, but several years later other experimenters began to examine the behavior of animals following manipulation of the early hormonal status. Some of the pioneering work was done with guinea pigs by Charles Phoenix and colleagues (1959). They found that when pregnant guinea pigs were injected with testosterone, the female offspring showed diminished female sexual behavior as adults and an increase in male sexual behavior. Geoffrey Harris and Seymour Levine (1962) found similar effects in rats.

It should be noted that there is a difference between *defeminization* and *masculinization*. It is not necessary for both to occur with early testosterone injections. These terms were introduced and defined by Beach and his associates (1972). Defeminization is defined as "partial or complete inhibition of traits normally well developed in females but absent or weakly developed in males." Masculinization of females "refers to the induction of anatomical, physiological, or behavioral characters or traits which normally are well developed in males but lacking or poorly developed in females" (Beach et al., 1972).

Likewise, several investigators (e.g., Whalen and Edwards, 1967) found that castration of male rats at birth resulted in increased lordosis when tested as adults with normal male partners. This *feminization* could be prevented by testosterone injections in the first few days of life. The male rats castrated at or near birth also showed *demasculinization*, evidenced by decreased male sexual behavior as adults when paired with receptive females. Feminization was defined by Beach and colleagues (1972) as the "evocation of traits usually characteristic of females and absent or only weakly developed in males." Demasculinization refers to "total or partial elimination of traits normally found in males but occurring rarely or not at all in females." The sort of behavior one sees depends on several factors, including the hormonal status during the critical period and the conditions of testing.

If sufficient testosterone is present during the critical developmental period, the sexual behavior of rodents tends to follow a masculine pattern. In rats this critical period includes a day or two prior to birth and perhaps as much as six days after birth. Hormonal manipulations in rats a week or so following birth generally have much less effect, although massive doses of testosterone may have some effect as late as 10 days after birth (Pfaff et al., 1974). In primate species the critical period seems to be entirely during fetal development.

Rat Studies

The conditions that prevail during the testing of animals also determine the kind of behavior seen. For example, one can administer either testosterone or estrogen to the subjects. Animals can be tested for female behavior by placing them with males and for male behavior by placing them with females. Many other conditions, such as time of day, previous testing experience, and nature of the apparatus, can be influential. Donald Pfaff and Richard Zigmond (1971) varied hormone regimes systematically and looked for both male and female behaviors in rats that had been manipulated hormonally at birth. They found that neonatally castrated male rats tested as adults showed diminished masculine behavior (compared with male rats castrated as adults) following either testosterone or estrogen administration. Thus these neonatal castrates were *demasculinized*. When tested for *female* behavior under various hormone conditions with a sexually vigorous male, the male neonatal castrates also showed more feminine behavior than males castrated as adults but otherwise treated in the same way. The neonatal castrates were mounted more by the males and responded by showing 40 times more lordosis responses than did adult castrates under identical experimental conditions. Thus, the neonatal castrates were *feminized* as well as demasculinized.

Female rats injected at birth with testosterone were also compared with females injected at birth with an inert oil. The neonatally testosterone-injected females showed significantly diminished female behavior when tested with vigorous males. They were *defeminized*. However, no consistent differences in malelike behavior were found between the female rats given testosterone at birth and the oil-injected controls. Both showed masculine behaviors at levels roughly comparable with those of neonatally castrated males. Thus no significant masculinization of the females by the neonatal testosterone treatment occurred. In general, subsequent experiments have supported these findings. Later in this chapter we shall discuss the effect of unusual fetal hormonal situations in human beings on later sexuality.

Primate Studies

Very few studies exist of prenatal hormonal manipulation in primates. The most systematic observations are those of Robert Goy and Charles Phoenix and their colleagues (Goy, 1970; Phoenix et al., 1983). Rhesus monkeys have a **gestation period** of about 168 days. Goy and Phoenix and co-work

gestation period (Jes-TAY-shun) The time from fertilization to birth.

ers produced masculinized female offspring by administering testosterone to pregnant female monkeys between day 40 and day 134 of gestation. The females born to mothers injected with testosterone had masculinized genitals. The internal organs were female, and these animals did menstruate, although puberty was delayed six months or so.

The social play of these animals as they grew from infancy to adulthood was intermediate in pattern compared with that of control male and female monkeys. In experiments done several years before, Leonard Rosenblum (1961) found that young male rhesus monkeys and young female rhesus monkeys display characteristic differences in play behavior. For example, prepubertal male monkeys show more wrestling, or rough-and-tumble play, initiate more chasing or tag games, and display more mock threat gestures than do prepubertal female monkeys. In observations of play group activities, Goy discovered that the masculinized female monkeys showed play patterns that were in between those of the normal male and female (see Figure 9.11).

These behavioral differences cannot be attributed to actual differences in gonadal hormone levels in the animals at the time the behaviors were seen, since all were prepubertal animals and blood levels of testosterone and estrogen were extremely low. Moreover, castration of normal male monkeys at birth does not prevent the appearance of perfectly normal malelike play behavior during the three to four years of prepubertal life.

Young male and female monkeys show strong sex differences in rough-and-tumble play and wrestling behavior, with males engaging in such behaviors much more frequently than females. Females whose mothers were injected with testosterone during pregnancy show levels of such behavior in between that of normal males and females.

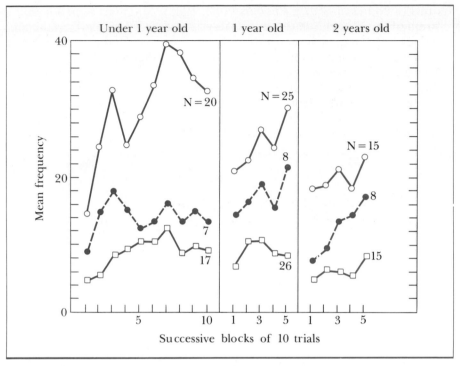

Figure 9.11
The frequency of rough-and-tumble play by normal male (○—○),
female (□—□), and masculinized female monkeys (●—●) (Goy, 1970).

It is possible that the prenatal exposure to testosterone in both the normal males (from their own testes) and the masculinized females (from the injections) altered the nervous system in such a way as to encourage the development of malelike play patterns.

   This conclusion must be somewhat tentative, because it is also possible that the masculinized appearance of the external genitals in the experimental female infants caused their mothers to respond differently to them, treating them more like male infants and influencing their behavior in that way. Gary Mitchell (1968) found that rhesus monkey mothers do treat male and female offspring differently, particularly during the first three months of life. Female infants are restrained more by their mother, are protected more, and are punished less than are male infants. In the Goy research, the first two masculinized females were removed from their mothers at birth, but all subsequent masculinized females, as well as all the controls, were kept with their mothers during the first three months of life. The mother's behavior toward the infants during the first few months of life may have contributed to the observed behavioral differences among the infants. More work along this line should clarify the role of various factors in the development of sex differences in primate play behavior.

   The masculinized monkeys have been tested for sexual behavior as

Müllerian inhibiting substance (MIS)   (mil-AIR-ee-an) Substance produced by the fetal testes. Inhibits the growth and development of the Müllerian (female) duct system.

adults (Eaton et al., 1973; Phoenix et al., 1983). Although some masculinization of the behavior in these animals was evident, particularly in the area of aggressive acts, wide individual differences were found and no clear pattern of masculinization of sexual behavior emerged. When evaluated specifically for female sexual behavior with sexually sophisticated males (who were not put off by a little aggressive behavior), the masculinized females did not differ from normal female monkeys in any important way. Thus, despite a certain degree of masculinization in the treated females, no significant defeminization was found.

Fetal Effects of Testosterone on Human Behavior

Figure 9.12 illustrates the way in which "chromosomal sex" is determined in human beings. If a Y chromosome is present in the developing fetus, the gonads develop as testes, and at about day 56 of gestation, these tiny testes begin to secrete substantial amounts of testosterone. This testosterone then masculinizes the external genitals and, along with **Müllerian inhibiting substance (MIS)** (also secreted by the testes), causes the internal reproductive system to differentiate along male lines. Figure 9.13 gives a

Figure 9.12 Determination of sex in the offspring.

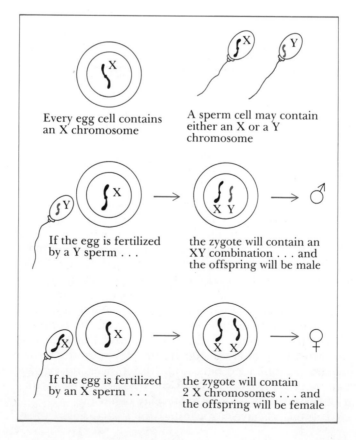

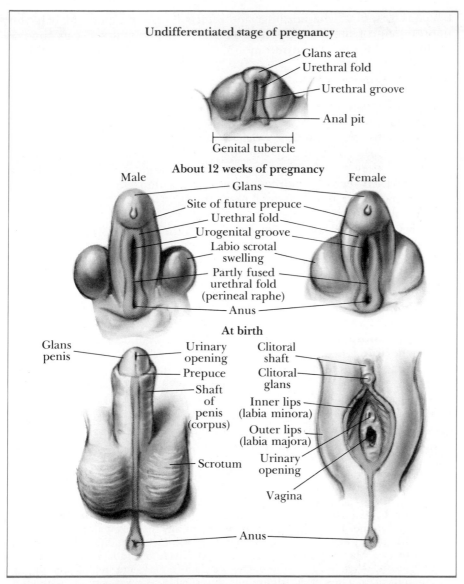

Undifferentiated stage of pregnancy

Glans area
Urethral fold
Urethral groove
Anal pit
Genital tubercle

About 12 weeks of pregnancy

Male   Female

Glans
Site of future prepuce
Urethral fold
Urogenital groove
Labio scrotal swelling
Partly fused urethral fold (perineal raphe)
Anus

At birth

Glans penis
Urinary opening
Prepuce
Shaft of penis (corpus)
Scrotum
Anus

Clitoral shaft
Clitoral glans
Inner lips (labia minora)
Outer lips (labia majora)
Urinary opening
Vagina
Anus

Figure 9.13   Three stages in the differentiation of human male and female genitals.
The top drawing shows the undifferentiated stage, which is present from conception until about the end of the first three months. Stage 2, shown in the middle drawing, begins at about three months. The bottom drawing shows the fully differentiated male and female genitals as they appear at birth.

brief overview of the differentiation of the reproductive structures in the human fetus.

Testosterone is also believed to masculinize the brain to suppress the inherent cyclic pattern of hormone secretion. In human beings the ques-

hypertrophy (hi-PER-tro-fee) Abnormal growth.

tion has arisen of whether lingering effects on some aspects of behavior may be found from fetal exposure to testosterone in males and its absence in females. Two human syndromes have been studied in some detail.

The CAH Syndrome

Some situations occur in which genetic females (XX chromosome pattern) are exposed to abnormal levels of androgens during fetal development. One such situation is called the *congenital adrenal* **hypertrophy** (CAH) syndrome. In this condition a genetic malfunction of the fetal adrenal glands occurs and they secrete large amounts of androgens rather than cortisol. This increased level of androgens causes masculinization of the external genitals and internal duct system. Once the child is born this condition can be controlled through medication and further masculinization can be prevented. Cosmetic surgery can be performed on the male-appearing genitals. These individuals are now usually raised as girls. Before the situation was recognized and treated, many CAH individuals were raised as males.

John Money, Anke Ehrhardt, and their colleagues have looked at the psychological and social development of these CAH individuals for many years (Money and Ehrhardt, 1972; Ehrhardt and Meyer-Bahlburg, 1981). In particular, they have been interested in the possible effects of fetal androgen exposure on such aspects of behavior as gender identity (feelings of maleness or femaleness), sex-related behaviors, and sexual orientation (homosexuality, heterosexuality). Those who have been recognized and treated at birth are perhaps most interesting from a theoretical point of view, since any masculinization is thought to be due to the effects of the fetal exposure and not to any social learning by the child. Three main generalizations concerning CAH syndrome individuals recognized and treated at birth and raised as females can be made.

1. Gender identity is female, with no unusual psychological problems. (This was most definitely not true in earlier, untreated cases.)
2. Gender-related behaviors in childhood are *somewhat* masculinized, with the CAH girls showing significantly higher levels of energy expenditure and higher levels of interest in more typically malelike games and sports. The CAH girls also show lessened interest in more traditional female activities. Many of these observations were made in the 1960s and early 1970s, when sex role stereotypes were more prevalent in child-rearing practices. The CAH girls are not abnormal in any way, simply more tomboyish [the term applied by Money and Ehrhardt (1972)].
3. Any effect on sexual orientation of the fetal androgen exposure is still uncertain. Such androgen exposure certainly does not determine that these women will be homosexual. A recent study did find, however, that a group of CAH women, now in their 20s and early 30s, show higher levels of homosexuality (as revealed by self-ratings) than either normal controls or controls born with abnormal vaginal structure (but not due to fetal androgenization—a condition known as Rokitansky's syndrome). Over a third of the CAH women (37 percent) rated themselves as bisexual or homosexual, compared with 7 percent of the Rokitansky girls (Money et al., 1984). Alfred Kinsey and colleagues (1953) placed the number of women who had had some homosexual contact with at least one partner by the age of 20 at 10 percent of the population.

The Androgen Insensitivity Syndrome

Another inherited condition occurs in which the body cells of genetic males (XY chromosome pattern) lack the capacity to respond to androgens. This *androgen insensitivity syndrome* causes the affected individuals to be born with no penis and no scrotum but with a somewhat enlarged **clitoris** and a shallow, pouchlike vagina. Testes are present, but they are located within the abdominal cavity, having failed to descend. Individuals with this syndrome are usually reared as females. Their insensitivity to androgens is often not discovered until they are in their teens, and nothing at present can be done to increase their sensitivity to them. However, plastic surgery can enlarge the vagina to accommodate sexual intercourse, and sufficient amounts of estrogen are secreted by the testes at puberty to bring about female breast development and body build (see Figure 9.14).

The degree of bodily feminization is so complete that some of these women have had successful careers as fashion models. From a study of the life histories of 14 such individuals, Money, Ehrhardt, and Masica (1968) concluded that "psychological differentiation is invariably feminine, with a strong degree of maternalism which makes for very good adoptive motherhood." Sexual orientation appears to develop along normal female lines.

clitoris (KLI-to-riss) Small erectile organ, part of female genitalia.

Figure 9.14 A patient with androgen-insensitivity syndrome.
Although a genetic XY male, this individual's body cells cannot respond normally to testosterone and develops female secondary sexual characteristics under the influence of the normal amounts of estrogen secreted at puberty by the testes.

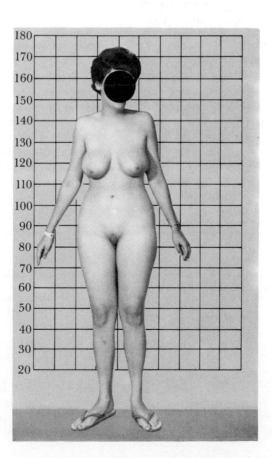

The Guevedoces *of Salinas*

Adolescence can be stormy enough without any extra complications. What would it be like if one had to change from being a girl to being a boy at puberty? For a small number of individuals this is a reality. A few years ago an unusual condition was discovered among the inhabitants of the village of Salinas in the Dominican Republic. Julianne Imperato-McGinley and colleagues (1974) reported a few genetic males who were born with female-appearing or ambiguous genitals. At puberty, however, dramatic changes in the genitals, particularly the growth of the "clitoris" into a penis, made it obvious that these individuals were, in fact, male. The villagers of Salinas gave the name *guevedoces* ("penis at twelve") to those individuals. The technical name for this condition is *5-alpha-reductase deficiency*. By 1979 38 cases were reported. These individuals came from 23 interrelated families in three rural villages, including Salinas (Imperato-McGinley, et al., 1979). A few cases from other parts of the world have also been found. Of the 38 Dominican individuals, 18 were unambiguously raised as girls. Yet during or after puberty, all but one changed to a male gender identity and all but two to a male gender role.

Guevedoces are born with the normal XY male chromosomal pattern, but because of an inherited genetic defect, they do not manufacture sufficient quantities of the enzyme 5-alpha-reductase, which is necessary to convert testosterone into another androgen, *dihydrotestosterone,* which is required during the fetal period for normal differentiation of the Wolffian system and male external genitalia. As a result of this enzyme deficiency, the affected males are born with ambiguous or female-appearing genitals. The *phallus* (embryonic tissue that develops into either the penis or the clitoris) is very small and looks like a clitoris. The urethral opening is positioned at the base of the phallus much as it would be in a normal female. The scrotum does not join down the midline and superficially resembles the outer lips of the vagina. There is no actual vagina, just a small pouch where the vagina would be in a female. Because of the appearance of the genitals, many of these individuals have been raised as females until puberty. This condition was first noted three generations back, and eight of these first-generation individuals are still alive. In the first generation, all of the affected males were raised as girls (Imperato-McGinley et al., 1979). In subsequent generations some of the *guevedoces* were raised as females, some as "males-to-be." The term *guevedoces* is a colloquial expression in the village that recognizes the special status of these children. Just over 1 percent of the male children born in this village over the last 100 or so years have been *guevedoces.*

At puberty, growth of the penis, deepening

Male–Female Differences in Nonreproductive Behavior

Several studies demonstrate that male and female animals show systematic differences in some nonreproductive behaviors. In many cases these differences have been shown to be partially determined by the presence or absence of testosterone during the critical periods of development of the organism. The great majority of these studies have been done with rodents, particularly rats, mice, and hamsters.

These behaviors include locomotor activity, intraspecies aggression, pheromone secretion, some learning tasks, and even response to brain damage (Beatty, 1979). In many of these cases, female rodents can be made to resemble males more closely in their behavior by injections of testoster-

of the voice and increase in muscle mass all depend directly on testosterone itself, which these individuals manufacture and secrete in normal amounts from their testes, which are undescended. With the increased secretion of testosterone at puberty, the scrotum takes on its normal wrinkled appearance, the testes descend, and the "clitoris" becomes a small but sexually functional penis. (Since the urethral opening is not in the penis, ejaculation takes place where the urethra does open, at the base of the penis. The penis, although small, is capable of erections, and most of these individuals include heterosexual intercourse as part of their sex life.)

According to Imperato-McGinley and colleagues, the great majority of these individuals eventually make a relatively normal adjustment to this profound change, but this does not happen overnight. "A male-gender identity gradually evolved over several years as the subjects passed through stages of no longer feeling like girls, to feeling like men and, finally, to the conscious awareness that they were indeed men. The change to a male-gender role occurred either during puberty or in the post-pubertal period, after the subjects were convinced that they were men (male-gender identity) and were experiencing sexual interest in women. The gender-role change took place at 16 years of age, on the average, with a range of 14 to 24 years"

(Imperato-McGinley et al., 1979).

It is not entirely clear what such radical psychosexual adjustments imply for the normal development of gender identity and gender role. Not all of these individuals have adopted male gender identities, although the great majority have. Likewise, most of these individuals prefer women as sexual partners, although again, this is not completely true. Although one may be tempted to argue that the genetic "maleness" and/or exposure to testosterone itself during the fetal period may be important in the ability of these individuals to adopt male gender identities, it should be remembered that in most cases, the family members and people in the community knew that these individuals would develop male genitalia at puberty, as their *guevedoces* label indicated. Such expectations, even if the child was raised tentatively as a girl, must have important effects on the individual's own views on his or her coming adult sexuality. This was probably not the case with the first generation of *guevedoces*, but their changeover was many years ago, and most of these individuals are now elderly. A psychological study of the first-generation *guevedoces* has not appeared. Perhaps the best generalization that can be made concerning these individuals is that human gender identity is multidetermined, and that the human spirit can often display amazing adaptive capacity.

one at or near birth, whereas males can be made to resemble females more closely by neonatal castration.

Structural Differences in Male and Female Brains

Since the early 1970s several studies have demonstrated structural differences in the brains of male and female animals. For some of these differences hormonal levels during the developmental period have been shown to be important. One of the first such demonstrations was that of Geoffrey Raisman and Pauline Field (1971; 1973b), who showed that systematic differences existed in the pattern of dendritic synapses in the preoptic area. This was a quite specific difference, as there was no such sex difference in the pattern of synapses in the nearby region of the ventromedial nucleus of the hypothalamus. A few years later similar findings were reported for hamsters and monkeys (Greenough et al., 1977; Ayoub et al., 1983).

Roger Gorski and colleagues (1978) found large sex differences in the size of the medial preoptic nucleus (MPON) in rats, with the male MPON being several times larger. Moreover, they found that this difference was related to the hormonal conditions during development. Males castrated at birth had smaller MPONs than normal males, whereas females injected with 1 mg of testosterone on day 4 following birth had larger MPONs than normal females. In neither case did the hormonal manipulations produce a reversal of MPON size, however. The increase in size of the MPON is due to a greater number of neurons being present in the male, as well as to the neurons being larger. Although it is tempting to speculate that the MPON is concerned with some aspect of reproductive or other sexually dimorphic behavior, this has yet to be clearly demonstrated. Several other sex-related structural differences in the nervous system have been reported as well (Arnold and Gorski, 1984).

Differences in the human brain have also been reported. D. F. Swaab and E. Fliers (1985) examined 13 male and 18 female human brains of individuals who ranged from 10 to 93 years of age at the time of their death. Swaab and Fliers measured what they called the "sexually dimorphic nucleus" of the preoptic region and reported that this nucleus is about 2.5 times larger in males than in females and contains over twice as many cells. The size of this nucleus decreases with age in both males and females. Although its function is unknown, it is in the region of the brain known to be involved with the control of GnRH secretion.

SUMMARY

1. Hormones are chemical messengers secreted into the bloodstream by various tissues, including the brain. The brain secretes hormones that regulate the production and secretion of hormones from the anterior pituitary. Cells of the body respond to a hormone only if they have the appropriate receptors for that particular hormone.

2. Hormones are classified into one of three groups: steroids, polypeptides, and a miscellaneous group. Steroids act primarily by binding with cytoplasmic receptors, migrating to the cell nucleus, and altering the production of some substance by interacting with the genetic machinery. Steroids can also act directly on cell membranes to alter the firing rate of neurons. Polypeptide hormones typically act through a "second messenger" system in which the hormone itself does not enter the cell, but instead binds with a receptor in the cell membrane. This in turn activates adenylate cyclase, which increases the levels of cyclic AMP within the cytoplasm of the cell. The cyclic AMP is the second messenger and alters the activity of the cell. Other second messenger systems also exist.

3. One of the basic distinctions between male and female mammals is that females secrete FSH, LH, and gonadal steroids on a cyclic basis, whereas

males do not. This is an example of sexual dimorphism. Sexual dimorphism can also be seen in behavior and in the structure of certain parts of the central nervous system. The male pattern of hormone secretion, behavior, and nervous system structure stems from the masculinizing effects of testosterone on the developing fetus. Female fetuses exposed to abnormal levels of testosterone or other similar hormones often show masculinizing effects in hormone secretion, behavior, body, and brain structure.

4. In mammals other than primates sexual behavior shows a clear relationship to gonadal steroid levels—estrogen and progesterone in the female, testosterone in the male. The picture is less clear in primates. In human beings social, cultural, and individual differences become increasingly important in sexual behavior.

5. Nursing depends on two hormones: prolactin, which causes milk production and secretion, and oxytocin, which is necessary for the secreted milk to be expelled to the outside of the body. The suckling reflex is an example of a neuroendocrine reflex.

6. Testosterone is important in producing male sexual behavior. Removal of the testes generally eliminates sexual behavior in animals below the levels of primates. In primates some elements of male sexual behavior may survive for many years following castration. No demonstrated relationship exists between testosterone levels in the bloodstream and measures of sexual vigor or level of activity in normal men. Extremely low levels of testosterone are typically accompanied by impotence. Antiandrogen medications are being used in the treatment of sex offenders in the United States and Europe.

7. Psychological studies of individuals with abnormal fetal hormonal conditions suggest that detectable effects on behavior may result from exposure to abnormally high levels of testosterone (or similar substances) in females and that detectable behavioral effects may be found in males with abnormally low levels of testosterone or cytoplasmic receptors for testosterone. Research with animals supports these findings. Thus hormones can affect behavior either indirectly, by their effects on the developing organism during the fetal period, or directly, through activational effects throughout the lifetime of the organism.

SUGGESTIONS FOR FURTHER READING

Adler, N. T. (Ed.) (1981). *Neuroendocrinology of reproduction.* New York: Plenum.

Arnold, A. O., and Gorski, R. A. (1984). Gonadal steroid induction of structural sex differences in the central nervous system. *Annual Review of Neuroscience, 7,* 413–442.

Ehrhardt, A. A., and Meyer-Bahlburg, H. F. L. (1981). Effects of prenatal sex hormones on gender-related behavior. *Science, 211,* 1312–1318. (This entire issue is devoted to the subject of sexual dimorphism.)

Feder, H. H. (1984). Hormones and sexual behavior. *Annual Review of Psychology, 35,* 165–200.

Money, J., and Ehrhardt, A. A. (1972). *Man and woman, boy and girl.* Baltimore: Johns Hopkins Press.

10

Sleep and Dreaming

Dreams are real as long as they last.
Can we say more of life?

HAVELOCK ELLIS

Preview

In the 1920s Hans Berger developed techniques to measure the spontaneous electrical activity of the brain and opened the way for the scientific study of sleep and dreaming. We now know that sleep and dreaming can be indexed clearly by electrical patterns (recorded from the scalp) quite different from those seen during waking. Actually, the electrical activity most commonly associated with dreaming resembles the waking pattern closely; this stage of sleep is sometimes called *paradoxical sleep* for that reason. Dreaming is also characterized by rapid movements of the eyes. The term *REM* (rapid eye movement) sleep is applied to this stage. Several different regions of the brain and several different neurotransmitters are involved in various stages of sleep.

Sleep and waking occur in regular cycles that are, in part, the product of neural mechanisms that generate biologic rhythms (termed *circadian* rhythms) of about 24 hours each. The neurons responsible for generating circadian rhythms have been identified tentatively as belonging to two tiny clusters of cells deep in the hypothalamus just superior to the optic chiasm, the *suprachiasmatic nuclei.* Removal of these nuclei in experimental animals disrupts many different biologic rhythms. Disruption of biological rhythms by changing time zones can produce "jet lag" and other disconcerting conditions in humans.

Although in general we all know what sleep is, it is useful to define it more formally. We shall consider sleep as a natural state of greatly reduced movements and diminished responsiveness to stimulation, characterized by distinctive patterns in the electrical activity of the brain and by maximal relaxation of the musculature. Such a definition helps to distinguish sleep from other states that resemble it superficially, such as those under anesthesia, coma, hypnosis, and various drugs.

Measuring Sleep—The EEG

How can we be sure that a person or an animal actually is asleep? We have all observed that sleeping organisms are harder to arouse than those that are awake. Sleepers also close their eyes, breathe in a regular rhythm, and relax their muscles. However, the most precise method of evaluating sleep is to measure brain waves, changes in the spontaneous electrical activity of the brain, which is generated by the constant flux of postsynaptic potentials in the neurons of the superficial layers of the cortex. This is measured by means of the **electroencephalogram** (**EEG,** for short).

Hans Berger

The first brain waves were recorded by a German psychiatrist, Hans Berger. Brilliant but withdrawn, he developed the basic techniques for measuring the electrical activity of the human brain from electrodes placed on the scalp. He first measured the brain activity of World War I veterans who had undergone partial skull removals. With these men he was able to record from the scalp just over the boneless areas where the signals were easier to detect because there was no skull to dampen them. Later he improved his techniques and was able to make scalp EEG recordings from normal subjects. He worked from 1924 to 1929 before publishing his results. When he did publish them in 1929, these so-called Berger waves were met with incredulity by the scientific community. Later, however, several other prestigious investigators confirmed his results and the EEG became a major tool in the analysis of brain function.

The frequency of the activity recorded in the human EEG, as in virtually all mammals, varies from less than 1 Hz (cycles per second) to 35–50 Hz. The amplitude of brain waves typically varies from 5 to 100 μV. Waves in which the frequency is 8 Hz or greater do not usually exceed 20 μV in amplitude. The EEG record of awake subjects shows two basic patterns. One is a regular, rather synchronized (smooth wave) pattern of 8–13 Hz. This is the **alpha rhythm,** so named because it is the first letter of the Greek alphabet and was the first clear pattern seen by Berger. **Beta** activity is characterized by higher-frequency (15–30 Hz), lower-voltage activity. Alpha waves are seen typically when the individual is relaxed, is awake, and has his or her eyes closed. Beta activity is seen when the person is alert, with eyes open (see Figure 10.1).

Stages of Sleep

Based on EEG records, sleep is usually divided into five stages, four of which are classified as *slow-wave sleep* (SWS), with frequencies of 7 Hz or

electroencephalogram (EEG) (e-lek-tro-en-CEF-a-low-gram) A recording of the spontaneous electrical activity of the brain. The instrument used in this procedure is called an *electroencephalograph,* the procedure is *electroencephalography* (e-lek-tro-en-cef-a-LOG-ra-fee).

alpha rhythm (AL-fa) Activity in the EEG characterized by regular waves at 8–13 Hz.

beta waves Activity in the EEG characterized by low-voltage waves at 15–30 Hz.

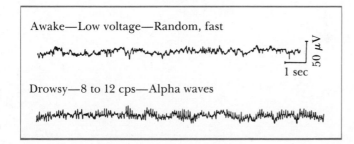

Figure 10.1 EEG records of an individual in two different waking states, alert and drowsy.

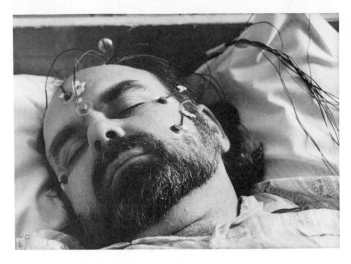

A subject in a sleep research experiment at the Montefiore hospital sleep and waking disorder center. The electrodes can measure both the electrical activity of the brain and eye movements such as those occur during REM sleep.

REM (rapid eye movement) sleep A stage of sleep characterized by low-voltage, fast EEG and low muscle tone (except for eye muscles). Associated with dreaming.

less. One stage of sleep is quite different. In this stage the EEG actually resembles that of the alert waking state. This phase is also accompanied by *rapid eye movements* and is, for this reason, called **REM sleep.** This stage of sleep is also sometimes called *paradoxical sleep,* since early investigators considered it paradoxical that such low-voltage, high-frequency brain waves would occur during sleep, which is generally characterized by much slower, larger waves. (Figure 10.2 shows these sleep stages.)

Stages 1 to 4 of slow-wave sleep (the sleep of each stage is deeper than the one preceding it) are marked by an increase in amplitude and a decrease in frequency of the brain waves. REM sleep occurs regularly throughout the night. During these periods breathing becomes faster and more irregular and heart rate and blood pressure increase. This stage of sleep was first reported by Nathaniel Kleitman and his colleagues (Aserinsky and Kleitman, 1953; Dement and Kleitman, 1955). Virtually all mam-

SUMMARY TABLE		
EEG Characteristics in Various Stages of Consciousness		
Consciousness State	**EEG Frequency**	**EEG Amplitude**
Alert waking	Quite variable (8–30 Hz)	Low
Awake–drowsy (alpha)	8–13 Hz (rhythmic)	Medium
Sleep—Stage 1	6–8 Hz	Low
Sleep—Stage 2	4–7 Hz (occasional bursts of 14-Hz "spindles")	Medium
Sleep—Stage 3	1–3 Hz	High
Sleep—Stage 4	Less than 2 Hz	Highest
REM sleep	Variable, mostly greater than 10 Hz	Low

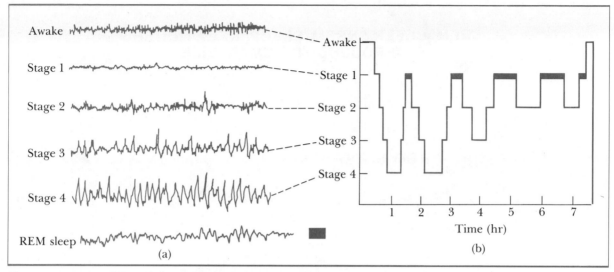

Figure 10.2 **(a) EEG recordings corresponding to the awake state and the four stages of slow-wave sleep. (b) A diagram of a typical night's sleep in a young adult human.**
Episodes of REM sleep are marked by dark bars. REM sleep periods tend to become longer during the night. The last REM period is interrupted by awakening. Dream recall would probably be good for this episode.

mals experience both slow-wave and REM sleep, although the proportions of time spent in the various stages of sleep vary considerably from species to species.

A Night's Sleep

A typical night's sleep is made up of several cycles, each lasting from 90 to 110 minutes, in which the sleeper goes through all four slow-wave sleep cycles and (at least after the first cycle) one episode of REM sleep. Laboratory studies have shown that everyone dreams, even those who claim they do not. Individuals awakened during REM sleep report dreams that are often quite vivid and complex and that, if the dreamers had not been awakened, could have been forgotten by the morning. This is what people do who believe they do not dream; they simply forget their dreams before morning. [A particularly interesting source on sleep and dreaming is William Dement's book *Some Must Watch While Some Must Sleep* (1974).]

Why Your Grandmother Always Hears You Come In Late

People of different ages seem to require different amounts of sleep. Newborn infants spend a large proportion of their sleep time in REM sleep,

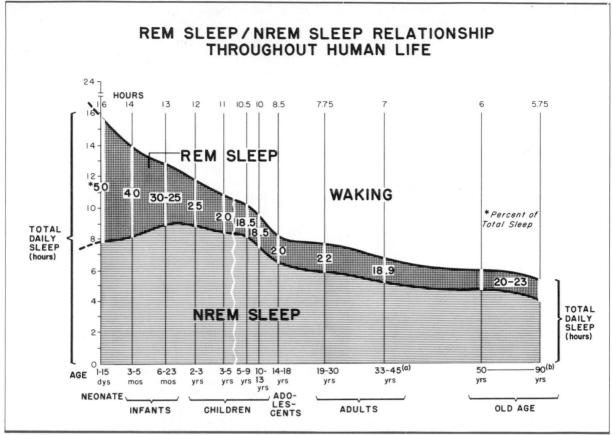

Figure 10.3 Graph showing the changes with age in the total amounts of sleep, REM sleep, and percentage of REM sleep to total sleep time during a typical 24-hour period.

As can be seen, the amount of REM sleep falls from about eight hours at birth to less than one hour in old age. Non-REM sleep decreases somewhat more gradually, from about eight hours at birth to about five hours in old age.

but this percentage declines to adult levels by about age 10. Total sleep time and proportion of REM sleep decline in the elderly, as does stage 4 sleep (deep sleep), which often disappears in persons over 60 years of age (D. D. Kelly, 1981). (This may explain why it is very hard to sneak in late without awakening your grandmother when she is staying at your house.) At present no accepted explanation exists for these changes in the sleep pattern with aging.

REM sleep has become well known outside of the textbooks because it is highly correlated with dreaming. The extent to which dreams occur in non-REM sleep is controversial. Dement (1974) has found that only about 14 percent of his subjects report that they were dreaming when wakened during periods of slow-wave sleep, contrasted with almost 80 percent who report that they had been dreaming when awakened during REM sleep. David Foulkes (1962), on the other hand, found that 51 percent of subjects awakened during non-REM sleep said that they had been dreaming, although even more of his subjects reported dreams when awakened during REM sleep. Thus researchers agree that REM sleep is more closely associated with dreaming than is non-REM sleep, but they disagree on the extent of dreaming that may take place in slow-wave sleep.

The discrepant results may depend somewhat on the definition of dreaming. REM sleep dreams (often called *imagery dreams*) are more likely to be filled with visual images and story lines that involve the dreamer. Non-REM dreams (called *static dreams*) are more like daytime "thinking," being more problem oriented and having less visual imagery and plot (Foulkes, 1966). Therefore some may not consider them to fall within the definition of a dream. In addition to the problem of how dreams are defined, discrepancies may arise because of differences in the way subjects are questioned. For example, some researchers may have asked their subjects, "Were you dreaming?" whereas others may have asked, "Was there anything going on in your mind?" These differences in wording could affect the answers.

In males REM sleep is associated with penile erections (Kiester, 1980); in females it is accompanied by vaginal secretions and clitoral engorgement. These changes tend to be independent of dream content, although, of course, they may be woven into the content of erotic dreams. The occurrence of erection during REM sleep provides sex therapists with an excellent way to distinguish between psychologically based and physiologically caused **impotence** (inability to achieve and/or maintain an erection). If an erection occurs during sleep, then the waking impotence cannot be due to physical causes.

REM sleep is also characterized by a dramatic decrease in muscle tone (except for the muscles that move the eyes). This "sleep paralysis" is produced by a group of neurons in the locus coeruleus (a nucleus in the brainstem) that send inhibitory input down to the neurons in the spinal cord innervating the skeletal musculature. This inhibition of the neurons that activate the body muscles would explain why sleepwalking or other acting out of dreams does not occur during REM sleep.

REM Deprivation and REM Rebound

What is the function of REM sleep? We still don't know, but the question has stimulated a great deal of research. For example, animals as well as human beings have been REM deprived by waking them during periods of REM sleep. Since such awakenings can also result in general sleep deprivation, control subjects in such experiments must be awakened for equal periods of time during slow-wave sleep. Although early reports suggested that effects might be dramatic, subsequent experiments have shown that the effects of REM deprivation are not spectacular. One clear result is that

impotence (IM-po-tents) Inability to achieve or maintain an erection long enough for satisfactory intercourse.

Randy Gardner's Vigil

What is the longest you have gone without sleep? Many people have stayed up all night once or twice, and a few have gone as long as 48 hours without proper sleep, but the longest sleepless vigil that has been documented is that of Randy Gardner, who went without sleep for 264 consecutive hours (about 11 days) as part of a science fair project. Sleep researchers George Gulevich and colleagues (1966) examined Randy both during and after his adventure in the waking zone, taking EEG recordings and administering neurologic and psychologic tests. Randy, described as a confident, self-assured 17-year-old at the time, was the oldest of four children. He was reported to be fascinated by extremes since early adolescence and undertook this project partly because people told him it couldn't be done. Randy had the support of two friends, one or another of whom was with him throughout his sleepless period.

Randy held up remarkably well during his record vigil. At about 90 hours of sleep deprivation he experienced his only illusion or hallucination while walking down a darkened street. At no time did he ingest any stimulant, not even coffee. He was irritable and had lapses of memory and "waking dreams" during days 4 and 5 of sleeplessness, but a psychiatric interview at 262 hours showed him to be well oriented as to time and place and in good contact with reality. Not surprisingly, toward the end of his sleepless period he reported being extremely tired and complained of burning eyelids. Minor increases in tremor and reflex responsiveness were noted. All these symptoms were virtually gone after the first night of sleep and he was back to normal a week later.

The researchers monitored Randy's brain activity continuously during the first three recovery nights and on three other nights 7 days, 6 weeks, and 10 weeks after his vigil. He slept for about 15 hours on his first night of sleep and a little over 10 hours on the second night and was back to near normal sleep time by the third night, having spent more time in REM sleep on the first few recovery nights. At the end of one week his sleep patterns were back to normal and he suffered no ill effects from his vigil.

The reasons someone goes without sleep may be important in determining the effects of sleep deprivation. If, like Randy, one is staying awake voluntarily for "science" or for some other worthy cause, the effects of sleep deprivation may be minimal. If, on the other hand, one is unable to sleep because of anxiety, worry, or depression, sleep deprivation may contribute to subsequent physical and emotional problems.

---

an individual who has been REM deprived tends to make up the debt by spending more time in REM sleep on the nights following REM deprivation. This REM rebound has been observed in both human beings and animals. No long-term effects have resulted from REM deprivation.

Sleep and Dreaming in Depression

Somewhat surprisingly, REM deprivation has been reported to be a successful treatment for some cases of depression (Vogel et al., 1980). Since REM deprivation has no known harmful effects, this type of depression

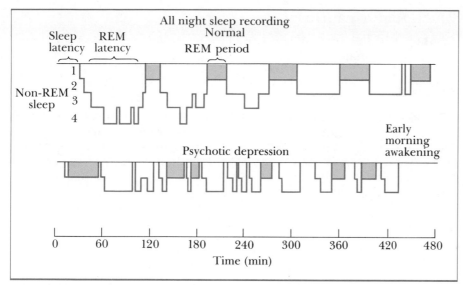

Figure 10.4   Sleep patterns of normal (top) and depressed patient (bottom).
Notice rapid onset of REM sleep in depressed individual.

therapy may prove very useful. The main differences between normals and depressives are not in total amount of REM sleep but in its distribution throughout the night. Moreover, the degree of improvement of the depressed patients (as measured with questionnaires) correlated with changes in the distribution of REM sleep episodes. The authors conclude that depressives may have a damaged or weakened sleep cycle oscillator and that improvement is due to some stimulation of this oscillator with REM deprivation. Virtually all drugs that are effective as antidepressants dramatically reduce the percentage of time cats spend in REM sleep, while slightly increasing overall sleep time (Scherschlicht et al., 1982). Figure 10.4 shows the differences in sleep pattern between a normal subject and a severely depressed patient (Gillin and Borbely, 1985).

The discovery that REM sleep is more highly correlated with reports of dreaming than non-REM sleep has resulted in a considerable amount of research on dreaming, but the function (if any) of dreams is still uncertain. Some information has emerged from these studies, however. For example, it is now thought that the notion of time compression in dreaming is not correct, for longer dreams seem to take longer real time (Dement, 1972). Moreover, bed-wetting is generally unrelated to dreaming and tends to occur primarily during slow-wave sleep. Sleepwalking occurs during stages 3 and 4 of non-REM sleep. Even some of the vivid, terrifying dreams (termed *night terrors*) that children (and some adults) occasionally experience can occur during non-REM sleep. Nightmares of the more usual kind occur during REM sleep as well.

benzodiazepines (ben-zo-die-AZ-e-peens) Family of drugs used to treat severe anxiety. Examples are Valium and Librium.

sleep apnea (AP-knee-ah) Disruptions in sleep due to blockage of airway or other causes.

Sleep Abnormalities

A number of sleep pathologies are known; *insomnia, sleep apnea,* and *narcolepsy* are the major ones.

Insomnia

As many as one person in five may experience severe difficulty in getting to sleep for a period of days or weeks. This is insomnia. Changes in sleeping habits, including insomnia, are sometimes indicators of mental depression and often occur in severely anxious individuals as well. Unfortunately, no "sleeping pill" is really effective. All the evidence suggests that sleeping pills only compound the problem; in fact, they may actually cause insomnia in healthy individuals. This can be a particular problem with aging, slightly anxious persons, who are often given "antianxiety" pills, such as the **benzodiazepines,** as sleeping pills, when they are simply in need of less sleep and are perhaps anxious because they believe that they aren't getting enough rest. Knowledge of the decreased need for sleep in the elderly and the harmful effects of medications to induce sleep would help to alleviate a lot of unnecessary worry and unhappiness. At present, the best advice that can be given about sleeping pills is simply, "Don't take them." Taking medication in order to get to sleep can initiate a vicious circle in which the person takes pills to get to sleep (which may only induce a heavily drugged state) and then becomes addicted to the point that he or she may experience real withdrawal symptoms, including even worse insomnia.

When some individuals who complain of insomnia are studied in sleep laboratories, they are often discovered to sleep a great deal more than they think they do. Moreover, some people who complain of insomnia actually do fall asleep but then *dream* that they are awake, trying to get to sleep. This is not to say that no genuine cases of insomnia exist, but the problem may not always be simple (Dement, 1974). Sleep requirements vary a great deal; for example, some healthy individuals may sleep as little as an hour or two each night.

Sleep Apnea

Sleep apnea, in which individuals stop breathing, is another serious sleep disturbance. Those who suffer from it wake up suddenly, catch their breath, and go back to sleep, and they may do this dozens or even hundreds of time a night. In adults sleep apnea usually does not pose a serious threat, although it is often quite annoying to the sleeper (and anyone sharing the same bed). It is sometimes caused by abnormalities in the throat or airway that can be corrected surgically. Although this phenomenon may underlie some cases of sudden infant death syndrome (SIDS), this is still just a hypothesis.

Narcolepsy

A small number of people suffer sudden attacks of sleepiness during the daytime and fall asleep for a few minutes, unable to control these "sleep seizures." This condition is known as **narcolepsy,** and no remedy is known. Obviously, this can have fatal consequences, if the individual is driving at the time, for example. Sometimes the person simply drops to the ground. Such attacks of extreme muscular weakness, termed **cataplexy,** often occur during states of violent emotion.

Sleep as an Active Brain Process

What changes in our brains underlie the various states of sleep and waking? Until a few years ago most investigators considered sleep to be a passive process—something that happens when we get tired and the brain cannot sustain normal operations. This is not the view held by most neuroscientists today. Ample evidence exists that both slow-wave and REM sleep are the result of *active* brain processes. Different stages of sleep are now seen as normal states of the brain.

As Berger's EEG techniques were adopted by other researchers, some of them began to record the electrical activity of the brains of sleeping animals. In general, the same sort of electrical patterns were found in animals of widely different species. This technique allowed the determination of waking or sleeping states in animals that were paralyzed or otherwise prevented from making normal movements. One early series of experiments was done by a Belgian neurophysiologist, Frederic Bremer (1936), who examined the cortical electrical activity in the forebrain of cats following transection of the brain at two different levels.

In the **cerveau isolé** (isolated forebrain) Bremer transected the brain just between the superior and inferior colliculi in the brainstem. In the **encephale isolé** (isolated brain) the transection is made at the caudal end of the brainstem, just ahead of the spinal cord (see Figure 10.5). In the cerveau isolé, recordings from the cortex of the cat showed no signs of normal waking activity, nor were there any eye movements or pupillary changes. The pupils remained constricted, and the EEG record was one of continuous slow-wave sleep.

In the encephale isolé preparation, in which the entire brainstem was still attached to the forebrain, the EEG record showed distinct cycles of waking and sleeping. Moreover, during the waking cycles the pupils were dilated and the eyes followed moving objects. Bremer concluded that sleep was a passive process caused by a reduction in sensory input. He reasoned that in the cerveau isolé preparation the forebrain was cut off from the sensory input from the fifth and eighth cranial nerves. In the encephale isolé preparation this input to the forebrain was preserved. These experiments appeared to confirm what most people assumed anyway, that the brain fell asleep when there was insufficient sensory input to keep it awake. Even at this time there should have been doubts about such a conclusion, because it was well known that people (and animals) can fall asleep in the presence of considerable light and noise and often fail to fall asleep even in quiet, dark surroundings. Nevertheless, the idea that sleep occurred as a result of decreased sensory input was not seriously challenged until the

narcolepsy (NAR-ko-lep-see) Abnormal sudden attacks of sleepiness during the day.

cataplexy (CAT-a-plex-ee) Sudden attacks of extreme muscular weakness, often associated with narcolepsy.

cerveau isolé (SAIR-vo eez-o-LAY) Experimental preparation in which the brain is transected in the brainstem between the anterior and posterior colliculi. See *encephale isolé.*

encephale isolé (On-seh-FAL eez-o-LAY) Experimental preparation in which the brain is transected at the caudal end of the brainstem, where it merges into the spinal cord. See *cerveau isolé.*

brainstem reticular formation (BSRF) (re-TIK-u-lar) Region of the brainstem packed with a network of cell bodies and dendrites. Important in many functions, including forebrain arousal.

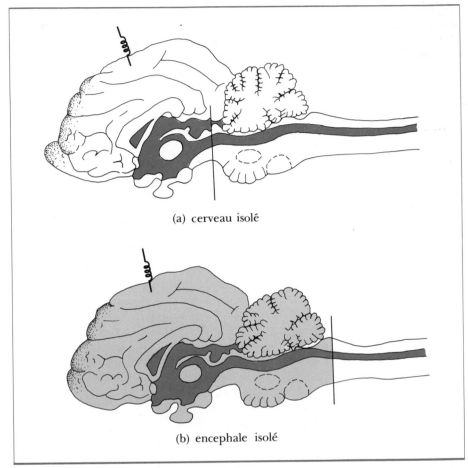

(a) cerveau isolé

(b) encephale isolé

Figure 10.5   The levels at which the brain is transected in the cerveau isolé preparation (a) and the encephale isolé (b).

pivotal experiments of Giuseppe Moruzzi and Horace W. Magoun over 10 years later (Moruzzi and Magoun, 1949).

The Brainstem Reticular Formation and Forebrain Arousal

The brainstem is not just the place where several cranial nerves enter the brain. It is packed with different nuclei and with axons of neurons coursing up and down between the brain and the spinal cord. Located along the central core of the brainstem is a small cylinder of neurons about the size of a person's little finger. Because of the netlike (reticulum) appearance of the dendrites and axons in this part of the brain, it is named the **brainstem reticular formation (BSRF).** Although more than 90 nuclei are recognizable in the BSRF, it is often viewed as having a single function.

In 1949 Moruzzi and Magoun discovered the capacity of the BSRF to arouse the rest of the brain. They found that direct electrical stimulation in the BSRF could waken a sleeping cat and change the EEG of a drugged animal to the waking, low-voltage, fast-activity pattern characteristic of the alert waking state. It may not seem surprising that one can waken an animal by passing electrical current into its brain, but under the conditions used by Moruzzi and Magoun, such stimulation was only successful in awakening the animals when the electrode tips were in the BSRF. Stimulation with similar current strength in other nearby regions of the brain did not awaken the cats. It was critical to their experiments that the cats were anesthetized with a nonbarbiturate drug—**chlorosane**—which does not severely depress the neurons of the BSRF, as do, for example, **barbiturates.** Using barbiturate drugs, electrical stimulation of the BSRF does not produce arousal.

Shortly after the study by Moruzzi and Magoun, Donald Lindsley and colleagues (1950) found that making lesions in the BSRF produced a permanently sleeping animal with an EEG pattern to match. However, destroying the surrounding regions of the brainstem but sparing the BSRF did not produce any significant changes in wake–sleep cycles. This last experiment was critical to disproving the hypothesis that sleep was a result of reduced sensory input, since these more lateral lesions *did* destroy the classical specific sensory input channels from the cochlea, vestibular system, and somesthetic system. Thus, Magoun and others reasoned, the input to the cortex from the BSRF, and *not* the specific sensory input, is critical in maintaining the waking state. Later experiments determined that clusters of neurons in the **intralaminar nuclei** of the thalamus were also involved in arousal of the forebrain.

The neurons of the BSRF get synaptic input from most of the specific sensory systems and from many other parts of the brain. Nevertheless, the specific sensory input was not critical in the maintenance of arousal, as lesions that interrupted these pathways showed. These findings shifted the view of sleep as due to a reduction of specific sensory input to a "reticular arousal" view of sleep, in which the nonspecific input of the BSRF and associated thalamic nuclei were seen as responsible for maintaining the necessary level of arousal for waking states. Although this was still a "passive" view of sleep, the focus of attention was now on the BSRF and away from specific sensory input. It was not long before an even more radical view of sleep emerged from further experiments on the operation of brainstem mechanisms in sleep.

Sleep-Producing Regions of the Brain

In the 1950s and 1960s a number of experiments, particularly from laboratories in Italy and France, demonstrated that centers existed in the brainstem that produced sleep. For example, workers in Moruzzi's laboratory in Italy examined cats in which the brainstem was cut just a few millimeters caudal to that known to produce the permanent "sleep" of the cerveau isolé. They discovered not only that episodes of normal-appearing wakefulness occurred in the cortical EEG but that some of these cats spent 70–90 percent of the time awake, in contrast to normal cats, which sleep 60 percent of the time. It soon became apparent that at least part of the expla-

chlorosane (KLOR-oh-sane) A nonbarbiturate anesthetic agent.

barbiturate (bar-BIT-u-rate) A central nervous system depressant.

intralaminar nuclei (in-tra-LAM-ih-nar) A system of nuclei *in between the layers* of other nuclei in the thalamus.

raphe system (rah-FEY) A string of nuclei along the midline of the brainstem (the term *raphe* means "seam" in Greek).

locus coeruleus (LOW-cus sir-RULE-ee-us) A system of neurons in the brainstem named because it stains blue (locus coeruleus means "the blue place") with appropriate dyes.

Parachlorophenylalanine (PCPA) (Para-klor-o-fen-nel-AL-ah-neen) A drug that blocks serotonin synthesis.

nation for this was that one or more sleep-producing centers existed below the level of the cut, in the region of the medulla (Batini et al., 1959).

Sleep can be induced in animals sometimes by electrical stimulation of these brainstem centers. This supported a new view, namely, that sleep is the result of *active brain processes* regulated by neurons in the brainstem. Sleep began to be viewed as a naturally occurring brain state produced by *different* (not just less) brain activity from that of the waking state. Subsequent experiments from many laboratories around the world have added supporting evidence. Single neuron recordings from the brains of sleeping animals show that overall levels of neuronal activity do not decrease during sleep. In fact, some neurons increase their activity, even in stage 4 slow-wave sleep. Sleep is characterized by *different patterns* of brain activity, not simply a reduction in the level of activity of either the specific sensory system, as suggested by Bremer, or the brainstem reticular formation, as suggested by the early experiments of Moruzzi and Magoun. Researchers are trying to determine the location of these sleep-inducing and wakeful-ness-inducing brain centers.

Jouvet's Theory of Sleep

In the 1960s and 1970s the dominant theory concerning the brain mechanisms in sleep was that of the French scientist Michel Jouvet. This theory involves two interrelated systems in the brainstem, the **raphe system** and a brainstem nucleus termed the **locus coeruleus** (Jouvet, 1967; 1974). The raphe system consists of a series of neuronal clusters along the midline of the brainstem. Jouvet found that selective lesions to the raphe system in cats brought about total insomnia lasting for several days. This insomnia gradually lessened, but his animals never again slept the 14–15 hours per day typical of normal cats.

Jouvet also reported that when cats were injected with the drug **para-chlorophenylalanine (PCPA)** they showed insomnia for about 40 hours, and normal sleep patterns did not return for over 200 hours (Jouvet, 1974). PCPA blocks the synthesis of serotonin, the neurotransmitter in the raphe system. On the basis of these and similar findings, Jouvet proposed that the raphe system is responsible for the induction of slow-wave sleep by inhibiting the neurons that maintain wakefulness. In his theory, which is an active view of the sleep process, wakefulness is mediated by neurons in the nearby brainstem reticular formation. The details of this hypothesis are weakened, however, by the finding that despite long-term suppression of serotonin levels in the brain with PCPA, sleep does eventually return to about 70 percent of normal levels (D. D. Kelly, 1981).

Jouvet also proposed an explanation for REM sleep. He suggested that a nearby brain region, the locus coeruleus, was responsible for suppressing the raphe system, thereby ending slow-wave sleep and initiating REM sleep. The neurotransmitter of the neurons in the locus coeruleus is norepi-nephrine. Jouvet found that lesions in the locus coeruleus prevented the appearance of REM sleep, and chemical suppression of norepinephrine had similar effects. However, other investigators have reported conflicting evidence, and as yet no clear picture has emerged of the role of the locus coeruleus and norepinephrine in producing REM sleep (Ramm, 1979).

Most researchers agree that sleep is the result of an active process, induced by neurons, probably in the brainstem and nearby hypothalamus. One representative modern theory is that of J. Allan Hobson and Robert McCarley (1977), which incorporates parts of Jouvet's theory but stresses the involvement of cholinergic neurons in the **nucleus gigantocellularis** (giant cells) of the pons as well. In cats the cells of the nucleus gigantocellularis are particularly active during REM sleep, firing in a phasic manner correlated with eye movements. Called **PGO** (pons-geniculate-occipital) **spikes,** these large bursts of electrical activity can be recorded from the pons, the lateral geniculate, and the occipital cortex during REM sleep. These PGO spikes are thought to be responsible for driving the rapid eye movements.

Sleep as a Circadian Rhythm

We sleep and wake with a certain rhythm, influenced, of course, by the demands of our lives. Although human beings tend to sleep when it is dark and become active when it is light (excluding college students on vacation), it does not necessarily follow that darkness puts us to sleep or that the light wakes us up. In fact, the evidence is now overwhelming that sleep–wake cycles in human beings (and, in fact, all vertebrates) are due to the existence of biologic clocks that generate a circadian sleep–wake rhythm. It is important to realize that circadian rhythms are not *driven* by events in the environment, such as sunrise and sunset, but by processes within the organism; that is, they are **endogenous** (originating within the organism). Normally, however, they are *synchronized* with some regularly occurring environmental event such as sunrise. The environmental event that captures or *entrains* an endogenous rhythm is called a **zeitgeber** (German for "time-giver").

The way to determine that a particular rhythm is endogenous and not simply driven by environmental events is to place the individual in an environment that lacks any cues to the environmental events, such as day length, and observe whether the rhythm persists. Figure 10.6 shows that the sleep–wake cycle in human beings is an endogenous circadian rhythm that "free-runs" in such constant conditions. Evidence on sleep–wake cycles has been gathered on human beings isolated from light, temperature, and other environmental cues in such places as the Mammoth caves in Kentucky and subterranean caves in the French Alps, as well as laboratories in various parts of the world.

Several interesting findings have emerged from such studies, one of which is that the human circadian sleep–wake cycle is actually about 25 (plus or minus 0.5) hours. Thus without alarm clocks, sunlight, or other environmental cues as to the time of day most human beings tend to go to bed about an hour later and get up about an hour later in every cycle. This natural period of 25 hours does not depend on either age or gender. The blind, either from birth or from early life, show 25-hour cycles in isolation just as sighted individuals do. Cycles of blind individuals in normal environments are a little more uneven than those of sighted individuals (Aschoff, 1980). The upper part of Figure 10.6 illustrates the entrainment

nucleus gigantocellularis (gi-GANT-o-sell-u-lair-iss) Nucleus in the pons thought to produce the PGO spikes seen in REM sleep.

PGO spikes (P-G-O) Bursts of electrical activity in the pons, lateral geniculate nucleus, and occipital lobe during REM sleep.

endogenous (en-DODGE-ih-nuss) Intrinsic.

zeitgeber (ZYTE-gay-ber) Some environmental event that captures or "entrains" a circadian rhythm.

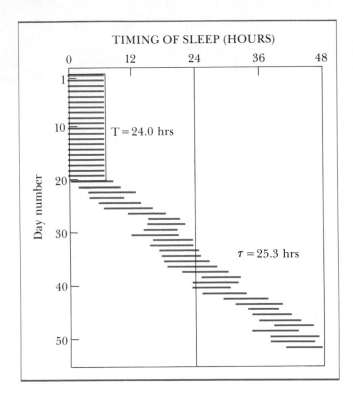

TIMING OF SLEEP (HOURS)

T = 24.0 hrs

τ = 25.3 hrs

Figure 10.6 Entrained (synchronized with environment) and free-running sleep–wake pattern of a normal 22-year-old male human subject living in an environment with no cues to the actual time and no periodic changes in the environment.

He spent about eight weeks in this environment. The horizontal bars indicate time spent in bed. Dark regions show actual sleep as measured by EEG recordings. During the free-running of the wake–sleep rhythm, the subject showed an endogenous period of about 25.3 hours. T = imposed period of rhythm; τ = endogenous period of free-running rhythm.

of the 25.3-hour cycle into the 24-hour day mandated by clocks and calendars. The normal zeitgeber for most individuals is probably a combination of daylight, alarm clocks, and social stimuli. On weekends and on vacations we can observe a little of our endogenous rhythm, however, as most of us tend to go to sleep and get up a little later each day unless we have a schedule to follow.

The sleep–wake cycle is not alone in displaying circadian rhythmicity. Body temperature, urine production, and the secretion of growth hormone, cortisol, and testosterone also display free-running circadian rhythms in constant environmental conditions. Circadian rhythmicity is potentially important in medicine too. William Hrushesky (1985) found that women undergoing chemotherapy for ovarian cancer responded differently to the drugs, depending on when they were administered during the patients' circadian rhythms.

Jet Lag

Upsetting bodily rhythms with respect to environmental time, which occurs during travel across several time zones, can have unpleasant effects—the fatigue, depression, and general malaise we call *jet lag*. Interestingly, our endogenous rhythm seems to be fairly adjustable for two hours either way around our natural period of 25 hours (i.e., from 23 to 27 hours). Since this is not symmetrical around our imposed 24-hour day, it follows that it should be easier to adapt to time shifts calling for sleep to be delayed than for shifts calling for sleep to begin before its usual time. Thus jet lag should be less severe in going from east to west ("gaining" time) than in going from west to east ("losing" time). Evidence supports this hypothesis, although other factors, such as sleep loss, changes in eating habits, and stress, may also be involved (Aschoff, 1980).

Resynchronizing the various rhythms to the "new time-givers" required by the different time can only take place gradually. Various techniques to combat jet lag have been developed. One suggestion is to make use of caffeine in resetting the biologic clock by carefully controlling and timing cups of coffee or tea. Caffeine has been demonstrated to either lengthen or shorten wake–sleep cycles in experimental rats, depending on when in the cycle it is administered (Moore-Ede et al., 1983). Changing the relationship between an endogenous rhythm and the environmental zeitgebers is termed *phase shifting*. The direction and magnitude of phase shifts depend on the nature of the zeitgeber and the point in the rhythm where it is applied.

A Clock in the Hypothalamus?

As the realization grew that various circadian rhythms were generated by the organism and not imposed on it from outside, various researchers began to search for the anatomic location of the biologic clocks. Without question the most industrious of the early researchers was Curt Richter (1965), who used blinded rats as subjects. Blind rats show a regular free-running locomotor activity rhythm. Richter tried a variety of procedures in an attempt to disrupt this pattern: "This included removal of the gonads, the pancreas, the adrenal, pituitary, thyroid, or pineal glands; electroshock, induced convulsions, prolonged anesthesia, and alcoholic stupor" (Moore-Ede et al., 1983). All these methods left the circadian running activity virtually unchanged. Eventually, after a series of experiments involving hundreds of brain lesions, Richter found that lesions near the ventral median nucleus of the hypothalamus would abolish not only the running rhythm but also the free-running circadian rhythms of drinking and eating that blind rats also display (Richter, 1967).

A few years later, two different laboratories identified the exact nuclei in the hypothalamus of rodents that were responsible for the abolition of these rhythms. The critical nuclei are the **suprachiasmatic nuclei (SCN),** a pair of small (about 10,000 neurons each) nuclei lying at the base of the brain just astride the optic chiasm. Robert Moore and Victor Eichler (1972) found that ablation of the SCN abolished the circadian rhythm of corticosterone (the main adrenal steroid in rats), and Friedrich Stephan and Irving Zucker (1972) found that similar lesions also abolished the circadian rhythms of drinking and locomotor activity in hamsters. Since that time considerable evidence has been published supporting the concept that the SCN contains the biologic clocks or neural oscillators that generate various circadian rhythms (Moore, 1982; Moore-Ede et al., 1983). Although the SCN appear to be the major components of a circadian system in the brain, evidence suggests that other components may exist outside of this hypo-

suprachiasmatic nuclei (su-pra-KY-as-mat-ik) A pair of small nuclei lying just on top of the optic chiasm. Involved in the generation of circadian rhythmicity in mammals.

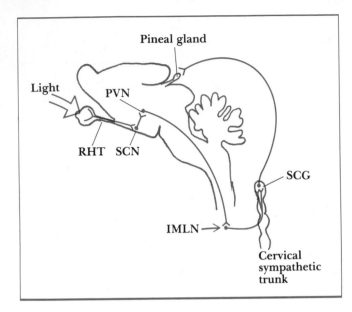

Figure 10.7   Summary diagram of current information concerning the neural pathways involving the retina, the SCN, and the pineal gland in rodents.
RHT = retinohypothalamic tract; SCN = suprachiasmatic nucleus; PVN = paraventricular nucleus of the hypothalamus; IMLN = intermediolateral nucleus of the spinal cord; SCG = superior cervical ganglion of the sympathetic nervous system.

retinohypothalamic tract (RET-in-o-hy-po-thal-AM-ik) A bundle of axons emerging from the optic tract and innervating the suprachiasmatic nuclei.

N-acetyltransferase   (N-ah-see-tul-TRANZ-fur-ase) The enzyme responsible for the production of melatonin in the pineal gland.

thalamic region in some species. For example, although SCN lesions abolish the circadian rhythm of body temperature in rats, neither this rhythm nor the circadian rhythm in cortisol secretion is apparently eliminated by SCN lesions in the rhesus monkey (Takahashi and Zatz, 1982).

The question of how light can influence (entrain) various endogenous rhythms has now been partly answered. A few retinal ganglion cells have axons that diverge from the optic nerve and course downward to enter the SCN, rather than going to the lateral geniculate nucleus. This tiny but important pathway is termed the **retinohypothalamic tract** and appears to be a general feature of the mammalian brain (Moore, 1982). (The circuitry involving the visual system and the SCN is discussed in more detail in Chapter 5.) Axons from the SCN go to other regions of the hypothalamus from which the neural signals that drive the various circadian rhythms are sent. There is also a circuitous pathway down into the spinal cord, out to the superior cervical ganglion of the sympathetic nervous system, and finally to the pineal gland. This pathway is responsible for driving the circadian rhythm of melatonin secretion from the pineal gland in mammals by regulating the rhythm of the enzyme responsible for melatonin production, ***N*-acetyltransferase.** (Figure 10.7 shows the major connections of this system.) The role of melatonin in mammalian behavior is still under investigation, but it appears that it is important in regulating the reproductive system in hibernating species such as the hamster, and perhaps in other species as well (Rusak and Zucker, 1979).

Melatonin levels rise in the dark and secretion of melatonin is suppressed with sufficient levels of light. Some researchers are investigating the possibility that abnormalties of melatonin secretion may be partially responsible for seasonal affective disorder (SAD), a severe depression that affects some individuals only during the short days of winter and early spring. Therapy involving exposure to very bright lights (in order to suppress melatonin secretion) is now being evaluated, and some beneficial effects have been reported (Lewy et al., 1982).

SUMMARY

1. The development of the EEG by Hans Berger opened the way for the investigation of the electrical activity of the brain in sleep and waking. Five stages of sleep are now recognized, using various EEG criteria. There are four stages of slow-wave sleep and a stage characterized by rapid eye movements and an EEG pattern that resembles that of waking. This stage of sleep is associated with more frequent reports of dreaming (REM sleep). A typical night's sleep is made up of several cycles of these stages, each cycle lasting a little over an hour and a half. People of different ages seem to require different amounts of sleep, and the distribution of different stages of sleep also varies with age. Individuals deprived of REM sleep tend to make up the deficit on subsequent nights.

2. Various sleep abnormalities exist, including insomnia, sleep apnea, and narcolepsy. For the most part these conditions are poorly understood. The effects of sleep deprivation probably depend on the circumstances involved. REM deprivation has shown promise as a therapy for depression.

3. Over the past half century research with experimental animals has led to the hypothesis that sleep is the result of active processes in the brain. Several different regions of the brain are involved in generating sleep and waking, including the brainstem reticular formation, thalamus, and regions of the hypothalamus, including the suprachiasmatic nuclei.

4. Sleep and waking are examples of circadian rhythms, rhythms inherent in the organism that have periods of *approximately* 24 hours. The sleep–waking rhythm in human beings seems to be close to 25 hours, when it is allowed to express itself under constant conditions such as those existing in an underground cave with no clocks. Naturally occurring events in the environment, such as sunrise and sunset, serve to synchronize these circadian rhythms to environmental rhythms. The suprachiasmatic nuclei are critical for generating many different circadian rhythms. Jet lag occurs when various bodily rhythms become desynchronized with environmental time-givers as the individual travels from one time zone to another.

SUGGESTIONS FOR FURTHER READING

Dement, W. C. (1974). *Some must watch while some must sleep.* San Francisco: W. H. Freeman.

Hobson, J. A., and McCarley, R. W. (1977). The brain as a dream state generator: An activation-synthesis hypothesis of the dream process. *American Journal of Psychiatry, 134,* 1335–1348.

Menaker, M., Takahashi, J. S., and Eskin, A. (1978). The physiology of circadian pacemakers. *Annual Review of Physiology, 40,* 501–520.

11

Emotion, Pleasure, and Pain

*Do we feel the pounding
in the blood — and love?
Or does the loving come first?*

D.P.K.

Preview

In the nineteenth century William James speculated that we experience emotion as a result of nerve impulses coming into our brains from the peripheral muscles and from such organs as the heart and stomach, many of which are innervated by neurons of the autonomic nervous system. So pervasive was this idea that it continues to stimulate research, and the autonomic nervous system is still considered important to emotion.

Other approaches to the study of emotion were stimulated by the discovery by James Olds and Peter Milner in the 1950s that rats would avidly seek to stimulate certain regions of their brains with electric current if given the chance. Study of such pleasure centers has enlarged our knowledge of the role of the brain in emotional experience, as have cases of loss of control brought about by damage to certain brain areas.

The discovery that our brains contain naturally occurring substances that mimic the effects of such opiate drugs as morphine and heroin has opened a new chapter in understanding pain. These so-called *endorphins* may be involved in pain suppression that occurs during strenuous exercise and stressful situations.

What Is Emotion?

Emotion has meant different things to different theorists. One commonly held idea is that it is a subjectively felt experience or **affect,** which we can usually label with some descriptive term such as fear, anger, anxiety, or joy. No one agrees on how many different emotions there are, and the lists of "basic emotional states" vary in number with different theorists from half a dozen to 10 or more (Plutchik, 1970; Izard, 1977; Ekman and Oster, 1979).

In addition to the subjective experience, at least three other components of emotion are known: physiologic arousal, expressive reactions of the body and face, and emotion-related behaviors. In the following section we discuss physiologic arousal in emotion, and the relationship between this arousal and subjective experience. The responses most commonly as-

Gestures and facial expressions are one way to assess emotional states. We may also suspect that the autonomic nervous systems in these individuals might reveal something about their on-going emotions.

sociated with emotional states, all of which are mediated by the autonomic nervous system, follow.

1. Changes in heart rate (racing pulse, palpitations).
2. Changes in the peripheral circulation, often experienced as clammy hands caused by constriction of peripheral blood vessels.
3. Activation of the sweat glands (nervous perspiration).
4. Inhibition of salivation (dry mouth). Anthropologists have reported that in certain cultures a test of guilt was to have a suspect chew a mouthful of rice. Since guilty persons would be likely to have dry mouths, they would have difficulty in chewing the rice and thereby reveal their guilt. Other techniques reportedly used in determining guilt or innocence have involved briefly touching a red-hot rod to the tongue of the suspect. If saliva was present, little or no harm would result, but a person with a dry mouth would receive a severe burn. (Of course the mere anticipation of having a red-hot rod placed on one's tongue might be enough to produce a dry mouth.)
5. Changes in gastric motility and digestive processes (butterflies in the stomach).

In addition, a variety of hormonal changes such as the release of adrenaline from the adrenal gland contribute to the physiologic arousal seen

psychophysiologist (SY-ko-fizz-e-OL-o-jist) Scientist interested in the relationships between the autonomic nervous system, behavior, and emotion.

in emotion. These sorts of responses are prominent not only in fear and anger, but in euphoria and joy as well. Although responses of the sympathetic division of the autonomic nervous system are often emphasized in reports of emotional arousal, parasympathetic responses are common as well. For example, heart rate increases are often noted in arousal, but heart rate decreases are also seen in fear and terror situations and may even contribute to heart failure in some panic situations. Increased secretion of stomach acids is characteristic of anxiety and stress and in some individuals may contribute to the formation of ulcers. Both heart rate deceleration and secretion of stomach acids are parasympathetic responses.

Scientists interested in the responses of the ANS are called **psychophysiologists.** Psychophysiologists have measured a wide variety of bodily responses trying to find the best windows through which to view the emotional life of human beings. The most commonly measured responses are heart rate, blood pressure, blood volume, and the electrical activity of the skin and muscles. Table 11.1 lists these responses. Other responses that have been used from time to time as measures of emotion include changes in respiration, temperature of the skin of hands and face, pupil size, and gastric motility (Grings and Dawson, 1978). Finally, in more elaborate studies, blood samples have been used to measure plasma levels of adrenaline, cortisol, testosterone, and free fatty acids.

These responses all have in common the fact that they are not normally under conscious control of the individual. Some of these responses, such as heart rate and blood pressure, however, can be modified significantly by the individual after biofeedback training. For most individuals under normal circumstances, however, the bodily responses underlying emotional arousal are *involuntary*.

TABLE 11.1   Summary of Major Nervous System Response Measures of Emotion

Response System	Primary Organ	Unit of Measurement	Sympathetic Effect	Parasympathetic Effect
1. Heart rate	Heart	Beats per minute	Increase	Decrease
2. Blood pressure	Heart and blood vessels	Millimeters of mercury pressure	Increase	Decrease
3. Peripheral blood volume	Blood vessels	Relative change in millimeters	Decrease	None
4. Electrodermal skin conductance	Sweat glands	Micromhos	Increase	None
5. Muscle potential	Skeletal muscles	Microvolts or millivolts	None	None
6. Electro-encephalogram	Brain	Microvolts	None	None

We See the Bear, We Run, and We Are Afraid

What is the relationship between bodily arousal and our subjective experience? Does the emotion-provoking stimulus cause the arousal we then experience as emotion, or are the conscious experience and bodily arousal both triggered more or less simultaneously? Questions such as these date back at least to 1884, when William James (1842–1910) proposed the counterintuitive idea that emotional experiences were the *result* of feedback from the physiologic arousal of the body. This arousal, in turn, James argued, happened *reflexively* to sudden threats or other emotion-producing stimuli. In his vivid phrasing, "we feel sorry because we cry, afraid because we tremble" (James, 1884). Instead of being afraid at the sight of a grizzly in Yellowstone Park, and *therefore* running away from it, James suggested, "we see the bear, we run, and we are afraid."

In 1885 a Danish physiologist, Carl Lange (1834–1900), independently published a similar theory. The idea that our emotions are the direct result of feedback from our internal organs, peripheral nervous system, and somatic musculature is now referred to as the *James–Lange theory* of emotion. Lange based his theory on changes in the vasculature, mediated by a presumed vasomotor center located somewhere in the brain: "We owe all the emotional side of our mental life, our joys and sorrows, our happy and unhappy hours, to our vasomotor system. If the impressions which fall upon our senses did not possess the power of stimulating it, we would wander through life unsympathetic and passionless, all impressions of the outer world would only enrich our experience, increase our knowledge, but would arouse neither joy nor anger, would give us neither care nor fear" (Lange, cited in Cannon, 1927). Although Lange published little else on this subject, James elaborated on his basic theory several times over the next few years and retained the basic ideas concerning the primacy of peripheral arousal in the generation of emotional experience for the rest of his life.

Although frequently criticized, the James–Lange theory was a dominant theory in psychology for 50 years. But in 1927 Walter Cannon (1871–1945) leveled his theoretical guns at it. His first objection was that "total separation of the viscera from the central nervous system does not alter emotional behavior." He cited the research of Sherrington, who had observed that spinal cord transections, along with **vagotomy** (cutting the vagus nerve), did not seem to alter the emotional responses of the dogs undergoing such surgery. Although such animals can move only their head and shoulders, Sherrington reported that one dog with a "markedly emotional temperament" still showed "her anger, her joy, her disgust, and when provocation arose, her fear." Although it is unclear how Sherrington interpreted this dog's head and shoulder responses to reach these conclusions, it is clear that he was talking about the *outward display* of emotion, not the emotional *experience*, which was the area about which James and Lange theorized. Nevertheless, Cannon found it unlikely that an animal incapable of feeling various emotions would still display movements consistent with them.

vagotomy (Vey-GOT-o-me) Cutting of the vagus nerves.

To test James's ideas directly, Cannon removed the sympathetic ganglia from a few cats. Animals with such operations can be kept healthy for several months following surgery, and they move and behave normally. Connections with the internal organs and vasculature normally provided by the sympathetic ganglia, however, are abolished. According to the James–Lange theory, such animals should be unable to experience emotion, since their brains were literally cut off from their internal organs and vasculature. Cannon pointed out that such animals *displayed* emotional responses: "all superficial signs of rage were manifested in the presence of a barking dog—hissing, growling, retraction of the ears, showing of the teeth, lifting of the paw to strike—*except* erection of the hairs, a response mediated by the sympathetic ganglia." While the relevance of these observations to the ideas of James and Lange is debatable, Cannon took the position that these operations "which in terms of the theory, largely or completely destroy emotional feeling, nevertheless leave the animals behaving as angrily, as joyfully, as fearfully as ever" (Cannon, 1927).

Cannon raised other objections to the James–Lange theory of emotion. He argued that the "same visceral changes occur in very different emotional states and in non-emotional states" and that therefore these bodily changes were unlikely to be able to provide the differential sensory input to allow us to experience *different* emotions (Cannon, 1927). He also cited the work of Marañon, who had injected adrenaline into subjects and found that they did not experience "true emotions" but only "as if" emotional feelings. That is, they reported feeling "as if I were afraid," or "as if awaiting a great joy" (Marañon, 1924).

The physiological arousal this young man is probably experiencing may be reinforcing his emotional state. What label would you place on this state, based on facial and postural clues?

Cognition-Arousal Theory of Emotion

Stanley Schacter and Jerome Singer (1962) reinvestigated the role of bodily responses in emotion in a study that has become famous in psychology. They proposed that people needed some sort of "cognition" about what was happening to them as well as physiologic arousal in order to label the experience as an emotion. They suggested that emotional experience was a joint product of cognition and feedback from the physiologic arousal.

Schacter and Singer devised an elaborate experiment in which subjects were given either injections of adrenaline or an inert placebo under the pretext that the injections were of a new vitamin that would improve visual acuity. As the subjects waited for their "vision test," stooges created an atmosphere of either euphoria or anger by acting either in a foolish, playful manner or in a surly, insulting manner. Within these two conditions various subgroups were informed about the probable physiologic effects of the injection they had received, were misinformed, or were given no information. The results of this experiment are difficult to interpret, but it provided sufficient support for the cognitive-arousal theory of emotion to make it the base for many subsequent experiments in the succeeding years.

Overall, the theory has not fared too well. In a recent review Rainer Reisenzein (1983) presents evidence against the Schacter–Singer idea that emotional states can result from the cognitive labeling of otherwise unexplained states of arousal. Feedback from arousal probably served to *intensify* the emotional state, but the arousal itself may or may not be necessary for emotion to occur. Moreover, experiments such as those of Marshall and Zimbardo (1979) have failed to replicate the original Schacter–Singer findings. Thus, although this experiment was the inspiration for two decades of research on the role of bodily states in emotion, the theory it produced appears to have only limited validity.

The Detection of Deception

Although the theoretical issues concerning the relationship between physiologic arousal and the experience of emotion remain unresolved, an applied technology of arousal measurements has developed in attempts to detect deception. The so-called lie detector, or polygraph, test has been widely used, particularly for interviewing prospective employees. As many as 500,000 people each year in the United States are required to take such tests as "conditions for securing employment, continuing employment, or promotion" (Tiner, 1983). In the following section we examine the assumptions, procedures, and validity of such tests.

Polygraph testing is based on two main assumptions: (1) The physiologic arousal observed in emotion is involuntary and (2) only individuals with "guilty knowledge" show such bodily responses when interviewed about the crime. Both of these assumptions are questionable, but the testing goes on. Although polygraph testing has many variations, two main techniques seem to be widespread—the *control question* technique and the *guilty-knowledge* technique (Grings and Dawson, 1978).

The control question technique involves an extensive pretest interview in which the questions to be used in the testing phase are first developed in cooperation between the tester and subject. In the test phase three types of questions are presented: (1) irrelevant questions (e.g., "How do you spell your last name?"); (2) control questions, which deal with issues similar to that under consideration but not directly relevant to the particular crime at hand (e.g., "Have you ever been accused of assault before?"); and (3) relevant questions, which deal directly with the matter at hand (e.g., "Did you assault this person on the night of April 7?"). The construction of the control questions is a critical part of this procedure, and they are designed to cause the subject to be concerned about them, perhaps even to lie about them. The questions are presented in unpredictable order, usually more than once, while various bodily responses are measured. It is assumed that the subject is being deceptive if arousal is consistently greater to the relevant questions than to the control questions. If the responses are consistently greater to the control questions than to the relevant questions, no deception is assumed. The results are considered inconclusive if no particular pattern emerges.

In practice, the control question procedure is more widely used than the guilty-knowledge procedure. The guilty-knowledge technique can be used only if it is assumed that the individual who is guilty of the crime has some knowledge an innocent person could not have. In this procedure various statements are read to the subject or various key words mentioned, but the person is not required to respond. Bodily arousal is monitored, and arousal to guilty-knowledge items is compared with arousal to irrelevant statements. If the guilty-knowledge items show a pattern of greater arousal, the person is considered to have failed the lie detector test.

Four widely used measures of physiologic arousal in such polygraph testing are the electrical resistance of the skin (galvanic skin response, or GSR), breathing patterns, heart rate, and blood pressure (Grings and Dawson, 1978). Putting to one side the ethical questions surrounding the use of such procedures, another critical question is, "Do such tests work?" The answer, found in many experiments over the years, is, "Certainly not perfectly, and maybe not very well at all." It is extremely difficult to evaluate such testing in the field, since one often does not know the true state of affairs about guilt and innocence. Even in the laboratory, where situations can be set up with "innocent" and "guilty" subjects, these procedures are not totally reliable. Some research showed that the guilty-knowledge procedure may identify innocent subjects in the laboratory rather well but only identifies guilty subjects 80–90 percent of the time (Grings and Dawson, 1978).

More recent reviews of polygraph testing emphasize the importance of the tester. Benjamin Kleinmuntz and Julian Szucko (1984) found that polygraph trainees with considerable experience may still label as guilty over half those known to be innocent. David Lykken (1981), who is extremely critical of the use of such tests, has concluded on the basis of his survey that the "polygraphic pens do no special dance when we are lying." Other investigators find that such techniques show promise, even though no current procedure is foolproof. The controversy is likely to continue.

Loss-of-Control Syndromes

Very little is actually known about how the brain mediates emotion. Some information about human emotion comes from patients with brain damage, such as that produced by tumors, trauma, and high fevers. In most such cases the damage is not very well localized in terms of anatomic landmarks, but sometimes an instructive case appears. Individuals who have experienced loss-of-control symptoms often have sustained damage to one or more structures of the limbic system, particularly the amygdala and hypothalamus. The septal area and, to a lesser extent, the hippocampus also have been implicated in some of these cases.

Julia

The following report comes from the work of Vernon Mark and Frank Ervin (1970).

In Julia's case, the relationship between brain disease and violent behavior was very clear. Her history of brain disease went back to the time, before the age of 2, she had a severe attack of encephalitis (brain infection) following mumps. When she was 10, she began to have epileptic seizures. . . . Most of the time they consisted of brief lapses of consciousness, staring, lip smacking, and chewing. Often after such a seizure she would be overcome by panic and run off as fast as she could without caring about destination. Her behavior between seizures was marked by severe temper tantrums followed by extreme remorse. Four of these depressions ended in serious suicide attempts. The daughter of a professional man, she was an attractive, pleasant, cherubic blonde who looked much younger than her age of 21.

On twelve occasions, Julia had seriously assaulted other people without any apparent provocation. By far the most serious attack had occurred when she was 18. She was at a movie with her parents when she felt a wave of terror pass over her body. She told her father that she was going to have another one of her "racing spells" and agreed to wait for her parents in the ladies lounge. As she went to it, she automatically took a small knife out of her hand bag. She had gotten into the habit of carrying this knife for protection because her "racing spells" often took her into dangerous neighborhoods where she would come out of her fugue-like ("trance") state to find herself helpless, alone and confused. When she got to the lounge, she looked in the mirror and perceived the left side of her face and trunk (including the left arm) as shriveled, disfigured, and "evil." At the same time, she noticed a "drawing" sensation in her face and hands. Just then another girl entered the lounge and inadvertently bumped against Julia's left arm and hand. Julia, in a panic, struck quickly with her knife, penetrating the other girl's heart and then screamed loudly. Fortunately, help arrived in time to save the life of her victim.

The next serious attack occurred inside the mental hospital to which Julia had been sent. Julia's nurse was writing a report, and when Julia said "I feel another spell coming on, please help me," the nurse replied, "I'll be with you in a minute." Julia dragged a pair of scissors out of the nurse's pocket and drove the point into the unfortunate woman's lungs. Luckily, the nurse recovered.

Subsequent investigation revealed the abnormal brain discharges that triggered Julia's epileptic attacks came from the amygdala. Eventually, Julia's condition was improved somewhat by neurosurgery, which removed much of the damaged amygdala, and the use of tranquilizing drugs.

Uncontrolled epileptic seizures also have been reported to result in intense emotional experiences that are interpreted by the individual as ecstasy of the highest order. The Russian writer Dostoyevsky, who had such seizures, is quoted as reporting:

All you, healthy people, do not even suspect what happiness is, that happiness which we epileptics experience during the second before the attack. In his Koran Mohammed assures us that he saw paradise and was inside. All clever fools are convinced that he is simply a liar and a fraud. Oh no! He is not lying! He really was in paradise during an attack of epilepsy from which he suffered as I do. I don't know whether this bliss lasts seconds, hours or months, yet take my word for it, I would not exchange it for all the joys which life can give [Voskuil, 1983].

Anxiety, Drugs, and the Brain

One of the more unpleasant emotions we all experience at one time or another is anxiety. Upcoming final exams or that five-minute talk you have to give in your speech class can cause a fear of what might happen. It does little good to be reminded that the chances of success are good and that everything will be fine. What do you do? In most of these situations the dreaded event comes fairly quickly, you get through it one way or another, and the crisis is over. But for some people anxiety is chronic and occurs not just in anticipation of a forthcoming situation but "in general." This is sometimes called *free-floating anxiety,* since there is no specific cause for it. Chronic anxiety does not float, though; it hangs like a heavy weight on one's back. Because of this type of anxiety many individuals have turned to drugs.

Historically, the most widely used drug to treat anxiety has been alcohol. Although alcohol can help to reduce anxiety temporarily, its costs are so great and so well known that no rational person would prescribe alcohol as a solution for anxiety. Despite the long history of alcohol use, pharmacologists still do not understand the effects of alcohol on the nervous system. However, its effects are known to be widespread in the brain and spinal cord, and it appears to interact with various neurotransmitters (Mancillas et al., 1986).

Beginning in the 1950s drug companies began to market "antianxiety" drugs to compete with the older barbiturates that had been available as "sleeping pills" and sedatives since the turn of the century. By the mid-1970s these new drugs had become so popular that one of them, *Valium,* was the most commonly prescribed drug in North America and Europe. Valium and the closely related drug *Librium* were being taken on a fairly regular basis by between 10 and 20 percent of adults in the Western world (Lickey and Gordon, 1983). Although use of these drugs has declined since the 1970s, they are still widely prescribed. Both Valium and Librium belong to a family of drugs called the **benzodiazepines.** The benzodiazepines (and the barbiturates that they have largely replaced) appear to interact with the postsynaptic receptors for **gamma-amino-butyric acid (GABA),** increasing the effectiveness of this neurotransmitter. GABA is widespread in the nervous system, and so far it has been found always to inhibit postsynaptic neurons. By increasing the inhibition generated by GABA, Valium and the other benzodiazepines may reduce neural activity in those brain circuits concerned with anxiety and fear. Both experimental and case study reports support the conclusion that these "tranquilizers" do reduce anxiety for some individuals. There are side effects, of course, including reduced mental acuity, increased sleepiness, and clumsiness. As a result, these drugs should not be taken before driving or operating machinery. They also can sometimes result in increased belligerence and hostility (as can alcohol). Although it is virtually impossible to kill oneself with an overdose of benzodiazepines *alone,* these drugs in combination with either barbiturates or alcohol can be lethal. Both the barbiturates and alcohol can produce death when taken by themselves in large amounts. When combined, they become much more deadly.

Of course, many ways of coping with anxiety do not involve drugs, and for most individuals, it seems wise to try these techniques. Some neuroscientists speculate that relaxation techniques, meditation, and so on, may be effective because they cause the release in the brain of some chemical substances chemically similar to the benzodiazepines, naturally occurring tranquilizers in the brain. Until we know much more about anxiety, drugs, and the brain, it is wise to be very cautious about using drugs to combat anxiety or other emotional problems.

Testosterone and Aggression

It often has been suggested that one cause of aggressive behavior is the level of testosterone in the blood. Testosterone is secreted from the gonads of both males and females, but males show much higher average levels in the blood. It is generally true that males of most species (not all) display higher levels of aggressive behavior than do females. In mice, rats, and hamsters it has been well documented that aggressive behavior declines following castration and can be restored to castrated males with testosterone injections (Beatty, 1979). Farmers have known for centuries that castration reduces aggression in a variety of domesticated animals, although the degree of taming is often quite variable. Moreover, it appears that testosterone at critical times in fetal development may be important for the later appearance of aggression in males of several species of rodents.

The relationship between testosterone and aggression in humans is not clear. This question has been approached in several ways. Testosterone levels have been measured in the blood plasma of male subjects who were also evaluated for aggression. Measures of both testosterone and aggression present methodological problems. Testosterone levels in the blood of normal men vary greatly, from 300 to 1200 ng/100 ml of plasma, and they vary with the time of day, state of health, degree of stress, and perhaps other variables. Obtaining reliable testosterone levels is not impossible, but it requires very good experimental design and careful selection of appropriate control groups and testing conditions. To date, few studies have satisfied all these criteria.

Measuring aggression can be even more difficult. Two basic procedures have been followed. One is to administer a paper and pencil self-evaluation questionnaire such as the Buss–Durkee (1957) inventory of aggression. This inventory, although of some use with normal populations for which it was developed, does not seem to assess, in an adequate fashion, the aggressive tendencies of individuals convicted of serious crimes. The second main technique for evaluating aggression is to use peer ratings, warden ratings, or arrest records. The definition of aggressive behavior is also in dispute. Is verbal abuse more or less aggressive than refusing to eat? Is armed robbery more or less a crime of aggression than rape? These questions are difficult to resolve, and progress in this area has been slow.

Despite all the preceding difficulties, dozens of attempts have been made to correlate levels of testosterone in the blood plasma with one or another measure of aggression. In general, the studies on normal male populations have found either no significant correlations or low but positive correlations (Monti et al., 1977; Rose, 1978; Rubin, 1982). Other studies have looked at testosterone levels in prison inmates, where typically little or no correlation with the Buss–Durkee inventory has been found. There is some suggestion that individuals convicted of particularly violent crimes (such as rape in which the victim was also beaten) do have significantly higher testosterone levels than other prisoners, convicted of less violent rapes (Rada et al., 1976). The number of such studies is small, as is the number of convicts taking part in them, and conclusions regarding the effect of testosterone on these individuals must be tentative. Neverthe-

benzodiazepines (Benz-o-die-AZ-eh-peens) Family of drugs used to treat severe anxiety.

gamma-amino-butyric acid (GABA) (GAM-ma a-meen-o bhu-tier-ik) (GAH-bah) An inhibitory neurotransmitter.

less, chemicals to reduce testosterone levels are being tried in Europe and the United States.

Of the individuals in the study by Rada and colleagues (1976), 32–46 percent could be considered alcoholic, as evaluated by their scores on screening tests for alcoholism. Many had been drinking at the time they committed the crime for which they were convicted (42–50 percent). Interestingly, the group that showed the *lowest* percentage of men who had been drinking at the time of the crime were the high-violence group with high testosterone levels. In this group only one individual out of five had been drinking at the time of the rape for which he was convicted. Although we remain largely ignorant about the role of testosterone in aggressive behavior of human males, it is oversimplistic to consider such behavior solely as testosterone driven.

Pleasure Centers in the Brain

One interesting chapter in the study of emotion began in a psychology laboratory at McGill University in Montreal. In 1954 James Olds (1922–1976) and Peter Milner published a paper called "Positive Reinforcement Produced by Electrical Stimulation of the Septal Area and Other Regions of the Rat Brain" (Olds and Milner, 1954). This experiment has led to a generation of research on what have often been called the pleasure centers of the brain. As is true for many important discoveries, an element of good fortune was involved. Olds, a postdoctoral fellow, and Milner were interested in concepts of drive and motivation as related to activity in the brainstem reticular formation. They decided to stimulate the presumed brainstem arousal system directly with electrical current to investigate the effects of such stimulation on learning.

Olds, whose Ph.D. was in social psychology, was not overly familiar with the rat brain. When he implanted the electrode in a particular rat, he miscalculated the brain coordinates of the brainstem from the brain atlas and, instead of inserting the electrode into the brainstem, penetrated the anterior part of the brain, with the tip winding up in the septal area, several millimeters away from its intended target. But by observation of the effects of stimulation of the septal area, Olds made the crucial discovery that this rat would avidly seek out such stimulation.

The experimental situation was such that the animal was unanesthetized and able to move more or less freely, as the electrode was connected with the current source by flexible wires. Olds discovered that the animal could be led to wherever it received brain stimulation. It reminded him, he later remarked, of a game of hide and seek, where someone guides the seeker by saying "hot, hotter, still hotter" as the hidden object is approached. Within a short period of time, Olds developed several different ways to test the reinforcing properties of electrical stimulation of the brain (see Figure 11.1). The standard way to test for such reinforcing effects is in a modified operant chamber, as shown in Figure 11.2.

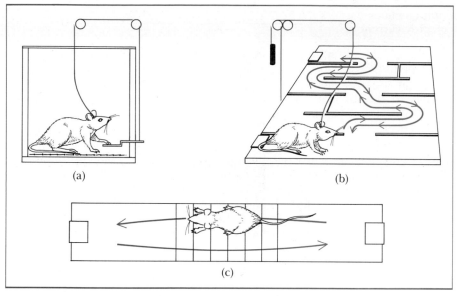

Figure 11.1 Various behaviors that rats perform in order to receive electrical stimulation of the brain.
(a) Bar-pressing in an operant chamber. (b) Maze running. In the maze the first three pedal presses deliver current to the rat's brain, but then the rat must go to the other pedal to receive additional stimulation. (c) In the runway the rat must cross an electrified grid in order to receive stimulation, as each pedal delivers only three pulses if the other pedal has not been activated just before.

Using this procedure, or similar ones adapted for use with other species, Olds and many other investigators have asked several questions about this phenomenon: (1) Do human beings also seek out such stimulation, and what do they say it feels like? (2) Is such stimulation always pleasant, or do some brain regions produce unpleasant feelings when electrically stimulated? (3) Do the rewarding properties of such stimulation mimic the rewarding characteristics of more naturally occurring rewards such as food, water, and sex? In addition, numerous more technical questions concerning optimal levels of current, location, and so on, have been raised, along with theoretical issues concerning the nature of the underlying neural activity that supports self-stimulation of the brain. A thorough review of these latter topics has been published (Gallistel et al., 1981).

To a psychologist, reports from human patients whose brains have been stimulated electrically are of particular interest. You may wonder how it is possible to stimulate the brain of a human being electrically and talk to the patient at the same time. Such procedures are not carried out on individuals except for medically sound reasons, such as in conjunction with diagnosis or therapy in such diseases as epilepsy and schizophrenia. However, it is not a particularly difficult or dangerous procedure. The brain

Figure 11.2 Rat in an operant chamber pressing a lever to deliver electric current to its brain.
The rate of bar pressing is a standard measure of the reinforcement properties of particular brain regions.

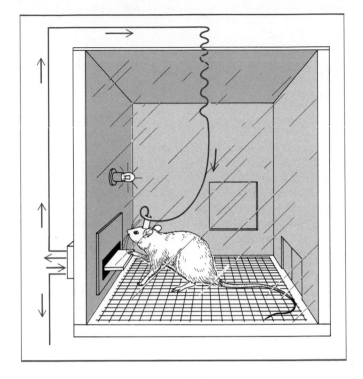

itself is not sensitive to pain when directly stimulated in this way, and only a local anesthetic is required to deaden any pain from stimulation of the scalp or dura mater. With chronically implanted electrodes, no anesthetic of any kind is required.

Interpretation of the remarks the individual makes on receiving such stimulation is not easy. This is illustrated by the following case, which comes from material published by the one scientist who has done more of this research than anyone else, C. W. Sem-Jacobsen of Norway. A few years ago, he reported on over 20 years of such cases with a total of 82 patients (Sem-Jacobsen, 1975). Even after this long experience, Sem-Jacobsen is very cautious in his conclusions:

> An emotional reward often has been designated as an explanation or motivation for self-stimulation. In humans, however, other incentives are also very strong and can sometimes be more potent than the simple pleasure received. The reasons given by patients for continuing stimulation seem as complex as man himself. *In man curiosity is probably the most dominant causative factor in initiating self-stimulation.* If a patient feels "something" he might wonder: Precisely what is the nature of this sensation? What am I feeling? Let me try it once more. Once more. Is it tickling? Is it real pleasure?

Interpretive problems can also arise because the experimenter does not always correctly understand the responses. For example, Sem-Jacobsen reports on a 50-year-old female patient for whom stimulation regularly evoked smiling and laughter.

phylogenetic (Fy-low-je-NET-ik) Related to evolutionary development.

> The striking effect was repeated at irregular intervals and at different times of the day with the patient basically in various moods. The result was always the same. This phenomenon was demonstrated to several colleagues, and all were convinced that the electrode being tested was in a strong, positive "pleasure region. . . ." Because of the patient's uniform reactions in repeated sessions, the author took it for granted that she liked it and discussed the significance of this response in her presence without eliciting any comment from her. Suddenly one day the patient became angry and told us she was "fed up," and "did not enjoy these stimulations at all." She asked us to stop and refrain from any further stimulation of this contact. She said she "had had enough." The stimulus did not give the patient any pleasure. Instead it created in some of her pelvic muscles a rhythmic contraction that tickled her and caused the laughter. It was evident that the author had not been stimulating either a "pleasure center" nor a center dealing with sensation. He had simply been stimulating muscles that contracted and caused the tickling and, in turn, forced the patient to smile and laugh [Sem-Jacobsen, 1968, p. 661].

Thus although there is some fragmentary evidence of pleasure areas in the human brain, this evidence is difficult to interpret unambiguously. The complexity of both human behavior and the human brain argue that even seemingly direct evidence must be evaluated carefully in the context of the situation, and the background and personality of the patient.

In the same year as Olds and Milner reported their results, another group of investigators (Delgado et al., 1954) reported seeing fearlike responses from electrical stimulation of three different regions of the cat's brain, the tectal area of the brainstem, the thalamus, and the hippocampus. Subsequent research has suggested that mammalian brains contain tissue that is either positive, negative, or neutral with respect to such stimulation.

Virtually all the cerebral cortex and cerebellum is essentially neutral. Animals neither press a lever to obtain such stimulation nor press one to avoid it. Most of the emotion-evoking parts of the brain seem to be in the limbic system, hypothalamus, and brainstem—regions of the brain that are **phylogenetically** older than the cortex. Stimulation of most of these sites is rewarding, but at least 5 percent are punishing, and animals will work to avoid or turn off stimulation of these regions. Such effects have been observed when the electrode is in the ventral region of the midbrain or in the *medial lemniscus,* a fiber tract implicated in the transmission of nerve impulses from the body concerned with pain sensations.

One reliable source of positive rewarding effects is the medial forebrain bundle, a large system of axons running in both directions along the ventral region of the brain. A map of positive and negative regions of the rat brain is shown in Figure 11.3.

Does the electrical stimulation of positive sites in the brain mimic the effects of more naturally occurring rewards? This question has been investigated almost exclusively with laboratory rats. In at least some regions of the brain a clear relationship seems to exist with some known reward; in other regions no such evidence is known. For example, self-stimulation

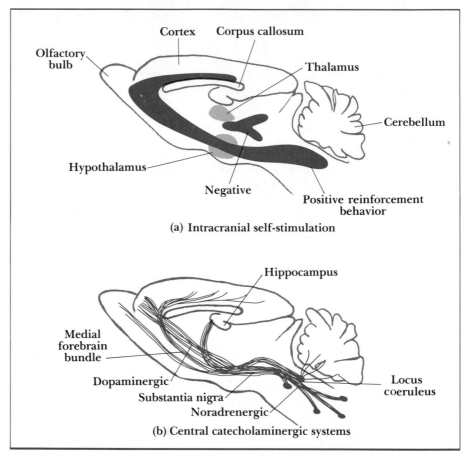

Figure 11.3   **(a) Regions of the rat brain from which positive and negative self-stimulation behavior can be obtained. (b) Monoamine neurotransmitter systems in the brain, showing a very similar distribution.**

of the lateral hypothalamus increases with hunger and decreases with feeding (Groves and Schlesinger, 1982). In fact, rats prefer the electrical stimulation to real food, since given a choice between self-stimulating in this region and eating, they usually choose to self-stimulate, even in the presence of food, until their body weight drops well below normal levels (Routtenberg and Lindy, 1965). Similar relationships have been observed between self-stimulation levels and thirst and access to sexual partners.

Pain

Pain, as we all know, hurts [although a few documented cases are known of individuals born without the ability to sense pain, who therefore incur severe injuries due to the lack of warning signals that normal pain provides (Melzack, 1973)]. But pain can also capture our attention, direct us to seek help, frighten us, and motivate us to escape the painful stimulus. As several theorists on pain have pointed out, pain is a sensation with two major components, a *discriminative* aspect ("Where does it hurt? What does it feel like?") and an *affective* or emotional aspect ("It hurts; I'm scared"). Although neither aspect of pain is well understood, each is important in dealing with patients' suffering.

Pain Pathways

Some understanding of the pathways of pain is available (see Figure 11.4). The peripheral nerves that convey pain sensations belong to one of two categories: the A delta or C fibers (discussed in Chapter 6). In most discussions the A delta fibers are simply called large (L) and the C fibers are called small (S). L fibers are finely myelinated and S fibers are unmyelinated. These two classes of fibers are thought to underlie the double-pain phenomenon, in which injury (such as a deep pin prick) produces first a

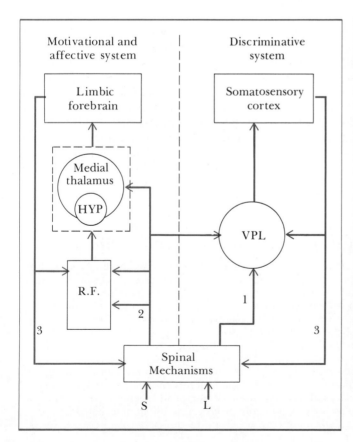

Figure 11.4 Diagram of central nervous system structures proposed to be involved in pain by Casey (1982).
Small-diameter afferents (S) and larger-diameter afferents (L) activate a spinal gating mechanism leading to the generation of impulses sent up the spinal cord to the brain. Figure 11.5 shows this spinal gating mechanism in more detail. Neurons in the ventral posterolateral nucleus of the thalamus (VPL) get input from the dorsal column-medial lemniscus (1) as well as from the spinothalamic tract (2). Projection of VPL neurons is proposed to underlie the discriminative aspects of pain. Other axons from the spinal cord project into the brainstem reticular formation (RF) and to the medial thalamus. Reticular formation neurons also project to the medial thalamus and hypothalamus (HYP). From here impulses may project to structures in the limbic forebrain (such as the hippocampus, cingulate cortex, and frontal lobes) where they are proposed to underly the affective and motivational components of pain. Both discriminative and affective-motivational systems are modulated by descending axons (3) acting on the thalamic, brainstem, and spinal neurons. Some of these modulating influences may be mediated by endorphins.

quick, sharp pain followed a second or two later by a more burning or aching pain. The L fibers are believed to be responsible for the first pain, giving a brief discharge of impulses that travel at about 15 m/sec, and the S fibers to be responsible for the second, longer-lasting pain, firing a prolonged burst of impulses that are conducted much more slowly, about 1 m/sec (Casey, 1982). Neither the L nor the S fibers are *exclusively* pain fibers, for they also carry information concerning touch and temperature. The contributions of the higher regions of the brain to the experience of pain remain largely unknown, but the reticular formation of the brainstem and related medial thalamic nuclei are likely to be important (Casey, 1982). In fact, neurons along the central axis of the brainstem and thalamus have been implicated in a variety of experiments concerning pain and pain suppression.

Gate-Control theory

Ronald Melzack and Patrick Wall (1965) proposed that L and S fibers interact in the transmission of pain impulses from the spinal cord to the brain. Their model is known as the *gate-control* theory of pain. This spinal gating mechanism for pain is, according to this theory, located in the dorsal horn of the cord. The term *gating* refers to the activity of the neural circuitry that either passes or blocks nerve impulses from reaching other regions of the brain. Transmission of pain impulses is regulated by the combined activity of the large and small fibers. Activity in the larger fibers tends to "close the gate," reducing traffic in the pain pathways, whereas activity in the smaller fibers tends to increase pain transmission in the pain pathways. Figure 11.5 illustrates the gate-control theory of pain. This theory suggests, for example, that the pain relief from acupuncture comes about by selectively stimulating the L fibers, closing the pain transmission gate. Several other implications of this theory for pain and pain relief are discussed in Ronald Melzack's book *The Puzzle of Pain* (1973).

The Endogenous Opioids: Pain-killers in Our Brains

I heard a shout. Starting, and looking half round, I saw the lion just in the act of springing upon me. I was upon a little height; he caught my shoulder as he sprang, and we both came to the ground below together. Growling horribly close to my ear, he shook me as a terrier does a rat. The shock produced a stupor similar to that which seems to be felt by a mouse after the first shake of the cat. It caused a sort of dreaminess in which there was no sense of pain nor feeling of terror, though I was quite conscious of all that was happening. It was like what patients partially under the influence of chloroform describe, who see all the operation, but feel not the knife. This singular condition was not the result of any mental process. The shake annihilated fear, and allowed no sense of horror in looking round at the beast. This peculiar state is probably produced in all animals killed by the carnivora, and if so, is a merciful provision by our benevolent creator for

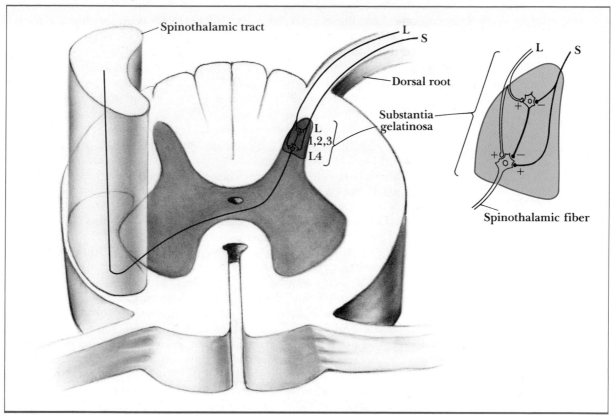

Figure 11.5 Diagram illustrating the main points of the Melzack–Wall theory of the gate control of pain.
The theory proposes that spinothalamic tract neurons carry pain sensations to the brain. Within a portion of the spinal cord termed the substantia gelatinosa [also called laminae (layers) 1, 2, 3 and 4], large (L)and small (S) afferent fibers interact to modulate the firing rate of the spinothalamic tract neurons. The theory suggests that L fibers *excite* the spinothalamic tract neurons directly and excite *inhibitory interneurons* that synapse on the same spinothalamic tract neurons. Activity in the L fibers can thus actually *reduce* overall firing rates in the spinothalamic fibers and thus reduce pain sensations. S fibers also excite the spinothalamic fibers directly, but S afferents *inhibit* the inhibitory interneurons, resulting in an increased rate of firing in the spinothalamic tract neurons and thus an increase in pain sensations.

lessening the pain of death . . . [David Livingstone, *Missionary Travels*, 1857; quoted in Kelly, 1981b].

The remarkable experience of Livingstone is a particularly vivid example of what is now termed stress-induced analgesia (SIA), a diminishing of pain produced by severe stress. Such analgesia may be due to the release of peptides in our body that have effects very much like that of members

endorphin (en-DOR-fin) A recently coined term, refers to the endogenous morphines—substances in the body that possess properties similar to the opiates.

enkephalin (en-KEF-a-lin) Term (meaning "in the head") used for two of the endogenous morphines. Both enkephalins are pentapeptides (i.e., made up of five amino acids).

leu-enkephalin (LEW-en-KEF-a-lin). One of the enkephalins. A small peptide with analgesic properties.

met-enkephalin (MET-en-KEF-a-lin) One of the enkephalins. A small peptide with analgesic properties.

proenkephalin (PRO-en-KEF-a-lin) Precursor molecule for one of the major families of endorphins.

prodynorphin (PRO-die-NOR-fin) Precursor molecule for one of the major families of endorphins.

proopiomelanocortin (POMC) (PRO-OPE-ee-o-muh-lan-o-KORT-in) Precursor molecule for one of the major families of endorphins.

beta-endorphin (BAIT-ah en-DOR-fin) Derived from POMC, has analgesic properties.

corticotropin-like intermediate lobe peptide (KORti-ko-TRO-pin) One of the constituents of POMC.

of the opium family of drugs, morphine and heroin. The term that has been coined for these ENDOgenous moRPHINES is **endorphins.** Endorphins may have a wide spectrum of activities in the brain, as well as elsewhere in the body. Research on these substances and their possible functions has been described as dizzying (Akil et al., 1984) and as an "incredible explosion" (Cooper et al., 1986). Over 7500 articles on endogenous opioids were published between 1976 and 1981 (Frederickson and Geary, 1982). We shall try to outline some of the basic facts that seem to be emerging and some of the lines that current research is taking.

In the early 1970s several laboratories had found specific receptors for opiate drugs such as morphine in the brain of experimental animals (e.g., Pert and Snyder, 1973). From these discoveries it was widely assumed that some naturally occurring substance must exist in the brain that resembles the opiates and for which specific opiate receptors have actually evolved. In a remarkably efficient piece of scientific research, workers at the University of Aberdeen in Scotland set out in the autumn of 1973 to find this natural opiate in the brain, and within two years they had found not one, but two such substances (Hughes, 1975; Hughes et al., 1975), which they named **enkephalins** ("in the head"). These two substances each contained five amino acids and differed in only one of the five. One of these substances is called **leu-enkephalin** and the other, **met-enkephalin.** These were the first of the endogenous morphines to be isolated, but several more were discovered in the frenzy of research that followed these reports. Within a year several other laboratories had discovered other endogenous morphines in the pituitary gland and in the brain. Since then endorphins have been discovered in the adrenal gland and in the intestine.

Three Endorphin Families

It is now thought that the opioid peptides naturally occurring in the body belong to one of three basic chemical families. The different endorphins are believed to be produced by the cleavage ("cutting up") of larger, precursor molecules (Akil et al., 1984; Khachaturian et al., 1985). The three endorphin families are named for one of the large precursor molecules from which the smaller molecules are cleaved.

Proenkephalin contains four copies of met-enkephalin, one copy of leu-enkephalin, and two "extended" met-enkephalins, each with other amino acids in addition to the basic five (see Figure 11.6). All seven of these peptides have opiatelike activity. A second group is the **prodynorphin** family, about which little is known. The third family is based on **proopiomelanocortin (POMC).** POMC is the precursor for **beta-endorphin,** ACTH, alpha, beta, and gamma-MSH (melanocyte-stimulating hormones), and a peptide termed **corticotropin-like intermediate lobe peptide (CLIP).** Proopiomelanocortin was first discovered in the anterior and intermediate lobes of the pituitary, but it is now known to exist in the brain as well, primarily in neurons whose cell bodies are in the arcuate nucleus of the hypothalamus and in the nucleus of the solitary tract in the brainstem (Akil et al., 1984).

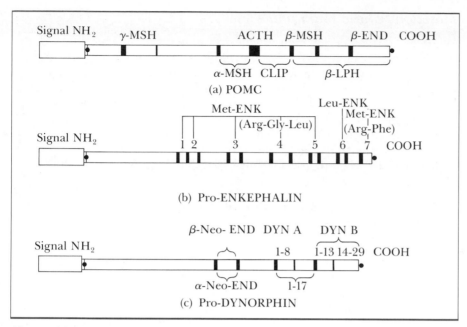

naloxone (nal-OX-own) An antagonist for opiate and opiate-related drugs.

naltrexone (nal-TREKS-own) An antagonist for opiate and opiate-related drugs.

Figure 11.6   Schematic representation of the three basic precursors for the major endorphin families.
POMC = proopiomelanocortin; γ-MSH = gamma-melanocyte stimulating hormone; α-MSH = alpha-melanocyte stimulating hormone; β-MSH = beta-melanocyte-stimulating hormone; ACTH = adrenocorticotropic hormone; β-END = beta-endorphin; COOH = carboxyl end of molecule; CLIP = corticotropin-like intermediate lobe peptide; β-LPH = beta-lipotropic hormone; Met-ENK = met-enkephalin; Leu-ENK = Leu-enkephalin; Arg = arginine; Gly = glycine; Phe = phenylalanine; α-Neo-END = alpha Neo-endorphin; β-Neo-END = beta Neo-endorphin; DYN A = Dynorphin A; DYN B = Dynorphin B.

Multiple Opiate Receptors

From pharmacologic experiments it is now known that there are at least four (and probably more) different receptors for the endogenous opiates. Four of the identified receptors are named for Greek letters (mu, kappa, delta, and sigma). The relationship between these different receptors and the various endorphins is not clear, although some opiate–receptor interactions are known (Akil et al., 1984). Solomon Snyder (1984) proposes that there are seven identified receptors for the endogenous opiates, but the true number is probably not yet known. The mu receptor is apparently specific for the main antagonist to morphine and related drugs—**naloxone.** The reversal of drug effects with naloxone is generally regarded as evidence that the effect was mediated by a morphinelike substance. However, since several opiate receptors do not bind naloxone, this argument is not infallible. Individuals who have taken an overdose of heroin can usually be revived by an injection of naloxone (or the closely related **naltrexone**), which displaces heroin from the mu receptors in the brain.

analogue   (AN-a-log) Substance with properties similar to those of another substance.

stimulation-produced analgesia (SPA)   Analgesia produced by electrical stimulation of certain regions of the brain.

stress-induced analgesia (SIA)   (ann-al-JEEZ-e-ah) Pain relief that occurs during some stressful situations.

periaqueductal gray matter (perry-AK-we-duct-al) Gray matter immediately surrounding the central canal or "aqueduct" in the brain.

analgesia   (an-al-JEEZ-e-ah) Pain relief without loss of consciousness.

Functions of the Endorphins

What are all these endogenous opiates, with their multiple receptors, doing in our brains? They probably contribute to a natural pain suppression system that comes into operation under extremely stressful conditions. That endophins should be involved in alleviating pain is not surprising, of course, since one of the characteristics of the opiates is their excellent pain-suppressing abilities. Sir William Osler called morphine "God's own medicine" (Jaffee and Martin, 1975). Morphine was named for Morpheus, the god of sleep, dreams, and forgetfulness. (Heroin was, believe it or not, named as the "heroic drug" that was to cure morphine and opium addiction.)

Evidence for Pain Suppression as a Result of Endorphin Release

The most direct demonstration that endorphins can suppress pain would be to administer them to individuals in pain and see if it was diminished. This is easier said than done, for we are faced with two major technical difficulties: The enkephalins are rapidly degraded enzymatically and therefore cannot be administered effectively, and beta-endorphin, although somewhat more long-lasting in the blood, crosses the blood–brain barrier into the brain only with difficulty. Therefore the practical use of these substances is limited, although longer-lasting chemical **analogues** of these substances are available and currently being tested experimentally. Some success in pain suppression with such analogues has been reported (Frederickson and Geary, 1982).

Despite the lack of direct evidence, considerable indirect evidence supports the view that the endorphins do play a role in pain suppression. Two main techniques have been used to investigate pain suppression: **stimulation-produced analgesia (SPA)** and **stress-induced analgesia (SIA).**

Stimulation-produced analgesia (SPA) is a profound reduction of pain sensibility produced by electrical stimulation of certain regions of the brain in unanesthetized animals or people. It was first reported by D. V. Reynolds in 1969, and subsequently by others (Mayer et al., 1971). Most of the brain sites that can produce SPA are in the **periaqueductal gray matter** surrounding the central canal of the brain and cerebral ventricles and in some nearby regions of the brainstem. Sufficient **analgesia** is produced in experimental animals to allow for abdominal surgery, although the usual tests involve the tail-flick or paw-removal response from a hot plate. SPA has also now been used successfully to relieve some types of chronic pain in human patients suffering from advanced cancer (Hosobuchi et al., 1977; Richardson and Akil, 1977). A few such patients have been implanted with electrodes with which they can "turn down" their pain. This technique offers some hope for patients who otherwise would need large doses of morphine (which has many unwanted side effects).

The fact that SPA can be eliminated by naloxone is strong evidence that the pain relief produced by direct electrical stimulation of the brain is mediated by endorphins (Akil et al., 1984). On the other hand, some of

Stress and Illness

Can stress make you sick? Had a bad cold lately? What do you think caused it? Germs? Not getting enough sleep? Being "run-down"? The model of illness that most of us use to explain illnesses such as colds and the flu is the germ model, or perhaps a germ plus lowered resistance model, in which we attribute the illness to "picking up a bug" or allowing ourselves to get run-down and become more susceptible to infection. There is no question that bacteria and viruses contribute to our illnesses, but it is also clear that we are often exposed to these viruses and do not become ill. What are the factors that determine whether we become ill or not?

For many years some theorists have proposed that stressful events, such as the death of a spouse or taking on a new and more difficult job, could contribute to the development of illness. This idea has been debated both within the medical community and (perhaps more so) in the popular press. One difficulty with such a theory was that the *mechanism* by which stress could contribute to the development of illness was unclear. How could being sad or "stressed out" make you sick? Recently, evidence has been accumulating that stress may contribute to the development of illness by interfering with the complex *immune system* in our bodies that fights foreign invaders such as bacteria and viruses. In the First International Workshop on Neuroimmunomodulation, held in November of 1984, several investigators reported on studies in which stress such as

recent bereavement or the taking of important examinations produced a measurable decrease in the activity of cells associated with the immune system (Marx, 1985). A recent review of the way in which naturally occuring stressful situations may contribute to illness also has concluded that there is considerable evidence linking stress to illness and to reductions in the effectiveness of the immune system (Jemmott and Locke, 1984).

The link between stress and illness may be through the release of *stress hormones,* such as *cortisol* from the adrenal cortex. During stressful events it is known that the brain signals the anterior pituitary to release ACTH, which circulates through the bloodstream and causes the release of cortisol and other hormones from the adrenal cortex. Many other bodily changes occur during stress, but the release of the adrenal hormones is one of the constant features of stress responses. One leading hypothesis is that the circulating steroid hormones from the adrenal cortex affect the immune system, reducing its effectiveness, perhaps by weakening or killing certain cells that are part of the body's defenses against infection. Since the levels of such stress hormones are elevated in individuals suffering from depression and other conditions, this explanation could be extended, if future evidence supports the proposed link between the brain, the endocrine system, and the immune system.

---

the pain relief mediated by brain stimulation is not eliminated by naloxone, demonstrating that nonopioid neuronal circuits also must underlie SPA (or that if this form of SPA is mediated by endorphins, the receptors involved are other than the mu receptors with which naloxone interacts).

SPA in human chronic pain patients also has been reported to cause a rise in enkephalin-like substances and beta-endorphin in the cerebrospinal fluid (Akil et al., 1984). This finding has been challenged, however, by a more recent report that the rise in such substances is produced as an artifact of the method used to take fluid samples from the ventricular system and is not strictly attributable to the pain suppression produced by SPA (Fessler et al., 1984).

A second line of evidence supporting the role of endorphins as pain suppressors comes from experiments with stress-induced analgesia (SIA). Stress, such as that induced by forced swims in cold water, can reduce an animal's response to painful stimulation. SIA can be as effective as large doses of morphine in reducing responsiveness to painful stimulation in rats. SIA is reversed by naloxone and is accompanied by an increase in brain endorphins (Akil et al., 1984). Evidence for SIA in humans (four men, two women) was published recently (Willer et al., 1981), with the finding that repetitive stress (defined as warning signals that shock was to occur) caused a significant increase in the threshold of a shock-induced reflex. This stress-induced analgesia was reversed by 5 mg of naloxone.

Certainly a great deal of anecdotal evidence exists to support the idea that during battles, accidents, athletic contests, and other emergency situations, severe injuries can be sustained with little immediate pain. Typically, such injuries begin to hurt when the emergency is over. Livingstone's experience with the lion is a real-life example of SIA. Not all SIA is reversed with naloxone, which leads to the conclusion that SIA comes in two forms, opioid and nonopioid. One factor that characterizes the opioid form of SIA is that the animal learns it has no control over the stressful situation. This is similar to the phenomenon of "learned helplessness," in which exposure to inescapable shock interferes with subsequent learning situations where escape from the shock is actually possible (Maier, 1983).

Many other situations produce analgesia, including trance states (as in

A patient undergoing acupuncture at the hospital for traditional medicine in Beijing. Some researchers now think that some of the effectiveness of such treatments in the relief of pain comes from the acupuncture procedures' release of endorphins in the patient's brain and bloodstream.

ritualistic dancing), hypnosis, acupuncture, sexual arousal, and prolonged exercise. In addition, the **placebo effect** occurs, in which a patient's belief that some treatment will be therapeutic produces real pain relief. Researchers have investigated a possible endorphin connection with these various kinds of pain suppression, with mixed results. This area of research is very new and our current thinking will probably change as further work is done, but at the moment it appears that **acupuncture** and the placebo effect are mediated through the release of endorphins (i.e., both are reversed by naloxone), whereas hypnotic analgesia probably is not. Evidence is insufficient to conclude that endorphins cause the analgesia produced by trance states and sexual arousal.

One experiment investigating the placebo effect is particularly interesting. Jon Levine and co-workers (1979) found that about one-third of young adults given a chemically inert placebo following dental surgery reported significant pain relief. All the patients had been told that they were being given a newly developed pain-killer. This placebo effect was reversed (pain was increased) by a subsequent injection of naloxone. The patients who received the placebo but who did not report significant pain relief reported no pain enhancement with naloxone either. More experiments such as this are needed, but it appears that some placebo effects may result from endorphin release.

Endorphins and the Runner's High

In the initial enthusiasm generated by endorphin research, many hypotheses have been put forward to suggest that such diverse phenomena as orgasm, "runner's high," and religious ecstasy are the result of endorphin release (Henry, 1982). One phenomenon that has been studied is the runner's high (the elevated mood produced in many experienced runners by a strenuous workout). Results in this area are mixed. One study did not support a role for endorphins, finding no naloxone reversal of runner's high (Markoff et al., 1982). This experiment was run in a **double-blind** fashion, which is necessary in such experiments. In double-blind experiments neither the experimenter giving the injection (naloxone or inert saline solution) nor the subject receiving it knows the identity of the material. This procedure reduces the problem of suggestibility or unconscious biasing of results due to the beliefs and expectations of either the experimenter or the subject. Another well-designed and executed study, however, has found evidence for endorphin-related pain suppression and mood changes in experienced distance runners following a strenuous workout and reported runner's high (Janal et al., 1984).

From a theoretical point of view the hypothesis that endorphins might be involved in sexual arousal and orgasm is attractive. The sudden release of a particular substance that (like morphine) has brief pleasurable effects seems plausible. The lack of sexual interest among narcotics addicts is well known and could be explained as the result of the drug's replacing some natural endorphin associated with sexual satisfaction. Sudden endorphin

placebo effect (pla-SEE-bo) (from the Latin, "I please") A drug or procedure that has some beneficial effect despite having no known biologic actions.

acupuncture (OK-oo-punk-shur) Technique for inducing analgesia developed in China involving insertion of fine needles into various regions of the skin.

double-blind Referring to an experimental design in which neither the subject nor the experimenter knows the nature of the treatment given to the subject until the results are complete.

The happiness of the long-distance runner may be due in part to the release of endorphins, although this point is far from proven. See text for further details on the possible connection between "runner's high" and endorphins.

release might be related to the phenomenon of a refractory period that follows orgasm in males. The evidence gathered to date is fragmentary and inconclusive. In general, naloxone seems to have little or no effect on human sexuality, but it has been reported to increase sexual activity in sexually inactive laboratory rats (Gessa et al., 1979). The same naloxone dose did not affect rats showing normal sexual behavior. Human volunteers administered long-lasting analogues of enkephalins do not report any pleasurable sensations (Frederickson and Geary, 1982). It is good to keep in mind, however, that this research is at an early stage.

SUMMARY

1. Both the peripheral and the central nervous system are active in emotional expression and experience. Psychophysiologists attempt to learn the relationships between physiologic arousal and emotional experience by measuring various bodily responses during emotional states.

2. The James–Lange theory of emotion proposes that the feedback from the vasculature, internal organs, and muscles provides the input that the brain interprets as emotion. This theory was criticized by Cannon, but it appears that such input may serve to intensify emotional states, even if it does not actually cause the emotion in the first place. The Schacter–Singer cognition-arousal theory of emotion suggests that the label we place on an aroused bodily state helps to define the emotion we experience, but the experimental evidence in support of this theory is not totally convincing.

3. The measurement of involuntary bodily responses underlies the development of lie detection devices. Despite evidence that such testing is not reliable, it is widespread in the United States. The most widely used indicators in such procedures include the electrical resistance of the skin, breathing patterns, and changes in heart rate and blood pressure. The two basic techniques used in polygraph testing are the control question technique and the guilty-knowledge procedure.

4. Various limbic system structures, particularly the amygdala, septal area, and hypothalamus seem to be involved more directly in emotion than more recently evolved tissue such as the cerebral cortex. Some of our information about the activity of the brain in emotion comes from case reports of individuals with brain damage or other brain abnormalities that result in outbursts of uncontrolled rage.

5. Studies of testosterone levels in human males do not reveal a strong relationship between these levels and aggressive behavior in normal populations. There are experimental difficulties yet to be overcome in this area, not the least of which is a satisfactory measure for aggression. There is some suggestion that men convicted of violent rapes may have higher than normal testosterone levels, but very few studies exist in this area. Nevertheless antiandrogen medications are sometimes used in the treatment of sex offenders.

6. Benzodiazepines such as Valium are widely used to combat anxiety. Antianxiety drugs seem to work by interacting with postsynaptic receptors for the inhibitory neurotransmitter GABA.

7. The discovery of "pleasure centers" in the brain by Olds and Milner in 1954 has been followed by a generation of research that indicates that the brains of human beings also contain such regions and that in at least some cases the sensation seems to be similar to that of sexual activity. In the estimation of Sem-Jacobsen, however, the main reason that most human patients electrically stimulate their own brains (a rare procedure) is curiosity, and the response of the individual can be misleading unless carefully analyzed.

8. The sensation of pain has two major components, a discriminative aspect ("Where does it hurt?") and an emotional aspect ("Ouch, it hurts."). Pain pathways consist of at least two different populations of sensory neurons, the larger A delta and the smaller C fibers. The type of sensation due to each of these two populations may be different. Melzack and Wall have proposed that these two fiber systems interact at the level of the spinal cord, and pain is the result of a complex neuronal gating mechanism.

9. In recent years many important discoveries have been made about substances in our bodies that possess analgesic properties similar to those of morphine and other opiates. These substances are termed *endorphins;* at present, three main endorphin families are recognized, each of which is named after a precursor molecule. These three are the *proenkephalin, prodynorphin,* and *proopiomelanocortin* families.

10. Experiments suggest that at least some types of stress-induced analgesia and analgesia produced by electrical stimulation of certain brain regions may be due to the release of endorphins. It is possible but still unproved that some placebo analgesic effects and pain suppression by acupuncture are also mediated by endorphin release.

SUGGESTIONS FOR FURTHER READING

Akil, H. (1982). On the role of endorphins in pain modulation. In A. L. Beckman (Ed.), *The neural basis of behavior* (pp. 311–333). Jamaica, NY: Spectrum Publications.

Grings, W. W. and Dawson M. E. (1978). *Emotions and bodily responses. A psychophysiological approach.* New York: Academic Press.

Sem-Jacobsen, C. W. (1968). Depth-electrographic stimulation of the human brain and behavior. From *Fourteen years of studies and treatment of Parkinson's disease and mental disorders with implanted electrodes.* Springfield, IL.: Charles C Thomas.

12

Learning and Memory

*You have to begin to lose your memory
if only in bits and pieces
to realize that memory is
what makes our lives.
Life without memory is no life at all...*

LUÍS BUÑUEL

Preview

engram (N-gram) The essential neural circuitry underlying a memory.

Understanding the neural basis of learning and memory is one of the thorniest problems facing behavioral neuroscientists, although good progress has been made in the last few years. The advances have come from research on quite different organisms: human beings, laboratory rats and rabbits, and the sea slug, or *Aplysia*. From amnesic patients we are learning more about the organization of the human brain and about those regions that may be involved in the storage and retrieval of memories. From the work with Aplysia and laboratory rats and rabbits we are learning about the synaptic changes that may be responsible for learning.

Where Is the Engram?

A few years ago Karl Lashley, one of the leading researchers in the search for the **engram** (a term used to identify the essential neural circuitry of learning), declared, only partly in jest: "I sometimes feel, in reviewing the evidence on the localization of the memory trace, that the necessary conclusion is that learning just is not possible" (Lashley, 1950). Things have improved since Lashley's time. We shall look at several different approaches to the question of where memory is stored.

Amnesia

Let us first consider individuals who have suffered brain damage and whose ability to learn and remember has been seriously impaired. The difficulty of being severely amnesic has been expressed well by one of these patients:

Every day is alone in itself, whatever enjoyment I've had, or whatever sorrow I've had. . . . Right now, I'm wondering, have I done or said anything amiss? You see, at this moment everything looks clear to me, but what happened just before? That's what worries me. It's like waking from a dream. I just don't remember. [H. M., quoted in Milner, 1970]

Human amnesics offer neuroscientists an opportunity to study pathologies of memory and make inferences about normal brain functions underlying memory. The study of people who have "lost their memory" goes back to the nineteenth century. Until recently, however, it was rare for the brains of amnesics to be examined by qualified neuroanatomists who could identify the site of injury accurately. It is still unusual to find case reports of amnesics who have been well studied from a behavioral standpoint and whose brains have come to autopsy.

What Is an Amnesic?

Amnesics display several symptoms, the first of which is a profound loss of memory. Amnesics are often very intelligent. For example, they can usually carry on ordinary conversations quite well. Only when one meets them a second time and they show no recollection of the first meeting, entering instead into the same conversation, does their problem become obvious. In amnesia memory loss can be either for past events or for ongoing events. Most amnesics show some loss in both categories. *Retrograde amnesia* refers to a loss of memory for past events, particularly episodes of the patient's life. *Anterograde amnesia* is an inability to store memories of current episodes. For an individual to be labeled as severely amnesic one leading team of researchers requires that the subject score at least two standard deviations below normal on a specially devised battery of memory tests (Warrington, 1984; Weiskrantz, 1985). Unfortunately, there are no generally accepted guidelines for inclusion or exclusion of subjects in studies of amnesia, a fact that has contributed to the controversy that surrounds amnesia.

To be categorized as amnesic, and not simply demented, patients must retain reasonable intelligence (excluding direct tests of memory), and some residual learning capacity on tasks that do not require access to specific personal events (Parkin, 1984). Some intelligence test part-scores may be normal, or even above normal. Thus, although individuals labeled as amnesic vary considerably, agreement exists concerning the main features of the syndrome: profound memory loss coupled with less severely disturbed or unimpaired intelligence. Paradoxically, amnesics also typically retain some residual capacity for learning. We shall return to this important point shortly.

What Causes Amnesia?

Amnesia can be produced in several ways: brain damage caused by strokes, infectious diseases, vitamin deficiency accompanying chronic alcoholism,

encephalitis (EN-sef-ah-LI-tis) Inflammation of the brain due to infection.

Korsakoff's psychosis (KOR-sa-koffs) A syndrome marked by profound memory loss. Usually preceded by chronic alcoholism.

accidents, or an unfortunate complication from brain surgery. Most amnesics belong to one of two basic diagnostic groups. Either they suffer from the aftereffects of **encephalitis** caused by the herpes simplex virus (post-encephalitic amnesics) or they are patients with **Korsakoff's psychosis,** a condition almost always preceded by chronic alcoholism. (Sergei Korsakoff was a nineteenth-century Russian neurologist whose insights into amnesia formed a solid basis for later work. He first described the amnesic syndrome that now bears his name.) It is believed that the cause of the brain damage seen in Korsakoff's patients is a vitamin B_1 deficiency associated with malnutrition. Alcohol may also impair the ability of the intestine to absorb vitamin B_1. A small number of extremely well-studied individuals became amnesic following either surgery or accidental injury. The two most famous such cases are known in the scientific literature only by their initials, H. M. and N. A.

H. M. is the patient quoted earlier in this section. He lives his life as if continually waking from a dream (Milner, 1970). He became amnesic after undergoing surgery at the age of 27 for life-threatening epilepsy. Although the surgery did save his life, it also left him with a global anterograde amnesia, some retrograde amnesia, and a variety of other symptoms, such as greatly diminished interest in sex and an indifference to the taste of food. Since his operation in 1953, H. M. has provided data for dozens of studies and is one of the most famous neurologic patients of all time. The surgery removed the medial surface of both temporal lobes, including the amygdala, the anterior two-thirds of the hippocampus, and surrounding white matter and neocortical tissue. (Figure 12.1 illustrates the extent of the surgery performed on H. M.) Over 30 years later, he remains severely amnesic. Despite above-average intelligence scores, he still "does not know where he lives, who cares for him, or what he ate at his last meal" (Corkin, 1984).

N. A. is not a global amnesic, as his memory deficit is largely confined to verbal material. He became amnesic following an accident in which a miniature fencing foil penetrated his nostril and pierced his brain (Teuber et al., 1968). He incurred damage to the thalamus as well as to brain tissue in the path of the foil as it penetrated to the middle of the brain. Moreover, he has an oculomotor disturbance, which indicates damage to the pretectal area. Since both H. M. and N. A. are still alive, the exact extent of their brain damage is still somewhat uncertain, although as more sophisticated methods of detecting brain damage in living patients are developed, more precise details will be available.

Several different theoretical issues have arisen in the past few years concerning amnesia. Two that have attracted considerable attention are: (1) Are different anatomic circuits and different symptoms involved in different types of amnesia? (2) What is the best way to characterize the defect in amnesia? That is, what is lost and what is preserved in the memory capacities of amnesics? Let us consider these issues in turn.

Are There Different Anatomies of Memory?

The fact that both H. M. and N. A. are amnesic with what appears to be damage to quite different areas of the brain has raised the issue of whether

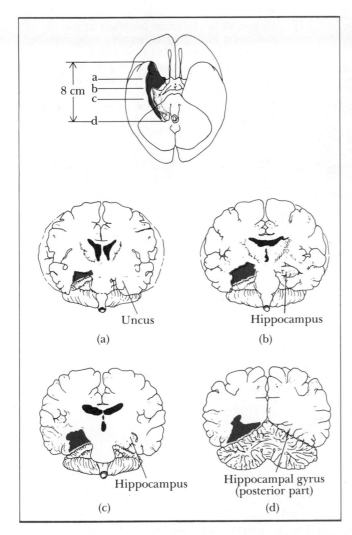

Figure 12.1 Drawings showing location of brain regions removed in H.M.
The underlying structures are shown on one side, overlying cortex on the other. Brain tissue was removed from the anterior tip of the temporal lobe to level d, a total distance of about 8 cm. (a) through (d) show cross sections at four levels within this region. (a) uncus; (b) anterior hippocampus. The amygdala would also be at about this point; (c) posterior hippocampus; (d) hippocampal gyrus, marking the posterior extent of H.M.'s lesion. The tissue removed is indicated on the left, and intact structures on the right, but H.M.'s surgery involved both sides.

two or more brain circuits may be involved in amnesia and memory. This suggestion is controversial. Those who favor the "two amnesias" hypothesis distinguish between **diencephalic** and *medial temporal lobe* amnesias. According to such theorists, the diencephalic type of amnesic is represented by Korsakoff's psychosis patients, in which the damage is thought to be primarily in the mammillary bodies of the hypothalamus, and possibly dorsomedial and midline nuclei of the thalamus. N. A. is considered a diencephalic amnesic (Squire, 1982).

The medial temporal lobe type of amnesia is thought to be represented by the postencephalitic patients, and by H. M. In fact, H. M. is often viewed as the prototype of the medial temporal lobe amnesic, although, as Lawrence Weiskrantz (1985) has pointed out, he may very well have neural degeneration in the mammillary bodies as a result of his surgery. (The

diencephalon (die-en-SEF-a-lon) That region of the brain that includes the thalamus and hypothalamus.

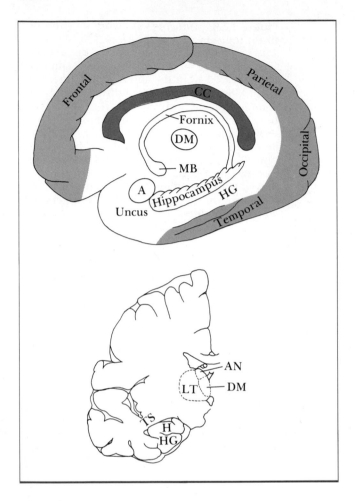

Figure 12.2   General location of the temporal lobe structures and diencephalic structures implicated in amnesia.
Top: Structures as seen in sagittal section. A = amygdala; HG = hippocampal gyrus; MB = mammillary bodies; DM = dorsomedial nucleus of the thalamus; CC = corpus callosum. Bottom: Frontal section through these structures in the right hemisphere. TS = temporal stem; H = hippocampus; LT = lateral thalamus; AN = anterior nucleus of thalamus.

confabulation (kon-FAB-u-la-shun) Falsifications that the patient accepts as true. Stories used to make up for lapses of memory. Characteristic of Korsakoff's psychosis patients, particularly in the earlier stages of the disease.

hippocampus is connected to the mammillary bodies via the fornix. Figure 12.2 shows these structures.) The issue cannot be resolved on the basis of existing information, because so few documented cases exist of the exact site of damage in amnesia, and in those cases that are known the areas of damage may overlap. On the basis of existing anatomic data, it is premature to conclude that two totally separate neural circuits underlie amnesia.

The issue of the existence of two or more types of amnesia has arisen on behavioral as well as anatomic grounds. Supporters of "two amnesias" suggest that these two groups of patients have behavioral or cognitive differences between them. For example, these theorists draw attention to the reports that diencephalic amnesics typically lack insight into their memory problems, and often employ **confabulation**—the replacement of memory gaps by falsifications that the patient accepts as correct. Confabulation is more characteristic of the early stages of Korsakoff's psychosis.

Medial temporal lobe patients rarely confabulate and usually have some insight into their memory problems, as indicated by the quote at the beginning of this section. It is important to remember that individual amnesics vary considerably, even within a particular diagnostic category, such as that of Korsakoff's patients. Different investigators have different criteria for including or excluding particular patients from their studies, a fact that also complicates generalizations about types of amnesia. Diencephalic amnesics also often display symptoms usually associated with damage to the frontal lobes. One such frontal symptom is *perseverative behavior,* in which patients have difficulty switching from one behavior to another. (Symptoms associated with frontal lobe damage are discussed in greater detail in Chapter 13.) Frontal lobe symptomatology is more characteristic of Korsakoff's patients than it is of postencephalitic patients. However, many of these differences between the different amnesic populations can be accounted for simply as differences in the *severity* of the amnesia. It is often difficult to determine whether the severity of amnesia is comparable in different studies. The evidence does not yet warrant the conclusion that two distinct types of amnesia exist.

consolidation (KON-sol-ih-DAY-shun) The concept that items in memory become less vulnerable to interference with time since learning.

What Is the Nature of the Deficit in Amnesia?

Let us consider the second issue. What is wrong with amnesics? The simple answer is that they cannot remember very well. But most researchers are not satisfied to leave the matter there. Memory is complicated. The brain performs at least three fundamental operations important in our ability to learn and remember: the *encoding, storage,* and *retrieval* of information.

Some theorists have proposed that the critical defect in Korsakoff's amnesics is in the encoding of information (Butters and Cermak, 1980). Others have suggested that the main difficulty in memory processing in amnesics has more to do with the consolidation of information into permanent memory (Milner, 1966). Still others have viewed the retrieval of information from memory as being faulty in amnesia (Warrington and Weiskrantz, 1970; Winocur and Weiskrantz, 1976). Many variants of these three basic positions also have been published. Of course amnesics may show defects in all the relevant memory processes, but most theorists have emphasized one of these processes over the others.

Encoding Deficit?

Although some amnesics, particularly Korsakoff's patients, do show some difficulty with encoding material, an explanation based on an encoding deficit is weakened by the fact that many amnesics do not have any such problem. Most of the controversy concerning the nature of the defect in amnesia is between those who favor a consolidation interpretation and those who support a retrieval explanation.

Consolidation Deficit?

Several theorists have proposed that a **consolidation** of memories takes place for some time after an event. This process is thought to strengthen memories of the event, making them more resistant to subsequent disruption. Patients who have received electroconvulsive shock therapy (ECT) or a severe blow to the head have been prevented from consolidating their memories and therefore do not remember the events immediately preceding the jolt or the blow. Animal experiments with convulsive shock also have demonstrated retrograde amnesia following such treatments. The time gradient of retrograde amnesia is often proposed as strong evidence for some consolidation process of memory.

Two German psychologists, G. E. Müller and A. Pilzecker, proposed the first consolidation theory in 1900. They suggested a consolidation process to account for the fact that subjects are better at remembering the first of two different lists of words if they learn the second list two days later than if they learn both lists on the same day. Müller and Pilzecker suggested that the memory for the first list somehow grew stronger, or became consolidated during the two-day period between tests in the first situation and thus became less vulnerable to the interference produced by the second list of words. The concept of memory consolidation has been of interest ever since.

A consolidation explanation for retrograde amnesia following traumatic head injury has gained considerable support (Russell and Nathan, 1946; McGaugh and Herz, 1972). According to this hypothesis, trauma to the brain interferes with the ongoing consolidation of memory, producing retrograde amnesia for the most recent experiences, those not yet consolidated. However, a major stumbling block for the consolidation theory is that the "lost memories" following blows to the head or ECT often return, at least in part.

Despite the problem concerning the return of some memories, H. M.'s amnesia has been interpreted by some theorists as a deficit in consolidation (Milner, 1966). This idea grew out of the observation that he can (with effort) remember things for a few minutes but cannot store these items in long-term memory. An anecdote illustrates this:

> Thus, he was able to retain the number 584 for at least 15 minutes, by continuously working out elaborate mnemonic schemes. When asked how he had been able to retain the number for so long, he replied: It's easy. You just remember 8, subtract it from 17 and it leaves 9. Divide 9 in half and you get 5 and 4, and there you are: 584. Easy." A minute or two later, H. M. was unable to recall either the number 584 or any of the associated complex train of thought; in fact, he did not know that he had been given a number to remember because in the meantime the examiner had introduced a new topic [Milner, 1970].

Although this finding does suggest a possible consolidation failure as the reason for H. M.'s amnesia, this explanation cannot be applied to all of H. M.'s memory problems or to those of other amnesics. For example, recently it has been reported that H. M. does have, after all, some retrograde amnesia stretching back 11 years or more prior to his surgery (Corkin, 1984). This fact strains any simple lack of consolidation explanation. Moreover, it turns out that H. M. (and other amnesics) can learn and retain something about ongoing events. It is difficult to reconcile the overall picture of amnesia with any existing version of the consolidation hypothesis.

Retrieval Deficit?

Another candidate for explaining amnesia is a *retrieval deficit* hypothesis, such as that of Elizabeth Warrington and Lawrence Weiskrantz (Warrington and Weiskrantz, 1970; Weiskrantz and Warrington, 1975). If a person cannot remember something, it does not prove that the information has been lost forever. It merely shows that the person cannot retrieve the memory at that moment. If the memory can be retrieved later, the momentary lapse is usually interpreted as a retrieval deficit.

A retrieval deficit interpretation for amnesia has several lines of support. In support of the concept that amnesics cannot retrieve items from memory in a normal fashion is the fact that almost half of amnesics recover their memory either completely or to a significant degree (Victor et al., 1971). Many patients with amnesia associated with ECT also show significant recovery. Improvements in either retrograde or anterograde amnesia strengthen a retrieval hypothesis.

Another line of support for a retrieval hypothesis is that prompts or partial cues can be very helpful to amnesics on various memory tasks. In such studies subjects are shown a series of incomplete figures. Each successive stimulus shows a little more of the figure. Eventually the subject can recognize the word or picture. On subsequent presentations normal subjects recognize the stimulus much earlier in the sequence of partial cues,

Humans can process and store remarkable amounts of information. Here Yeshiva students are probably reading and listening to their instructor at the same time.

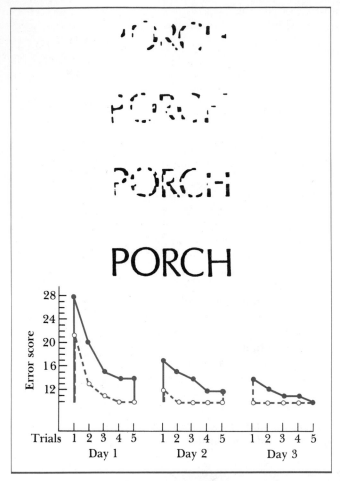

Figure 12.3   An example of incomplete word prompt or cue stimulus and learning curves for both amnesics and normal controls. Note that although amnesics do not perform as well as controls, they improve their performance on successive days, despite the fact that they do not remember having encountered the learning task before ●—●—● = amnesics; ○—○—○ = controls.

because these partial cues or prompts have been stored in memory and aid in recognizing the total picture. Interestingly, amnesics, although not quite as good as normals overall, also show correct recognition of these stimuli with fewer partial cues on subsequent days. However, they typically do not consciously remember seeing the stimuli before and often do not even remember the experimenter. Such *learning without awareness* has been noted in amnesics for several different types of tasks, as will be discussed. (Figure 12.3 shows some of the prompt type cues that can be used by amnesics.)

Learning without Memory

One complication in any attempt to explain amnesia is that amnesics have been shown repeatedly to be capable of new learning, even though they typically do not remember it! This learning without awareness poses some thorny theoretical puzzles. Even global amnesics such as H. M., who has both verbal and nonverbal memory problems, can learn and remember, although H. M. does not consciously remember seeing the tasks before.

Figure 12.4   Schematic drawing of the Tower of Hanoi puzzle.
The task consists of moving the five circular blocks in (a) onto the peg in (c) by moving only one block at a time and never placing a larger block on top of a smaller one.

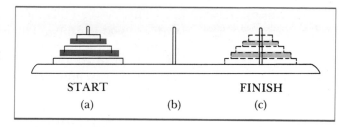

START   FINISH

(a)   (b)   (c)

For example, it was learned many years ago that H. M. could learn to make fewer and fewer errors when tracing a star and looking in a mirror. Moreover, he showed *savings* on successive days, as do normal individuals. (*Savings* is defined as a reduction in errors or trials to reach some criterion when given the same task on successive occasions.) Unlike normals, however, and despite his obvious retention of the mirror-drawing task, H. M. could not remember having done the task before and had to be reinstructed each time (Milner, 1966).

Other amnesics display similar retention without awareness (Squire, 1982), one example of which has been demonstrated repeatedly with several different amnesic patients. This is the so-called Tower of Hanoi puzzle, which involves learning a complicated series of moves in order to solve the problem efficiently, with fewer and fewer moves. Amnesic patients typically show good learning of this task, solving the problem better each time, very much like normal controls. They retain this learning across several days or weeks. Nevertheless, they do not remember learning the task, approaching it each time as if it were new to them and expressing surprise when told how well they are doing (Cohen et al., 1985). (Figure 12.4 shows the Tower of Hanoi puzzle, and Figure 12.5 shows the performance on the puzzle for a group of amnesics and a group of normal controls.)

Figure 12.5   Performance of normals and matched controls on the Tower of Hanoi puzzle shown in Figure 12.4.
The puzzle was presented four times each day for four consecutive days. Although there was clear-cut improvement over days among the amnesics, they did not recall having seen the puzzle before and expressed surprise when told they were doing well.

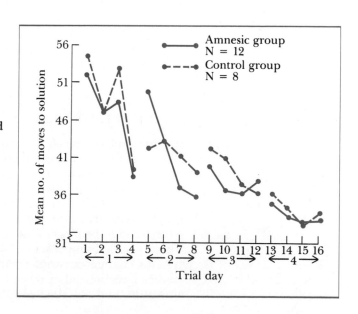

episodic memory (EP-ih-sod-ik) Memory of events in an individual's life.

semantic memory (suh-MAN-tik) Organized knowledge about words, symbols, world events, and so on.

habituation (ha-BIT-shu-a-shun) Decrease in the strength of a response with repeated presentations.

sensitization (senz-ih-tuh-ZA-shun) Increase in the strength of all responses to sudden stimuli for some time following exposure to a potentially threatening stimulus.

classical conditioning Experimental procedures for producing a learned association between two stimuli. Developed by Ivan Pavlov.

The Tower of Hanoi puzzle is not the only task at which amnesics display good learning. There is a diverse list of examples of tasks that can be learned by amnesics, including greatly improved recognition and recall of both pictures and words with prompts, retention of various unusual visual patterns, and learning of math problems (Weiskrantz, 1985).

Episodic and Semantic Memory Distinctions

No one label seems to cover all examples of spared learning in amnesics. Many psychologists think it may be useful, particularly in discussing amnesics, to consider long-term memory as consisting of two basic types. The labels for these two types vary considerably. The original idea comes primarily from Endel Tulving (1972), who proposed that there was a fundamental distinction between **episodic memory** and **semantic memory.** Episodic memory is organized around the personal history of the individual, importantly related to time and often influenced by emotion. Other terms for this sort of personal memory system include autobiographical memory and declarative memory. If you say, "I went to a party last Friday and met a young woman from China," this is an example of episodic memory. Semantic memory, on the other hand, deals more with organized knowledge about the world, including knowledge of words, symbols, and general logical thought. It is not necessarily concerned with the individual, is less related to time, and less influenced by emotion. An example of semantic memory would be, "China is a large, densely populated country in Asia."

Several theorists have suggested that episodic memory is more vulnerable to loss in amnesics than semantic memory. Many other theorists have also proposed differences between fundamental memory types. There is, of course, a tension between the demands of parsimony, which motivates theorists to use as few postulates as possible, and the pressures from the data, which are difficult to explain within any single memory theory. Mammalian nervous system functions provide many examples of parallel systems; it may be that memory also involves not one but several different processes in several different locations in the brain.

A Search for Simpler Systems

In addition to research with human cases of amnesia, researchers interested in the biology of memory also have generated a large body of research concerned with learning and memory in animals. One relatively new development is that investigators have begun to study learning in simple organisms, usually invertebrates such as the marine sea slug Aplysia in which there are fewer neurons to contend with, and the neurons themselves tend to be larger and easier to manipulate than those of vertebrates. These so-called simple systems have provided important clues to how nervous systems change during learning. In general, the most successful of these studies have looked at three basic learning phenomena: **habituation, sensitization,** and **classical conditioning.**

Jimmie, Forever 19 Years Old

The world of profound amnesia can be almost surreal in its strangeness. Consider the case of Jimmie R. As described by Oliver Sacks, a British-born neurologist now living in New York, Jimmie is frozen in time at the age of 19, even though he is now more than 60 years old. Because of his almost complete amnesia for events since 1945, he lives each day as if it were the same one, over and over again.

Jimmie is a bright and talkative man, and he remembers his life until the age of 19 in vivid detail. After that, however, his memory is blank. Sacks interviewed Jimmie for the first time in 1975 and was impressed with the freshness and animation with which Jimmie was recounting his days in the United States Navy during World War II, 30 years before. Jimmie was using the present tense, as if these old events were actually happening at the present time. As Sacks then writes:

> A sudden, improbable suspicion seized me.
> "What year is this, Mr. R?" I asked, concealing my perplexity under a casual manner.
> "Forty-five, man. What do you mean?" He went on, "We've won the war, FDR's dead, Truman's at the helm. There are great times ahead."
> "And you, Jimmie, how old would you be?"
> Oddly, uncertainly, he hesitated a moment, as if engaged in calculation.
> "Why, I guess I'm 19, Doc. I'll be 20 next birthday."
> Looking at the grey-haired man before me, I had an impulse for which I have never forgiven myself—it was, or would have been, the height of cruelty had there been any possibility of Jimmie's remembering it.
> "Here," I said, and thrust a mirror toward him. "Look in the mirror and tell me what you see. Is that a 19-year-old looking out from the mirror?"
> He suddenly turned ashen and gripped the sides of the chair. "Jesus Christ," he whispered. "Christ, what's going on? What's happened to me? Is this a nightmare? Am I crazy? Is this a joke?"—and he became frantic, panicky" [Sacks, 1985].

Fortunately, Sacks was able to calm Jimmie down and two minutes later, not only had Jimmie forgotten the mirror incident, but did not recognize Sacks, who had left the room for a few seconds. This was to be the permanent condition of Jimmie, forever locked into a memory that admitted no new events and kept him forever 19 years old, living a day in 1945 over and over again. As his story was pieced together by Sacks, Jimmie had actually stayed in the navy until 1965, performing his duties without difficulty. However, after he left the navy he began to drink heavily, and in 1970 he began to show serious symptoms of delirium and memory loss characteristic of Korsakoff's psychosis. As the disease progressed, Jimmie's retrograde amnesia wiped out his memories back to 1945, and his anterograde amnesia was complete. He remains institutionalized under Sacks' care to this day. Jimmie has found some solace in religion, and finds peace in the contemplation of art and nature, and in listening to music. As Sacks concludes, "however great the organic damage . . . there remains the undiminished possibility of reintegration by art, by communion, by touching the human spirit: and this can be preserved in what seems at first a hopeless state of neurological devastation."

Your Shoes Are Full of Feet

The American psychologist Karl Dallenbach was fond of pointing out, when introducing the concept of habituation to psychology students, that until he drew it to their attention, they were probably not aware that their shoes were full of feet. When it was mentioned, however, they became aware of

dishabituation (DIS-ha-BIT-shu-a-shun) Elimination of habituation.

the slight pressure of their shoes, which they had ceased to notice. Another common example of habituation is the ticking of the clock or the sound of the air conditioner that we "tune out" of our consciousness but that we can readily hear when our attention is redirected to it. Habituation has been observed in many animal species and is considered a universal and primitive form of learning. Habituation is learning not to respond to stimuli that are of little consequence. We do not habituate to all repetitive stimuli. For example, we would not habituate to the ticking of a time bomb.

Habituation is not simply fatigue. It can be observed with repetition rates far below those required to produce fatigue of the response, and slight changes in the stimulus can quickly bring about a return of the response to the stimulus—a phenomenon know as **dishabituation.** One effective way to bring about dishabituation is the missing stimulus effect. If habituation occurs to a series of regularly spaced stimuli, the absence of a stimulus at its usual time often dishabituates the response to the following stimulus in the series.

Sensitization

Another form of primitive, nonassociative learning is sensitization, which is an increase in the strength of responses to new stimuli for some time after the animal has been exposed to a potentially threatening or noxious stimulus. Makers of horror movies are well aware of the power of sensitization. By presenting plot details that inform the viewers that a particular character is in reality an axe murderer, even innocent statements or acts by this character later in the movie make our pulse race. A horse that has been "spooked" by a rattlesnake will, for a time, shy at any sudden noise. Sensitization is nonassociative, since there is no particular association between the sensitizing stimulus and the stimuli to which the organism subsequently shows exaggerated responses. Instead, there is a widespread increase in response to stimuli that otherwise would attract little attention.

Classical Conditioning: Pavlov's Legacy

Ivan Pavlov (1849–1936) was responsible for a large body of work that demonstrated most of the basic phenomena of what we now call classical conditioning. Pavlov was a Russian physiologist whose initial interest was in the digestive system (in fact, his Nobel prize in 1904 was for his work on digestion, not the conditioned reflex). In the early stages of his work, he noticed that his experimental dogs began to salivate *before* food was placed in their mouths. In fact, they often started salivating as they were being placed into the restraining harness used in the experiments. This only happened after they had been in such experiments for several days. Pavlov quickly recognized the potential importance of what he called *psychic secretions* for investigating brain function. He then spent the remainder of his life exploring conditioning, which he believed would unlock the secrets of the brain. Although his theories of brain function in conditioning are now primarily of historical interest, his basic experimental techniques are still used in laboratories around the world.

Basic Conditioning Terms

In classical conditioning, learning occurs as an association between some innate response of the organism, called the *unconditioned response* (UCR), and a new, learned stimulus, the *conditioned stimulus* (CS). The UCR is made to occur by presenting an appropriate stimulus (the *unconditioned stimulus*, or UCS). In a typical Pavlov experiment the UCS was meat powder in the mouth, which produced the UCR—reflex salivation. The meat powder was then presented in close association with a neutral stimulus, such as a bell or light. After repeated pairings, the bell or light (the CS) elicited the salivation, the *conditioned response* (CR). The UCR and the CR usually have slight differences, but they need not concern us here.

Pavlov discovered that it was crucial in such procedures to keep distracting stimuli to a minimum. (Pavlov sought and obtained sophisticated sound-proofed laboratories from a suspicious and impoverished government following the Russian revolution.)

Habituation, Sensitization, and Conditioning in the Aplysia

Eric Kandel and his colleagues have adapted Pavlov's conditioning techniques for use with the sea slug **Aplysia,** a large invertebrate that lives in the intertidal zones of warm waters. Although its behavioral repertoire is somewhat limited, the Aplysia does seek and find food, squirts a purple ink to confuse potential predators, reproduces, lays eggs, and shows distinct rhythms of activity and rest.

Kandel and his colleagues have examined habituation, sensitization, and conditioning of one innate response shown by the Aplysia, the gill withdrawal reflex (Kandel and Schwartz, 1982; Carew et al., 1983). (Figure 12.6 shows an Aplysia.) These creatures extract oxygen from seawater through delicate gills that are protected by a sheet of tissue, the mantle shelf, which ends in a fleshy spout termed the siphon. The gill, mantle shelf, and siphon are normally extended out from the body as the animal slithers about its daily routine. If either the siphon or mantle shelf is touched lightly, siphon, mantle shelf, and gill all withdraw. What makes this gill withdrawal particularly useful as a model response system is that the neural circuitry underlying this reflex is now known in considerable detail.

The gill withdrawal reflex is controlled largely by one of the nine neural ganglia of the Aplysia, the abdominal ganglion, which contains about 2000 neurons. Moreover, virtually all the neurons in this ganglion are recognizable from animal to animal. Many of these cells have been identified and given names (numbers, actually, such as L28 or M7). The entire animal has only about 20,000 neurons. With a fairly well-known circuitry

Aplysia (ah-PLEASE-ee-ah) Marine invertebrate widely used in neuroscience because of its recognizable, large neurons and relatively simple neural circuits.

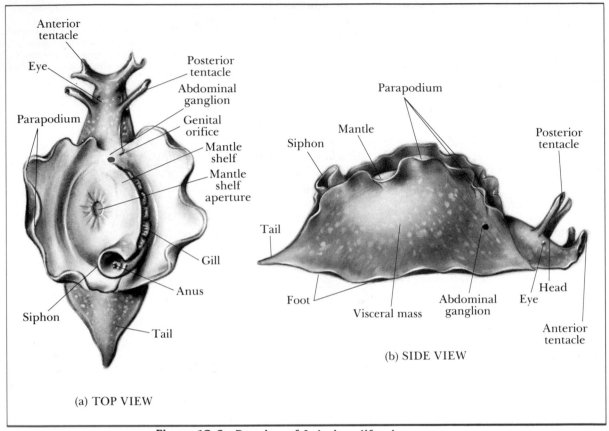

Figure 12.6   Drawing of Aplysia californica.

and large, identifiable neurons, the Aplysia has yielded considerable information concerning the cellular mechanisms underlying habituation, sensitization, and classical conditioning of the gill withdrawal reflex. In a series of experiments over several years Kandel and his associates have concluded that the primary site of change underlying learned alterations in the gill withdrawal reflex is in the *axon terminals of the sensory neurons that synapse on the motor neurons controlling the reflex.*

Habituation of Gill Withdrawal

If the siphon or mantle is briefly squirted with a mild jet of water, the gill, mantle, and siphon withdraw. Habituation to the water jet can be obtained within 10–15 trials, so that the gill, mantle, and siphon are retracted only about one-third as far as before habituation. This habituation lasts for an hour or so. Kandel has termed this *short-term habituation.* If repeated habituation sessions are held, say 4 sessions of 10 stimulus presentations each, habituation can still be seen weeks later. This is termed *long-term habituation*. (Kandel's original experimental setup for studying the behavioral habituation of the gill withdrawal reflex is shown in Figure 12.7.)

In later experiments, using microelectrodes, Kandel and associates were able to produce habituation within the neurons that produce the gill withdrawal reflex by stimulating the sensory neuron at levels just above threshold for firing the motor neuron. Thus they were able to study the neural changes underlying changes in the withdrawal reflex directly. They found neuronal habituation was characterized by smaller excitatory postsynaptic potentials (EPSPs) in the motor neurons activated by the sensory neurons. The smaller EPSPs resulted in fewer action potentials and thus diminished contractions in the muscles of the mantle, siphon, and gill. The smaller EPSPs, in turn, were caused by smaller amounts of neurotransmitter being released by the sensory neurons, which was caused by a decrease in the Ca^{2+}

Figure 12.7 **Drawing showing experimental setup for studying habituation and sensitization of gill withdrawal reflex.**
The reflex is produced by a tactile stimulus (water jet) to the siphon. The sensitizing stimulus is a shock to the tail. (a) Gill prior to withdrawal. (b) The gill after partial withdrawal. Recordings of degree of gill withdrawal after 1, 6, 11, and 13 habituation trails and on trial 14, following the first presentation of the sensitizing stimulus. The interstimulus interval was 1.5 sec (Kandel and Schwarts, 1982).

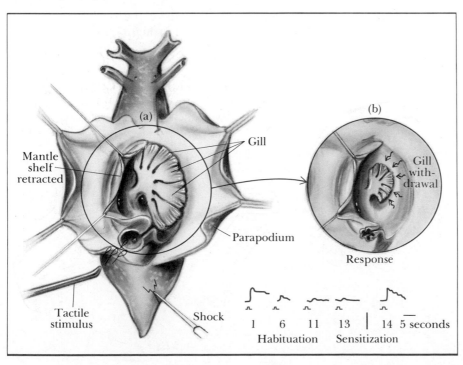

influx required to cause transmitter release. Thus the basic cause of habituation in this situation was a decrease in Ca^{2+} entry. Research is now aimed at "peeling the onion" one more layer to discover what is responsible for the decrease in the amount of Ca^{2+} that enters the axon terminals with repeated stimulation.

Sensitization

Sensitization of the gill withdrawal reflex can be accomplished with a strong electric shock to the tail, which produces an enhancement of the withdrawal reflex to stimuli presented immediately after the tail shock. Kandel and his co-workers also studied the sensitization of this reflex directly, using microelectrodes in the sensory and motor neurons, as they had done in examining habituation. The duration of sensitization also varies from hours to weeks, depending on the intensity of the shock and how often it is applied. As is true for habituation, the neural locus for the sensitization of the reflex was found to be in the axon terminals of the sensory neurons. In many ways sensitization appears to be a mirror image of habituation. It is associated with an *increase* in the size of the EPSPs in the motor neuron, caused by an increase in transmitter release, which is caused by an increase in Ca^{2+} influx.

One major difference in the circuitry underlying habituation and sensitization is that a "facilitatory interneuron" is involved in sensitization. This neuron carries impulses produced by the tail shock to the sensory neuron. The terminals of the facilitatory interneuron synapse on the axon terminals of the sensory neurons. (A simplified diagram of the neuronal circuitry underlying the gill withdrawal reflex is shown in Figure 12.8.) Thus both

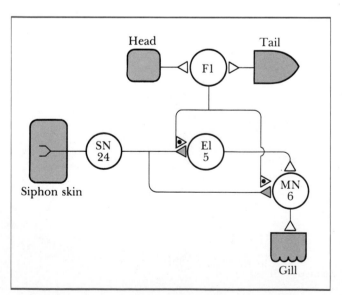

Figure 12.8 Simplified diagram of the basic neuronal circuitry underlying the gill withdrawal reflex in the Aplysia.
SN 24 = sensory neuron 24; FI = facilitating interneuron; EI = excitatory interneuron 5; MN 6 = motor neuron 6.

habituation and sensitization of this reflex appear to be produced by modulations in the Ca^{2+} influx.

Classical Conditioning of the Gill Withdrawal Reflex

The gill withdrawal reflex also has been classically conditioned (Carew et al., 1983). The CS in these studies was a brief touch to the siphon with a nylon bristle, whereas the UCS was an electric shock to the tail that produces a gill withdrawal reflex. Prior to conditioning, this CS produced only a feeble gill withdrawal reflex. Since the tail shock could also produce sensitization, which would increase all subsequent responses, including that of gill withdrawal, the appropriate control groups are animals that receive either *paired* (conditioning) or *unpaired* (sensitization) presentations of the CS and UCS. For conditioning to be demonstrated, the animals receiving paired presentations of stimuli must show greater gill withdrawal to the CS than animals presented with unpaired stimuli.

Using such procedures, conditioning lasting for several days was obtained with as few as 15 trials. The cellular mechanisms for conditioning seem to be similar to those for sensitization, but the timing of CS and UCS is critical. Robert Hawkins and his associates (1983) found that with paired presentations of the CS and UCS, the sensory neuron released more transmitter in response to the CS if it had just been activated by the UCS than when it had been unstimulated.

Although the exact explanation of these results is sure to undergo revision with further experimentation, we have sufficient evidence to conclude that the gill withdrawal reflex in the Aplysia is an extremely useful system in which to explore the cellular mechanisms underlying habituation, sensitization, and classical conditioning. By exploiting the behavioral capacities of the Aplysia and taking advantage of its relatively simple neuronal circuitry, these researchers have advanced our understanding of the possible cellular changes underlying simple learning.

You may be wondering if changes in Ca^{2+} influx also underlie the learning that takes place in *your* brain when you learn about the gill withdrawal reflex in Aplysia. We do not know. It does seem, however, that evolution has been conservative as larger and more complex brains have appeared. For example, the basic mechanisms underlying the nerve impulse and synaptic communication are fundamentally similar in the squid and in the brains of higher mammals. A similar conservation of mechanism may be true for learning as well. Obviously, many complications and unknown changes must accompany the rapid and sophisticated learning shown by advanced mammals, but these changes may build on the sort of synaptic changes revealed in simpler nervous systems.

Classical Conditioning in a Vertebrate Brain

Pavlov's conditioning procedures have also been used in the investigation of learning in vertebrates. One such series of experiments has been done

nictitating membrane
(NIK-ti-ta-ting) The tough
"third" eyelid present in
cats, rabbits, and some
other species.

**dentate-interpositus nu-
cleus**   (DEN-tate in-ter-
POZ-i-tuss) A nucleus in
the cerebellum found to be
important in conditioning
of the nictitating mem-
brane.

by Richard F. Thompson and his colleagues. They have found that there
are restricted regions of the brain (in the cerebellum, hippocampus, and
brainstem) that are apparently part of the neural circuit underlying the
classical conditioning of an eyeblink response in the rabbit (Thompson et
al., 1983; McCormick and Thompson, 1984; Thompson et al., 1984). The
conditioned response (CR) in these studies is a contraction (blink) of the
nictitating membrane or "third eyelid" present in rabbits, cats, and many
other animals. Actually the response measured in these studies involves
not only that of the nictitating membrane but the outer eyelids and some
of the nearby muscles of the face as well (McCormick and Thompson,
1984). The UCS in these studies is a puff of air to the cornea of the eye.
The CS is typically a tone.

In several different experiments these researchers found that lesions
in the **dentate-interpositus nucleus** of the cerebellum abolish both previous and subsequent CRs to the tone. Such lesions do not interfere with
the production of the eyeblink produced by the UCS, demonstrating a
disruption of the *learned* response but no interference with the unlearned
response. This suggests that the cerebellum (or this part of it anyway) is
involved in the learning of this simple motor response. Neurons in the
nearby brainstem also appear to be involved.

Other research has also implicated the cerebellum in learning. Animals
use a number of reflex eye movements to compensate for head movements
and thus maintain a stable retinal image of the visual field even when
running, jumping, and so on. One such reflex is the vestibulo-ocular reflex,
which adjusts to systematic changes in visual input produced, for example,
by placing distorting prisms over the animal's eyes. This adjustment by the
animals of their vestibulo-ocular reflex is a form of learning. It too is abolished by small cerebellar lesions. The reflex itself remains intact, but it no
longer can be altered by changes in the sensory input such as those produced by the prisms (Miyashita, 1981).

We should not conclude that all learning involves the cerebellum, but
if one is studying reflex adjustments of the eyes, the basic wiring of the
vertebrate nervous system suggests that the cerebellum should be a prime
location for any learning involving ocular reflexes. The entire brain probably contains neurons that may be involved in some type of learning or
another. The trick is to demonstrate this involvement.

Hippocampus Involvement in Trace Conditioning

Pavlov's basic conditioning technique has several different variations. For
example, the experimenter can present the CS and UCS so that they overlap in time (termed *delayed conditioning*) or with a pause between the two
(termed *trace conditioning*). The introduction of a slight time delay between
the CS and UCS introduces the necessity for a brief "memory load" on the
animal if conditioning is to occur. In Pavlov's terms the animal learns to
associate the occurrence of the UCS with the *memory trace* of the CS. Figure
12.9 shows the difference between delayed and trace conditioning procedures.

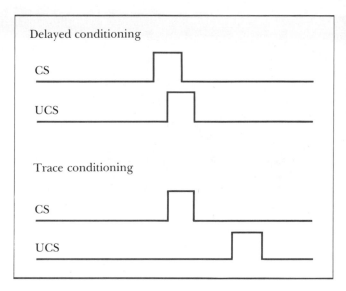

Figure 12.9 Diagram illustrating the time relationships between presentation of the conditioned stimulus (CS) and the unconditioned stimulus (UCS) in delayed and trace conditioning.
Note that in trace conditioning there is a pause between the offset of the CS and the onset of the UCS.

Thompson and his colleagues have found that when a memory demand is placed on the animal in an eyeblink conditioning situation, the hippocampus becomes part of the critical neural circuitry. With delayed conditioning procedures hippocampal lesions do not interfere with learning, but when trace conditioning techniques are used, hippocampal lesions abolish eyeblink conditioning. These same animals can still be conditioned using delayed conditioning procedures. *What* must be learned in part determines *where* in the brain learning occurs.

long-term potentiation (LTP) (po-ten-she-A-shun) An increased neuronal response to a standard stimulus following intense stimulation of an afferent pathway to those neurons.

Long-Term Potentiation (LTP)

As discussed previously, Eric Kandel and James Schwartz (1982) have proposed that the critical site of change underlying learning in the Aplysia is *presynaptic*. In particular, they believe the critical changes take place in the axon terminals of the sensory neurons that activate the motor neurons triggering the gill withdrawal reflex. A quite different view of the critical locus of change underlying learning is offered by Lynch and Baudry (1984), who suggest that the *postsynaptic* side of the synapse shows significant changes associated with memory storage.

Gary Lynch and Michel Baudry base their hypothesis mainly on data concerning a phenomenon known as **long-term potentiation (LTP).** LTP is an increase in the size of an evoked potential produced by a standard strength electrical stimulus following brief but intense electrical stimulation of the afferent pathway to the neurons producing the evoked potential. An evoked potential is the combined response of a cluster of neurons to the activation of an afferent pathway. Such potentials can be recorded in

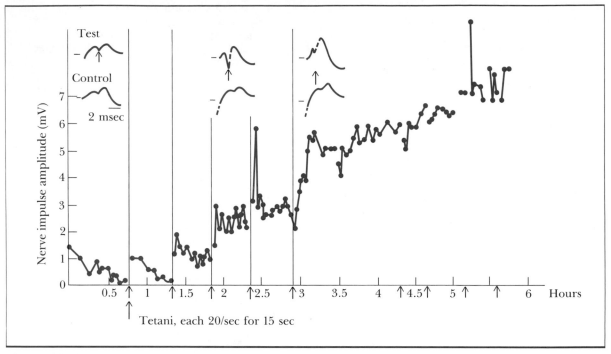

Figure 12.10 Long-term potentiation (LTP) of the response of a group of granule cells in the dentate gyrus.
Tetanic (rapid) stimulation of perforant path neurons, which excite neurons in the dentate gyrus, was applied at 20 impulses/sec for 15 sec. The amplitude of the evoked potential increased following such tetanic stimulations across the six hours of the experiment.

perforant pathways (PER-for-ant) A major afferent tract from the entorhinal cortex to the dentate gyrus.

dentate gyrus (DEN-tate JY-russ) Part of the hippocampal formation in the mammalian brain.

calpain (KAL-pain) A protein in the postsynaptic spine.

fodrin (FOE-drin) A protein in the postsynaptic spine.

the dentate gyrus (part of the hippocampal formation) by stimulation of one of the main afferent paths, the **perforant pathways.** The perforant pathways are made up of axons of neurons in the nearby entorhinal cortex that synapse on the granule cells of the **dentate gyrus.** Figure 12.10 shows LTP (Bliss and Lomo, 1973). LTP can last for months and may be related to long-term changes that underlie learning.

Gary Lynch and Michel Baudry (1984) have marshaled evidence to support the hypothesis that LTP involves the activation of a substance called **calpain** in the *postsynaptic* terminals of the granule cells. Calpain, they suggest, degrades or breaks up a structural protein, called **fodrin,** on the inner side of the postsynaptic membrane. As fodrin is degraded, Lynch and Baudry propose, it uncovers more postsynaptic receptors for the neurotransmitter at these synapses. This process is more or less permanent, they argue, and therefore the next time that the circuit is activated, the response capability of the postsynaptic neuron will be enhanced by the presence of more receptor sites (see Figure 12.11).

This hypothesis differs from that of Kandel and Schwartz primarily in

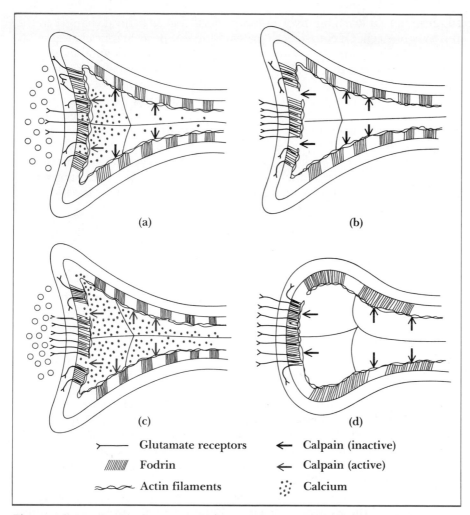

(a)   (b)

(c)   (d)

⊱—	Glutamate receptors	← Calpain (inactive)
▨	Fodrin	← Calpain (active)
⌇	Actin filaments	⁝ Calcium

Figure 12.11   Lynch–Baudry (1984) hypothesis concerning the molecular changes that may underlie LTP.
Diagram shows a dendritic spine that undergoes changes with tetanic stimulation as shown in Figure 12.10. The neurotransmitter at this synapse is glutamate. (a) Neurotransmitter release (small, unfilled circles) causes an increase in free Ca^{2+} within the postsynaptic receptive region of the spine. This increase in Ca^{2+} activates one protein, calpain, which in turn degrades another protein, fodrin, uncovering previously occluded glutamate receptors. (b) Calcium is removed from spine, inactivating the calpain. (c) Subsequent episodes of tetany produce an even larger influx of Ca^{2+} because more postsynaptic receptors are available for the transmitter to activate. The increased Ca^{2+} activates still more calpain, which degrades still more fodrin, eventually leading to a structural change in the shape of the spine. (d) Ca^{2+} is again eliminated from the spine following activation, but structural changes in the dendritic spine remain.

suggesting that learning involves biochemical and structural changes in the postsynaptic cell. Of course both presynaptic and postsynaptic changes may occur in brain tissue in various learning situations. Both hypotheses agree that synapses are the critical sites in the neuronal circuitry underlying learning. The idea that learning is due to the modification of existing synapses has a long history, going back at least to Ramón y Cajal. A rich and detailed theory that learning involves the recruitment of neurons into cell assemblies that constitute the physical manifestation of memories and habits appeared in an influential book written by Donald Hebb in 1949 titled *The Organization of Behavior*. Although it has been difficult to put Hebb's precise ideas to experimental tests, the general concepts and suggestions in this book have contributed significantly to thinking about learning and the brain.

SUMMARY

1. Studies of human amnesia patients suggest that the medial temporal lobe and portions of the thalamus and hypothalamus are important for the storage and retrieval of memories of past experiences. Amnesics are particularly poor at remembering events from their own lives (termed *episodic memory*) and somewhat less impaired on their more general knowledge of the world (called *semantic memory*). Most amnesia is caused either by a brain infection, such as that incurred in encephalitis, or by alcoholism accompanied by vitamin B_1 deficiency. This latter condition is termed *Korsakoff's psychosis*. Injury to the brain, such as that incurred in neurosurgery or accidental trauma, can also cause amnesia.

2. Different hypotheses have been offered to account for the memory loss seen in amnesics. This loss is not total, since some new tasks can be learned, despite the fact that the amnesic patient does not remember having learned the new task. The consolidation deficit and the retrieval deficit hypotheses are the leading hypotheses put forward to account for the facts of amnesia. A retrieval hypothesis of some sort would appear to be more likely.

3. Several simple forms of learning have proved useful in trying to uncover the neural basis of learning and memory. These include habituation (learning not to respond to repeated, inconsequential stimuli), sensitization (increase in all responses following the presentation of a potentially threatening stimulus), and classical conditioning (as discovered by Ivan Pavlov). All these forms of behavioral change have been examined in the laboratory with animal subjects.

4. In a search for simpler systems in which to investigate learning and memory, neuroscientists have turned to creatures such as the Aplysia. The gill withdrawal reflex of Aplysia has proved useful for studies involving habituation, sensitization, and classical conditioning. According to the research program generated by Eric Kandel and his colleagues, the main site of change for these various phenomena appears to be in

the presynaptic terminals of the sensory neurons that produce the gill withdrawal reflex. The changes in these terminals appear to follow from changes in the ion channels that allow for either increased or decreased levels of Ca^{2+} to enter the terminals. The amount of neurotransmitter and hence the amplitude and duration of postsynaptic potentials depend on the amount of Ca^{2+} that enters the presynaptic terminals.

5. The investigation of learning in vertebrates has followed several different paths. One of the more productive research programs is that of Richard F. Thompson and his colleagues, who have found evidence that the dentate-interpositus nucleus of the cerebellum and regions of the nearby brainstem are critical for the classical conditioning of the nictitating membrane in rabbits. The hippocampus is also involved in conditioning situations in which a delay occurs between the presentation of the to-be-conditioned stimulus and the unconditioned stimulus.

6. Another approach to learning in the vertebrate brain involves a phenomenon known as long-term potentiation (LTP). LTP is an increase in the size of an evoked potential to a standard stimulus following brief but intense electrical stimulation of an afferent pathway to the neurons producing the evoked potential. Much of this research has been done in the dentate gyrus of the hippocampal formation. Lynch and Baudry have proposed that LTP involves the appearance of an increased number of postsynaptic receptors. Although the details of the Kandel hypothesis and that of Lynch and Baudry differ, both focus on the synapse as the site of change in the brain underlying learning and memory.

SUGGESTIONS FOR FURTHER READING

Bailey, C. H., and Kandel, E. P. (1985). Molecular approaches to the study of short-term and long-term memory. In C. W. Coen (Ed.), *Functions of the brain* (pp. 98–129). Oxford, England: Clarendon Press.

Corkin, S. (1984). Lasting consequences of bilateral medial temporal lobectomy: Clinical course and experimental findings in H. M. *Seminars in Neurology, 4,* 249–259.

Zechmeister, E. B., and Nyberg, S. E. (1982). *Human memory.* Monterey, CA: Brooks/ Cole.

13

Hemispheric Specializations in the Human Brain

I felt a cleavage in my mind
As if my brain had split;
I tried to match it, seam by seam
But could not make them fit.

EMILY DICKINSON

Preview

One feature that distinguishes the human brain from that of other advanced mammalian brains, it has been proposed recently, is the differences it displays between the left and right hemispheres. We now know this is not true, but the degree of such *functional asymmetry* seems to be greater in our brains than in the brains of our closely living primate relatives. This specialization between the hemispheres has been observed in several different experimental situations, but the most vivid examples have been in epileptic patients who have undergone surgery that severed the corpus callosum, the main neural link between the two cerebral hemispheres. From careful observation of these people, and observations on patients with brain damage restricted to one hemisphere, it now appears that the left hemisphere is usually better at producing language than the right and that the right hemisphere is better than the left in the recognition of visual, somesthetic, and auditory *patterns*. The fact that differences exist between the left and right hemispheres should not cause us to forget that our two cerebral hemispheres work together in a coordinated fashion.

For more than 100 years the frontal lobes have been viewed as particularly responsible for our ability to plan for the future and maintain normal emotional responses, although conclusions regarding the functions of the frontal lobe are made difficult by the anatomic complexity of this region of the brain.

Is Your Left Hemisphere Different from Your Right?

If you were to hold a human brain in your hands, you would notice that the two large cerebral hemispheres are attached to each other by a large bundle of shiny white myelinated axons—the **corpus callosum.** If you were to look down at the top of the brain and gently pry the two hemispheres apart, you would see the corpus callosum a centimeter or two down in the

Corpus
callosum

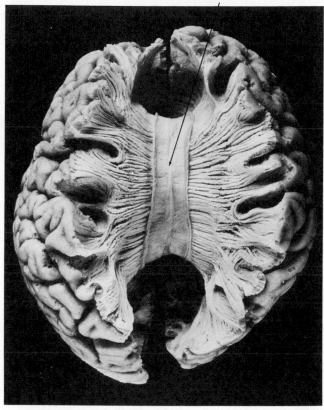

Figure 13.1 Photo of human brain as seen from above, looking down on partially split corpus callosum.

space between the hemispheres (see Figure 13.1). In this imaginary investigation let us gently cut through the corpus callosum with a scalpel until the thalamus is exposed. In addition to the corpus callosum, three other **commissures** allow the two hemispheres to communicate with each other—the anterior, the posterior, and the hippocampal commissures. If we were to continue our midline section of the brain through the thalamus, we would reach the hypothalamus and then the brainstem. If we were to lay the two brain halves on the table, it might appear at first that we had divided the brain into two identical, mirror-image halves.

For many years neuroanatomists concluded that the two halves of the brain were indeed mirror images. More recently, detailed examination has shown that most human brains show slight structural differences between the left and right hemispheres. The best-known left–right asymmetry is in the temporal lobe, in an area known as the **planum temporale.** This asymmetry was discovered by Norman Geschwind and Walter Levitsky in 1968 (see Figure 13.2). The planum temporale is part of the cortex that is important for language comprehension (as will be discussed in greater detail

commissure (KOM-i-sure) A band of axons crossing from one hemisphere to the other.

planum temporale (PLAY-num tem-po-RAL-e) A region of the temporal lobe found to exhibit right–left asymmetry.

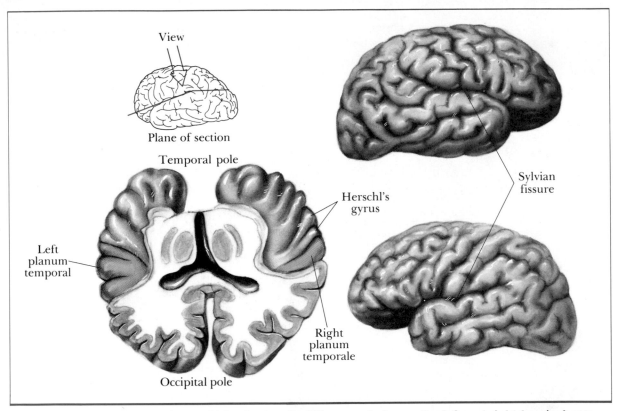

Figure 13.2 Anatomic differences between the left and right hemispheres in the temporal lobes.
Notice the larger area of the planum temporale in the left hemisphere. The slope of the Sylvian fissure in the left hemisphere (top) is gentler than that on the right.

in the following chapter) and thought to be concerned with the production of voluntary movement sequences.

Geschwind and Levitsky examined 100 adult brains and found that in 65 the planum temporale was clearly larger in the left hemisphere, in 11 cases it was larger in the right hemisphere, and in 24 cases no significant difference occurred. Several follow-up studies have confirmed this original finding. Sandra Witelson (1983) reviewed seven anatomic studies on adult brains (including the 1968 study by Geschwind and Levitsky). The total number of brains surveyed was 420. Overall, different researchers found that the planum temporale is larger in the left hemisphere in 71 percent of the brains, larger in the right hemisphere in 15 percent, and about the same size in both hemispheres in the remaining 14 percent.

Although brain asymmetry appears to be most highly developed in human beings, it is not a unique characteristic of the human brain. Marjorie Le May and Geschwind (1975) examined the brains of 28 great apes and found that in 17 (61 percent) of them the planum temporale was larger in the left hemisphere. The species included in this study were gorilla, chimpanzee, and orangutan. (No animals were killed just for this study; the brains were from animals that had died of other causes.) In a similar study of monkeys and lesser apes (gibbon, siamang), structural asymmetries were found in only 7 percent of the brains examined. Birds also display left–right differences in brain structure, particularly in those nuclei related to song production (Nottebohm, 1977).

The left–right difference in the size of the planum temporale is the most reliable anatomic asymmetry so far observed in human brains. Unfortunately, at present no other way to evaluate the size of the planum temporale is known except at autopsy. Quite recent developments, however, have shown other anatomic differences may be revealed by brain scanning techniques. Some of the differences that may prove to be of theoretical significance include the structure of the large middle cerebral artery, the width of the frontal and occipital lobes, and the length of the posterior horns of the lateral ventricles (Witelson, 1983; Kolb and Whishaw, 1985).

Hemispheric Specialization

Let us return to the question asked earlier: "Is your left hemisphere different from your right?" We have seen that the odds are about two to one that your left planum temporale is larger than your right one. A more intriguing question is, "In addition to any structural differences, do the left and right hemispheres have functional specializations? The answers to this question have been accumulating for over a century. At present, the general conclusion is that there are differences in the functions of the left and right hemispheres, but what these differences are, their magnitude, and their significance for understanding normal behavior are topics of debate. Both normal and brain-damaged subjects have been examined in a variety of ways to determine the nature and extent of hemispheric specialization. In this section we shall consider the evidence from individuals who have undergone surgical separation of the two hemispheres.

Hemispheric Deconnection: "Split-Brain" Patients

The most dramatic demonstration that the two cerebral hemispheres are not functionally identical has come from examining a small number of patients who have undergone a remarkable brain operation in order to relieve uncontrollable epilepsy. In such operations the main connections between the hemispheres are severed to prevent the spread of epileptic seizures from one hemisphere to the other. (This is, of course, a treatment of last resort.) The first attempts to treat epilepsy in this manner were made during the late 1930s by an American neurosurgeon, William Van

Wagenen. Some of these early "split-brain" patients were given some psychological tests, but no significant effects were observed (Van Wagenen and Herren, 1940; Akelaitis, 1944). In most cases Van Wagenen did not completely sever the corpus callosum, and as these operations were only marginally helpful in reducing seizures, he did not continue them.

In the 1950s Roger Sperry and Ronald Myers began a series of experiments with cats in which the two hemispheres were isolated from each other by section of the commissures and a splitting of the optic chiasm. This allowed the experimenters to train the cat to perform visual discriminations with each hemisphere independent of the other. Sperry and Myers found that, indeed, each hemisphere could control the responses of the animal independent of the other hemisphere's experience. These experiments encouraged a team of neurosurgeons in California to try the Van Wagenen technique again with epileptic patients, as Myers and Sperry's cats showed no general ill effects from such radical surgery (Myers, 1956; Myers and Sperry, 1958). The neurosurgeons, Joseph Bogen and Phillip Vogel, made complete sections of the corpus callosum, as well as the anterior commissure, hippocampal commissure, and in some cases part of the thalamus as well (Bogen and Vogel, 1962).

These surgeons have been much more successful at reducing the intensity and frequency of the patient's seizures than Van Wagenen. However, because of the radical nature of the surgery, only a small number of such operations have been done. [By 1983 the "California series" totaled 15. Another 28 such patients were operated on elsewhere (Gazzaniga, 1983). Only a small number have been suitable for psychological testing (many have quite low IQs and widespread brain abnormalities).] Our knowledge of the deconnection syndrome in human beings rests on the examination of fewer than 10 individuals, some repeatedly tested over a period of years. Although it is not possible to draw sweeping generalizations from the results with these patients, they do present a unique opportunity to assess the capacities and characteristics of each hemisphere in human beings. The California patients have been tested primarily by Roger Sperry and his colleagues. Other patients have been examined primarily by Michael Gazzaniga (Sperry, 1968; 1974; Gazzaniga, 1967; Gazzaniga and LeDoux, 1978).

Communicating with One Hemisphere at a Time

Many of the insights into the deconnection syndrome have emerged from studies in which the researchers have exploited the anatomy of the human visual system. As outlined in Chapter 5, each optic nerve divides, so that about half of the axons in the nerve cross over and project to the opposite side of the brain (see Figure 13.3). The result is that objects flashed briefly to the left of a point directly out from the tip of the nose (as the subject looks straight ahead) are processed by the right hemisphere. This is the left visual field. Objects flashed to the right of this point (right visual field) are processed in the left hemisphere. Of course, if the object remains in

Figure 13.3
The anatomy of the human visual system is such that things in the visual field to the left of a central fixation point are projected to the right hemisphere and vice versa.

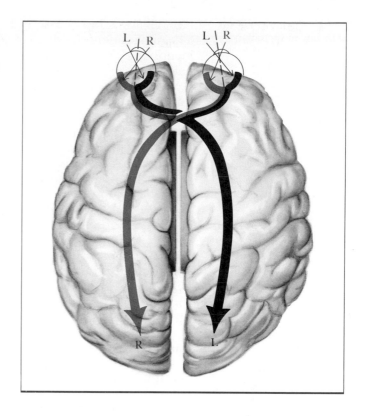

either visual field for more than about 200 msec, the subject can shift his or her gaze and thus cause the object to be processed by both hemispheres. A device called a **tachistoscope** is used in such studies to control the location and duration of the visual stimuli.

This technique is popular not only with split-brain researchers, but in the study of perception more generally, and well over 1000 experiments have been reported using tachistoscopic presentation of stimuli (Beaumont, 1983). Somewhat similar studies can be done using the sense of touch, since the shape and identity of objects held in the left hand are sensed primarily by the right hemisphere and vice versa. However, this hemispheric "separation of channels" is not as clear-cut for touch recognition as it is for vision, as some ipsilateral connections appear to exist in the somesthetic system.

Some of the most startling findings appeared quite early in this research. Sperry and his colleagues (including Michael Gazzaniga at that time) found that when words were flashed into the right visual field, the patients had no difficulty in reading them correctly out loud. However, if the same words were flashed to the left visual field (processed by the right hemisphere), the patient could not call out the word or verbally identify a picture of the object corresponding to the word flashed on the screen. A typical response to a left visual field presentation of the word *spoon* might

tachistoscope (Ta-KISS-ta-scope) Device for the presentation of visual stimuli for controlled periods of time and in specific regions on the visual field.

aphasia (Ah-FAZE-e-ah)
Difficulty in speech and
language performance due
to brain damage.

be, "That was just a flash of light," or, "I didn't see anything that time." The same patient could, however, read out loud the word *spoon* or correctly identify the picture of a spoon when it was presented to the right visual field.

One might conclude that the right hemisphere is simply stupid and can neither read nor recognize pictures of simple objects. That, however, would be incorrect, as Sperry demonstrated. If, instead of being asked to *name* or *read aloud* the word or picture, the patient is asked to retrieve with the left hand an object that *matches* the word or picture seen from a group of objects placed out of sight, the person can do this with almost 100 percent accuracy using the sense of touch. It must have been quite remarkable to observe these patients correctly choosing the appropriate object time and time again and each time denying that he or she had seen anything. Moreover, both responses were correct. The right hemisphere could make the identification by touch but not produce the appropriate words. The left hemisphere, in fact, did not see anything, since the stimulus was presented in the left visual field, which projects only to the right hemisphere.

Subsequent studies confirmed that the two cerebral hemispheres in these patients were, under such circumstances, processing and remembering things independently of the other. Sperry has described the situation thus:

> Instead of the normally unified single stream of consciousness, these patients behave in many ways as if they have two independent streams of conscious awareness, one in each hemisphere, each of which is cut off from and out of contact with the mental experience of the other. In other words, each hemisphere seems to have its own separate and private sensations; its own perceptions, its own concepts; and its own impulses to act, with related volitional, cognitive, and learning experiences. Following the surgery, each hemisphere also has thereafter its separate chain of memories that are rendered inaccessible to the recall processes of the other [Sperry, 1968].

(It should be remembered, of course, that except for these specialized laboratory experiments, both hemispheres go to the same parties, meet the same people, and in general are exposed to the same environmental stimuli.)

Right Hemisphere Language: An Ongoing Controversy

The inability of the right hemisphere to speak, even though it could "read" simple words, fits well with the fact that almost always the left hemisphere controls speech production and, to a large extent, speech comprehension as well. The basic support for the conclusion that the production of language is a left hemisphere specialization comes from **aphasia** cases, in which brain damage produces difficulty with language comprehension, language production, or both.

In most cases aphasia is caused by damage to the left hemisphere, although right hemisphere aphasia cases are well known. With the exception of one individual, all the split-brain patients so far examined have left hemisphere dominance for language. The exception is an individual with some language capacity in both hemispheres. Although it was not surprising that the left hemisphere was dominant for language in the cases examined by Sperry and Gazzaniga, it was somewhat surprising that, given an opportunity to respond *nonverbally,* the right hemisphere of these individuals could read a substantial number of simple words. Moreover, at least two of these patients could select (with their left hand) the appropriate object from a group of hidden test objects when they were given such verbal instructions as, "Find a measuring instrument" (left hand retrieves a ruler) or, "Select a container for liquids" (left hand retrieves a cup). These findings, however, have been made ambiguous by the fact that there is a small projection from neurons in the left hand to the left hemisphere as well as the major projection from the left hand to the right hemisphere (Gazzaniga, 1983).

The extent of language capacity in the right hemisphere is controversial. (It is important to emphasize that being able to *produce* language, either by speaking or writing, and *comprehending* it, for which the evidence may be obtained in other ways, are separate aspects of language and are often affected unequally by brain damage.) The right hemisphere generally has been found to be much better at language comprehension than at language production (Searleman, 1977; 1983).

Although the left hemisphere is usually language dominant (better at language production), this is not always true. About 90–99 percent of all right-handed individuals have their main language centers in the left hemisphere, whereas only about 50–70 percent of non-right-handed individuals (left-handed and ambidextrous) have their main language centers there. For ease of discussion, we generally use the term *left hemisphere* for the hemisphere dominant for language production.

The strongest case for significant language comprehension ability in the right hemisphere comes from two California patients. Eran Zaidel (1975) developed a system of presenting visual material to one hemisphere by projecting the stimuli onto a sort of contact lens worn by the patient. This device allows longer messages to be transmitted than is true of a tachistoscope. Zaidel found that the two patients he examined had substantial right hemisphere capacity to comprehend language. In fact, he concluded that the "reading level" of the right hemisphere was only about two years behind that of the left hemisphere.

In addition, at least two additional patients appear to have developed virtually normal language *comprehension* in the right hemisphere, although this hemisphere still is severely deficient at speech *production.* These two patients can respond appropriately verbally in many cases with short answers. For example, when the picture of a man holding a pistol was flashed to the right hemisphere, one of these patients said, "Holdup" (Gazzaniga, 1983).

Michael Gazzaniga believes that language in the right hemisphere is limited to comprehension and probably not widely distributed in the general population, since so few individuals seem to have significant right hemisphere speech capacity. Zaidel (1983) argues that right language capacity is not unusual among the split-brain population and may be relatively common among normal individuals as well. Finally, Jay Myers (1984) has pointed out some of the difficulties in drawing any firm conclusion on the basis of evidence with the split-brain patients, since so many have low IQs, widespread brain damage, or both. Although the controversy remains lively, it seems reasonable to summarize the situation at the present by saying that the left hemisphere is clearly superior to the right, particularly in language production. It is less superior in language comprehension.

Right Hemisphere Specializations

Is the right hemisphere generally inferior in intellectual capacity to the left, or is it superior at some tasks? Evidence on this question comes from split-brain patients, from patients with brain damage to only one hemisphere, and from special testing techniques with normal subjects. This evidence suggests that the right hemisphere is superior to the left at some tasks.

It is somewhat misleading to pose questions strictly in terms of left versus right hemisphere abilities for normal brains. After all, in the normal brain massive interhemispheric connections allow continuous communication between the two hemispheres. In addition, our visual world is not usually presented to us through tachistoscopes.

Eye movements and head movements bring our visual environment to us in a unified manner. Thus only with special testing techniques can we glimpse possible differential capacities of the two hemispheres.

Pattern Recognition: A Right Hemisphere Specialization?

On the basis of his work with split-brain cases Sperry has suggested that the right hemisphere is superior to the left in the ability to *recognize and construct patterns,* particularly visual patterns. In some early work Gazzaniga and Sperry (1967) noticed that their patients were much more adept at drawing a cube in three-dimensional perspective or arranging blocks to match two-dimensional geometric patterns with their *left* hand. This was true despite the fact that all their early patients were right-handed. In one instance they filmed a patient struggling ineffectually with his right hand to arrange the blocks to match a relatively simple geometric design. As he fumbled, the patient's left hand, as if controlled by another person, reached out and began to arrange the blocks correctly. When the left hand was gently removed from the blocks by the experimenter, the right hand (controlled by the left hemisphere) went back to its fumbling, unable to benefit from the right hemisphere's ability to construct the pattern.

Similar evidence was gathered on these patients for drawings of houses, cubes, and so on, in perspective. All such drawings were done better by the left hand, guided by the right hemisphere. Figure 13.4 summarizes Sperry's conclusions regarding hemispheric specializations of the human brain, based on his work with split-brain patients.

Left handers are found in disproportionate numbers in certain activities that require good spatial perceptual skills, such as tennis. This is John McEnroe, one of many fine left-handed tennis players.

More recent research with normal subjects suggests that hemispheric differences in visual pattern recognition may be quite subtle. Justine Sergent (1982) used human faces as her stimuli and normal young adult males as her subjects. Using a tachistoscope, she presented unfamiliar faces at exposure durations of 40, 120, and 200 msec. Subjects were required simply to identify the face as being either male or female. The answers were given by pushing one of two buttons, and reaction time was taken. Overall error rate was about the same (about 6 percent) regardless of which visual field was used. Sergent found that at the short exposure, responses were faster (568 msec to 582 msec) when the faces were flashed into the left visual field and thus projected directly only to the right hemisphere. (The information, of course, can be relayed from the right hemisphere to the left via the interhemispheric connections.) When there was a relatively long exposure time (200 msec), the advantage shifted to the left hemisphere. Faces flashed into the right visual field were identified more quickly than those flashed into the left visual field (480–492 msec.) Sergent concluded that the right hemisphere may be more competent at the early visual processing of "low-resolution" stimuli but that when more information is available (with "high-resolution" stimuli), the left hemisphere becomes slightly faster at face recognition.

Some theorists have suggested that it is not the type of stimuli to which the two hemispheres are differentially tuned that is important, but the *mode*

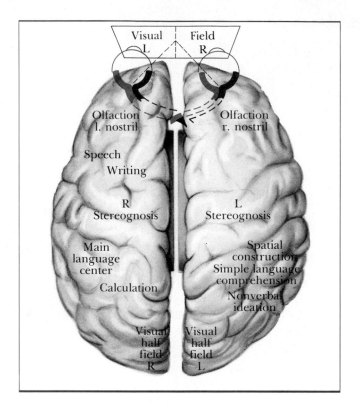

Figure 13.4
Summary diagram of Sperry (1968) showing the functional lateralization of the two hemispheres as revealed by experiments with split-brain patients.

of processing for which the two hemispheres are specialized. They tend to regard the left hemisphere as operating in an "analytic–sequential" manner, characteristic of language and mathematical reasoning, and the right hemisphere as operating in a "spatial–synthetic" mode, more characteristic of pattern appreciation and "holistic" thinking (Levy-Agresti and Sperry, 1968; Sperry, 1968). In such models the left hemisphere is characterized as being specialized for the analysis of "discrete items in reference to their *temporal* arrangement," whereas the right hemisphere is thought to produce a "synthesis of stimuli into a holistic percept in which the *spatial* aspects of the stimuli take precedence over the temporal aspects" (Witelson, 1983). Whether such characterizations are sufficient to describe the fundamental and complicated specializations of the two hemispheres remains to be seen.

A great deal of information on hemispheric function has come from the study of patients who have suffered unilateral brain damage. One such series of experiments has been conducted by Brenda Milner on patients at the Montreal Neurological Institute (Milner, 1967; 1974; 1982). These patients underwent surgery to remove diseased brain tissue that was causing epileptic seizures. They were not "split-brain" patients, but patients in which the abnormal tissue is localized primarily to one side of the brain. The surgical rationale is to remove the abnormal brain tissue completely, sparing as much normal tissue as possible. Often the abnormal tissue is in the temporal lobes. In analyzing such temporal lobe patients Milner and others have found that deficits in the recognition of visual patterns, including faces, is much more common following right temporal lobe surgery than following left temporal lobe surgery. Patients with removals of portions of the right temporal lobe are not blind. In fact, their visual acuity as measured with standard eye charts is unchanged by the surgery. However, they display subtle but readily detected deficits in the perception of visual patterns that cannot be easily "recoded" into verbal terms. Such a visual "nonsense" pattern is shown in Figure 13.5.

In another experiment Milner found that right temporal lobe patients were quite poor at remembering whether they had been shown a photograph of a face (taken from an unfamiliar school yearbook). Other types of neurologic patients, including patients with left temporal lobe damage, do much better at such face recognition tasks. Elizabeth Warrington and her colleagues in England have found related deficits in patients with damage to the right **parietal lobe.** In what Warrington has termed the "right parietal imperception syndrome," she found that subjects with right parietal damage had great difficulty in recognizing common objects when they were viewed from an unusual perspective (see Figure 13.6). Warrington (1982) believes this difficulty represents a failure of perceptual categorization "whereby a set of two or more stimulus inputs are allocated to the same perceptual category." She suggests that in normals, the right hemisphere is particularly specialized for such perceptual categorization, a necessary step in the storage of visual memories.

Researchers have also found right hemisphere superiority in a variety of other recognition and mental manipulation tasks involving visual stimuli. These tasks include map reading, judging the size of circles from small arcs, recognizing correct transformations of visual designs, and finding hidden figures embedded in other figures (Sperry, 1982; Beaumont, 1983; Milner, 1982). The theme that ties these results together is rapid and accurate perception of visual *pattern,* a skill at which the right hemisphere seems superior.

In addition to right hemisphere specialization for *visual* pattern recognition, the right hemisphere may be better than the left at two other related skills at least. One of these is the recognition of objects by their

parietal lobe   (Pa-RY-et-al) One of the four main lobes of the brain.

Figure 13.5 A nonsense figure. Patients with right temporal lobe damage have great difficulty recognizing such figures, whereas patients with left temporal lobe lesions have no more difficulty than normals.

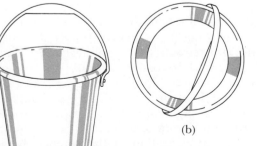

(b)

(a)

Figure 13.6 Unconventional Views of Objects Test. Patients with right temporal lobe lesions have difficulty in recognizing common objects such as the pail (a) when it is shown from an unusual angle as in (b).

Left-handed individuals appear to be over-represented among artists, athletes, and architects, occupations in which spatial skills are of particular importance.

dyslexia (diz-LEKS-e-ah) Unusual difficulty in learning to read and spell.

autism (AW-tizm) A condition that appears early in childhood, primarily in boys. Autism is marked by failure to relate to others, language disorders, and other symptoms.

feel. The other is memory for musical patterns. Sandra Witelson (1983) has developed a test for touch recognition in which subjects are given three-dimensional objects of "meaningless shape," one in each hand, and asked to choose the correct match from a series of two-dimensional display cards. With normal subjects, objects placed in the left hand (for which the touch receptors project mainly to the right hemisphere) are identified more accurately than objects placed in the right hand.

One interesting feature of this experiment was that Witelson found boys showed this hemispheric specialization as early as 6–10 years of age, whereas girls did not display a left-hand superiority until about age 13. Witelson believes for a variety of reasons, including the preceding finding, that females experience later specialization of the hemispheres. This longer period of plasticity may be related to the fact that fewer girls than boys suffer from developmental **dyslexia** (profound difficulty in reading) and that boys suffer more from **autism,** a condition marked by social withdrawal that may be related to severe difficulty in using language. Witelson suggests that since hemispheric specialization proceeds more slowly in girls, they are better than boys at withstanding various conditions that adversely affect left hemisphere functions.

Finally, evidence suggests that the right hemisphere may be specialized for the recognition of a sequence of tones (i.e., "melody"). Brenda Milner (1967) found that patients with right temporal lobe removals were quite deficient, compared with left temporal lobe patients, for certain tests of musical abilities, including tests of memory for short sequences of notes. Right temporal lobe patients were also deficient at *timbre discrimination*, having more trouble than normals or left temporal lobe patients at discriminating the same note played on different instruments.

We have much to learn about specialization of the cerebral hemispheres. The differences that have been uncovered have inspired a flood of research on normal subjects, as well as continued work with the split-brain patients and patients with unilateral brain damage. There has also been wide popular interest in hemispheric specializations, and many

"*I Just Can't Place Your Face*"

One of the most curious conditions to result from brain damage in humans is the selective inability to recognize faces. A recent review by Antonio Damasio (1985) details many of the basic facts about this rare phenomenon. People with this condition suddenly can no longer recognize the faces of family members or friends. In fact, in some cases, such individuals do not even recognize their own face in the mirror. Otherwise, they are relatively normal and have few other neurologic symptoms. This condition is called *prosopagnosia* (from the Greek *proso*, for "face"; *a*, "not"; and *gnosis*, "perception"). The specificity of the problem is impressive. These patients do not have difficulty *discriminating* among different unfamiliar faces; they can perform normally in matching unfamiliar faces, for example, nor do they have difficulty in drawing complex figures or other perceptual tasks. Their visual acuity is normal, but they become permanently unable to recognize people by simply looking at their faces. They do recognize familiar individuals as soon as they speak, indicating that the difficulty has to do with the triggering of appropriate memories by the *visual stimuli* associated with the person's face. In addition, all the memories these patients have of friends and relatives remain intact, but they can no longer recognize them by sight.

Recent evidence reviewed by Damasio shows that difficulty with visual recognition in these patients is not restricted solely to human faces. They also have difficulty recognizing different makes of automobiles (they cannot recognize their own car, for example), different animals within groups, or clothes of the same type (e.g., dresses, shirts, etc.). They know that a car is a car and a horse is a horse, but cannot tell individual members of a given class from one another, even with extended practice. Analysis of these patients has led to the tentative conclusion that the perceptual process must proceed normally but that the connection between the stimulus and the memory for that specific item cannot be activated. At the present no satisfactory explanation for proso-pagnosia exists.

The precise anatomic basis for prosopagnosia is still somewhat controversial. Although some theorists favor a right hemisphere location for the critical site of damage (e.g., Kolb and Whishaw, 1985), Damasio (1985) presents evidence that the damage must be bilateral, located in the occipito-temporal region. Even if Damasio is correct, as it appears he is, this does not mean that the two hemispheres make equal contributions to face recognition. In fact, it would be surprising if they did, based on what else we know about the functional asymmetry of the human brain.

---

oversimplified and/or erroneous ideas have been published in newspapers, magazines, and "pop psychology" paperback books. It is a good idea to maintain a perspective in the area of brain research. At the present, we know that our hemispheres work in a cooperative and unified fashion, even though the right and left hemispheres may contribute in different ways.

The Frontal Lobes

The frontal lobes have interested brain scientists since the time of Phineas Gage, who, in the middle of the nineteenth century, became the first well-studied individual with severe damage in that region. Gage was a 25-year-old foreman on a railroad construction crew. The crew was using blasting powder to remove some rock and Gage was injured while tamping down the blasting powder with a long iron bar. As later reported by the physician who treated him, "Phineas P. Gage, an efficient and capable foreman, was injured on September 13, 1848, when a tamping iron was blown through the frontal region of his brain" (Harlow, 1868). The tamping iron, over 3 feet long, entered Gage's head just below one eye and exited through the top of his skull, destroying virtually all his frontal lobes. Miraculously, he survived. In fact, he only briefly lost consciousness and was able to talk to his men within minutes after the accident. (Figure 13.7 shows Gage's skull and a reconstruction of his head.)

Harlow's report of the profound changes in Gage's personality are still descriptive of the "frontal-lobe personality." Prior to the accident, Gage had the reputation as a sober, hard-working, family-oriented man, but following his accident, he was described as follows:

> He is fitful, irreverent, indulging at times in the grossest profanity (which was not previously his custom), manifesting but little deference to his fellows, impatient of restraint or advice when it conflicts with his desires, at times pertinaciously obstinate yet capricious and vacillating, devising many plans for future operation which no sooner are arranged than they are abandoned in turn for others appearing more feasible. His mind was radically changed so that his friends and acquaintances said that he was no longer Gage [Harlow, 1868].

Gage survived for another 12 years, and spent part of his later years traveling with a circus, displaying the tamping bar and retelling over and over the details of the accident.

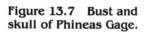

Figure 13.7   Bust and skull of Phineas Gage.

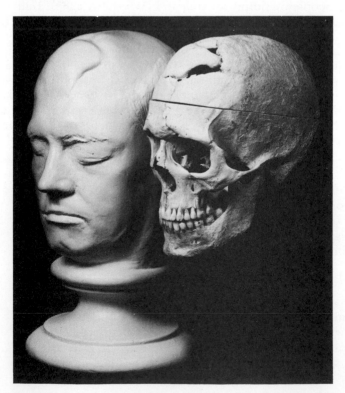

Although not all individuals with damage to the frontal lobes show the same personality changes, lack of awareness of social customs, poor planning, and erratic behavior are common. In the years since Gage's spectacular accident, a great deal of information has accumulated on the behavior of patients with damage to the frontal lobes. Because of their great size and complexity, the contributions of the frontal lobes to behavior are still difficult to understand. Not the smallest part of the difficulty is their anatomic complexity.

Anatomy of the Frontal Lobes

Figure 13.8 illustrates the location and subdivisions of the human frontal lobes. The frontal lobes have been subdivided in many different ways (Stuss and Benson, 1984). The frontal lobes contain the primary motor area (Brodmann area 4), as well as an area just anterior to area 4, termed the premotor area (Brodmann area 6 and part of 8). In addition, there is a region termed the frontal eye-fields, important in the control of eye movements. The remainder of the frontal lobes is generally divided into three parts, the dorsolateral area, the mesial area, and the orbital area. These areas have reciprocal connections with many other parts of the brain, including much of the remainder of the cerebral cortex, the basal ganglia, hypothalamus, and amygdala (Milner and Petrides, 1984). At present no clear relationship has been found between various frontal lobe symptoms

Figure 13.8 **Major subdivisions of the frontal lobes in humans.**

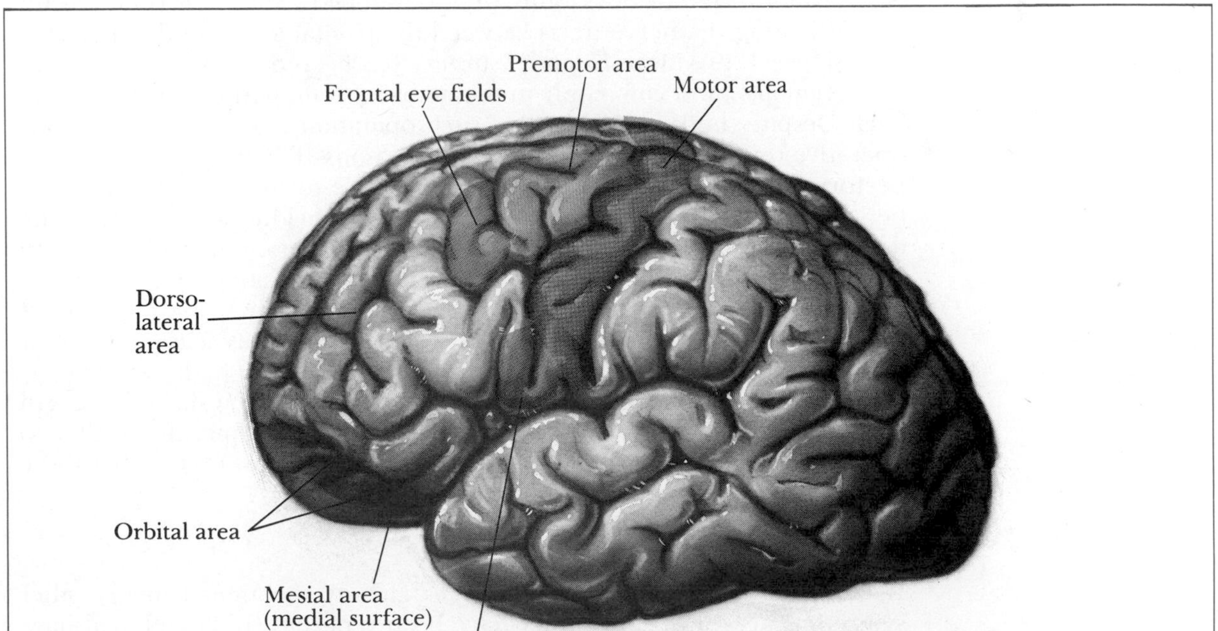

frontal lobotomy (low-BOT-o-me). A surgical procedure in which portions of the frontal lobes are removed and connections between the frontal cortex and the thalamus are severed.

frontal leukotomy (lew-KOT-o-me). A surgical procedure in which the neural connections between the thalamus and the frontal lobe are severed.

apraxia (Ah-PRAKS-ee-eh) Difficulty in performing simple movements in response to commands. Caused by brain damage.

and these anatomic subdivisions. Bryan Kolb and Ian Whishaw (1985) have summarized the available information.

The Patient Population

The uncertainty regarding frontal lobe function does not arise out of a shortage of patients to study. Gunshot wounds, tumors, and strokes have contributed to a large number of patients with frontal lobe injury. In addition, in a most misguided period in the history of psychiatry, approximately 35,000 patients underwent frontal lobe surgery in the years between 1936 and 1958 (Valenstein, 1980). It was hoped that such "psychosurgery" would improve the condition of individuals with schizophrenia, depression, and other mental illnesses.

The history of the rise and fall of psychosurgery has been documented by Elliot Valenstein (1973). Although a few psychosurgical operations are still performed, such procedures are now rare and highly regulated. During the years when it was popular, individual neurosurgeons performed hundreds of such operations a year. The technique was developed by a Portuguese neurosurgeon in 1935, after hearing a talk at an international meeting of neurologists concerning the "calming" effect such an operation had on a single chimpanzee. Introduced and popularized in this country by Walter Freeman and James Watts (1950), **frontal lobotomies** or **leukotomies** soon became a fad among psychiatrists desperate to try to improve the lot of mental patients for whom they had no satisfactory treatment.

Several different operations were developed. The most common involved cutting the nerve tracts between the frontal lobe and the thalamus (see Figure 13.9). More recently, surgery has been done on various other brain regions, most commonly in the limbic system, particularly the amygdala. Despite the large number of such operations, very few useful post-operative reports are available, for many reasons. The neurosurgeons who performed the operations were not always able to follow up on their patients and since the surgeons were also the individuals who judged the degree of "recovery," many of these reports were not totally objective. In other cases, the analysis of the outcome of such operations was so shallow or brief that no real information was in the reports. Moreover, the patients were not normal to begin with. Most were diagnosed as schizophrenic or had some other serious mental disorder. Even in the better studies, by objective and careful investigators, problems of patient availability, length of time since operation, and other difficulties made it almost impossible to reach any generalization about frontal lobe operations, except that there is no overall result (Benson et al., 1981).

Frontal Lobe Symptoms

In addition to the personality changes already mentioned, many other symptoms of frontal lobe injury have been reported (Kolb and Whishaw, 1985; Milner and Petrides, 1984; Stuss and Benson, 1984). Some of the motor difficulties (such as various **apraxias** and changes in overall activity levels) may be related to damage to the motor area and premotor area.

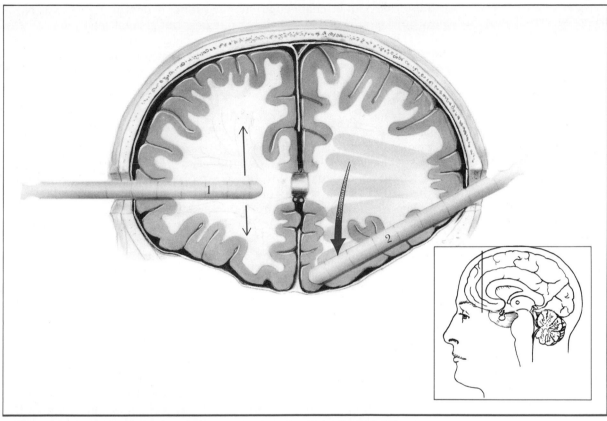

Figure 13.9 The surgical method of Freeman and Watts for frontal leukotomy.
The initial incision in 1 is deepened in 2.

(Apraxia, discussed in greater detail in the following chapter, is difficulty in performing simple movements in response to commands, in the absence of paralysis or sensory deficits.) Difficulties in visual tracking and in paying appropriate attention to visual stimuli also have been noted with frontal lobe damage. It is difficult to find a common denominator for these various perceptual changes, but deficits in attention are often suggested as partly responsible for frontal lobe symptoms.

Somewhat surprisingly, no clear-cut decrease is found in scores on standard intelligence tests by frontal lobe patients (Kolb and Whishaw, 1985). Such patients require very careful testing, as their attention may wander and they tend to become overly engrossed in some small part of the test. In other cognitive tasks they do typically show abnormalities (Milner and Petrides, 1984). They often display *perseverative behavior;* that is, they do not change strategies in various tests as do normals. In one commonly used test, patients with frontal lobe damage tend to keep on sorting a deck of cards with various stimuli on them according to rules that worked earlier in the test but that have become incorrect. In this test the cards can be sorted by color, form, or number of the geometric stimuli on the cards,

Capgras syndrome (CAP-grass) An unusual condition in which the patient is convinced that close relatives are actually imposters. Occurs with damage to the frontal lobe in a small number of cases.

and the rules can be changed arbitrarily suddenly by the investigator. Normals quickly adjust their sorting strategies, but frontal lobe patients are slow to change. Sometimes this perseverative behavior continues even though the patient verbalizes his or her knowledge that the rules have changed. For example, he or she may say, continuing to make errors, "Now I know this will be wrong again."

Frontal lobe patients typically are poor in various word fluency measures, such as generating words starting with a particular letter. They have unusual difficulties in the *Stroop test,* in which the subject is shown the names of various colors ("red," "blue," etc.) printed in different colors of ink. In this test subjects are asked to name the *color of the ink,* not the color name. A variety of other tests tend to reveal a pattern of perseverative thinking on the part of frontal lobe patients, such that they have unusual difficulty in giving up one type of response and switching to another one. They may show some memory difficulties, but this is not always true. Some patients show some very unusual difficulties in their mental life. For example, a few frontal lobe patients display the **Capgras syndrome.** Patients with this rare condition believe that close relatives (spouse, children) are actually imposters who look and talk like the actual relatives (Stuss and Benson, 1984).

The symptoms of frontal lobe damage are so varied and involve so many potential functions that it may not be possible to assign particular roles to this region of the cortex. This is just the conclusion that one researcher has come to, based on measurements of glucose consumption and regional cerebral blood flow in the frontal lobes. Per Roland (1984) says: "It is absurd now to speak about *the function* of the prefrontal cortex. The prediction that arises from these experiments is that in man one or more prefrontal areas participate in any structured treatment of information by the brain in the awake state." The same conclusion could be reached for the frontal lobes as a whole.

SUMMARY

1. In seeking explanations for human behavior that may be related to special features of the human brain, investigators have become particularly interested in the anatomic and functional asymmetries between the left and right cerebral hemispheres. The structural asymmetry of the two hemispheres is particularly obvious in the temporal lobe, where the planum temporale is larger in the left hemisphere about 71 percent of the time, larger in the right hemisphere about 15 percent of the time, and of equal size in the two hemispheres about 14 percent of the time. Other left–right differences have also been reported. To a lesser extent this anatomic asymmetry can be seen in the brains of great apes as well.

2. Some of the most dramatic evidence regarding functional differences between the left and right hemispheres has come from the study of epileptic patients who have had their cerebral hemispheres deconnected

as a last resort for the control of their disease. The evidence from these patients, according to Roger Sperry, suggests that "these patients behave in many ways as if they have two independent streams of conscious awareness, one in each hemisphere, each of which is cut off from and out of contact with the mental experience of the other."

3. The deconnection patients, as well as patients with unilateral brain damage, have demonstrated that in the majority of cases the left hemisphere is superior to the right in speech and language production and comprehension. The right hemisphere, however, is usually superior to the left in the appreciation of spatial relations and in tactile and tonal pattern recognition. These relationships hold in general, even in left-handed individuals, although there is usually greater right hemisphere language capacity in left-handed persons. Even in individuals with the left hemisphere dominant for language production and comprehension, the right hemisphere can understand some language.

4. Some theorists have suggested that the two hemispheres are fundamentally different in the mode of mental processing. Such theorists generally regard the left hemisphere as operating in an analytic, sequential manner, being particularly designed to appreciate stimuli in temporal order (of critical importance for language comprehension). These theorists view the right hemisphere as operating in a more spatial-synthetic mode, better suited to the rapid and accurate appreciation of spatial patterns. It is important to emphasize that the two hemispheres work together in normal individuals, despite the fact that they may have functional specializations that may be uncovered by brain damage or special testing.

5. Prosopagnosia is a very rare condition in which individuals can no longer recognize people by looking at their face. Sometimes they cannot recognize their own face in the mirror. Similar difficulties exist in telling one type of car from another, or one dress from another, even though there is no difficulty in visual acuity. The area of damage responsible for this curious difficulty appears to be on both sides of the brain in the occipital-temporal region.

6. Patients with frontal lobe injury show difficulty in planning for the future, shifting from one problem-solving strategy to another, and in maintaining normal attention. They often show profound personality changes. Many of the existing frontal lobe injury patients underwent psychosurgery during the hey-day of frontal lobotomies, which was from about 1936 to 1958.

SUGGESTIONS FOR FURTHER READING

Beaumont, J. G. (1983). *Introduction to neuropsychology.* New York: Guilford.
Gazzaniga, M. S., and LeDoux, J. E. (1978). *The integrated mind.* New York: Plenum.
Kolb, B., and Whishaw, I. Q. (1985). *Fundamentals of human neuropsychology* (2d ed.). New York: W. H. Freeman.

14

Speech and Language

Preview

Cerebral Dominance and Handedness
The Wada Test
Evidence from Other Species

Aphasia
Expressive Aphasia
Receptive Aphasia
The Disconnection Theory of Aphasia
Recovery from Aphasia

The Development of Cerebral Dominance

Other Language-Related Difficulties with Cerebral Damage
Apraxia: Disorders in Planned Movements

The Cortical Column as the Basic Module of the Cortex

Summary

Suggestions for Further Reading

*The limits of my language
mean the limits of my world.*

LUDWIG WITTGENSTEIN

Preview

aphasia (ah-FAY-zee-ah) Loss of the ability to produce normal speech due to brain damage. There are two basic types of aphasia, expressive and receptive.

Language difficulties that result from brain damage can provide important clues to understanding the organization of the brain. It is important in discussions of the language centers of the brain to distinguish between speech production and speech comprehension, because different regions of the brain seem to be concerned with these two aspects of language. The main speech and language comprehension circuits of about 95–99 percent of all right-handed individuals are in the left hemisphere, but a smaller percentage, 60–70 percent, of non-right-handers have their language centers there.

Much of our knowledge of the location of brain regions involved in speech production and language comprehension comes from examining patients with aphasia. Aphasia has two basic types, expressive and receptive. Expressive aphasia is characterized by a difficulty with speech production and is associated with damage to an area of the left frontal lobe known as Broca's area. Receptive aphasia is characterized by difficulty in both comprehending language and producing meaningful speech. It is associated with damage to a region in the left temporal and parietal lobes known as Wernicke's area.

Recovery from aphasia varies. Children tend to recover better than adults. Two main therapies are the *stimulation* technique and the *programmed* technique. The evidence now tends to support the concept that human beings are born with one hemisphere (usually the left) dominant for speech and language, but that the right hemisphere can take over many of these functions if the left hemisphere is damaged early in childhood. However, as children get older this takeover ability apparently diminishes.

The chapter concludes with a discussion of Vernon Mountcastle's theory of the cortical column as a basic functional module in the cortex. This theory suggests that the development of sophisticated skills in primate brains results from a dramatic increase in the number of such modules.

Cerebral Dominance and Handedness

The first decisive evidence that **aphasia** is more commonly associated with damage to the *left* hemisphere was presented by a French physician, Paul Broca, in 1861, although 25 years earlier another French physician, M.

We converse not only with words, but with gestures, facial expressions, and other bodily cues. In most individuals, the neural circuits important for actual speech production are housed in the left hemisphere, but both hemispheres are involved in communicating fully.

Dax, had also called attention to the association of language difficulties and left hemisphere damage (Dax, 1836). (Dax, however, published in an obscure journal and had no autopsy reports to back up his claim.) Since the time of Broca, the evidence from brain damage cases has been overwhelming in its support of his finding that the left hemisphere is responsible for speech production in most individuals. To a somewhat lesser extent, this is also true for speech comprehension.

The main language production center of most people is in the left hemisphere, whether they are right- or left-handed, but non-right-handed people are more likely than right-handers to have some speech production capacity in the right hemisphere or in both hemispheres. The evidence from aphasics indicates that in right-handed individuals, damage to the left hemisphere is responsible for the aphasia in 95–99 percent of the cases. Aphasia caused by right hemisphere damage—called *crossed aphasia* (Le May and Geschwind, 1978)—occurs in right-handed individuals in 1–5 percent of cases.

Among *non-right-handers* (which includes individuals who are clearly left-handed and those for whom handedness is difficult to determine) lateralization of speech and language functions is less than it is for right-handers. For example, Marjorie Le May and Norman Geschwind (1978) found that only about 60 percent of non-right-handed aphasics have damage to the left hemisphere and 40 percent have right hemisphere damage. The aphasia evidence, then, is good that non-right-handers are more likely than right-handers to have some language capacity in the right hemisphere.

The Wada Test

Wada test (WAH-dah) A procedure for discovering which cerebral hemisphere is dominant for speech production developed by Juhn Wada. An anesthetic is injected into either the left or right carotid artery. Speech is disrupted only when the drug is injected into the hemisphere responsible for speech production. This technique does not test for language comprehension.

In addition to the evidence from aphasia, data on the relationship between handedness and hemispheric dominance for language have been obtained from the **Wada test**. This procedure was developed by neurosurgeon Juhn Wada (1949) and involves anesthetizing one hemisphere at a time so that the dominant hemisphere for speech production can be determined prior to brain surgery. Once the neurosurgeon has this information, the exact details of the surgery can be designed to spare this region if possible.

To perform the Wada test, a small tube is inserted into the left or right carotid artery, the main blood vessels supplying the hemispheres of the brain. Then, with the patient lying on his or her back, sodium amytal (a powerful central nervous system depressant) is injected, almost instantly anesthetizing that side of the brain but leaving the other hemisphere awake. During this procedure the patient is instructed to count out loud. If the drug is injected into the hemisphere that contains the neural circuitry underlying speech production, the patient stops counting and remains speechless for the duration of the drug's effect, usually about five minutes. If the hemisphere receiving the drug is not the one responsible for speech production, the patient hesitates briefly and then continues counting. This is the most sensitive test of hemispheric lateralization for speech production available (Wada and Rasmussen, 1960), but it does not test for speech *comprehension* (Searleman, 1977). The accompanying summary table shows the results of one such study (Rasmussen and Milner, 1975).

Theodore Rasmussen and Brenda Milner (1975) performed the Wada test on 262 patients (140 right-handers and 122 non-right-handers), none of whom had suffered early brain damage to the left hemisphere, which is known to increase the likelihood of right hemisphere dominance for speech and language comprehension. This subject population was not a random sample, since all were neurologic patients. Rasmussen and Milner found that 96 percent of the right-handers showed a left hemisphere dominance for speech production, whereas the other 4 percent showed right hemi-

---

SUMMARY TABLE
Relationships Between Handedness and Cerebral Lateralization for Speech Production*

Handedness	Hemisphere Most Likely to Control Speech Production (%)
Right-handed	Left (96%)
Non-right-handed	Left (70%)
Right-handed, early left hemisphere damage	Left (81%)
Non-right-handed, early left hemisphere damage	Right (51%)

*From Rasmussen and Milner (1975).

sphere dominance. Among the non-right-handers, only 70 percent showed a left hemisphere dominance for speech production, 15 percent showed a right hemisphere dominance, and 15 percent showed evidence for speech production capacity in both hemispheres.

In an examination of 109 other patients who *had* suffered left hemisphere damage early in life, a much higher proportion of right hemisphere dominance was found. Not surprisingly, this sample showed a high percentage of non-right-handers (only 31 right-handers to 78 non-right-handers). The speech of right-handers was centered mainly in the left hemisphere, but the percentage was only 81 percent. Thirteen percent showed right hemisphere dominance and 6 percent showed bilateral representation of speech production. Only 30 percent of the non-right-handers showed left hemisphere dominance, 51 percent showed right hemisphere dominance, and 19 percent had some speech production capacity in both hemispheres.

The results of Rasmussen and Milner show that right-handers and non-right-handers alike tend to have speech production mechanisms centered in the left hemisphere, but the proportion decreases in non-right-handers. Moreover, dominance for speech is more likely to be located in the right hemisphere in individuals who have suffered early brain damage to the left hemisphere.

Evidence from Other Species

As discussed in the previous chapter, structural asymmetry in the brains of some of the great apes has been found. Does evidence exist that brain mechanisms underlying vocalizations in other primates show hemispheric asymmetry? That is, to the extent that one can speak of language in other primates, do these species exhibit hemispheric dominance as well? The evidence on this point is not conclusive, but to date the answer appears to be yes.

To place this discussion in perspective, generally it has been found that unilateral brain lesions in animals do not have profound effects either on overall sensory abilities or on learning or memory tasks. Naturally, such unilateral lesions can affect sensory discriminations or motor tasks involving those areas of the body related to the brain damage (usually contralateral body parts). Very few research projects have even attempted to investigate right–left functional differences, presumably because of the prevailing belief that finding them would be unlikely. In fact, at least one series of experiments supports the concept that no significant difference exists in the functions of the left and right hemispheres in one monkey species (Hamilton, 1977). These experiments were conducted with split-brain rhesus monkeys in which the optic chiasm was also severed to allow each cerebral hemisphere to be tested separately. In a series of tests involving facial recognition (at which monkeys are quite adept), no left–right differences were seen. This task was chosen because it is one at which the right hemisphere is superior in human beings.

One interesting aspect of these studies was that although no left–right difference was found for visual *recognition* tasks, a left–right difference in *preference* of what to look at did exist. When given a choice between viewing a blank screen or color photos (particularly of other monkey faces), the left hemispheres of these monkeys showed a clear preference for the photographs. Their right hemispheres, however, displayed no such preference. No external reward of any sort was associated with the preference test.

A few studies bear on the question of hemispheric specialization for vocalization, two of which concern the species-specific calls of the Japanese macaque monkey. Like most primate species, Japanese macaques have several different calls. In one study Michael Peterson and colleagues recorded some of these calls and presented them to either the left or right ears of five monkeys (Peterson et al., 1978). All five discriminated more accurately among calls presented to the right ear.

This result is very similar to the "right-ear advantage" found in human beings (Geffen and Quinn, 1984). Human subjects correctly identify words more often when they are presented to the right ear than when they are presented to the left ear. This is believed to be because of a combination of left hemisphere dominance for language comprehension and a slight advantage for the contralateral over ipsilateral auditory pathways. It is important to point out that although this difference is generally reliable, it is seen in only 65–85 percent of subjects and amounts to just 2–6 percent better overall accuracy rate for the right ear compared with the left (Searleman, 1977). When these Japanese macque calls were presented in the same way to five monkeys *of other species*, only one of the five showed a right ear advantage. The authors suggest that the left hemisphere may be dominant for comprehending these species-characteristic vocalizations in the Japanese macaque.

Support for this conclusion comes from a study by Henry and Rickye Heffner (1984), who also used recorded calls, teaching 11 Japanese macaques to discriminate among 15 different calls. They then ablated either the left or right superior temporal gyrus in all but one of these monkeys. (Figure 14.1 illustrates the region removed.) Five monkeys with left temporal lobe lesions could not discriminate among the various calls following surgery, whereas five monkeys with right temporal lobe lesions showed no postoperative problems. The area of brain removed constitutes the primary and secondary auditory areas. In human beings the corresponding area includes cortex known to be involved in speech comprehension. Although these studies report preliminary findings on a small number of animals, they do support the concept that primates other than human beings display hemispheric lateralization with respect to the comprehension of sounds that carry significant meaning for members of that species.

Aphasia

Aphasia is a catch-all term that refers to a language disturbance resulting from brain injury. It can vary from mild hesitations in speech to profound

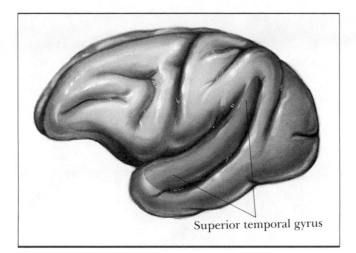

Superior temporal gyrus

Figure 14.1 Outline drawing of the left cerebral hemisphere of the macaque monkey.
The superior temporal gyrus lesioned by Heffner and Heffner (1984) is indicated in red.

inability to talk or understand written or spoken language. The most common causes of aphasia are strokes and traumas. (Strokes are cerebral hemorrhages that kill some neurons and damage others.) Recovery is variable, depending on a variety of factors, not all of them known.

Until recently, our knowledge of the actual areas damaged in aphasia was based almost exclusively on autopsy reports. However, in 1973 a major new tool for examining living soft tissue such as the brain was introduced (Hounsfield et al., 1973). This technique is called **computerized transaxial tomography**, or CT scanning. Although x-ray techniques have been known for many years, regular x rays are not very useful for examining soft tissues, because the density of such tissues does not vary much from one region to another and thus shows up as a uniform gray, unlike such hard tissues as bones, which appear white, since they absorb much of the x radiation.

In CT scanning a much finer grain analysis of the brain can be achieved by using a computer to combine x-ray scans taken from many different angles as the radiation detectors are rotated through 180 degrees around the head. The combined scan reveals an x ray of a slice through a particular region of the brain. Tumors and areas of increased vascularization (typically associated with tumors) can be visualized much more easily, as can regions of cell destruction (Brust, 1981). CT images can be enhanced further with intravenous injections of radio-opaque iodine for even greater contrast between healthy and damaged tissue. Figure 14.2 shows a CT scan of a human brain containing a benign tumor in the patient's right hemisphere.

A related technique developed in the last few years is **positron emission tomography (PET scanning)**, which gives a detailed view of blood flow in the living brain. (PET scanning is described more fully in Chapter 1.) Both CT scanning and PET scanning have dramatically increased the ability to evaluate the location and extent of brain damage in the living brain. In general, while adding much needed detail and clarity, these tech-

computerized transaxial tomography (toe-MA-graf-ee) (CT scanning) A procedure for examining living brain tissue involving computer analysis of x-ray pictures.

positron emission tomography (POZ-ih-tron ee-MISH-un toe-MA-graf-ee) (PET scanning) A procedure for measuring the blood flow patterns in living brain tissue. Blood flow patterns can then be the basis for inferences concerning function of those brain regions.

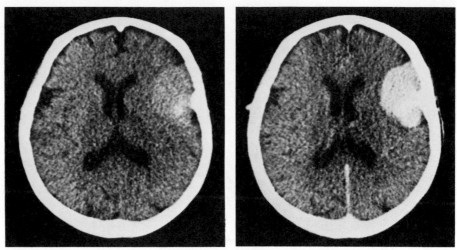

Figure 14.2   CT scan of a brain with a benign tumor in the right hemisphere.
In (a) the tumor is harder to detect than in (b), in which the contrast is enhanced by an injection of iodine into the patient's bloodstream.

niques tend to support the earlier conceptions of the regions of the brain associated with the various aphasia syndromes. The evidence continues to support the concept "different lesions, different aphasias" (Damasio and Geschwind, 1984). (Figure 14.3 shows a PET scan of the brains of normal, schizophrenic, and depressed patients.)

A recently developed imaging device, which appears to be even more sensitive to variations in brain density, uses **nuclear magnetic resonance**

Figure 14.3   PET scans of the left hemisphere in three individuals, a normal subject, a schizophrenic patient, and a depressed patient.
The normal subject shows greater activity in the frontal lobe than either of the other two subjects.

Normal control   Schizophrenic   Depressive

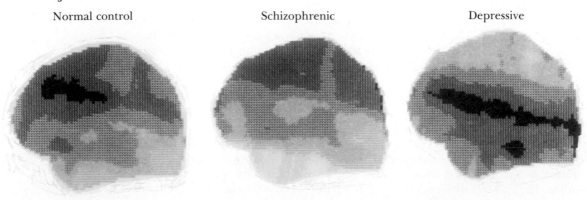

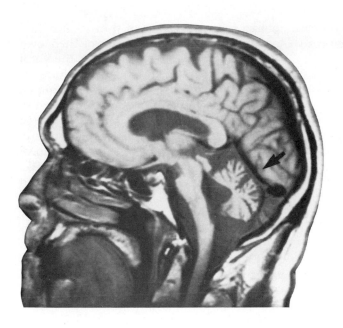

Figure 14.4   A photograph of a human brain as seen using the nuclear magnetic resonance (NMR) technique.

(NMR) imaging and may replace both CT scans and PET scans for some purposes. This technique capitalizes on the fact that hydrogen atoms behave like tiny spinning magnets. Radio waves are used to cause the hydrogen atoms in the brain to rotate synchronously and measurements are made of the tiny voltages set up by the magnetic field so produced. These are sent to a computer, which constructs clear images of the living brain. NMR imaging is particularly useful in detecting certain brain diseases such as multiple sclerosis. (Figure 14.4 shows a NMR image of the human brain.)

Expressive Aphasia

Many different schemes exist for classifying aphasia, but the most widely accepted distinction is between *expressive aphasia* (also called **Broca's aphasia**) and *receptive aphasia* (also called **Wernicke's aphasia**). Patients with expressive aphasia cannot speak properly, typically retaining little of their previous speaking vocabulary and articulating only with difficulty those words they do retain. They cannot form syntactically complete sentences. Pronouns, verb inflections, and connectives are usually lost, resulting in "telegraphic" speech. For example, Norman Geschwind described the utterances of one patient with expressive aphasia trying to talk about a dental appointment: "Yes . . . Monday . . . Dad and Dick . . . Wednesday nine o'clock . . . ten o'clock . . . doctors . . . and . . . teeth." Such patients can be considered to have function word deficits and difficulties with syntax but experience less difficulty with content words, although no characterization exactly fits all patients.

nuclear magnetic resonance (NMR)   A technique for gaining images of the living human brain. The technique is based on the fact that hydrogen atoms act like tiny spinning magnets that can be made to generate an electrical field that can be used by a computer to create images.

Broca's aphasia   (BRO-ka) A form of aphasia characterized by poor speech fluency but good language comprehension. Also termed *expressive aphasia*.

Wernicke's aphasia (VERN-ik-ee) A form of aphasia characterized by poor understandability and comprehension but good speech fluency. Also termed *receptive aphasia*.

Patients with expressive aphasia can *understand* much of what is said to them or what they read and therefore are usually aware of their own difficulties. It is critical in understanding aphasia to know that the vocal cords and other speech muscles are not paralyzed or weak. A dramatic example of this is provided by the many patients with expressive aphasia who can *sing* words they cannot use in speech. Presumably this is because the neural mechanisms underlying singing are not the same as those in ordinary speech, and they may even be located in the opposite hemisphere.

One instructive case is that of a woman who underwent total removal of her cancerous left hemisphere and consequently became severely aphasic. However, she retained her singing ability. When asked to define the word *spangled*, she responded by placing her hand over her heart and singing "God Bless America" in its entirety. Then she said, "Now that is what it is" (Searleman, 1977). (Of course, the word *spangled* occurs in the "Star-Spangled Banner," not in "God Bless America," but we may assume the woman may have had this phrase in mind when she sang out her response.) This type of aphasia was first reported by Broca and is therefore also referred to as Broca's aphasia. It is associated with damage to the posterior and inferior portion of the frontal lobe in the left hemisphere, as illustrated in Figure 14.5. (This region of the brain is called Broca's area.)

Receptive Aphasia

In 1874, just a few years after Broca had presented his evidence for a speech center in the left frontal lobe, a young German physician named Carl Wernicke reported a quite different sort of language disturbance associated primarily with brain damage in the left temporal lobe. This type of aphasia is now known as *receptive aphasia* or *Wernicke's aphasia*, and the region of the temporal (and parietal) lobes where damage produces this aphasia is termed *Wernicke's area*. In receptive aphasia no particular hesitation or difficulty is seen in articulation and the patient has nearly normal fluency, or "flow of speech." However, what the patient does say makes little sense. These aphasics can be described as showing content word deficits, with less function word difficulties than expressive aphasics display. For example, a patient with receptive aphasia, when asked, "How are you?" responded, "I think that I am no so safe than now much with others to some extent directly." Another patient responded to the same question by saying, "I felt worse because I can no longer keep in mind from the mind of the minds to keep me from mind and up to the ear which can be to find among ourselves." Still another patient, asked to identify some keys, responded, "Indication of measurement in piece of apparatus or intimating the cost of apparatus in various forms" (Brain, 1961). (There is no truth to the rumor that this patient was later hired by the Internal Revenue Service to compose tax form instructions).

Patients with receptive aphasia typically have a poor understanding of their own speech problems because they have difficulty *comprehending* speech,

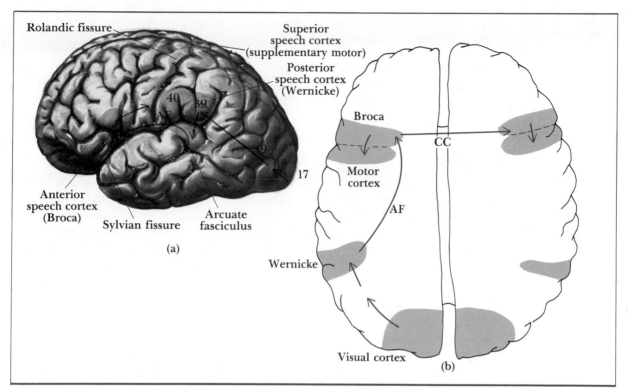

Figure 14.5   Summary diagram of the Wernicke–Geschwind theory disconnection theory of speech and language.
(a) Lateral view of the left hemisphere, showing postulated functional connections among visual cortex, Wernicke's area, Broca's area, and the motor cortex. (b) Overhead view of both hemispheres. AF = arcuate fasciculus; CC = corpus callosum. Numbers refer to Brodmann areas.

including their own. They do not understand complicated or lengthy conversations, cannot follow written instructions, and cannot form coherent sentences, either in speech or writing. Communicating with such patients is extremely difficult.

Another characteristic of receptive aphasia is the insertion of nonsense words. For example:

EXAMINER: (*pointing to a picture of a man on a bicycle*). What's he doing?
PATIENT: Goin' togowi. She's . . . got . . . a . . . rabliun. I . . . think . . . I wanta . . . oh . . . he.

Although the rhythm and general flow of speech are often better than

arcuate fasciculus   (ARK-u-ate fah-SIK-u-lus) A nerve tract connecting Wernicke's area with Broca's area.

those of expressive aphasics, the overall ability to communicate is generally poorer.

What do cases of aphasia tell us about the organization of the brain? The fact that lesions in different regions of the brain produce different types of aphasia has important implications for how the brain might be organized to comprehend language and produce speech.

The Disconnection Theory of Aphasia

One leading theory of brain organization is based on ideas first put forward by Wernicke in 1874 and updated by Geschwind (1965a, b). It proposes that different regions of the neocortex control different aspects of speech and language and that aphasia can be understood as a disconnection of one or more of these regions from other areas. For example, this theory distinguishes between the *underlying structure* of a particular utterance and its *neural program for expression*. The neural circuitry for the comprehension of language is proposed to reside in those regions of the left hemisphere numbered by Brodmann as areas 22 and 40, now termed Wernicke's area (see Figure 14.5). Input can reach this region from the nearby auditory cortex (Brodmann areas 41 and 42) as well as from the visual cortex of the occipital lobe (Brodmann areas 17, 18, 19). The axons of these neurons project to Wernicke's area through a region of cortex known as the *angular gyrus*. Also traversing the angular gyrus, according to this theory, are axons of neurons from the parietal lobe that carry commands for the writing of language.

The neural circuitry necessary to transform the underlying structure of an utterance into actual speech is postulated by the disconnection theory to be located in Broca's area. These two regions, Wernicke's area and Broca's area, are connected by the **arcuate fasciculus**. Finally, from Broca's area, neurons project to the nearby motor cortex, which activates the vocal cords and associated speech apparatus. Other regions of the brain also have access to this region of the motor cortex, such as those containing the neural programs for singing.

According to the disconnection theory, strokes or brain damage disconnect these various parts of the speech and language system from each other, producing different types of aphasia. Since accidental damage very rarely cuts this system at precise boundaries, mixed aphasias, with both expressive and receptive symptoms, are the most common. In theory, expressive aphasics have a more or less intact Wernicke's area and can form the underlying structures for language. That is, they know what they mean to say but cannot transform this underlying structure into a speech program suitable for normal expression. Since Wernicke's area is intact in such individuals, they can comprehend either spoken or written language. Their problem is in forming the instructions for speech that must then be sent to the motor cortex for execution.

				Auditory
SUMMARY TABLE *Types of Aphasia*				
Aphasia	**Lesion Location**	**Speech Fluency**	**Understand-ability**	**Auditory Compre-hension**
Broca's (expressive)	Posterior frontal lobe, left hemisphere (Brodmann 44, 45)	Poor	Fair	Good
Wernicke's (receptive)	Temporal lobe, left hemisphere (Brodmann 22, 40)	Good	Poor	Poor
Conduction	Arcuate fasciculus	Good	Poor	Good

However, this theory considers receptive aphasics to have incurred damage to the brain mechanisms necessary to *comprehend* language. In addition, it holds that Wernicke's area contains the neural circuits required to compose the underlying meaningful structure of speech. Without information concerning this underlying structure being sent to it, the execution circuits in Broca's area can only churn out nonsense speech, interspersed with speech fragments, or short "canned programs" of commonly used word combinations. The patient cannot correct this "nonsense talk" because of the damage to the comprehension circuits in Wernicke's area.

Support for the disconnection theory is found in a type of aphasia termed *conduction aphasia*. The speech of individuals with this aphasia sounds very much like that of patients with receptive aphasia: relatively fluent but largely nonsensical. Unlike receptive aphasics, however, language comprehension of conduction aphasics is reasonably good. It has been found that in conduction aphasia the apparatus for forming the underlying structure of speech is intact, as is the neural apparatus for programming this underlying structure, but the *connection* between Wernicke's area and Broca's area, the arcuate fasciculus, is damaged. Thus the two processing centers are isolated from each other, with conduction aphasia the result (Damasio and Geschwind, 1984). The left thalamus and perhaps other subcortical centers also may play a role in aphasia, but the contribution of these regions is still poorly understood (Crosson, 1984).

Recovery from Aphasia

Some aphasic patients recover, at least in part. The recovery process is so poorly understood that there is no single agreed-on therapy, no satisfactory explanation for success or failure, and no understanding of the brain changes underlying recovery. One of the most systematic approaches to aphasia therapy is that of Andrew Kertesz (1979). He and his colleagues have developed a scale for aphasia (the *aphasia quotient*, or AQ) that allows for comparisons among patients at different stages of recovery. They found that in one group of adult aphasics about 21 percent recovered in the first year. Many other patients recovered some aspects of speech and language comprehension but still scored below normal on the AQ test.

Recovery is best in the first few months following injury, with only very gradual improvement being seen after the first year. Children tend to recover more completely than adults. In one study of 32 cases of aphasia in children, Alajouanine and Lhermitte (1965) found that about one-third of the children they examined showed almost total spontaneous recovery within six months of injury and 75 percent recovered within a year.

Types of Therapy

"There are as many varieties of aphasia treatment as there are aphasics" (Kertesz, 1979). Most rehabilitation workers adjust their therapy to the individual patient. Nevertheless, several schools of thought on aphasia therapies exist. Two common ones employ the stimulation technique and the programmed instruction therapy. The stimulation technique relies on the principle of surrounding the patient with language and language-related stimuli.

One example of the stimulation approach is that of author Roald Dahl (*Charlie and the Chocolate Factory* among other books), whose wife, actress Patricia Neal, suffered severe paralysis on her right side and severe aphasia after a stroke to the left hemisphere. Dahl nagged and cajoled Neal, making her try to talk. He hired a nurse to continue working with her when he and their friends became exhausted. They were successful in bringing Neal to a level of recovery where she could resume her acting career.

The programmed instruction method is based on systematically learning basic words and language skills, rather than simply flooding the patient with language. Thus, patients are retaught words and simple sentences, gradually working up to more complex conversations. Still other approaches take advantage of the residual ability of most aphasic patients to sing. This *melodic intonation therapy* encourages patients to sing what they want to say, much as in operatic conversations (Sparks et al., 1974).

The Development of Cerebral Dominance

The belief that children recover somewhat more readily from brain damage than adults has led to the idea that the speech and language dominance of one hemisphere over the other is not finally established until several years after birth. But there are two different views of this matter. One suggests that cerebral dominance develops with age; the other holds that cerebral dominance is present from birth but that the nondominant hemisphere retains a plasticity that allows it to take over in case of damage to the dominant hemisphere and that it is this plasticity that gradually diminishes with age.

For many years the main body of evidence relevant to this issue came from children who had undergone brain surgery or suffered brain damage early in life. In cases where such injury occurred prior to the time most children learn to talk (about two years of age), it was widely reported that whether the damage was to the left or the right hemisphere did not much affect whether speech would be delayed. That is, cerebral dominance for speech did not seem to be present, or was very weak in infants (Basser, 1962). Other reports of early brain damage supported the belief that the earlier in life the injury occurred, the better the chances that the child would recover (or develop) normal speech and language skills. The interpretation of these cases most commonly given was that infants start life with both the left and right hemispheres more or less equal in speech and language capacity and that, for unknown reasons, the left hemisphere usually becomes dominant for language.

More recently, the equal-at-birth hypothesis concerning the cerebral hemispheres has come under attack. Substantial evidence suggests that the left hemisphere is probably dominant for language from birth. To account for the fact that children recover better from left hemisphere damage than adults, the dominant-at-birth hypothesis suggests that the child's brain is more plastic than that of the adult and that its right hemisphere can take over language functions more readily than the adult's when the left is damaged. This plasticity diminishes with age.

Several lines of evidence support the dominance-at-birth hypothesis, although the argument is far from over. First, various researchers have reexamined the earlier reports of childhood brain damage and found that these studies do not support the gradual development of dominance as originally claimed (Kinsbourne, 1975; Springer and Deutsch, 1981). In addition, in a recent survey of 65 children with unilateral cerebral damage, Woods (1983) found that in 34 cases of damage to the left hemisphere, 25 (73 percent) showed symptoms of aphasia, whereas in 31 cases of damage to the right hemisphere, only 4 (13 percent) showed such symptoms. These figures are comparable to those of adults and suggest that cerebral dominance for speech and language is present in young children much as it is in adults.

Second, evidence gathered with normal children also supports the dominance-at-birth hypothesis. A. W. Young (1982) has reviewed evidence that the right ear advantage for the detection of words appears in children as early as they can be tested (about three years of age). Furthermore, no evidence has been found that this right ear advantage changes as children get older. Similar findings are available for a left hemisphere advantage for words presented visually.

alexia   (a-LEK-see-ah)
Profound difficulty in understanding written or printed words caused by brain trauma. Different from dyslexia.

dyslexia   (dis-LEK-see-ah)
Unusual difficulty in learning to read and spell.

agraphia   (a-GRAF-ee-ah)
Inability to write normally, because of brain trauma.

Finally, some anatomic support can be found for the dominance-at-birth hypothesis, although it is not overwhelming. Sandra Witelson and Wazir Pallie (1973) found that the left planum temporale was larger in 79 percent of their sample of brains of infants that came to autopsy before the age of three months. Other investigators found similar but less dramatic results. Juhn Wada and colleagues (1975) examined 100 brains of infants who had died at ages ranging from seven months of gestation to 18 months postnatally. They found that the planum temporale was larger in the left hemisphere in 56 percent of those studied, larger in the right hemisphere in 12 percent, and the same in the remaining 32 percent.

In fetal brains (10–44 weeks of gestation), Je Chi and colleagues (1977) found the planum temporale larger in the left hemisphere in 54 percent of their cases, larger in the right in 18 percent, and the same in the other 28 percent. Of course, it is not known that anatomic differences in the planum temporale are related to cerebral dominance for language, although such a relationship is quite plausible. Moreover, these anatomic measurements are not easy. Different investigators employ different procedures to make their measurements (Witelson, 1983). Thus, although the anatomic data are compatible with the dominance-at-birth hypothesis, they do not prove the point.

Other Language-Related Difficulties with Cerebral Damage

As mentioned earlier, damage to the language centers of the left hemisphere not only produces deficits in speech and spoken language comprehension, but also typically affects reading and writing. The term **alexia** refers to the inability to comprehend written or printed language, because of brain damage. [**Dyslexia** is a different condition and refers to the developmental difficulties encountered by some children in learning to read and write properly. Dyslexia appears to be a linguistic deficiency and not due to defects in visual perception, as is often assumed from the difficulty dyslexic children have in writing letters of the alphabet correctly (Vellutino, 1987). Norman Geschwind and Albert Galaburda (1985) believe that it may be related to a failure of normal migration or aggregation of neurons in the planum temporale, as discussed in Chapter 4.]

Agraphia refers to the inability to write, because of brain damage. Alexia, agraphia, and aphasia often occur to one degree or another in individuals with brain damage to the language dominant hemisphere. Such difficulties can also appear more or less independently, a fact compatible with the disconnection theory. One rather startling example is *pure alexia*, in which there is a profound inability to read but no other symptoms. In such rare cases an individual can write meaningfully but cannot read what he or she has just written! D. Frank Benson and Norman Geschwind (1969)

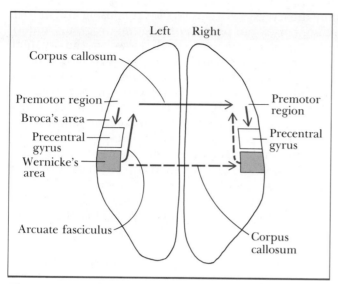

Figure 14.6   Diagram of human brain as viewed from above showing probable pathways for voluntary movements in response to verbal commands.

apraxia (a-PRAK-see-ah) Profound disability in carrying out purposeful movements in the absence of any paralysis.

report just such a case from the records of a physician writing in the year 1588. (More recent cases are also known.)

Apraxia: Disorders in Planned Movements

Imagine you are a physician examining a patient who has recently suffered a stroke. As part of your examination you ask the patient to pretend to blow out a match. Although you have already determined that this patient does not have a hearing problem and that he is cooperative, he cannot comply with your request. You then light an actual match and hold it in front of him, and he promptly blows it out. This sequence of events is repeated. Is this patient playing a game with you, or is this some unusual symptom of brain damage?

Actually, what you have just observed is a symptom of **apraxia.** According to Geschwind (1975), apraxia is a "disorder of learned movement which cannot be accounted for either by weakness, incoordination, sensory loss or by incomprehension of or inattention to commands." Apraxia patients may suffer little or no loss of language comprehension. An explanation for their curious inability must be sought elsewhere. In the just described patient the CT scan showed that the stroke had damaged the premotor region of the left hemisphere (see Figure 14.6).

The disconnection theory explains apraxia by proposing that either the left or right premotor cortex can produce the neural programs underlying facial movements such as blowing out a match. However, the situation becomes more complicated when a verbal instruction must be followed. According to the theory, the critical neural pathway for executing such commands starts in the auditory comprehension region of the left temporal lobe. The axons of the neurons carrying the message to the motor cortex travel in the arcuate fasciculus to the left premotor region. From there neurons send axons across the corpus callosum to the right premotor region. But the left premotor region in this patient was incapacitated by the damage caused by the stroke, which also disconnected the left from the right premotor region. The auditory command, although understood by the patient, could not result in a message to the remaining right premotor region because the critical neural pathway was destroyed. Thus the patient could not follow a verbal instruction for even simple movements. However, when an actual match was presented, the visual stimulus of the burning match could initiate a blowing response, using the undamaged right premotor region.

Although these cases provide a valuable framework for understanding the organization of the brain with respect to speech and language capacity, they do not give us much insight into possible neural mechanisms that allow for these skills. Indeed, although speculation about these matters is widespread, very litle hard information exists. One lead toward understanding neocortical function is the recognition that the cortex appears to be composed of *functional columns*.

The Cortical Column as the Basic Module of the Cortex

Vernon Mountcastle (1979) has proposed that mammals have a basic functional module in the cerebral cortex consisting of a column of functionally related cells. He marshals considerable evidence to support the idea that, across wide regions of the cortex, a basic structure exists that he terms the *cortical column*. He suggests that the neural mechanisms underlying all cortical function may be related to the interaction of these functional columns.

Different neocortical regions vary in their function primarily because of their different extrinsic connections, not because of different rules of their internal organization. "This suggests that neocortex is everywhere functionally much more uniform than hitherto supposed and that its avalanching enlargement in mammals and particularly in primates has been accomplished by replication of a basic neural module, without the appearance of wholly new neuron types of qualitatively different modes of intrinsic organization" (Mountcastle, 1979).

Careful counts indicate that there are about 110 neurons from surface to underlying white matter in a column of cortex 30 μm in diameter. Mountcastle calls this a *minicolumn*. Based on various pieces of evidence, he estimates that about 400 million such minicolumns, containing about 44 billion neurons, can be found in the human cortex. Different regions of the cortex, of course, contain different numbers of such columns. Within a given column the neurons all share very similar functional properties, such as responding to line segments of a given orientation or to tones of similar frequency. Such functionally similar columns have now been reported for visual cortex, auditory cortex, and somesthetic cortex. The motor cortex also seems to be organized into such functional columns, as stimulation of neurons in a given vertical column causes movements of the same or closely related body parts. Columns that are somewhat spatially separated could still be linked functionally by lateral connections to form distributed systems serving some particular function. Individual columns could be members of several different distributed systems. Thus brain damage could disconnect various organizations of these columns, resulting in the conditions observed in neurologic patients. It is a challenge still unmet to relate such useful ideas as functional columns to the symptoms of aphasia and apraxia, but at the present, this lead may prove insightful.

SUMMARY

1. Aphasia is a difficulty in language use caused by brain damage. In right-handed individuals the left hemisphere controls speech production in about 96 percent of the cases. In non-right-handed individuals the left hemisphere controls speech production in only about 70 percent of cases. Early brain damage to the left hemisphere results in greater reliance on the right hemisphere for speech production. Cerebral lateralization for language comprehension can be seen in nonhuman primates, with the left hemisphere being dominant.

2. Various techniques have been developed recently to scan the human brain, including CT scanning, PET scanning, and NMR imaging. These procedures promise to provide much greater detail on the areas of brain damage following stroke and trauma. They have already proved to be of great value in the study of brain localization in aphasia.

3. Damage to an area of the posterior portion of the left frontal lobe results in expressive (Broca's) aphasia, characterized by halting, impoverished speech but fairly good language comprehension. Damage to a region in the posterior temporal lobe of the left hemisphere results in receptive (Wernicke's) aphasia, characterized by speech that is very hard to understand despite nearly normal fluency. Speech comprehension is also severely impaired in Wernicke's aphasia.

4. The leading theory of brain organization is that of Norman Geschwind, based on a theory proposed by Carl Wernicke in 1874. This theory proposes that different regions of the neocortex control different aspects of speech and language production and comprehension and that different forms of aphasia can be understood best as the result of the disconnection of one or more of these regions from the others.

5. Some aphasic patients recover significant language capacity, but the mechanisms underlying this recovery are not understood. Most recovery occurs in the first few months after injury. There are many different forms of aphasia therapy. Two common ones are the stimulation technique and programmed instruction therapy.

6. Two different views are held regarding the development of cerebral dominance for language. One proposal is that such dominance is present from birth but that the nondominant hemisphere (usually the right) retains some capacity to take over language function in the event of severe damage to the left hemisphere. This hypothesis states that this capacity of the nondominant hemisphere diminishes with age. The other view is that at birth the two hemispheres are nearly equal in their capacity for language and that the dominance of the left hemisphere for language function develops with age. The evidence favors the "left dominance at birth" hypothesis, but the issue is not yet settled.

7. Other language difficulties related to brain damage include alexia (inability to read) and agraphia (inability to write). Dyslexia is a developmental difficulty in learning to read encountered by a significant fraction of children. It is not thought to be caused by brain damage, but may be related to a failure of neurons in the planum temporale to migrate and form proper synaptic connections, as discussed in Chapter 4.

8. Apraxia is, according to Norman Geschwind, a "disorder of learned movement which cannot be accounted for either by weakness, incoordination, sensory loss, or by incomprehension of or inattention to commands." Such difficulty appears to be accounted for by an extension of the disconnection theory.

9. According to Vernon Mountcastle, the cortex can be viewed as being constructed of functional columns of neurons that are synaptically linked together in various ways to form "distributed systems." This model of cortical organization is compatible with Geschwind's disconnection theory, despite the fact that these ideas come from different traditions within neuroscience.

SUGGESTIONS FOR FURTHER READING

Beaumont, J. G. (1983). *Introduction to neuropsychology*. New York; Guilford.

Geschwind, N., and Galaburda, A. M. (Eds.). (1984). *Cerebral dominance: The biological foundations*. Cambridge, MA: Harvard University Press.

Mountcastle, V. B. (1979). An organizing principle for cerebral function: The unit module and the distributed system. In F. O. Schmitt and F. G. Worden (Eds.), *The neuroscience fourth study program*. (pp. 21–42). Cambridge, MA: MIT Press.

Searleman, A. (1983). Language capabilities of the right hemisphere. In A. Young (Ed.), Functions of the right cerebral hemisphere (pp. 87–111). New York: Academic Press.

15

Disorders of Brain and Behavior

If I should return during my absence,
keep me here until I come back.

MENTAL PATIENT QUOTED IN MACSWEENEY, 1984

Preview

chlorpromazine (klor-PRO-mah-zeen) Generic name for one of the phenothiazine family of drugs (trade name Thorazine) used in the treatment of schizophrenia.

Increasingly, mental illness is being viewed as brain disease, and hundreds of thousands of mental patients are being treated with drugs that directly affect brain function. Since the introduction of such drugs the number of mental patients in hospitals has dropped dramatically. Drug therapy has not necessarily cured these patients, but it has changed attitudes about hospitalizing them. The result is that fewer patients are institutionalized and more are treated on an outpatient basis, which has had mixed results. Too often they simply are released and drift on the streets of our big cities, where they receive little or no care.

This chapter focuses on the way these drugs interact with neurotransmitter systems in the brain. In particular, we shall examine two major ideas concerning the biology of mental illness, the *dopamine hypothesis of schizophrenia* and the *monoamine hypothesis of depression.*

Most of the drugs used to treat mental illness appear to produce their therapeutic effects by interacting at synapses in the brain. Often a particular drug acts very selectively on the synapses that use a particular neurotransmitter. The synaptic effects of other drugs are much more widespread. (Figure 15.1 illustrates some of the major steps in synaptic transmission, any one of which can be altered by drugs.)

The number of steps in synaptic transmission is somewhat arbitrary, depending on what one identifies as a step. See Chapter 2 for further details on chemical synaptic transmission. Many drugs affect one or more of the following synaptic events: synthesis of the transmitter, release of transmitter, reuptake of transmitter, metabolic destruction of transmitter, and blocking of the postsynaptic transmitter sites. It is important to remember, however, that drugs have two classes of effects: those we know about and those we do not.

The Drug Revolution in Psychiatry

Since the 1950s a drug revolution has occurred in psychiatry, a sign of which has been the dramatic decrease in the number of patients in mental hospitals. From about 1900 to 1950 the number of hospitalized mental patients in the United States increased to over 600,000. The major antipsychotic drug, **chlorpromazine,** was introduced in the mid-1950s. By 1975

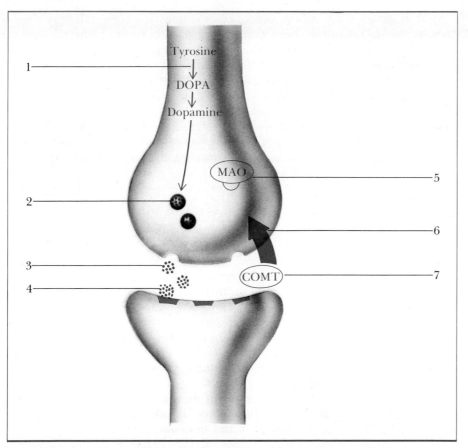

Figure 15.1 Some major steps in synaptic transmission, any one of which can be influenced by drugs.
(1) Conversion of substrate (in this case, tyrosine) into transmitter. In dopaminergic cells DOPA is an intermediate product. (2) Storage of the transmitter in synaptic vesicles. (3) Transmitter release. (4) Transmitter–postsynaptic receptor interaction. (5) Intracellular destruction of transmitter not protected by vesicles; in this case destruction is by monoamine oxidase (MAO). (6) Reuptake of the transmitter by the presynaptic neuron. (7) Extracellular metabolism of transmitter—in this case by catechol-O-methyltransferase (COMT).

fewer than 250,000 mental patients still were hospitalized in the United States. However, this statistic is deceptive. It reflects not only the effectiveness of the drugs, but also a profound change in the attitudes toward hospitalization of mental patients. This change is toward shorter-term hospitalization and increased outpatient treatment. Unfortunately, many of the mentally ill who have been released from long-term hospitalization face bleak futures, either on the streets of our cities or in nursing homes staffed by individuals who may not be well trained in their care (Bassuk and Gerson, 1978).

DSM-III   (D-S-M three) The
third edition of the *Diagnostic and Statistical Manual,*
published by the American
Psychiatric Association in
1980.

schizophrenia   (skits-o-
FREEN-ee-ah) Mental ill-
ness, characterized by
thought disorder, emo-
tional withdrawal, and delusions.

How do we know when someone is mentally ill? We often may think that someone "must have been crazy to do that," but in fact, the variability in human behavior is so great that many seemingly strange and bizarre behaviors are not the result of mental illness. It is not easy to diagnose mental illness. For many years the American Psychiatric Association has tried to clarify the criteria by which someone can be judged mentally ill. The current source for these criteria is the third edition of the *Diagnostic and Statistical Manual* (1980), widely referred to simply as **DSM-III.** The main purpose of the manual is to allow for more standard diagnoses. *DSM-III* was based on field tests involving over 12,000 patients and 550 psychiatrists (Lickey and Gordon, 1983).

Schizophrenia

Mental illness comes in many varieties, but most cases fall into one of three categories: **schizophrenia,** unipolar depression, or bipolar depression. *DSM-III* has several pages of diagnostic criteria for schizophrenia. These include:

1. *Delusions,* such as the belief that one's thoughts are being controlled by signals from a distant planet, or that one is the identical twin of a famous person. Such delusions are often accompanied by *auditory hallucinations,* "voices" that talk to the patient, often scolding or suggesting that he or she do certain things. These voices can contribute to the bizarre behaviors displayed by schizophrenics.

Several individuals have written about their psychotic experiences. One such record (written after the patient recovered) follows, in which the woman refers to her "voice" as her resident and her companion:

> I first went to Out-Patients at a mental hospital accompanied by a very voluble devil. How we ever reached there at all I don't know, because he would keep buzzing the wrong directions at me. But we found the place at last, and after walking three times round the building, an entrance grew up where there had not been one before. . . . Once inside there was a long wait during which we argued the best way to deal with the doctor. He turned out to be a dark sallow man with a quite extraordinary likeness to Satan himself. "You'll be a fool," warned my companion, "if you tell this one anything. He's as bad as me. Worse, probably." We were hurriedly passed on to another doctor. He was more fortunate with his face and I liked him at once. There was a cosiness all around him. My resident, who had been bullying me for days about this appointment and threatening death, destruction and lunacy if I breathed so much as a word about him, suddenly went all sulky and muttered: "Oh tell him what you like. He won't believe it anyway, so why should I care?" [Cecil, 1956]

2. A second diagnostic criterion for schizophrenia is *disordered thinking,* marked by illogical chains of associations or incoherent speech, often intermingled with the content of delusions and hallucinations.

3. *Flat affect* is a third schizophrenic symptom; it often appears as an absence of emotions in situations where they would appear called for, such

as when a relative or close friend dies. Inappropriate emotional responses are also considered to be diagnostic of schizophrenia, if of sufficient intensity and duration.

4. A fourth major criterion for the diagnosis of schizophrenia is *social withdrawal,* often accompanied by increased difficulty with work or school and with taking care of oneself. Finally, symptoms must be present for a considerable time, generally at least six months, must not be due to some known physical cause such as syphilis, and must have begun prior to age 45. Males tend to be first diagnosed as schizophrenic when they are in their early 20s. Women typically are first determined to be schizophrenic in their late 20s or early 30s. By age 65, however, approximately equal numbers of men and women have been diagnosed schizophrenic. The incidence of schizophrenia is very similar among those countries where accurate records are kept, about 1 percent of the population.

Risks of Developing Schizophrenia

The causes of schizophrenia are not known, but a tendency to develop the disease probably is inherited. For example, although the incidence of schizophrenia in the general population is about 1 percent, the risk of developing it if you have a brother or sister who is schizophrenic is 10 times greater, and almost 50 times greater if your identical twin is diagnosed as schizophrenic (Nicol and Gottesman, 1983). (Figure 15.2 illustrates some of the risks of developing schizophrenia.) Since over half the identical twins of schizophrenics *do not* develop the disease, environmental factors also must play an important role in individuals with inherited predispositions to develop schizophrenia.

It is uncertain what these environmental factors are. Stressful situations within the family, at school or at work may be responsible. It has also been suggested that a virus related to the herpes virus may be involved. About one in nine schizophrenics has an antibody to the **cytomegalovirus (CMV)** in his or her cerebrospinal fluid, whereas normal controls do not (Torrey et al., 1982). Equal numbers of schizophrenics and controls had the antibody in their blood plasma, suggesting that some individuals may be genetically more vulnerable to this virus entering the brain, although the viral hypothesis of schizophrenia remains largely untested.

Drug Treatments for Schizophrenia—Drug Names

One important distinction in the way drugs are named is between generic drug names, such as chlorpromazine, and the trade name for that generic drug used by a given manufacturer. For example, chlorpromazine is marketed under the trade name Thorazine. It is one of a family of the so-called antipsychotic drugs, the **phenothiazines.** Other phenothiazines are *triflupromazine* (Vesprin) and *thoridazine* (Mellaril). Other families of drugs

cytomegalovirus (CMV) (SY-toe-meg-ah-low-virus) A virus related to the herpes virus that may be involved in schizophrenia.

phenothiazines (fen-o-THY-a-zines) A family of drugs used in the treatment of schizophrenia.

Drug-Induced Hallucinations

The hallucinations experienced by schizo-phrenics are not caused by drugs, but a variety of substances and situations can cause abnormal perceptual experiences, including hallucin-ations (perceptual experiences for which there is no external stimulus). Perceptions can also be so distorted as to appear to the individual as visions or apparitions. One of the most powerful hallucination-causing drugs is *lysergic acid diethylamide (LSD),* or "acid." The *hallucino-genic* properties of LSD were discovered in 1943 by a Swiss chemist, A. Hofmann, who accidentally ingested a small amount of LSD while working with this new, unknown drug. Noting that it had unusual effects on his perceptions, Hofmann deliberately took a second dose of 0.25 mg, an amount we now know to be several times that necessary to produce vivid hallucinations. He described his experience as follows:

> ". . . my field of vision swayed before me, and objects appeared distorted like images in curved mirrors. I had the impression of being unable to move from the spot, although my assistant told me afterwards that we had cycled at a good pace. . . . As far as I remember, the following were the most outstanding symptoms: vertigo, visual disturbances; the faces of those around me appeared as grotesque masks. . . . Occasionally I felt as if I were out of my body. . . . When I closed my eyes, an unending series of colorful, very realistic and fantastic images surged in upon me" [Hofmann, quoted in Byck, 1975].

The exact nature of LSD's effects on the brain are still uncertain. Its chemical structure is similar to that of the neurotransmitter serotonin (see Figure 15.3) and evidence suggests that it blocks serotonin receptors in the raphe system of the brainstem, but LSD's pharmacology is so complex and so poorly understood that authoritative pharmacologists are reluctant to speculate on the behavioral implications of the LSD–serotonin connection (Cooper et al., 1986).

One interesting hypothesis is that naturally occurring substances related to LSD may have played a role in the hallucinations reported by young girls that led to the Salem witch trials (Caporael, 1976; Matossian, 1982). LSD is an *ergot alkaloid,* related to several naturally occurring hallucinogens that can be isolated from *ergot,* a substance produced by a fungus that grows on many different grains. Rye is particularly vulnerable to ergot growth. Ergot poisoning, in which hallucinations of various types appear, has been observed, sometimes as epidemics, since at least 600 B.C., although its cause has only recently been understood (Brazeau, 1975). Two main forms of ergot poisoning exist, *gangrenous ergotism* and *convulsive ergotism.* Gangrenous ergotism is now believed to account for the reports of a disease known in the Middle Ages as St. Anthony's fire, or *ignis sacer* ("holy fire"). In this condition gangrene of the hands and feet is common, usually accompanied by intense burning sensations and, in some cases, loss of the affected parts. Convulsive ergotism, in which various bodily sensations and convulsions occur, has been suggested as the main cause of the symptoms afflicting the eight young girls who were the key witnesses in the witchcraft accusations in Salem, Massachusetts, in 1692, in which 20 men and women were executed for witchcraft. Data on the climate at the time (favorable for ergot growth) and the fact that rye was a common crop in Salem led Caporael (1976) to make a circumstantial case for ergot poisoning of the girls, although these conclu-sions have been vigorously disputed (Spanos and Gottlieb, 1976).

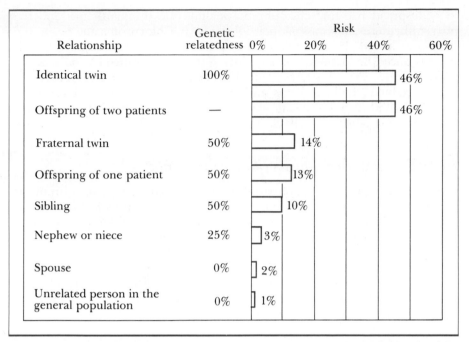

Relationship	Genetic relatedness	Risk
Identical twin	100%	46%
Offspring of two patients	—	46%
Fraternal twin	50%	14%
Offspring of one patient	50%	13%
Sibling	50%	10%
Nephew or niece	25%	3%
Spouse	0%	2%
Unrelated person in the general population	0%	1%

Figure 15.2   Lifetime risks of developing schizophrenia for individuals with different genetic relatedness.
With an individual having two schizophrenic parents, genetic relatedness cannot be expressed in terms of percentage, but the regression of the individual's "genetic value" on that of the parents is 1, the same as that for identical twins (Nicol and Gottesman, 1983).

Figure 15.3   Chemical structures of LSD and serotonin.

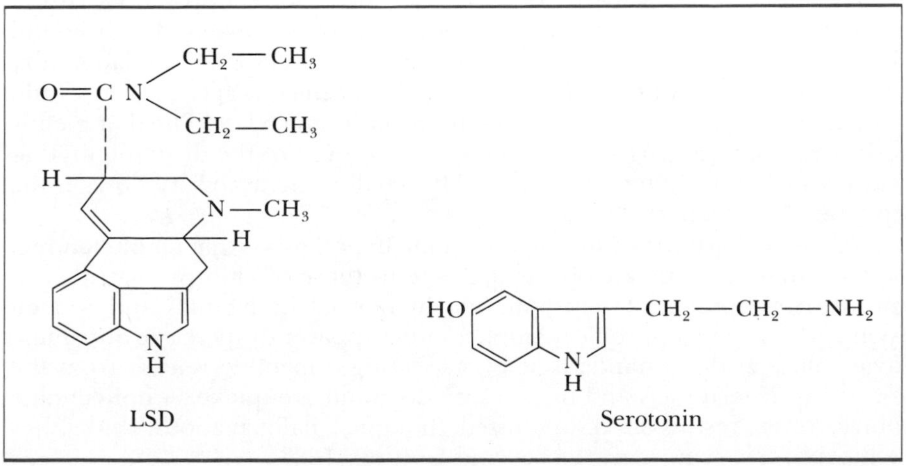

thioxanthenes (thy-o-ZAN-thenes) A family of drugs used in the treatment of schizophrenia.

butyrophenones (beauter-o-fuh-NONES) A family of drugs used in the treatment of schizophrenia.

neuroleptic (nur-o-LEP-tik) Term for the various antipsychotic drugs.

amphetamine (am-FET-a-meen) A stimulant drug that affects dopamine synapses.

in widespread use for schizophrenia include the **thioxanthenes** and the **butyrophenones,** such as haloperidol (Haldol). Chlorpromazine began the drug revolution. Henri Laborit, a French surgeon, discovered that this drug reduced his patients' anxiety during the preoperative period. Shortly thereafter two French psychiatrists, Jean Delay and Pierre Deniker, found that it reduced hallucinations and thought disorders in chronic schizophrenics. Within a few years chlorpromazine was being prescribed for schizophrenia worldwide (Byck, 1975).

The Dopamine Hypothesis of Schizophrenia

The leading hypothesis about the brain dysfunction in schizophrenia is that it results from an abnormality in neural circuits in which *dopamine* is the neurotransmitter. The major piece of evidence in favor of the dopamine hypothesis of schizophrenia is that the drugs most effective for treating schizophrenia are also the most effective dopamine blockers.

Chlorpromazine apparently works by blocking dopamine receptors (Cooper et al., 1986). Dopamine has at least two different types of postsynaptic receptor molecules, D_1 and D_2. The evidence suggests that many of the antipsychotic drugs have their main effect at the D_2 receptor.

How Do the Neuroleptics Take Hold?

Antipsychotic, or **neuroleptic,** drugs such as chlorpromazine are effective blockers of dopamine synapses. We know this from experiments performed with animal brain tissue. How do we know that this dopamine blocking action observed in animal brain tissue is related to the therapeutic effect of these drugs in schizophrenics? Strictly speaking, we do not know from direct evidence that the therapeutic properties of chlorpromazine are due to the ability of this drug to block D_2 receptors. Chlorpromazine may work primarily through some other action on the brain. Nevertheless, evidence suggests that D_2 blockade is the main effect of various antipsychotic drugs. First, the correlation between the therapeutic effectiveness of a drug and its ability to block dopamine transmission at D_2 receptor sites in laboratory experiments is very high. The correlation between clinical effectiveness and a drug's ability to block D_1 synapses, however, is much less. The therapeutic effectiveness of a drug is measured by the amount of the drug required to suppress the unwanted symptoms. The smaller the necessary dosage, the greater the effectiveness.

A second argument for the dopamine hypothesis is that **amphetamine,** a drug that has synaptic effects opposite to those of chlorpromazine, can produce symptoms of schizophrenia in normal individuals and worsen symptoms in schizophrenics. Amphetamine apparently increases dopamine availability in the synaptic cleft by increasing dopamine release from the presynaptic terminals and by blocking dopamine reuptake. Amphetamine abuse often results in disorganized thoughts, hallucinations, and other schizophrenic symptoms (Lickey and Gordon, 1983).

Chlorpromazine blocks not only the postsynaptic (D_2) receptors for dopamine, but also the **autoreceptors** for dopamine. Autoreceptors are located on the axon terminals, axon, cell body, and dendrites of the presynaptic dopamine-releasing neuron; their function is unclear. Autoreceptors may affect the synthesis and release of dopamine by the neuron through negative feedback (Cooper et al., 1986). Autoreceptor blockade causes an increase in the firing rate of dopamine-releasing neurons when they are squirted with chlorpromazine in laboratory experiments. However, with continued use in patients, it is believed that this initial activation gives way to a "depolarization blockade" that occurs with continued depolarization of the presynaptic neurons. This process may contribute to the suppression of dopamine transmission, along with the direct blocking effect on the postsynaptic D_2 receptors. Depolarization blockade takes several days to develop, which may account for the "therapeutic lag" between the time a patient is first placed on neuroleptic medication and the time the symptoms begin to lessen, as will be discussed (Creese, 1983).

The dopamine hypothesis of schizophrenia rests principally on drug data. Several attempts have been made to examine possible abnormalities either in the level of dopamine or in the number of dopamine receptors in the brains of schizophrenics. Some recent research has uncovered evidence that D_2 dopamine receptors are more numerous in the basal ganglia of the brains of schizophrenics that had never been treated with neuroleptics (Wong et al., 1986).

In addition, the dopamine hypothesis presents a theoretical problem because of the "therapeutic lag" time. The dopamine-blocking effects in the brain occur within hours of a patient's being placed on drugs, but generally at lest two weeks pass before psychotic symptoms begin to diminish. The explanation offered by Ian Creese (1983) (see earlier) may account for this lag, but this is still just a hypothesis.

Side Effects of the Neuroleptics

Despite the convincing evidence that, compared with other therapies, the antipsychotic drugs do indeed reduce and control schizophrenic symptoms, a "counterrevolution" in reaction to their prolonged use is growing. The main problem is that serious side effects often occur, the most disturbing of which are abnormal, involuntary movements, particularly of the tongue and face. These movement disorders can take several forms and range from mild to virtually incapacitating. The worst form of this disorder is **tardive dyskinesia** ("tardy," or late-appearing, movement disorder). With prolonged use of neuroleptics (patients must stay on the medications to suppress their schizophrenic symptoms), these movement disorders become more likely. They begin as "jerky, ticlike movements in the tongue and face. As the disease progresses, the entire body may become affected, making either ticlike or writhing movements. These movements are virtually continuous during waking hours but cease during sleep" (Lickey and Gordon, 1983).

autoreceptors Neurotransmitter receptors located on the neuron secreting the neurotransmitter.

tardive dyskinesia (TARdive dis-kin-EASE-ee-ah) Late-appearing movement disorders caused by prolonged use of neuroleptics.

Estimates of the number of patients who will develop tardive dyskinesia vary, but with prolonged use and increased age, it is possible that those affected will be more than 30 percent of the total treated. Obviously, such severe side effects raise the question of which is worse, schizophrenia or tardive dyskinesia. This is a question that will probably be answered on a case-by-case basis, but it may lessen doctors' willingness to prescribe these drugs. Obviously, we need antipsychotic drugs without such severe side effects. [Although extremely rare, several deaths have been reported from the use of neuroleptics. This condition, called neuroleptic malignant syndrome (NMS), is characterized by extremely high fever and circulatory collapse. About 60 deaths from NMS had been reported by 1980 (Garfield, 1983b).]

Dopamine Circuits in the Brain.

The dopamine circuits in the brain are complex, but the cell bodies of most are restricted to just a few locations. These include the substantia nigra and tegmental area of the midbrain and the arcuate nucleus of the hypothalamus. The axons of neurons of the substantia nigra and tegmental area are quite long and innervate regions of the basal ganglia, medial frontal cortex, cingulate and entorhinal cortex, as well as nuclei in and around the septum. For a variety of reasons it is believed that the movement disorders of tardive dyskinesia are due to an abnormal *increase of sensitivity* of dopaminergic synapses in the basal ganglia brought about by chronic chemical denervation due to the neuroleptic drug.

This concept of *denervation supersensitivity* has been suggested by similar phenomena observed in muscles that have been deprived of their neural input. For example, denervated muscles become supersensitive to acetylcholine, the transmitter at nerve–muscle junctions. Whether a denervation supersensitivity explanation is correct remains to be proved. Suppression of schizophrenic symptoms is (with considerably less certainty) thought to be related to blocking of dopamine transmission in the prefrontal cortex, septal area, or other brain regions. Figure 15.4 shows the distribution of the main dopaminergic circuits in the human brain (Iversen, 1979).

Depression

Schizophrenia is one of the two major types of mental illness. Depression is the other. Depression is much more common than schizophrenia. *DSM-III* describes diagnostic criteria for two main subtypes of depression, unipolar and bipolar. *Unipolar* ("one pole") depression is characterized by profound sadness and loss of pleasure in one's usual activities. In terms of *DSM-III* criteria, four of the following symptoms also must be present for at least two weeks: significant changes in appetite and/or weight, changes in sleeping pattern, psychomotor agitation or slowness, loss of interest in sex, loss of energy, feelings of worthlessness or self-reproach, inability to

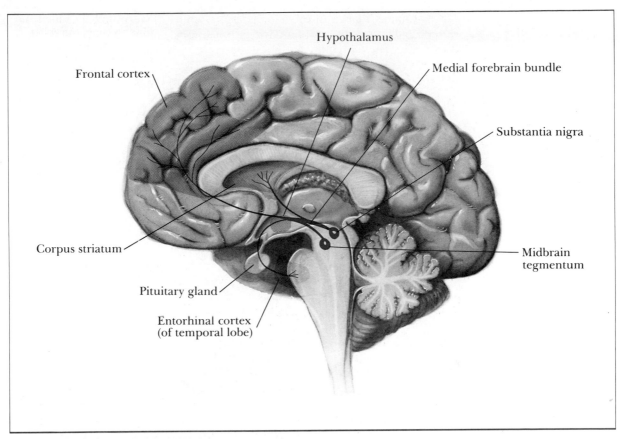

Figure 15.4 Dopamine pathways in the human brain.
The entorhinal cortex is actually behind the midbrain in this figure.

concentrate, slowed thought processes, and recurrent thoughts of death and suicide.

To illustrate the depths to which depression can go, here is an excerpt from the diary of a depressed patient.

> I had by now become quite convinced that I was finished for good and all. There was no possible chance of my coming out of the Hospital alive. In fact though not actually dead, I was as good as dead. For some inscrutable reason, perhaps because I had committed "the unforgivable sin" or just because I was such an appalling sinner, the worst man who had ever existed, I had been chosen to go alive through the portals of Hell, in an ordinary English lunatic-asylum. Therefore it was obviously too late for repentance. It was, I knew, quite unsound theology to imagine that people got another chance after they were dead. Obviously when they saw what they were in for they would repent; anybody would. But they would be cast into outer darkness and the Lord would not bother about them any more, however much they wept and gnashed their teeth [Custance, 1952].

Everyone feels blue from time to time, but when the symptoms of depression become severe, as outlined in the text, some therapy is indicated.

A second type of depression is termed *bipolar* ("two-pole") *depression*. (An older term is "manic depression.") This illness is marked by episodes of mania and periods of depression. In these manic states the person has bizarre ideas, often engages in strange and erratic behavior, takes unnecessary risks, initiates uncharacteristic bouts of sexual activity or sexually oriented conversations, and is typically irritable and difficult. For example, the previously quoted patient, "the worst man who ever existed," was a bipolar depressive. He describes himself in one of his manic periods.

> It seemed to me that I had found a mission. I could and must serve these women—any harlot who called; it would certainly not be right to exercise any choice. Those I met soon found the trick to get my money; all they had to do was to pretend that they wanted to leave the life of the streets, but needed money to pay their debts and so on. I gave money away until my bank warned me about my overdraft, but I was convinced that God would give me money to carry on the good work . . . [Custance, 1952].

The activity level maintained by individuals in such manic states is so high that they may collapse with exhaustion. At some point these wild highs end and the patient falls into profound depression, paralyzed with self-loathing and guilt, in which thoughts of death and suicide dominate.

About 10 percent of men and 20 percent of women in the United States are likely to suffer at least one clinically significant episode of depression sometime during their life. Bipolar illness is much less common than unipolar depression, occurring in about 1 percent of the population, a figure similar to that of schizophrenia.

The Monoamine Hypothesis of Depression

Just as schizophrenia has been linked to dopamine, depression has been linked theoretically with presumed abnormalities in neurons that share a common neurotransmitter. The particular neurotransmitter responsible for depression, however, is uncertain. The two leading hypotheses that attempt to explain this focus attention on norepinephrine and serotonin.

Norepinephrine, like dopamine, is a **catecholamine,** containing both an amine group (NH$_2$) and a catechol nucleus (see Figure 15.5). Serotonin is an **indolamine,** since it contains an indol ring as well as an amine group (see Figure 15.6). Both the catecholamines and the indolamines are classified as **monoamines** ("one-amine group"). Therefore the proposal that one or the other (or both) of these neurotransmitters is involved in depression is referred to as the *monoamine hypothesis of depression.* Like the dopamine hypothesis of schizophrenia, the monoamine hypothesis of depression came primarily from clinical findings with drugs. In its simplest form this hypothesis states that unipolar depression is due to lowered availability of one or more of the monoamine transmitters in the synaptic cleft. Mania is considered to result from an excess or other abnormality of monoamine synaptic transmission. To gain some perspective on the general idea that abnormalities in monoamine neurotransmission underlie depression, let us look at how this idea began.

The monoamine hypothesis first arose in the 1950s, when it was noticed that a drug used in the treatment of high blood pressure, **reserpine,** caused severe depression in 10–15 percent of the patients to whom it was administered. (No one knows why the other 85–90 percent were unaffected.) At about the same time physicians and nurses noted that a drug

catecholamine (cat-e-KOLE-a-meen) A substance that contains both an amine (NH$_2$) and a catechol group. Catecholamines include dopamine, norepinephrine, and epinephrine.

indolamine (IN-dole-a-meen) A substance that contains both an amine (NH$_2$) and an indol ring (e.g., serotonin).

monoamine (MO-no-a-meen) A substance with a single amine (NH$_2$) group. Includes the catecholamines (e.g., dopamine and norepinephrine) and the indolamines (e.g., serotonin).

reserpine (RES-ur-peen) A drug that can precipitate depression; contributed to development of monoamine theory of depression.

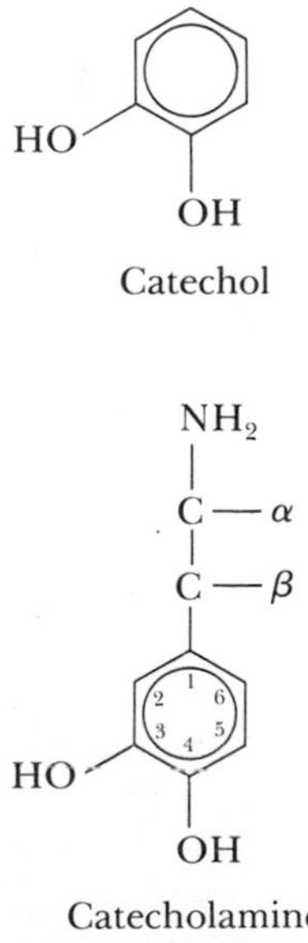

Catechol

Catecholamine

Figure 15.5 Basic catechol and catecholamine structure.
NH$_2$ is an amine group. α and β represent various side chains.

Figure 15.6 Structure of serotonin, an indolamine transmitter.
The indol ring contains a nitrogen atom (N).

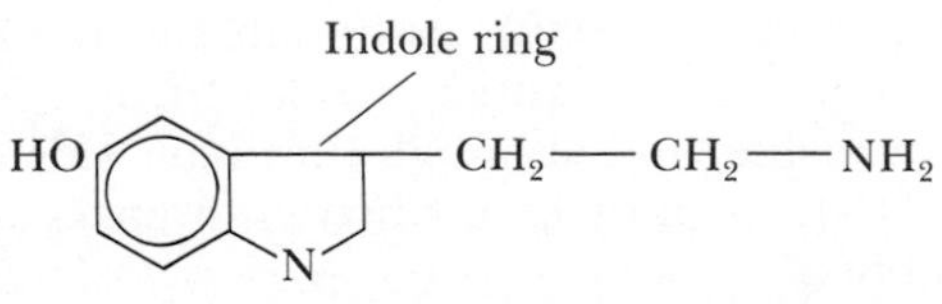

iproniazid (ip-ro-NYE-ah-zid) A drug used in the early years of drug treatment for unipolar depression. A monoamine oxidase inhibitor.

monoamine oxidase inhibitor (MAOI) (MO-no-a-meen OX-i-dace) A family of drugs that inhibit monoamine oxidase, the substance that helps to remove monoamines from the synapse. The effect of MAOIs is to increase the availability of monoamines at the synapse.

monoamine oxidase (MAO) (MO-no-a-meen OX-i-dace) An enzyme that metabolizes monoamines.

tricyclics (try-CY-kliks) A major family of drugs used for unipolar depression.

imipramine (im-IP-rah-meen) The generic name for one of the major tricyclics.

desipramine (dez-IP-rah-meen) The generic name for one of the major tricyclics.

isocarboxazid (ice-o-car-BOX-a-zid) The generic name for one of the monoamine oxidase inhibitors.

iprindole (IP-rin-dole) A tricyclic. Effective as an antidepressant.

SUMMARY TABLE
Suspected Transmitter Abnormalities in Mental Illness

Condition	Suspected Transmitter System	Prescribed Drugs
Schizophrenia	Dopamine	Chlorpromazine, haloperidol
Unipolar depression	Norepinephrine? Serotonin?	Tricyclics, MAOI's
Bipolar depression	Norepinephrine?	Lithium

---

being used for the treatment of tuberculosis, **iproniazid,** caused several patients to be particularly high-spirited. The catecholamine hypothesis of depression was born when researchers realized that reserpine *reduced* the amount of available catecholamines in the synapse (by impairing the ability of the presynaptic vesicles to store the transmitter adequately) and iproniazid *increased* it (Schildkraut, 1965; Bunney and Davis, 1965). Iproniazid is a **monoamine oxidase inhibitor (MAOI)**; as such, it inhibits the action of the enzyme **monoamine oxidase (MAO)**, which normally decreases the supply of monoamines by oxidizing them to inactive metabolites.

Antidepressant Drugs

Two main families of drugs are used as antidepressants, **tricyclics** [e.g., **imipramine** (Tofranil) or **desipramine** (Pertofrane)] and the *monoamine oxidase inhibitors* (MAOIs) [e.g., **isocarboxazid** (Marplan)]. Iproniazid itself is seldom used today because of its side effects. The tricyclics, like the MAOIs, are believed to relieve depression by increasing monoamine availability at critical synapses in the brain. The effectiveness of the tricyclics is thought to rely on the ability of these drugs to block the reuptake of monoamines, thereby increasing their synaptic availability. As with the dopamine hypothesis, however, this hypothesis must contend with the serious problem of "therapeutic lag." The drugs block reuptake within a few minutes of administration, but it takes one to two weeks for the depression to lift. Even more damaging to the simpler version of the monoamine hypothesis is the finding that some new tricyclics that are very effective in treating depression (e.g., **iprindole**) do not alter reuptake significantly of either norepinephrine or serotonin and that several drugs that do block reuptake are not antidepressants (Cooper et al., 1986). Although the theoretical controversy continues, so does the use of antidepressant drugs. Several effective antidepressants are available, and although they have side effects (particularly true of the MAOIs), in most cases their drawbacks do not outweigh the therapeutic benefits.

The main side effects of the tricyclics involve heart rate and blood pressure changes. The side effects of the MAOIs can be much more serious, however, and include dangerous and sudden increases in blood pressure, increasing the danger of strokes. [Fatalities are rare even with MAOIs, however—about one for every 250,000 patients (Lickey and Gordon, 1983).] Consequently, tricyclics are usually chosen over MAOIs.

The main alternative physical treatment for severe depression is *electroconvulsive therapy* (ECT), introduced in 1937. It is still useful for patients who do not respond to drugs or in situations where the individual is in real danger of committing suicide before drugs can take effect. The use of ECT is controversial, but most professionals who deal with severe depression view it as necessary for some individuals. It is not known how ECT works, but its usefulness in relieving depression, at least for a while, is overwhelming. (Behavioral treatments for depression are also valuable but discussing them is beyond the scope of this chapter.)

The main treatment for bipolar depression is to administer **lithium,** first used for bipolar illness by an Australian psychiatrist, John Cade. In 1949 he observed that lithium calmed the normal agitated behavior in a handful of guinea pigs. He promptly administered lithium to manic patients. Fortunately, his guess proved remarkably insightful. Lithium is now virtually the only treatment for bipolar depression. In the great majority of cases it is extremely therapeutic, although some 20 percent of those suffering from this illness are not helped by it (Lickey and Gordon, 1983). We do not know how lithium works. It has complex biochemical effects at noradrenergic synapses, but how or whether these effects are responsible for the improvement in bipolar patients is still uncertain. It is probable that lithium has effects at synapses where norepinephrine is not the transmitter as well.

Lithium is administered as a salt, lithium carbonate; the Li^+ ion (similar to Na^+ in many respects) is the effective agent. When taken in appropriate dosages, lithium therapy can return individuals suffering from bipolar depression to a productive and nearly normal life. It is particularly effective at bringing patients down from their mania without plunging them into depression. Careful medication with lithium can control both the manic and depressive phases of most patients' disease.

lithium (LITH-e-um) The lithium ion (Li^+) is the effective agent in the lithium salts used as medication for bipolar depression.

Disorders of Brain and Behavior in Childhood

Attention Deficit Disorder with Hyperactivity

One of the leading behavioral problems in children is a condition characterized by inattention, impulsivity, restlessness, and poor self-control. In the past few years, children who display these symptoms have been called *hyperactive, minimally brain damaged, learning disabled,* and a variety of other names. Gradually, diagnostic criteria and some convergence of thinking have resulted in the widely used classification *attention disorder deficit* (ADD) for this syndrome. If hyperactivity is also part of the syndrome, the label is *ADDH (DSM-III,* 1980). Different investigators working with behavior disorders in children emphasize one or more of the preceding four characteristics, and many add symptoms of their own, such as an "increased tendency to seek immediate reinforcement" (Douglas, 1983). Diagnostic problems are still formidable. Not everyone agrees that such a condition should be classified as a syndrome, but in general, most people who have worked with or studied such children agree that some classification scheme is useful. Most children classified as having ADD or ADDH are boys.

Now a common treatment, the use of stimulant drugs for ADD–ADDH syndromes began in the 1930s, when Charles Bradley and others used benzedrine to treat hyperactive children (Bradley, 1937). Three drugs are used commonly to treat ADD–ADDH today: methylphenidate (trade name Ritalin), dextroamphetamine, and magnesium pemoline. Over 600,000 children are treated with one of more of these drugs each year. These drugs are effective for inattention, restlessness, and distractibility in about 75 percent of patients, (unfortunately, one ADD child in four is not helped by these or other drugs). As is true for virtually all drugs, these drugs have undesirable side effects, such as slowing the growth rate (Zametkin and Rapoport, 1987).

It may strike you as paradoxical that stimulant drugs should prove effective for hyperactive children. In fact, this unexpected result of stimulant drugs is still not well understood. Children often respond to drugs in a manner different from (in some cases opposite to) that of adults. Such findings provide theoretical and practical puzzles for scientists and physicians. One known mode of action for the stimulant drugs involves activation of synapses at which the catecholamines norepinephrine and dopamine are released. This fact has given rise to the *catecholamine hypothesis of ADD*. As is true for the catecholamine hypothesis of depression, this idea comes in several versions, but the basic theme is that of an abnormality of synaptic transmission in the brain involving dopamine, norepinephrine, or both.

Treatment with such stimulant drugs as Ritalin tends to increase the availability of catecholamines in the synaptic cleft. This could occur at noradrenergic synapses, dopaminergic synapses, or both. Assuming that this is the case, at least four different interpretations for ADD–ADDH have been suggested (Kalat, 1984):

1. ADD–ADDH children actually suffer from low levels of brain arousal, and their behavior is a form of overcompensation. Stimulants are effective by producing increased levels of arousal by increasing the activity at catecholaminergic synapses.
2. Stimulant effects may be "rate dependent," lowering very high levels and raising very low levels of behavioral responding. Such an idea is supported by data gathered in experiments with rats and other laboratory animals.
3. Stimulants may reduce the number or effectiveness of catecholamine receptors ("down regulation"), thereby normalizing arousal levels.
4. Stimulants may alter catecholamine production and destruction through complex biochemical effects.

All these ideas have arguments against them, but all survive as possibilities because of our fundamental lack of information about chemical transmission in the brain. The importance of basic neuroscience research for understanding human problems is nowhere more apparent than in the area of attention deficit disorders.

infantile autism (AW-tizm) A condition that appears early in childhood, primarily in boys. Autism is marked by failure to relate to others, language disorders, and other symptoms.

Infantile Autism

One of the most puzzling and difficult to treat disorders of brain and behavior is **infantile autism,** a rare (one in about 2500 children) condition marked by inadequate language development, socialization, and various other abnormalities. Most autistic children are boys. First described and named by Leo Kanner in 1943, infantile autism has baffled researchers; no adequate explanation for it exists. Although the diagnosis of this condition is often controversial and individual children display one or more of the symptoms to different degrees, most autistic children fail to show normal affection toward others. This emotional indifference is displayed at very early ages. An early sign of autism is the absence of snuggling or cuddling normally displayed by infants. Autistic children tend to become rigid when held and generally do not respond to touching or hugging, although some eventually do respond more normally, particularly after behavioral training that rewards hugging. This lack of interest in contact with others can be a very heavy load for parents and relatives to bear and may discourage others from hugging or touching an autistic child.

Typically, autistic children either do not develop language or develop only a few words (usually nouns and a few verbs). Even when it seems clear that an autistic child understands language, he or she does not use it in socially effective ways. In most cases, autistic children are very "set in their ways" and are very upset with even the slightest change in routine. They often engage in repeated, stereotyped behavior for long periods of time. Other symptoms include abnormal responses to sensory stimulation (e.g., increased sensitivity to cold or decreased sensitivity to pain). Although by some measures these children might be termed retarded, they often display normal or even superior skills in areas such as music, art, and even mathematical calculations. Although some have suggested that autism may be caused by faulty parenting, this idea currently has few supporters. For example, brothers and sisters of autistic children are generally normal. Most researchers assume that autism has a biological basis, but so far this hypothesis is unproved.

Several suggestions concerning the possible brain abnormality underlying autism have been made. For example, the language abnormalities in autism led to the hypothesis that the left hemisphere of autistic children developed in a faulty way, but careful examination of the evidence and the logic of this hypothesis has caused it to be rejected (Fein et al., 1984; Kinsbourne and Hiscock, 1983).

Some autistic children show abnormal electrical responses to auditory stimuli (clicks) in scalp EEG records. This activity, although measured on the scalp, is due to brain activity in the brainstem and reflects transmission time for the processing of auditory stimulation from brainstem centers to the cortex. (See Chapter 6 for a diagram of these pathways.) These evoked potentials are called *brainstem auditory evoked potentials (BAEP)* and may prove of use in the early diagnosis of autistic children (Fein et al., 1981).

SUMMARY

1. Mental illness can be viewed as the result of abnormal brain function. Since the 1950s and the introduction of chlorpromazine, various drugs have been used to treat schizophrenia and depression, the two most common forms of mental illness. Most of these drugs affect chemical synaptic transmission.

2. Drugs can affect one or more synaptic events, including synthesis, release, reuptake, and metabolic destruction of the neurotransmitter or blocking of the receptors for the transmitter. The use of these drugs has created a revolution in the care of psychiatric patients, with many more mentally ill patients being treated on an out-patient basis or allowed to live on their own, often without adequate supervision.

3. Diagnosis of mental illness is not easy. Diagnostic criteria for mental illness have been published by the American Psychiatric Association in the *Diagnostic and Statistical Manual,* the most recent edition coming out in 1980 (*DSM-III*). Diagnostic criteria for schizophrenia include delusions, disordered thinking, flat affect, and social withdrawal.

4. The risks of developing schizophrenia are greater if one has a relative who has it. The risk increases from about 1 percent of the general population to close to 50 percent if one has an identical twin who is schizophrenic. This sort of evidence indicates a genetic factor in the tendency to develop schizophrenia. The causes of schizophrenia are unknown. Development of symptoms may be due to stress or even a virus.

5. Drugs such as LSD can induce hallucinations, which may result from the interaction of the drug with serotonin synapses, although the evidence for this is not compelling.

6. The drugs used to treat schizophrenia belong to the phenothiazine family. One common drug is chlorpromazine, marketed under the trade name Thorazine. Drugs used to treat schizophrenia are classified as *neuroleptics.*

7. Most neuroleptics work to reduce schizophrenic symptoms by blocking one of the receptors for dopamine, the D_2 receptor. Neuroleptics may also block autoreceptors for dopamine that are on the presynaptic (dopamine releasing) neuron itself. It is unclear why D_2 receptor blockade reduces the schizophrenic symptoms. The correlation between the effectiveness of a given neuroleptic and its ability to block D_2 dopamine receptors is very high. This sort of evidence has led to the *dopamine hypothesis of schizophrenia,* which, simply stated, holds that abnormalities

in neural circuits involving dopamine are responsible for schizophrenia.

8. Serious and often irreversible side effects occur with prolonged use of neuroleptics such as chlorpromazine. The most serious side effect is a syndrome of movement disorders termed *tardive dyskinesia,* which can virtually cripple the individual for normal life. This aspect of drug treatment for mental illness may pose the cruel choice between the disease and the side effects of its treatment. At present no successful nondrug treatment exists for schizophrenia. Not all patients develop side effects, but as many as 30 percent may do so. Tardive dyskinesia may be related to the development of *denervation supersensitivity* of neurons sensitive to dopamine brought about by the receptor blocking actions of the drug.

9. The other main type of mental illness is depression. At least two major types of depression exist, unipolar and bipolar. Unipolar depression is the most common form of mental illness. Its symptoms include profound sadness and loss of pleasure in one's usual activities and pastimes, and at least four of the following additional symptoms: significant changes in appetite or weight, changes in sleeping pattern, psychomotor agitation or slowing down, loss of interest in sex, loss of energy, feelings of worthlessness or self-reproach, inability to concentrate, slowed thinking, and recurrent thoughts of death and suicide.

10. Bipolar depression is the term for depression coupled with bouts of manic, hyperactive, bizarre behavior. This condition was at one time called *manic depression.* In manic states the person has bizarre ideas, often engages in strange and erratic behavior, takes unnecessary risks, and may initiate uncharacteristic bouts of sexual activity or sexually oriented conversations. Patients in manic states often become irritable and difficult to deal with. Differential diagnosis of bipolar depression from other forms of mental illness, such as unipolar depression or schizophrenia, is crucial, as the drugs prescribed for these conditions are quite different.

11. Depression has been linked to abnormalities in the monoamine neurotransmitter systems, particularly serotonin and norepinephrine. This *monoamine hypothesis of depression* comes in several varieties, and the evidence in support of it is complex and not completely convincing. Nevertheless, the drugs used to treat unipolar depression are believed to work by increasing the availability of monoamines at the synapse. Two main families of antidepressants are used to treat unipolar depression, the tricyclics, such as *imipramine,* and monoamine oxidase inhibitors, such as *isocarboxazid.*

12. Bipolar depression is treated by administering lithium salts. No one is quite sure why this treatment is so successful, but it is very useful in controlling the symptoms of at least 75 percent of all cases of bipolar depression.

13. Attention deficits in children, often accompanied by hyperactivity, are generally treated with stimulant drugs such as methylphenidate

(Ritalin). How such drugs act is unknown, but the leading hypothesis is that some deficit in catecholamine neurotransmitters underlies childhood attention deficits and hyperactivity.

14. Infantile autism is a rare and puzzling disorder characterized by inadequate language development, poor socialization, and other abnormalities. Autistic children may display superior abilities in restricted areas such as mathematics, music, or art. Some abnormal EEG activity has been seen in autistic children, suggesting that abnormalities may occur in processing auditory stimulation from the brainstem to the cortex.

SUGGESTIONS FOR FURTHER READING

Cooper, J. R., Bloom, F. E., and Roth, R. H. (1986). *The biochemical basis of neuropharmacology.* (5th ed.). New York: Oxford University Press.

Lickey, M. E., and Gordon, B. (1983). *Drugs for mental illness. New York:* W. H. Freeman.

McNeal, E. T., and Cimbolic, P. (1986). Antidepressants and biochemical theories of depression. *Psychological Bulletin, 99,* 361–374.

Glossary

abducens nerve (Ab-DEW-sens)   The sixth cranial nerve. Concerned with eye movements.

absolute refractory period   The period of time immediately following a nerve impulse during which a second impulse cannot be initiated at that site.

acetylcholinesterase (ah-SEE-tul-ko-leen-ESS-ter-ace)   An enzyme that breaks down acetylcholine in the synaptic cleft.

acupuncture (OK-oo-punk-shur)   The technique for inducing analgesia that was developed in China and that involves insertion of fine needles into various regions of the skin.

adenine (ADD-i-neen)   One of the bases of DNA.

adipose tissue (ADD-ih-pose)   Fat tissue.

adenylate cyclase (ah-DEE-nil-ate CY-klase)   An enzyme in the membrane of target cells for hormones using the second messenger system. When activated by a hormone, adenylate cyclase activates cyclic AMP, the second messenger.

adrenaline   See *epinephrine*.

affect (Aa-fekt)   Feeling or emotion.

afferent (AF-er-ent)   Leading toward a center. (In the nervous system, axons that bring sensory information into the brain and spinal cord are afferent neurons.)

agonist (AG-o-nist)   A substance that mimics the action of a naturally occurring neurotransmitter.

agraphia (a-GRAF-ee-ah)   Inability to write normally, because of brain trauma.

alexia (a-LEK-see-ah)   Profound difficulty in understanding written or printed words caused by brain trauma. (Different from dyslexia.)

all-or-none law   The "law" that states a nerve impulse either occurs or does not. When it does occur, it is of a fixed amplitude. (This law does not hold for synaptic potentials.)

alpha motor neurons (AL-fa)   The main motor neurons to striated muscles.

alpha rhythm (AL-fa)   Activity in the EEG characterized by regular waves at 8–13 Hz.

alveoli (al-VEE-o-ly) (singular, *alveolus*)   Sacs or ducts surrounding the nipples.

Alzheimer's disease (ALLS-hymers)   Severe mental and emotional deterioration caused by abnormal changes in the brain.

amacrine cell (AM-ih-krin)   A major cell type in the retina.

amblyopia ex anopsia (am-blee-OPE-e-ah ex an-OPE-see-ah)   A deterioration in vision in one eye resulting from the underutilization of that eye.

amino acids   Basic components of proteins.

amphetamine (am-FET-a-meen)   Stimulant drug that affects catecholamine synapses.

ampulla (am-PUL-lah) [plural, *ampullae* (am-PUL-lie)]   Describes a "jar" or "flask-like" enlargement in a tubular structure. In the semicircular canals the ampullae contain the sense receptors for balance.

amygdala (ah-MIG-dah-la) [plural, *amygdalae* (ah-MIG-dah-lie)]   A group of brain nuclei in the tip of the temporal lobe.

amyloid (AIM-ih-loyd)   A substance found in the senile plaques often observed in the brains of patients with Alzheimer's disease.

analgesia (an-al-JEEZ-e-ah)   Pain relief without loss of consciousness.

analogue (AN-a-log)   A substance with properties similar to those of another substance.

androgens (AN-dro-jens)   Hormones that produce masculinizing effects. (Distinctions between androgens and estrogens have become somewhat blurred with new discoveries. The two types of hormones are closely related chemically.)

angiotensin II (anj-ee-o-TEN-sin two)   A hormone made from the action of renin on angiotensinogen.

angiotensinogen (anj-ee-o-ten-SIN-o-jen)   A liver product converted into angiotensin II by renin.

anion (AN-eye-on)   An ion with one or more negative charges.

anorexia nervosa (ann-or-EKS-ee-ah nur-VOSE-ah)   A condition in which patients do not eat enough to sustain normal body weight.

antagonist (ann-TAG-o-nist)   A muscle opposing the movement under consideration.

antagonist   A substance that blocks the action of a neurotransmitter.

anterograde (ANN-tur-o-grade)   Forward-going.

anterolateral system   One of two major nerve tracts serving somesthesis.

antidiuretic hormone (ADH) (An-tie-die-ur-ET-ik)   Another name for vasopressin. A posterior pituitary hormone that acts on the kidney to cause more concentrated urine, thus conserving body water.

aphasia (ah-FAY-zee-ah)   Inability to produce normal speech resulting from brain damage. (There are two basic types of aphasia, expressive and receptive.)

Aplysia (ah-PLEASE-ee-ah)   Marine invertebrate widely used in neuroscience because of its recognizable large neurons and relatively simple neural circuits.

apraxia (a-PRAK-see-ah)   Profound disability in carrying out purposeful movements in the absence of any paralysis.

aqueous humor (AH-kwee-us)   A waterlike material in the anterior part of the eye.

arachnoid layer (a-RACK-noid)   The middle of the three layers of membranes covering the brain and spinal cord.

arcuate fasciculus (ARK-u-ate fah-SIK-u-lus)   A nerve tract connecting Wernicke's area with Broca's area.

atrophy (AH-tro-fee)   To grow smaller, generally through disuse.

autism (AW-tizm)   A condition that appears early in childhood, primarily in boys. Autism is marked by failure to relate to others, language disorders, and other symptoms.

autoreceptors   Neurotransmitter receptors located on the neuron secreting the neurotransmitter.

axoaxonic synapses (AKS-o-ax-ON-ik)   Synapses on the axonal end feet of the postsynaptic neuron.

axodendritic synapses (AKS-o-den-DRIT-ik)   Synapses on the dendrites of the postsynaptic neuron.

axon (AKS-on)   The part of the neuron that carries the nerve impulse. (Usually a long process extending from the cell body.)

axosomatic synapses (AKS-o-so-ma-tik)   Synapses on the soma (cell body) of the postsynaptic neuron.

ballistic movements (ball-ISS-tik)   Movements made rapidly to a particular point in space, too fast for feedback to be an effective guide.

barbiturate (bar-BIT-u-rate)   A central nervous system depressant.

baroreceptors (BARE-owe-re-sep-tors)   Pressure receptors in the heart and large arteries that respond to changes in blood volume.

basal ganglia (BAY-zal GANG-lee-ah)   A group of brain structures near the thalamus and hypothalamus, including the caudate nucleus, the putamen, and the globus pallidus.

base   A substance capable of giving up electrons. There are four bases in DNA from which the genetic code is composed—thymine, cytosine, adenine, and guanine. In RNA there are also four bases—cytosine, adenine, guanine, and uracil.

basilar membrane (BAZ-i-lar)   The membrane to which the hair cells are attached in the organ of Corti.

benzodiazepines (ben-zo-die-AZ-e-peens)   The family of drugs used to treat severe anxiety (e.g., Valium and Librium).

beta-endorphin (BAIT-ah en-DOR-fin)   Derived from POMC, has analgesic properties. (See POMC.)

beta waves   Activity in the EEG characterized by low-voltage waves at 15–30 Hz.

Betz cell (BETS)   A type of large neuron in the motor cortex whose axons descend in the pyramidal tract. Also called *giant pyramidal cells.*

blindsight   The ability of some individuals with visual cortex damage to "guess" at better than chance levels the identity of stimuli in parts of their visual field that correspond to their scotomata.

blood–brain barrier   A term given to the series of membranes and specialized capillaries that act as filters between the general circulation and the fluid that bathes the neurons.

brainstem reticular formation (BSRF) (re-TIK-u-lar)   The region of the brainstem that is packed with a network of cell bodies and dendrites. Important in many functions, including forebrain arousal.

Broca's aphasia (BRO-ka)   A form of aphasia characterized by poor speech fluency but good language comprehension. Also termed *expressive aphasia.*

Brodmann numbering system   A system for identifying various regions of the cortex on the basis of microscopic appearance of the tissue.

bulimia (bu-LEEM-e-ah)   Binge eating.

butyrophenones (beaut-er-o-fuh-NONES)   A family of drugs used in the treatment of schizophrenia.

calpain (KAL-pain)   A protein in the spines of dendrites.

Capgras syndrome (CAP-grass)   An unusual condition in which the patient is convinced that close relatives are actually imposters. (Occurs with damage to the frontal lobe in a small number of cases.)

cataplexy (CAT-a-plex-ee)   Sudden attacks of extreme muscular weakness, often associated with narcolepsy.

catecholamine (cat-e-KOLE-a-meen)   A substance that contains both an amine (NH_2) and a catechol group. (Catecholamines include dopamine, norepinephrine, and epinephrine.)

cation (CAT-eye-on)   An ion with one or more positive charges.

caudal (CAW-dul)   Toward the tail; posterior.

caudate nucleus (CAW-date)   One of the basal ganglia.

cephalic (suh-FAL-ik)   Pertaining to the head.

cerebrospinal fluid (CSF) (sir-E-bro-spy-nal)   Fluid in the ventricles and central canal of the central nervous system.

cerveau isolé (SAIR-vo eez-o-LAY)   Experimental preparation in which the brain is transected in the brainstem between the anterior and posterior colliculi. See *encephale isolé.*

cervical nerves (SERV-i-kal)   One of the divisions of the spinal nerves.

chemically gated ion channel An ion channel whose permeability to one or more ions is regulated by the presence of certain chemical substances such as neurotransmitters.

chemoaffinity hypothesis (KEY-mo-a-FIN-uh-tee) The concept that neurons make appropriate synaptic connections during development and regeneration due to guidance by specific molecules.

chlorosane (KLOR-oh-sane) A nonbarbiturate anesthetic agent.

chlorpromazine (klor-PRO-mah-zeen) Generic name for one of the phenothiazine family of drugs (trade name Thorazine) used in the treatment of schizophrenia.

cholecystokinin (COLA-sis-toe-kine-in) A term for several peptides secreted by the duodenum of the small intestine that have satiety-producing effects in several species, including human beings.

choline (KO-leen) A precursor of acetylcholine.

choline acetyltransferase (ChAT) (KO-leen ah-see-tul-TRANZ-fur-ace) The enzyme involved in the synthesis of acetylcholine from its precursors, choline and acetyl-coenzyme A.

chromaffin cell (KROME-a-fin) The main secretory cell type in the adrenal medulla.

chromatolysis (krome-a-TOL-a-sis) The change in the color of a neuron's cell body when it is stained with standard dyes (a result of cutting its axon).

circadian (sir-KAY-dee-an) Referring to endogenous rhythmic changes in some process or behavior. A circadian rhythm peaks once about every 24 hours, even in the absence of environmental changes.

classical conditioning Experimental procedures for producing a learned association between two stimuli. Developed by Ivan Pavlov.

clitoris (KLIT-o-riss) Small erectile organ, part of female genitalia.

coccygeal nerves (KOKs-a-jee-al) The most caudal pair of spinal nerves.

cochlea (KOK-lee-ah) That portion of the inner ear concerned with hearing.

colloid (KOL-oyd) A gelatinous substance that does not diffuse through cell membranes but that can absorb water.

commissure (KOM-i-sure) A band of axons crossing from one hemisphere to the other.

computerized transaxial tomography (toe-MA-graf-ee) (CT scanning.) A procedure for examining living brain tissue involving computer analysis of x-ray pictures.

confabulation (kon-FAB-u-la-shun) Falsification that the patient accepts as true, used to make up for lapses in memory. (Characteristic of Korsakoff's psychosis patients, particularly in the earlier stages of the disease.)

consolidation (KON-sol-uh-DAY-shun) The concept that learned items become less vulnerable to forgetting with the passage of time.

corpus callosum (KORE-pus Ka-LO-sum) A band of about 200 million axons (in the human being) that connects the right and left cerebral hemispheres.

corollary discharge (KORE-o-lar-ee) Hypothetical signals from motor cortex to the cerebellum and possibly other brain regions informing them of coming movement commands.

corticosteroid (kor-ti-ko-STE-royd) Any of the steroids produced by the cortex of the adrenal gland.

corticotropin-like intermediate lobe peptide (KOR-ti-ko-TRO-pin) One of the constituents of POMC. (See *proopiomelanocortin*.)

cretinism (KREE-tin-ism) Physical and mental stunting due to insufficient thyroid secretion during fetal development.

crista (KRIS-ta) (plural, *cristae*) The sensory organs in the semicircular canals. Formed from a cluster of hair cells.

cupula (KOOP-you-lah) ("Little cup.") The gelatinous mass in which the cilia of the hair cells in the vestibular organs are embedded.

cyclic (SY-clik) On a regularly occurring basis.

cyclic AMP (cAMP) (SY-klik) An enzyme found in many cells and activated by adenylate cyclase. cAMP is the second messenger for many hormones, carrying out the activities within the cell that are initiated by substances utilizing the second messenger system.

cyproterone (Cy-PRO-ter-own) A chemical with antiandrogen properties.

cytoarchitecture (sigh-toe-ARK-i-tek-shur) Microscopic appearance of cortical tissue.

cytomegalovirus (SY-toe-meg-ah-low-virus) A virus related to the herpes virus that may be involved in schizophrenia.

cytosine (SY-toe-seen) One of the bases in DNA.

decerebrate rigidity (dee-SAIR-ih-brate) An enhancement of the normal degree of contraction of the antigravity muscles following transection of the brainstem at the anterior level of the pons.

decibel (DES-ih-bel) Unit of measurement for the intensity of the pressure in sound waves.

decussate (de-KUS-ate) To cross over to the opposite side.

dementia (de-MEN-sha) Deterioration in mental abilities.

dendrites (DEN-drites) Branchlike extensions of the neuron's cell body that form the main sites for synapses.

dentate gyrus (DEN-tate JY-russ) Part of the hippocampal formation in the mammalian brain.

dentate-interpositus nucleus (DEN-tate in-ter-POZ-i-tuss) A nucleus in the cerebellum found to be important in conditioning the nictitating membrane.

deoxyribonucleic acid (DNA) (de-OX-e-rye-bo-new-CLAY-ik) The molecule that contains the genetic information in virtually all living cells. The genetic code is constructed from combinations of the four bases—thymine, cytosine, adenine, and guanine.

depolarization A change in the resting potential in the direction of a smaller voltage difference across the membrane.

dermatome A segment of the body associated with a particular spinal nerve.

desipramine (dez-IP-rah-meen) Generic name for one of the major tricyclics. Used as an antidepressant.

diencephalon (die-en-SEF-a-lon) The region of the brain that includes the thalamus and hypothalamus.

dishabituation (DIS-ha-BIT-tu-a-shun) Elimination of habituation.

disinhibition Release from inhibition.

DNA See *Deoxyribonucleic acid.*

double-blind An experimental design in which neither the subject nor the experimenter knows the nature of the treatment given to the subject until the results are complete.

Down's syndrome Condition marked by mental retardation and physical abnormalities due to the presence of an extra chromosome (three rather than the normal two copies of chromosome number 21).

DSM-III (D-S-M three) The third edition of the *Diagnostic and Statistical Manual,* published by the American Psychiatric Association in 1980.

dura mater (DUR-ah MAH-ter) The outermost membrane covering the brain and spinal cord.

dyslexia (dis-LEK-see-ah) Unusual difficulty in learning to read and spell.

ectopic (ek-TOP-ik) Out of its normal place.

efferent (EF-er-ent)   Leading away from a center. (In the nervous system axons that carry impulses away from the brain and spinal cord are termed *efferent*.)

electroencephalogram (EEG) (e-lek-tro-en-CEF-a-low-gram)   A recording of the spontaneous electrical activity of the brain. [The instrument used in this procedure is called an *electroencephalograph*; the procedure itself is *electroencephalography* (e-lek-tro-en-cef-a-LOG-ra-fee).]

encephale isolé (on-suh-FAL eez-o-lay)   Experimental preparation in which the brain in transected at the caudal end of the brainstem, where it merges into the spinal cord. See *cerveau isolé*.

encephalitis (EN-sef-ah-LI-tis)   Inflammation of the brain due to infection.

endocrine system (END-o-krin)   The collection of glands in the body that secrete hormones into the bloodstream.

endogenous (en-DODGE-ih-nuss)   Intrinsic.

endoplasmic reticulum (ER) (EN-do-plas-mik re-TIK-u-lum)   A network (reticulum) of membranes within the cell body concerned with the production and transportation of cellular products. The prefix *endo* means "within" or "inner." (ER with associated ribosomes is called *rough ER*. ER without associated ribosomes is called *smooth ER*.)

endorphin (en-DOR-fin)   A recently coined term referring to the endogenous morphines. Substances in the body that possess properties similar to the opiates.

engram (N-gram)   The essential neural circuitry underlying a memory.

enkephalin (en-KEF-a-lin)   ("In the head.") Term used for two of the endogenous morphines. Both enkephalins are pentapeptides (made up of five amino acids).

enzyme (N-zyme)   A substance that produces or speeds up a biochemical reaction.

epinephrine (ep-ee-NEF-rin)   A catecholamine neurotransmitter and a hormone secreted from the adrenal medulla. Synonymous with *adrenaline*.

episodic memory (EP-ih-sod-ik)   Memory of events in an individual's life.

epithelium (ep-uh-THEE-lee-um)   The sheet of cells covering a particular surface. The olfactory epithelium is the sheet of receptor cells for olfaction in the nose.

estradiol (ESS-tra-DY-all)   A potent estrogen.

estrogens (ESS-tro-jens)   Hormones that produce feminizing effects. See *androgens*.

estrus (ESS-trus)   Period of sexual receptivity in female mammals. Not applicable to human beings. (The associated adjective is *estrous*.)

excitatory postsynaptic potential (epsp)   Graded depolarization across the postsynaptic membrane at an excitatory synapse.

extrafusal muscles (EX-tra-fuse-al)   The main muscles that produce movement. Activated by the alpha motor neurons.

extrapyramidal system (EX-tra-peer-AM-i-dal)   Those neurons concerned with movement that are not part of the pyramidal system.

fascicle (FAS-i-kul)   Small bundle of axons.

fetal alcohol syndrome (FAS)   Mental retardation, facial abnormalities, and other symptoms in the child, produced by alcohol ingested by the mother while pregnant.

fimbria-fornix (FIM-bree-ah-FOR-nicks)   A major nerve tract in the mammalian brain, connecting the hippocampus and other parts of the brain.

fistula (FIS-tue-la)   An abnormal passage in the body, generally made to divert the flow of material from its normal course, typically to the outside of the body.

fodrin (FOE-drin)   A protein in the postsynaptic spine apparatus of neurons.

fovea (FOE-vee-ah)   A cone-rich region of the central retina in which most daylight vision is initiated in animals with both rods and cones.

frontal leukotomy (lew-KOT-o-me)   A surgical procedure in which the neural connections between the thalamus and the frontal lobes are severed.

frontal lobotomy (low-BOT-o-me)   A surgical procedure in which portions of the frontal lobes are removed and connections between the frontal cortex and the thalamus are severed.

gamma-amino-butyric acid (GABA) (GAM-ma a-meen-o bhu-tier-ik) (GAH-bah)   An inhibitory neurotransmitter.

gamma motor neurons (GAM-ma)   Motor neurons in the ventral root that activate the intrafusal muscles of the muscle spindle organs.

gestation (jes-TAY-shun)   The time from fertilization to birth.

glabrous (GLA-brus)   Hairless.

glia (glee-ah)   Satellite cells that, along with neurons, make up the two main types of cells in the nervous system. Also termed *neuroglia*.

globus pallidus (GLOBE-us PAL-i-dus)   One of the basal ganglia.

glomerulus (glo-MARE-u-lus) [plural, *glomeruli* (glo-MARE-u-lie)]   A cluster or ball of cells.

glossopharyngeal nerve (GLOSS-o-fair-en-JEE-al)   Ninth cranial nerve. A mixed nerve concerned with mouth and throat.

glycogen (GLY-ko-jen)   A form of stored glucose.

Golgi body (GOAL-gee)   A series of membranes in the cell body important in the production of various substances. Synonymous term is *Golgi complex*.

Golgi tendon organs (GOAL-jee)   Sense organs in the tendons attached to muscles, concerned with signaling degree of tension in the muscle.

guanine (GWA-neen)   One of the bases in DNA.

habituation (ha-BIT-shu-a-shun)   Decrease in the strength of a response with repeated presentations.

hippocampus (hip-po-KAM-pus)   A region of the brain whose functions, although probably concerned with memory, are still under active investigation.

homeostasis (home-ee-oh-STAY-sis)   The tendency of a system to maintain internal stability.

homunculus (huh-MUN-kew-lus)   "Little man" cartoon representing the proportion of the motor cortex devoted to the regulation of various muscles in the body.

Huntington's disease   Disease of the basal ganglia, produces uncontrollable movements and dementia.

hyperphagia (high-per-FAYJ-ee-ah)   Overeating.

hyperpolarization   A change in the resting potential in the direction of a greater voltage difference across the membrane.

hyperreflexia (high-per-re-FLECKS-ee-ah)   Exaggerated reflex movements that can occur following the period of spinal shock.

hypertonic (high-per-TON-ik)   A solution that is more concentrated with respect to dissolved substances than the comparison solution. Often refers to a solution with more than 0.9 percent concentration of Na^+ and Cl^- ions, the concentration in blood plasma.

hypertrophy (hi-PER-tro-fee)   Abnormal growth.

hypothalamic–pituitary portal system (hi-poe-tha-LAM-ik pih-TOO-ih-tare-ee)   The private circulatory system between the hypothalamus and the anterior pituitary.

hypothalamus (high-po-THAL-ah-muss)   A region at the base of the brain just below the thalamus.

hypotonic (high-po-TON-ik)   A solution that is less concentrated than a comparison solution. Often refers to a solution with less than 0.9 percent concentration of Na^+ and Cl^- ions, the concentration in blood plasma.

hypovolemia (high-po-vol-EEM-ia)   Reduced blood volume.

imipramine (im-IP-rah-meen)   Generic name for one of the major tricyclics. Used as an antidepressant.

impedance (im-PEED-ance)   Resistance to the flow of energy.

impotence (IM-po-tents)   Inability to achieve or maintain an erection long enough for satisfactory intercourse.

indolamine (IN-dole-a-meen)   A substance that contains both an amine (NH_2) and an indol ring. (Serotonin is an indolamine.)

inferior colliculus (kul-IK-u-lus) [plural, *colliculi* (kul-IK-u-lie)]   A region of the midbrain concerned with audition.

inhibitory postsynaptic potential (ipsp)   Graded hyperpolarization across the postsynaptic membrane at an inhibitory synapse.

insulin (IN-sool-in)   Hormone secreted by the pancreas.

interstitial fluid (in-ter-STISH-al)   The fluid of the body located between the cells.

intrafusal muscles (in-tra-FUSE-al)   Small muscle fibers in the muscle spindle organs. Activated by gamma motor neurons.

intralaminar nuclei (in-tra-LAM-ih-nar)   A system of nuclei "in between the layers" of other nuclei in the thalamus.

intromission   Penetration of the vagina by the penis.

ion (EYE-on)   An electrically charged particle formed when a substance breaks apart or dissociates. The ions that are particularly important for neuronal signaling are Na^+, K^+, Cl^-, and Ca^{2+}.

ion channels   Passages in the neuronal membrane through which ions can pass under certain conditions.

iprindole (IP-rin-dole)   A tricyclic. Used as an antidepressant.

iproniazid (ip-ro-NYE-ah-zid)   A drug used in the early years of drug treatment for unipolar depression. A monoamine oxidase inhibitor.

isocarboxazid (ice-o-car-BOX-a-zid)   Generic name for one of the monoamine oxidase inhibitors. Used to treat depression.

isomer (ICE-o-mer)   One of two or more different chemical compounds with the same molecular formula. Isomers differ because of the different spatial arrangement of identical atoms.

kinocilium (kine-oh-SIL-ee-um)   A large cilium (extension of the cell body) in "hair" cells of the vestibular organs.

Klüver—Bucy syndrome (CLUE-ver Bhu-see)   Psychic blindness and emotional changes seen after temporal lobe removal in monkeys.

Korsakoff's psychosis (KOR-sa-koffs)   A syndrome marked by profound memory loss. Usually preceded by chronic alcoholism.

lanugo hair (lah-NU-go)   A fine, downy hair often found on skin of the fetus. Sometimes develops in anorexia nervosa patients.

lecithin (LES-ih-thin)   The main dietary source of choline. Found in foods such as egg yolk and liver.

lemniscal system (lem-NISK-al)   One of two major nerve tracts serving somesthesis.

leu-enkephalin (LEW-en-KEF-a-lin)   One of the enkephalins. Possesses analgesic properties.

Librium (LIB-ree-um)   An antianxiety drug.

limbic system (LIM-bick)   A group of brain structures that probably do not actually form a coherent system but that are often grouped together. Usually includes the hippocampus, septal nuclei, and amygdala.

lipid   Fat molecules that are insoluble in water and thus can only be extracted from tissue with a "fat solvent" such as alcohol. One of the main constituents of living things, lipids form the basic matrix of cell membranes.

lithium (LITH-e-um)   The lithium ion (Li^+) is the effective agent in the lithium salts used as medication for bipolar depression.

locus coeruleus (LOW-cus sir-RULE-ee-us)   A system of neurons in the brainstem named because it stains blue (locus coeruleus means "the blue place") with appropriate dyes.

long-term potentiation (LTP) (po-ten-she-A-shun)   An increased neuronal response to a standard stimulus following intense stimulation of an afferent pathway to those neurons.

lordosis (lore-DOSE-us) [plural, lordoses (lore-DOSE-ease)]   The posture adopted by some female mammals, such as rats and cats, when they are sexually receptive.

lordosis quotient (lore-DOSE-us KWO-shunt)   The number of times the female adopts the lordosis posture divided by the number of mounts by the male. A standard measure of female receptivity in laboratory animals such as the rat.

L-DOPA   A precursor of the catecholamines.

luteinizing hormone (LH) (LU-tin-eyes-ing)   Anterior pituitary hormone responsible for ovulation in the female. Stimulates testosterone production in the male.

medroxyprogesterone (med-ROK-see-pro-JES-ter-own)   A chemical used as an anti-androgen. Also a synthetic progesterone.

melatonin (mel-ah-TONE-in)   A hormone made and secreted by the pineal gland.

meninges (men-IN-jees)   The membranes covering the brain and spinal cord.

menstrual cycle (MEN-stral)   Cyclic sloughing off of the uterine walls. Only occurs in primates.

met-enkephalin (MET-en-KEF-a-lin)   One of the enkephalins. Possesses analgesic properties.

microfilaments   See *microtubules*.

microtubules (mike-ro-TUBE-yools)   Tube-shaped proteins within the cell body and axon of neurons. Important in the transport of nutrients and other substances within the cell. Other similar structures are called *neurofilaments* and *microfilaments*.

mitochondria (my-toe-KON-dree-ah)   Rod-shaped structures in cells that are the principal sites of the generation of energy.

mitotic cycle (my-TOT-ik)   Describes the events in cell division, or *mitosis* (my-TOE-sis).

monamine (MO-no-a-meen)   Substance with a single amine (NH_2) group. Includes the catecholamines such as dopamine and norepinephrine and indolamines such as serotonin.

monamine oxidase (MAO) (MO-no-a-meen OX-i-dace)   Enzyme that metabolizes monoamines.

monoamine oxidase inhibitor (MAOI) (MO-no-a-meen OX-i-dace)   A family of drugs that inhibit monamine oxidase, the substance that helps to remove monoamines from the synapse. Effect of MAOIs is to increase the availability of monoamines at the synapse.

monosynaptic reflex (MOAN-o-sin-AP-tik)   Reflex involving only one set of synapses.

motor unit   One alpha motor neuron and the muscle cells it innervates, which all contract simultaneously.

MPP$^+$ (methylphenylpyridine) (meth-ul-FEN-ul-PEER-uh-deen)   Substance produced in the body from MPTP. Selectively destroys neurons in the substantia nigra, causing Parkinson's disease.

MPTP (methylphenyltetrahydropyridine) (meth-ul-FEN-ul-tet-rah-high-dro-PEER-uh-deen)   A substance found as a contaminant in some "designer drugs." Causes Parkinson's disease by destroying neurons in the substantia nigra after being converted into MPP$^+$ in the body.

Müllerian inhibiting substance (MIS) (mull-AIR-ee-an)   Substance produced by the fetal testes. Inhibits the growth and development of the Müllerian (female) duct system.

muscle spindle organs   Sense organs embedded in the muscles, concerned with signaling the length of the muscle.

mutant (mew-tant)   Organism that has undergone a sudden change in its DNA that is inherited by any offspring.

myelin (MY-lin)   A fatty substance, actually the cell body of a satellite cell (either glia or Schwann cell) that provides the "insulation" around myelinated axons.

N-acetyltransferase (N-ah-see-tul-TRANZ-fur-ase)   The enzyme responsible for producing melatonin in the pineal gland.

naloxone (nal-OX-own)   An antagonist for opiate and opiate-related drugs.

naltrexone (nal-TREKS-own)   An antagonist for opiate and opiate-related drugs.

narcolepsy (NAR-ko-lep-see)   Abnormal sudden attacks of sleepiness during the day.

Nernst equation   An equation based on the work of Walter Nernst, a German chemist. The Nernst equation allows for the calculation of the membrane voltage that would be present, given the internal and external concentrations of a particular ion, assuming the ion is free to move across the membrane. That membrane voltage is called the *equilibrium potential* for that ion.

neuroblasts (NUR-o-blasts)   Neurons prior to differentiation.

neurofibrillary tangles (nur-o-FIB-rih-lar-ee)   Distorted neurotubules and neurofilaments seen in some brain cells of individuals with Alzheimer's disease.

neurofilaments.   See *microtubules*.

neuroleptic (nur-o-LEP-tik)   Referring to the various antipsychotic drugs.

neuromelanin (nur-o-MEL-ah-nin)   A black substance in certain neurons, such as in the substantia nigra.

neuromodulator   A chemical substance that amplifies or dampens neuronal activity but is not strictly a neurotransmitter.

neuron (NUR-on)   An individual nerve cell, the main components of which include the cell body, nucleus, dendrites, axon, and end feet.

neuronal oscillator (OS-sil-a-tor)   Term for neural circuitry underlying the production of rhythmic activities, such as walking, swallowing, and flying.

neuroregulator.   General term for any substance that affects neuronal activity. Includes both neurotransmitters and neuromodulators.

neurotransmitter.   A chemical substance manufactured, stored, and released by neurons. Neurotransmitters are the messenger chemicals between neurons at chemical synapses.

nerve growth factor (NGF)   Naturally occurring protein that stimulates the growth of neurons.

nictitating membrane (NIK-ti-ta-ting)   The tough "third" eyelid present in cats, rabbits, and some other species.

nocioceptor (NO-see-o-sep-tor)   A receptor sensitive to noxious or pain-related stimuli.

nodes of Ranvier (ron-vee-AY)   Gaps in the myelin sheath in myelinated axons.

norepinephrine (NOR-ep-ee-nef-rin)   A catecholamine neurotransmitter and a hormone secreted from the adrenal medulla. Synonymous with *noradrenaline*.

nuclear magnetic resonance (NMR)   A technique for gaining images of the living human brain, based on the fact that hydrogen atoms act like tiny spinning magnets that can be made to generate an electrical field, which in turn can be used by a computer to create images.

nucleotide (NEW-klee-o-tide)   One of the units of DNA, containing a sugar, phosphoric acid, and a base.

nucleus (NEW-klee-us)   A structure in the cell body containing the genetic material. The term *nucleus* is also used to refer to a cluster of neurons and their associated dendrites and glial cells.

nucleus basalis of Meynert (nbM) (NEW-klee-us ba-SAL-is of MAY-nurt)   A small region of the forebrain with a high concentration of cholinergic neurons. Undergoes profound cell loss in Alzheimer's disease.

nucleus gigantocellularis (gi-GANT-o-sell-u-lair-iss)   Nucleus in the pons thought to produce the PGO spikes seen in REM sleep.

nucleus hyperstriatum ventralis pars caudalis (HVc) (hy-per-stree-A-tum ven-TRALL-iss parz kaw-DAL-iss)   A region of the brain of some song birds to which new neurons are added and subtracted each fall.

oculomotor nerve (OCK-u-low-motor)   The third cranial nerve, regulates eye movements and pupil size.

opsin (OPP-sin)   The protein component of rhodopsin.

organ of Corti (KORE-tee)   The actual sense organ of hearing in the cochlea.

osmoreceptors (OZ-mo-re-cep-tors)   Neurons in the brain (thought to be primarily in the lateral preoptic region) that are sensitive to cellular dehydration and that can signal changes in osmotic pressure.

osmosis (oz-MOE-sis)   When two solutions varying in concentration of some substance are separated by a membrane permeable to water, but not to the dissolved substance, water flows from the region of lesser concentration of the substance to the region of higher concentration. This movement of water is called *osmosis.* The pressure that would be required to stop this flow of water completely is the *osmotic pressure* of the solution.

osmotic pressure (oz-MOT-ik)   See *osmosis.*

ossicles (OS-sik-uls)   The three tiny bones involved in hearing—the malleus, incus, and stapes.

otoconia (oh-toe-CONE-ee-ah)   (singular, *otoconium*) Crystals of calcium carbonate atop the otolithic membrane in the semicircular canals.

ovarian follicles (o-VAR-ee-an FOL-ik-ul)   Many-celled structure in the ovary that contains and nourishes the ovum. Also produces hormones such as the estrogens.

ovulation (ov-u-LAY-shun)   Expulsion of the ripe ovum from the ovary.

oxytocin (ox-e-TOSE-in)   One of the two hormones secreted by the posterior pituitary.

Pacinian corpuscle (pa-SIN-ee-an KOR-pus-ul)   A sense receptor for deep touch or pressure.

parietal lobe (pa-RY-et-al)   One of the four main lobes of the cerebral cortex.

Parkinson's disease   Deterioration in motor control and movement initiation, sometimes accompanied by cognitive impairments.

parachlorophenylalanine (PCPA) (para-klor-o-fen-nel-AL-ah-neen)   A drug that blocks serotonin synthesis.

perforant pathways (PER-for-ant)   A major afferent tract from the entorhinal cortex to the dentate gyrus.

periaqueductal gray (perry-AK-we-duct-al)   Gray matter immediately surrounding the central canal or "aqueduct" in the brain.

PGO spikes (P-G-O)   Bursts of electrical activity in the pons, lateral geniculate nucleus, and occipital lobe during REM sleep.

phenothiazines (fe-no-THI-a-zines)   A family of drugs used in the treatment of schizophrenia.

phenylalanine (fen-ul-AL-a-neen)   An amino acid.

pheromone (FEAR-oh-moan)   A chemical substance secreted by an animal that carries a specific message to others of its species.

photon (FOE-ton)   Elementary particle of radiant energy.

phylogenetic (fy-low-je-NET-ik)   Related to evolutionary development.

physostigmine (fy-zo-STIG-meen)   A drug that inhibits acetylcholinesterase.

pia mater (PEE-ah MAH-ter)   The innermost membrane covering the brain and spinal cord.

pineal gland (pin-NEEL)   An unpaired organ in the brain whose functions in mammals are still poorly understood. Secretes melatonin.

piracetam (purr-ASS-ih-tam)   A drug that releases acetylcholine from presynaptic terminals.

pituitary gland (pih-TOO-ih-tare-ee)   A complex gland closely associated with the hypothalamus. Manufactures and secretes a variety of hormones.

placebo effect (pla-SEE-bo)   (From the Latin, "I please.") A drug or procedure that may produce some beneficial effect despite having no known biologic action.

planum temporale (PLAY-num tem-po-RAL-e)   A region of the temporal lobe often found to exhibit right–left asymmetry in human beings.

polypeptide (polly-PEP-tide)   A molecule composed of two or more amino acids.

polysynaptic reflex (POLLY-sin-AP-tik)   Reflex involving two or more sets of synapses.

positron emission tomography (POZ-ih-tron ee-MISH-un toe-MA-graf-ee)   PET scanning. A procedure for measuring the blood flow patterns in living brain tissue. Blood flow patterns then can be the basis for inferences concerning function of those brain regions.

prandial drinking (PRAN-dee-al)   Drinking initiated by eating dry food.

proceptive behavior (PRO-sep-tive)   Behaviors that are initiated by the female that increase the likelihood of sexual contact.

prodynorphin (PRO-die-NOR-fin)   Precursor molecule for one of the major families of endorphins.

proenkephalin (PRO-en-KEF-a-lin)   Precursor molecule for one of the major families of endorphins.

progestins (pro-JES-tins)   Steroid hormones such as progesterone. Progestins affect the wall of the uterus to prepare it for implantation of the fertilized egg.

prolactin (pro-LAK-tin)   A protein hormone secreted by the anterior pituitary. Supports lactation in the female.

proopiomelanocortin (POMC) (PRO-OPE-ee-o-muh-lan-o-KORT-in)   Precursor molecule for one of the major families of endorphins.

prosopagnosia (pro-zo-pag-NOSE-ee-ah)   An inability to recognize familiar faces. Caused by brain damage in the temporal and occipital lobes.

protein   One of the basic types of molecules in living matter. Proteins are synthesized from amino acids.

psychophysiologist (SY-ko-fizz-e-OL-o-jist)   Scientist interested in the relationship between the autonomic nervous system, behavior, and emotion.

Purkinje cell (purr-KIN-jee)   The main output neuron of the cerebellum.

putamen (pew-TAY-men)   One of the basal ganglia.

pyramidal tract (peer-AM-i-dal)   Those axons that cross over in the medulla, forming the medullary pyramids.

raphe system (rah-FEY)   A group of nuclei along the midline of the brainstem. (The term *raphe* means "seam" in Greek.)

reactive synaptogenesis (sin-nap-toe-JEN-uh-sis)   Synapse formation in reaction to axon terminal degeneration at nearby receptor sites.

receptive field   The receptive field of a neuron is that region of the sensory surface in which appropriate energy changes produce an alteration in the firing rate of that neuron.

relative refractory period   The period of time following the absolute refractory period when another nerve impulse can be produced only if the second stimulus is of the suprathreshold intensity.

REM sleep (Rapid eye movement sleep.) A stage of sleep characterized by low-voltage, fast EEG, low muscle tone (except for eye muscles). Associated with dreaming.

renin (REN-in) An enzyme produced by the kidney that, when released into the general circulation, converts a liver hormone, angiotensinogen, into angiotensin II.

reserpine (RES-ur-peen) A drug that can precipitate depression, a fact that contributed to development of the monoamine theory of depression.

resting potential The electrical potential across the neuronal membrane when the neuron is not producing a nerve impulse.

retina (RET-in-ah) The sheet of cells in the eye in which transduction of light to nerve activity occurs.

retinal (RET-in-al) A component of rhodopsin, derived from vitamin A. Also called *retinene*.

retinitis pigmentosa (ret-in-EYE-tis pig-men-TOE-sah) An eye disease in which debris shed by rods is not removed, as is normally done.

retinohypothalamic tract (RET-in-o-hy-po-thal-AM-ik) A small bundle of axons that emerge from the optic tract and innervate the suprachiasmatic nuclei.

ribonucleic acid (RNA) (rye-bo-new-CLAY-ik) Complex molecules within cells that are concerned with the translation of genetic information into the synthesis of proteins.

rhodopsin (ro-DOP-sin) The photosensitive substance in rods.

ribosomes (RYE-bo-somes) Structures associated with endoplasmic reticulum. Ribosomes are made of protein and ribonucleic acid (RNA). Important for protein synthesis.

rostral (ROS-trul) Toward the head; anterior.

saccade (Sah-KAD) Rapid voluntary eye movement.

saccule (SACK-yule) A sense organ in the inner ear concerned with the sense of balance.

saltatory conduction (SAL-ta-tor-ee) Conduction of the nerve impulse in myelinated axons. The impulse jumps from node to node, skipping the internodal regions.

satiety (sah-TY-ih-tee) The feeling of having had enough, particularly of food or water.

schizophrenia (skits-o-FREEN-ee-ah) A mental illness characterized by thought disorder, emotional withdrawal, and delusions.

Schwann cell An accessory cell that forms the myelin sheath around the axons of peripheral neurons.

scotomata (sko-TOE-mah-tah) [singular, *scotoma* (sko-TOE-mah)] Regions of severely decreased vision or blindness due to damage in the visual cortex.

sella turcica (SEL-lah tur-KEE-ka) The pocket of bone in which the pituitary gland is encased.

semantic memory (suh-MAN-tik) Organized knowledge about words, symbols, world events, and so on.

sensitization (senz-ih-tuh-ZA-shun) Increase in the strength of all responses to stimuli for some time following exposure to a potentially threatening stimulus.

septal nuclei Clusters of cell bodies in the septum, a thin wall of brain tissue in the midline of the forebrain.

septum A thin wall of brain tissue in the midline of the forebrain. Contains the septal nuclei.

sexual dimorphism (di-MORF-ism) Refers to differences in structure or behavior that distinguish male and female patterns.

sleep apnea (AP-nee-ah) "Not breathing" sleep. Disruptions in sleep caused by blockage of airway or other causes. Often correctable.

sodium inactivation Cessation of Na$^+$ flow across neuronal membrane due to change in shape of Na$^+$ channels.

sodium–potassium pump (Na$^+$–K$^+$ pump) An enzyme that causes the active transport or "pumping" of Na$^+$ and K$^+$ ions across the membrane from regions of lower concentration to regions of higher concentrations.

somesthesis (som-ess-THEE-sis) Collective term for the skin and muscle senses, including touch, temperature, and pain.

sone A unit of loudness; the loudness of a 1000-Hz tone at 40 dB above a listener's threshold.

spike-initiating region The part of the neuron that has the lowest threshold for producing a nerve impulse.

spinal shock Loss of spinal reflexes below the level of the spinal cord transection. Lasts for varying periods of time in different species.

steroid (STE-royd) One of three main chemical families of hormones. Includes the reproductive hormones such as testosterone and estrogen.

stimulation-produced analgesia (SPA) Analgesia produced by electrical stimulation of certain regions of the brain.

strabismus (strah-BIZ-mus) A deviation of one eye.

stress-induced analgesia (ann-al-JEEZ-e-ah) Decreased pain sensations during stressful situations.

striate cortex (STRY-ate) Visual cortex, area 17.

striated muscle (STRY-ate-ed) "Striped" muscle, such as those that move the limbs.

subfornical organ (SFO) (sub-FORN-ih-kal) Structure in the brain that projects into the lateral ventricle below the fornix.

substantia gelatinosa (sub-STAN-sha je-LAT-uh-nos-ah) A region of the dorsal spinal cord in which pain-related impulses are processed.

substantia nigra (sub-STAN-sha NYE-gra) Nucleus in the brainstem containing the cell bodies of dopamine-secreting neurons that project to the basal ganglia and other forebrain structures.

superior colliculus (kul-IK-u-lus) [plural, *colliculi* (kul-IK-u-lie) A region in the midbrain concerned with orientation and response to visual stimuli.

suprachiasmatic nuclei (su-pra-KY-as-mat-ik) A pair of small nuclei lying just on top of the optic chiasm. Involved in the generation of circadian rhythmicity in mammals.

synapse (SIN-naps) Junctions between neurons. Synapses can be either electrical or chemical. Most of the synapses in mammalian brains are thought to be chemical.

synaptic cleft (sin-AP-tik) The small space between the presynaptic end foot and the postsynaptic receptor site.

synaptic receptors (sin-AP-tik) Molecules in the neuronal membrane that bind the neurotransmitter.

synaptogenesis (sin-nap-toe-JEN-uh-sis) Synapse formation.

synergist (SIN-er-jist) A muscle cooperating in the movement under consideration.

tachistoscope (ta-KISS-ta-scope) Device for the presentation of visual stimuli for controlled periods of time and in specific regions of the visual field.

tardive dyskinesia (TAR-dive dis-kin-EASE-ee-ah) "Late-appearing" movement disorders caused by prolonged use of neuroleptics.

tectorial membrane (tek-TOR-ee-al) The membrane into which the cilia of the hair cells in the organ of Corti are embedded.

temporal summation The algebraic addition of postsynaptic potentials across some period of time.

testosterone (tes-TOS-ter-own)   A major androgen.

tetrodotoxin (TTX) (te-TRO-doe-TOK-sin)   A substance found in a few animal species such as the Puffer fish. TTX selectively blocks the Na$^+$ channels in the neuronal membrane.

thalamus (THAL-a-muss)   A complex collection of nuclei in the center of the mammalian brain.

thioxanthenes (thy-o-ZAN-thenes)   A family of drugs used in the treatment of schizophrenia.

threshold   The level of depolarization required to initiate a nerve impulse some percentage of the time (e.g., 50 percent).

thymine (THIGH-meen)   One of the bases in DNA.

thyrotropin releasing hormone (TRH) (thigh-ro-TRO-pin)   A hypothalamic hormone that causes the production and release of the hormone thyrotropin from the anterior pituitary. A tripeptide.

timbre (TIM-ber or TAM-ber)   The musical quality of a sound. The quality that allows a listener to tell the difference in two sounds having the same pitch and loudness.

tonotopic (TONE-o-top-ik)   Referring to the orderly projection from particular locations in the basilar membrane on higher auditory centers.

trabecula (tra-BECK-u-la) [plural, *trabeculae* (tra-BECK-you-lie)]   Strands of connective tissue in the arachnoid layer of the nervous system.

tricyclics (try-CY-liks)   A major family of drugs used for unipolar depression.

trigeminal nerve (try-JEM-in-al)   The fifth cranial nerve. Mixed afferent and efferent nerve concerned with the face and mouth.

tympanic membrane (tim-PAN-ik)   The eardrum.

trochlear nerve (TROK-lee-ar)   The fourth cranial nerve, regulates eye movements.

tyrosine (TIE-ro-seen)   One of the amino acids. (The catecholamines are derived from tyrosine.)

utricle (U-trik-ul)   A sense organ in the inner ear concerned with the sense of balance.

vagotomy (vey-GOT-o-me)   Cutting of the vagus nerves.

Valium (VAL-e-um)   An antianxiety drug.

vasopressin (vas-o-PRES-in)   One of the two hormones secreted by the posterior pituitary.

vesicle (VESS-ik-ul)   One of the small, round structures in the axonal end feet that contain the neurotransmitter.

vitreous humor (VIT-ree-us)   A gellike material just in front of the retina of the eye.

voltage-gated ion channel   An ion channel whose permeability to one or more ions is regulated by the voltage across it.

vomeronasal organ (VOME-er-o-naze-al)   Accessory olfactory organ present in some species.

W cell   Cell type in the optic nerve and LGN.

Wada test (WAH-dah)   A procedure for discovering which cerebral hemisphere is dominant for speech production. Developed by Juhn Wada. An anesthetic is injected into either the left or the right carotid artery. Speech is disrupted only when the drug is injected into the hemisphere responsible for speech production. This technique does not test for language comprehension.

Wernicke's aphasia (VERN-ik-eez)   A form of aphasia characterized by poor understandability and comprehension but good speech fluency. Also termed *receptive aphasia*.

X cell   Cell type in the optic nerve and LGN.

Y cell   Cell type in the optic nerve and LGN.

zeitgeber (ZYTE-gay-ber)   ("Time-giver.") An environmental event that captures or "entrains" a circadian rhythm.

References

Adler, N. T. (Ed.) (1981). *Neuroendocrinology of reproduction*. New York: Plenum.

Adolph, E. F. (1950). Thirst and its inhibition in the stomach. *American Journal of Physiology, 161,* 374–386.

Akelaitis, A. J. (1944). A study of gnosis, praxis, and language following section of the corpus callosum and anterior commissure. *Journal of Neurosurgery, 1,* 94–102.

Akil, H. (1982). On the role of endorphins in pain modulation. In A. L. Beckman (Ed.) , *The neural basis of behavior* (pp. 311–333). Jamaica, NY: Spectrum.

Akil, H., Watson, S. J., Young, E., Lewis, M. E., Khachaturian, H., and Walker, J. M. (1984). Endogenous opioids: Biology and function. *Annual Review of Neuroscience, 7,* 223–255.

Alajouanine, T., and Lhermitte, F. (1965). Acquired aphasia in children. *Brain, 88,* 653–662.

Altman, J. (1967). Postnatal growth and differentiation of the mammalian brain, with implications for a morphological theory of memory. In G. C. Quarton, T. Melnechuk, and F. O. Schmitt (Eds.), *The neurosciences: A study program* (pp. 723–743). New York: Rockefeller University Press.

American Psychiatric Association (1980). *Diagnostic and statistical manual of mental disorders* (3d ed.). Washington, DC: APA.

Anand, B. K., and Brobeck, J. R. (1951). Hypothalamic control of food intake in rats and cats. *Yale Journal of Biology and Medicine, 24,* 123–140.

Andersson, B. (1953). The effect of injections of hypertonic NaCl solutions in different parts of the hypothalamus of goats. *Acta Physiologica Scandinavica, 28,* 188–201.

Angevine, J. B., and Cotman, C. W. (1981). *Principles of neuroanatomy*. New York: Oxford University Press.

Antin, J., Gibbs, J., Holt, J., Young, R. C., and Smith, G. P. (1975). Cholecystokinin elicits the complete behavioral sequence of satiety in rats. *Journal of Comparative and Physiological Psychology, 89,* 784–790.

Arnold, A. P., and Gorski, R. A. (1984). Gonadal steroid induction of structural sex differences in the central nervous system. *Annual Review of Neuroscience, 7,* 413–442.

Aschoff, J. (1980). The circadian system in man. In D. T. Krieger and J. C. Hughes (Eds.), *Neuroendocrinology* (pp. 77–83). Sunderland, MA: Sinauer.

Aserinsky, E., and Kleitman, N. (1953). Regularly occurring periods of eye motility, and concomitant phenomena during sleep. *Science, 118,* 273–274.

Ayoub, D. M., Greenough, W. T., and Juraska, J. M. (1983). Sex differences in dendritic structure in the preoptic area of the juvenile macaque monkey brain. *Science, 219,* 197–198.

Backlund, E. O., Granberg, P. O., Hamberger, B., Knutsson, E., Martensson, A., Sedvall, G., Seiger, A., and Olsen, L. (1985). Transplantation of adrenal medullary tissue to striatum in parkinsonism—First clinical trials. *Journal of Neurosurgery, 62,* 169–173.

Bailey, C. H., and Kandel, E. P. (1985). Molecular approaches to the study of short-term and long-term memory. In C. W. Coen (Ed.), *Functions of the brain.* Oxford, England: Clarendon Press.

Banks, M. S., Aslin, R. N., and Letson, R. D. (1975). Sensitive period for the development of human binocular vision. *Science, 190,* 675–677.

Barchas, J. D., Akil, H., Elliott, G. R., Holman, R. B., and Watson, S. J. (1978). Behavioral neurochemistry: Neuroregulators and behavioral states. *Science, 200,* 964–973.

Barlow, H. B. (1982). General principles: The senses considered as physical instruments. In H. B. Barlow and J. D. Mollon (Eds.), *The Senses* (p. 1–33). Cambridge, England: Cambridge University Press.

Bartus, R. T., Dean, R. L., Beer, B., and Lippa, A. S. (1982). The cholinergic hypothesis of geriatric memory dysfunction. *Science, 217,* 408–417.

Bartus, R. T., Dean R. L., Pontecorvo, M. J., and Flicker, C. (1985). The cholinergic hypothesis: A historical overview, current perspective, and future directions. In D. S. Olton, E. Gamau, and S. Corkin (Eds.), *Memory dysfunctions: An integration of animal and human research from preclinical and clinical perspectives* (pp. 332–358). New York: New York Academy of Sciences.

Basser, L. S. (1962). Hemiplegia of early onset and the faculty of speech with special reference to the effects of hemispherectomy. *Brain, 85,* 427–460.

Bassuk, E. L., and Gerson, S. (1978). Deinstitutionalization and mental health services. *Scientific American, 238,* 46–53.

Batini, C., Magni, F., Palestini, M., Rossi, G. F., and Zanchetti, A. (1959). Neural mechanisms underlying the enduring EEG and behavioral activation in the midpontine pretrigeminal cat. *Archives Italiennes de Biologie, 97,* 13–25.

Baylor, D. A., Lamb, T. D., and Yau, K.-W. (1979). The membrane current of single rod outer segments. *Journal of Physiology, 288,* 589–611.

Beach, F. A. (1976). Sexual attractivity, proceptivity, and receptivity in female mammals. *Hormones and Behavior, 7,* 105–138.

Beach, F. A., Kuehn, T. E., Sprague, R. H., and Anisko, J. J. (1972). Coital behavior in dogs—XI. Effects of androgenic stimulation during development on masculine mating responses in females. *Hormones & Behavior, 3,* 143–168.

Beatty, W. W. (1979). Gonadal hormones and sex differences in nonreproductive behaviors in rodents: Organizational and activational influences. *Hormones and Behavior, 12,* 112–163.

Beaumont, J. G. (1983). *Introduction to neuropsychology.* New York: Guilford.

Békésy, G. von (1960). *Experiments in hearing.* New York: McGraw-Hill.

Bellows, R. T. (1939). Time factors in water drinking in dogs. *American Journal of Physiology, 125,* 87–97.

Benson, D. F., and Geschwind, N. (1969). The alexias. In P. J. Vinken and G. W. Bruyn (Eds.), *Handbook of clinical neurology* (Vol. 4, pp. 112–140). Amsterdam: North-Holland.

Benson, D. F., Stuss, D. T., Naeser, M. A., Weir, W. S., Kaplan, E. F., and Levine, H. (1981). The long-term effects of prefrontal leukotomy. *Archives of Neurology, 338,* 165–169.

Berger, H. (1929). Über das Elektrenkephalogramm des Menschen. *Archiv für Psychiatrie und Nervenkrankheiten, 87,* 527–570.

Bermant, G., and Davidson, J. M. (1974). *Biological bases of sexual behavior.* New York: Harper & Row.

Björklund, A., and Stenevi, U. (1984). Intracerebral neural implants: Neuronal replacement and reconstruction of damaged circuitries. *Annual Review of Neuroscience, 7,* 279–308.

Blakemore, C., and Cooper, G. F. (1970). Development of the brain depends on the visual environment. *Nature, 228,* 477–478.

Blakemore, C., and Sutton, P. (1969). Size adaption: The new aftereffect. *Science, 166,* 245–247.

Bliss, T. V. P., and Lomo, T. (1973). Longlasting potentiation of synaptic transmission in the dentate area of the anaesthetized rabbit following stimulation of the perforant path. *Journal of Physiology, 232,* 331–356.

Bogen, J. E., and Vogel, P. J. (1962). Cerebral commissurotomy: A case report. *Bulletin of the Los Angeles Neurological Society, 27,* 169.

Boring, E. G. (1950). *A history of experimental psychology* (2d ed.). New York: Appleton-Century-Crofts.

Bradley, C. (1937). The behavior of children receiving benzedrine. *American Journal of Psychiatry, 94,* 577–585.

Brain, R. (1961). *Speech disorders.* London: Butterworths.

Braitman, L. E., Adlin, E. V., and Stanton, J. L., Jr. (1985). Obesity and caloric intake: The national health and nutrition examination survey of 1971–1975. *Journal of Chronic Diseases, 38,* 727–732.

Brazeau, P. (1975). Oxytocics. In L. S. Goodman and A. Gilman (Eds.), *The pharmacological basis of therapeutics* (5th ed., pp. 867–880). New York: Macmillan.

Bremer, F. (1936). Nouvelles recherches sur le mécanisme du sommeil. *Comptes Rendus des Séances de la Société de Biologie et de Ses Filiales, 122,* 460–464.

Broca, P. (1861). Remarques sur le siège de la faculté du langage articulé. *Bulletin of the Society of Anatomy, Paris* (Ser. 2), *6,* 330–357.

Brodmann, K. (1909). *Vergleichende Lokalisationslehre der Grosshirnrinde.* Leipzig: Barth.

Brody, H. (1955). Organization of the cerebral cortex III. A study of aging in the human cerebral cortex. *Journal of Comparative Neurology, 102,* 511–556.

Brown, S., and Schaefer, E. A. (1888). An investigation into the functions of the occipital and temporal lobes of the monkey's brain. *Philosophical Transactions of the Royal Society of London. Series B: Biological Sciences, 179,* 303–327.

Bruce, C., Desimone, R., and Gross, C. G. (1981). Visual properties of neurons in a polysensory area in superior temporal sulcus of the macaque. *Journal of neurophysiology, 46,* 369–384.

Bruch, H. (1973). *Eating disorders: Obesity, anorexia nervosa, and the person within.* New York: Basic Books.

Brust, J. C. M. (1981). Stroke: Diagnostic, anatomical and physiological considerations. In E. R. Kandel and J. H. Schwartz (Eds.), *Principles of neural science* (pp. 667–679). New York: Elsevier.

Buell, S. J., and Coleman, P. D. (1979). Dendritic growth in the aged human brain and failure of growth in senile dementia. *Science, 206,* 854–856.

Bunney, W. E., Jr., and Davis, J. M. (1965). Norepinephrine in depressive reactions. *Archives of General Psychiatry, 13,* 483–494.

Buss, A. H., and Durkee, A. (1957). An inventory for assessing different kinds of hostility. *Journal of Consulting Psychology, 21,* 343–349.

Butters, N., and Cermak, L. S. (1980). *Alcoholic Korsakoff's syndrome: An information processing approach to amnesia.* New York: Academic Press.

Byck, R. (1975). Drugs and the treatment of psychiatric disorders. In L. S. Goodman and A. Gilman (Eds.), *The pharmacological basis of therapeutics* (5th ed., pp. 152–200). New York: Macmillan.

Cabanac, M. (1971). Physiological role of pleasure. *Science, 173,* 1103–1107.

Campbell, F. W. (1974). The transmission of spatial information through the visual system. In F. O. Schmitt and F. G. Worden (Eds.), *The neurosciences third study program* (pp. 95–103). Cambridge, MA: MIT Press.

Campbell, F. W., and Robson, J. G. (1968). Application of Fourier analysis to the visibility of gratings. *Journal of Physiology, 197,* 551–566.

Campenot, R. B. (1977). Local control of neurite development by nerve growth factor. *Proceedings of the National Academy of Sciences of the United States of America, 74,* 4516–4519.

Cannon, W. B. (1919). The physiological basis of thirst. *Proceedings of the Royal Society of London. Series B: Biological Sciences, 90,* 283–301.

Cannon, W. B. (1927). The James–Lange theory of emotions: A critical examination and an alternative theory. *American Journal of Psychology, 39,* 106–124.

Cannon, W. B., and Washburn, A. L. (1912). An explanation of hunger. *American Journal of Physiology, 29,* 441–454.

Caporael, L. R. (1976). Ergotism: The Satan loosed in Salem? *Science, 192,* 21–26.

Carew, T. J. (1981). Spinal cord II: Reflex action. In E. R. Kandel and J. H. Schwartz (Eds.), *Principles of neural science* (pp. 293–304). New York: Elsevier.

Carew, T. J., Hawkins, R. D., and Kandel, E. R. (1983). Differential classical conditioning of a defensive withdrawal reflex in *Aplysia californica. Science, 219,* 397–400.

Carlson, N. R. (1986). *Physiology of behavior* (3d ed.). Boston: Allyn and Bacon.

Casey, K. L. (1982). Neural mechanisms in pain and analgesia: An overview. In A. L. Beckman (Ed.) , *The neural basis of behavior* (pp. 273–283). Jamaica, NY: Spectrum.

Cecil, M. (1956, December). Through the looking glass. *Encounter,* pp. 18–29.

Chi, J. G., Dooling, E. C., and Gilles, F. H. (1977). Left–right asymmetries of the temporal speech areas of the human fetus. *Archives of Neurology, 34,* 346–348.

Cohen, N. J., Eichenbaum, H., Deacedo, B. S., and Corkin, S. (1985). Different memory systems underlying acquisition of procedural and declarative knowledge. *Annals of the New York Academy of Sciences, 444,* 54–71.

Colangelo, W., and Jones, D. G. (1982). The fetal alcohol syndrome: A review and assessment of the syndrome and its neurological sequelae. *Progress in Neurobiology, 19,* 271–314.

Cooper, J. R., Bloom, F. E., and Roth, R. H. (1986). *The biochemical basis of neuropharmacology* (5th ed.). New York: Oxford University Press.

Corkin, S. (1981). Acetylcholine, aging and Alzheimer's disease. Implications for treatment. *Trends in Neurosciences, 4,* 287–290.

Corkin, S. (1984). Lasting consequences of bilateral medial temporal lobectomy: Clinical course and experimental findings in H. M. *Seminars in Neurology, 4,* 249–259.

Côté, L. (1981a). Aging of the brain and dementia. In E. R. Kandel and J. H. Schwartz (Eds.), *Principles of neural science* (pp. 547–556). New York: Elsevier.

Côté, L. (1981b). Basal ganglia, the extrapyramidal motor system, and diseases of transmitter metabolism. In E. R. Kandel and J. H. Schwartz (Eds.), *Principles of neural science* (pp. 347–357). New York: Elsevier.

Cotman, C. W., and Lynch, G. S. (1976). Reactive synaptogenesis in the adult nervous system: The effects of partial deafferentation on new synapse formation. In S. Barondes (Ed.) , *Neuronal recognition* (pp. 69–108). New York: Plenum.

Cotman, C. W., and McGaugh, J. L. (1980). *Behavioral neuroscience.* Orlando, FL: Academic Press.

Cotman, C. W., and Nadler, J. V. (1978). Reactive synaptogenesis in the hippocampus. In C. W. Cotman (Ed.) , *Neuronal Plasticity* (pp. 227–272). New York: Raven Press.

Cowan, W. M. (1979a). The development of the brain. *Scientific American, 241,* 112–133.

Cowan, W. M. (1979b). Selection and control in neurogenesis. In F. E. Schmitt and F. G. Worden (Eds.), *The neurosciences fourth study program* (pp. 59–79). Cambridge, MA: MIT Press.

Cowan, W. M., Fawcett, J. W., O'Leary, D. D. M., and Stanfield, B. B. (1984). Regressive events in neurogenesis. *Science, 225,* 1258–1270.

Coyle, J. T., Price, D. L., and DeLong, M. R. (1983). Alzheimer's disease: A disorder of cortical cholinergic innervation. *Science, 219,* 1184–1190.

Creese, I. (1983). Classical and atypical antipsychotic drugs: New insights. *Trends in Neurosciences, 6,* 479–481.

Crook, T. (1985). Clinical drug trials in Alzheimer's disease. In D. S. Olton, E. Gamzu, and S. Corkin (Eds.), *Memory dysfunctions: An integration of animal and human research from preclinical and clinical perspectives* (pp. 428–436). New York: New York Academy of Sciences.

Crosson, B. (1984). Role of the dominant thalamus in language: A review. *Psychological Bulletin, 96,* 491–517.

Custance, J. (1952). *Wisdom, madness, and folly; the philosophy of a lunatic.* New York: Pellegrini and Cudahy.

Damasio, A. R. (1983). Pure alexia. *Trends in Neurosciences, 6,* 93–96.

Damasio, A. R. (1985). Prosopagnosia. *Trends in Neurosciences, 7,* 132–135.

Damasio, A. R., and Geschwind, N. (1984). The neural basis of language. *Annual Review of Neuroscience, 7,* 127–147.

Damassa, D. A., Smith, E. R., Tennent, B., and Davidson, J. M. (1977). The relationship between circulating testosterone levels and sexual behavior. *Hormones and Behavior, 8,* 275–286.

D'Amato, R. J., Lipman, Z. P., and Snyder, S. H. (1986). Selectivity to the Parkinsonian neurotoxin MPTP: Toxic metabolite MPP$^+$ binds to neuromelanin. *Science, 231,* 987–989.

Darwin, C. (1965). *The expression of the emotions in man and animals.* Chicago: The University of Chicago Press. (Original work published in 1872.)

Das, G. D., and Altman J. (1971). Transplanted precursors of nerve cells: Their fate in the cerebellums of young rats. *Science, 173,* 637–638.

Davidson, J. M. (1980). Hormones and sexual behavior in the male. In D. T. Krieger and J. C. Hughes (Eds.), *Neuroendocrinology* (pp. 232–238). Sunderland, MA: Sinauer.

Davidson, J. M., Kwan, M., and Greenleaf, W. J. (1982). Hormonal replacement and sexuality in men. *Clinics in Endocrinology and Metabolism, 11,* 599–623.

Dax, M. (1836). *Lésions de la moitié gauche de l'encephale coincident avec l'oubli des signes de la pensée.* Montpellier, France: Montpellier Presse.

Delgado, J. M. R., Roberts, W. W., and Miller, N. E. (1954). Learning motivated by electrical stimulation of the brain. *American Journal of Physiology, 179,* 587–593.

DeLong, G. R., and Sidman, R. L. (1970). Alignment defect of reaggregating cells in cultures of developing brains of reeler mutant mice. *Developmental Biology, 22,* 584–599.

Dement, W. C. (1974). *Some must watch while some must sleep.* New York: W. H. Freeman.

Dement, W. C., and Kleitman, N. (1955). Incidence of eye motility during sleep in relation to varying EEG pattern. *Federation Proceedings, 14,* 216.

Dennis, W. (Ed.) . (1948). *Readings in the history of psychology.* East Norwalk, CT: Appleton-Century-Crofts.

Der Heydt, R. von, Peterhaus, E., and Baumgartner, G. (1984). Illusory contours and cortical neuron responses. *Science, 224,* 1260–1262.

De Valois, R. L., and De Valois, K. K. (1975). Neural coding of color. In E. C.

Carterette and M. P. Friedman (Eds.), *Handbook of perception: Seeing* (Vol. 5, pp. 117–166). Orlando, FL: Academic Press.

De Valois, R. L., and De Valois, K. K. (1980). Spatial vision. *Annual Review of Psychology, 31,* 309–341.

De Valois, R. L., and Jacobs, G. H. (1968). Primate color vision. *Science, 162,* 533–540.

De Valois, R., Morgan, H., and Snodderly, D. (1974). Psychophysical studies of monkey vision. III. Spatial luminance contrast sensitivity tests of macaque and human observers. *Vision Research, 14,* 75–81.

Doty, R. L., Shaman, P., Applebaum, S. L., Giberson, R., Sikorski, L., and Rosenberg, L. (1984). Smell identification ability: Changes with age. *Science, 226,* 1441–1443.

Doty, R. W. (1951). Influence of stimulus patterns on reflex deglutition. *American Journal of Physiology, 166,* 142–158.

Doty, R. W., and Bosma, J. F. (1956). An electromyographic analysis of reflex deglutition. *Journal of Neurophysiology, 19,* 44–60.

Douglas, V. I. (1983). Attentional and cognitive problems. In M. Rutter (Ed.) , *Developmental neuropsychiatry* (pp. 280–329). New York: Guilford.

Dowling, J. E. (1979). Information processing by local circuits: The vertebrate retina as a model system. In F. O. Schmitt and F. G. Worden (Eds.), *The neuroscience fourth study program* (pp. 163–179). Cambridge, MA: MIT Press.

Dowling, J. E., and Boycott, B. B. (1966). Organization of the primate retina: Electron microscopy. *Proceedings of the Royal Society of London. Series B: Biological Sciences, 166,* 80–111.

Duggan J. P., and Booth, D. A. (1986). Obesity, overeating, and rapid gastric emptying in rats with ventromedial hypothalamic lesions. *Science, 231,* 609–611.

Dunnett, S. B. Toniolo, G., Fine, A., Ryan, C. N., Björklund, A., and Iversen, S. D. (1985). Transplantation of embryonic ventral forebrain neurons to the neocortex of rats with lesions of nucleus basalis magnocellularis II. Sensorimotor and learning impairments. *Neuroscience, 16:*787–797.

Eaton, G. G., Goy, R. W., and Phoenix, C. H. (1973). Effects of testosterone treatment in adulthood on sexual behavior of female pseudohermaphrodite rhesus monkeys. *Nature, 242,* 119–120.

Eayrs, J. T. (1964). Endocrine influence on cerebral development. *Archives of Biology, 75,* 529–565.

Ehrhardt, A. A., and Meyer-Bahlburg, H. F. L. (1981). Effects of prenatal sex hormones on gender-related behavior. *Science, 211,* 1312–1318.

Ekman, P., and Oster, H. (1979). Facial expressions of emotions. In M. R. Rosenzweig and L. W. Porter (Eds.), *Annual review of psychology* (pp. 527–554). Palo Alto: Annual Reviews.

Enroth-Cugell, C., and Robson, J. G. (1966). The contrast sensitivity of retinal ganglion cells of the cat. *Journal of Physiology, 187,* 517–552.

Epstein, A. N. (1971). The lateral hypothalamic syndrome: Its implications for the physiological psychology of hunger and thirst. In E. Stellar and J. M. Sprague (Eds.), *Progress in physiological psychology* (Vol. 4, pp. 263–317). Orlando, FL: Academic Press.

Epstein, A. N., Fitzsimons, J. T., and Rolls, B. J. (1970). Drinking induced by injection of angiotensin into the brain of the rat. *Journal of Physiology, 210,* 474.

Epstein, A. N., Kissileff, H. R., and Stellar, E. (Eds.) (1973). *The neuropsychology of thirst.* Washington, DC: V. H. Winston.

Erickson, R. P., Covey, E., and Doetsch, G. S. (1980). Neuron and stimulus typologies in the rat gustatory system. *Brain Research, 196,* 513–519.

Evans, E. F. (1982a). Basic physics and psychophysics of sound. In H. B. Barlow and J. D. Mollen (Eds.), *The senses* (pp. 239–250). Cambridge, England: Cambridge University Press.

Evans, E. F. (1982b). Functional anatomy of the auditory system. In H. B. Barlow and J. D. Mollen (Eds.), *The senses* (pp. 251–306). Cambridge, England: Cambridge University Press.

Evarts, E. V. (1979). Brain mechanisms of movement. *Scientific American, 241,* 164–179.

Feder, H. H. (1981a). Hormonal actions on the sexual differentiation of the genitalia and the gonadotropin-regulating systems. In N. T. Adler (Ed.) , *Neuroendocrinology of reproduction* (pp. 89–126). New York: Plenum.

Feder, H. H. (1981b). Perinatal hormones and their role in the development of sexually dimorphic behaviors. In N. T. Adler (Ed.) , *Neuroendocrinology of reproduction* (pp. 127–157). New York: Plenum.

Feder, H. H. (1984). Hormones and sexual behavior. *Annual Review of Psychology, 35,* 165–200.

Fein, D., Skoff, B., and Mirsky, A. F. (1981). Clinical correlates of brainstem dysfunction in autistic children. *Journal of Autism and Developmental Disorders, 11,* 303–315.

Fein, D., Humes, M., Kaplan, E., Lucci, D., and Waterhouse, L. (1984). The question of left hemisphere dysfunction in infantile autism. *Psychological Bulletin, 95,* 258–281.

Fessler, R. G., Brown, F. D., Rachlin, J. R., Mullan, S., and Fang, V. S. (1984). Elevated β-endorphin in cerebrospinal fluid after electrical brain stimulation: Artifact of contrast infusion? *Science, 224,* 1017–1019.

Fitzsimons, J. T. (1971). The physiology of thirst: A review of the extraneural aspects of the mechanisms of drinking. In E. Stellar and J. M. Sprague (Eds.), *Progress in physiological psychology* (Vol. 4, pp. 119–201). Orlando, FL: Academic Press.

Foulkes, W. D. (1962). Dream reports from different stages of sleep. *Journal of Abnormal and Social Psychology, 65,* 14–25.

Foulkes, W. D. (1966). *The psychology of sleep.* New York: Scribner's.

Frederickson, R. C. A., and Geary, L. E. (1982). Endogenous opioid peptides: Review of physiological, pharmacological and clinical aspects. *Progress in Neurobiology, 19,* 19–69.

Freeman, W., and Watts, J. W. (1950). *Human psychosurgery* (2d ed.). Springfield, IL: Charles C Thomas.

Friedman, M. I., and Stricker, E. M. (1976). The physiological psychology of hunger: A physiological perspective. *Psychological Review, 83,* 409–431.

Gage, F. H., and Björklund, A. (1986). Cholinergic septal grafts into the hippocampal formation improve spatial learning and memory in aged rats by an atropine-sensitive mechanism. *J. Neuroscience, 6:*2837–2847.

Galaburda, A. M., and Kemper, T. L. (1979). Cytoarchitectonic abnormalities in developmental dyslexia: A case study. *Annals of Neurology, 6,* 94–100.

Gallistel, C. R., Shizgal, P., and Yeomans, J. S. (1981). A portrait of the substrate for self-stimulation. *Psychological Review, 88,* 228–273.

Ganong, W. F. (1977). *The nervous system.* Los Altos, CA: Lange Medical Publications.

Garcia, J., Hankins, W. G., and Rusiniak, K. W. (1974). Behavioral regulation of the milieu interne in man and rat. *Science, 185,* 824–831.

Garfield, E. (1983a). What do we know about the group of mental disorders called schizophrenia? Part 1: Etiology. *Current Contents, 25,* 5–13.

Garfield, E. (1983b). What do we know about the group of mental disorders called schizophrenia? Part 2: Diagnosis and treatment. *Current Contents, 27,* 5–16.

Garfield, E. (1984). Anorexia nervosa: The enigma of self-starvation. *Current Contents: Life Sciences*, pp. 3–13.

Garner, D. M., Garfinkel, P. E., Schwartz, D., and Thompson, M. (1980). Cultural expectations of thinness in women. *Psychological Reports, 47*, 483–491.

Gash, D. M., Collier, T. J., and Sladek, J. R., Jr. (1985). Neural transplantation: A review of recent developments and potential applications to the aged brain. *Neurobiology of aging, 6*, 131–150.

Gaze, R. M. (1970). *The formation of nerve connections*. Orlando, FL: Academic Press.

Gazzaniga, M. S. (1967). The split brain in man. *Scientific American, 217*, 24–29.

Gazzaniga, M. S. (1983a). Reply to Levy and to Zaidel. *American Psychologist, 38*, 547–549.

Gazzaniga, M. S. (1983b). Right hemisphere language following brain bisection. *American Psychologist, 38*, 525–537.

Gazzaniga, M. S., and Le Doux, J. E. (1978). *The integrated mind*. New York: Plenum.

Gazzaniga, M. S., and Sperry, R. W. (1967). Language after section of the cerebral hemispheres. *Brain, 90*, 131–148.

Geffen, G., and Quinn, K. (1984). Hemispheric specializations and ear advantages in processing speech. *Psychological Bulletin, 96*, 273–291.

Gelfand, S. A. (1981). *Hearing*. New York: Marcel Dekker.

Geschwind, N. (1965a). Disconnexion syndromes in animals and man: Part 1. *Brain, 88*, 237–294.

Geschwind, N. (1965b). Disconnexion syndromes in animals and man: Part 2. *Brain, 88*, 585–644.

Geschwind, N. (1975). The apraxias: Neural mechanisms of disorders of learned movement. *American Scientist, 63*, 188–195.

Geschwind, N., and Galaburda, A. M. (Eds.) (1984). *Cerebral dominance: The biological foundations*. Cambridge, MA: Harvard University Press.

Geschwind, N., and Galaburda, A. M. (1985). Cerebral lateralization. Biological mechanisms, associations, and pathology. I. A hypothesis and a program for research. *Archives of Neurology, 42*, 428–459.

Geschwind, N., and Levitsky, W. (1968). Human brain: Left–right asymmetries in temporal speech region. *Science, 161*, 186–187.

Gessa, G. L., Paglietti, E., and Pellegrini Quarantotti, B. (1979). Induction of copulatory behavior in sexually inactive rats by naloxone. *Science, 204*, 203–205.

Ghez, C., and Fahn, S. (1981). The cerebellum. In E. R. Kandel and J. H. Schwartz (Eds.), *Principles of neural science* (pp. 334–346). New York: Elsevier.

Gillin, J. C., and Borbely, A. A. (1985). Sleep: A neurobiological window on affective disorders. *Trends in Neurosciences, 8*, 537–542.

Glaser, J. H., Rubin, B. S., and Barfield, R. J. (1983). Onset of the receptive and proceptive components of feminine sexual behavior in rats following the intravenous administration of progesterone. *Hormones and Behavior, 17*, 18–27.

Gluhbegovic, N., and Williams, T. H. (1980). *The human brain: A photographic atlas*. New York: Harper & Row.

Goldberg, M. E., and Wurtz, R. H. (1972). Activity of superior colliculus in behaving monkey. II. Effect of attention on neuronal responses. *Journal of Neurophysiology, 35*, 560–574.

Goldfoot, D. A., Krevetz, M. A., Goy, R. W., and Freeman, S. K. (1976). Lack of effect of vaginal lavages and aliphatic acids on ejaculatory responses in rhesus monkeys: Behavioral and chemical analyses. *Hormones and Behavior, 7*, 1–28.

Goldman, S. A., and Nottebohm, F. (1983). Neuronal production, migration, and differentiation in a vocal control nucleus of the adult female canary brain. *Proceedings of the National Academy of Sciences of the United States of America, 80*, 2390–2394.

Goldstein, E. B. (1984). *Sensation and perception* (2d ed.). Belmont, CA: Wadsworth.

Goodman, H. M. (1974). The pituitary gland. In V. B. Mountcastle (Ed.) , *Medical physiology* (13th ed., Vol. 2, pp. 1609–1631). St. Louis: C. V. Mosby.

Gorski, R. A., and Barraclough, C. A. (1963). Effects of low dosages of androgen on the differentiation of hypothalamic regulatory control of ovulation in the rat. *Endocrinology, 73,* 210–216.

Gorski, R. A., Gordon, J. H., Shryne, J. E., and Southam, A. M. (1978). Evidence for a morphological sex difference within the medial preoptic area of the rat brain. *Brain Research, 148,* 333–346.

Gorski, R. A., and Wagner, J. W. (1965). Gonadal activity and sexual differentiation of the hypothalamus. *Endocrinology, 76,* 226–239.

Gouras, P. (1981). Visual system. IV: Color vision. In E. R. Kandel and J. H. Schwartz (Eds.), *Principles of neural science* (pp. 249–257). New York: Elsevier.

Goy, R. W. (1970). Experimental control of psychosexuality. *Philosophical Transactions of the Royal Society of London. Series B: Biological Sciences, 259,* 149–162.

Green, D. M. (1976). *An introduction to hearing.* Hillsdale, NJ: Lawrence Erlbaum.

Greenough, W. T. (1975). Experiential modification of the developing brain. *American Scientist, 63,* 37–46.

Greenough, W. T., Carter, C. S., Steerman, C., and De Voogd, T. J. (1977). Sex differences in dendritic patterns in hamster preoptic area. *Brain Research, 126,* 63–72.

Grings, W. W., and Dawson, M. E. (1978). *Emotions and bodily responses. A psychophysiological approach.* Orlando, FL: Academic Press.

Gross, C. G., Rocha-Miranda, C. E., and Bender, D. B. (1972). Visual properties of neurons of inferotemporal cortex of the macaque. *Journal of Neurophysiology, 35,* 96–111.

Grossman, S. P. (1967). *A textbook of physiological psychology.* New York: Wiley.

Grossman, S. P., Dacey, D., Halaris, A. E., Collier, T., and Routtenberg, A. (1978). Aphagia and adipsia after preferential destruction of nerve cell bodies in hypothalamus. *Science, 202,* 537–539.

Groves, P. M., and Schlesinger, K. (1982). *Biological psychology.* Dubuque, IA: W. C. Brown.

Growdon, J. H., and Corkin, S. (1980). Neurochemical approaches to the treatment of senile dementia. In J. O. Cole and J. E. Barrett (Eds.), *Psychopathology in the aged* (pp. 281–294). New York: Raven Press.

Guillemin, R. (1980). Hypothalamic hormones: Releasing and inhibiting factors. In D. T. Krieger and J. C. Hughes (Eds.), *Neuroendocrinology* (pp. 23–32). Sunderland, MA: Sinauer.

Gulevich, G., Dement, W. C., and Johnson, L. (1966). Psychiatric and EEG observations on a case of prolonged (264 hours) wakefulness. *Archives of General Psychiatry, 15,* 29–35.

Gustavson, C., Garcia, J., Hankins, W., and Rusiniak, K. (1974). Coyote predation control by aversive conditioning. *Science, 184,* 581–583.

Gustavson, C. R., and Gustavson, J. C. (1985). Predation control using conditioned food aversion methodology: Theory, practice, and implications. In N. S. Braveman and P. Bronstein (Eds.), *Experimental assessments and clinical applications of conditioned food aversion* (pp. 348–356). New York: New York Academy of Sciences.

Hamilton, C. R. (1977). An assessment of hemispheric specialization in monkeys. In S. Dimond and D. Blizzard (Eds.), *Evolution and lateralization of the brain* (pp. 222–232). New York: New York Academy of Sciences.

Harlow, J. M. (1868). Recovery from the passage of an iron bar through the head. *Publications of the Massachusetts Medical Society (Boston), 2,* 327–346.

Harris, G. W. (1955). *The neural control of the pituitary gland.* Baltimore: Williams and Wilkins.

Harris, G. W., and Jacobsohn, D. (1952). Functional grafts of the anterior pituitary gland. *Proceedings of the Royal Society of London. Series B: Biological Sciences, 139,* 263–276.

Harris, G. W., and Levine, S. (1962). Sexual differentiation of the brain and its experimental control. *Journal of Physiology, 163,* 42–44.

Hawkins, R. D., Abrams, T. W., Carew, T. J., and Kandel, E. R. (1983). A cellular mechanism of classical conditioning in Aplysia: Activity-dependent amplification of presynaptic facilitation. *Science, 219,* 400–405.

Hebb, D. O. (1949). *The organization of behavior.* New York: Wiley.

Heffner, H. E., and Heffner, R. S. (1984). Temporal lobe lesions and perception of species-specific vocalizations by macaques. *Science, 226,* 75–76.

Henry, J. L. (1982). Circulating opioids: Possible physiological roles in central nervous function. *Neuroscience and Biobehavioral Reviews, 6,* 229–245.

Hetherington, A. W., and Ranson, S. W. (1942). The spontaneous activity and food intake of rats with hypothalamic lesions. *American Journal of Physiology, 136,* 609–617.

Hill, R. G. (1981). The status of naloxone in the identification of pain control mechanisms operated by endogenous opioids. *Neuroscience Letters, 21,* 217–222.

Hirsch, H. V. B., and Spinelli, D. N. (1971). Modification of the distribution of field orientation in cats by selective visual exposure during development. *Experimental Brain Research, 12,* 509–527.

Hirsch, J. (1984). Hypothalamic control of appetite. *Hospital Practice, 19*(2), 131–138.

Hobson, J. A., and McCarley, R. W. (1977). The brain as a dream state generator: An activation-synthesis hypothesis of the dream process. *American Journal of Psychiatry, 134,* 1335–1348.

Hodgkin, A. L. (1964). *The conduction of the nerve impulse.* Liverpool: Liverpool University Press.

Hodgkin, A. L., and Huxley, A. F. (1952). A quantitative description of membrane current and its application to conduction and excitation in nerves. *Journal of Physiology, 117,* 500–544.

Hosobuchi, Y., Adams, J. E., and Linchitz, R. (1977). Pain relief by electrical stimulation of the central gray matter in humans and its reversal by naloxone. *Science, 197,* 183–186.

Hounsfield, G., Ambrose, J., Perry, J., and Bridges, C. (1973). Computerized transverse axial scanning. *British Journal of Radiology, 46,* 1016–1051.

Hoyt, M. (1975, February 5). Noise: how to muffle it. *Christian Science Monitor,* p. 4.

Hrushesky, W. J. M. (1985). Circadian timing of cancer chemotherapy. *Science, 228,* 73–75.

Hubel, D. H. (1967). Effects of distortion of sensory input on the visual system of kittens. *The Physiologist, 10,* 17–45.

Hubel, D. H. (1982). Exploration of the primary visual cortex. *Nature, 299,* 515–524.

Hubel, D. H., and Wiesel, T. N. (1962). Receptive fields, binocular interaction, and functional architecture in the cat's visual cortex. *Journal of Physiology, 160,* 106–154.

Hubel, D. H., and Wiesel, T. N. (1963). Receptive fields of cells in striate cortex of very young, visually inexperienced kittens. *Journal of Neurophysiology, 26,* 944–1002.

Hubel, D. H., and Wiesel, T. N. (1965a). Binocular interaction in striate cortex of kittens reared with artificial squint. *Journal of Neurophysiology, 28,* 1041–1059.

Hubel, D. H., and Wiesel, T. N. (1965b). Receptive fields and functional architecture in two non-striate visual areas (18 and 19) of the cat. *Journal of Neurophysiology, 28,* 229–289.

Hubel, D. H., and Wiesel, T. N. (1977). Ferrier lecture: Functional architecture of macaque monkey visual cortex. *Proceedings of the Royal Society of London, Series B: Biological Sciences, 198,* 1–59.

Hubel, D. H., and Wiesel, T. N. (1979). Brain mechanisms of vision. *Scientific American, 241,* 150–162.

Hudspeth, A. J. (1983). The hair cells of the inner ear. *Scientific American, 248,* 42–52.

Hughes, J. (1975). Isolation of an endogenous compound from the brain with pharmacological properties similar to morphine. *Brain Research, 88,* 293–308.

Hughes, J., Smith, T. W., Kosterlitz, H. W., Fothergill, L. A., Morgan, B. A., and Morris, H. R. (1975). Identification of two related pentapeptides from the brain with potent opiate agonist activity. *Nature, 258,* 577–579.

Imperato-McGinley, J., Guerrero, L., Gautier, T., and Peterson, R. E. (1974). Steroid 5 alpha-reductase deficiency in man: An inherited form of male pseudohermaphroditism. *Science, 186,* 1213–1215.

Imperato-McGinley, J., Peterson, R. E., Stoller, R. and Goodwin, W. E. (1979). Male pseudohermaphroditism secondary to 17β-Hydroxysteroid dehydrogenase deficiency: Gender role change with puberty. *Journal of Clinical Endocrinology and Metabolism, 49,* 391–395.

Ito, M. (1970). Neurophysiological aspects of the cerebellar motor control system. *International Journal of Neurology, 7,* 162–176.

Iversen, L. L. (1979). The chemistry of the brain. *Scientific American, 241,* 134–149.

Izard, C. E. (1977). *Human emotions.* New York: Plenum.

Jacobson, M. (1978). *Developmental neurobiology* (2d ed.). New York: Holt, Rinehart and Winston.

Jaffe, J. H. and Martin, W. R. (1975). Narcotic analgesics and antagonists. In L. S. Goodman and A. Gilman (Eds.), *The pharmacological basis of therapeutics* (5th ed., pp. 245–283). New York: Macmillan.

James, W. (1884). What is an emotion? *Mind, 9,* 188–205.

James, W. (1890). *Principles of psychology.* New York: Holt.

James, W. (1894). The physical basis of emotion. *Psychological Review, 1,* 516–529.

Janal, M. N., Colt, E. W. D., Clark, W. C., and Glusman, M. (1984). Pain sensitivity, mood and plasma endocrine levels in man following long-distance running: Effects of naloxone. *Pain, 19,* 13–25.

Jasper, H. H., and Sourkes, T. L. (1983). Nobel laureates in neuroscience: 1904–1981. *Annual Review of Neuroscience, 6,* 1–42.

Jemmott, J. B., and Locke, S. E. (1984). Psychosocial factors, immunologic mediation, and human susceptibility to infectious diseases: How much do we know? *Psychological Bulletin, 95,* 78–108.

Jensen, E. V., and DeSombre, E. R. (1973). Estrogen–receptor interaction. *Science, 182,* 126–134.

Johnson, W. G., and Wildman, H. E. (1983). Influence of external and covert food stimuli on insulin secretion in obese and normal persons. *Behavioral Neuroscience, 97,* 1025–1028.

Jones, K. L., and Smith, D. W. (1973). Recognition of the fetal alcohol syndrome in early infancy. *Lancet, 2,* 999–1001.

Jouvet, M. (1967). The states of sleep. *Scientific American, 216,* 62–72.

Jouvet, M. (1974). Monoaminergic regulation of the sleep–waking cycle in the cat. In F. O. Schmitt and F. G. Worden (Eds.), *The neurosciences: Third study program* (pp. 499–508). Cambridge, MA: MIT Press.

Jung, R. (1984). Sensory research in historical perspective: Some philosophical foundations of perception. In J. M. Brookhart and V. B. Mountcastle (Eds.), *Handbook of physiology, Section 1: The nervous system* (Vol. 3, pt. 1, pp. 1–74). Bethesda, MD: American Physiological Society.

Kaas, J. H., Nelson, R. J. Sur, M., and Merzenich, M. M. (1981). Organization of somatosensory cortex in primates. In F. O. Schmitt, F. G. Worden, G. Adelman, and S. G. Dennis (Eds.), *The organization of the cerebral cortex* 237–261). Cambridge, MA: MIT Press.

Kalat, J. W. (1984). *Biological psychology* (2d ed.). Belmont, CA: Wadsworth.

Kandel, E. R., and Schwartz, J. H. (Eds.) (1981). *Principles of neural science.* New York: Elsevier.

Kandel, E. R., and Schwartz, J. H. (1982). Molecular biology of learning: Modulation of transmitter release. *Science, 218,* 433–443.

Kanner, L. (1943). Autistic disturbances of affective contact. *Nervous Child, 2,* 217–250.

Katsuki, Y. (1961). Neural mechanism of auditory sensation in cats. In W. A. Rosenblith (Ed.), *Sensory Communication* (pp. 561–583). Cambridge, MA: MIT Press.

Katsuki, Y., Norgren, R., and Sato, M. (1981). *Brain mechanisms of sensation.* New York: Wiley.

Keesey, R. E., Boyle, P. C., Kemnitz, J. W., and Mitchel, J. S. (1976). The role of the lateral hypothalamus in determining the body weight set point. In D. Novin, W. Wyrwicka, and G. A. Bray (Eds.), *Hunger: Basic mechanisms and clinical implications* (pp. 243–255). New York: Raven Press.

Keesey, R. E., and Powley, T. L. (1975). Hypothalamic regulation of body weight. *American Scientist, 63,* 558–565.

Kelly, D. D. (1981). Disorders of sleep and consciousness. In E. R. Kandel and J. H. Schwartz (Eds.), *Principles of neural science* (pp. 486–499). New York: Elsevier.

Kelly, J. P. (1981a). Auditory system. In E. R. Kandel and J. H. Schwartz (Eds.), *Principles of neural science* (pp. 258–268). New York: Elsevier.

Kelly, J. P. (1981b). Reactions of neurons to injury. In E. R. Kandel and J. H. Schwartz (Eds.), *Principles of neural science* (pp. 138–146). New York: Elsevier.

Kennedy, G. C. (1950). The hypothalamic control of food intake in rats. *Proceedings of the Royal Society of London. Series B: Biological Sciences, 137,* 535–548.

Kennedy, G. C. (1966). Food intake energy balance and growth. *British Medical Bulletin, 22,* 216–220.

Kertesz, A. (1979). Recovery and treatment. In K. M. Heilman and E. Valenstein (Eds.), *Clinical neuropsychology.* New York: Oxford University Press.

Keverne, E. B. (1982). Chemical senses: Smell. In H. B. Barlow and J. D. Mollen (Eds.), *The senses* (pp. 409–427). Cambridge, England: Cambridge University Press.

Khachaturian, H., Lewis, M. E., Schafer, M. K.-H., and Watson, S. J. (1985). Anatomy of the CNS opioid systems. *Trends in Neurosciences, 8,* 111–119.

Khanna, S. M. and Leonard, D. G. B. (1982). Basilar membrane tuning in the cat cochlea. *Science, 215,* 305–306.

Kiester, E., Jr. (1980). Images of the night. *Science 80, 1,* 36–43.

Kimble, D. P., BreMiller, R., and Stickrod. G. (1986). Fetal brain implants improve maze performance in hippocampal-lesioned rats. *Brain Research, 363,* 358–363.

Kimura, K., and Beidler, L. M. (1961). Microelectrode study of taste receptors of rat and hamster. *Journal of Cellular and Comparative Physiology, 58,* 131–139.

King, W. J. and Greene, G. L., (1984). Monoclonal antibodies localize oestrogen receptors in the nuclei of target cells. *Nature, 307,* 745–747.

Kinsbourne, M. (1975). The ontogeny of cerebral dominance. In D. Aaronson and R. W. Rieber (Eds.), *Developmental psycholinguistics and communication disorders* (pp. 244–250). New York: New York Academy of Sciences.

Kinsbourne, M., and Hiscock, M. (1983). The normal and deviant development of functional lateralization of the brain. In M. M. Haith and J. J. Campos (Eds.), P. H. Mussen (Series ed.), *Handbook of child psychology: Vol. II. Infancy and developmental psychobiology* (4th ed., pp. 157–280). New York: Wiley.

Kinsey, A. C., Pomeroy, W. B., and Martin, C. E. (1948). *Sexual behavior in the human male*. Philadelphia: W. B. Saunders.

Kinsey, A. C., Pomeroy, W. B., Martin, C. E., and Gebhard, P. H. (1953). *Sexual behavior in the human female*. Philadelphia: W. B. Saunders.

Kissileff, H. R., Pi-Sunyer, F. X., Thornton, J., and Smith, G. P. (1981). C-terminal octapeptide of cholecystokinin decreases food intake in man. *The American Journal of Clinical Nutrition, 34,* 154–160.

Kleinmuntz, B., and Szucko, J. J. (1984). Lie detection in ancient and modern times. A call for contemporary scientific study. *American Psychologist, 39,* 766–776.

Kluver, H., and Bucy, P. C. (1939). Preliminary analysis of functions of the temporal lobe in monkeys. *Archives of Neurology and Psychiatry, 42,* 979–1000.

Kolata, G. (1984). New neurons form in adulthood. *Science, 224,* 1325–1326.

Kolb, B., and Whishaw, I. Q. (1985). Fundamentals of human neuropsychology (2d ed.). New York: W. H. Freeman.

Kornhuber, H. H. (1974). Cerebral cortex, cerebellum, and basal ganglia: An introduction to their motor functions. In F. O. Schmitt and F. G. Worden (Eds.), *The neurosciences: Third study program* (pp. 267–280). Cambridge, MA: MIT Press.

Kuehn, R. E., and Beach, F. (1963). Quantitative measurement of sexual receptivity in female rats. *Behavior, 21,* 282–299.

Kuffler, S. W. (1953). Discharge patterns and functional organization of mammalian retina. *Journal of Neurophysiology, 16,* 37–68.

Kuffler, S. W., Nicholls, J. G., and Martin, A. R. (1984). *From neuron to brain* (2d ed.). Sunderland, MA: Sinauer.

Kurz, E. M., Sengelaub, D. R., and Arnold, A. P. (1986). Androgens regulate the dendritic length of mammalian motoneurons in adulthood. *Science, 232,* 395–398.

Lange, C. G. (1885). *Om Sindsbevaegelser*. Kjøbenhavn.

Langston, J. W., Ballard, P., Tetrud, J. W., and Irwin, I. (1983). Chronic Parkinsonism in humans due to a product of meperidine-analog synthesis. *Science, 219,* 979–980.

Lashley, K. S. (1950). In search of the engram. In *Society for experimental biology symposium. No. 4: Mechanisms in animal behaviour* (pp. 454–482). Cambridge, England: Cambridge University Press.

Le Douarin, N., Renaud, D., Teillet, M., and Le Dourin, G. (1975). Cholinergic differentiation of presumptive adrenergic neuroblasts in interspecific chimeras after heterotopic transplantation. *Proceedings of the National Academy of Sciences of the United States of America, 72,* 728–732.

Le Magnen, J. (1985). *Hunger,* Cambridge, England: Cambridge University Press.

Le May, M., and Geschwind, N. (1975). Hemispheric differences in the brains of great apes. *Brain, Behavior and Evolution, 11,* 48–52.

Le May, M., and Geschwind, N. (1978). Asymmetries of the human cerebral hemispheres. In A. Caramazza and E. B. Zurif (Eds.), *Language acquisition and language breakdown* (pp. 311–328). Baltimore: Johns Hopkins University Press.

LeVay, S., Wiesel, T. N., and Hubel, D. H. (1980). The development of ocular dominance columns in normal and visually deprived monkeys. *J. Comparative Neurology, 191,* 1–51.

Levi-Montalcini, R. (1966). The nerve growth factor: Its mode of action on sensory and sympathetic nerve cells. *Harvey Lectures, 60,* 217–259.

Levi-Montalcini, R., and Hamburger, V. (1951). Selective growth-stimulating effects of mouse sarcoma on the sensory and sympathetic nervous system of the chick embryo. *Journal of Experimental Zoology, 116,* 321–362.

Levine, J. D., Gordon, N. C., and Fields, H. L. (1979). Naloxone dose dependently produces analgesia and hyperalgesia in post-operative pain. *Nature, 278,* 740–741.

Levy-Agresti, J., and Sperry, R. W. (1968). Differential perceptual capacities in major and minor hemispheres. *Proceedings of the National Academy of Sciences of the United States of America, 61,* 1151.

Lewy, A. J., Kern, H. E., Rosenthal, N. E., and Wehr, T. A. (1982). Bright artificial light treatment of a manic-depressive patient with a seasonal mood cycle. *American Journal of Psychiatry, 139,* 1496–1498.

Lickey, M. E., and Gordon, B. (1983). *Drugs for mental illness.* New York: W. H. Freeman.

Lindsley, D. B., Schreiner, L. H., Knowles, M. S., and Magoun, H. W. (1950). Behavioral and EEG changes following chronic brainstem lesions in the cat. *Electroencephalography and Clinical Neurophysiology, 2,* 483–498.

Llinas, R. R. (1982). Calcium in synaptic transmission. *Scientific American, 247,* 38–47.

Logue, A. W. (1985). Conditioned food aversion learning in humans. In N. S. Braveman and P. Bronstein (Eds.), *Experimental assessments and clinical applications of conditioned food aversions* (pp. 316–329). New York: New York Academy of Sciences.

Lorenz, D. N., and Goldman, S. A. (1982). Vagal mediation of the cholecystokinin satiety effect in rats. *Physiology and Behavior, 29,* 599–604.

Lowenstein, W. R. (1971). Mechano-electric transduction in the Pacinian corpuscle. Initiation of sensory impulses in mechanoreceptors. In W. R. Lowenstein (Ed.) *Handbook of sensory physiology: Vol. 1. Principles of receptor physiology* (pp. 269–290). New York: Springer-Verlag.

Lund, R. D., and Hauschka, S. D. (1976). Transplanted neural tissue develops connections with host rat brain. *Science, 193,* 582–584.

Lykken, D. T. (1981). *A tremor in the blood: Uses and abuses of the lie detector.* New York: McGraw-Hill.

Lynch, G., and Baudry, M. (1984). The biochemistry of memory: A new and specific hypothesis. *Science, 224,* 1057–1063.

Macko, K. A., Jarvis, C. D., Kennedy, C., Miyaoka, M., Shinohara, M., Sokoloff, L., and Mishkin, M. (1982). Mapping the primate visual system with $[2-^{14}C]$ Deoxyglucose. *Science, 218,* 394–397.

Macsweeney, D. (1982). *The crazy ape.* London: Peter Owen.

Maddison, S., Wood, R. J., Rolls, E. T., Rolls, B. J., and Gibbs, J. (1980). Drinking in the rhesus monkey: peripheral factors. *Journal of Comparative and Physiological Psychology, 94,* 365–374.

Maffei, L., and Fiorentini, A. (1973). The visual cortex as a spatial frequency analyser. *Vision Research, 13,* 1255–1267.

Maier, S. F., Sherman, J. E., Lewis, J. W., Terman, G. W., and Liebeskind, J. C. (1983). The opioid/nonopioid nature of stress-induced analgesia and learned helplessness. *Journal of Experimental Psychology: Animal Behavior Processes, 9,* 80–90.

Mancillas, J. R., Siggins, G. R., and Bloom, F. E. (1986). Systemic ethanol: Selective enhancement of responses to acetylcholine and somatostatin in hippocampus. *Science, 231,* 161–163.

Marañon, G. (1924). Contribution à l'étude de l'action émotive de l'adrénaline. *Revue Française d'Endocrinologie, 2,* 301–325.

Mark, V. H., and Ervin, F. R. (1970). *Violence and the brain.* New York: Harper & Row.

Markoff, R. A., Ryan, P., and Young, T. (1982). Endorphins and mood changes in long-distance running. *Medicine and Science in Sports and Exercise, 14,* 11–15.

Marlowe, W. B., Mancall, E. L., and Thomas, J. J. (1975). Complete Klüver–Bucy syndrome in man. *Cortex, 11,* 53–59.

Marr, D. (1969). Theory of cerebellar cortex. *Journal of Physiology, 202,* 437–470.

Marr, D. (1980). *Vision.* New York: W. H. Freeman.

Marshall, G., and Zimbardo, P. G. (1979). Affective consequences of inadequately explained physiological arousal. *Journal of Personality and Social Psychology, 37,* 970–988.

Marx, J. L. (1985). The immune system "belongs in the body." *Science, 227,* 1190–1192.

Matossian, M. K. (1982). Ergot and the Salem witchcraft affair. *American Scientist, 70,* 355–357.

Mayer, D. J., Wolfe, T. L., Akil, H., Carder, B., and Liebeskind, J. C. (1971). Analgesia from electrical stimulation in the brainstem of the rat. *Science, 174,* 1351–1354.

Mayer, J. (1953). Glucostatic mechanisms of regulation of food intake. *New England Journal of Medicine, 249,* 13–16.

Mayer, J. (1955). Regulation of energy, intake and the body weight: The glucostatic theory and the lipostatic hypothesis. *Annals of the New York Academy of Sciences, 63,* 15–43.

McClurkin, J. W., and Marrocco, R. T. (1984). Visual cortical input alters spatial tuning in monkey lateral geniculate nucleus cells. *Journal of Physiology, 348,* 135–152.

McCormick, D. A., and Thompson, R. F. (1984). Cerebellum: Essential involvement in the classically conditioned eyelid response. *Science, 223,* 296–299.

McEwen, B. S. (1980). The brain as a target organ of endocrine hormones. In D. T. Krieger and J. C. Hughes (Eds.), *Neuroendocrinology* (pp. 33–43). Sunderland, MA: Sinauer.

McGaugh, J. L., and Hertz, M. J. (1972). *Memory consolidation.* San Francisco: Albion.

McNeal, E. T., and Cimbolic, P. (1986). Antidepressants and biochemical theories of depression. *Psychological Bulletin, 99,* 361–374.

McWilliams, J. R., and Lynch, G. (1983). Rate of synaptic replacement in denervated rat hippocampus declines precipitously from the juvenile period to adulthood. *Science, 221,* 572–574.

Meadows, J. C. (1974). Disturbed perception of colours associated with localized cerebral lesions. *Brain, 87,* 615–632.

Melzack, R. (1973). *The puzzle of pain.* New York: Basic Books.

Melzack, R., and Wall, P. D. (1965). Pain mechanisms: A new theory. *Science, 150,* 971–979.

Menaker, M., Takahashi, J. S., and Eskin, A. (1978). The physiology of circadian pacemakers. *Annual Review of Physiology, 40,* 501–526.

Meredith, M. A., and Stein, B. E. (1985). Descending efferents from the superior colliculus relay integrated multisensory information. *Science, 227,* 657–659.

Merzenich, M. M., and Harrington, T. (1969). The sense of flutter-vibration evoked by stimulation of the hairy skin of primates: Comparison of human sensory capacity with the responses of mechanoreceptive afferents innervating the hairy skin of monkeys. *Experimental Brain Research, 9,* 236–260.

Merzenich, M. M., and Kaas, J. H. (1980). Principles of organization of sensory-perceptual systems in mammals. In J. M. Sprague and A. N. Epstein (Eds.),

Progress in psychobiology and physiological psychology (Vol. 9, pp. 1–42). Orlando, FL: Academic Press.

Merzenich, M. M., Nelson, R. J., Stryker, M. P., Cynader, M. S., Schoppmann, A., and Zook, J. M. (1984). Somatosensory cortical map changes following digit amputation in adult monkeys. *Journal of Comparative Neurology, 224,* 591–605.

Michael, R. P., and Keverne, E. B. (1970). Primate sex pheromones of vaginal origin. *Nature, 225,* 84–85.

Milner, B. (1966). Amnesia following operation on the temporal lobes. In C. W. M. Whitty and O. L. Zangwill (Eds.), *Amnesia* (pp. 109–133). London: Buttersworths.

Milner, B. (1967). Brain mechanisms suggested by studies of temporal lobes. In F. L. Darley (Ed.) , *Brain mechanisms underlying speech and language* (pp. 122–145). New York: Grune & Stratton.

Milner, B. (1970). Memory and medial temporal regions of the brain. In K. H. Pribram and D. E. Broadbent (Eds.), *Biology of memory* (pp. 29–50). Orlando, FL: Academic Press.

Milner, B. (1974). Hemispheric specialization: Scope and limits. In F. O. Schmitt and F. G. Worden (Eds.), *The neurosciences third study program* (pp. 75–89). Cambridge, MA: MIT Press.

Milner, B. (1982). Some cognitive effects of frontal-lobe lesions in man. *Philosophical Transactions of the Royal Society of London. Series B: Biological Sciences, 298.* 211–226.

Milner, B., and Petrides, M. (1984). Behavioural effects of frontal-lobe lesions in man. *Trends in Neurosciences, 7,* 403–407.

Mitchell, D. E. (1980). The influence of early visual experience on visual perception. In C. S. Harris (Ed.) , *Visual coding and adaptability* (pp. 1–50). Hillsdale, NJ: Lawrence Erlbaum.

Mitchell, G. D. (1968). Attachment differences in male and female infant monkeys. *Child Development, 39,* 611–620.

Miyashita, Y. (1981). Differential roles of the climbing and mossy fiber visual pathways in vision-guided modification of the vestibulo-ocular reflex. In H. Flohr and W. Precht (Eds.), *Lesion-induced neuronal plasticity in sensorimotor systems* (pp. 305–313). Berlin: Springer-Verlag.

Money, J., and Ehrhardt, A. A. (1972). *Man and woman, boy and girl.* Baltimore: Johns Hopkins Press.

Money, J., Ehrhardt, A. A., and Masica, D. N. (1968). Fetal feminization induced by androgen insensitivity in the testicular feminizing syndrome: Effect on marriage and maternalism. *The Johns Hopkins Medical Journal, 123,* 105–114.

Money, J., Schwartz, M., and Lewis, V. G. (1984). Adult erotosexual status and fetal hormonal masculinization and demasculinization: 46, XX congenital virilizing adrenal hyperplasia and 46, XY androgen-insensitivity syndrome compared. *Psychoneuroendocrinology, 9,* 405–414.

Monti, P. M., Brown, W. A., and Corriveau, D. P. (1977). Testosterone and components of aggressive and sexual behavior in man. *American Journal of Psychiatry, 134,* 692–694.

Moore, R. Y. (1982). The suprachiasmatic nucleus and the organization of a circadian system. *Trends in Neurosciences, 5,* 404–407.

Moore, R. Y., and Eichler, V. B. (1972). Loss of a circadian adrenal corticosterone rhythm following suprachiasmatic lesions in the rat. *Brain Research, 42,* 201–206.

Moore-Ede, M. C., Czeisler, C. A., and Richardson, G. S. (1983). Circadian timekeeping in health and disease. *New England Journal of Medicine, 309,* 469–476.

Moruzzi, G., and Magoun, H. W. (1949). Brain stem reticular formation and activation of the EEG. *Electroencephalography and Clinical Neurophysiology, 1,* 455–473.

Mountcastle, V. B. (1968). *Medical physiology* (12th ed.). St. Louis: C. V. Mosby.

Mountcastle, V. B. (1979). An organizing principle for cerebral function: The unit module and the distributed system. In F. O. Schmitt and F. G. Worden (Eds.), *The neuroscience fourth study program* (pp. 21–42). Cambridge, MA: MIT Press.

Mozell, M. M. (1970). Evidence for a chromatographic model of olfaction. *Journal of General Physiology, 56,* 46–63.

Myers, J. J. (1984). Right hemisphere language: Science or fiction? *American Psychologist, 39,* 315–320.

Müller, G. E., and Pilzecker, A. (1900). Experimentelle beitrage zur lehre vom gedachtniss. *Zeitschrift für Psychologie und Physiologie der Sinnesorgane, Erganzungsband 1,* 1–288.

Myers, R. E. (1956). Function of corpus callosum in interocular transfer. *Brain, 79,* 358–363.

Myers, R. E., and Sperry, R. W. (1958). Interhemispheric communication through the corpus callosum. Mnemonic carry-over between the hemispheres. *Archives of Neurology and Psychiatry, 80,* 298–303.

Nabekura, J., Oomura, Y., Minami, T., Mizuno, Y., and Fukuda, A. (1986). Mechanism of the rapid effect of 17-β-Estradiol on medial amygdala neurons. *Science, 233,* 226–228.

Nauta, W. J. H., and Feirtag, M. (1986). *Fundamental neuroanatomy.* New York: W. H. Freeman.

Nicol, S. E., and Gottesman, I. I. (1983). Clues to the genetics and neurobiology of schizophrenia. *American Scientist, 71,* 398–404.

Niijima, A. (1969). Afferent impulse discharges from glucoreceptors in the liver of the guinea pig. *Annals of the New York Academy of Sciences, 157,* 690–700.

Noback, C. R., and Demerest, R. J. (1975). *The human nervous system: Basic principles of neurobiology* (2d ed.). New York: McGraw-Hill.

Norris, D. O. (1980). *Vertebrate endocrinology.* Philadelphia: Lea & Febiger.

Nottebohm, F. (1977). Asymmetries in neural control of vocalization in the canary. In S. Harnad, R. W. Doty, L. Goldstein, J. Jaynes, and G. Krauthamer (Eds.), *Lateralization in the nervous system* (pp. 23–44). Orlando, FL: Academic Press.

Novin, D. (1976). Visceral mechanisms in the control of food intake. In D. Novin, W. Wyrwicka, and G. A. Bray (Eds.), *Hunger, basic mechanisms and clinical implications* (pp. 357–367). New York: Raven Press.

Novin, D. (1979). Some expected and unexpected effects of glucose on food intake. In G. A. Bray (Ed.) , *Recent advances in obesity research: II* (pp. 27–32). Westport, CT: Food and Nutrition Press.

Nunn, B. J., and Baylor, D. A. (1982). Visual transduction in retinal rods of the monkey *Macaca fascicularis. Nature, 299,* 726–728.

Olds, J., and Milner, P. (1954). Positive reinforcement produced by electrical stimulation of the septal area and other regions of the rat brain. *Journal of Comparative and Physiological Psychology, 47,* 419–427.

Oomura, Y., Ohta, M., Ishibashi, S., Kita, H., Okajima, T., and Ono, T. (1979). Activity of chemosensitive neurons related to the neurophysiological mechanisms of feeding. In G. A. Bray (Ed.) , *Recent advances in obesity research: II* (pp. 17–26). Westport, CT: Food and Nutrition Press.

Orsini, J. C. (1985). Direct effects of androgens on lateral hypothalamic activity in the male rat: II. A pressure ejection study. *Brain Research Bulletin, 15,* 547–552.

Parkin, A. J. (1984). Amnesic syndrome: A lesion-specific disorder? *Cortex, 20,* 479–508.

Paton, J. A., and Nottebohm, F. N. (1984). Neurons generated in the adult brain are recruited into functional circuits. *Science, 225,* 1046–1048.

Patterson, P. H., Potter, D. D., and Furshpan, E. J. (1978). The chemical differentiation of nerve cells. *Scientific American, 239,* 38–47.

Pearson, K. (1976). The control of walking. *Scientific American, 235,* 72–86.

Peck, J. W., and Novin, D. (1971) Evidence that osmoreceptors mediating drinking in rabbits are in the lateral preoptic area. *Journal of Comparative and Physiological Psychology, 74,* 134–147.

Penfield, W., and Perot, P. (1963). The brain's record of auditory and visual experience. *Brain, 86,* 595–696.

Perrett, D. I., Smith, P. A. J., Potter, D. D., Mistlin, A. J., Head, A. S., Milner, A. D., and Jeeves, M. A. (1985). Visual cells in the temporal cortex sensitive to face view and gaze direction. *Proceedings of the Royal Society of London. Series B: Biological Sciences, 223,* 293–317.

Pert, C. B., and Snyder, S. H. (1973). Opiate receptor: Demonstration in nervous tissue. *Science, 179,* 1011–1014.

Petersen, M. R., Beecher, M. D., Zoloth, S. R., Moody, D. B., and Stebbins, W. C. (1978). Neural lateralization of species-specific vocalizations by Japanese macaques. *Science, 202,* 324–326.

Pfaff, D., Diakow, C., Zigmond, R. E., and Kow, L. M. (1974). Neural and hormonal determinants of female mating behavior in rats. In F. O. Schmitt and F. G. Worden (Eds.), *The neurosciences third study program* (pp. 621–646). Cambridge, MA: MIT Press.

Pfaff, D. W., and McEwen, B. S. (1983). Actions of estrogens and progestins on nerve cells. *Science, 219,* 808–814.

Pfaff, D. W., and Zigmond, R. E. (1971). Neonatal androgen effects on sexual and non-sexual behavior of adult rats tested under various hormone regimes. *Neuroendocrinology, 7,* 129–145.

Pfaffmann, C. (1959). The afferent code for sensory quality. *American Psychologist, 14,* 226–232.

Pfeiffer, C. A. (1936). Sexual differences in the hypophyses and their determination by the gonads. *American Journal of Anatomy, 58,* 195–225.

Phoenix, C. H. (1976). Sexual behavior of castrated male rhesus monkeys treated with 19-hydroxytestosterone. *Physiology and Behavior, 16,* 305–310.

Phoenix, C. W., Goy, R. W., Gerall, A. A., and Young, W. C. (1959). Organizing action of prenatally administered testosterone propionate on the tissue mediating mating behavior in the female guinea pig. *Endocrinology, 65,* 369–382.

Phoenix, C. H., Jensen, J. N., and Chambers, K. C. (1983). Female sexual behavior displayed by androgenized female rhesus macaques. *Hormones and Behavior, 17,* 146–151.

Pickard, G. E. (1985). Bifurcating axons of retinal ganglion cells terminate in the hypothalamic suprachiasmatic nucleus and the intergeniculate leaflet in the thalamus. *Neuroscience Letters, 55,* 211–217.

Pirke, K. M., and Kockott, G. (1982). Endocrinology of sexual dysfunction. In J. Bancroft (Ed.) , *Clinics in endocrinology and metabolism, diseases of sex and sexuality* (Vol. 11, pp. 599–624). Philadelphia: W. B. Saunders.

Pi-Sunyer, X., Kissileff, H. R., Thornton, J., and Smith, G. P. (1982). C-terminal octapeptide of cholecystokinin decreases food intake in obese men. *Physiology and Behavior, 29,* 627–630.

Plutchik, R. (1970). Emotion, evolution and adaptive processes. In M. Arnold (Ed.) *Feelings and emotions.* New York: Academic Press.

Pöppel, E., Held, R., and Frost, D. (1973). Residual visual function after brain wounds involving the central visual pathways in man. *Nature, 243,* 295–296.

Powell, T. P. S., and Mountcastle, V. B. (1959). Some aspects of the functional organization of the cortex of the postcentral gyrus of the monkey: A correlation of findings obtained in a single unit analysis with cytoarchitecture. *Bulletin of the Johns Hopkins Hospital, 105,* 133–162.

Powley, T. L. (1977). The ventromedial hypothalamic syndrome, satiety, and a cephalic phase hypothesis. *Psychological Review, 84,* 89–126.

Price, D. L, Cork, L. C., Struble, R. G., Whitehouse, P. J., Kitt, C. A., and Walker, L. C. (1985). The functional organization of the basal forebrain cholinergic system in primates and the role of this system in Alzheimer's disease. In D. S. Olton, E. Gamzu, and S. Corkin (Eds.), *Memory dysfunction: An integration of animal and clinical perspectives* (pp. 287–295). New York: New York Academy of Sciences.

Rada, R. T., Laws, D. R., and Kellner, R. (1976). Plasma testosterone levels in the rapist. *Psychosomatic Medicine, 38,* 257–268.

Raichle, M. E. (1983). Positron emission tomography. *Annual Review of Neuroscience, 6,* 249–267.

Raisman, G. (1969). Neuronal plasticity in the septal nuclei of the adult rat. *Brain Research, 14,* 25–48.

Raisman, G., and Field, P. M. (1971). Sexual dimorphism in the preoptic area of the rat. *Science, 173,* 731–733.

Raisman, G., and Field, P. M. (1973a). A quantitative investigation of the development of collateral reinnervation after partial deafferentation of the septal nuclei. *Brain Research, 50,* 241–264.

Raisman, G., and Field, P. M. (1973b). Sexual dimorphism in the neuropil of the preoptic area of the rat and its dependence on neonatal androgen. *Brain Research, 54,* 1–29.

Rakic, P. (1978). Neuronal migration and contact guidance in the primate telencephalon. *Postgraduate Medical Journal, 54,* 25–40.

Rakic, P. (1981). Developmental events leading to laminar and areal organization of the neocortex. In F. O. Schmitt (Ed.) , *The organization of the cerebral cortex* (pp. 7–28). Cambridge, MA: MIT Press.

Rakic, P. (1985). Limits of neurogenesis in primates. *Science, 227,* 1054–1056.

Rakic, P., and Sidman, R. L. (1973). Sequence of developmental abnormalities leading to granule cell deficit in cerebellar cortex of weaver mutant mice. *Journal of Comparative Neurology, 152,* 103–132.

Ramm, P. (1979). The locus coeruleus, catecholamines, & REM sleep: A critical review. *Behavioral and Neural Biology, 25,* 415–448.

Ramón y Cajal, S. (1937). Recollections of my life (E. H. Craigie, Trans.). *Memoirs of the American Philosophical Society: Vol. 8.* Philadelphia: American Philosophical Society. (Translated from 1923 edition of original work.)

Rasmussen, T., and Milner, B. (1975). Clinical and surgical studies of the cerebral speech areas in man. In K. J. Zulch, O. Creutzfeldt, and G. C. Galbraith (Eds.), *Cerebral localization* (pp. 238–257). Berlin: Springer-Verlag.

Reisenzein, R. (1983). The Schachter theory of emotion: Two decades later. *Psychological Bulletin, 94,* 239–264.

Reynolds, D. V. (1969). Surgery in the rat during electrical analgesia induced by focal brain stimulation. *Science, 164,* 444–445.

Richardson, D. E., and Akil, H. (1977). Pain reduction by electrical brain stimulation in man: Part 2. Chronic self-administration in the periventricular gray matter. *Journal of Neurosurgery, 47,* 184–194.

Richter, C. P. (1965). *Biological clocks in medicine and psychiatry.* Springfield, IL: Charles C Thomas.

Richter, C. P. (1967). Sleep and activity: Their relation to the 24-hour clock. *Research Publication—Association for Research in Nervous and Mental Disease, 45,* 8–27.

Rodin, J. (1976). The relationship between external responsiveness and the development and maintenance of obesity. In D. Novin, W. Wyrwicka, and G. A. Bray (Eds.), *Hunger, basic mechanisms and clinical implications* (pp. 409–419). New York: Raven Press.

Rodin, J. (1978). Has the distinction between internal versus external control of feeding outlived its usefulness? In G. Bray (Ed.) , *Recent advances in obesity research: II* (pp. 75–85). Westport, CT: Food and Nutrition Press.

Roffwarg, H., Muzio, J., and Dement, W. (1966). Ontogenetic development of the human sleep–dream cycle. *Science, 152,* 604–619.

Rogel, M. J. (1978). A critical evaluation of the possibility of higher primate reproductive and sexual pheromones. *Psychological Bulletin, 85,* 810–830.

Roland, P. E. (1984). Metabolic measurements of the working frontal cortex in man. *Trends in Neurosciences, 7,* 430–435.

Rolls, B. J., and Rolls, E. T. (1982). *Thirst.* Cambridge, England: Cambridge University Press.

Rolls, E. T. (1984). Neurons in the cortex of the temporal lobe and in the amygdala of the monkey with responses selective for faces. *Human Neurobiology, 3,* 209–222.

Roots, B. I. (1984). Evolutional aspects of the structure and function of the nodes of Ranvier. In J. C. Zagoren and S. Federoff (Eds.), *The node of Ranvier* (pp. 1–29). Orlando, FL: Academic Press.

Rose, R. M. (1978). Neuroendocrine correlates of sexual and aggressive behavior in humans. In M. A. Lipton, A. DiMascio, and K. F. Killam (Eds.), *Psychopharmacology: A generation of progress* (pp. 541–552). New York: Raven Press.

Rosenblum, L. A. (1961). *The development of social behavior in the rhesus monkey.* Unpublished doctoral dissertation, University of Wisconsin, Madison.

Rosenzweig, M. R., and Leiman, A. L. (1982). *Physiological psychology.* Lexington, MA: D. C. Heath.

Routtenberg, A., and Lindy, J. (1965). Effects of the availability of rewarding septal and hypothalamic stimulation on bar-pressing for food under conditions of deprivation. *Journal of Comparative and Physiological Psychology, 60,* 158–161.

Rowland, L. P. (1981). Diseases of the motor unit: The motor neuron, peripheral nerve, and muscle. In E. R. Kandel and J. H. Schwartz (Eds.), *Principles of neural science* (pp. 147–154). New York: Elsevier.

Rubin, R. T. (1982). Testosterone and aggression in men. In J. V. Beaumont and G. D. Burrows (Eds.), *Handbook of psychiatry and endocrinology* (pp. 353–366). New York: Elsevier Biomedical Press.

Rusak, B., and Zucker, I. (1979). Neural regulation of circadian rhythms. *Physiological Reviews, 59,* 449–526.

Russek, M. (1971). Hepatic receptors and the neurophysiological mechanisms controlling feeding behavior. In S. Ehrenpreis (Ed.) , *Neurosciences Research* (Vol. 4, pp. 213–282). Orlando, FL: Academic Press.

Russell, W. R., and Nathan, P. W. (1946). Traumatic amnesia. *Brain, 69,* 280–300.

Sacks, O. (1985). *The man who mistook his wife for a hat.* New York: Summit Books.

Samorajski, T. (1976). How the human brain responds to aging. *Journal of American Geriatrics Society, 24,* 4–11.

Schachter, S. (1971). Some extraordinary facts about obese humans and rats. *American Psychologist, 26,* 129–144.

Schachter, S., and Singer, J. E. (1962). Cognitive, social, and physiological determinants of emotional state. *Psychological Review, 69,* 379–399.

Scheibel, A. B., and Tomiyasu, U. (1978). Dendritic sprouting in Alzheimer's presenile dementia. *Experimental Neurology, 60,* 1–8.

Scheibel, M. E., Lindsay, R. D., Tomiyasu, U., and Scheibel, A. B. (1975). Progressive dendritic changes in aging human cortex. *Experimental Neurology, 47,* 392–403.

Scheibel, M. E., Tomiyasu, U., and Scheibel, A. B. (1977). The aging human Betz cell. *Experimental Neurology, 56,* 598–609.

Scherschlicht, R., Polc, P., Schneeberger, J., Steiner, M., and Haefely, W. (1982). Selective suppression of rapid eye movement sleep (REMS) in cats by typical and atypical antidepressants. In E. Costa and G. Racagni (Eds.), *Typical and atypical antidepressants: Molecular mechanisms* (pp. 359–364). New York: Raven Press.

Schiffman, S. S., and Erickson, R. P. (1980). The issue of primary tastes versus a taste continuum. *Neuroscience and Biobehavioral Reviews, 4,* 109–117.

Schildkraut, J. J. (1965). The catecholamine hypothesis of affective disorders: A review of supporting evidence. *American Journal of Psychiatry, 122,* 509–522.

Schmitt, F. O. (1984). Molecular regulators of brain function: A new view. *Neuroscience, 13,* 991–1001.

Schnapf, J. L., and Baylor, D. A. (1987). How photoreceptor cells respond to light. *Scientific American, 256,* 40–47.

Schwartz, M. F., Kolodny, R. C., and Masters, W. H. (1979). Plasma testosterone levels of sexually functional and dysfunctional men. Paper presented at Eastern Association for Sex Therapy, Philadelphia, Pennsylvania, March 23–25.

Searleman, A. (1977). A review of right hemisphere linguistic capabilities. *Psychological Bulletin, 84,* 503–528.

Searleman, A. (1983). Language capabilities of the right hemisphere. In A. Young (Ed.) , *Functions of the right cerebral hemisphere* (pp. 87–111). Orlando, FL: Academic Press.

Segal, S. J., and Johnson, D. C. (1959). Inductive influence of steroid hormones on neural system. *Archives d'Anatomie Microscopique, 48,* 261–273.

Seifert, W. (1983). Epilogue. In W. Seifert (Ed.) , *Neurobiology of the hippocampus* (pp. 624–627). London: Academic Press.

Sem-Jacobsen, C. W. (1968). Depth-electrographic stimulation of the human brain and behavior. From *Fourteen years of studies and treatment of Parkinson's disease and mental disorders with implanted electrodes.* Springfield, IL: Charles C Thomas.

Sergent, J. (1982). Theoretical and methodological consequences of variations in exposure duration in visual laterality studies. *Perception and Psychophysics, 31,* 451–461.

Shapiro, D. (1977). A monologue on biofeedback and psychophysiology. *Psychophysiology, 14,* 213–227.

Shepherd, G. M. (1979). *The synaptic organization of the brain* (2d ed.). New York: Oxford University Press.

Shepherd, G. M. (1983). *Neurobiology.* New York: Oxford University Press.

Sherrington, C. S. (1906). *Integrative action of the nervous system.* New Haven, CT: Yale University Press.

Sidman, R. L., Green, M. C., and Appel, S. H. (1965). *Catalog of the neurological mutants of the mouse.* Cambridge, MA: Harvard University Press.

Simpson, J. B., and Routtenberg, A. (1973). Subfornical organ: Site of drinking elicitation by angiotensin II. *Science, 181,* 1172–1174.

Smith, G. P., Jerome, C., Cushin, B. J., Eterno, R., and Simansky, K. J. (1981). Abdominal vagotomy blocks the satiety effect of cholecystokinin in the rat. *Science, 213,* 1036–1037.

Snyder, S. H. (1984). Drug and neurotransmitter receptors in the brain. *Science, 224,* 22–31.

Sokoloff, L. (1977). Relation between physiological function and energy metabolism in the central nervous system. *Journal of Neurochemistry, 27,* 13–26.

Spanos, N. P., and Gottlieb, J. (1976). Ergotism and the Salem Village witch trials. *Science, 194,* 1390–1394.

Sparks, R., Helm, N., and Albert, M. (1974). Aphasia rehabilitation resulting from melodic intonation therapy. *Cortex, 10,* 303–316.

Sperry, R. W. (1951). Mechanisms of neural maturation. In S. S. Stevens (Ed.) , *Handbook of experimental psychology* (pp. 236–280). New York: Wiley.

Sperry, R. W. (1963). Chemoaffinity in the orderly growth of nerve fiber patterns and connections. *Proceedings of the National Academy of Sciences of the United States of America, 50,* 703–710.

Sperry, R. W. (1968). Hemispheric deconnection and unity in conscious awareness. *American Psychologist, 23,* 723–733.

Sperry, R. W. (1974). Lateral specialization in the surgically separated hemispheres. In F. O. Schmitt and F. G. Worden (Eds.), *The neurosciences third study program* (pp. 5–19). Cambridge, MA: MIT Press.

Sperry, R. (1982). Some effects of disconnecting the cerebral hemispheres. *Science, 217,* 1223–1226.

Springer, S. P., and Deutsch, G. (1981). *Left brain, right brain.* New York: W. H. Freeman.

Squire, L. R. (1982). The neuropsychology of human memory. *Annual Review of Neuroscience, 5,* 241–273.

Stenevi, U., Bjorklund, A., and Svendgaard, N-A. (1976). Transplantation of central and peripheral monoamine neurons to the adult rat brain: Techniques and conditions for survival. *Brain Research, 114,* 1–20.

Stephan, F. K., and Zucker, I. (1972). Circadian rhythms in drinking behavior and locomotor behavior of rats are eliminated by hypothalamic lesions. *Proceedings of the National Academy of Sciences of the United States of America, 69,* 1583–1586.

Stephan, H. (1972). Evolution of primate brains: A comparative anatomical investigation. In T. Tuttle (Ed.) , *The functional and evolutionary biology of primates* (pp. 155–174). Chicago: Aldine-Atherton.

Stevens, C. F. (1979). The neuron. In *The brain* (a Scientific American book, pp. 15–25). New York: W. H. Freeman.

Stone, J., and Hoffmann, K-P. (1972). Very slow-conducting ganglion cells in the cat's retina: A major new functional type? *Brain Research, 43,* 610–616.

Stricker, E. M., and Zigmond, M. J. (1976a). Brain catecholamines and the lateral hypothalamic syndrome. In D. Novin, W. Wyrwicka, and G. A. Bray (Eds.), *Hunger: Basic mechanisms and clinical implications* (pp. 19–32). New York: Raven Press.

Stricker, E. M., and Zigmond, M. J. (1976b). Recovery of function following damage to central catecholamine-containing neurons: A neurochemical model for the lateral hypothalamic syndrome. In J. M. Sprague and A. N. Epstein (Eds.), *Progress in psychobiology and physiological psychology* (Vol. 6, pp. 121–188). Orlando, FL: Academic Press.

Stryker, M. P., and Sherk, H. (1975). Modification of cortical orientation selectivity in the cat by restricted visual experience: A re-examination. *Science, 190,* 904–906.

Stuss, D. T., and Benson, D. F. (1984). Neuropsychological studies of the frontal lobes. *Psychological Bulletin, 95,* 3–28.

Sutherland, E. W. (1972). Studies on the mechanism of hormone action. *Science, 177,* 401–408.

Swaab, D. F., and Fliers, E. (1985). A sexually dimorphic nucleus in the human brain. *Science, 228,* 1112–1115.

Takahashi, J. S., and Zatz, M. (1982). Regulation of circadian rhythmicity. *Science, 217,* 1104–1111.

Tanabe, T., Iino, M., Oshima, Y., and Takagi, S. F. (1974). An olfactory area in the prefrontal lobe. *Brain Research, 80,* 127–130.

Tarsy, D., and Baldessarini, R. J. (1984). Tardive dyskinesia. *Annual Review of Medicine, 35,* 605–623.

Tennant, B. J., Smith, E. R., and Davidson, J. M. (1982). Effects of progesterone implants in the habenula and midbrain on proceptive and receptive behavior in the female rat. *Hormones and Behavior, 16,* 352–363.

Teitelbaum, P., and Epstein, A. N. (1962). The lateral hypothalamic syndrome: Recovery of feeding and drinking after lateral hypothalamic lesions. *Psychological Review, 69,* 74–90.

Teuber, H.-L., Milner, B., and Vaughn, H. G. (1968). Persistent anterograde amnesia after stab wound of the basal brain. *Neuropsychologia, 6,* 267–282.

Thoenen, H., and Edgar, D. (1985). Neurotrophic factors. *Science, 229,* 238–242.

Thompson, C. I. (1980). *Controls of eating.* New York: SP Medical and Scientific Books.

Thompson, R. F., Berger, T. W., and Madden, J. (1983). Cellular processes of learning and memory in the mammalian CNS. *Annual Review of Neuroscience, 6,* 447–491.

Thompson, R. F., Clark, G. A., Donegan, N. H., Lavond, D. G., Madden, J., Mamounas, L. A., Mauk, M. D., and McCormick, D. A. (1984). Neuronal substrates of basic associative learning. In L. R. Squire and N. Butters (Eds.), *Neuropsychology of memory* (pp. 424–442). New York: Guilford.

Tiner, M. L. (1983, May 9). Polygraph tests: Two views [Letters to the editor]. *Washington Post,* p. A10.

Torrey, E. F., Yolken, R. H., and Winfrey, C. J. (1982). Cytomegalovirus antibody in cerebrospinal fluid of schizophrenic patients detected by enzyme immunoassay. *Science, 216,* 892–894.

Tulving, E. (1972). Episodic and semantic memory. In E. Tulving and W. Donaldson (Eds.), *Organization of memory* (pp. 382–403). Orlando, FL: Academic Press.

Valenstein, E. (1973). *Brain control.* New York: Wiley.

Valenstein, E. S. (Ed.) 1980. The *psychosurgery debate.* New York: W. H. Freeman.

Van der Loos, H., and Woolsey, T. A. (1973). Somatosensory cortex: Structural alterations following early injury to sense organs. *Science, 179,* 395–398.

Van Essen, D. C., and Maunsell, J. H. R. (1983). Hierarchical organization and functional streams in the visual cortex. *Trends in Neuroscience, 6,* 370–375.

Van Wagenen, W. P., and Herren, R. Y. (1940). Surgical division of commissural pathways in the corpus callosum. *Archives of Neurology and Psychiatry, 44,* 740–759.

Vaughn, I. (1984). Living with Parkinson's disease: Learning the tactics of coping. *The Listener, 112,* 13–14.

Vellutino, F. R. (1987). Dyslexia. *Scientific American, 256,* 34–41.

Victor, M., Adams, R. D., and Collins, G. H. (1971). *The Wernicke–Korsakoff Syndrome.* Oxford: Blackwell.

Vogel, G. W., Vogel, F., McAbee, R. S., and Thurmond, A. J. (1980). Improvement of depression by REM sleep deprivation. *Archives of General Psychiatry, 37,* 247–253.

Voskuil, P. H. A. (1983). The epilepsy of Fyodor Mikhailovitch Dostoevsky (1821–1881). *Epilepsia, 24,* 658–667.

Wada, J. (1949). A new method for the determination of the side of cerebral speech dominance: A preliminary report on the intracarotid injection of sodium amytal in man. *Medicine and Biology, 14,* 221–222.

Wada, J., and Rasmussen, T. (1960). Intracarotid injection of sodium amytal for lateralization of cerebral speech dominance. *Journal of Neurosurgery, 17,* 266–282.

Wada, J. A., Clarke, R., and Hamm, A. (1975). Cerebral hemisphere asymmetry in humans. *Archives of Neurology, 32,* 239–246.

Wagensteen, O. H., and Carlson, A. J. (1931). Hunger sensations of a patient after total gastrectomy. *Proceedings of the Society for Experimental Biology and Medicine, 28,* 545–557.

Wald, G. (1968). Molecular basis of visual excitation. *Science, 162,* 230–239.

Wald, G., Brown, P. K., and Gibbons, I. R. (1963). The problem of visual excitation. *Journal of the Optical Society of America, 53,* 20–35.

Warrington, E. K. (1982). Neuropsychological studies of object recognition. *Philosophical transactions of the Royal Society of London. Series B: Biological Sciences, 298,* 15–33.

Warrington, E. K. (1984). *Recognition memory test.* Windsor, England: NFER-Nelson.

Warrington, E. K., and Weiskrantz, L. (1970). The amnesic syndrome: Consolidation or retrieval? *Nature, 228,* 628–630.

Watson, J. D., and Crick, F. H. C. (1953). Molecular structure of nucleic acid. A structure for deoxyribose nucleic acid. *Nature, 171,* 737–738.

Webster, W. G. (1975). *Principles of research methodology in physiological psychology.* New York: Harper & Row.

Weiskrantz, L. (1985). On issues and theories of the human amnesic syndrome. In N. M. Weinberger, J. L. McGaugh, and G. Lynch (Eds.), *Memory systems of the brain: Animal and human cognitive processes* (pp. 380–415). New York: Guilford.

Weiskrantz, L., and Warrington, E. K. (1975). The problem of the amnesic syndrome in man and animals. In R. L. Isaacson and K. H. Pribram (Eds.), *The hippocampus: Vol. 2. Neurophysiology and behavior* (pp. 411–428). New York: Plenum.

Weiskrantz, L., Warrington, E. K., Sanders, M. D., and Marshall, J. (1974). Visual capacity in the hemianopic field following a restricted occipital ablation. *Brain, 97,* 709–728.

Wellman, P. J. (1986). *Laboratory exercises in physiological psychology* (3d ed.). Boston: Allyn and Bacon.

Wever, E. G. (1949). *Theory of hearing.* New York: Wiley.

Whalen, R. E., and Edwards, D. A. (1967). Hormonal determinants of the development of masculine and feminine behavior in male and female rats. *Anatomical Record, 157,* 173–180.

Wiesel, T. N., and Hubel, D. H. (1966). Spatial and chromatic interactions in the lateral geniculate body of the rhesus monkey. *Journal of Neurophysiology, 29,* 1115–1156.

Willer, J. C., Dehen, H., and Cambier, J. (1981). Stress-induced analgesia in humans: Endogenous opioids and naloxone-reversible depression of pain reflexes. *Science, 212,* 689–691.

Winblad, B., Hardy, J., Backman, L., and Nilsson, L-G. (1985). Memory function and brain biochemistry in normal aging and in senile dementia. In D. S. Olton, E. Gamzu, and S. Corkin (Eds.), *Memory dysfunctions: An integration of animal and human research from preclinical and clinical perspectives* (pp. 255–268). New York: New York Academy of Sciences.

Winocur, G., and Weiskrantz, L. (1976). An investigation of paired-associate learning in amnesic patients. *Neuropsychologia, 14,* 97–110.

Wirtshafter, D., and Davis, J. D. (1977). Set points, settling points, and the control of body weight. *Physiology and Behavior, 19,* 75–78.

Witelson, S. F. (1983). Bumps on the brain: Right–left anatomic asymmetry as a key to functional lateralization. In S. J. Segalowitz (Ed.) , *Language functions and brain organization* (pp. 117–144). Orlando, FL: Academic Press.

Witelson, S. F., and Pallie, W. (1973). Left hemisphere specialization for language in the newborn: Neuroanatomical evidence of asymmetry. *Brain, 96,* 641–646.

Woods, B. T. (1983). Is the left hemisphere specialized for language at birth? *Trends in Neuroscience, 6,* 116–117.

Wong, D. F., Wagner, H. N. Jr., Tune, L. E., Dannals, R. F., Pearlson, G. D., Links, J. M., Tamminga, C. A., Broussolle, E. P., Ravert, H. T., Wilson, A. A., Toung, J. K. T., Malat, J., Williams, J. A., O'Tuama, L. A., Snyder, S. H., Kuhar, M. J., and Gjeddet, A. (1986). Positron emission tomography reveals elevated D_2 dopamine receptors in drug-naive schizophrenics. *Science, 234,* 1558–1563.

Wurtz, R. H. (1969). Visual receptive fields of striate cortex neurons in awake monkeys. *Journal of Neurophysiology, 32,* 727–742.

Wurtz, R. H., and Albano, J. E. (1980). Visual-motor function of the primate superior colliculus. *Annual Review of Neuroscience, 3,* 189–226.

Young, A. W. (1982). Asymmetry of cerebral hemispheric function during development. In J. W. T. Dickerson and H. McCurk (Eds.), *Brain and behavioral development* (pp. 168–202). Surrey, England: Surrey University Press.

Zaidel, E. (1975). A technique for presenting lateralized visual input with prolonged exposure. *Vision Research, 15,* 283–289.

Zaidel, E. (1983). A response to Gazzaniga: Language in the right hemisphere, an empirical perspective. *American Psychologist, 38,* 542–546.

Zametkin. A. J., and Rapoport, J. L. (1987). The pathophysiology of attention deficit disorder with hyperactivity: A review. In B. B. Lahey and A. Kazdin (Eds.), *Advances in Clinical Child Psychology: Vol. 9* (pp. 177–216). New York: Plenum.

Zechmeister, E. B., and Nyberg, S. E. (1982). *Human memory.* Monterey, CA: Brooks/Cole.

Zeki, S. (1980). The representation of colours in the cerebral cortex. *Nature, 284,* 412–418.

Name Index

Subject Index

Pacinian corpuscle, 196–199
Pain, affective, discriminative aspects, 324–325
  gate-control theory, 326
  pathways in the nervous system, 325–326
Parachlorophenylalanine (PCPA), 302
Parkinson's disease, 114, 219–221
Perforant pathways to dentate gyrus, 358
Peripheral nervous system, cranial nerves, 64–65
  spinal nerves, 65–66
Perseverative behavior, 343
PET scanning (Positron emission tomography) 20, 391–393
PGO spikes (pons-geniculate-occipital), 303
Phenothiazines, 411
Phenylalanine, 55
Pheromones, 194–195
Photons, 126
Photopigments, 132–133
Photoreceptors, 127
Phrenology, 84
Physostigmine, 121
Pia mater, 74
Pineal gland, 5, 75, 77, 261
Piracetam, 121
Pituitary gland, 262–264
Placebo effects, 333
Planum temporale, 365–367
Plaques, senile, 119
Pleasure centers in the brain, 320–324
Positron, 20
Positron emission tomography (PET scanning), 20, 391–393
Postnatal neurogenesis, 93, 103
Potassium ion (K^+), 34, 37–49
Prandial drinking, 246
Precocious puberty, 276
Preoptic area, 285–286
Prepiriform cortex, 194
Proceptive behavior, 270
Prodynorphin, 328
Proenkephalin, 328
Progesterone, 271–272
Prolactin, 265, 272
Proliferative zone, 96
Pronase, 44
Proopiomelanocortin, 328–329
Prosopagnosia, 162, 377
Protein synthesis, 31

Psychic blindness, 159–160
Psychopharmacology, 52
Psychophysiology, 312
Puberty, 276
Pupil, 127
Purkinje cell, 217
Putamen, 219
Pyramidal cells, 81
Pyramidal tracts, 73, 223–224

Radial glia, 96
Raphe system, 302
Reactive synaptogenesis, 113
Readiness potential, 226
Receptive behavior, 270–271
Receptive fields in vision, 136, 140–143
Reciprocal inhibition, 209–210
Reflexes, 206–208
Refractory periods, 48–49
Regeneration of neural tissue, 103–105
Relative refractory period, 48–49
REM (rapid eye movement) sleep, 290, 292–297
REM (rapid eye movement) sleep deprivation, 295–296
Renaissance, 9, 22
Reserpine, 419
Retina, cell types in, 135–136
  cone types in, 145–146
  potentials in, 136–139
  transduction, 132–134
Retinal, 132–134
Retinene, 132
Retinitis pigmentosa, 133
Retinohypothalamic tract, 164, 306
Reuptake of neurotransmitter substance, 56
Rhodopsin, 132–134
Ribonucleic acid (RNA), 28, 30
Ribosomes, 28
Right cerebral hemisphere, language, 370–372
  pattern recognition, 372–377
Right-ear advantage, 390
Right parietal lobe imperception syndrome, 375
Ritalin (methylphenidate), 422
RNA (ribonucleic acid), 28, 30
Rods, 127
Rokitansky's syndrome, 282
Runner's high, 333

Saccades, 165, 218
Saccule, 184
Sacral nerves, 65
Salem witch trials, 412
Saltatory conduction, 46
Schizophrenia, diagnostic criteria, 410–411
  dopamine hypothesis, 408
  drug side effects, 415–416
  drug therapy, 411, 414–415
  risks of developing, 411
Schwann cells, 29, 46
Scotomata, 162
Second messenger system, 261
Self-stimulation of the brain, 320–324
Sella turcica, 268
Semicircular canals, 184–185
Sensitization, 348
Septal nuclei, 79
Serotonin, 16, 302
Set point for body weight, 230, 247–248, 250–252
Sexual dimorphism, behavior, 276–281
  brain structure, 285–286
  defined, 265–266
  hormonal cyclicity, 266–268
Sexual orientation, 282–285
Simple cells, 149–150
Single-unit recording, 17–18
Sleep, abnormalities, 298–299
  brain regions in, 299–302
  depressed patients, 296–297
  deprivation, 296–297
  elderly, 293–294
  REM (rapid eye movement) 290, 292–297
  slow wave, 291–292
Sleep apnea, 298
Sleep-wake cycles in the blind, 303
Sleeping pills, 298
Sodium inactivation, 38, 43–45
Sodium ion (Na^+), 34, 37–49
Sodium-potassium pump, 40–41
Somesthesis, cortical maps, 201–202
  receptor types, 195–199
Spatial frequency model of visual cortex neurons, 151–152
Spike-initiating region of neurons, 43, 48
Spinal shock, 215
Spinocerebellar tract, 73
Split-brain patients, 367–372

Acknowledgments

Figure 1.2 From Nauta, W.J.H. & Feirtag, M. (1986). *Fundamental neuroanatomy*, p. 159. By permission of the authors and W.H. Freeman and Company. *Figure 1.4* Photo courtesy the Warren Grant Magnuson Clinical Center, National Institutes of Health.

Figure 2.1 From Bloom, William and Fawcett, Don. W. (1968). *A textbook of histology* (9th ed.), pp 305, 314, 315. By permission of W.B. Saunders Company. *Figure 2.4* From Bloom and Fawcett, p. 338. *Figure 2.5* From Solomon, E.P. & Davis, P.W. (1983). *Human anatomy and physiology*, p. 730. By permission of Holt, Rinehart and Winston, Inc. *Figure 2.6* From Bloom and Fawcett, p. 322. *Figure 2.7* From Solomon and Davis, fig. 2-11. *Figure 2.8* From Solomon and Davis, p. 262. *Figure 2.10* From Solomon and Davis, p. 263. *Figure 2.12* Redrawn from Kuffler, S.W., Nicholls, J.G., & Martin, A.R. (1984). *From neuron to brain* (2d ed.), p. 156. By permission of Sinauer Associates, Inc. *Figure 2.15* From Bloom and Fawcett, p. 220. *Figure 2.16* From Solomon and Davis, p. 267. *Figure 2.17* From Bloom and Fawcett, p. 341. Photo courtesy Sanford L. Palay. *Figure 2.19* From Schmidt, R.F. and Thews, G., eds. (1983). *Human physiology*, p. 67. By permission of Springer-Verlag, Heidelberg, West Germany.

Figure 3.1 From Solomon and Davis, p. 328. *Figure 3.2* From Kandel, E.R. & Schwartz, J.H., eds. (1981). *Principles of neural science*, p. 309. By permission of Elsevier Science Publishing Co., Inc., New York. *Figure 3.5* From Johnson, E.M., Schmidt, R.R., Solomon, E.P., & Davis, P.W. (1985). *Human anatomy*, p. 253. By permission of Holt, Rinehart and Winston, Inc. *Figure 3.7* From Gardner, E. (1975). *Fundamentals of neurology* (6th ed.), p. 130. By permission of W.B. Saunders Company. *Figure 3.17* From Angevine, J.B. & Cotman, C.W. (1981) *Principles of neuroanatomy*, fig. 13-4, p. 290. Copyright © 1981 Oxford University Press, Inc. Reprinted by permission. *Figure 3.18* From Bloom and Fawcett, fig. 12.11, p. 215.

Figure 4.1 Courtesy of Dr. K.W. Tosney, University of Michigan. *Figure 4.4* From Harris, W.A. et al. Growth cones of developing retinal cells in vivo, on culture surfaces, and in collagen matrices. *Journal of Neuroscience Research* 13 (1985): fig. 6, p. 113. By permission of Alan R. Liss, Inc., New York. *Figure 4.5* From Pytkowicz-Streissguth, A. et al. Teratogenic effects of alcohol in humans and laboratory animals. *Science* 209 (18 July 1980): fig. 4, p. 357. By permission of the authors and the American Association for the Advancement of Science. Copyright © 1980 by the AAAS. *Figure 4.6* Adapted from Patterson et al. The chemical differentiation of nerve cells. *Scientific American* (July 1978), p. 59. Copyright © 1978 by Scientific American, Inc. All rights reserved. *Figure 4.8* From Cowan, W. Maxwell. The development of the brain. *Scientific American* (September 1979), p. 132. Copyright © 1979 by Scientific American, Inc. All rights reserved. *Figure 4.13* From Scheibel, M.E. et al. Progressive dendritic changes in aging human cortex. *Experimental Neurology* 47 (1975): fig. 6, p. 402. *Figure 4.14* From Scheibel, A.B. & Tomiyasu, U. Dendritic sprouting in Alzheimer's presenile dementia. *Experimental Neurology* 60 (1978): fig. 1, p. 3.

Figure 5.2 From Solomon and Davis, p. 367. *Figure 5.4* From Gluhbegovic, N. and Williams, T.H. (1980). *The human brain: A photographic guide*. Philadelphia: Lippincott. Fig. 5-24, p. 147. *Figure 5.5* Photo courtesy Richard T. Marrocco. *Figure 5.7* From Kandel and Schwartz, p. 217. *Figure 5.8* From Kandel and Schwartz, p. 219. *Figure 5.11* From Boycott, B.B. Aspects of the comparative anatomy and physiology of the vertebrate retina. In Bellairs, R. & Gray, E.G., eds. (1974). *Essays on the nervous system* (London: Oxford University Press): fig. 10.19, p. 252. *Figure 5.12* From Kandel and Schwartz, p. 223.

Figure 5.13 From Kandel and Schwartz, p. 239. *Figure 5.14* From Chapani, A., Garner, W.R., & Morgan, C.T. (1949). *Applied experimental psychology* (New York: Wiley): fig. 15, p. 68. *Figure 5.18* From Kanizsa, Gaetano. Subjective contours. *Scientific American* (April 1976), p. 48. Copyright © 1976 by Scientific American, Inc. All rights reserved. *Figure 5.20* From Maffei, L. & Fiorentini, A. The visual cortex as a spatial frequency analyser. *Vision Research* 13 (1973): fig. 3, p. 1259. Reprinted with permission. Copyright © 1973 Pergamon Press, Ltd. *Figure 5.21* From Blakemore, C. and Sutton, P. Size adaption: A new aftereffect. *Science* 166 (10 October 1979): fig. 1, p. 245. By permission of the authors and the American Association for the Advancement of Science. Copyright © 1979 by the AAAS. *Figure 5.22* From Hubel, D.H. Effects of distortion of sensory input on the visual system of kittens. *The Physiologist* 10 (1967): fig. 7, p. 28. *Figure 5.23* From Hubel: fig. 17, p. 41. *Figure 5.24* From Neil R. Carlson, *Physiology of Behavior*, 3d ed. Copyright © 1986 by Allyn and Bacon, Inc. Used with permission. *Figure 5.25* From Gross, C.G., Rocha-Miranda, C.E., & Bender, D.B. Visual properties of neurons in inferotemporal cortex of the macaque. *Journal of Neurophysiology* 35 (1972): fig. 6, p. 104. *Figure 5.26* From Bruce, C., Desimone, R., & Gross, C.G. Visual properties of neurons in a polysensory area in superior temporal sulcus of the macaque. *Journal of Neurophysiology* 46 (1981): fig. 7, p. 379. *Figure 5.27* From Merzenich, M.M. & Kaas, J.H. (1980). Principles of organization of sensory-perceptual systems in mammals. In Sprague, J.J. & Epstein, A.A., eds. *Programs in psychobiology and physiological psychology*, vol. 9; fig. 1, p. 8. *Figure 5.28* From Merzenich and Kaas, fig. 4, p. 12.

Figure 6.1 From Solomon and Davis, p. 370. *Figure 6.4 (a)* From Zemlin, W.R. (1981). *Speech and hearing science: Anatomy and physiology* (2d ed.), p. 604. Copyright © 1981. Reprinted by permission of Prentice-Hall, Inc., Englewood Cliffs, N.J. *(b)* From Tonndorf, J. Shearing motion in scala media of cochlear models. *Journal of the Acoustical Society of America* 32 (1960). *Figure 6.5* From Figure 6-9, p. 153, from *Introduction to Physiological Psychology* by Thomas Bennett. Copyright © 1982 by Wadsworth, Inc. Reprinted by permission of Brooks/Cole Publishing Company, Monterey, California 93940. *Figure 6.7* Figure 2, p. 566, from Katsuki, Y. Neural mechanisms of auditory sensations in cats. In W.A. Rosenblith, ed. (1961). *Sensory communication*. By permission of the MIT Press, Cambridge, Mass.

Figure 7.4 From Kandel and Schwartz, p. 275. *Figure 7.9* Photo © Tom Miller, London. *Figure 7.12* Figure 1, p. 268, from Kornhuber, H.H. Cerebral cortex, cerebellum, and basal ganglia: An introduction to their motor functions, figure 1, p. 268. In F.O. Schmitt and F.G. Worden, eds., *The neurosciences: The third study program*. Published by the MIT Press, 1974. By permission of the MIT Press, Cambridge, Mass.

Figure 8.2 From Gamble, J.L. (1954) *Chemical anatomy, physiology and pathology of extracellular fluid* (6th ed.), chart 1, p. 3. Reprinted by permission of Harvard University Press. *Figure 8.3* Based on Figure 2, p. 130, Rolls, B.J. & Rolls, E.T. The control of drinking. *British Medical Bulletin* 37 (1981). *Figure 8.5* From Teitelbaum, P. & Epstein, A.N. The lateral hypothalamic syndrome: Recovery of feeding and drinking after lateral hypothalamic lesions. *Psychological Review* 69 (1963), p. 83. Copyright 1963 by the American Psychological Association. Reprinted by permission of the author.

Figure 9.3 Based on Solomon and Davis, p. 387. *Figure 9.4* Based on Solomon and Davis, p. 387. *Figure 9.7* From Figure 4, p. 237, Gorski, R.A. & Wagner, J.W. Gonadal activity and sexual differentiation of the hypothalamus. *Endocrinology* 76 (1965). *Figure 9.8* Based on Figure 26.3, p. 288, of Brown-Grant (1971), The role of steroid hormones in gonadtotropin secretion in adult female mammals. In C.H. Sawyer and R.A. Gorski (eds.), *Steroid hormones and brain function*. Berkeley, Calif.: University of California Press, 1971. *Figure 9.9* From Solomon and Davis, p. 696. *Figure 9.11* From Figure 2, p. 156, in Goy, R.W. Experimental control of psychosexuality. *Philosophical Transactions of the Royal Society (London)*, Series B (1970), 259. *Figure 9.12* From Solomon and Davis, p. 701. *Figure 9.14* From Money, J. & Ehrhardt, A.A. (1973) *Man and woman, boy and girl*, fig. 6.4, p. 116. Baltimore: The Johns Hopkins University Press. By permission of publisher and author.

Figure 10.2 After Kandel & Schwartz, Fig. 40-2, p. 475. *Figure 10.3* From H. Roffwarg et al. Ontogenetic development of the human sleep-dream cycle. *Science* 152 (29 October 1982), 604–619: fig. 1. By permission of the authors and the American Association for the Advancement of Science. Copyright © 1980 by the AAAS. *Figure 10.4* After J.C. Gillin & A.A. Borbely. Sleep: a neurobiological window on affective disorders. *Trends in Neuroscience* (December 1985), fig. 1, p. 537. By permission of Elsevier Publications Cambridge, Cambridge, England. *Figure 10.6* From C.A. Czeisler et al. Chronotherapy: Resetting the circadian clocks of patients with delayed sleep phase insomnia. *Sleep* 4 (1981): p. 4, fig. 1. Reproduced with the permission of the authors and Raven Press, New York. *Figure 10.7* From G.E. Pickard & F.W. Turek. Effects of partial destruction of the suprachiasmatic nuclei, etc. *J. comp. physiol. A* 156 (1985): fig. 5, p. 811. Used by permission of the authors and Springer-Verlag, Heidelberg, West Germany.

Figure 11.4 Reprinted by permission of the publisher, based on Figure 1, page 277, Chapter 13 in *The Neural Basis of Behavior* by Alexander L. Beckman (ed.). Copyright 1982, Spectrum Publications, Inc., Jamaica, New York.

Figure 12.3 From E.K. Warrington and L. Weiskrantz. New method of testing long-term retention with special reference to amnesic patients. *Nature* 217: figs. 2 and 3, p. 972. Reprinted by permission from *Nature*, vol. 217, no. 5132. Copyright © 1968 Macmillan Journals Limited, London. *Figures 12.4, 12.5* Figures 1 (p. 57) and 5 (p. 63) from Olton, Gamzu, & Corkin (eds.). *Memory dysfunctions: An integration of animal and human research from preclinical and clinical perspectives*. Vol. 444, *Annals of the New York Academy of Sciences*. By permission of the editors and the New York Academy of Sciences. *Figure 12.8* From E.R. Kandel & J.H. Schwartz. Molecular biology of learning. . . . *Science* 218 (29 October 1982): fig. 3, p. 435. By permission of the authors and the American Association for the Advancement of Science. Copyright © 1982 by the AAAS. *Figure 12.11* After G. Lynch and M. Baudry. The biochemistry of memory: a new and specific hypothesis. *Science* 224 (8 June 1984): fig. 2, p. 1060. By permission of the authors and the American Academy for the Advancement of Science. Copyright © 1984 by the AAAS.

Figure 13.1 From Gluhbegovic and Williams, fig. 5-21, p. 141. *Figure 13.5* From D. Kimura. Right temporal lobe damage. *Archives of Neurology* 8 (1963), fig. 8-3, p. 217. Copyright 1963, American Medical Association. Reprinted by permission of Dr. Kimura and the AMA. *Figure 13.6* Redrawn from Fig. 5-3, p. 92 in Beaumont, J.G. (1983). *Introduction to Neuropsychology*. New York: Guilford Press. *Figure 13.9* After Figure 15, page 42, from Freeman, W. and Watts, J.W. (1950). *Psychosurgery*, 2nd ed. Courtesy of Charles C Thomas, Springfield, Illinois.

Figure 14.2 CAT scan photographs reproduced by permission of Fred J. Hodges III, MD, Washington University Medical Center, St. Louis, two of a series that appeared in S.S. Kety, Disorders of the human brain. *Scientific American* 241 (September 1979), 203. *Figure 14.3* PET scan images courtesy

M.S. Buchsbaum, MD. From Buchsbaum et al. Positron emission tomographic image measurement in schizophrenia and affective disorders. *Annals of Neurology* 15 (April 1984): fig. 6, p. S163. *Figure 14.4* NMR image courtesy Dr. Robert Grimm, Portland, Oregon.

Figure 15.2 From S.E. Nichol & I.I. Gottesman. Clues to the genetics and neurobiology of schizophrenia. *American Scientist* 71 (1983): fig. 1, p. 399. Reprinted by permission of *American Scientist*, journal of Sigma Xi.

Photographic Credits:

Chapter Openers *One:* Leonardo da Vinci. *The Vitruvian Man*, c.1490. Accademia, Venice. Photo: Art Resource. *Two:* Neurons in cerebral cortex of cat. Pyramidal cells. Golgi stain. Photo: M. Abbey/Photo Researchers. *Three:* Leonardo da Vinci. Sketches of the brain. 1504–1507. Side view and view of bases. The two other figures are of unknown significance. Photo: The Bettmann Archive. *Four:* Leonardo da Vinci. Fetus in Utero. 1452–1519. Windsor Castle Royal Library. Photo: The Bettmann Archive. *Five:* Leonardo da Vinci. Studies of the eye and visual relations. Biblioteca Ambrosiana, Milan and Institut de France, Paris. Photo: The Bettmann Archive. *Six:* Robert Fludd, an alchemist. c.1619. Illustration from Historia—Oppenheim for J. T. de Bry. By H. Galler, Frankfurt e Kempffer. 1619–1621. From the collection of the University of California library, Berkeley. *Seven:* Edgar Degas, Dancer with tambourine and studies of legs. Musée d'Orsay, Paris. Photo: Réunion des Musées Nationaux, Paris. *Eight:* Pieter Bruegel. *Peasant Wedding Feast*. c.1520–1569. Kunsthistorisches Museum, Vienna. Photo: Bildarchiv Foto Marburg/Art Resource. *Nine:* Edvard Munch. *The Kiss*. 1902. Oslo Kommunes Kunstsamlinger, Munch Museet, Oslo, Norway. *Ten:* William Blake. *Queen Katherine's Dream*. The Fitzwilliam Museum, Cambridge, England. *Eleven:* Leonardo da Vinci. Study of heads for the *Battle Of Anghiari*. c.1503. Szépmüvészeti Museum of Fine Arts, Budapest, Hungary. *Twelve:* Leonardo da Vinci. An old man in profile seated on a rocky ledge (detail). Windsor Castle, Royal Library. Photo by permission of Her Majesty Queen Elizabeth II. *Thirteen:* The human mind: Brain with three cavities (as interpreted by Albertus Magnus in his *Philosophia Naturalis*). Photo: The Bettmann Archive. *Fourteen:* Michelangelo. Portrait of Leonardo da Vinci. The British Museum. Photo: Anderson/Archivi Alinari, Florence. *Fifteen:* Edvard Munch. *The Scream*. 1895. Oslo Kommunes Kunstsamlinger, Munch Museet, Oslo, Norway.

Photos *P. 9,* From De Fabrica (1543) by Andreas Vesalius. Photo from The Wellcome Institute for The History Of Medicine, London; *P. 13,* Ap/Wide World; *P. 35,* Jen & Des Bartlett/Photo Researchers; *P. 39* (left), A. W. Ambler/National Audubon Society/Photo Researchers; (right), Jack Dermid/National Audubon Society/Photo Researchers; *P. 115,* Charles Harbutt/Archive Pictures; *P. 144,* National Audubon Society/Photo Researchers; *P. 177,* Shelby Grossman/Photo Researchers; *P. 185,* The Bettmann Archive; *P. 192,* Jen & Des Bartlett Photo Researchers; *P. 198,* Suzanne Arms/Jeroboam; *P. 207,* UPI/Bettmann; *P. 251,* Roy Ellis/Photo Researchers; *P. 250,* Zimbel/Monkmeyer Press; *P. 266,* Barrett Gallagher/Animals, Animals; *P. 278,* Harlow Primate Laboratory, University of Wisconsin, Madison; *P. 292,* Michal Heron/Woodfin Camp; *P. 311,* Chester Higgins Jr./Photo Researchers; *P. 314,* Abigail Heyman/Archive Pictures; *P. 332,* Paolo Koch/Photo Researchers; *P. 333,* Bill Bachman/Photo Researchers; *P. 345,* Joan Liftin/Archive Pictures; *P. 373,* Leslie Wong/Archive Pictures; *P. 376,* Susan Wong Wagner/Photo Researchers; *P. 387,* Roswell Angier/Archive Pictures; *P. 418,* Monkmeyer Press.